FEDORA
LINUX

Other Linux resources from O'Reilly

Related titles
SUSE Linux
Knoppix Hacks™
Linux Annoyances for Geeks
Linux Cookbook™
Linux Desktop Hacks™
Linux in a Nutshell
Linux Network
   Administrator's Guide

Linux Multimedia Hacks™
Linux Security Cookbook™
Linux Server Hacks™
Linux Server Security
Running Linux
Ubuntu Hacks™

Linux Books Resource Center
linux.oreilly.com is a complete catalog of O'Reilly's books on Linux and Unix and related technologies, including sample chapters and code examples.

ONLamp.com is the premier site for the open source web platform: Linux, Apache, MySQL and either Perl, Python, or PHP.

Conferences
O'Reilly brings diverse innovators together to nurture the ideas that spark revolutionary industries. We specialize in documenting the latest tools and systems, translating the innovator's knowledge into useful skills for those in the trenches. Visit *conferences.oreilly.com* for our upcoming events.

Safari Bookshelf (*safari.oreilly.com*) is the premier online reference library for programmers and IT professionals. Conduct searches across more than 1,000 books. Subscribers can zero in on answers to time-critical questions in a matter of seconds. Read the books on your Bookshelf from cover to cover or simply flip to the page you need. Try it today for free.

FEDORA LINUX

Chris Tyler

O'REILLY®

Beijing · Cambridge · Farnham · Köln · Paris · Sebastopol · Taipei · Tokyo

Fedora Linux
by Chris Tyler

Published by O'Reilly Media, Inc., 1005 Gravenstein Highway North, Sebastopol, CA 95472.

O'Reilly books may be purchased for educational, business, or sales promotional use. Online editions are also available for most titles (*safari.oreilly.com*). For more information, contact our corporate/institutional sales department: (800) 998-9938 or *corporate@oreilly.com*.

Editor: Brian Jepson	**Indexer:** Lucie Haskins
Production Editor: Sanders Kleinfeld	**Cover Designer:** Karen Montgomery
Copyeditor: Derek Di Matteo	**Interior Designer:** David Futato
Proofreader: Sanders Kleinfeld	**Illustrators:** Robert Romano and Jessamyn Read

Printing History:

October 2006:   First Edition.

RepKover™ This book uses RepKover™, a durable and flexible lay-flat binding.

ISBN-10: 0-596-52682-2
ISBN-13: 978-0-596-52682-5

[M]

Table of Contents

Preface

Welcome to *Fedora Linux*: *A Complete Guide to Red Hat's Community Distribution*. I've based this book on the premise that the best way to learn Linux is to use it; each lab deals with a specific task or problem and starts with solutions. It then expands the discussion to explain the principles underlying the solutions and shows you where you can learn more about the topic if you want to dig deeper. Although the labs do build on each other in some small ways, I expect that most readers will jump from lab to lab according to their needs and interests rather than read the book linearly from front to back. Where appropriate, I have have included both graphical user interface and command-line techniques; use whichever approach suits your needs and style.

This book is written for experienced computer users, regardless of their previous experience with Linux. It covers both desktop and server configurations, and is ideally suited to an administrator or power user migrating to Fedora Linux from another environment, such as Windows, Mac OS X, or Unix.

This book is targeted at Fedora Core 6 but will also be useful to users of Fedora Core 5 and Fedora Core 7. Fedora is more than an operating system; it includes a wide range of applications, programming languages, and tools, and many of these packages are the subject of their own books. This book does not cover each topic in exhaustive detail; instead, it is designed to give you the most critical information in an accessible format and show you how the packages work within the context of Fedora.

 At the time of writing, Fedora Core 6 was being finalized; my apologies for the inevitable little discrepancies between the screenshots and descriptions in this book and the final version of Fedora Core 6.

How This Book Is Organized

Each chapter in this book contains a number of labs. Each lab covers a task or problem and contains four sections:

How Do I Do That?
> A description of techniques that may be used to accomplish the task or solve the problem

How Does It Work?
> An explanation of how the solution and the underlying technology work

What About...
> An exploration of related concepts and ideas

Where Can I Learn More?
> Pointers to additional information if you want to dig into the topic in greater detail

The labs are grouped into 10 chapters:

Chapter 1, *Quick Start: Installing Fedora*
> Covers the installation of Fedora Core using a variety of installation media and methods.

Chapter 2, *Using Fedora on Your Desktop*
> Introduces the use of Fedora on the desktop, including the use and customization of the GNOME and KDE graphical user interfaces and the configuration of basic features such as the display and printing.

Chapter 3, *Using Fedora on Your Notebook*
> Deals with the issues specific to using Fedora on a notebook computer, including power management, hopping between networks, and configuring external video for presentations.

Chapter 4, *Basic System Management*
> Covers basic system management tasks, including user and group administration, file management, remote access, and service configuration.

Chapter 5, *Package Management*
> Discusses package management—adding, removing, and updating software—and shows you how to take advantage of the thousands of packages available through Fedora's software repositories.

Chapter 6, *Storage Administration*
> Deals with storage administration using logical volume management and RAID arrays. It also covers data backup, including unattended overnight backups.

Chapter 7, *Network Services*
> Is the server chapter. It covers the Samba file server (compatible with Windows systems), as well as DHCP, DNS, web, email, and print services. Web-based applications including Wikis and webmail round out the coverage.

Chapter 8, *Securing Your System*
> Deals with security using Fedora's security facilities including SELinux, PAM, and ACLs.

Chapter 9, *The Fedora Community*
> Discusses the Fedora community and how you can become involved.

Chapter 10, *Advanced Installation*
> Deals with advanced installation options, including resizing a Windows partition to make room for Fedora, automating the installation process with Kickstart, and using Xen virtualization.

What You Need to Use This Book

Since this is a hands-on book, you'll want to have a computer available on which to run Fedora. Although you can use these labs with a production system, it's a good idea to use a noncritical machine so that you can freely experiment. And although it's not required, a good Internet connection is very helpful because it makes it easy to obtain software updates.

If you have Fedora installed, that's great—but if you don't, Chapter 1 will take you through the process.

Conventions Used in This Book

The following typographical conventions are used in this book:

Italic
> Indicates new terms, URLs, email addresses, filenames, file extensions, pathnames, and directories.

Constant width
> Indicates commands, options, switches, the contents of files, or the output from commands.

Constant width bold
> Shows commands or other text that should be typed literally by the user. Also used to highlight key portions of code or files.

Constant width italic
> Shows text that should be replaced with user-supplied values.

$
> This is the shell prompt for a regular user, which indicates that the command interpreter is ready to accept a new command. The normal Fedora shell prompt includes additional information before the dollar sign, including the username, hostname, and current directory; I've left those out to reduce clutter in the examples.

#
This is the shell prompt for the system administrator, known as *root* or the *superuser*. Use the command su - to switch from a normal account to the superuser account.

This icon signifies a tip, suggestion, or general note.

This icon indicates a warning or caution.

Using Code Examples

This book is here to help you get your job done. In general, you may use the code in this book in your programs and documentation. You do not need to contact O'Reilly for permission unless you're reproducing a significant portion of the code. For example, writing a program that uses several chunks of code from this book does not require permission. Selling or distributing a CD-ROM of examples from O'Reilly books *does* require permission. Answering a question by citing this book and quoting example code does not require permission. Incorporating a significant amount of example code from this book into your product's documentation *does* require permission.

We appreciate, but do not require, attribution. An attribution usually includes the title, author, publisher, and ISBN. For example: "*Fedora Linux* by Chris Tyler. Copyright 2007 O'Reilly Media, Inc., 978-0-596-52682-5."

Safari® Enabled

When you see a Safari® Enabled icon on the cover of your favorite technology book, that means the book is available online through the O'Reilly Network Safari Bookshelf.

Safari offers a solution that's better than e-books. It's a virtual library that lets you easily search thousands of top tech books, cut and paste code samples, download chapters, and find quick answers when you need the most accurate, current information. Try it for free at *http://safari.oreilly.com*.

How to Contact Us

Please address comments and questions concerning this book to the publisher:

O'Reilly Media, Inc.
1005 Gravenstein Highway North
Sebastopol, CA 95472
800-998-9938 (in the United States or Canada)
707-829-0515 (international or local)
707-829-0104 (fax)

There is a web page for this book, which lists errata, examples, and any additional information. You can access this page at:

http://www.oreilly.com/catalog/fedoralinux

To comment on or ask technical questions about this book, send email to:

bookquestions@oreilly.com

For more information about books, conferences, software, Resource Centers, and the O'Reilly Network, see the O'Reilly web site at:

http://www.oreilly.com

Acknowledgments

Thank you to the open source community and to Red Hat and the Fedora community in particular for developing, integrating, and supporting such a powerful collection of software.

I'd like to thank my editor, Brian Jepson, for his patient and skillful work and many suggestions; to David Brickner for getting me started on this project; and to Behdad Esfahbod for his thoughtful and detailed technical review.

My deep gratitude to my loving wife Diane and my girls Saralyn and Laura, who have patiently kept the family going without me for the past eight months. And above all, my humble thanks to God for the skills and understanding he has given me—may they be used to His glory.

## CHAPTER 1

Quick Start: Installing Fedora

Fedora is a powerful, fast-changing, freely available operating system. It can be used as a productive desktop or server environment, or it can be used to learn about Linux and experiment with new technologies.

1.1 Choosing Fedora: Is It Right for You?

There are many different Linux distributions, each with a different set of features, aimed at a different type of user. Before you invest time and effort in Linux, you need to decide if Fedora is the right distribution for you.

How Do I Do That?

Fedora Core is a collection of software that provides a complete working environment for a desktop or a server computer. It is often called an *operating system*, but, like other Linux distributions, it provides a lot more functionality than operating systems such as Microsoft Windows or Mac OS X because it includes desktop productivity applications and server software. Fedora Extras is a collection of software that is compatible with and extends the functionality of Fedora Core.

Fedora is developed and supported by a large community of developers, testers, package maintainers, documentation writers, marketers, and advocates. Many leading community members are also employees of Red Hat, Inc., which provides servers, *build systems* (the computers that compile and test the thousands of packages included with Fedora) and some funding for the project. In return, Red Hat gains the opportunity to receive feedback on new software and features before incorporating them into its commercial product line, called Red Hat Enterprise Linux.

What compatibility do you need?

If you want (or need) to run Windows games or a specific Windows application, Fedora may not be the right OS for you—although Wine will let you run some

Windows applications when you're in a pinch. Two commercial products based on Wine are available: Cedega, for Windows games, and CrossOver Office, for Microsoft Office and other business applications.

What level of stability do you need?

A new Fedora release is made approximately every four to nine months, and only the current and next-to-current releases are actively maintained by the project (beyond this time frame, security and bug fixes are supplied by the Fedora Legacy project).

If you need a platform with long-term stability, consider using Red Hat Enterprise Linux (RHEL) instead (or CentOS, which is a nonaffiliated project based on RHEL that does not have commercial support). Each RHEL release is supported with updates and security enhancements for a full seven years.

Because Fedora serves as a testbed for new technologies, it can be used to gain a preview of the new technologies that will be incorporated into future Red Hat Enterprise Linux releases.

What kind of support do you need?

As a *community* distribution, support for Fedora is provided by the Fedora community rather than a commercial entity. That means that most questions receive a quick and friendly answer, but since no one is being paid to help you, you may not receive any answers to unique or unusual questions.

If you like Fedora but need commercial support, consider using RHEL, which is Red Hat's fully supported commercial Linux product.

Does your equipment meet Fedora's system requirements?

Fedora will install on PCs with Intel and AMD 32- and 64-bit processors, as well as compatible processors from Transmeta, Via, and others. You will need a minimum of 256 MB of memory, 7 GB of disk space, and a processor speed of 400 MHz to obtain reasonable performance with the graphical user interface. A broadband Internet connection is desirable for obtaining software updates but is not necessary.

 You can install a very basic version of Fedora Core without a graphical user interface on a system with as little as 64 MB of memory, 1 GB of disk space, and a processor speed of 200 MHz. However, this is not recommended for desktop usage.

You can also install Fedora Core on a system with a PowerPC processor, such as an Apple Mac produced after 1999 and before 2006, or an IBM RS/6000 system.

How Does It Work?

Fedora Core includes over 2,200 software packages, and Fedora Extras (a library of compatible software) includes hundreds more. All of these packages are open source (*http://www.opensource.org/*), which means that the human-readable version of the software (*source code*) is distributed along with the ready-to-run *binaries*. Each package is licensed under one of a set of open source licenses that permits the software to be modified, adapted, and redistributed.

Most of these packages are developed and maintained by a team that may include developers, documentation writers, and testers, and most of the packages are not specific to Fedora; they're also distributed with other Linux distributions and non-Linux operating systems (for example, the excellent Firefox web browser is used on Linux, Windows, Mac OS X, and many other operating systems).

Each of these pieces of software is packaged for Fedora by another maintainer. To distinguish the two groups, the original developers and maintainers of the software are called the *upstream maintainers*, while the people responsible for integrating the package into Fedora are called *Fedora maintainer*s. The Fedora packages use the RPM package format for ease of management by package tools such as *yum*.

The current development version of Fedora is called *Rawhide* (see Lab 9.4, "Running Rawhide") and is highly unstable; people using Rawhide expect a steady flow of changes, along with features that appear and disappear, and work and then stop working again. Rawhide serves as the testing and proving ground for the software that will become the next Fedora release.

A similar process is used for Fedora Core updates and Fedora Extras: software is released to a testing repository, where it is tested by volunteers on the bleeding edge, and once the bugs are worked out, the software is moved to the Fedora Core updates or Fedora Extras repository.

What About...

...trying Fedora but also keeping Windows?

Fedora Core can be configured for *dual booting*, as long as you have sufficient disk space for both operating systems. You will be given the opportunity to select the default operating system during the Fedora installation, and you can override this default during the boot process, selecting the operating system you wish to use from a menu.

If Windows is currently using your entire hard disk, you will need to resize the Windows partition (see Lab 10.1, "Resizing a Windows Partition") or add an extra disk drive. If Windows is not yet installed on your computer, you should install it before Fedora; otherwise, it may overwrite your Fedora bootloader (or, in some cases, the entire Fedora installation).

...other Linux distributions?

There are dozens and dozens of Linux distributions, each aimed at a different audience. For details about specific distributions, visit *http://distrowatch.com*.

...seeing a list of the software packages included in Fedora Core?

Visit *http://download.fedora.redhat.com/pub/fedora/linux/core/6/i386/os/repodata/*, and you'll see a browsable display of all of the packages in Fedora Core. Click on a package name to see a detailed description of the package.

Where Can I Learn More?

- The Fedora Project: *http://fedora.redhat.com/* and *http://fedoraproject.org*
- The Fedora Legacy Project: *http://www.fedoralegacy.org/*
- The Open Source Initiative: *http://www.opensource.org/*
- About Fedora: *http://fedora.redhat.com/About*
- Red Hat Enterprise Linux: *http://redhat.com/rhel*
- CentOS: *http://www.centos.org/*
- Linux distributions: *http://distrowatch.com/*

1.2   Obtaining Fedora Core Software

The Fedora software exists in two parts: *Fedora Core*, a Linux distribution that includes base applications for desktop and server systems, and *Fedora Extras*, a repository of additional applications that can be added easily to a Fedora Core system.

The first step is to obtain a copy of the Fedora Core software itself.

How Do I Do That?

The Fedora Core installer is a bare-bones configuration of Linux designed specifically for the installation process. Once the installer is running, it configures and installs the Fedora Core software on your system.

There are, therefore, two parts to the software: the software used to boot up the system for the installation session, and the software that is installed on your system. These may be on the same media, or they may be separated into *boot media* and *installation media*.

Determining your architecture

Before selecting the media and obtaining the software, you must determine which architecture (machine type) you are using. Fedora Core is available for three different architectures:

i386

All Intel-compatible 32-bit systems with a standard BIOS, including all Intel 32-bit Celeron, Pentium, Centrino, and Core systems; AMD 32-bit Athlon, Duron, and Turion systems; and VIA CPUs such as the C3 and Eden processors. Older processors such as 80386, 80486, and K6 processors will also work. Fedora Core may be installed on Apple Mac systems with an Intel processor by using Apple's Boot Camp software (included in Mac OS X 10.5 and available in beta form for Mac OS X 10.4).

x86_64

All AMD-compatible 64-bit systems, including Opteron, Athlon 64, Duron 64, and Turion 64 systems, and Intel 64-bit Pentium 4, Xeon, and Core 2 systems. These systems can also run the i386 version but will do so in 32-bit mode.

PPC

Systems based on the PowerPC G3/POWER4 and later PowerPC processors, including recent PPC-based Apple Macs (manufactured between 1999 and 2006), IBM eServer pSeries, and IBM RS/6000 systems.

This chapter focuses on the i386 and x86_64 platforms, but the PPC installation procedure is quite similar.

Choosing boot and installation media

The Fedora Core installation boot software is usually started from a CD or DVD disc. It's also possible to boot from a USB flash disk drive if the system's BIOS supports it, or to boot from a network boot server using the PXE protocol. Table 1-1 outlines the boot media requirements.

Table 1-1. Boot media requirements for installing Fedora Core 6

Media type	Media count	Size	Notes
DVD	1	4.7 GB (or larger)	All of the software will fit on one disc (which serves as both the boot and installation medium), so this is usually the fastest and most convenient installation option.
CD	1	8 MB (any CD)	A single CD or mini-CD can be used to start a network or hard disk installation. If you will be using CDs for both the boot and installation media, five 700 MB discs are required (see Table 1-2).
USB flash drive	1	8 MB or higher	Requires a Linux system to configure the drive. Useful for network or hard disk installation. The BIOS of some systems will not permit booting from a USB flash key (beware of BIOS versions that permit booting only from a USB floppy or Zip drive).
PXE Server (Network Boot)	1	6.5 MB	Requires an existing system to serve as the PXE server (see Lab 10.3, "Preparing Alternate Installation Media").

Once the system has been booted, the rest of the installation software can be on a DVD, several CDs, an existing hard drive partition on the computer (or an external hard disk drive), or an FTP, NFS, or HTTP server. Table 1-2 outlines the requirements.

Table 1-2. Installation media requirements for Fedora Core 6

Media type	Media count	Size	Notes
DVD	1	4.7 GB or higher	Same media used for booting.
CD	5	700 MB	The images will not fit on 650 MB discs, such as some CD-RWs or old CD-Rs.
Network server (HTTP, NFS, or FTP)	1	3.5 GB of disk space on the server	HTTP is the lightest of the three protocols and is often the easiest to set up.
Hard disk partition	1	3.5 GB of disk space	Only ext2 and ext3 (Linux) and FAT (Windows/DOS) partitions are supported, on an internal or external disk drive. NTFS and LVM-based partitions will *not* work. This option is useful when adding Fedora to a computer that already has an operating system installed; the existing OS can be used to download the installation images. Note that the file size exceeds the maximum for FAT16 filesystems (2 GB).

Creating Fedora Core CDs or DVDs

To create a Fedora Core CD or DVD set, you must obtain the *ISO image files*.

To download the entire Fedora Core distribution for installation direct from disc, use one of these two procedures:

- Go to the web page *http://fedora.redhat.com/Download/mirrors.html* and select an HTTP or FTP site for direct download. Select the directory for the desired Fedora Core version number (6), then the directory for your machine architecture (i386, PPC, or x86_64), and then select the *iso* directory. You will probably not need the files containing "SRPM" in the name. If you want the CD images, get the files containing "disc1," "disc2," and so forth in the name; to obtain the DVD image, get the file containing "DVD" in the name.

- Use BitTorrent (*http://www.bittorrent.com*) to obtain the files from one of the Fedora torrents listed on *http://torrent.fedoraproject.org/*.

 Some download tools have problems with files over 2 GB in size. Most of the time, these problems affect only the download size, progress, or time-remaining displays during the download process, but some versions of the Lynx browser will not successfully download files over 2 GB. Older versions of *wget* also have a 2 GB limitation. If you are downloading onto a Windows system that is formatted with the FAT file system, the maximum file size may be 2 GB (FAT16) or 4 GB (FAT32).

To download only the boot disk ISO (for use with a network or hard disk installation):

- Go to the web page *http://fedora.redhat.com/Download/mirrors.html* and select an HTTP or FTP site for direct download. Select the directory for the desired Fedora Core version number (6), then the directory for your machine architecture (i386, PPC, or x86_64), select the *os* directory, and then select the *images* directory. Download the file named *boot.iso*. (You can also find this file in the *images* directory of the Fedora Core DVD or CD disc 1).

Once you have the image files, burn them onto optical media using the CD-creator program available on the platform used for downloading. For example, on Windows you could use Nero or Roxio Easy Media Creator; on a Linux system (such as Fedora Core 4), right-click on the file and select "Write to disc," or use a tool such as *K3B*, *xcdroast*, or *growisofs*.

 When burning a CD or DVD, use the ISO image file as the disc filesystem, but do not place the ISO image inside another filesystem on the disc. You will usually get the correct results if you save the ISO file to the desktop and then double-click on it.

To verify that the disk was created correctly, open it after you burn it: you should see several files and directories. If you see a single file with a *.iso* extension, the disc was not created correctly.

Buying Fedora Core CDs or DVDs

Depending on the speed of your Internet connection, it may be faster and cheaper to purchase a set of Fedora discs than to download the software. A list of online Fedora Core vendors is available at *http://fedoraproject.org/wiki/Distribution/OnlineVendors*, and a list of local retailers carrying Fedora Core is at *http://fedoraproject.org/wiki/Distribution/LocalVendors*.

Preparing files for a hard disk installation

To install Fedora Core from a FAT, ext2, or ext3 partition, simply copy the ISO image files for the DVD or CD set onto that disk partition. For example, on a Windows system with a FAT32 disk partition *D:*, download the DVD image file as though you were going to burn it onto a DVD but place the image file on drive *D:* (be sure to record the name of the directory/folder containing the images!).

Preparing a USB flash disk, network installation server, or PXE boot server

Each of these tasks is most easily performed on a running Linux system; see Chapter 10 for instructions. (Similar software is available for other platforms.)

How Does It Work?

An ISO image file is an exact copy of the contents of an optical disk. The name comes from the fact that data on optical discs is stored using a standard known as *ISO 9660*.

Each type of boot media has a unique standard for specifying how boot data is stored. On optical discs, the El Torito standard permits the system BIOS to find the boot software. For USB disks, a standard hard disk boot sector is used. For PXE network booting, a *boot protocol* (bootp) server is used to identify the boot files, and a *trivial file transfer protocol* (TFTP) server is used to serve them to the client system.

The first piece of software that loads from the boot media is the bootloader: *isolinux* for optical discs, *syslinux* for USB flash drives, or *pxelinux* for PXE boot servers.

After accepting boot parameters from the user, the bootloader subsequently loads two files:

vmlinuz
> A compressed Linux kernel; the heart of the Fedora Core operating system.

initrd.img
> A filesystem image that is loaded into memory and used as a ramdisk. This provides the drivers, startup scripts, and programs to get the system started.

Once these files have been loaded, the kernel is executed and begins the install process.

What About...

...installing from a floppy disk?

The Fedora installer has grown to the point that it no longer fits on a floppy disk. The USB flash disk method has replaced the floppy-disk boot procedure.

Where Can I Learn More?

- The Fedora Core release notes: *http://fedora.redhat.com/docs/release-notes/* or in the root directory of Fedora Core CD disc 1 or DVD
- The Fedora Core installation guide: *http://fedora.redhat.com/docs/fedora-install-guide-en/*
- Documentation on *syslinux*, *isolinux*, and *pxelinux*: *http://syslinux.zytor.com/*
- Burning ISO images to CD/DVD: *http://www.linuxiso.org/viewdoc.php/howtoburn.html*
- Fedora on Macintel: *http://fedoraproject.org/wiki/FedoraOnMactel*

1.3 Installing Fedora Core

Installing Fedora Core is a simple and straightforward task on most modern computers.

How Do I Do That?

To install Fedora Core, you'll need the installation media and your computer. If you are going to use a local area network or broadband Internet connection, it's recommended that you have it connected during the installation process.

A Fedora installation will usually take 15 to 90 minutes, depending on the speed of your computer and the amount of optional software you choose to install.

> Be sure to check the system requirements in the release notes at *http://fedora.redhat.com/docs/release-notes/* or in the root directory of the Fedora Core DVD or CD disc 1.
>
> On your system, if you have any data that you want to preserve, back it up before installing Fedora Core, and test the integrity of the backup copy.

Preparing for dual-boot

If your system already has Windows installed, and you intend to continue to use Windows, you will need to free up some space on the hard disk for Fedora Core. See Lab 10.1, "Resizing a Windows Partition," for instructions on shrinking a Windows disk partition (or deleting one that is unused).

There is an alternative to repartitioning your disk: you can install an additional disk drive in your system and use that drive for Fedora, or use an external USB or Fire-Wire drive.

Starting the installation

Insert your installation media (DVD, CD, or USB stick, or plug your system into a network with a PXE network boot server) and turn your system on. If it does not boot from the installation media, change your system BIOS settings to boot from it.

The first thing you will see is the boot screen shown in Figure 1-1.

The boot: prompt at the bottom of the screen lets you configure special options. You can press Enter for a standard, graphical installation, or you can type **linux** followed by any of the keywords in Table 1-3 to specify particular options for the installation session. Table 1-4 lists hard disk device names.

> Additional installation boot options are discussed in Chapter 10.

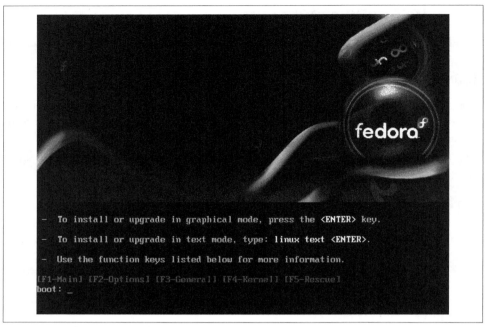

Figure 1-1. Fedora Core installation boot screen

Table 1-3. Fedora Core basic installation options

Option	Description	Notes
lowres	Uses 640 × 480 screen resolution.	Use if you are installing with a very old monitor.
resolution= 1024 × 768	Specifies a standard video resolution.	Use if the installer does not correctly detect your monitor capabilities and the video signal is out of range.
text	Uses text mode for installation (no graphics mode or mouse access).	Use this if graphics are garbled or slow when using the regular installer.
askmethod	Ask the user for the installation method (source of the software to be installed).	The installer will automatically ask if the boot media is a USB flash drive or a network boot. For a CD or DVD installation, the installer will assume that you're installing from the CD or DVD unless the askmethod or method= options are specified.

method=*method*	Specifies the installation *method*:
	
	cdrom
	    Install from optical disc (CD or DVD)
	
	http://*server*/*path*
	    Install from HTTP server
	
	ftp://*server*/*path*
	    Install from FTP server
	
	nfs:*server*/*path*
	    Install from a NFS server
	
	hd://*partition*/*path*
	    Install from an ISO file on a hard disk partition
		For the hd installation method, take the hard disk device name from Table 1-4 and add the partition number at the end. For example, if the ISO file is in the folder *fc6* on the 2nd partition of the primary master hard disk, use: method=hd://dev/hda2/fc6/.

Table 1-3. Fedora Core basic installation options (continued)

Option	Description	Notes
expert	Enables the use of a driver disk with additional device driver modules.	Use this to install onto hardware that requires driver modules not included in Fedora Core 6.

Table 1-4. Hard disk device names

Device name	Disk type	Controller	Unit
/dev/hda	Parallel ATA (IDE)	Primary	Master
/dev/hdb	Parallel ATA (IDE)	Primary	Slave
/dev/hdc	Parallel ATA (IDE)	Secondary	Master
/dev/hdd	Parallel ATA (IDE)	Secondary	Slave
/dev/hde	Parallel ATA (IDE)	Auxiliary #1	Master
/dev/hdf	Parallel ATA (IDE)	Auxiliary #1	Slave
/dev/hdg	Parallel ATA (IDE)	Auxiliary #2	Master
/dev/hdh	Parallel ATA (IDE)	Auxiliary #2	Slave
/dev/sd<X>	SATA, SCSI, IEEE1394, or USB	<X> is a for the first disk found, b for the second disk found, c for the third disk, and so forth. With USB and IEEE1394 (FireWire) devices, the assignments may change between reboots.	

For example, if you are using a CD for booting, and you want to use text mode and to be asked for the installation method, enter this boot string:

```
boot: linux text askmethod
```

In most cases, you should simply press Enter at the boot prompt. The Linux kernel and ramdisk (*initrd.img*) will load, as shown in Figure 1-2, and then start executing, as shown in Figure 1-3.

Testing the installation media

At this point—if you are installing from DVD or CD set—a media-check tool enables you to test the DVD or CD set, as shown in Figure 1-4. Press Enter to test the discs (optional), or press Tab and then Enter to skip the media check. The tests will take 2–6 minutes per CD or 8–12 minutes per DVD on a modern computer.

 Some disc burning programs will *pad* the image before burning it, adding additional data to the end of the disc. This will cause the disc to fail the media check even though the disc is valid.

Selecting the installation method

The screen shown in Figure 1-5 will appear only if you did not *not* boot from an optical disc, or if you entered the method or askmethod keywords at the boot prompt (Figure 1-1).

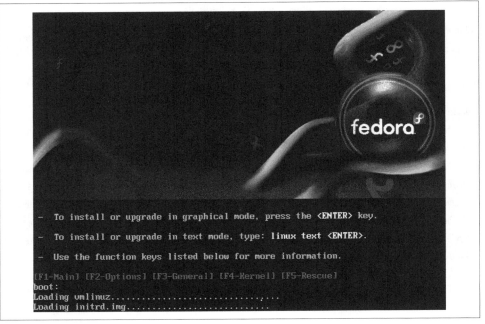

Figure 1-2. Loading the kernel and initrd (ramdisk)

```
io scheduler cfq registered (default)
Limiting direct PCI/PCI transfers.
ACPI: Processor [CPU0] (supports 8 throttling states)
isapnp: Scanning for PnP cards...
isapnp: No Plug & Play device found
Real Time Clock Driver v1.12ac
Linux agpgart interface v0.101 (c) Dave Jones
agpgart: Detected an Intel 440BX Chipset.
agpgart: AGP aperture is 64M @ 0xf0000000
PNP: PS/2 Controller [PNP0303:KBC,PNP0f13:MOUS] at 0x60,0x64 irq 1,12
serio: i8042 AUX port at 0x60,0x64 irq 12
serio: i8042 KBD port at 0x60,0x64 irq 1
Serial: 8250/16550 driver $Revision: 1.90 $ 4 ports, IRQ sharing enabled
serial8250: ttyS0 at I/O 0x3f8 (irq = 4) is a 16550A
serial8250: ttyS1 at I/O 0x2f8 (irq = 3) is a 16550A
00:09: ttyS0 at I/O 0x3f8 (irq = 4) is a 16550A
00:0a: ttyS1 at I/O 0x2f8 (irq = 3) is a 16550A
RAMDISK driver initialized: 16 RAM disks of 16384K size 1024 blocksize
Uniform Multi-Platform E-IDE driver Revision: 7.00alpha2
ide: Assuming 33MHz system bus speed for PIO modes; override with idebus=xx
PIIX4: IDE controller at PCI slot 0000:00:07.1
PIIX4: chipset revision 1
PIIX4: not 100% native mode: will probe irqs later
    ide1: BM-DMA at 0x1058-0x105f, BIOS settings: hdc:DMA, hdd:pio
```

Figure 1-3. The Linux kernel starting up

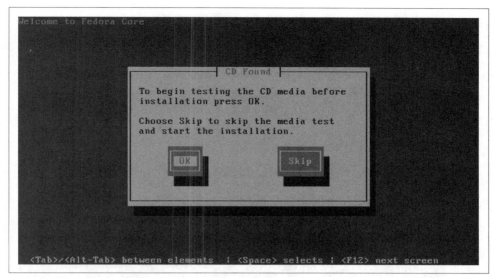

Figure 1-4. DVD/CD media check

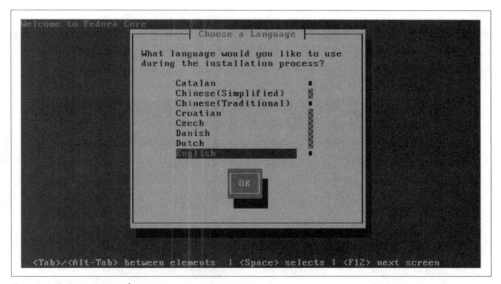

Figure 1-5. Language selection screen

Select the language to use during installation using the up/down cursor keys, and then press Enter to proceed. The keyboard selection screen shown in Figure 1-6 will appear.

Select the entry that matches your keyboard and press Enter.

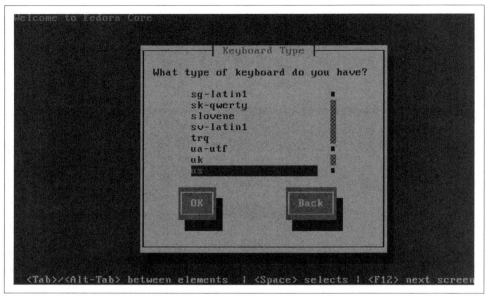

Figure 1-6. Keyboard selection screen

If you included the askmethod keyword at the boot prompt or booted from a USB flash disk or a PXE boot server, the installation method dialog shown in Figure 1-7 will appear next.

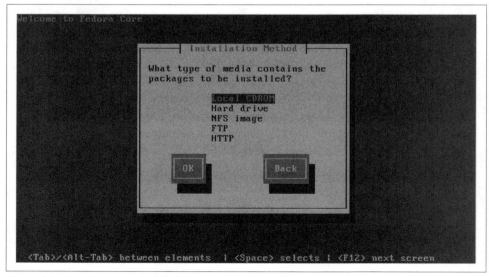

Figure 1-7. Installation method dialog

If you select an installation method that is network-based (NFS, FTP, or HTTP), you will be presented with a network configuration screen where you can enable automatic IP configuration through DHCP and select IPV4 (used on most networks) and/or IPV6. If you do not enable DHCP support, an additional page will appear to collect the IP settings (IP address, netmask, DNS server, and gateway). In most established networks (including small business or home networks with a broadband Internet connection through a router/gateway device), the IP settings can be obtained from a DHCP server. If in doubt, try the DHCP server option; if it fails, you will be given the opportunity to enter the network information manually.

If you select the hard disk installation method, you will be prompted to select the disk device and path to the Fedora Core ISO images. Use Table 1-4 to determine the disk device, and append the partition number to the device name (for example, use /dev/hda2 for partition 2 on the IDE primary master disk); for the path, enter the pathname of the directory containing the ISO images, using the forward-slash (/) character to separate directories instead of the Windows-style backslash (\).

Installation stage 2

At this point, control of the system passes from the boot media to the installation media. For example, if you've used a USB flash drive to boot and HTTP for the installation method, it is at this point that the system switches over to software from the HTTP server.

If you're using a graphical installation, the graphical environment will be started now, and the splash screen shown in Figure 1-8 will appear. Click Next to proceed.

 If your mouse is not working, you can activate a graphical button on the installation screen by using the keyboard; just press Alt and the letter underlined in the button label. For example, to view the release notes while on the splash screen in Figure 1-8, press Alt-R (because R is underlined on the Release notes button).

If you are using a text-mode installation, you will see a text-based version of each of the following screens; the layout may be slightly different to accommodate the available screen space and the absence of a mouse pointer. Use the Tab key to navigate among the controls on the text screen.

 You cannot manually create a new Logical Volume configuration using the text-mode installer.

If you have not already selected your language and keyboard type, the screens shown in Figures 1-9 and 1-10 are presented to collect this information.

Figure 1-8. Fedora Core graphical-installation splash screen

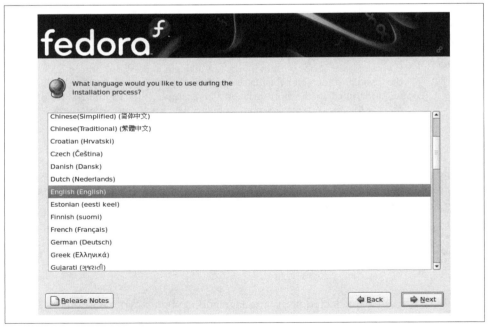

Figure 1-9. Graphical language selection

Figure 1-10. Graphical keyboard selection

Upgrading a Fedora installation

The installation program will check to see if you have an existing Fedora installation; if you do, it will offer you the option of upgrading the current system instead of performing a new installation (Figure 1-11).

Choose Install Fedora Core if you want to replace your existing installation, or "Upgrade an existing installation" if you want to upgrade your existing Fedora system to Fedora Core 6. Click Next.

This dialog may appear if you previously started a Fedora installation, but aborted the installation process before it was finished (producing a partially installed system). In that case, choose Install rather than Upgrade to ensure that the new system is complete.

If you have an existing Fedora installation and you want to replace it with Fedora Core 6, but you wish to preserve the data in your home directories, and the home directories have their own filesystem or partition, you can choose Upgrade.

If you choose Install, skip to the next section titled "Performing a New Fedora Installation." Otherwise, the screen shown in Figure 1-12 will appear, asking what you want to do with the bootloader configuration.

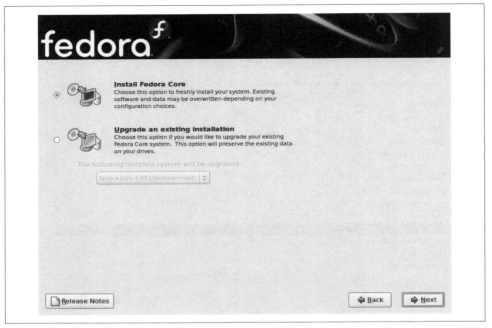

Figure 1-11. Upgrade option

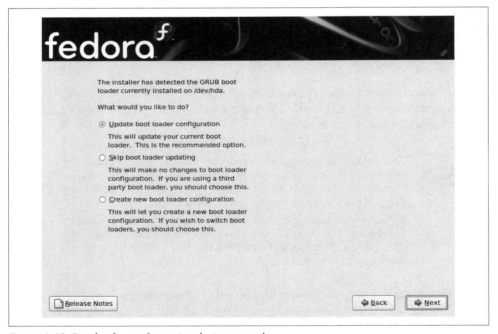

Figure 1-12. Bootloader configuration during upgrade

Choose an option based on your current bootloader:

Update boot loader configuration
> Use this if your previous installation installed the GRUB bootloader (the default for recent versions of Fedora Core).

Skip boot loader updating
> Use this if you are using a third-party bootloader program. You will need to refer to your bootloader documentation to determine how to update the bootloader manually.

Create new boot loader configuration
> Select this option if you are using the older LILO bootloader. The installation system will replace LILO with GRUB.

Click Next. After a few seconds, the screen shown in Figure 1-13 will appear.

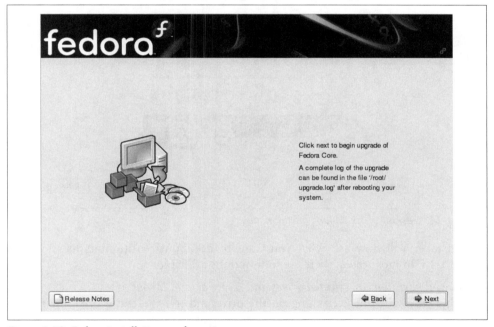

Figure 1-13. Fedora installation confirmation screen

This is the point of no return. Click Next to proceed with the upgrade, but remember that the upgrade process must run to completion and cannot be safely interrupted. The Fedora installer will analyze the software installed in your existing Fedora system, determine what needs to be updated, and install the new packages.

Performing a new Fedora installation

If any of your hard disks are empty and have not been previously used, the warning message displayed in Figure 1-14 will appear. If the drive contains data that you wish to preserve, abort the installation and boot into your existing operating system, figure out why the disk does not show a partition table, and restart the installation. Otherwise, click Yes to continue the installation.

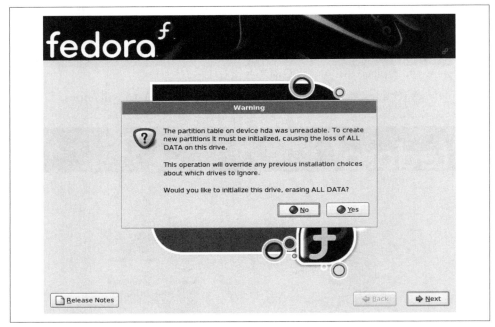

Figure 1-14. Warning about a blank partition table

The installer will now ask what you want to do about partitioning, as shown in Figure 1-15. In most cases, there are four options available:

Remove all partitions on selected drives and create default layout
> This will wipe out everything on the drive and use the entire drive for Fedora Core. Select this option on a new computer or a computer you want to convert for use entirely with Fedora Core. This is also the right option to use when you are installing Linux on a second (or third) disk drive, leaving the software and data on the other drives untouched—but be careful that only the Fedora Core drive is selected in the list of available disks.

Remove Linux partitions on selected drives and create default layout
> Use this option if you are replacing an existing Linux installation and want to leave other operating systems (such as Windows) untouched.

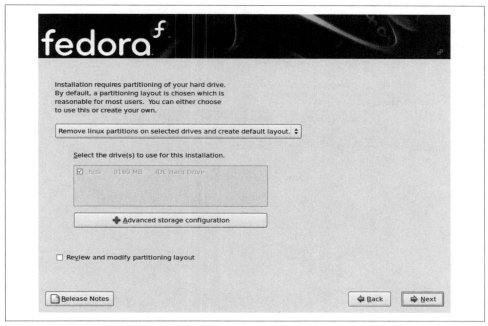

Figure 1-15. Disk and partition strategy selection

Use free space on selected drives and create default layout
    If you have unused space on your disk drive, or you have shrunk a Windows partition to free up some space, select this option.

Create custom layout
    If you are familiar with partitioning and have special requirements—for example, you wish to preserve only one filesystem (such as */home*) from a previous Linux installation—select this option.

If you have more than one disk drive installed, you will be able to select the drive(s) to be used for Fedora using the checkboxes in the rectangle labeled "Select the drive(s) to use for this installation." Refer to Table 1-4 for Linux disk names.

At the bottom of this screen, be sure to select the checkbox labeled "Review and modify partitioning layout" so that you will have an opportunity to see the proposed disk layout before it is used. Click Next to continue.

If you have selected an option that involves removing an existing partition, you will see the partition-removal warning shown in Figure 1-16. Review the information shown, and then click Yes to confirm that you are prepared to remove the partitions listed.

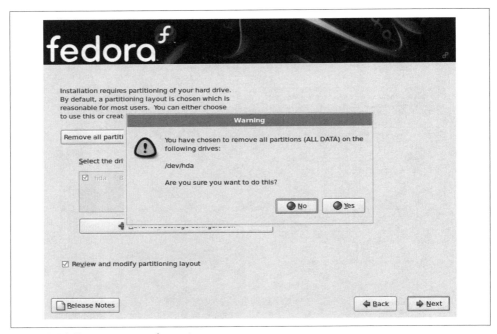

Figure 1-16. Partition removal warning

Partitioning layout

By default, Fedora Core uses a system called *Logical Volume Management* (LVM). A partition managed using LVM is called a *physical volume* (PV). Storage space from one or more PVs is used to create a pool of storage called a *volume group* (VG). Out of this pool of storage, one or more virtual partitions are created; each virtual partition is a *logical volume* (LV). Figure 1-17 illustrates the relationship between these components.

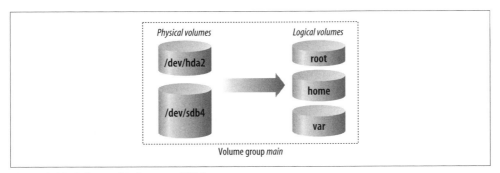

Figure 1-17. Relationship between LVM components

LVM has several advantages over traditional partitioning:

- Logical volumes can be resized, enabling you to shift space between filesystems without reinstalling the system.
- Logical volumes can span multiple physical volumes, enabling the use of filesystems that are larger than one physical disk.
- Additional storage can be added to existing filesystems—for example, you can add a new disk drive and add that storage space to the *home* filesystem.
- Data can be migrated from one drive to another.

Chapter 6 delves into more detail regarding LVM.

Although logical volumes can be enlarged or reduced at any time, the ext3 filesystem that Fedora uses can be enlarged only while it is in use. It must not be in use when it is reduced in size. This can make it fairly complicated to shrink an ext3 partition. Because it's difficult to determine how much disk space each filesystem will require in the future, it is a good idea to make Fedora filesystems no larger than necessary at first, and then add space to them as required. This avoids the need to reduce the size of one LV in order to increase the size of another.

Unfortunately, the LVM system is too complex to use during the early stages of the booting process, so a system configured to use LVM must also have a small traditional partition for boot files.

 In order to use Fedora Core's *hibernate* feature, you will also need a swap partition (either instead of or in addition to swapspace on a logical volume). See Lab 3.1, "Power Management," for more information on hibernation.

If you have selected a partitioning option that includes the default layout and have selected the checkbox to review and modify the layout, the screen in Figure 1-18 will appear at this point in the installation.

The table on the bottom half of the screen contains two sections: one for LVM volume groups and one for hard disks. The default layout creates a 100 MB boot partition, and takes all remaining available disk space on all drives and places it in a single volume group named *VolGroup00*. The space in this volume group is then divided into two logical volumes: *LogVol00* for the root filesystem and *LogVol01* for swap space (virtual memory).

There are three improvements that we are going to make to the default Fedora Core partition/LVM layout:

- A separate LV will be used for the */home* filesystem, so that users' home directories are separated from the operating system. This will enable you to wipe out the operating system and reinstall it (or install another distribution of Linux or a later version of Fedora Core) without affecting the users' files.

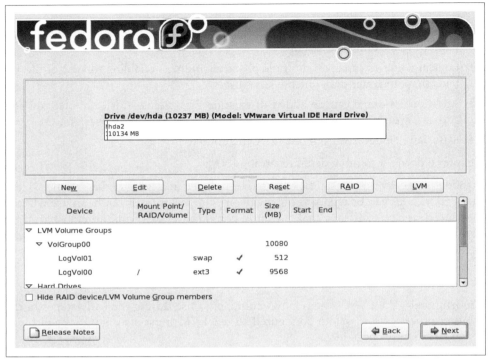

Figure 1-18. Fedora Disk Druid partitioning screen

- The LVs will be reduced in size so that they are no larger than necessary. Surplus disk space can be left unassigned within the volume group and added to logical volumes as needed; this eliminates the need to perform complex operations to shrink one volume group in order to grow another.

- The volume group and logical volume names will be replaced with more descriptive text.

To make these changes, double-click on the line in the table that reads VolGroup00 and then click the Edit button. The Edit LVM Volume Group window will appear, as shown in Figure 1-19.

Start by changing the Volume Group Name at the top of this window from VolGroup00 to main. Next, click on the entry that has a mount point of / and click Edit; the Edit Logical Volume window shown in Figure 1-20 will appear.

Change the Logical Volume Name to root, and change the size to a value that is closer to the size of the installation. I recommend 8,000 MB (i.e., 8 GB; most server and desktop systems will take 2–6 GB of space to install, so 8 GB gives a modest amount of headroom). Click OK when you are done.

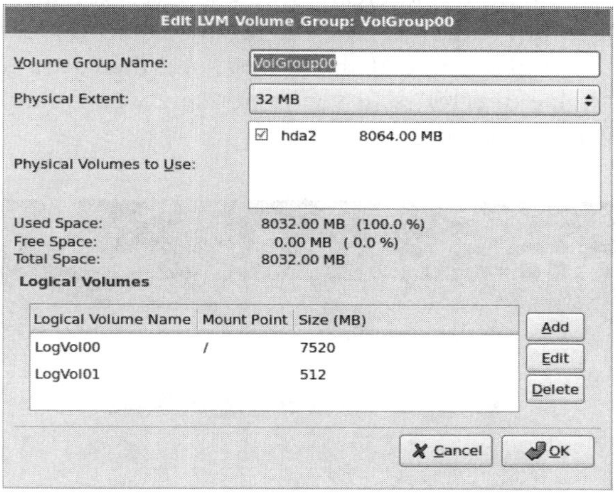

Figure 1-19. Edit LVM Volume Group window

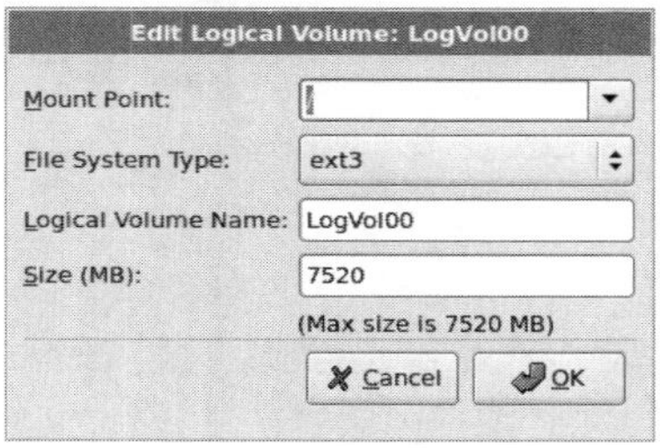

Figure 1-20. Edit Logical Volume window for the root LV

Figure 1-21 shows the settings that repeat the process for the other predefined LV: click on this LV and then click Edit. Change the Logical Volume Name to swap, leaving the size at the default value. Click OK when you are done.

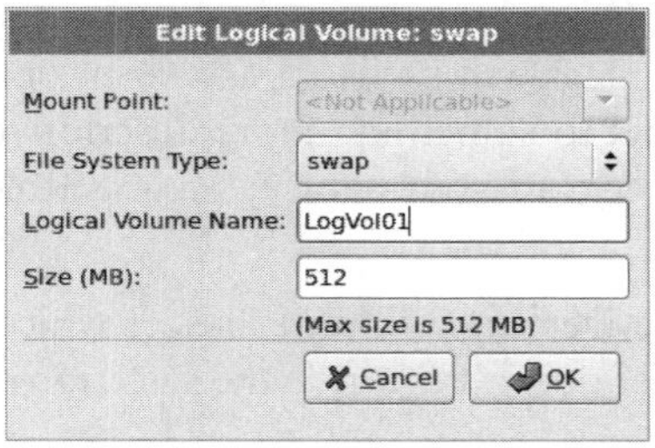

Figure 1-21. Edit Logical Volume window for the swap LV

Finally, click the Add button and create a new Logical Volume to hold the home directories, as shown in Figure 1-22. Set the Mount Point to /home, the File System Type to ext3, the Logical Volume Name to home, and then set a reasonable size for storing the users' home directories (if you're not sure what value to use, start with 1000). Click OK when you are done.

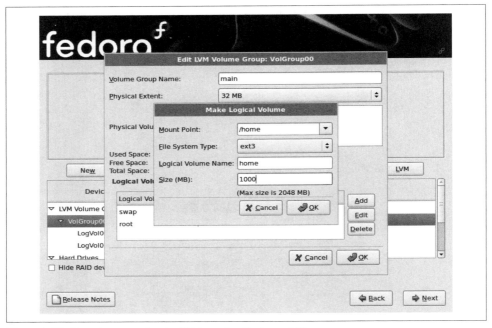

Figure 1-22. Creating a new Logical Volume for the home LV

Review the final disk partition and LVM layout, and then click Next. The bootloader configuration screen will appear, as shown in Figure 1-23.

The default bootloader configuration replaces any existing bootloader installed on the main hard disk. If you have more than one operating system installed, the bootloader will ask you which OS to boot when the system is started. If you have a Windows boot partition present, it will be listed as a boot option, but it will be labeled Other. To change this label to something more descriptive, click on that entry, and then click Edit. Enter the text of your choice, such as Windows XP Professional, and then click OK.

Use the checkboxes in the Default column to select which operating system will be loaded by default if the user doesn't override the selection at boot time.

It is a good idea to install a bootloader password. Without this, any person with physical access to your machine will be able to easily override all security by booting

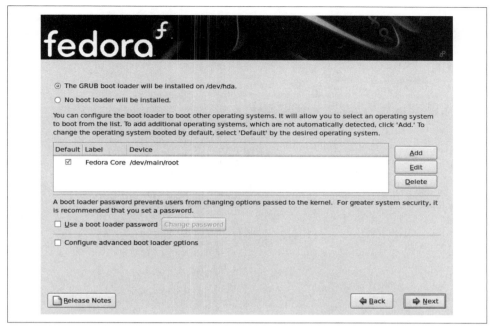

Figure 1-23. Bootloader configuration screen

the system into single-user mode. Click "Use a boot loader password" and then enter your selected password twice when prompted.

> The bootloader password is a critical piece of information—don't lose it!

Click Next to proceed.

General questions

If you have not already configured the network, and you have a network adapter installed in your system, the network configuration screen appears next, as shown in Figure 1-24.

If you have a DHCP server on your network—which is the case in most large networks and in most small office and home networks that have a broadband Internet gateway/router device—then you will only need to change the "Set the hostname" option to "manually" and then enter the hostname of your choice (unless your DHCP server sets the hostname for you). If you have a registered domain, choose a hostname within that domain, such as *bluesky.fedorabook.com* (which specifies the

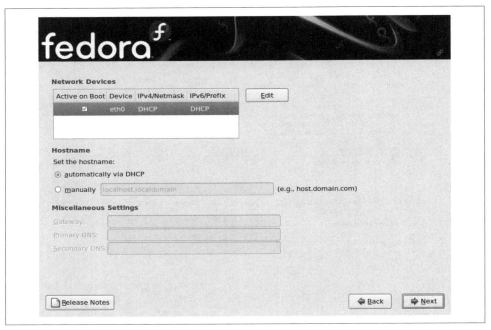

Figure 1-24. Network configuration screen

host *bluesky* within the domain *fedorabook.com*); otherwise, choose a hostname and append *.localdomain* to the end of the name.

If you do not have a DHCP server on your network, select your primary Ethernet card from the Network Devices list and then click Edit. You will see the Edit interface window shown in Figure 1-25. Click on the "Configure using DHCP" option to deselect that checkbox, then enter the IP address and netmask. Click OK to save this information, and enter the hostname, gateway, and DNS server information in the blanks provided (it is necessary only to enter a Primary DNS server).

Click Next to proceed to the next step in the installation, which is time zone selection, as shown in Figure 1-26.

Click on your region of the map to zoom in, and then click on the major city closest to your location—or use the pull-down menu to select your time zone.

You can choose to configure the system's hardware clock to store information in local time or in Coordinated Universal Time (UTC). This is controlled by the checkbox labeled "System clock uses UTC." If you are using multiple operating systems on your computer (dual-boot), to use local time, deselect the checkbox so that the other operating system will interpret the time correctly.

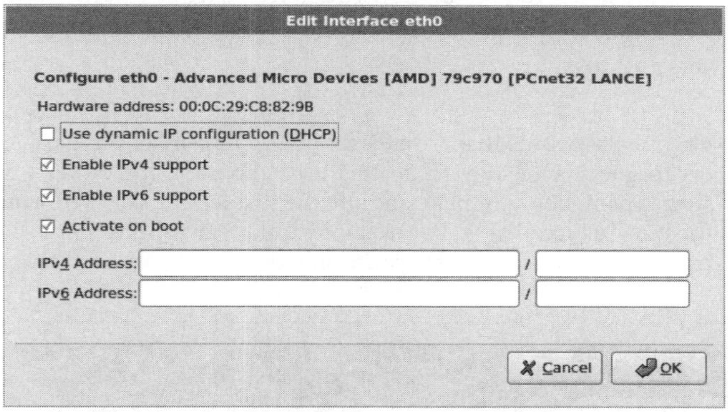

Figure 1-25. Edit interface window

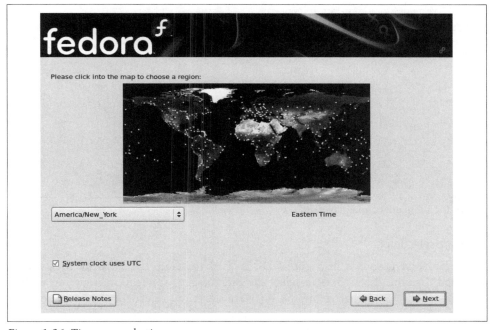

Figure 1-26. Time zone selection

If you are using only Fedora, or Fedora and another distribution of Linux, choose UTC by selecting the checkbox. This will avoid multiple adjustments of the clock when entering or exiting daylight savings time.

Click Next to proceed.

The screen in Figure 1-27 requests that you enter a *root password* for the system (twice). This is the master system administration password, so be sure to safeguard it against both theft and loss.

Choose passwords that are easy for you to remember but hard for others to guess. One way to do this it to choose a line or verse from a song, poem, book, or play, and use the first letter from each word plus the punctuation marks. For example, from Shakespeare's line "Do you bite your thumb at us, sir?" you would derive the password *Dybytau,s?*

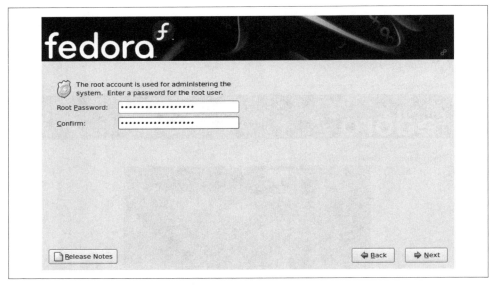

Figure 1-27. Creating a root password

Software selection

The next screen, shown in Figure 1-28, is used to select the software that will be installed. Use the checkboxes to select the categories of applications that you wish to have installed. To further refine the software selection, select the "Customize now" option; this is recommended if you are installing on a system with minimal disk space or a slow Internet connection.

When installing from DVD or CD, the button labeled "Add additional software repositories" can be used to add a Fedora Updates network repository to ensure that the latest versions of the Fedora Core packages are installed. This can be somewhat faster than installing the disc version of all packages and then updating the software after installation, but it requires a good Internet connection (or local repository). See Lab 5.3, "Using Repositories," for more information.

Figure 1-28. Software selection screen

Click Next to continue. If you selected "Customize now," you will see the screen shown in Figure 1-29. Otherwise, skip ahead two paragraphs.

Select a category on the left side to see the package groups within that family on the right side. Use the checkboxes provided to select the groups you want. For even finer control, you can select a package group, click the "Optional packages" button, then select the individual packages you wish to include from the window shown in Figure 1-30.

Click Next to continue. After a short time for dependency processing, the screen shown in Figure 1-31 will appear.

This is the point of no return; once you click Next, the partition table, filesystems, and bootloader will all be modified. Once the installation process begins, it cannot be safely interrupted and must be allowed to run to completion. During the installation, a progress bar similar to the one in Figure 1-32 will be shown.

 Bored? You can read the release notes during the installation; just click on the button in the lower-left corner of the screen.

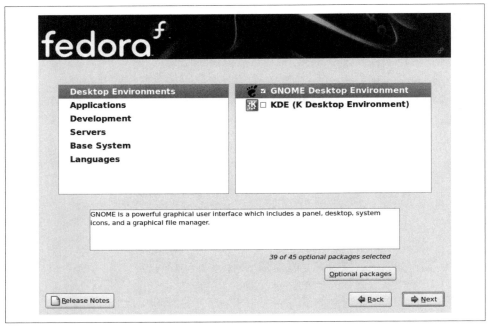

Figure 1-29. *Software customization screen*

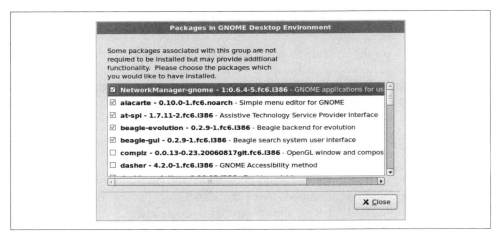

Figure 1-30. *Optional package selection screen*

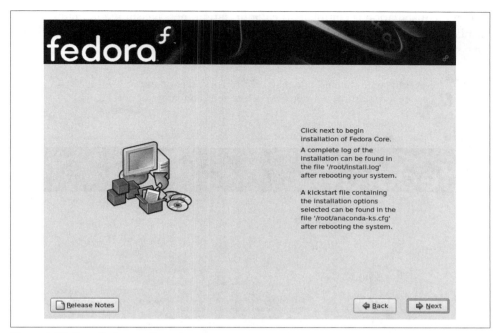

Figure 1-31. Installation confirmation

Figure 1-32. Installation progress indicator

When the installation is complete, the confirmation message shown in Figure 1-33 is displayed. Remove the installation boot media, and then click Reboot to start up the new system.

 On some systems, you may need to click Reboot and wait for the system to start the boot process before you can remove optical media.

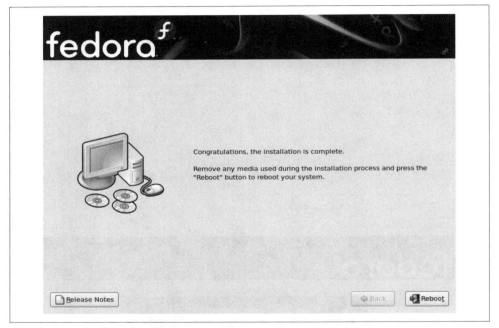

Figure 1-33. Completed installation

First boot

The first time you boot your freshly installed Fedora system, you will be asked a few questions to finish up the initial configuration. The display shown in Figure 1-34 will greet you; as you work through the questions, the arrow on the lefthand side of the screen will move downward to indicate your progress.

Click Forward to proceed to the license-agreement screen. Read the license carefully, and then click Yes or No to indicate whether you accept the license terms.

Click Forward to enter the firewall configuration screen. I strongly recommend that you leave the firewall enabled, and that you initially select only *ssh* as a trusted service. You can loosen your firewall to permit other inbound services later, as you set those services up.

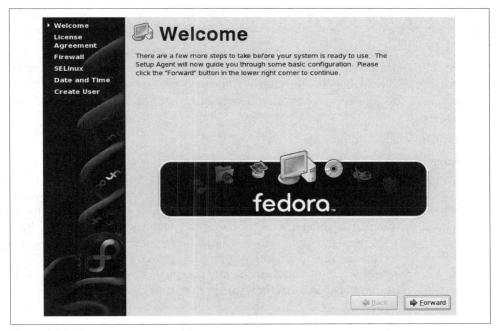

Figure 1-34. First boot welcome screen

Click Next to proceed to SELinux configuration. SELinux hardens the Linux kernel against attack. Although it can be a bit difficult to configure at times, the protection that it provides is well worth the extra effort. SELinux is covered in more detail in Lab 8.2, "Using SELinux." For now, leave the Modify SELinux Policy option at its default setting; you can always adjust SELinux later.

Click Forward to proceed to the date and time configuration screen. Select the current date by clicking on the calendar, and enter the current time into the fields provided.

If you have an always-on Internet connection, click on the Network Time Protocol tab. Select the checkbox labeled Enable Network Time Protocol. This will configure your system to communicate with *timeservers* on the Internet to keep the clock closely synchronized to official time. This is valuable because it ensures that time and date stamps on your system are always accurate.

You can edit the list of timeservers that can be contacted using the Add, Edit, and Remove buttons beside the server list. The NTP Server Pool Project maintains a pool of publicly accessible timeservers; the default server list (*0.fedora.pool.ntp.org*, *1.fedora.pool.ntp.org*, and *2.fedora.pool.ntp.org*) configures your system to randomly select up to three timeservers from the pool at boot. To use a timeserver in your country, use your ISO country code as the hostname within the *pool.ntp.org* domain; I'm in Canada, so a server in my country could be found using the name *ca.pool.ntp.org.*

Click Next to proceed on to creating the first user. The root password that you entered during installation is used only for system administration and should not be used for day-to-day work. This screen lets you create the first user account; you can create as many additional accounts as you want later (see Lab 4.7, "Managing Users and Groups").

Fill in the four fields on this screen:

Username
> Choose a username that contains no spaces and starts with a letter. This name will be used for logging in and will also serve as the user's local email address (typically, this is not intended to replace the email address you got from your ISP or mail provider; it is generally used to receive system notices and other local messages). I recommend using only lowercase letters, digits, underscores, and periods. If you are setting up a home or personal system, first names work well; for a corporate server, full names in *firstname.lastname* form reduce the likelihood of confusion between users (now and in the future).

Full name
> Enter the user's full name (for example, Chris Tyler).

Password
> Enter a password that is easy to remember and hard to guess. Just like the root password, using the first letter from each word plus the punctuation from an obscure line of text can be helpful (for example, FL:AcgtRHcd. for "Fedora Linux: A complete guide to Red Hat's community distribution.").

If the button in the lower-righthand corner of the screen reads Forward, there is one more step. Click on that button to proceed to the the sound card check screen.

On this screen, click on the Play button (labeled ▶) and adjust the volume slider until you hear a guitar strum on the right, left, then the center channel of your sound system. If you don't hear anything, check your speaker power, physical volume control, and sound connections (if you have multiple sound cards, use the device tabs on the left side to switch between them), clicking Play after each adjustment (or just select the Repeat checkbox).

If you can't get sound working at this point, don't worry; you may just need access to some of the advanced mixer controls, which you can experiment with later (see Lab 2.6, "Configuring Sound").

Click Finish. Congratulations, Fedora is installed and ready to use!

How Does It Work?

The Fedora Core installer is named *Anaconda*. It shares code and technology with several other tools, including:

yum, pup, and pirut
> Tools for adding and removing software (see Chapter 5).

kudzu
> A tool that checks the system at boot time to see if any hardware has been added or removed, and adjusts the system configuration appropriately.

system-config-component
> Graphical tools to configure individual system components.

Because the hard disk is in an unknown state and the CD is not writable during the installation session, Anaconda uses a *ramdisk*—an area of memory configured to act like a disk drive—as the filesystem while it is running. After interacting with you to get the configuration details, Anaconda partitions and formats the hard disks and mounts them. It then starts installing RPM packages containing the selected software. Finally, it reboots the system.

Each time the system boots, the init script */etc/rc.d/init.d/firstboot* is executed. If the file */etc/sysconfig/firstboot* does not exist, the Python script */usr/sbin/firstboot* is executed to ask the initial configuration questions.

Once the configuration details have been saved, the *firstboot* script exits and the normal boot sequence continues.

What About...

...rerunning the firstboot process to reset the system configuration?

You can rerun the *firstboot* script by adding `reconfig` to the boot parameters when the system is started (boot parameters are entered in the same way as runlevels are during the boot process; see Lab 4.5, "Using Runlevels"). The sequence of steps used during a reconfiguration is slightly different and longer from that used when the script executes for the first time; for example, you can change the system's default language during reconfiguration.

 If you are not using a bootloader password, then any user with physical access to your computer can reset the password of any account on the system using the `reconfig` boot argument.

…getting help if I encounter problems during (or after) installation?

Fedora is a community-based project, and the Fedora community is very helpful. The best places to turn for help are the Fedora Forum and the Fedora mailing lists. You can also access help using IRC (see Lab 9.2, "Using IRC," for more information).

Where Can I Learn More?

- The Fedora Core release notes: *http://fedora.redhat.com/docs/release-notes/*
- The Anaconda web page: *http://fedora.redhat.com/projects/anaconda-installer/*
- The manpages for *kudzu* and *yum*
- The Fedora Forum: *http://fedoraforum.org*

## CHAPTER 2

Using Fedora on Your Desktop

Fedora Linux provides a solid desktop computing environment—including a graphical user interface, communication tools, and office applications—that goes well beyond the traditional definition of an operating system. This chapter focuses on using Fedora in the desktop role.

Where possible, the labs in this book include instructions for performing tasks using both the graphical user interface and the command line. If you are not familiar with entering Linux commands, see Lab 4.1, "Using the Command Line."

2.1 Getting Started Using the Fedora Graphical User Interfaces

Fedora Core provides two attractive and easy-to-use *graphical user interfaces* (GUIs): KDE and GNOME. Each of these GUIs should be a comfortable adjustment for the majority of Windows and Mac users because basic operations are similar. However, there are some capabilities that are unique to Linux, and learning to use these features will enable you to take full advantage of the Fedora GUIs.

How Do I Do That?

Fedora Linux can boot into graphical mode or text mode, depending on the default runlevel (see Lab 4.5, "Using Runlevels"); when installed using the graphical installation program, Fedora's default is to present the graphical login display shown in Figure 2-1.

In the middle of the screen are four clickable controls:

Language
    Displays a dialog enabling you to select the default language for the session. This will not change the messages on the login display, but it will change the default for messages after you successfully log in. Where possible, messages will appear

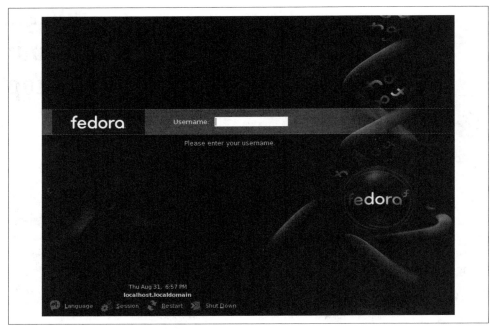

Figure 2-1. Fedora default login screen

in this selected language, but when no translation for the selected language is found, messages will appear in the default language for the application (usually English). After you enter a username and password, you will be given the choice of making the selected language the permanent default for that username, or using it only for one session.

Session

Permits you to select the session type: GNOME (the default) or a fail-safe session. If you install additional software for other desktop environments, such as KDE or Xfce, they will also appear on this menu.

Restart

Presents a confirmation dialog, then restarts the computer. Except for the kernel (the core of the operating system), almost everything in Fedora can be restarted without a reboot, so this option is usually used only when switching between operating systems in a dual-boot configuration.

Shut Down

Presents a confirmation dialog, then shuts down the system and turns the computer off.

If you press F10, a menu containing most of these options appears.

After you enter your username and password, the system will check to see if you have selected a session type or language different from your normal settings. If so, you will be asked if the change is temporary ("Just for This Session") or permanent ("Make default"). Click on one of the buttons to make your selection.

KDE or GNOME?

GNOME and KDE are built upon different technology and have been designed with different philosophies—as a GNOME or KDE advocate will quickly tell you. However, the most common operations are the same in both environments, and the GNOME and KDE communities collaborate on a number of key issues through freedesktop.org (*http://freedesktop.org*). The friendly rivalry between the groups spurs them on to develop innovations and refinements for both desktop environments.

Fedora installs and uses GNOME by default, and it is the best choice for most Fedora users. However, KDE is provided on the installation CDs/DVD, and it's worthwhile experimenting with both desktops to find the one that suits your style.

 Regardless of which GUI environment you use, you can run both KDE and GNOME programs and have them side by side on your display. For example, you can fire up Evolution (the GNOME email/calendar/scheduling application) and Konqueror (the KDE web browser) and cut and paste data between them. This interoperability is enabled by the X Window System, which provides the foundation for both GUIs.

Using the desktop

Once you have logged in, you will see the GNOME desktop, shown in Figure 2-2, or the KDE desktop, shown in Figure 2-3. The same default visual theme has been installed in both environments to provide a fairly consistent appearance and style.

Although the two desktop environments have some significant differences, their main features are very similar. Here is a summary; where KDE and GNOME differ in their naming conventions, I've used a unified terminology (which will mortify GNOME or KDE purists but allow the rest of us to talk about the desktop in a sane way):

Panel bar (panel)
   Fedora's default configuration of the GNOME desktop includes two panel bars, one at the top of the screen and one at the bottom. Fedora's KDE configuration includes one panel bar at the bottom of the screen. In both cases, you can move the panels to any edge of the screen by clicking on them (in an empty area of the panel) and dragging them. You can move an item within a panel by clicking on it with the middle mouse button (on a mouse with a wheel, depress the wheel; on a two-button mouse, press both buttons simultaneously) and dragging it to the desired location. To shove other items along while dragging an item, hold down the Shift key.

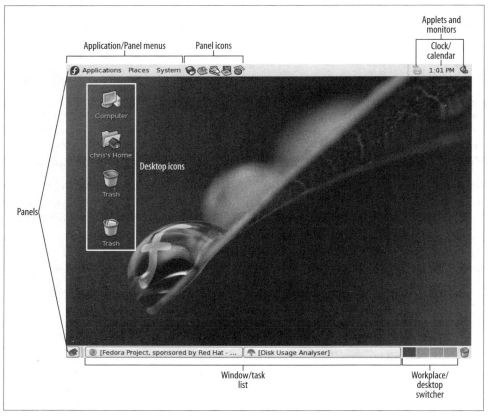

Figure 2-2. Fedora GNOME desktop.

 You can lock an item to a specific location within the panel by right-clicking and selecting the checkbox labeled "Lock to panel"; to unlock the item, deselect the checkbox.

Application/panel menus

GNOME's application menus appear on the left side of the top panel bar. Three menus are provided: Applications, which contains various useful programs; Places, which contains a list of location-oriented options, such as viewing your home directory or desktop, searching for files, or going to a recently edited document; and System, which includes preferences, administration, help, and options to log out or lock the display.

KDE's main panel menu is called the *K menu* (it's customized to look like an F in Fedora) and is located at the left side of the panel bar. It includes roughly the same applications as the GNOME menus, with some KDE programs replacing

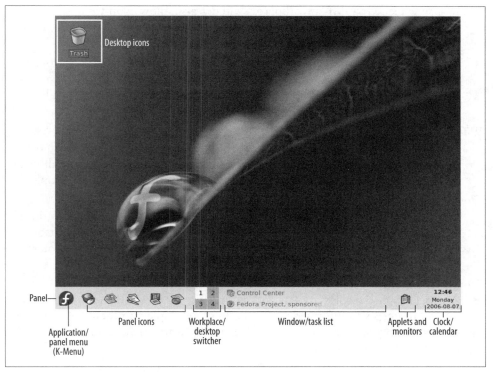

Figure 2-3. Fedora KDE desktop

GNOME programs (such as the KDE Control Center instead of the GNOME Preference options).

Both environments permit you to access the application menu by pressing Alt-F1.

Panel icons

Common applications have icons on the panel bar. To add an icon for another program to the panel, find the program on the application menu, then right-click and select "Add this Launcher to Panel" or "Add Item to Main Panel."

Desktop icons

A default set of icons appears on the desktop, including your Home directory, Computer, and Trash. You can create additional icons by dragging files from a file manager or links from a web browser and dropping them on the desktop. Desktop icons are stored in the directory named *~/Desktop*.

Workplace/desktop switcher

Both GNOME and KDE include *virtual desktop* (or *workspace*) capability, which means that the visible screen represents only one of several desktop workspaces. To switch between desktops, click on one of the desktop icons in the desktop switcher, or place your mouse pointer over the desktop switcher and roll the mouse wheel. GNOME's workplace switcher also allows you to drag a window outline from one desktop to another. GNOME's workspaces are initially arranged in a horizontal row, while KDE's are arranged in a 2×2 grid.

The virtual desktop facility provides a lot of screen area to arrange your windows; many users arrange their open applications according to tasks—for example, having email and messaging programs open on one desktop, a web browser on another, and OpenOffice.org on a third.

Window/task list
> When an application is running, an entry appears in the *window list* (or *task list*) in the bottom panel. KDE's default task list includes the windows in all virtual desktops; GNOME's includes only windows in the current virtual desktop.

Clock/calendar
> Click on the clock/calendar to display a calendar of the current month. The GNOME version of the calendar will also show you to-do list items from the Evolution scheduler program, and double-clicking on a date will take you to the Evolution schedule for that date.

Applets and monitors
> A panel can also display applets and monitors to let you perform operations easily and to keep you informed. To add additional applets to the panel bar, right-click an empty spot on the panel and select "Add to Panel," and then select the applet or monitor from the list displayed.

Managing windows

When you start a program by clicking on an icon or application menu item, one or more windows will appear. Almost all windows have a title bar and window controls, as shown on the window in Figure 2-4.

These are the basic controls:

Window border
> When you position the mouse cursor over any edge or corner of a resizable window, it will change to a double-ended arrow. Click and drag to resize the window.

Title bar
> Clicking and dragging the title bar will move the window. Double-clicking the title bar can be configured to maximize the window to fill the entire screen (the default for GNOME, similar to Windows) or to roll up the window into the title bar like a window shade (the default for KDE, similar to Mac OS 9).

Window menu
> Clicking on the icon on the left side of the titlebar will bring up the window menu. You can also view the window menu by right-clicking anywhere on the window border.

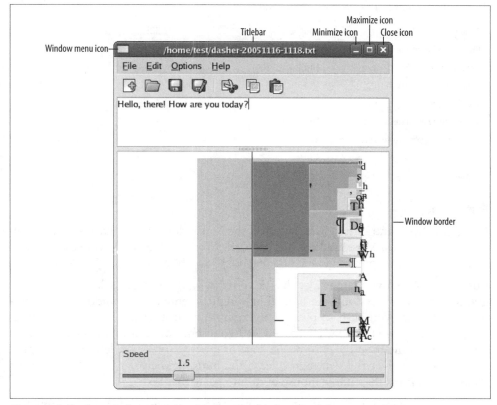

Figure 2-4. Dasher window, showing title bar and window controls

The window menu contains options for placing the window on top of all other windows; maximizing, minimizing, and closing the window; and placing the window on a specific workspace/desktop or making it appear on all workspaces.

Minimize, maximize, and close icons

There are three icons on the right side of the titlebar. Clicking the leftmost one will minimize the window (you can then access through the window list); clicking the middle one will maximize or unmaximize the window, and clicking on the rightmost one will close the window.

You can also minimize a window by clicking on its entry in the window list.

Table 2-1 lists a number of useful keyboard shortcuts available for window management.

Table 2-1. Keyboard shortcuts for window management

Action	GNOME	KDE
Display window menu	Alt-Space	Alt-F3
Close window	Alt-F4	Alt-F4
Unmaximize (Restore)	Alt-F5	—
Task list menu	—	Alt-F5
Move window using cursor keys	Alt-F7	—
Resize window using cursor keys	Alt-F8	—
Minimize	Alt-F9	—
Maximize	Alt-F10	—

Fast pasting

KDE, GNOME, and other GUIs based on the X Window System have standard cut-and-paste features. Most applications use Ctrl-X for cut, Ctrl-C for copy, and Ctrl-V for paste, which is compatible with the keyboard shortcuts on other platforms.

But the X Window System also has a faster way of pasting: select the text (or graphic) you want to duplicate by highlighting it, then click the middle mouse button at the point you wish to paste. For example, to fast-paste a web address from Firefox into an email being composed in Evolution, you can highlight the text in Firefox (place the mouse cursor at the start of the text, press the left mouse button, drag the cursor over the text, and release the button), then move to the Evolution window and press the middle mouse button to paste that text.

Taking this one step further, all of the Fedora web browsers allow you to highlight a web address in any application's window, then middle-click on a blank spot in the browser window to go directly to that page (with Firefox, you can also search using this technique, by highlighting a search term instead of an address—as long as there's no period in your search term).

> The clipboard used for cut/copy-and-paste operations is not used for fast pasting; instead, the *selection* (highlighted text or graphics) is directly duplicated (pasted) into the destination, and the clipboard contents are left intact.

Logging out

To log out of the desktop, press Ctrl-Alt-Delete. A confirmation dialog will appear, and then you will be logged out. You can also select the Log Out option from the application menu (System menu in GNOME).

How Does It Work?

The Fedora GUI is built in seven layers plus some toolkits or user-interface libraries, as shown in Figure 2-5.

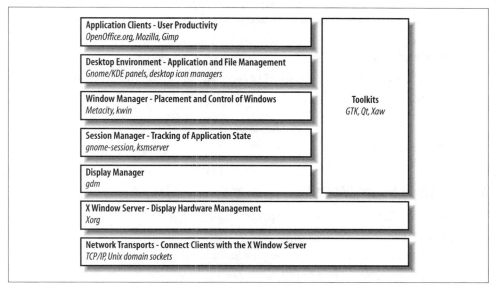

Figure 2-5. Layers in the Fedora GUI

This architecture fits in well with the Unix/Linux philosophy of writing programs that each do one task and do it well. The layers can be mixed and matched to serve various needs; for example, in the standard Fedora configuration, selecting a GNOME or KDE session changes the software used for the Session Manager, Window Manager, and Desktop Environment layers, even though the Display Manager and Application Clients remain the same. Likewise, if the system is configured for character-mode login, but the user starts the GUI after she has logged in, then the Display Manager layer is not used at all.

The X server manages all of the display hardware and is the only program that directly accesses the hardware. Client programs—which include any program that needs to communicate with the user, including the Display Manager, Session Manager, Window Manager, Desktop Environment, and Application Clients—communicate with the X server using the X protocol over a network connection. That means that any application that can be used on a local display can also be used on a remote display. This provides powerful flexibility for remote access.

The Toolkits are function libraries used to simplify development of GUI applications. GTK+ is the toolkit used by GNOME, and Qt is used by KDE applications (though not all applications that use these toolkits are full-blown GNOME or KDE applications, because both environments provide additional services).

What About...

...other desktops/GUIs?

Many other desktop/GUI environments are available—for example, Xfce, a nice but lightweight desktop environment included in the Fedora Extras repository. To install Xfce:

```
# yum groupinstall XFCE
```

You'll see an entry for Xfce in the Display Manager's Session menu (shown in Figure 2-1).

See Chapter 5 for more information on using *yum*.

Where Can I Learn More?

- The GNOME Project: *http://gnome.org*
- The KDE Project: *http://kde.org*
- The freedesktop.org project: *http://freedesktop.org*
- X.org, developers of the X Window System: *http://x.org*
- Information about many different window managers and desktop environments (both current and old): *http://xwinman.org/*

2.2 Customizing GNOME

Fedora's version of the GNOME desktop provides a convenient and attractive desktop environment, but by customizing it for the way you work you can increase your comfort and productivity.

How Do I Do That?

Almost all of the Fedora GNOME desktop, as well as desktop options that are not part of GNOME or KDE, can be configured using the System → Preferences menu; other portions of the desktop can be configured by right-clicking on a GNOME component.

This lab looks at the GNOME settings most commonly used to customize the desktop.

Most GNOME settings take effect immediately; you do not need to click an Apply button for a change to take effect.

Customizing the desktop appearance using themes

The GNOME desktop and the Metacity window manager (the default GNOME window manager) use themes to configure appearance. Each *theme* is a combination of configuration information, images, and software that provides a particular visual effect and behavior.

Three types of component themes are used on the desktop:

Application (or control) themes
> Configure the appearance of the controls: elements used by applications to build the graphical user interface, such as buttons, sliders, scrollbars, and text-entry fields.

Window border themes
> Used by the Metacity window manager to control the appearance of the window borders, title bar, and title bar buttons.

Icons
> Control the appearance of icons on the panel, desktop, application toolbars, and Nautilus file manager.

One component theme from each category can be combined into an overall *desktop theme*.

To change themes, select System → Preferences → Theme from the panel menu. The window shown on the left of Figure 2-6 will appear.

You can select a desktop theme from this list by clicking on it. The theme will start to load immediately, and the appearance of your desktop will change in a few seconds.

To create a custom combination of component themes, click the Theme Details button. The window shown on the right of Figure 2-6 will be displayed. There is a tab for each of the three component theme types. You can select a different theme for any of the components, and when you do, a Custom Theme entry will appear in the main Theme Preferences window. Your selection will take effect immediately so that you can preview the effect. Once you are satisfied with a combination of component themes, click on the Save Theme button to name the combination and save it as a desktop theme.

To install additional component themes, open a browser and go to *http://art.gnome.org/*, and open the Theme Preferences window in an adjacent part of the screen. When you find a theme on *art.gnome.org* that you wish to install, simply drag the download icon (a small floppy disk) from the browser window to the Theme Preferences window, and it will automatically be installed. You can then combine that component theme with others to produce a new desktop theme as described earlier.

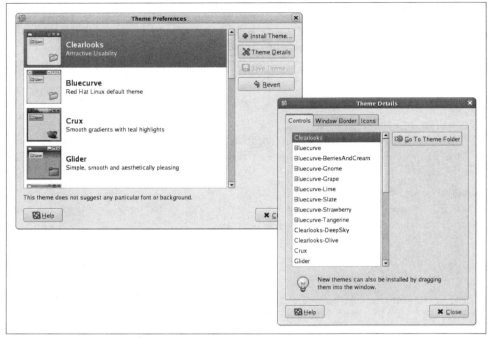

Figure 2-6. Theme preferences tool

Customizing the panels

Fedora's desktop is configured with two panels by default: one at the top of the screen containing the menus, icons, and applets, and one at the bottom of the screen containing the task list.

You can add another panel by right-clicking on an existing one and selecting New Panel. The new panel will appear on an edge of the screen that doesn't have a panel, or at the top of the screen if all of the edges are occupied. You can move it to another location by dragging it with the mouse.

To delete a panel, right-click on it and select "Delete this Panel." If there is anything on the panel, a confirmation dialog will appear before the panel is deleted.

To add items to a panel, right-click on the panel and select "Add to Panel." Although most of the options presented are applets or monitors, you can also add a *drawer*, which is like a panel that can be unfolded from another panel. A drawer is managed in the same way as a panel, by right-clicking on it.

To move an item around a panel, or move it to another panel, middle-click on the item and drag it (or right-click and use the Move menu option). To push along other icons, hold the shift key while dragging.

To delete an item from the panel, right-click on it and select "Remove from Panel."

To set a panel's properties, right-click it and select Properties. A small window will appear, containing two tabs, General and Background.

The General tab contains these settings:

Orientation

Selects one of the four screen edges for panel placement.

Size

Sets the panel size in pixels. 48 pixels is the default; the minimum size is 23 pixels, and the maximum is 120. Reducing this number will make the panel smaller and leave more screen space for your applications, while increasing this number will increase the panel size, making the icons bigger so that they are easier to see and click on. Experiment to find a value that works well for you; I find that 24 pixels is right for my eyes.

Expand

Selecting this checkbox makes the panel expand to fill the entire edge of the screen; deselecting it makes the panel just large enough to hold its contents.

Autohide

When selected, most of the panel will slide off the screen when not in contact with the mouse pointer, freeing up space for applications. To unhide the panel, place your mouse pointer over the part of the panel that is still visible.

Show hide buttons

Enables buttons at the end of the panel that can be clicked to make the panel slide off the screen (endwise). The "Arrows on Hide Buttons" checkbox will make the hide buttons bigger and add a graphical arrow to each one.

The Background tab lets you set the background color to the default for the current desktop theme, a solid color (which can have a pseudo-transparency effect applied using the Style slider), or a background image. This is almost always left at the default setting, which uses the desktop theme.

Customizing the desktop background

The menu option System → Preferences → Desktop Background is used to adjust the desktop background color and image—but most Fedora users get there using the shortcut of right-clicking on the desktop and selecting Change Desktop Background. Both methods cause the Desktop Background Preferences window to appear, shown in Figure 2-7.

You can change to any of the listed background images by clicking on it. To add your own image, drag and drop an image file from the Nautilus file manager, or click the Add Wallpaper button and enter the filename; to remove an image, highlight it and click the Remove button. If you don't want a background image, select the No Wallpaper option.

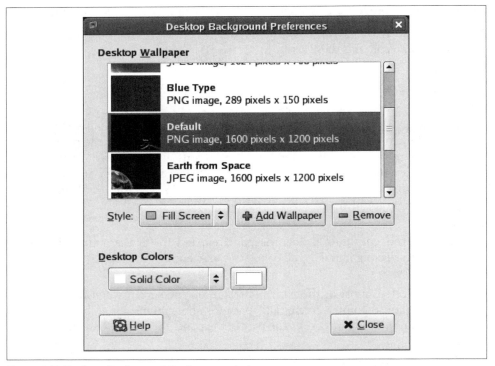

Figure 2-7. Desktop Background Preferences window

The Style control determines how the selected image will be displayed:

Centered

> The image is placed, full-size, in the center of the screen. If it's smaller than the screen, the remaining space is filled with the desktop color; if it's larger than the screen, it is automatically cropped.

Fill Screen

> The image is scaled in both the horizontal and vertical dimensions to fill the screen. This may result in some distortion of the image if its rectangular proportions (*aspect ratio*) don't match those of the screen.

Scaled

> The image is scaled, keeping the original aspect ratio, until it fills the screen. Any remaining space is filled with the desktop color. For photographs, this is a better choice than Fill Screen.

Tiled

> The image is placed in the upper-left corner of the screen and repeated as many times as necessary (both horizontally and vertically) to fill the screen.

The Desktop Colors control sets the desktop color style (*solid*, *horizontal gradient*, or *vertical gradient*) and the colors used for that style. The color or gradient selected here will fill any part of the background not covered by an image and will show through background images that have transparency.

Customizing the window manager's behavior

Select the menu option System → Preferences → Window to modify the behavior of the window manager, Metacity. Three options are presented in a window:

Select windows when the mouse moves over them
> This behavior is called *focus-follows-mouse* and is very popular with some long-time users of the X Window System. Normally, you need to click on a window to give it *focus*—in other words, the last window clicked is the window that receives keyboard input. If you select this checkbox, you can focus a window simply by placing your mouse pointer over it. This is convenient, but if your mouse pointer drifts to another window, you may end up typing into the wrong window.
>
> If you select "focus-follows-mouse," then you can optionally configure the window manager to automatically raise focused windows after a brief pause, so that they are on top of other windows.

Titlebar Action
> Configures the window manager to maximize or shade a window when the titlebar is double-clicked.

Movement Key
> This setting selects the modifier key for moving windows. If you hold down the selected modifier and click on a window, you can drag it to a new location.

Customizing Nautilus

The Nautilus file manager is configured using the Edit → Preferences option in any Nautilus window, or through the panel menu option System → Preferences → File Management. A configuration window will appear with five tabs, containing lots of options.

Here are some common customizations for Nautilus:

- The appearance of folder contents can be separately configured for each folder using the Nautilus toolbar. To configure default settings, set the View New Folders Using and the Arrange Items options on the Views tab.

- To disable the spatial behavior of Nautilus, select the Behavior tab and select the "Always Open in Browser Windows" checkbox.

- To enable the direct deletion of files (instead of placing them in the trash, which requires the trash to be emptied before the disk space is freed up), select

"Include a Delete Command that Bypasses Trash" on the Behavior tab. Right-clicking on a file will now expose both the normal "Move to Trash" option and a new Delete option.

Customizing keyboard shortcuts

Both mice and keyboards are effective input devices—but switching between them can significantly slow you down. A good set of keyboard shortcuts enables you to perform common operations without switching to the mouse.

Fedora's GNOME configuration contains a good set of keyboard shortcuts. To change shortcuts or add new ones, select the menu option System → Preferences → Keyboard Shortcuts, which displays the window shown in Figure 2-8.

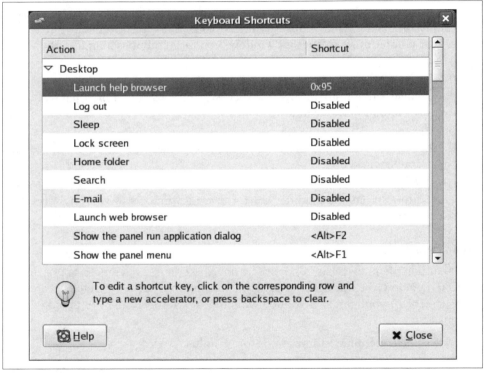

Figure 2-8. GNOME Keyboard Shortcuts window

This window shows a number of actions on the desktop and the shortcut key for each. To change a shortcut, click on an entry. The shortcut for that entry will change to read New Accelerator. Press the key or key combination that you wish to use for that keyboard shortcut; if the shortcut is not already in use, it will be assigned to the selected action, and if it is in use, the conflict will be displayed in an error dialog.

To remove a keyboard shortcut, click on an entry, and then press Backspace.

 If you have a "multimedia" keyboard with keys for sound control and common applications, you can in most cases use those keys as shortcuts. However, the Keyboard Shortcuts window will show these keys as hexadecimal codes, as shown in the highlighted line in Figure 2-8. Not all keys can be used as shortcuts because some multimedia keyboards are internally divided to act as two separate keyboards, with multimedia keys being sent to a different output. In a few rare cases, the multimedia keys don't generate normal keyboard scancodes at all.

How Does It Work?

GNOME stores most of its configuration in hidden directories in each user's home directory. Most configuration options and settings are stored, using the Gconf system, in XML files located in ~/.gconf.

Themes consist of a large number of files, stored in specific directories according to the type of theme and whether the theme is installed for personal use or system-wide use, as shown in Table 2-2. The GNOME theme configuration tools perform a personal installation of themes.

Table 2-2. Directories for themes and icons

Theme type	Personal installation	System-wide installation
Icon themes	~/.icons	/usr/share/icons/
Application/control and Window Manager themes	~/.themes	/usr/share/themes/

When a new user is created, the files and directories in */etc/skel* are copied to the new user's home directory; you can include default configuration settings by placing them into that directory. For example, files in */etc/skel/.gconf* are placed in ~/.gconf when a new account is created.

GNOME panels are managed by the *gnome-panel* program, and the desktop is managed by Nautilus.

What About...

...making a theme available to all users?

After testing component themes, you can move them from your personal theme directories to the system-wide directories:

```
# mv /home/yourusername/.icons/* /usr/share/icons/
# mv /home/yourusername/.themes/* /usr/share/themes/
# chown -R root:root /usr/share/{icons,themes}
```

Where Can I Learn More?

- The GNOME desktop manual; press F1 in any GNOME application, select System → Help, or enter the command yelp.
- GNOME homepage: *http://gnome.org*
- freedesktop.org: *http://freedesktop.org*

2.3   Customizing KDE

Fedora's KDE defaults are altered from the original upstream developers' version—even more so than GNOME is modified from its upstream version. For this reason, some die-hard KDE fans don't like working on a Fedora system.

Like GNOME, KDE can be tweaked, fiddled, and configured to look and work just the way you want.

How Do I Do That?

Most KDE configuration is performed through the KDE Control Center, which is found on the K menu. The Control Center is shown in Figure 2-9.

 If you do not have KDE installed, you can install it; see Lab 5.3, "Using Repositories."

Along the lefthand side of this window, there is a collapsible menu of configuration categories; each category contains several subcategories, which can be revealed or hidden by clicking on the +/- icon in front of the category name. Each subcategory is handled by a separate *configuration module*. When you click on a configuration category, the configuration module for that category is shown on the righthand side of the window.

You can also configure some desktop components by right-clicking on them. For example, right-clicking on the desktop and selecting Configure Desktop will bring up a subset of the Control Center options, which is useful for changing the appearance of the desktop.

Unlike GNOME, KDE settings are not usually automatically applied; you must click on the Apply button before your changes take effect.

 An alternative, express way to change basic KDE desktop settings is to select Settings → Desktop Settings Wizard (or enter the command kpersonalizer), which will walk you through the process of setting the most common desktop options.

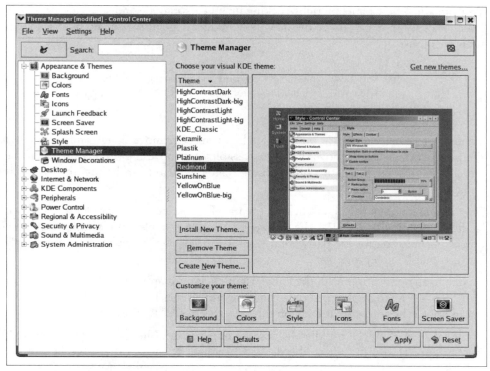

Figure 2-9. KDE Control Center

Customizing the desktop appearance using themes

To configure KDE themes, select Appearance & Themes → Theme Manager in the Control Center (Figure 2-9). You can select a theme from among the options listed by clicking on it and then clicking Apply.

To install a new theme, click the "Get new themes…" link in the upper-right corner to open the Konqueror web browser with the *kde-look* home page (*http://kde-look.org*). Select a theme that is packaged into a *.kth* file and download it to your system. Click the Install New Theme button within the KDE Control Center and open the downloaded file to install it into the list of available themes.

> Relatively few themes are packaged in the *.kth* format required by the Theme Manager. Themes supplied in source format cannot be installed by the Theme Manager and must be configured manually.

Customizing the panels

KDE panels are configured in much the same way as GNOME panels.

You can add a new panel by right-clicking on an existing one and selecting Add New Panel → Panel. You can move the new panel to any edge of the screen by dragging it with the mouse.

 The Add New Panel facility can add special panel types that are pre-populated with specific tools; for details, right-click on a panel and select Help.

To delete a panel, right-click on any panel and select Remove Panel, and then select the panel you wish to remove. It is not possible to remove the original panel. If the panel contains anything, a confirmation dialog will appear before the panel is deleted.

To add items to a panel, right-click on the panel and select "Add Applet to panel" or "Add Application to panel"—the difference being that *applets* run within the panel, displaying information or performing useful actions, while *applications* are simply buttons that launch programs.

To delete an application from the panel, right-click on it and select "Remove application." To delete an applet, place your mouse cursor over it, which will cause a small bar to appear beside it; right-click on this bar, and select "Remove applet."

To move a panel object, middle-click on the object (or on the bar beside the object if it is an applet) and drag it to the desired location. To push other objects around, hold down the Shift key while dragging; to move between bars, left-click and drag.

To set a panel's properties, right-click on a panel and select Configure Panel, which displays the window in Figure 2-10. You can also start the KDE Control Center and select Desktop → Panels, in which case the window arrangement is modified slightly to fit into the design of the Control Center.

In either case, you will have buttons or tabs for Arrangement, Hiding, Menus, and Appearance.

The Arrangement section contains these settings:

Position
> The location of the panel on the screen. There are twelve buttons, enabling you to place the panel in the center or either corner of any edge of the screen (for example, if you place the panel on the bottom edge of the screen, you can place it in the left corner, the center, or the right corner). The position along an edge has no effect if the panel length has been set to 100%.

Length
> The percent of the screen edge that will be occupied by the panel. The default is 100%, where the panel fills the entire length of one side of the screen. The checkbox labeled "Expand as required to fit contents" makes the specified length the minimum.

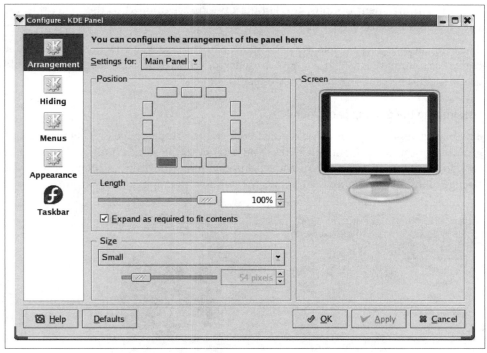

Figure 2-10. KDE panel configuration window

Size

> The thickness of the panel in pixels. The Fedora default is rather big, so I usually set this to Small or Tiny.

The settings affect the panel selected by the "Settings for" drop-down menu. As you adjust the settings, the preview in the Screen section is updated to show your changes.

The Hiding section contains three settings:

Hide Mode

> Configures the panel to be displayed all the time unless manually hidden, to hide itself after a period of time, or to be coverable by other windows. To reveal an automatically hidden panel, place the mouse cursor along the edge of the screen where the panel would normally appear.

Panel-Hiding Buttons

> Allows you to add buttons to the left and right (or top and bottom) ends of the panel.

Panel Animation

> Configures the animated sliding of the panel when it is hidden or revealed. The panel animation is a cute effect, and it serves the practical purpose of helping the user understand what's happening to the panel.

Like the Arrangement options, the Hiding options are applied to the panel selected with the "Settings for" control.

The Appearance section lets you configure icon mouseover effects (which include really big, animated tool tips), tool tips helps, colored or patterned button backgrounds, and a pseudo-transparency effect for panels.

Customizing the desktop background

The background image or color is adjusted using the Appearance & Themes → Background option in the Control Center. You can get to the same configuration module by right-clicking on the desktop and selecting Configure Desktop, then selecting the Background button. Figure 2-11 shows the window that appears.

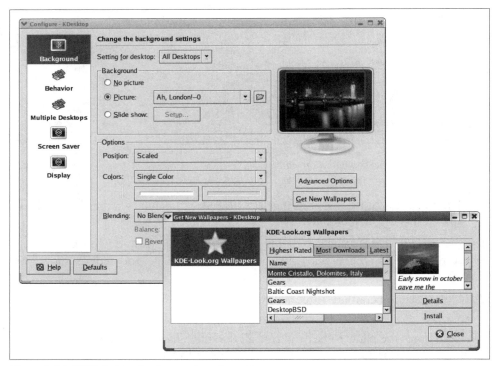

Figure 2-11. KDE desktop background configuration

You can individually configure the desktop background for each virtual desktop. This can make it easier to identify which virtual desktop is currently displayed, but it can use a lot of memory and increases the amount of time it takes to switch desktops. The "Settings for Desktop" control selects the desktop to be configured; use All Desktops to use the same image on all of the virtual desktops.

In this configuration module, there are two sections:

Background
> Selects a picture or slideshow to use for the image background.

Options
> Sets the background image position, scaling, and tiling (repeat) options; background colors, patterns, and gradients; and blending between the background image and background colors/patterns.

There are also two special buttons:

Advanced Options
> Permits you to use a program to draw the desktop background (such as *kwebdesktop*, which uses a web page for the desktop background), to set the color and shadow for the desktop icon text, and to set the size of the background cache.

Get New Wallpapers
> Provides a simple way to download wallpapers from *http://kde-look.org*, using the window shown at bottom right in Figure 2-11. A list of available wallpapers appears (you can use the tabs to change the sort order); clicking on one will present a preview, and clicking Install will add that wallpaper to the Picture list in the KDesktop Background window.

Customizing the window manager's behavior

To configure window-manager behavior, right-click on a title bar and select Configure Window Behavior. Figure 2-12 shows the window that appears. You can access the same options through the Control Center using the Appearance & Themes → Window Decorations, Desktop → Window Behavior, and the Desktop → Window-Specific Settings options.

The KDE window manager, *kwin*, offers extensive configuration options:

Window Decorations
> Enables you to select the window-manager theme and the buttons that will be placed in the title bar. Some themes have additional customization options, such as adjustable border width.

Actions
> Configures the actions performed when the various mouse buttons are clicked on the title bar and active or inactive windows. The Titlebar Actions tab contains settings for the action that will be taken when the user clicks on the window title bar, frame, and maximize button.

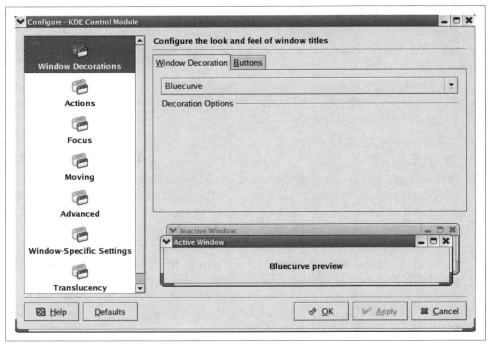

Figure 2-12. KDE window-manager behavior configuration

Focus

The window with focus—also called the *active* window—receives keyboard input. This section selects the focus policy:

Click to Focus

Click on a window to give it focus.

Focus Follows Mouse

Place the mouse cursor over a window to give it focus. You can also change focus with Alt-Tab or Shift-Alt-Tab.

Focus Under Mouse

Same as Focus Follows Mouse, but Alt-Tab/Shift-Alt-Tab does not change the window focus (though it will raise other windows to the top), and new windows will not receive focus.

Focus Strictly Under Mouse

Same as Focus Under Mouse, but moving the mouse pointer over the desktop background (not over any window) will unfocus *all* windows instead of leaving the last window focused.

If you select a focus policy other than "Click to Focus," you can configure a delay between when a window receives focus and when it raises, as well as whether focused windows are raised at all (placed in front of other windows).

The Navigation section enables you to set options related to keyboard navigation between windows (Alt-Tab/Shift-Alt-Tab).

Moving

Configures behavior when windows are moved. For best performance on a slower system (or a remote connection), disable the options "Display content in moving windows," "Display content in resizing windows," and "Animate minimize and restore"—but on a fast machine, these options can provide useful user feedback. The Snap Zone settings make it easier to align windows with other windows or with the edge of the screen.

Advanced

Configures Shading (window roll-up) animation and automatic unrolling when under the mouse; Active Desktop Borders, which permit you to move off the desktop onto an adjacent virtual desktop; and Focus Stealing Prevention, which attempts to eliminate unpleasant surprises when you're typing and a new window appears (which in normal circumstances would automatically get focus). Right-click on the control and select "What's This?" to see a detailed description of the options.

Window-Specific Settings

Enables you to configure *kwin* to handle some applications differently than others. To create special settings for a window, ensure that the window is presently on the screen, and then click New in that window. A window labeled Edit Window-Specific Settings will appear; click the Detect button, and then click on the window you wish to configure. You can then use the provided tabs to configure your desired settings, such as specific window geometry (size and location) or preferences (e.g., causing the window to stay above or below other windows).

Translucency

Enables transparency and shadow effects for windows. This uses the COMPOSITE capability of the X server, which requires a modern graphics card for good operation; you can then use these settings to configure the transparency, shadows, and fade effects. To enable the COMPOSITE extension, see Lab 2.4, "Fine-Tuning Your Display Configuration."

Customizing Konqueror

Since Konqueror was designed as both a web browser and a file manager, it offers many options for customization. You can access these configuration options by selecting Settings → Configure Konqueror from within Konqueror, or within the KDE Control Panel by selecting KDE Components → File Manager. The arrangement of the configuration options is slightly different, depending on the route you take get there; Figure 2-13 shows both layouts.

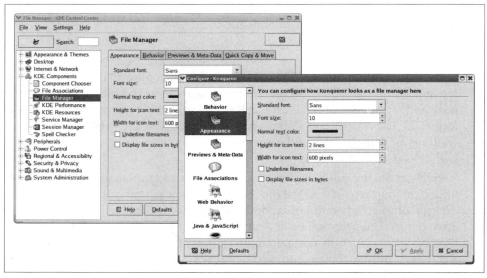

Figure 2-13. Konqueror configuration window; Control Panel version (left) and Konqueror Settings version (right)

Here are some of the most useful customizations:

- On the Behavior tab/button, the checkbox "Open folders in separate windows" enables a mode similar to the Nautilus spatial mode, which displays each folder separately—but, unlike Nautilus, window locations are not remembered on a per-directory basis by Konqueror.

- Also on the Behavior tab/button, the checkbox "Show 'Delete' context menu entries which bypass the trashcan" enables you to directly delete files without the two-step process of moving them to trash and then emptying the trash (two-step deletion gives you a chance to review deletions before finalizing them but does not free up disk space right away).

- The Previews tab/button configures the types of files and the maximum size of files for which previews will be generated. Setting the maximum size to a lower value will speed up the display of large directories of big files. Enabling "Show file tips" and "Show previews in file tips" on the Behavior tab/button will make Konqueror display an extended preview whenever you hover the mouse pointer over a file icon.

- The Quick Copy & Move tab (Control Center only) enables "Copy to" and "Move to" options on context menus. This is a useful feature that offers recent and common directories as copy/move targets.

Customizing keyboard shortcuts

Keyboard shortcuts are configured using the Control Center option Regional & Accessibility → Keyboard Shortcuts, shown in Figure 2-14. To add or change a shortcut, double-click on an action in the list of actions under the Shortcut Schemes tab or a command under the Command Shortcuts tab. Enter the new shortcut (such as Ctrl-Shift-H) and click OK, or click on the whisk-like icon beside the Shortcut field to clear it.

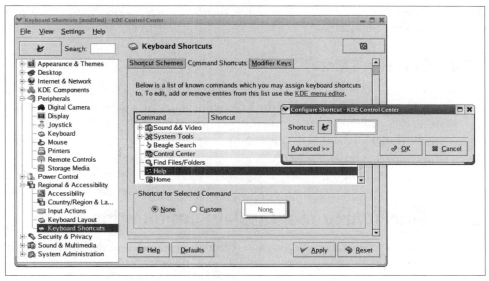

Figure 2-14. KDE keyboard shortcut configuration

How Does It Work?

KDE configuration options are stored in text files in ~/.kde/share/config. The format of these files varies slightly, but most take the form of name and value pairs divided into sections denoted by section titles in square brackets:

```
[$Version]
update_info=kfmclient_3_2.upd:kfmclient_3_2

[HTML Settings]
AutomaticDetectionLanguage=0

[KonqMainWindow Toolbar Speech Toolbar]
IconText=IconOnly
Index=4

...(snip)...

[SearchBar]
Mode=1
```

Since these are text files, they may be copied from one account to another.

What About...

...setting the defaults for new users?

The directory */etc/skel* acts as a template, or *skeleton*, for new account creation. Any KDE configuration files placed in */etc/skel/.kde/share/config* will get copied to new user accounts automatically.

Where Can I Learn More?

- Start with the KDE online manual, accessed through the Help option on the K menu. The first time you access the KDE online manual, you will be asked if you wish to create the index; select the Application Manual and click Build Index to create the index (this takes only a minute or two).
- KDE home page: *http://kde.org*
- freedesktop.org: *http://freedesktop.org*

2.4   Fine-Tuning Your Display Configuration

Fedora's Anaconda installer detects and configures most display hardware optimally. However, there are some situations where it's necessary to override the default configuration to set up a desired display resolution and color depth.

How Do I Do That?

Fedora's display configuration program is called *system-config-display*.

If you have a working graphical display, you can start this program by selecting System → Administration → Display from the panel menus (System Settings → Display in KDE). You'll need to enter the root password when prompted.

If you don't have a working graphical display, or you've booted into character mode (see Lab 4.5, "Using Runlevels"), you can start this program from the command line:

```
$ system-config-display
You are attempting to run "system-config-display" which requires administrative
privileges, but more information is needed in order to do so.
Password for root: secret
```

The graphical display will be started in a very basic mode so that the graphical configuration dialog can be displayed.

 system-config-display uses the existing display configuration as a starting point. If the existing configuration does not work at all, you may need to delete it to force *system-config-display* to start from scratch:

```
# rm /etc/X11/xorg.conf
```

Whether started from the menu or the command line, the window shown in Figure 2-15 will be displayed.

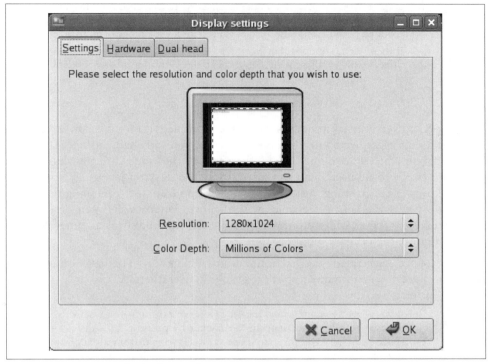

Figure 2-15. system-config-display window

This dialog has three tabs:

Settings

Selects the default resolution and color depth for the system. The maximum display resolution is limited by the monitor setting on the Hardware tab; the color depth should almost always be set to "Millions of Colors," which enables 24-bit color.

Hardware

Selects the monitor and video card type installed in your system. The Anaconda installer will have preselected the best match in most cases, but in some display configurations—including those with keyboard-video-mouse (KVM) switches, video splitters, or old monitors—the monitor type cannot be determined automatically. If your monitor does not appear on the list, select the closest option from the Generic CRT or Generic LCD categories.

In most cases, the exact video card model is not important; it's the chipset that counts. From your video card documentation, find out the chipset manufacturer and model (such as NVIDIA GeForce 4 MX) and select that option from the list. In many cases, an exact match is not required because one video driver is used for a wide range of chipsets.

If there are no options that work for your video card, select the VESA driver, which will provide basic capabilities on almost any modern video card.

Dual head

The X.org server used in Fedora can drive multiple monitors. If you have a second monitor connected to a *second video card*, you can enable it here. Select the checkbox labeled "Use dual head," then specify the video card, resolution, and color depth to be used. You can also specify the desktop layout as "Individual desktops" or "Spanning desktops"; for most applications, "Spanning desktops" is most versatile, since it enables you to move windows between desktops or even have a window fill both desktops. The second monitor is assumed to be to the right of the primary monitor.

Once you have selected the desired configuration, click OK. The new configuration will take effect the next time you start the graphical user interface.

If you logged in graphically, the GUI won't restart until you restart the system. You can force it to restart sooner by pressing Ctrl-Alt-Backspace—but you will lose any unsaved data, so exit from all applications first. (This key sequence abruptly aborts the X server process and normally should not be used to exit from a graphical session).

How Does It Work?

system-config-display changes the X server configuration file, */etc/X11/xorg.conf*. If necessary, it creates an entirely new file. Most of the information for this file is determined from the hardware by probing.

The *xorg.conf* file contains configuration information for four types of devices:

- Video card
- Monitor
- Keyboard
- Pointer (typically a mouse, but possibly a trackball, graphics tablet, touch screen, light pen, or some other positional input device)

The *xorg.conf* file is a plain-text file and can be edited by hand (see Lab 4.4, "Basic Text Editing Using vi"). Be sure to make a backup copy before making any changes.

You can find a detailed description of the configuration options in *xorg.conf*'s manpage (see Lab 4.2, "Accessing Online Documentation"):

```
$ man xorg.conf
```

The file is divided into sections, each of which looks like this:

```
Section "SectionName"
    Configuration Directives
EndSection
```

The most commonly used sections in this file are shown in Table 2-3.

Table 2-3. Common xorg.conf section names

Name	Description
Monitor	Monitor specifications.
InputDevice	Keyboard configuration.
	Pointer device configuration (mice, graphics tablets, touch screens).
Device	Video card configuration.
Screen	Associates a Device with a Monitor and defines the available resolutions and color depth.
ServerLayout	Associates one or more Screen sections with two or more InputDevice sections. Different ServerLayouts can be defined to combine devices in different ways for use at different times; for example, a laptop can have a ServerLayout that specifies that the internal+external displays should be used, and another one that specifies only the internal display.
Files	Location of auxiliary files such as fonts, drivers, and color tables.
ServerFlags	Flags to control the overall operation of the X server. The flags may alternatively be placed in the ServerLayout sections if they apply to some ServerLayouts but not to others.
Extensions	Enables/disables extensions to the server capabilities.
Module	Loads additional modules. (Modules may provide extensions, but extensions don't have to exist as separate modules.)
Modes	Defines special video modes (rarely required).
DRI	Direct Render Interface (DRI) device configuration, used for some 3-D gaming.

Here is a typical *xorg.conf* file:

```
Section "ServerLayout"
        Identifier     "single head configuration"
        Screen      0  "Screen0" 0 0
        InputDevice    "Keyboard0" "CoreKeyboard"
        InputDevice    "Synaptics" "CorePointer"
        InputDevice    "Mouse0"    "AlwaysCore"
EndSection

Section "Files"
        FontPath       "unix/:7100"
EndSection
```

```
Section "Module"
        Load   "glx"
        Load   "dri"
        Load   "synaptics"
EndSection

Section "InputDevice"
        Identifier   "Keyboard0"
        Driver       "kbd"
        Option       "XkbModel" "pc105"
        Option       "XkbLayout" "us"
EndSection

Section "InputDevice"
        Identifier   "Mouse0"
        Driver       "mouse"
        Option       "Device" "/dev/input/mice"
        Option       "Protocol" "IMPS/2"
        Option       "ZAxisMapping" "4 5"        # Scrollwheel support
        Option       "Emulate3Buttons" "yes"     # L+R buttons count as middle
EndSection

Section "InputDevice"
        Identifier   "Synaptics"                 # Laptop touchpad
        Driver       "synaptics"
        Option       "Device" "/dev/input/mice"
        Option       "Protocol" "auto-dev"
        Option       "Emulate3Buttons" "yes"
EndSection

Section "Monitor"
        Identifier   "Monitor0"
        VendorName   "Monitor Vendor"        # Just for reference
        ModelName    "LCD Panel 1400x1050"   # Just for reference
        HorizSync    31.5 - 90.0             # Horiz. sync in kHz
        VertRefresh  59.0 - 75.0             # Vert. refresh in Hz
        Option       "dpms"                  # Enables power management
EndSection

Section "Device"
        Identifier   "Videocard0"
        Driver       "nv"
        VendorName   "Videocard vendor"      # Just for reference
        BoardName    "nVidia Corporation NV34M [GeForce FX Go5200]"  # Ditto
EndSection

Section "Screen"
        Identifier "Screen0"
        Device      "Videocard0"             # Associates the video card
        Monitor     "Monitor0"               # with this monitor
        DefaultDepth    24                   # Default is 24-bit colour
        SubSection "Display"
                Viewport   0 0               # "0 0" is almost always used
                Depth     24                 # This section used by default
                Modes      "1400x1050" "1280x1024" "1024x768" "800x600" "640x480"
```

```
                                        # Change modes with Ctrl-Alt-+/-
         EndSubSection

# This next SubSection is not selected by default (because of the
# DefaultDepth line in the previous section). However, it would be used if the
# -depth option was specified on the X server command line,
# overriding the DefaultDepth setting.

         SubSection "Display"
                 Viewport   0 0
                 Depth      16                    # Because default is 24-bit,
                 Modes      "800x600" "640x480"   # ...this will usually be ignored
         EndSubSection

EndSection

Section "DRI"                                     # Configures DRI devices...
       Group        0                             # Root (user ID 0) owns them
       Mode         0666                          # Readable/writable by all
EndSection

Section "Extensions"
       Option "Composite" "Enabled"               # Enables transparency, etc.
EndSection
```

To change the default color depth, edit the DefaultDepth line in the Screen section (make sure that a SubSection for that depth exists in the Screen section of the file). Values that work with most video cards include 8, 16, and 24 bits; the number of colors available is 2^{depth}.

Similarly, the default resolution is controlled by the Modes entry in SubSection "Display" with the same Depth as DefaultDepth.

For example, to change the configuration in this example from a 24-bit (16-million-color) to 16 bit (65,536 color) depth, and to change the resolution to 800×600, change the DefaultDepth to 16 and then change the Modes line in the SubSection for 16-bit color:

```
Section "Screen"
        Identifier "Screen0"
        Device     "Videocard0"                   # Associates the video card
        Monitor    "Monitor0"                      # with this monitor
        DefaultDepth    16                         # Default is 16-bit colour
        SubSection "Display"
                Viewport   0 0                     # "0 0" is almost always used
                Depth      24                      # This section used by default
                Modes      "1400x1050" "1280x1024" "1024x768" "800x600" "640x480"
                                                   # Change modes with Ctrl-Alt-+/-
        EndSubSection
        SubSection "Display"
                Viewport   0 0
                Depth      16
                Modes      "800x600"
        EndSubSection
EndSection
```

The Composite extension, enabled in the Extensions section of the file, powers the use of advanced visual effects, including transparency. Not all video drivers support Composite.

What About...

...per-user display resolution settings?

The GNOME menu option System → Preferences → Screen Resolution sets the default resolution and refresh rate for a particular user (in KDE, select Control Center from the panel menu, then click on Display under Peripherals; be sure to select the checkbox labeled "Apply settings on KDE startup").

The system-wide resolution setting will be used for the user login display; individual user settings will take effect after the user logs in. The color depth can't be set this way because the architecture of the X Window System requires the color depth to be a system-wide setting.

...creating the xorg.conf file without using system-config-display?

The X server itself is capable of generating a reasonable *xorg.conf* file, which you can then fine-tune by manually editing it:

```
# X -configure :1
```

 The system will automatically start an X server using display number :0. Additional X servers can be started as long as they each use a unique display number—which is why :1 was used in this command.

The new configuration file will be placed in */root/xorg.conf.new*. In order to use it, you'll need to link the name */dev/mouse* to the default mouse device:

```
# ln -s /dev/input/mice /dev/mouse
```

You can then test the new configuration:

```
$ X -config /root/xorg.conf.new
```

This will present a blank display with an X-shaped mouse pointer. If the display looks right and you can move the pointer with your mouse, then go ahead and install this new configuration file as the default configuration:

```
# mv /root/X11/xorg.conf /root/X11/xorg.conf.backup
# mv /root/xorg.conf.new /etc/X11/xorg.conf
```

You can fine-tune this configuration either manually or by using tools such as *system-config-display*.

…using multiple mice and keyboards with one display?

The default X server configuration will work with all USB pointer devices and keyboards plugged into the system. The devices will work in parallel; for example, if you have two mice, moving either one will move the onscreen pointer, and if you have two keyboards, typing on either will send characters to the display.

Most keyboards will be detected as soon as they are plugged in, but other keyboards will be detected only when the system starts. For example, I have a secondary French Canadian USB keyboard and a USB calculator/numeric keypad; the French Canadian keyboard is detected as soon as it is plugged in, but the numeric keypad must be plugged in during boot in order to be detected properly. Special features of advanced pointers (such as touchpads) will not be configured automatically unless those devices are plugged in when *system-config-display* is run.

…a nonstandard monitor, such as a widescreen laptop display?

In most cases, these displays can be probed automatically using VESA standard protocols. If not, edit */etc/X11/xorg.conf*, find the Monitor section, and enter the HorizSync (horizontal scan frequency) and VertRefresh (vertical scan/refresh frequency) values specified in your monitor documentation:

```
Section "Monitor"
        Identifier     "Monitor0"
        VendorName     "Monitor Vendor"
        ModelName      "Unknown Monitor"
        HorizSync      32.00 - 72.0              # Horiz. sync in kHz
        VertRefresh    58.0 - 62.0               # Vert. refresh in Hz
EndSection
```

Next, edit the default resolution to match your hardware:

```
Section "Screen"
        Identifier "Screen0"
        Device     "Videocard0"
        Monitor    "Monitor0"
        DefaultDepth     24
        SubSection "Display"
                Depth     24
                Modes        "1280x800"
        EndSubSection
EndSection
```

Where Can I Learn More?

- The manpages for X (general information about the X Window System), Xserver (general information about the X window server), Xorg (specific information about the X.org version of the Xserver used in Fedora Core), and *xorg.conf* (information about the X server configuration file).

2.5 Configuring Printing

In order to print from your Fedora system, you have to configure at least one *print queue* to manage documents waiting to be printed. For printers directly connected to your computer, this process is fully automatic, and for other printers (such as those on your network), it is very simple.

How Do I Do That?

Select the menu option System → Administration → Printing (in KDE, it is Administration → Printing). You will be prompted to enter the root password, and then the printer configuration window will appear, as shown in Figure 2-16. If any print queues have been previously defined, they will be listed on the left side of the window, grouped according to connection type; if you click on one of these printers, the configuration details for that printer will appear on the right.

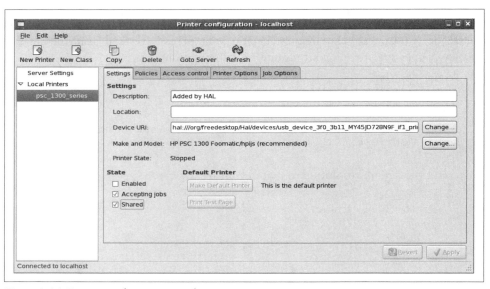

Figure 2-16. Printer configuration window

Add a new print queue

USB and parallel printers, as well as network printers that use the Internet Print Protocol (IPP), will be detected and configured automatically; you can adjust the printer configuration by editing the values in the main printer-configuration window (Figure 2-16) and then clicking Apply.

Other printers must be configured manually. Click on the New Printer icon to access the window shown in Figure 2-17.

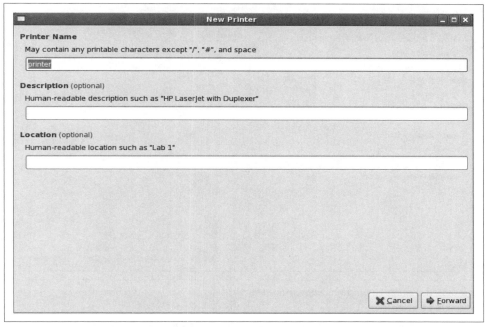

Figure 2-17. New Printer window

Enter the name of the printer, which should be short and contain no spaces. I recommend using the generic printer type followed by a number (e.g., *laser3* or *inkjet0*); even if you only have one printer now, you may add more in the future. If desired, you can add verbose description and location information. Click Forward to proceed to the connection configuration step, shown in Figure 2-18.

The Devices list shows all detected local printers, plus serial ports and common network printing protocols. Select the appropriate option; for network printers, you will need to enter the IP address or hostname as well as the printer or queue name. Press Forward to proceed to the driver configuration step, shown in the left side of Figure 2-19. Select the printer manufacturer, then click Forward; on the next display (shown on the right side of Figure 2-19), select the printer model. Use the Comments buttons to display information about the printer, driver, or PPD file.

The Drivers list may present more than one driver option. In almost all cases, it is best to use the default driver.

Click Forward, then click Apply on the confirmation dialog that appears.

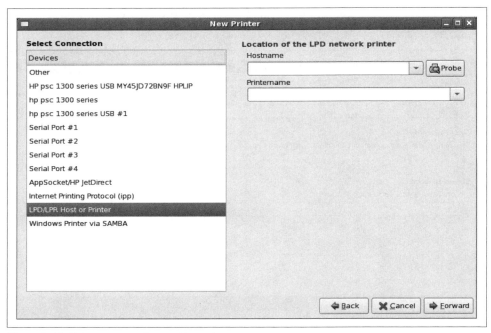

Figure 2-18. Printer connection configuration

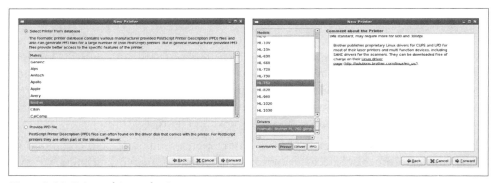

Figure 2-19. Printer driver selection

Edit an existing print queue

To change an existing queue configuration, select the printer in the main window
(Figure 2-16) and edit the option values on the tabs:

Settings

Configures the printer description, location, connection details, printer driver,
and printer status (enabled/accepting/shared). *Enabled* means the the queue
contents will be sent to the printer; *accepting* means that new print requests may
be enqueued.

Policies

> Configures starting and ending banner pages (which identify each print job) and the action to be taken when a printer error occurs.

Access control

> Used to restrict printer access to specific users, or to prevent specific users from accessing the printer.

Printer options

> Configures the default settings for printer features such as stapling, duplexing, media, ink cartridge type, and resolution.

Set the default print queue

The default print queue is used for all print requests that do not specify a queue. To set the default, select a printer and then click Make Default Printer. Click Apply to activate your change.

Printing

The command *lpr* (line printer requester) is used to place a print request into a queue. When used from the command line, *lpr* can accept input from standard input or from a specified file. For example, to print the file *output.ps*:

```
$ lpr output.ps
```

Or to print the calendar for the year, generated by the cal -y command:

```
$ cal -y | lpr
```

To specify a specific print queue (such as *laser3*), add the -P argument along with the name of the queue:

```
$ lpr -P laser3 output.ps
$ cal -y | lpr -P laser3
```

You can view the status of a print queue, including the documents in the queue, by clicking on the printer icon that appears in the notification area of the GNOME panel bar. The window shown in Figure 2-20 will appear; this window shows all print requests made by you on all print queues. To delete a document from the queue, right-click on it and select the Cancel document option.

The lpq command provides another way of viewing a queue's contents:

```
$ lpq
inkjet0 is ready
no entries
```

While the graphical Document print-status window shows requests by one user on all queues, lpq shows requests by all users on a single queue. The output in the previous example shows that there are no documents in the default queue *inkjet0*. You can specify a specific printer queue using the -P argument:

```
$ lpq -P laser3
laser3 is ready and printing
```

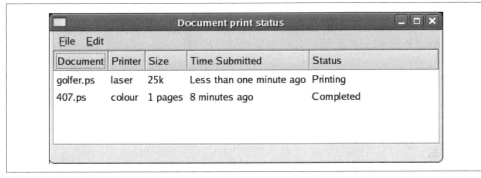

Figure 2-20. Document print-status window

```
Rank    Owner   Job     File(s)                 Total Size
active  chris   91      report.ps               124928 bytes
2       jason   92      spreadsheet.ps          523423 bytes
```

In this case, there are two jobs in the queue; job 91 is printing, and job 92 is scheduled to be printed next.

You can delete a document using the *lprm* command, which accepts a job number (the default is the active job) and the -P option to specify the print queue. This command will delete job 92 on the print queue *laser3*:

```
$ lprm -P laser3 92
```

How Does It Work?

Fedora's printing system combines four fairly complex tools into a comprehensive print solution. The Common Unix Printing System (CUPS) provides queue management and printer sharing; the Foomatic system provides access to the large database of printer configuration information and notes maintained by *linuxprinting.org*; Ghostscript converts PostScript, the most common printer output format used by Linux applications, into other formats for use by non-PostScript printers; and the *system-config-printer* script provides the user interface for printer configuration.

system-config-printer manipulates the CUPS configuration files in */etc/cups* and restarts the CUPS server (*cupsd*) to load configuration changes. These files can be edited by hand, but this is not recommended.

CUPS provides queue management, storing queued documents in */var/spool/cups* until they are printed. It is heavily tied into the Internet Print Protocol (IPP), which is based on the web protocol HTTP. You can connect to the CUPS server's administrative interface by accessing the address *http://localhost:631/* through a web browser; however, if you do any configuration through that interface, you may no longer be able to use *system-config-printer*, which is generally a better configuration tool.

Applications vary enormously in the quality of their interface into the print system:

- Programs with the most advanced print control, such as OpenOffice.org, load the list of queues from CUPS, including each queue's capabilities. They also let you set print options—such as duplexing, ink mode, paper type, and resolution—using the Properties button in the print dialog.

- Other applications, such as Firefox and Evince, load the queue list but don't permit full control over print options. You can select the queue from a drop-down list in the print dialog.

- Many other programs such as xpdf simply allow you to specify the *lpr* command to be used; queue selection is performed using *lpr*'s -P option.

The printer icon in the GNOME panel's notification area is provided by the *eggcups* program.

What About . . .

. . . creating a group of similar printers that are accessed on a first-available-printer basis?

This is called a printer class; to create one, use the New Class button in the graphical configuration tool. Add the desired printers to the printer class and click Apply; you can then print to the printer class instead of a specific printer, and the first available printer will be used to print your document.

. . . setting up more than one queue for a printer?

Not only is it possible to set up more than one queue for a printer, it's a good idea, because each queue can have a different driver configuration.

For example, I have a color inkjet printer, which is used in text mode with plain paper and in a photo mode with photo paper. I have created three separate queues: *color0-draft* for fast, low-quality printing that saves ink; *color0* for regular printing; and *color0-photo* for photo printing. The appropriate driver options have been set for each. Although it is possible to create just one queue and set the resolution and paper type within some applications, not all applications are capable of setting those options, and it's simply faster and more convenient to have preconfigured queues. Similarly, I have single- and double-sided queues for my laser printer.

 Printer queues are created with default driver options. To adjust the driver options, create the queue, and then use the Printer Options tab to access the driver settings.

. . . making a PDF instead of printing?

Many applications that don't provide PDF output do provide the ability to print to a file instead of printing to an output queue; this feature can be used to save a

PostScript copy of the print request, which you can then convert to a PDF by using Ghostscript via the *ps2pdf* script.

For example, you could "print" from Firefox to the file *bankstatement.ps* and then convert *bankstatement.ps* to *bankstatement.pdf* with this command:

```
$ ps2pdf bankstatement.ps
```

The resulting PDF file can be viewed with Evince, xpdf, or Adobe Acrobat Reader (not installed by default).

...using an HP multifunction printer?

HP produces several lines of multifunction printer/copier/scanner devices that use a multiplexed communication protocol; the printer and scanner are accessed through a single connection. The software necessary to access these devices is built into Fedora Core; just ensure that the *hplip* service is running.

Where Can I Learn More?

- The manpages for *lpr*, *lpq*, and *lprm*
- LinuxPrinting.org (home of Foomatic and compatibility reports for hundreds of different printers): *http://www.linuxprinting.org*
- CUPS web site: *http://www.cups.org*
- Ghostscript web site: *http://www.ghostscript.com*
- Configuring your firewall to permit remote access to CUPS printers: "Preventing Unwanted Connections"
- Configuring the print service to start automatically (or not to start): Lab 4.5, "Using Runlevels"
- Sharing printers using Microsoft Windows File & Print sharing: "Configuring Samba to Share Files with Windows"

2.6   Configuring Sound

Fedora Core contains drivers for many different types of sound cards. However, it may be necessary to configure the sound path or select from different sound devices before your sound output is usable.

How Do I Do That?

Fedora provides two tools for configuring sound: the Soundcard Detection tool and the audio mixer.

To access the Soundcard Detection tool, select System → Administration → Sound-card Detection (or Administration → Soundcard Detection in KDE). The window shown in Figure 2-21 will appear.

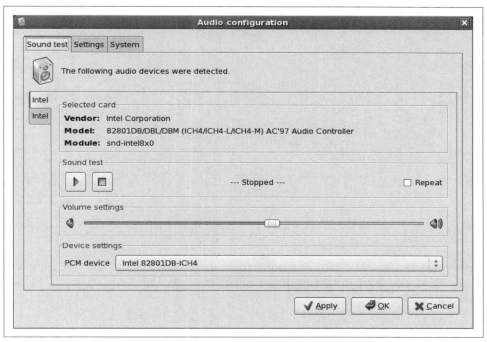

Figure 2-21. Soundcard Detection window

This window offers a minimal set of options: basically, you can select the default device to be used, and you can play a test sound.

To test your sound card, make sure that your speakers are plugged in and turned on, then click the Play button. You should hear a guitar chord played on the right, then the left, and then the right+left channels. If you don't, try selecting different device tabs (on the left side of the window) and PCM Device settings (at the bottom of the window) until you find a combination that works. Your system may have multiple sound cards (e.g., both a motherboard and PCI sound card), or there may be sound devices on your sound card that are not connected to a sound path that goes to your speakers; they may instead go to a modem, headphone jack, or thin air.

If you still don't hear anything, then it's time to break out the Volume Control/Mixer. In GNOME, you can do this either by right-clicking on the volume-control panel applet (the icon that looks like a speaker, shown way back in Figure 2-2) and select-ing Open Volume Control, or by selecting the menu option System → Preferences → Volume Control; the window shown on the right in Figure 2-22 will appear. In KDE, select Sound and Video → KMix or, if there's a volume-control icon in your panel, right-click it and select Show Mixer Window. The KMix window is shown on the left in Figure 2-22.

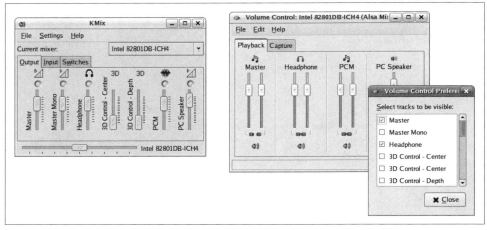

Figure 2-22. KDE KMix (left) and GNOME Volume Control (right)

To change which sound device is being configured, click File → Change Device and select the device from the list (in KMix, select the device using the "Current mixer" control).

 Make sure the sound device you are configuring with the Volume Control/Mixer is the same device you are testing with the Soundcard Detection tool!

Modern sound chips have many different inputs, outputs, and processing sections, but not all sound card designs implement all of these features, and even if the features are implemented, some of the inputs and outputs may not be connected to anything, or they may be connected to an input or output labeled with a different name. KMix presents controls for almost every available input, output, sound path routing option, and switch; GNOME's Volume Control lets you configure which controls you wish to display. This reduces clutter on the screen, but it also means that required controls may not be visible until you enable them.

To change the configuration of the Volume Control, select its menu option Edit → Preferences. The small checkbox list shown in Figure 2-22 will appear. Until you know which control does what, I'd recommend enabling all of the controls.

With all of the sound card controls in front of you, you can now experiment to see which control is preventing the test sound from reaching your ears. After each adjustment, test the result by clicking on the Play button in the Soundcard Detection tool.

First, check to make sure that your Pulse Code Modulation (PCM), Master, Headphone, and Master Mono outputs are turned up and not muted (i.e., the Volume Control speaker icons are not crossed out or the KMix LEDs are illuminated). If that doesn't solve the problem, experiment with the switches (such as External Amplifier) and the PCM output path/3-D processing.

After you have set the options you want, they will be saved and restored by default the next time you log in, so for most users this is a one-time (per user) configuration step.

Once you have found the correct sound device, select the Settings tab in the Audio Configuration window (Figure 2-21) and set the Default Audio Card and Default PCM Device. Click OK to save your configuration and exit.

Once you have sound working, you can change the volume level by placing your mouse over the volume-control panel applet and rolling the mouse wheel: away from you increases the volume; toward you decreases the volume. If you don't have a mouse wheel, click on the volume panel applet to reveal a slider control. To mute the sound, right-click on the panel applet and select Mute.

To configure sound when using a text console, type:

```
$ alsamixer
```

The AlsaMixer display is shown in Figure 2-23. Use the left/right cursor keys to select a control, up/down to set levels, Tab to switch between the Playback/Capture (Output/Input) views, M to mute, and Escape to exit.

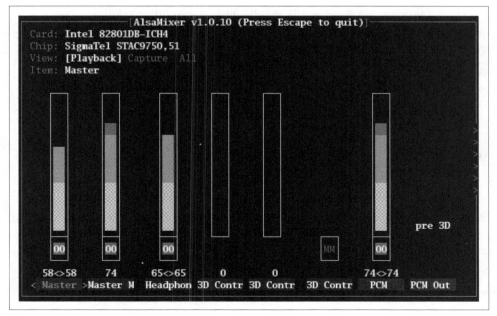

Figure 2-23. AlsaMixer display

How Does It Work?

Fedora uses the Advanced Linux Sound Architecture system (ALSA), which has replaced the Open Sound System (OSS) used in older Linux kernels. The ALSA interface is generally more advanced than the OSS interface; however, OSS is used on many Unix systems, so ALSA also provides an OSS-compatible sound interface for the convenience of cross-platform software developers.

ALSA uses devices in the */dev/snd* directory such as */dev/snd/controlC0*, which is used by the Volume Control and KMix tools to control the first sound card (*C0*). Devices for OSS compatibility are in the */dev* directory and include */dev/dsp*, */dev/audio*, and */dev/mixer*.

Most sound chips have several inputs—in some cases, a few dozen inputs—which are routed through various sound paths to arrive at one or more outputs. Most of these inputs have a description assigned by the chip designer, but it's not necessary for the sound card designer to use a particular input for its designated purpose, and it's also not guaranteed that the system builder will connect a given signal source to the appropriate input on the sound card. Since the ALSA drivers generally use the designations provided by the chip documentation, you may find situations where the Video control manages the CD-ROM volume, or the Headset control affects the main speaker output.

It's not uncommon for different sound card models to use the same chipsets, with the support circuitry for some features left off of the budget models. In these cases, ALSA has no idea which features are wired up and which ones have been omitted, which explains why there are so many controls that don't do anything.

The Soundcard Detection tool is a Python script named *system-config-soundcard*. This script configures the file */etc/asound.conf* with the selected default PCM device.

When the system is shut down, the script */etc/rc.d/init.d/halt* saves the sound configuration (including mixer settings) to */etc/asound.state*. The state is restored by the Udev subsystem using the program */etc/dev.d/sound/alsa.dev* when the sound devices are detected during system boot.

What About...

...allowing multiple users to use a sound device at the same time?

When a user logs in, Fedora assigns ownership of the sound devices to that user and sets the permissions so that only that user can open them. If you want to allow several users (including those remotely logged in) to use sound at the same time, you can change the permissions of the sound devices so that they're universally accessible:

```
$ chmod 0777 /dev/snd/* /dev/mixer* /dev/audio* /dev/dsp*
```

To make this the default configuration, add this line to the end of the system-wide login script, */etc/profile*.

...controlling the volume levels from the command line or a script?

The *amixer* utility provides command-line access to the sound controls. Run without arguments, it will tell you all of the current settings (which can run into hundreds of lines of output):

```
$ amixer
Simple mixer control 'Master',0
  Capabilities: pvolume pswitch pswitch-joined
  Playback channels: Front Left - Front Right
  Limits: Playback 0 - 31
  Mono:
  Front Left: Playback 17 [55%] [on]
  Front Right: Playback 17 [55%] [on]
Simple mixer control 'Master Mono',0
  Capabilities: pvolume pvolume-joined pswitch pswitch-joined
  Playback channels: Mono
  Limits: Playback 0 - 31
  Mono: Playback 14 [45%] [on]
Simple mixer control 'Headphone',0
  Capabilities: pvolume pswitch pswitch-joined
  Playback channels: Front Left - Front Right
  Limits: Playback 0 - 31
  Mono:
  Front Left: Playback 20 [65%] [on]
  Front Right: Playback 20 [65%] [on]
...(Lines snipped)...
```

You can generate a more compact list of just the simple mixer control names using the scontrols subcommand as an argument:

```
$ amixer scontrols
Simple mixer control 'Master',0
Simple mixer control 'Master Mono',0
Simple mixer control 'Headphone',0
Simple mixer control '3D Control - Center',0
Simple mixer control '3D Control - Depth',0
Simple mixer control '3D Control - Switch',0
Simple mixer control 'PCM',0
...(Lines snipped)...
```

To get the setting for a single control, use the get subcommand:

```
$ amixer get Master
Simple mixer control 'Master',0
  Capabilities: pvolume pswitch
  Playback channels: Front Left - Front Right
  Limits: Playback 0 - 31
  Mono:
  Front Left: Playback 20 [65%] [on]
  Front Right: Playback 20 [65%] [on]
```

To change a setting, use the set subcommand:

```
$ amixer set Master 31
Simple mixer control 'Master',0
  Capabilities: pvolume pswitch
  Playback channels: Front Left - Front Right
  Limits: Playback 0 - 31
  Mono:
  Front Left: Playback 31 [100%] [on]
  Front Right: Playback 31 [100%] [on]
```

...playing or recording an audio file from the command line?

There are many different audio file formats, and Fedora includes many different media players so that you can listen to them (including Totem, Mplayer, and Xine). Fedora Core also includes the *sox* utility to convert between formats; the *sox* package also includes a handy script named *play* that can be run from the command line. It converts just about any file into an appropriate format for output and sends the sound to your speakers:

```
$ play /usr/share/sounds/KDE_Startup_2.ogg
```

You can also apply various *sox* effects to the output. To play a file backward at a reduced volume:

```
$ play /usr/share/sounds/KDE_Startup_2.ogg -v 0.2 reverse
```

The sox package also includes the *rec* script to record sound:

```
$ rec /tmp/x.ogg
Send break (control-c) to end recording
Ctrl-C
```

Where Can I Learn More?

- The ALSA web site: *http://www.alsa-project.org/*
- The manpages for *alsactl*, *alsamixer*, *amixer*, *speaker-test*, *sox*, *play*, and *rec*

2.7   Adding and Configuring Fonts

Although Fedora ships with a good set of basic fonts, many users find it useful to add more fonts. Fortunately, this is very easy to do, either graphically or from the command line.

How Do I Do That?

Fonts can be easily added or removed by manually copying the font files or by using the file managers: Nautilus (GNOME) or Konqueror (KDE).

Adding and removing fonts using GNOME Nautilus

GNOME's Nautilus file manager has a special URI for viewing and managing fonts. To access it:

1. Start Nautilus; use the My Computer or Home desktop icons, the panel bar icons, or any folder in the Places menu.
2. Select Open Location from the Nautilus File menu, or press Ctrl-L. An Open Location dialog will appear.
3. Enter *fonts:/* in the location text box.

Figure 2-24 shows the Nautilus font display.

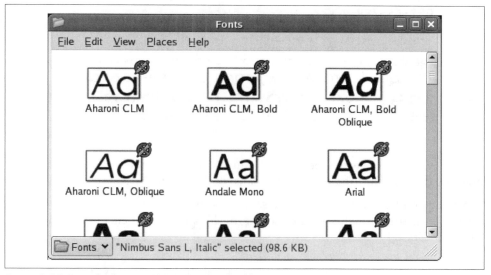

Figure 2-24. Font display in GNOME's Nautilus file manager

The lower- and uppercase letter A of each font are displayed, if the font has those characters. Double-clicking on a font (or right-clicking and selecting "Open with GNOME Font Viewer") will display some basic information about the font—including the license, file size, and font style—along with an extended font sample, as shown in Figure 2-25.

To install fonts into your personal font directory (*~/.fonts*), simply drag and drop them into the Nautilus font window. The fonts may not show up in the Nautilus display until you log out and log in again, but they will be installed and immediately accessible to applications when they start (if an application is already running, just restart that application to gain access to the new fonts).

To install fonts that are in a compressed archive, such as those from *http://www.1001freefonts.com*, click on the *.zip* archive link (i.e., for the Windows font) in your

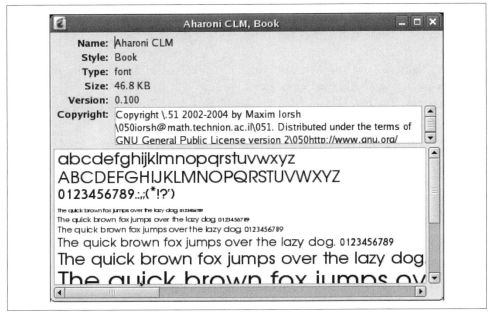

Figure 2-25. GNOME font viewer

web browser, then select "Open with Archive Manager" as the action. You can then drag and drop the file from the Archive Manager window to the Nautilus font window.

A personal font can be deleted in the same way that a file is deleted using Nautilus: drag it from the Nautilus window to the trash can, or right-click on it and select "Move to Trash."

> Nautilus does not permit you to install or delete system-wide fonts. However, Konqueror does, and it is possible to run Konqueror within a GNOME session. One easy way of doing this is to type Ctrl-F2 and enter **konqueror** in the dialog that appears.

Adding and removing fonts using KDE Konqueror

KDE's Konqueror file and web browser enables you to view, install, and delete fonts from both the system-wide font directories and your personal font directory. To access this mode:

1. Start Konqueror, using the Home or Web Browser panel icons, or the K menu.

2. Enter *fonts:/* into the location field.

The window will show icons labeled Personal and System; double-click on the group you wish to see, and the display shown in Figure 2-26 will appear (the System group is shown here).

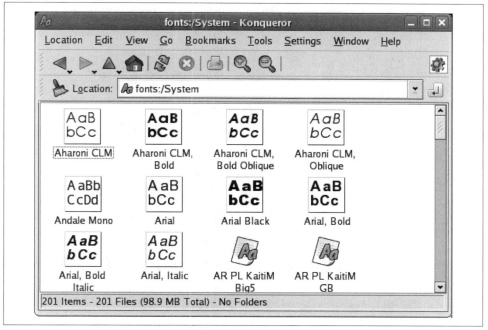

Figure 2-26. Konqueror system font display

Double-clicking on a font will present the KFontView window shown in Figure 2-27, showing an extended font sample. Clicking on the *T* icon will enable you to change the sample sentence; the default sentence is same pangram used in the GNOME font viewer.

To add fonts, simply drag and drop them into the font window. If you drop them into the system font window, you will be prompted to enter the root password.

To delete a font, treat it like a file: drag and drop it onto the trash can, or right-click and select Delete. As with installation, you will be prompted for the root password if the font is from the system font window.

 You can also install and remove fonts through the KDE Control Panel.

Adding and removing fonts from the command line

When an application starts, the font configuration system automatically scans *~/.fonts* (your personal font directory) as well as */usr/share/fonts* (which is the system-wide font directory). Any changes to the fonts contained in those directories are detected automatically, so adding fonts is simply a matter of placing files into those directories, and removing fonts is simply a matter of deleting them.

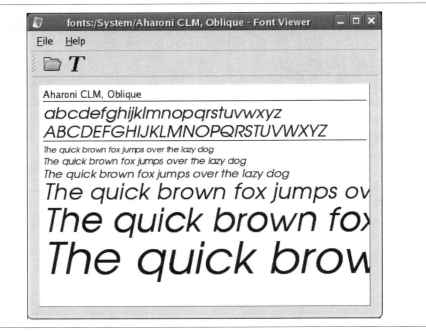

Figure 2-27. KFontView window

For example, if you have a compressed tar file named */tmp/newfonts.tgz* containing a folder named *newfonts* full of TrueType fonts and wish to install them for your own private use, you can use these commands:

```
$ cd ~/.fonts
$ tar xvzf /tmp/newfonts.tgz "*.ttf" "*.TTF"
```

Or, to install the fonts so that they are accessible to all users system-wide:

```
# cd /usr/share/fonts
# mkdir newfonts
# cd newfonts
# tar xvzf /tmp/newfonts.tgz "*.ttf" "*.TTF"
```

To delete all of your personal fonts:

```
$ rm -rf ~/.fonts/*
```

And to delete the system-wide fonts installed in *newfonts*:

```
# rm -rf /user/share/fonts/newfonts
```

Installing the Microsoft fonts

Web pages and documents created on Microsoft systems often use fonts that are distributed with Windows. For a time, Microsoft made these fonts available free of charge on its web site; although they are no longer available directly from Microsoft, they are available from *fontconfig.org* under Microsoft's fairly simple licensing terms, documented in *http://fontconfig.org/webfonts/Licen.TXT*.

Installing these fonts makes it possible to view Word and Excel documents and web pages created under Windows as they were originally designed. Mozilla, Firefox, OpenOffice, and other applications can all use these fonts.

In order to install these fonts, you'll need to obtain a copy of the *cabextract* program to extract the fonts from archives created in Microsoft's proprietary CAB format:

```
# yum install cabextract
```

Once *cabextract* is installed, you can easily install the Microsoft fonts from the command line:

```
# wget http://fontconfig.org/webfonts/webfonts.tar.gz
# tar xvzf webfonts.tar.gz
# cd msfonts
# cabextract *.exe
# mkdir /usr/share/fonts/microsoft
# cp *.[tT]* /usr/share/fonts/microsoft
# cd ..
# rm -rf msfonts
# fc-cache
```

Using newly installed fonts

Applications load their font lists at startup time, so simply relaunching an application is usually all that is required before you can start using new fonts.

The command `fc-cache` will create an index cache to speed application startup. To use it:

```
$ fc-cache
# fc-cache
```

Running `fc-cache` as a regular user will create the index cache for *~/.fonts*, which is not really necessary because the index cache will be created automatically. Running it as *root* will create the index cache for */usr/share/fonts* and is strongly recommended; otherwise, an index of the system-wide fonts will be created for each individual user, wasting time and storage space.

Configuring font rendering options

Font rendering can be tuned to adjust the font appearance to suit user preferences and the display hardware in use. Both GNOME and KDE provide configuration tools to configure font rendering.

The GNOME configuration window shown in Figure 2-28 is accessed from the menu item System → Preferences → Font. The KDE rendering configuration panel shown in Figure 2-29 is accessed through the KDE Control Panel under Appearance & Themes → Fonts.

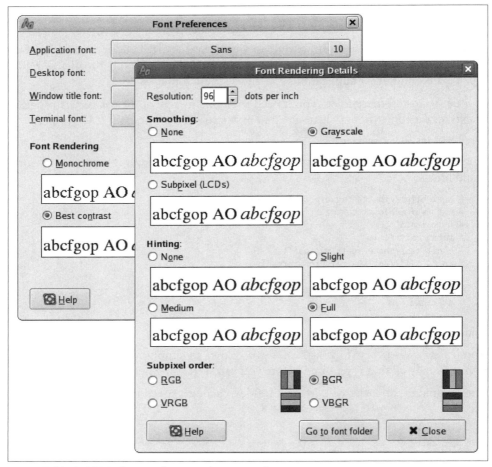

Figure 2-28. GNOME font-rendering preferences tool

In both cases, you can enable or disable antialiasing, adjust the level of antialiasing hinting, and set subpixel order.

On an older system with a slow CPU and/or low memory resources, turning off antialiasing can make enough of a performance difference to turn an unbearably slow system into one that performs reasonably.

When antialiasing is enabled, the hinting level can be set according to user preference—experiment and see what looks best.

If you have an LCD screen, select "Smoothing: Subpixel (LCD)" in GNOME or "Use Subpixel Smoothing" in KDE. You'll also need to select the order of the red, green, and blue elements on your screen; since this information is almost never documented

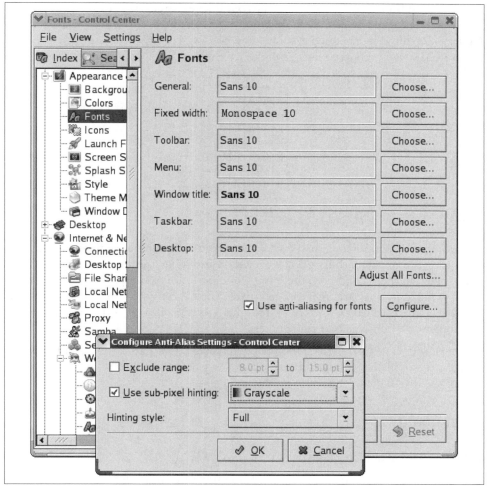

Figure 2-29. KDE font rendering preferences tool

in the hardware specifications, use a large magnifying glass or experiment until you find the setting that looks the best.

How Does It Work?

X Window System programs use one of two different font systems. The old system, known as *core fonts*, is still used by a few applications and is needed to start the X server. Almost all current applications use a system comprising two components: *FreeType* and *fontconfig*, two software libraries that provide high-quality font rendering and font matching. Since these are client-side libraries accessed by applications, each application separately handles its own font operations.

FreeType's sub-pixel rendering capability is, by and large, useful only on LCDs. It involves treating each of the RGB color elements in a pixel as a partial pixel. Figure 2-30 shows an enlarged diagonal line border between black and white regions on an LCD screen, rendered using subpixel hinting.

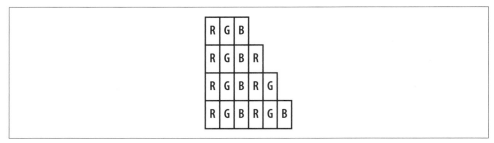

Figure 2-30. Subpixel rendering on an LCD panel

Note that each pixel is comprised of a red, green, and a blue element; on this display, they are arranged horizontally in R-G-B order. In the first row, there is one white pixel. In the second row, there is a white pixel followed by one-third of a white pixel—which, in this case, means a red pixel. The third row consists of a white pixel followed by two-thirds of a pixel—a red-plus-green pixel, which displays as yellow. The fourth row contains two white pixels.

It seems odd that a color pixel would be perceived as a partial pixel, but it works because of sophisticated algorithms and the fact that the subpixels are a continuation of the R-G-B element pattern on the line.

What About...

...getting a list of available fonts?

The *fc-list* program (a utility provided with Fontconfig) will list all of the fonts available through the Xft/Fontconfig system:

```
$ fc-list
Luxi Serif:style=Regular
MiscFixed:style=Regular
Utopia:style=Bold Italic
Nimbus Sans L:style=Regular Italic
Bitstream Vera Sans Mono:style=Bold
Webdings:style=Regular
Console:style=Regular
URW Palladio L:style=Roman
Century Schoolbook L:style=Bold Italic
Luxi Serif:style=Bold
...(snip)...
```

The list isn't in any sort of order, and it contains a lot of information about the styles available for each font, so it's not very readable. Using some arguments and the sort command will produce a much more readable list of available font faces:

```
$ fc-list : family|sort -u
Andale Mono
Arial
Arial Black
Bitstream Charter
Bitstream Vera Sans
Bitstream Vera Sans Mono
Bitstream Vera Serif
Century Schoolbook L
Comic Sans MS
Console
console8x8
Courier
...(snip)..
```

...specifying a font name?

Fontconfig font names are very easy to use: just specify the font face you wish to use. You can optionally include a size (separated by a hyphen) or font attribute name/value pairs (after a colon).

For matching purposes, you can specify multiple values for the font name or size, separated by commas. The first matching value will be selected.

Table 2-4 lists some font names expressed using this notation.

Table 2-4. Fontconfig font names

Font name	Meaning
Courier-12	Courier face, 12-point size
Utopia:style=italic	Utopia face in italics
Helvetica,Arial,Swiss-12	Helvetica, Arial, or Swiss face (preferred in that order), 12-point size
Fixed-12,16,10	Fixed face in 12-, 16-, or 10-point size (preferred in that order)

For a complete list of font properties that can be used in font names, see the documentation on the Fontconfig web site at *http://fontconfig.org*. Note that many of the properties mentioned in the documentation are not used; on most systems, style is the only property specified for most of the fonts.

xterm has support for Fontconfig/Xft and can be used to test a Fontconfig font name. The command-line option to use is -fa (face); if the font name contains spaces, be sure to quote it on the command line. Here are some examples:

```
$ xterm -fa courier
$ xterm -fa courier-12
$ xterm -fa courier-18:style=italic
```

```
$ xterm -fa "Bitstream Vera Sans Mono-16:style=bold"
$ xterm -fa foo,bar,baz,utopia,courier,qux-12,18,10:style=italic
```

If the selected font does not use character-cell spacing, xterm will add considerable spacing between characters (the last example demonstrates this).

Where Can I Learn More?

- The manpages for *fc-list*, *fc-cache*, and *Xft*
- The Fontconfig web site: *http://fontconfig.org*
- freedesktop.org: *http://freedesktop.org*
- Keith Packard's Xft tutorial: *http://www.keithp.com/~keithp/render/Xft.tutorial*

2.8   Using USB Storage

USB is a widely used interface for peripherals. It's intelligent, fast, hot-pluggable, uses a compact and foolproof connector, and even provides a couple of watts of power for small devices.

Many USB devices fall into the *storage* class, including cameras, portable music players, and storage card readers. These devices can easily be used with Fedora.

How Do I Do That?

Using USB storage in Fedora Core is easy: simply insert the USB storage device into any available USB port.

If you're using GNOME, the device will be mounted, an icon will appear on the desktop, and a window will open showing the contents of the device.

When you insert a USB storage device while running KDE, the dialog in Figure 2-31 appears with two options: "Open in New Window" and "Do Nothing." Choose one of the options and click OK. If you want to skip this dialog next time you insert a storage device, select the checkbox labeled "Always do this for this type of media."

The action performed when a new USB storage device is detected is configurable in both GNOME and KDE.

Safely removing a USB drive

Before unplugging a USB drive, you should unmount it to prevent data loss. In GNOME and KDE, right-click on the drive's desktop icon and select the menu option Unmount Volume or Remove Safely. Wait until the activity lights stop blinking and then unplug the drive.

Figure 2-31. KDE USB Storage action dialog

Configuring default actions in GNOME

To configure the action taken when GNOME detects a new USB storage device, select the menu option System → Preferences → "Removable Drives and Media." The window shown in Figure 2-32 will appear.

The first tab, Storage, contains four checkboxes for USB storage devices:

Mount removable drives when hot-plugged
Freshly inserted USB drives will be mounted, and a corresponding icon will appear on the desktop.

Mount removable media when inserted
Freshly inserted media such as CDs and DVDs will be mounted, and an icon will appear on the desktop.

 This option does not apply to media inserted into a memory-card reader! Use the "Mount removable drives when hot-plugged" option for memory cards.

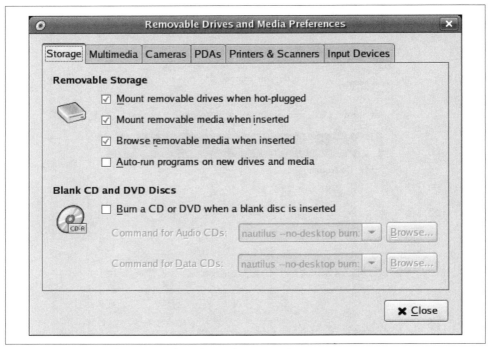

Figure 2-32. Removable Drives and Media Preferences tool

Browse removable media when inserted

Removable drives and removable media will be displayed in a Nautilus window when they are mounted, regardless of whether they are mounted automatically (depending on the settings of the checkboxes) or manually.

Auto-run programs on new drives and media

Searches for a file named *autorun* on newly mounted media, prompts the user for confirmation, and then executes that file. The file may be a script or a compiled program.

 The auto-run feature does not work with automatically mounted media because GNOME takes the precaution of mounting media with the noexec option, which prevents direct execution of files (including *autorun* files). It does work with manually mounted media.

The third tab, Cameras, has a checkbox labeled "Import digital photos when connected." When checked (which is the default), GNOME will look for a directory named *dcim* on any newly mounted USB media. If found, it will run the specified command (the default is *gthumb-import*).

Configuring default actions in KDE

To configure the behavior of KDE when storage devices are inserted, open the KDE Control Center and select the configuration category Peripherals → Storage Media. The window shown in Figure 2-33 will appear.

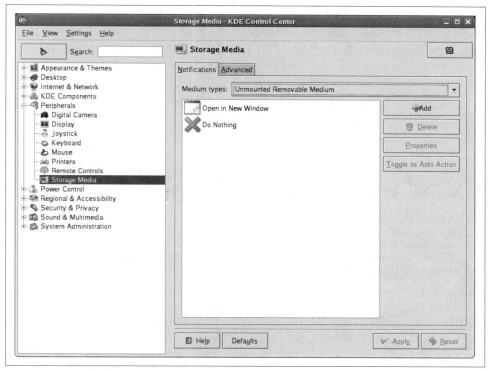

Figure 2-33. KDE Removable Media configuration

Select Unmounted Removable Medium in the "Medium types" menu. Two actions will be displayed: "Open in New Window," which mounts the drive and opens a Konqueror browse window, and Do Nothing, which causes a drive icon to be displayed on the desktop, which, when clicked, will mount and browse the drive.

To set one of these actions as the default, click on it, then click "Toggle as Auto Action," and then Apply. The selected action will take place automatically when new media is detected.

How Does It Work?

When a USB storage device is detected by the USB drivers, the *hal* subsystem takes note and sends a message on the *dbus*, a messaging system for desktop applications.

GNOME or KDE desktop applications listen for messages on the dbus and then perform the action you have configured, such as mounting the drive or displaying the drive contents in a window.

USB devices use a set of data items called *descriptors* to inform the controlling host of their capabilities. The Class descriptor is used to identify storage devices. These devices, which understand the same commands used to control SCSI disk drives, are given a device name in the form */dev/sd<x>* where *<x>* is a sequential drive letter (*sd* stands for *SCSI disk*). Partitions within a USB storage device, if present, are given device names in the form */dev/sd<xp>* where *<p>* is the partition number (1 is the first partition).

When a drive is mounted in a Fedora system, a record of the mount is made in */etc/ mtab*, which can be viewed with the *mount* command:

```
$ mount
/dev/mapper/main-root on / type ext3 (rw)
/dev/proc on /proc type proc (rw)
/dev/sys on /sys type sysfs (rw)
/dev/devpts on /dev/pts type devpts (rw,gid=5,mode=620)
/dev/md0 on /boot type ext3 (rw)
/dev/shm on /dev/shm type tmpfs (rw)
/dev/mapper/main-home on /home type ext3 (rw)
/dev/mapper/main-var on /var type ext3 (rw,acl)
/dev/sda on /media/spreadsheet type ext2 (rw,noexec,nosuid,nodev)
/dev/sdb on /media/disk type vfat (rw,noexec,nosuid,nodev,shortname=winnt,uid=500)
```

This particular single USB storage device appears as two separate devices, highlighted in bold in this example: a disk drive, mounted using the filesystem label as the mount point (*/media/<fslabel>*), and a floppy disk (mounted as */media/disk* in the output above). This is a common configuration used on older USB keys; the emulated floppy disk device is intended to store encryption or password software for accessing the main storage device. Removable media is mounted under the */media* directory.

A more useful way of looking at the */etc/mtab* table is to use df:

```
# df -h
Filesystem            Size  Used Avail Use% Mounted on
/dev/mapper/main-root
                       30G  8.9G   20G  32% /
/dev/md0              251M   33M  205M  14% /boot
/dev/shm              506M     0  506M   0% /dev/shm
/dev/mapper/main-home
                       31G  5.9G   25G  20% /home
/dev/mapper/main-var   36G   26G  9.3G  74% /var
/dev/sda              120M  1.6M  112M   2% /media/spreadsheet
/dev/sdb              1.4M   70K  1.4M   5% /media/disk
```

This shows most of the information displayed by mount, but with a nice column layout showing the total size, amount of storage used, and the available space.

/proc/mounts contains the same information as */etc/mtab* but is generated directly from the kernel's data structures (and is therefore more reliable).

The kernel uses memory as a buffer, writing data to disk periodically. Unmounting a disk flushes the buffer to disk immediately and updates the disk control structures to indicate that the drive is in a consistent (clean) state. If a drive is removed while mounted, some data (including parts of files) may not be written to the disk, resulting in data corruption.

What About...

...partitioning a flash drive?

You can use the standard *fdisk* utility to partition a flash drive (after unmounting it, if necessary). Here is an example in which *fdisk* is used to divide a 64 MB flash drive into two partitions:

```
# fdisk /dev/sdb
```

Since *fdisk* is an interactive tool, it's necessary to enter single-letter commands to specify the changes that should be made to the partition table. First, print the partition table on the screen so you can review it:

```
Command (m for help): p

Disk /dev/sdb: 65 MB, 65536000 bytes
3 heads, 42 sectors/track, 1015 cylinders
Units = cylinders of 126 * 512 = 64512 bytes

   Device Boot      Start         End      Blocks   Id  System
/dev/sdb1               1        1015       63924   83  Linux
```

This table shows a 64 MB device (64,512 bytes) with one partition.

If the display does not match the device you are trying to partition, you may be partitioning the wrong device; enter **q** to exit immediately!

Delete the old partition:

```
Command (m for help): d
Selected partition 1
```

Create a new primary partition number 1 that is 30 MB in size:

```
Command (m for help): n
Command action
   e   extended
   p   primary partition (1-4)
p
Partition number (1-4): 1
```

```
First cylinder (1-1015, default 1): ENTER
Using default value 1
Last cylinder or +size or +sizeM or +sizeK (1-1015, default 1015): +30M
```

Create a new primary partition number 2, taking up the rest of the drive:

```
Command (m for help): n
Command action
   e   extended
   p   primary partition (1-4)
p
Partition number (1-4): 2
First cylinder (467-1015, default 467): ENTER
Using default value 467
Last cylinder or +size or +sizeM or +sizeK (467-1015, default 1015): ENTER
Using default value 1015
```

Print the partition table to check it:

```
Command (m for help): p

Disk /dev/sdb: 65 MB, 65536000 bytes
3 heads, 42 sectors/track, 1015 cylinders
Units = cylinders of 126 * 512 = 64512 bytes

   Device Boot      Start         End      Blocks   Id  System
/dev/sdb1               1         466       29337   83  Linux
/dev/sdb2             467        1015       34587   83  Linux
```

Set the type code for the two partitions:

```
Command (m for help): t
Partition number (1-4): 1
Hex code (type L to list codes): L

 0   Empty           1e  Hidden W95 FAT1 80  Old Minix       be  Solaris boot
 1   FAT12           24  NEC DOS         81  Minix / old Lin bf  Solaris
 2   XENIX root      39  Plan 9          82  Linux swap / So c1  DRDOS/sec (FAT-
...(snip)...
 9   AIX bootable    4f  QNX4.x 3rd part 8e  Linux LVM       df  BootIt
 a   OS/2 Boot Manag 50  OnTrack DM      93  Amoeba          e1  DOS access
 b   W95 FAT32       51  OnTrack DM6 Aux 94  Amoeba BBT      e3  DOS R/O
 c   W95 FAT32 (LBA) 52  CP/M            9f  BSD/OS          e4  SpeedStor
 e   W95 FAT16 (LBA) 53  OnTrack DM6 Aux a0  IBM Thinkpad hi eb  BeOS fs
...(snip)...
1c   Hidden W95 FAT3 75  PC/IX
Hex code (type L to list codes): c
Changed system type of partition 1 to c (W95 FAT32 (LBA))

Command (m for help): t
Partition number (1-4): 2
Hex code (type L to list codes): c
Changed system type of partition 2 to c (W95 FAT32 (LBA))
```

Write (save) and exit:

```
Command (m for help): w
The partition table has been altered!

Calling ioctl() to re-read partition table.

Syncing disks.
```

The partition type used, c, indicates that the partition will contain a FAT filesystem. This enables compatibility with Windows and Mac OS X systems and is also necessary for most camera flash-memory cards and digital music players.

Once the partitions have been created, they can be formatted with *mkfs*:

```
# mkfs -t vfat -n spreadsheet -F 32 /dev/sdb1
mkdosfs 2.10 (22 Sep 2003)
# mkfs -t vfat -n database -F 32 /dev/sdb2
mkdosfs 2.10 (22 Sep 2003)
```

 You may need to remove and reinsert the drive to force the kernel to load the new partition table before you can format the partitions.

The option -F 32 forces the use of 32-bit file allocation tables, which is not strictly necessary for drives under 512 MB in size but is required for larger drives and matches the filesystem type assigned to the partition by the previous *fdisk* command. The -n *labelname* option sets the filesystem label, which will be used to determine the mount points for the filesystem.

 If you have ever used your USB drive without a partition table (formatting */dev/sda* instead of */dev/sda1*, for example), erase the *master boot record* (MBR) before partitioning to prevent *udev* from later detecting the drive as unpartitioned and mounting it incorrectly:

```
# dd bs=1k count=1 if=/dev/zero of=/dev/sdb
```

…using a Linux filesystem such as ext2 on a USB storage device?

You can use ext2 or any other filesystem on a USB storage device, but that will reduce compatibility with other systems. To format the partition */dev/sdb2* with an ext3 filesystem:

```
# mkfs -t ext3 /dev/sdb2
```

…accessing USB storage from a nongraphical application?

Automatically mounted storage media are mounted to the directory */media/<label>* if the filesystem has a volume label, or to */media/disk<-N>* if there is no volume label, where *<-N>* is a sequentially assigned number (the first disk mounted is simply called */media/disk*).

...manually mounting a USB storage device?

When you're in runlevel 3 (character mode), your USB storage devices won't be automatically mounted. You can still use USB storage; you just have to mount it by hand:

```
# mkdir /mnt/usbdisk1
# mount /dev/sda1 /mnt/usbdisk1
```

The SCSI disk IDs are sequentially assigned (the first USB disk found since boot is */dev/sda*, the second is */dev/sdb*, and so forth) but you may need to experiment to find the right value.

When you're done with the storage device, unmount it before unplugging it:

```
# umount /mnt/usbdisk1
```

 The unmount command is spelled *umount*; there's only one *n*.

Where Can I Learn More?

- The USB Implementors Forum, Inc. (USB standards): *http://www.usb.org/home*
- The Linux USB project: *http://www.linux-usb.org/*
- The Udev project: *http://www.kernel.org/pub/linux/utils/kernel/hotplug/udev.html*
- Fedora documentation on Udev: *http://fedora.redhat.com/docs/udev/*
- The GNOME and KDE online manuals

## CHAPTER 3

Using Fedora on Your Notebook

Notebook systems are becoming more like desktop systems with each generation, and many notebooks have CPU, memory, disk, and video capabilities that make them true desktop replacements. But the compact, mobile nature of notebooks requires more complex configurations in order to handle power management, mobile networking, and frequently changing hardware configurations.

Many of the topics in this chapter apply to both desktop and notebook systems (and, to a lesser extent, server systems), but become more complex in a mobile environment.

3.1 Power Management

When you're on the go, you have to carry your power with you. Notebook power management therefore receives a lot more attention than desktop power management, even though attention to these issues on the desktop can result in significant savings in electrical costs, system wear, and heat production.

For many years, power-management interfaces have been proprietary and required custom software supplied by the hardware vendor in order to function well (even when they purportedly adhered to industry standards). The situation is slowly improving, and Fedora contains good tools for power management on well-behaved systems.

How Do I Do That?

Fedora uses the Advanced Configuation and Power Interface (ACPI) specification to monitor and manage the current power configuration. This approach requires support from the motherboard and CPU as well as the operating system; fortunately, most systems built in the last decade have some level of ACPI support, though many BIOS implementations are nonstandard.

Using gnome-power-manager to conserve power

Fedora's main power-management tool is *gnome-power-manager*. You can access the *gnome-power-manager* configuration window using the menu option System → Preferences → More Preferences → Power Management.

 Fedora Core does not include the KDE ACPI modules. However, you can use *gnome-power-manager* in KDE by starting it manually: press Alt-F2 or open a terminal, and type:

```
$ gnome-power-manager
```

A second power-management icon will appear in the KDE panel. You can disable KDE's icon through the Control Center menu option; go to Power Control → Laptop Battery and deselect the checkbox labeled "Show battery monitor."

gnome-power-manager will automatically be started next time you enter KDE.

The same program controls the power-management icon in the panel bar, which may or may not appear depending on the system configuration (it will usually appear by default on a system that has a battery, including most notebooks, but will not appear by default on a system with no battery). The symbol used for the icon will change according to the power supply: it will show a battery when discharging the battery, a battery plus a power cord when charging the battery, or just a power cord on a system with no battery. You can access the *gnome-power-manager* configuration window by right-clicking on the icon and selecting Preferences.

Regardless of how you access the configuration window, you will see the display shown in Figure 3-1.

This window contains three tabs: one that configures power management when the system is running on AC or charging the battery, one that configures power management when the system is running on (and discharging) the battery, and one for general power-management settings.

The controls on first two tabs are almost identical:

Sleep
Configures the conditions under which the display and the whole system is put to sleep. For the display, "sleep" is defined as a low-power mode; for the system, the definition of "sleep" is taken from the setting on the General tab. You can set either to a value between 11 and 60 minutes (in one-minute intervals), or you can disable sleep by moving the slider all the way to the right (Never).

When laptop lid is closed
Specifies the action to be taken when a lid closure event is signaled by ACPI. The options include: do nothing, which causes the system to continue to use full power, to be available the moment you open the screen; blank the screen, which

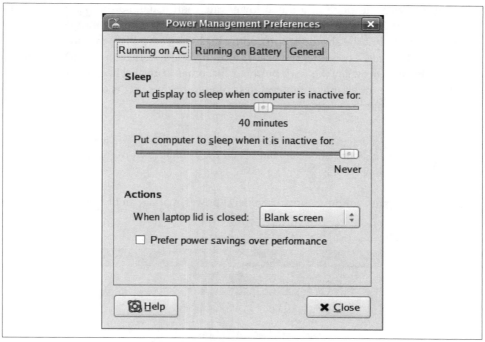

Figure 3-1. Power Manager Preferences window

is similar to doing nothing but will use slightly less power and delay system startup for a few seconds; or suspend or hibernate the system.

Configuring the screen to blank without suspending or hibernating the system whenever the lid is closed is ideal for listening to digital music.

Prefer power savings over performance

If you are performing a task that is not very demanding, such as editing a document, instruct *gnome-power-manager* to maximize the battery life (or, on AC, reduce power consumption) by selecting the checkbox. On the other hand, if you need optimal performance without regard to the power consumption—such as when you are giving an important presentation—leave the checkbox for this option unselected.

When battery power critical

This button appears only on the "Running on Battery" tab, and it configures the action to be taken if the battery runs down to the point that it will power the system for only a few minutes. The options are to do nothing, to suspend or hibernate, or to shut down the system. For most users, doing nothing is a poor choice because the system will abruptly shut off within a few minutes; suspend continues to use power, although at a much lower rate than usual, so the battery will ultimately go dead in due course (causing the loss of any data in memory). Shutdown in an option, but the shutdown procedure itself may take a few minutes and uses a fair bit of power. Therefore, the best choice (if your system supports it) is to hibernate the system when the battery power becomes critical. Hibernation takes less than a minute to complete and even less time to resume, yet it uses no power during the time that the system is in hibernation.

 Depending on the hardware installed on your system, you may see different combinations of controls on the "Running on AC" and "Running on Battery" tabs.

The third tab in this window controls general power-management options, as shown in Figure 3-2.

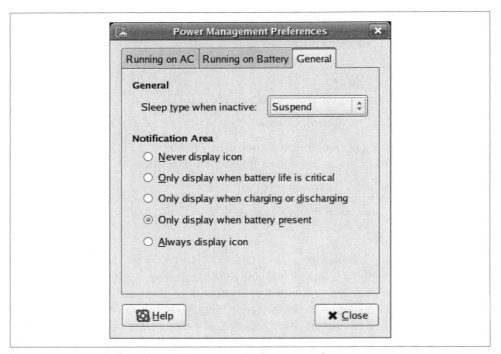

Figure 3-2. General tab on Power Management Preferences window

The options in this window control how the system is put to sleep when the inactivity period set in the other tabs is reached (do nothing, suspend, or hibernate). It also configures the times that the the power-management icon is displayed in the Notification Area; the default is to display it only when the battery is present, so if you want to easily access the power-management controls on an AC-only system, set this to "Always display icon."

It's important to understand the difference between the *suspend* and *hibernate* options: in both cases, the system is effectively off, but in suspend mode the memory is still operating (and consuming power), while in hibernate mode the memory is transferred to swapspace. This means that suspend state will eventually run your battery down, and then the information in RAM will be lost—but until that time, the system will be able to quickly resume its operation. On the other hand, your system can be in hibernate state forever without any power and still resume successfully, but it will take a little longer to do so.

In order to hibernate or suspend successfully, the drivers for all of the devices attached to the system must be able to save and restore the device state. There's no simple way to predict if this will be the case, so it's best to try suspend and resume operations when you have nothing critical happening on the system. For hibernation, it's also necessary to have a swap partition instead of (or in addition to) swapspace on a logical volume.

To manually provoke a suspend or hibernate operation, right-click on the power-management icon in the status bar and use the menu options that appear. To resume from a suspend, use the *wake-up* key defined for your system (you may have to consult the system documentation or experiment to find this). To resume from hibernation, turn your system power on with the power button, then let it start a normal boot cycle. The kernel will recognize the hibernation state and attempt to resume; if this fails, a normal boot will take place (but you may lose changes to any files that were opened when you hibernated your computer, so it's a good idea to save changes before you hibernate).

A password is required to unlock the screen after a resume if passwords are configured in the screensaver (which is the default).

Resuming from hibernation will fail if the kernel has been upgraded since the last boot.

Viewing power information

If your system has a battery, *gnome-power-manager* provides a number of interesting graphs showing your power state. To view them, right-click on the power management icon on the panel, then select Information. The window shown in Figure 3-3 will be presented.

The tabs across the top provide access to the available information and graphs:

Device Information
> Displays the current battery state. Clicking on More presents the battery technology, serial number, and a capacity rating showing the percentage of the original design capacity that the battery is now capable of holding (the higher the number, the better the battery condition).

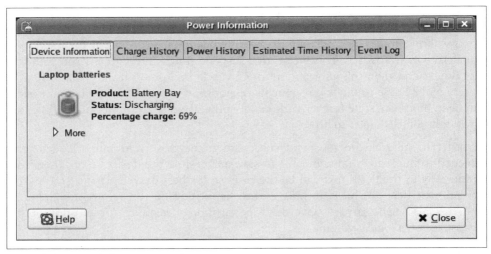

Figure 3-3. Power Information window

Charge History

This graph shows the battery charge (as a percentage of its current maximum) over time. The graphs are automatically scaled horizontally.

Power History

Displays the battery charge and discharge rates over time, as shown in Figure 3-4. If the battery is fully charged and the system is on external power, the discharge rate will be shown as zero, but if the battery is charging, the system will show the rate at which it is charging. When running on battery power, this graph shows the rate of discharge. Power events are marked on this graph, including transitions to and from AC power, suspend and hibernate events, lid closures, and display idle periods. You can use the information in this graph to see the impact of your usage patterns on the system's power consumption.

Estimated Time History

Shows the history of the calculated time to charge the battery, when you're on AC power, or to discharge the battery, when you're running only on the battery. Power events are also shown on this log.

Event Log

Displays a more verbose listing of the same power events shown on the graphs.

On an AC-only system, the graphs will all be flat lines, but power events will still be displayed.

Changing the CPU speed

If CMOS semiconductors were perfect, they would consume power only when they changed state. They're not perfect, so they leak energy and consume power when idle, but that's a tiny fraction of the power they consume when changing state.

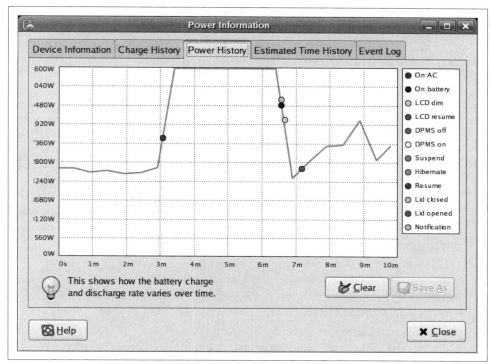

Figure 3-4. Power History graph

The system *clock* is a pulse generator that controls the speed at which the CPU changes state, and therefore controls the amount of energy used by the CPU and related system components. Therefore, there is a trade-off between performance and power consumption.

Fedora can balance power usage against performance automatically according to system workload. This feature is provided by the *cpuspeed* service and is enabled by default.

The default parameters used by this service work well in most cases, but can be adjusted by editing the file */etc/cpuspeed.conf*, which looks like this:

```
VMAJOR=1
VMINOR=1

# uncomment this and set to the name of your CPUFreq module
#DRIVER="powernow-k7"

# Let background (nice) processes speed up the cpu
OPTS="$OPTS -n"

# Add your favorite options here
#OPTS="$OPTS -s 0 -i 10 -r"
```

```
# uncomment and modify this to check the state of the AC adapter
#OPTS="$OPTS -a /proc/acpi/ac_adapter/*/state"

# uncomment and modify this to check the system temperature
#OPTS="$OPTS -t /proc/acpi/thermal_zone/*/temperature 75"
```

 Usually the DRIVER, VMAJOR, and VMINOR lines should not be changed.

Uncomment the OPTS lines that contain additional options you wish to use. The pre-configured lines have these meanings:

-n

Allow processes that have been marked as low priority using the *nice* command to run at full speed. The default is to slow down the processor when only low-priority processes are running.

-s 0 -i 10 -r

Manages only CPU 0 (-s 0), making speed change decisions once a second instead of the default of once every two seconds (-i 10), and restore the original speed when *cpuspeed* exits (-r).

-a /proc/acpi/ac_adapter/*/state

Monitors the AC adapter and switches to minimum speed when AC power is removed. Adding -C will force the system to operate at maximum speed when AC power is connected.

-t /proc/acpi/thermal_zone/*/temperature 75

Watches the system temperature and slows down the CPU when the temperature exceeds 75 degrees Celsius (167 degrees Fahrenheit).

To see a list of all available options, run this command:

```
$ /usr/sbin/cpuspeed --help 2>&1|less
```

After editing */etc/cpuspeed*, restart the *cpuspeed* service:

```
# service cpuspeed restart
Stopping cpuspeed:                                          [  OK  ]
Starting cpuspeed:                                          [  OK  ]
```

You can monitor the CPU speed by installing a monitor on your panel. Right-click on your GNOME panel, then select "Add to Panel." Choose the CPU Frequency Scaling Monitor and click Add. The icon shown in Figure 3-5 will appear; the bar graph will rise and fall as the CPU clock speed is adjusted, and hovering your mouse cursor over the display will show the current frequency setting (the box that appears below the icon in Figure 3-5).

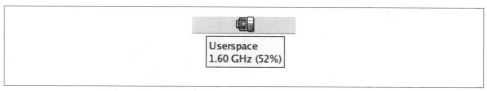

Figure 3-5. CPU Frequency Scaling Monitor

Managing power from the command line

If you are using your system through a text-mode console, you can still access the important power-management tools.

To suspend the system, execute the *pm-suspend* script:

```
$ pm-suspend
```

To hibernate, use the *pm-hibernate* script:

```
$ pm-hibernate
```

To view the battery status, access ACPI through the */proc* filesystem:

```
$ cat /proc/acpi/battery/*/state
present:               yes
capacity state:        ok
charging state:        charging
present rate:          3079 mA
remaining capacity:    2912 mAh
present voltage:       16273 mV
```

Battery details are also available from ACPI:

```
$ cat /proc/acpi/battery/*/info
present:                 yes
design capacity:         6450 mAh
last full capacity:      5154 mAh
battery technology:      rechargeable
design voltage:          14800 mV
design capacity warning: 515 mAh
design capacity low:     156 mAh
capacity granularity 1:  5 mAh
capacity granularity 2:  5 mAh
model number:            DELL 0017F
serial number:           14639
battery type:            LION
OEM info:                Sony
```

By dividing the last full capacity by the design capacity, you can determine the condition of the battery. In this case, the battery can presently store 5154/6450 mAh, or about 80 percent of its design capacity, indicating that it's in reasonably good condition.

Other ways to extend battery life

To further reduce power consumption:

- Dim your screen as much as the ambient lighting conditions will allow. The backlight for the screen draws a huge amount of power; one of my systems draws 31 percent more power in total when the screen is at maximum brightness than when it is set to minimum brightness.
- Turn off all unneeded services, reducing CPU and disk activity.
- Use a lightweight desktop environment such as Xfce instead of GNOME or KDE.

 Xfce can be easily installed (see Lab 5.3, "Using Repositories"). To select your desktop environment, use the Session menu on the graphical login screen.

- Unplug any unneeded external devices, including USB devices, headphones, mice, and keyboards. Each USB device can consume up to 2.5 watts of power, increasing your power consumption by as much as 20 percent.
- Turn off your wireless network radio when it is not in use. Most laptops have a wireless kill switch (sometimes labeled *airplane* or *flight mode*) that turns off the radio portion of the wireless card. This can cut your power consumption by up to 5 percent.

How Does It Work?

The ACPI specification enables a system's BIOS to supply data and program code to the operating system. The code is written in a unique, processor-independent pseudo-machine language called ACPI Machine Langauge (AML). The Linux kernel interpretively executes the AML code to access certain features of the host hardware system. You can think of the AML code as a type of device driver that is downloaded from the BIOS to the operating system.

The Linux kernel uses the ACPI data and code to collect data that is then exposed through the */proc/acpi* directory. Information received through the */proc/acpi* directory—such as instructions to change the CPU frequency—is passed to the ACPI code.

Applications such as *cpuspeed* and *gnome-power-manager* monitor the ACPI information and combine it with other information (such as current process load) and then make power management decisions. These decisions cause actions to be taken by various subsystems such as the ACPI, the X Window server, storage, and loadable modules.

The Fedora power-management system is in active development. To stay informed of the latest developments, subscribe to the *fedora-laptop-list* (see Lab 9.1, "Participating in the Fedora Mailing Lists").

What About...

...stopping the hard drive motors when the drives are not in use?

The *hdparm* program can be used to stop a drive immediately or to configure it to stop if it is idle for a certain length of time; this is called a *spin-down* (and restarting the drive is called a *spin-up*). This does save some power; however, the drive is rarely idle for very long and the length of time (and amount of energy) required to spin-up the drive is significant (and hard on some hardware), so opinion is divided on whether it makes sense to use this feature.

In the case of a two-drive system where the second drive is rarely used, an idle spin-down timeout is a good idea. Configure it with the *hdparm* command:

```
# hdparm -S 6 /dev/[hs]d[a-z]
```

The -S option configures the amount of time that the drive must be idle before spin-down is triggered. The scheme used to encode the timeout period is a bit convoluted (it is described in detail on the manpage for *hdparm*), but 0 means that spin-down is disabled, and a value from 1 to 240 sets the idle timeout in multiples of 5 seconds (5 seconds to 20 minutes). The value of *6* used here indicates a 30-second idle timeout.

...turning the computer on and off (or hibernating and resuming) at certain times automatically?

Some important operations are best performed when a system is not in normal use, such as backup, software updating, and data indexing. It's not necessary to keep a system running 24×7 in order to schedule nighttime tasks.

Most modern system BIOSes contain an *alarm wake* feature, which causes the system to turn on at a preset time. This feature can be used with the hibernate state or a full system shutdown to automate nocturnal activities.

The BIOS configuration utility varies from system to system; consult your system or motherboard documentation.

Some BIOS versions permit the wake time to be set through ACPI. To see if this is possible on your system, enable the *alarm wake* feature using your BIOS configuration utility, then boot Fedora and examine the */proc/acpi/alarm* file:

```
$ cat /proc/acpi/alarm
2007-03-17 00:00:00
```

Attempt to set this to a time in the future (the date portion of the time may be ignored by your system). If your system clock is maintained in UTC, be sure to also specify this time in UTC:

```
# echo "2007-03-17 16:45:00" >/proc/acpi/alarm
$ cat /proc/acpi/alarm
2007-03-17 16:45:00
```

Shut down your system and see if it turns on at the specified time.

Regardless of whether you can set the alarm time using Linux, you can use the wake-up feature in conjunction with *cron* to configure automatic boot and shutdown.

Configure your system to turn on at a specified time using either the BIOS or Linux ACPI methods. Create a *nocturnal* script that performs the work you wish to do at boot time:

```
#!/bin/bash
#
# /usr/local/bin/nocturnal :: script for nighttime processing

# Place whatever commands you wish to execute at night here
/usr/local/bin/backup-scp
yum -y update

# Shut the system back off - you can use pm-hibernate here
# if it works on your system
shutdown -h now
```

Replace the last line with pm-hibernate if hibernation works on your system and you wish to reduce the startup time in the morning.

Edit your *crontab*:

```
# crontab -e
```

Add a line to execute the *nocturnal* script a few minutes after your preset wake-up time:

```
# Perform nighttime processing after the 4:30 wake-up
35 4 * * * /usr/local/bin/nocturnal
```

If you shut down the system at the end of your working day, it will wake up at night, perform the processing you have configured, and then shut down.

If your system supports changing the alarm time through ACPI, you can schedule multiple wake-up times: have your system start up in the middle of the night and perform the operations described above, and then have it schedule the next wake-up time before shutting down:

```
#!/bin/bash
#
# /usr/local/bin/nocturnal :: script for nighttime processing
```

```
# Please whatever commands you wish to execute at night here
/usr/local/bin/backup-scp
yum -y update

# Schedule another wake-up
date "+%Y-%m-%d 07:50:00" >/proc/acpi/alarm

# Shut the system back off; you can use pm-hibernate here
# if it works on your system
shutdown -h now
```

This sets the next wake-up for 7:50 a.m. the same day, just in time to start work at 8 a.m. If your nocturnal processing takes place before midnight, schedule the wake-up for the following day:

```
# Schedule another wake-up
date +"%Y-%m-%d 07:50:00" -d tomorrow >/proc/acpi/alarm
```

Where Can I Learn More?

- *gnome-power-manager* home page: *http://www.gnome.org/projects/gnome-power-manager/*
- ACPI Promoters' web site, including the ACPI specification: *http://www.acpi.info/*
- "Linux ACPI-Howto, The Sequel": *http://www.columbia.edu/~ariel/acpi/acpi_howto.html*
- The manpage for *hdparm*

3.2   Configuring Networking

The majority of modern computer system are connected to a network. While server and desktop systems are often configured for one network at installation time and remain plugged into that same network for weeks, months, or years, laptop systems are frequently on the move and may connect to several different networks in one day. Fortunately, Fedora provides a good set of network configuration tools that enable you to easily swing from one network to another like a digital Tarzan.

How Do I Do That?

There are three ways to configure networking on Fedora. Each approach has its advantages and disadvantages:

Graphical configuration tool
>   The best approach for desktop and server systems that will connect to one or two networks and rarely require changes to the network configuration

NetworkManager
   Excellent for laptops that will be connecting to a variety of different networks, but only compatible with certain network hardware

Network configuration commands
   Good for experimentation, remote administration, and very complex configurations

Configuring networking graphically

Select the menu option System → Administration → Networking to access the GUI network configuration tool shown in Figure 3-6. Alternatively, you can type the command system-config-network into a shell (or use the traditional nickname for this program, *neat*).

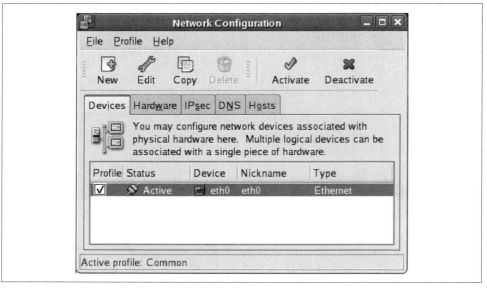

Figure 3-6. Network Configuration window

To add a network connection, click on the New icon. The window in Figure 3-7 will appear, enabling you to select the connection type.

Use the default Ethernet connection option for any LAN connection, including cable modem connections as well as all DSL connections made through a router or gateway device. Click Forward to proceed to the device-selection window in Figure 3-8.

All of the Ethernet devices that have been automatically detected (or previously configured manually) will be listed, with the device name in parentheses (such as *eth0*). Select the device you wish to configure and click Forward.

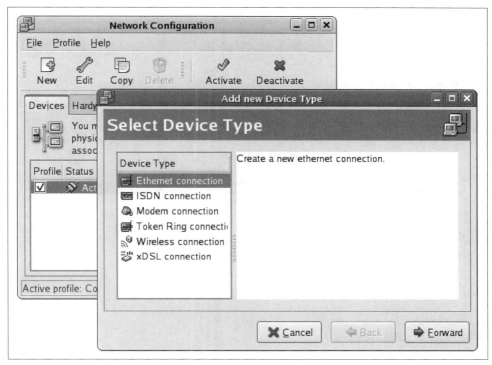

Figure 3-7. New Device Type window

If the device is not in the list, select Other Ethernet Card from the bottom of the list and click Forward. The window shown in Figure 3-9 will appear; select the Adapter type (which selects the device driver to be used), the device name to be used (the default is usually OK), and any resources the card will use (this area should almost always be left blank). Click Forward.

You will now see the window shown in Figure 3-10. Select one of the two options to assign the IP address for this network connection:

Automatically obtain IP address settings
    Use this option if you wish to use an IP address assigned by a system on your network (such as another computer running a DHCP server, a gateway or router device, or a cable modem). Set the adjacent protocol control to DHCP unless your network uses the older BOOTP protocol (rare).

Statically set IP addresses
    Select this option to manually configure the IP address. Fill in the IP address, subnet mask, and gateway (router) address in the labeled fields.

Click Forward to proceed.

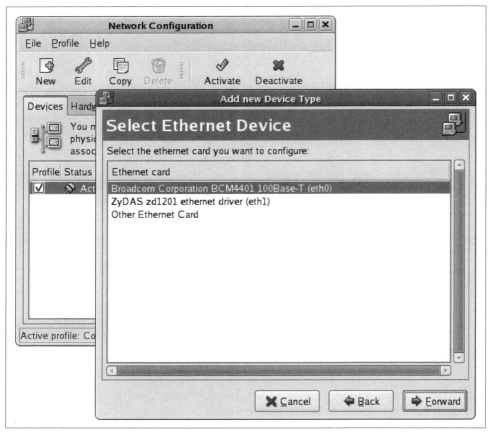

Figure 3-8. Device-selection window

Figure 3-11 shows the final confirmation window that appears. Review the information for accuracy and then click Apply.

Changing a device configuration. To edit an existing network device, double-click on it in the main Network Configuration window (shown earlier in Figure 3-6), or select it and click the Edit icon. Figure 3-12 shows the editing window that appears.

 The editing window includes some options that are unavailable when the device is first created.

There are three tabs in this window. The first tab, General, provides fields for basic device configuration:

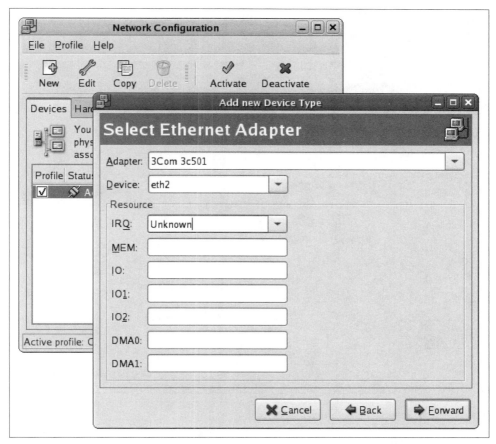

Figure 3-9. New device-setup window

Nickname

Any name of your choice. This is provided only for your reference; for example, if you have two Ethernet cards, you might nickname one *Internet* and the other *Corporate* to identify the networks to which they are connected.

Activate device when computer starts

Most network devices will have this box checked, but you should leave it unchecked for unused devices and for devices that are used only in certain contexts—for example, a wireless card on a laptop that is used only at home.

Allow all users to enable and disable this device

If selected, this feature enables any user to activate or deactivate the network device without the *root* password.

Enable IPv6 configuration for this interface

If your network supports IP version 6 (which is rare but becoming more common), select this box.

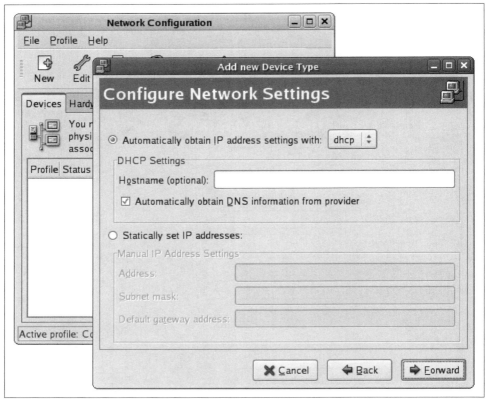

Figure 3-10. IP address configuration

IP address settings

These fields replicate the fields used during the initial device setup.

 Changing the hostname field and then saving the network configuration will prevent you from opening any new GUI applications because the X Window System uses the hostname in the security key used to control access to the display. To correct this problem, log out and then log in again after changing the hostname, or enter this command before doing so:

```
$ xhost +localhost
```

Figure 3-13 shows the Route tab, which is used to configure network routes when there is more than one gateway (router) available to your system.

For single-gateway networks—including most home and office networks—use the Default Gateway field on the Devices tab and do not fill in any information on the Route tab.

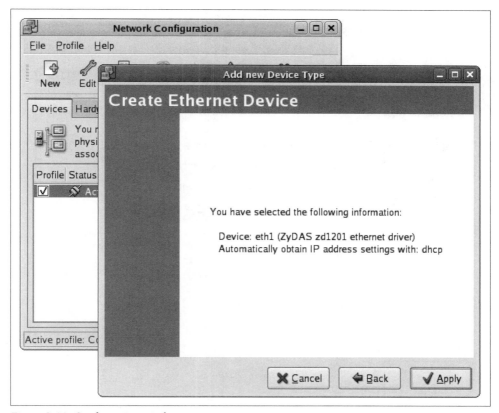

Figure 3-11. Confirmation window

To add a new route, click the Edit button, then enter the network to be routed as an IP network address and a netmask, and then enter the Gateway (router) to which packets destined for that network are to be sent.

Figure 3-13 shows a new routing entry for an 8-bit subnet: the network number is 172.16.4.0, and the netmask is 255.255.255.0, which means that any packets addressed to an IP address that starts with 172.16.4 must be sent through the gateway associated with this route, which has been set to 172.16.97.200.

 The gateway must be on the same subnet as the network interface device.

To edit or delete existing routes, select the route and click on the Edit or Delete buttons.

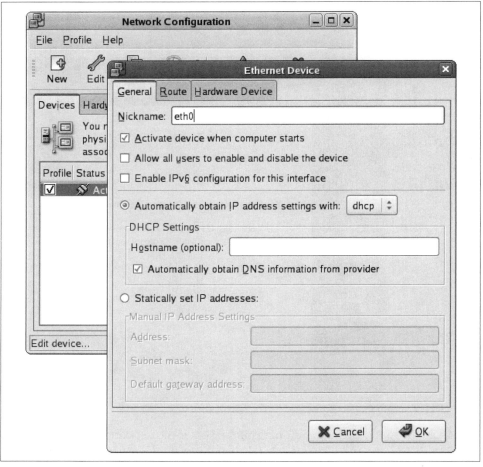

Figure 3-12. Network Configuration device-editing window

Figure 3-14 shows the third tab, labeled Hardware Device, which contains three groups of fields:

Hardware

Selects the physical network device used for this interface.

Device alias number

Used to configure multiple IP addresses for one device. If you have one Ethernet card and wish to assign it the IP addresses 192.168.4.13 and 10.0.17.42, one IP address could be assigned to the base device (*eth0*), and the other IP address could be assigned to a different interface device entry connected to the same hardware (which would result in a device alias, such as *eth0:1*). This field is used to set the alias number (*1* in this example).

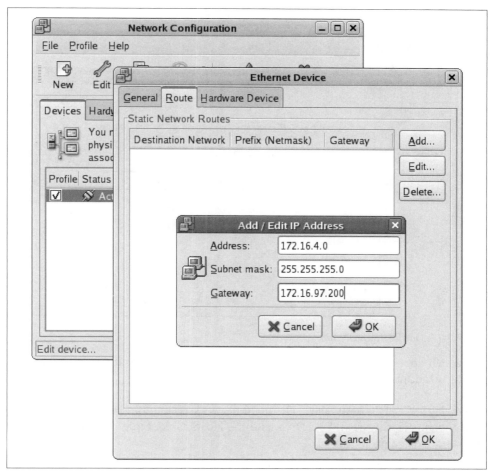

Figure 3-13. Routing configuration

 To create alias devices, use the same procedure that you use to create physical interfaces. The configuration tool will set the alias number for you automatically.

Bind to MAC address

This field associates this device entry with a specific physical network interface card via the MAC address (electronic serial number) of the network card. This is desirable in most cases because it prevents the network interfaces from being renumbered if network hardware is later added to the system, shifting (for example) *eth0* into *eth1*. However, this can cause problems if you replace a network card with a different card of the same model, or if you are using removable disks that are moved between systems (such as hard drives in removable drive trays,

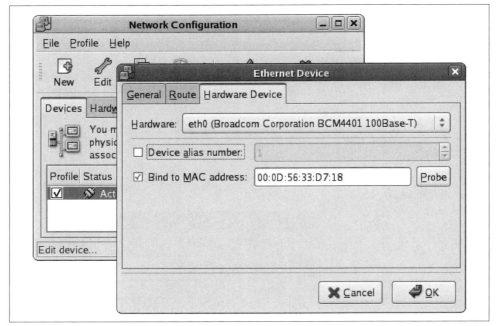

Figure 3-14. Hardware Device tab

which are often used in testing environments and schools). If you do expect the MAC address to change, deselect this checkbox.

Configuring DNS and the Hosts table. The main network configuration window also contains tabs for Hardware, IPSec, DNS, and the Hosts table. I'm going to focus on the DNS and Hosts tabs in this lab.

The DNS tab shown in Figure 3-15 is used to configure *nameservers*, computers that are configured to translate hostnames such as *google.com* into IP addresses. When using DHCP, this information is usually configured automatically. If your DHCP server does not supply this information or you're not using DHCP, enter up to three DNS servers using the Primary, Secondary, and Tertiary DNS fields. In the Hostname field, enter the name of the server you are configuring; this should be part of a valid domain, or localhost.localdomain if you don't have a domain.

> If you are running a nameserver on the same computer, enter 127.0.0.1 (the loopback address that connects to the local host) as the Primary nameserver. Optionally, enter another nameserver as the Secondary DNS just in case your local nameserver is ever down.
>
> If a nameserver times out on you frequently (a problem that is common on slow or congested links, and which causes name lookups to fail the first time and succeed the second time they are requested), enter the nameserver twice (for example, make it both the primary and secondary nameserver).

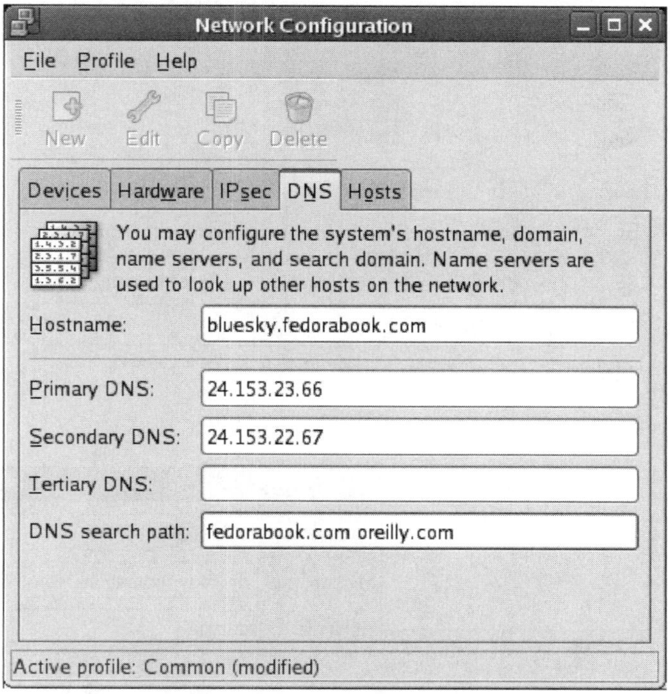

Figure 3-15. DNS tab

The "DNS search path" field is used to specify the domains to be searched when looking up a hostname that does not have a domain-name component. For example, if this field contained myorganization.ca fedorabook.com, then the hostname bluesky would be looked up as *bluesky.myorganization.ca*, and if no IP address could be found for that name, it would be looked up as *bluesky.fedorabook.com*.

The Hosts tab shown in Figure 3-16 is used to configure *static mappings*, which define the relationship between hostnames and IP addresses without using DNS. This is useful if you have only a handful of hosts and wish to refer to them by hostname without going to the trouble of configuring a DNS nameserver.

To add a static mapping, click the New button, and then enter the IP address, hostname, and (optionally) any aliases or alternate hostnames for that particular IP address. In Figure 3-16, the address 172.16.97.143 is being associated with the hostname *darkday.fedorabook.com* as well as the (shorter) alias of just *darkday*. Click OK to save the mapping.

As you would expect, the Edit and Delete buttons may be used to change or remove a selected static mapping.

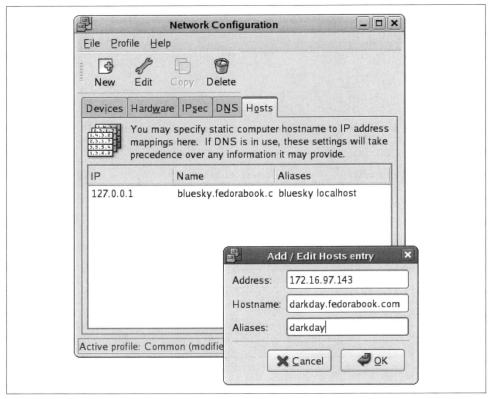

Figure 3-16. Hosts tab

 Do not delete the entry for 127.0.0.1 or ::1, or your system will not work properly. Both the system's hostname and localhost must appear as the hostname or alias for this entry. If you change this entry and save the configuration, it may not be possible to open new programs on the graphical display until you log out and then log in again.

Saving and using the network configuration. To save the network configuration that you have configured using the GUI tool, select the menu option File → Save. This will update the network configuration files with your changes but will not immediately activate those changes.

To enable or disable network interfaces, go to the Devices tab (Figure 3-6), select the interface you wish to change, and click Activate or Deactivate. Alternately, you can exit from the network configuration tool and restart the Network service graphically (see Lab 4.6, "Managing and Configuring Services") or by entering this command:

```
# service network restart
Shutting down interface eth0:                        [  OK  ]
Shutting down loopback interface:                    [  OK  ]
```

```
Bringing up loopback interface:                      [  OK  ]
Bringing up interface eth0:                          [  OK  ]
```

Network interface devices which are set to activate at boot will automatically start up when the network interface is started. Other devices may be started and stopped using the network configuration tool.

However, if the option labeled "Allow all users to enable and disable the device" has been set in the interface device configuration (Figure 3-12), any user can activate or deactivate the device using the GNOME menu option Application → System Tools → Network Device Control (in KDE, System → Network Device Control).

This option may not appear on your GNOME menu; to make it available, right-click on the GNOME application menu and select Edit Menus. Figure 3-17 shows the menu editor that appears.

Figure 3-17. The GNOME menu editor

Select Applications → System Tools in the left pane, select the checkbox labeled Network Device Control in the right pane, and then click on the Close button.

When you start the Network Device Control program, either through the menu or by typing **system-control-network** in a shell, the window shown in Figure 3-18 will appear.

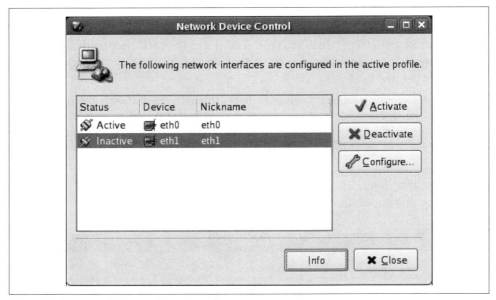

Figure 3-18. Network Device Control window

To activate or deactivate network interface devices using this program, select the interface and click on the Activate or Deactivate buttons. Click Close when you are done with the window.

You can also activate and deactivate network interfaces from the command line using the ifup and ifdown commands:

```
# ifconfig eth1
eth1      Link encap:Ethernet  HWaddr 00:0C:2D:00:2B:DB
          BROADCAST MULTICAST  MTU:1500  Metric:1
          RX packets:794 errors:0 dropped:0 overruns:0 frame:0
          TX packets:195 errors:0 dropped:0 overruns:0 carrier:0
          collisions:0 txqueuelen:1000
          RX bytes:115671 (112.9 KiB)  TX bytes:19491 (19.0 KiB)


# ifup eth1

Determining IP information for eth1... done.


# ifconfig eth1
eth1      Link encap:Ethernet  HWaddr 00:0C:2D:00:2B:DB
          inet addr:172.16.97.101  Bcast:172.16.97.255  Mask:255.255.255.0
          inet6 addr: fe80::20c:2dff:fe00:2bdb/64 Scope:Link
          UP BROADCAST RUNNING MULTICAST  MTU:1500  Metric:1
          RX packets:802 errors:0 dropped:0 overruns:0 frame:0
          TX packets:213 errors:0 dropped:0 overruns:0 carrier:0
          collisions:0 txqueuelen:1000
          RX bytes:117520 (114.7 KiB)  TX bytes:22579 (22.0 KiB)
```

```
# ifdown eth1
# ifconfig eth1
eth1      Link encap:Ethernet  HWaddr 00:0C:2D:00:2B:DB
          BROADCAST MULTICAST  MTU:1500  Metric:1
          RX packets:802 errors:0 dropped:0 overruns:0 frame:0
          TX packets:213 errors:0 dropped:0 overruns:0 carrier:0
          collisions:0 txqueuelen:1000
          RX bytes:117520 (114.7 KiB)  TX bytes:22579 (22.0 KiB)
```

Using network profiles. The graphical network configuration tool supports the concept of *profiles* to permit easy roaming between different networks. You can configure a separate profile for each network that you use (such as *home*, *office*, and *coffeeshop*).

A standard profile named *Common* is created when your system is installed. The Common profile is automatically selected at boot time, and it's the only profile that can define interfaces that will be started when the system boots.

To create additional profiles, use the Profile → New menu option. The dialog shown in Figure 3-19 will appear; enter the name of the new profile. You can then select a specific profile from the Profile menu, use the checkboxes in front of the network devices to configure which interfaces are active in that profile, and then select File → Save to save the configuration of that profile.

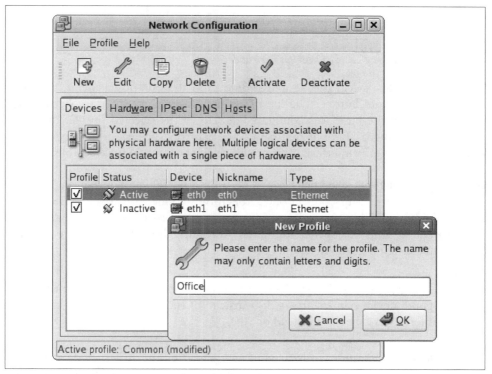

Figure 3-19. Creating a new Network Configuration profile

Once you have created at least one profile in addition to the standard Common profile, the Network Device Control window will gain a new pull-down menu that enables you to select the active profile, as shown in Figure 3-20 (compare with Figure 3-18).

Figure 3-20. The Active Profile control has been added

To change profiles, select the desired profile from the pull-down menu, and then click on the Activate button. The list of configured network interface devices will change to reflect the interfaces configured as part of the selected profile. Interfaces that are part of the profile but that cannot be activated or deactivated by ordinary users will appear in the interface list, but will be grayed out and unselectable.

Configuring other network connection types. The procedure for configuring an ISDN or analog telephone dial-up connection, a token-ring connection, or an xDSL (DSL, ADSL, SDSL, or IDSL) connection is identical to the procedure for configuring an Ethernet connection, except that additional (or slightly different) details are required in order to configure the connection:

Token Ring

> This configuration is almost identical to Ethernet configuration, except that the configured device name starts with *tr* instead of *eth* (for example, the first token ring interface is called tr0 instead of eth0).

Wireless

> Wireless configuration adds a window right after the Ethernet device driver selection and resource settings. This window requests the management mode

(Auto, Managed [for normal communication with a permanent network], or Ad Hoc [for temporary networks of peer systems]), network name (set this to the SSID or ESSID of the network to which you are connecting), channel, transmit rate, and WEP encryption key. In most cases, entering the network name and WEP key is all that is required.

xDSL

All varieties of DSL lines require just one screen to set up. The configuration tool will ask you for the Ethernet device (such as *eth0*) that is connected to the DSL modem, the Internet service provider name (such as Bell Sympatico, which is recorded only for your reference), the account type (normal or T-Online), and the PPOE login name and password provided by your ISP.

ISDN and Modem Dial-Up Connections

Although ISDN and analog modems use very different technology, the configuration process is similar. First, you'll need to enter the device details. For an ISDN line, this is the ISDN adapter type and resources (usually left blank), as well as the D-channel type (leave this set to Euro ISDN in all countries except Germany, where it should be set to 1TR6). For a modem, this includes the modem device, baud rate, and flow control (these settings are usually all left at their defaults), plus volume and touch-tone settings (adjust these according to your preferences). For both types of dial-up connections, the next window asks you to select your Internet service provider and enter the phone number, username, and password that were provided by your ISP; the last window asks for the encapsulation mode (usually Sync PPP) and IP settings (whether to obtain these from the provider or manually configure them).

Using GNOME NetworkManager

The GNOME NetworkManager facility provides an alternative to the use of profiles. NetworkManager is a service that automatically detects network configuration changes and determines available options. A small GUI application permits you to quickly select the network option you wish to use. It's ideal for laptop users because it permits rapid switching between multiple wired and wireless networks.

> At this time, NetworkManager is a work in progress. When it works, it works well, but some hardware that works fine with other configuration techniques does not work at all with NetworkManager. It is proposed that NetworkManager will eventually become the configuration tool of choice.

The NetworkManager service is enabled in the same way as every other service (see Lab 4.6, "Managing and Configuring Services"). You can configure it to start at the next boot by choosing the menu option System → Administration → Services, and then selecting the checkboxes labeled NetworkManger (the related

NetworkManagerDispatcher service is not usually required); to start the services immediately, select each of them in turn and then click the Start button.

From the command line, you can start the service immediately using the service command, and you can configure it to start at boot time using *chkconfig*:

```
# service NetworkManager start
Setting network parameters...
Starting NetworkManager daemon:                    [  OK  ]
# chkconfig NetworkManager on
```

 Notice the nonstandard use of capital letters in the name Network-Manager.

As soon as the NetworkManager starts, an icon should appear in your panel's notification area, which is shown in Figure 3-21. This icon will indicate the type of IP connection currently in use. To switch to a different connection, click on the icon; a list of available connections will appear (including all broadcast local network names if you have a wireless card, plus a little signal-strength bar graph for each wireless network). Click on the network you wish to connect to, and NetworkManager will attempt to make the connection. You will be prompted to enter WEP or WPA encryption keys if necessary.

Figure 3-21. NetworkManager icon (left), showing that a wired Ethernet connection is active

NetworkManager will establish connections with wired networks automatically, but it will not automatically connect to wireless networks to which you have not previously connected because they may belong to your neighbor, or to companies that you are passing if you are in a vehicle. It will also detect the loss of network connectivity when a wireless signal is no longer usable or a network cable is unplugged.

You can also view the NetworkManager status from the command line by using *nm-tool*:

```
# nm-tool

NetworkManager Tool

State: connected

- Device: eth0 -----------------------------------------------------------
  NM Path:              /org/freedesktop/NetworkManager/Devices/eth0
  Type:                 Wired
  Driver:               b44
  Active:               yes
```

```
HW Address:        00:0D:56:33:D7:18

Capabilities:
   Supported:       yes
   Carrier Detect:  yes
   Speed:           100 Mb/s

Wired Settings
   Hardware Link:   yes

IP Settings:
   IP Address:      172.16.97.100
   Subnet Mask:     255.255.255.0
   Broadcast:       172.16.97.255
   Gateway:         172.16.97.254
   Primary DNS:     24.153.23.66
   Secondary DNS:   24.153.22.67
```

Configuring networking from the command line

The GUI network configuration tool and NetworkManager both work well for desktop users, but when you're logged in to a server that is a few time zones away or need to make a fast change, it's useful to be able to configure networking from the command line.

The main interface configuration command is *ifconfig* (for *interface configuration*). Executed by itself, it displays the basic configuration of active interfaces:

```
$ /sbin/ifconfig
eth0      Link encap:Ethernet  HWaddr 00:0D:56:33:D7:18
          inet addr:172.16.97.100  Bcast:172.16.97.255  Mask:255.255.255.0
          inet6 addr: fe80::20d:56ff:fe33:d718/64 Scope:Link
          UP BROADCAST RUNNING MULTICAST  MTU:1500  Metric:1
          RX packets:289 errors:0 dropped:0 overruns:0 frame:0
          TX packets:228 errors:0 dropped:0 overruns:0 carrier:0
          collisions:0 txqueuelen:1000
          RX bytes:45844 (44.7 KiB)  TX bytes:27193 (26.5 KiB)
          Interrupt:177

lo        Link encap:Local Loopback
          inet addr:127.0.0.1  Mask:255.0.0.0
          inet6 addr: ::1/128 Scope:Host
          UP LOOPBACK RUNNING  MTU:16436  Metric:1
          RX packets:2258 errors:0 dropped:0 overruns:0 frame:0
          TX packets:2258 errors:0 dropped:0 overruns:0 carrier:0
          collisions:0 txqueuelen:0
          RX bytes:2884024 (2.7 MiB)  TX bytes:2884024 (2.7 MiB)
```

The two interfaces displayed here are eth0, the first Ethernet interface, and lo, the loopback interface used when a client and a server that are both on the local machine need to communicate. For each interface, the information displayed includes the IP version 4 address (inet addr), IP version 6 address (inet6 addr), netmask (Mask), status flags (such as UP and RUNNING), and transmit, receive, and error statistics.

You can narrow down the report to a single interface by specifying that interface name as an argument:

```
$ /sbin/ifconfig eth0
eth0      Link encap:Ethernet  HWaddr 00:0D:56:33:D7:18
          inet addr:172.16.97.100  Bcast:172.16.97.255  Mask:255.255.255.0
          inet6 addr: fe80::20d:56ff:fe33:d718/64 Scope:Link
          UP BROADCAST RUNNING MULTICAST  MTU:1500  Metric:1
          RX packets:331 errors:0 dropped:0 overruns:0 frame:0
          TX packets:261 errors:0 dropped:0 overruns:0 carrier:0
          collisions:0 txqueuelen:1000
          RX bytes:49667 (48.5 KiB)  TX bytes:32047 (31.2 KiB)
          Interrupt:177
```

To see both active and inactive interfaces, use the -a option:

```
$ /sbin/ifconfig -a
eth0      Link encap:Ethernet  HWaddr 00:0D:56:33:D7:18
...(Lines snipped)...
lo        Link encap:Local Loopback
...(Lines snipped)...
sit0      Link encap:IPv6-in-IPv4
          NOARP  MTU:1480  Metric:1
          RX packets:0 errors:0 dropped:0 overruns:0 frame:0
          TX packets:0 errors:0 dropped:0 overruns:0 carrier:0
          collisions:0 txqueuelen:0
          RX bytes:0 (0.0 b)  TX bytes:0 (0.0 b)

wlan0     Link encap:Ethernet  HWaddr 00:0C:2D:00:2B:DB
          BROADCAST MULTICAST  MTU:1500  Metric:1
          RX packets:0 errors:0 dropped:0 overruns:0 frame:0
          TX packets:0 errors:0 dropped:0 overruns:0 carrier:0
          collisions:0 txqueuelen:1000
          RX bytes:0 (0.0 b)  TX bytes:0 (0.0 b)
```

In this case, there are two interfaces here that didn't show up when *ifconfig* was run without the -a argument: sit0, used for IPv6 tunneling, and wlan0, a Wi-Fi (802.11a/b/g) interface.

ifconfig is also used to configure interfaces. The wlan0 interface can be given an IP address, broadcast address, netmask, and state (up or down):

```
# ifconfig wlan0 up 192.168.9.37 netmask 255.255.255.0 broadcast 192.168.9.255
# ifconfig wlan0
wlan0     Link encap:Ethernet  HWaddr 00:0C:2D:00:2B:DB
          inet addr:192.168.9.37  Bcast:192.168.9.255  Mask:255.255.255.0
          inet6 addr: fe80::20c:2dff:fe00:2bdb/64 Scope:Link
          UP BROADCAST RUNNING MULTICAST  MTU:1500  Metric:1
          RX packets:1 errors:0 dropped:0 overruns:0 frame:0
          TX packets:18 errors:0 dropped:0 overruns:0 carrier:0
          collisions:0 txqueuelen:1000
          RX bytes:268 (268.0 b)  TX bytes:2922 (2.8 KiB)
```

In almost all cases, the broadcast address can be left out because it can be determined from the IP address and netmask. The netmask can also be omitted if it is the default value for the network class indicated by the IP address. Table 3-1 lists the standard netmasks.

 Although the use of network classes has been made obsolete by the introduction and widespread use of classless interdomain routing (CIDR), the network class values are still used to determine the default netmask. This generates the correct value for most private networks.

Table 3-1. Netmasks by IP address class (not including Multicast addresses)

First octet of IP address	Example	Network class	Netmask	Number of IP addresses in subnet
0–127	3.15.97.4	A	255.0.0.0	16,777,216
128–191	132.2.2.9	B	255.255.0.0	65,536
192–255	204.99.3.8	C	255.255.255.0	256

The up argument is also unnecessary if an IP address is being specified.

The previous command can therefore be written much more simply:

```
# ifconfig wlan0 192.168.9.37
# ifconfig wlan0
wlan0     Link encap:Ethernet  HWaddr 00:0C:2D:00:2B:DB
          inet addr:192.168.9.37  Bcast:192.168.9.255  Mask:255.255.255.0
          inet6 addr: fe80::20c:2dff:fe00:2bdb/64 Scope:Link
          UP BROADCAST RUNNING MULTICAST  MTU:1500  Metric:1
          RX packets:1 errors:0 dropped:0 overruns:0 frame:0
          TX packets:18 errors:0 dropped:0 overruns:0 carrier:0
          collisions:0 txqueuelen:1000
          RX bytes:268 (268.0 b)  TX bytes:2922 (2.8 KiB)
```

Configuring wireless networks from the command line. For wireless interfaces, there are two additional commands that are useful for configuration: *iwconfig*, which sets wireless parameters—such as the channel, encryption, and ESSID—and *iwlist*, which can be used to scan for available networks.

iwconfig will display current settings if no parameters are given:

```
# iwconfig
lo        no wireless extensions.

eth0      no wireless extensions.

sit0      no wireless extensions.

wlan0     IEEE 802.11b  ESSID:""  Nickname:"zd1201"
          Mode:Managed  Channel:6  Access Point: 00:90:4C:7E:00:29
          Bit Rate:11 Mb/s
```

```
Retry:off    RTS thr:off    Fragment thr:off
Encryption key:off
Power Management:off
Link Quality:0/128  Signal level=60/128  Noise level:0/128
Rx invalid nwid:0  Rx invalid crypt:0  Rx invalid frag:0
Tx excessive retries:0  Invalid misc:0   Missed beacon:0
```

Here you can see that this interface has associated with an access point with a MAC address of 00:90:4C:7E:00:29, and which is apparently an 802.11b network (11 Mb/s).

To scan for available networks, use *iwlist* with the scan argument:

```
# iwlist scan
lo          Interface doesn't support scanning.

eth0        Interface doesn't support scanning.

sit0        Interface doesn't support scanning.

wlan0       Scan completed :
            Cell 01 - Address: 00:90:4C:7E:00:29
                      ESSID:"fedorabook"
                      Mode:Master
                      Channel:11
                      Bit Rates:1 Mb/s
                      Bit Rates:2 Mb/s
                      Bit Rates:5.5 Mb/s
                      Bit Rates:11 Mb/s
                      Encryption key:off
                      Quality=60/128  Signal level=-76 dBm  Noise level=-100 dBm

            Cell 02 - Address: 00:87:29:13:c0:71
                      ESSID:"tylers"
                      Mode:Master
                      Channel:2
                      Bit Rates:1 Mb/s
                      Bit Rates:2 Mb/s
                      Bit Rates:5.5 Mb/s
                      Bit Rates:11 Mb/s
                      Bit Rates:18 Mb/s
                      Bit Rates:24 Mb/s
                      Bit Rates:36 Mb/s
                      Bit Rates:54 Mb/s
                      Encryption key:on
                      Quality=59/128  Signal level=-76 dBm  Noise level=-99 dBm
```

To select which network wlan0 associates with, set the *extended service set identifier* (ESSID) of the interface:

```
# iwconfig wlan0 essid fedorabook
# iwconfig wlan0
wlan0       IEEE 802.11b  ESSID:"fedorabook"  Nickname:"zd1201"
            Mode:Managed  Channel:6  Access Point: 00:90:4C:7E:00:29
            Bit Rate:11 Mb/s
            Retry:off   RTS thr:off    Fragment thr:off
```

```
Encryption key:off
Power Management:off
Link Quality:0/128  Signal level=76/128  Noise level:0/128
Rx invalid nwid:0  Rx invalid crypt:0  Rx invalid frag:0
Tx excessive retries:0  Invalid misc:0   Missed beacon:0
```

To disable an interface, turn it down using *ifconfig*:

```
# ifconfig wlan0 down
# ifconfig wlan0
wlan0     Link encap:Ethernet  HWaddr 00:0C:2D:00:2B:DB
          inet addr:192.168.9.37  Bcast:192.168.9.37  Mask:255.255.255.0
          BROADCAST MULTICAST  MTU:1500  Metric:1
          RX packets:476 errors:0 dropped:0 overruns:0 frame:0
          TX packets:18 errors:0 dropped:0 overruns:0 carrier:0
          collisions:0 txqueuelen:1000
          RX bytes:84965 (82.9 KiB)  TX bytes:2922 (2.8 KiB)
```

Notice that the *ifconfig* display no longer shows the UP flag for the interface.

Netmasks and routing. The netmask is used to determine which computers are on the local network, and which ones are remote and must therefore be reached through a gateway or router. These rules create the default routing table, which can be displayed with *route*:

```
# route
Kernel IP routing table
Destination     Gateway         Genmask         Flags Metric Ref    Use Iface
172.16.97.0     *               255.255.255.0   U     0      0        0 eth0
default         172.16.97.254   0.0.0.0         UG    0      0        0 eth0
```

Notice that two routes have been configured. The first one states that local machines (those with IP addresses starting with 172.16.97) can be reached directly on the local network (gateway * and no G in the Flags column), and the second entry states that packets destined to any other IP address are to be sent through the router 172.16.97. 254 (which is on the local network and therefore directly reachable).

The default route can be removed and added back in, pointing to a different gateway/router:

```
# route delete default
# route add default gw 172.16.97.253
# route
Kernel IP routing table
Destination     Gateway         Genmask         Flags Metric Ref    Use Iface
172.16.97.0     *               255.255.255.0   U     0      0        0 eth0
default         172.16.97.253   0.0.0.0         UG    0      0        0 eth0
```

When the wlan0 interface is configured, a new route is added for hosts directly accessible through that interface:

```
# ifconfig wlan0 192.168.9.37
# route
Kernel IP routing table
```

```
Destination     Gateway        Genmask         Flags Metric Ref    Use Iface
172.16.97.0     *              255.255.255.0   U     0      0        0 eth0
192.168.9.0     *              255.255.255.0   U     0      0        0 wlan0
default         172.16.97.253  0.0.0.0         UG    0      0        0 eth0
```

If other networks are available through additional gateways, these can be configured
by using *route* with the -net and netmask arguments. For example, if your corporate
network 10.x.x.x in London were accessible through the gateway 192.168.9.1 on
your wireless network, you could configure the route with this command:

```
# route add -net 10.0.0.0 netmask 255.0.0.0 gw 192.168.9.1
# route
Kernel IP routing table
Destination     Gateway        Genmask         Flags Metric Ref    Use Iface
172.16.97.0     *              255.255.255.0   U     0      0        0 eth0
192.168.9.0     *              255.255.255.0   U     0      0        0 wlan0
10.0.0.0        192.168.9.1    255.0.0.0       UG    0      0        0 wlan0
default         172.16.97.253  0.0.0.0         UG    0      0        0 eth0
```

DNS and hostnames. DNS resolution is controlled by the file */etc/resolv.conf*, which
looks something like this:

```
search fedorabook.com oreilly.com
nameserver 127.0.0.1
nameserver 216.183.93.224
```

There are three common option keywords used in this file:

search

> A space- or tab-delimited list of domains to be searched when attempting to
> resolve a hostname without a domain component. In this example, if the DNS
> resolver were given the hostname *bluesky*, it would attempt to resolve the host-
> name *bluesky.fedorabook.com*, and if that failed, it would attempt to resolve
> *bluesky.oreilly.com*. There is a limit of six domains in the search list.

domain

> A rarely used alternative to search that can specify only one domain. The domain
> and search options are mutually exclusive and cannot be used at the same time.

nameserver

> The IP address of a nameserver available to resolve DNS queries. Listing multi-
> ple nameservers provides redundancy in case one of the servers is unavailable. In
> this example, the address for localhost (this computer) is given first, with a sec-
> ond nameserver entry providing the IP address of a remote nameserver as
> backup.

If the DNS settings are configured by DHCP, this file is overwritten automatically
with the values provided by the DNS server. In that case, an additional comment line
will appear at the top of the file:

```
; generated by /sbin/dhclient-script
```

To change the DNS configuration, simply edit this file with a text editor, adding or removing domains in the search line or adding or removing nameserver lines as necessary.

The */etc/hosts* file contains a list of IP and hostname mappings. As initially set up by Anaconda (the Fedora installation system), the file will look like this:

```
# Do not remove the following line, or various programs
# that require network functionality will fail.
::1             bluesky.fedorabook.com  localhost
```

The one entry in this file associates the system's name and the localhost alias with the loopback device (which may be expressed as ::1 in IPv6 notation, or 127.0.0.1 in IPv4 notation). This entry *must* exist in the file, or many system services will fail to operate.

You can add additional entries to */etc/hosts* if you want to refer to local computers by name but don't want to go through the effort of setting up DNS (see Lab 7.3, "Configuring a Domain Name Server"). Simply place the IP address at the start of the line and then list the names and aliases for that host, separated by spaces or tabs:

```
# Do not remove the following line, or various programs
# that require network functionality will fail.
::1             bluesky.fedorabook.com     localhost
172.16.97.60    darkday.fedorabook.com     darkday    frank
172.16.97.73    accounting.fedorabook.com  accounting susan
172.16.97.207   samba.fedorabook.com
```

To change the system's hostname, edit the */etc/hosts* file and change the entry for the loopback line (do not remove the localhost alias):

```
# Do not remove the following line, or various programs
# that require network functionality will fail.
::1             beige.fedorabook.com       localhost
```

Then edit the HOSTNAME entry in */etc/sysconfig/network*:

```
NETWORKING=yes
NETWORKING_IPV6=yes
HOSTNAME=beige.fedorabook.com
```

The change will take effect next time you boot. To make the change take effect immediately, use the hostname command:

```
# hostname beige.fedorabook.com
# hostname
beige.fedorabook.com
```

Configuring networking from the command line using DHCP. Fedora Core provides the *dhclient* program to configure network interfaces based on information received from Dynamic Host Configuration Protocol (DHCP) servers. Simply run this program as *root*, specifying the interface(s) that you wish to configure:

```
# dhclient wlan0
# ifconfig wlan0
```

```
wlan0      Link encap:Ethernet  HWaddr 00:0C:2D:00:2B:DB
           inet addr:10.144.12.160  Bcast:10.144.255.255  Mask:255.255.0.0
           inet6 addr: fe80::20c:2dff:fe00:2bdb/64 Scope:Link
           UP BROADCAST RUNNING MULTICAST  MTU:1500  Metric:1
           RX packets:3 errors:0 dropped:0 overruns:0 frame:0
           TX packets:18 errors:0 dropped:0 overruns:0 carrier:0
           collisions:0 txqueuelen:1000
           RX bytes:1222 (1.1 KiB)  TX bytes:3442 (3.3 KiB)
```

Since information supplied by a DHCP server is considered a lease that expires after a preset time, *dhclient* continues to run in the background so that it can renew the lease when necessary. If you move the machine to a new network and attempt to run *dhclient* again, the existing background process will be detected, and the new copy of *dhclient* will exit immediately without obtaining a new network configuration. To work around this problem, kill the background copy of *dhclient* before running it for the second time:

```
# killall dhclient
# dhclient wlan0
```

dhclient may be running even if you didn't start it manually, since boot-time network activation or activation through *system-config-network* or *system-control-network* may have launched it.

Using wireless adapters that require firmware

Fedora's distribution policies do not permit the inclusion of binary software without source code, and that includes firmware. Unfortunately, some very popular wireless network cards require firmware for which the vendor will not release source code.

The most common wireless adapter family affected by firmware issues is the Intel Pro Wireless (IPW) series—often integrated into systems under the Centrino moniker, but also sold as add-on units with Mini-PCI, CardBus, or USB interfaces.

If you find that your wireless network card is not working, it is possible that a driver is present, but the firmware file is not. Use *grep* to search the system logfile for messages related to firmware:

```
# grep firmware /var/log/messages
Jun 29 04:11:57 beige kernel: usb 2-1: Failed to load zd1201.fw firmware file!
Jun 29 04:11:57 beige kernel: usb 2-1: Make sure the hotplug firmware loader
    is installed.
Jun 29 04:11:57 beige kernel: usb 2-1: zd1201 firmware upload failed: -2
Jun 29 04:11:57 beige firmware_helper[14394]: Loading of
    /lib/firmware/zd1201.fw for usb driver failed: No such file or directory
```

These messages clearly show that the system attempted to load firmware for a USB wireless adapter but failed because the firmware file was not found (No such file or directory).

To find more information, view the */var/log/messages* file using a text editor or the *less* program, and search for the date and time identified by the previous *grep* command:

```
# less /var/log/messages
...(Lines skipped)...
Jun 29 04:11:57 beige kernel: usb 2-1: new full speed USB device using
    uhci_hcd and address 5
Jun 29 04:11:57 beige kernel: usb 2-1: configuration #1 chosen from 1 choice
Jun 29 04:11:57 beige kernel: usb 2-1: Failed to load zd1201.fw firmware file!
Jun 29 04:11:57 beige kernel: usb 2-1: Make sure the hotplug firmware
    loader is installed.
Jun 29 04:11:57 beige kernel: usb 2-1: Goto http://linux-lc100020.sourceforge.net
    for more info
Jun 29 04:11:57 beige kernel: usb 2-1: zd1201 firmware upload failed: -2
```

Notice the message directing you to the driver web site. Visit that web site and download the firmware file provided (in this case, the file was named *zd1201-0.14-fw.tar.gz*, which was downloaded to the */tmp* directory through a web browser). The next step is to unpack this file and then install the firmware by copying the **.fw* files to */lib/firmware*:

```
# cd /tmp
# tar xvzf zd1201-0.14-fw.tar.gz
zd1201-0.14-fw/
zd1201-0.14-fw/zd1201.fw
zd1201-0.14-fw/README
zd1201-0.14-fw/makefile
zd1201-0.14-fw/zd1201-ap.fw
# cd zd1201-0.14-fw
# cp *.fw /lib/firmware
```

You can now use the wireless device after resetting the device driver, which you can do by physically disconnecting and reconnecting the adapter (if it is a removable device, such as a USB or CardBus adapter), rebooting the system, or using *modprobe* to remove and then reload the device driver.

In this case, the driver name is *zd1201*, so the driver can be reloaded with these commands:

```
# modprobe -r zd1201
# modprobe zd1201
```

After pausing for a moment to permit the interface to be configured, you can view */var/log/messages* and the output of *ifconfig* to see whether the driver loaded successfully and brought up the interface:

```
# tail -50 /var/log/messages
...(Lines snipped)...
Jun 29 04:25:58 beige kernel: usbcore: deregistering driver zd1201
Jun 29 04:26:04 beige kernel: usb 2-1: wlan0: ZD1201 USB Wireless interface
Jun 29 04:26:04 beige kernel: usbcore: registered new driver zd1201
Jun 29 04:26:05 beige dhclient: DHCPREQUEST on eth1 to 255.255.255.255 port 67
```

```
Jun 29 04:26:10 beige dhclient: DHCPREQUEST on eth1 to 255.255.255.255 port 67
Jun 29 04:26:11 beige dhclient: DHCPACK from 172.16.97.254
Jun 29 04:26:11 beige NET[15776]: /sbin/dhclient-script : updated /etc/resolv.conf
Jun 29 04:26:11 beige dhclient: bound to 172.16.97.101 -- renewal in 39113 seconds.
# ifconfig
eth0      Link encap:Ethernet  HWaddr 00:0D:56:33:D7:18
          inet addr:172.16.97.100  Bcast:172.16.97.255  Mask:255.255.255.0
          inet6 addr: fe80::20d:56ff:fe33:d718/64 Scope:Link
          UP BROADCAST RUNNING MULTICAST  MTU:1500  Metric:1
          RX packets:18181 errors:0 dropped:0 overruns:0 frame:0
          TX packets:3263 errors:0 dropped:0 overruns:0 carrier:0
          collisions:0 txqueuelen:1000
          RX bytes:2561730 (2.4 MiB)  TX bytes:375878 (367.0 KiB)
          Interrupt:177

lo        Link encap:Local Loopback
          inet addr:127.0.0.1  Mask:255.0.0.0
          inet6 addr: ::1/128 Scope:Host
          UP LOOPBACK RUNNING  MTU:16436  Metric:1
          RX packets:4936 errors:0 dropped:0 overruns:0 frame:0
          TX packets:4936 errors:0 dropped:0 overruns:0 carrier:0
          collisions:0 txqueuelen:0
          RX bytes:2973825 (2.8 MiB)  TX bytes:2973825 (2.8 MiB)

wlan0     Link encap:Ethernet  HWaddr 00:0C:2D:00:2B:DB
          inet addr:172.16.97.101  Bcast:172.16.97.255  Mask:255.255.255.0
          inet6 addr: fe80::20c:2dff:fe00:2bdb/64 Scope:Link
          UP BROADCAST RUNNING MULTICAST  MTU:1500  Metric:1
          RX packets:10 errors:0 dropped:0 overruns:0 frame:0
          TX packets:13 errors:0 dropped:0 overruns:0 carrier:0
          collisions:0 txqueuelen:1000
          RX bytes:1026 (1.0 KiB)  TX bytes:2384 (2.3 KiB)
```

Using private networks

Any IP address that is publicly accessible must be assigned by a central authority in order to prevent address collisions. For private networks, addresses can be freely assigned from pools reserved for this purpose, as listed in Table 3-2; these addresses are guaranteed not to conflict with any public IP addresses. Many home and small business gateway products default to assigning addresses in the 192.168.1.x range. If your computer is assigned one of these addresses, it will not normally be accessible from machines that are on different networks (unless you are using the *port forwarding* feature of your router or wireless access point).

Table 3-2. Private network address pools

Address range	Available IP addresses	Treatment using default netmask
10.0.x.x	16,777,216	One Class A network of 16,777,216 addresses
172.16.x.x–172.31.x.x	1,048,576	16 class B networks of 65,536 addresses each
192.168.x.x	65,536	256 class C networks of 256 addresses each

How Does It Work?

The Linux kernel keeps track of network devices in the form of *interfaces*. Each interface is assigned a unique name, such as eth0, eth1, eth2, tr0, tr1, tr2, and so forth. The interface name is initially assigned by the device driver and kernel but may be overridden using *ifrename*. Each interface has a number of flags, statistics, and configuration settings; these values are exposed through */proc/net* and */sys/class/net*, and are displayed and manipulated by *ifconfig*. Interface *aliases* such as eth0:1 and eth0:2 permit multiple interfaces to be assigned to one physical network device.

Packet routing is also performed by the kernel; the kernel routing table is exposed through */proc/net/route* and */proc/net/ipv6_route*, and is displayed and manipulated by the *route* command (netstat -r displays the same information).

The DNS information stored in */etc/resolv.conf* is used by the resolver libraries loaded by applications. Since most resolvers load the contents of */etc/resolv.conf* only when an application is started, it is usually necessary to restart your applications after changing the resolver configuration.

 As an exception to the rule, Firefox does not need to be restarted after */etc/resolv.conf* is changed.

The *system-config-network* tool is a Python script that manipulates the file */etc/sysconfig/network* and the contents of the directory */etc/sysconfig/network-scripts* (in addition to the */etc/hosts* and */etc/resolv.conf* files). These files are then read by the system init script to configure the boot-time network environment, and they are also used by other utilities such as *ifup*, *ifdown*, and *system-control-network*.

The NetworkManager service consists of a single binary, */usr/sbin/NetworkManager*, which attempts to keep a network running at all times. The NetworkManager-Dispatcher service can be used to launch scripts in */etc/NetworkManager/dispatcher.d* as interfaces are brought up and down, but this capability is not used by Fedora Core, so you can leave this service disabled. The GUI component of NetworkManager is provided by *nm-applet* (*/usr/bin/nm-applet*); the two components communicate through the *desktop bus* (dbus) mechanism.

Wireless interface drivers provide an extended set of control and monitoring functions called the *wireless extensions*. There are many versions of the wireless extensions in use, and not all of the extensions are supported by each driver. The current version of the wireless extensions is version 20, and it is expected that this version will remain stable for some time. When a wireless card can be configured by the GUI or command line but not by NetworkManger, it's usually due to incomplete or out-of-date wireless extension support in the interface device.

What About...

...using a Fedora system as a router?

A router passes packets from one interface to another, and Fedora is capable of doing this. */proc/sys/net/ipv4/ip_forward* controls packet forwarding; writing a 1 to this path enables forwarding:

```
# echo 1 >/proc/sys/net/ipv4/ip_forward
```

Likewise, writing a 0 disables forwarding:

```
# echo 0 >/proc/sys/net/ipv4/ip_forward
```

...renaming a network interface, or configuring a "wlan" interface using the GUI configuration tool?

The *ifrename* utility can be used to rename a network interface. The -i option specifies the old interface name, and -n sets the new name. To rename wlan0 to eth1, for example:

```
# ifrename -i wlan0 -n eth1
eth1
# ifconfig wlan0
wlan0: error fetching interface information: Device not found
# ifconfig eth1
eth1      Link encap:Ethernet  HWaddr 00:0C:2D:00:2B:DB
          BROADCAST MULTICAST  MTU:1500  Metric:1
          RX packets:0 errors:0 dropped:0 overruns:0 frame:0
          TX packets:0 errors:0 dropped:0 overruns:0 carrier:0
          collisions:0 txqueuelen:1000
          RX bytes:0 (0.0 b)  TX bytes:0 (0.0 b)
```

The GUI network configuration program (*system-config-network*) will sometimes refuse to configure interfaces that start with wlan; after renaming the interface, you can use the GUI configuration tool to permanently set up the interface.

Where Can I Learn More?

- The manpages for *ifconfig, route, netstat, iwconfig, iwlist, resolver, resolv.conf, hosts, dhclient, NetworkManager, NetworkManagerDispatcher, nm-applet, nm-tool,* and *modprobe.*

- The home pages for wireless firmware projects on SourceForge, including *http:// ipw2100.sf.net/, http://ipw2200.sourceforge.net/, http://ipw3945.sf.net/,* and *http:// linux-lc100020.sourceforge.net/*

- RFC1918, Address Allocation for Private Internets: *http://tools.ietf.org/html/1918*

- Documentation on the files in */etc/sysconfig: /usr/share/doc/initscripts*/sysconfig.txt*

3.3   Configuring a Touchpad

Many laptops use a Synaptics TouchPad (or an Alps GlidePoint, which can use the same driver). By default, a touchpad will emulate a PS/2 mouse, so it should work fine with the default driver, but if you use the Synaptics-specific driver, you can exquisitely fine-tune the touchpad's extended features.

How Do I Do That?

You will need to manually edit the X server configuration file, */etc/X11/xorg.conf*, to make two changes.

 It's a good idea to get into the habit of making a backup of configuration files before modifying them, just in case something goes wrong:

```
# cp /etc/X11/Xorg.conf /etc/X11/Xorg.conf.backup
```

First, add an InputDevice line to the ServerLayout section:

```
Section "ServerLayout"
        Identifier    "Default Layout"
        Screen      0 "Screen0" 0 0
        InputDevice   "Mouse0" "CorePointer"
        InputDevice   "TouchPad0" "AlwaysCore"
        InputDevice   "Keyboard0" "CoreKeyboard"
EndSection
```

Next, add a new InputDevice section (you can add this to any part of the file that is not between Section and EndSection lines):

```
Section "InputDevice"
        Identifier  "Touchpad0"
        Driver      "synaptics"
        Option      "SHMConfig"        "on"
EndSection
```

When you restart the X server by restarting the system or pressing Ctrl-Alt-Backspace (save any work first!), the Synaptics driver will be loaded with a default configuration that will permit you to:

- Click the left mouse button by tapping one finger in the middle area or by tapping the upper-left corner.
- Drag with the left mouse button by tapping and then dragging one finger (touch-release-touch, then drag).
- Click the middle mouse button by tapping two fingers in the middle area or by tapping the upper-right corner (this will usually perform a fast-paste of selected text).

- Click the right mouse button by tapping three fingers in the middle area or by tapping the lower-right corner.
- Scroll up and down by running your finger up and down the right side (if supported by your application).
- Scroll left and right by running your finger across the bottom (if supported by your application). Some web browsers, such as Firefox, use this for history navigation (left for previous page, right for next page).

These default options work well for most users, but the driver is incredibly customizable. It's also one of the few X drivers that can be adjusted without restarting the X server, through the use of the *synclient* program.

Running *synclient* with the -1 option will list the current driver settings:

```
$ synclient -l
Parameter settings:
    LeftEdge                = 1900
    RightEdge               = 5400
    TopEdge                 = 1900
    BottomEdge              = 4000
    FingerLow               = 25
    FingerHigh              = 30
    MaxTapTime              = 180
    MaxTapMove              = 220
    MaxDoubleTapTime        = 180
    ClickTime               = 100
    FastTaps                = 0
    EmulateMidButtonTime    = 75
    VertScrollDelta         = 100
    HorizScrollDelta        = 100
    MinSpeed                = 0.09
    MaxSpeed                = 0.18
    AccelFactor             = 0.0015
    EdgeMotionMinZ          = 30
    EdgeMotionMaxZ          = 160
    EdgeMotionMinSpeed      = 1
    EdgeMotionMaxSpeed      = 400
    EdgeMotionUseAlways     = 0
    UpDownScrolling         = 1
    LeftRightScrolling      = 1
    UpDownRepeat            = 1
    LeftRightRepeat         = 1
    ScrollButtonRepeat      = 100
    TouchpadOff             = 0
    GuestMouseOff           = 0
    LockedDrags             = 0
    RTCornerButton          = 2
    RBCornerButton          = 3
    LTCornerButton          = 0
    LBCornerButton          = 0
    TapButton1              = 1
    TapButton2              = 2
```

```
TapButton3            = 3
CircularScrolling     = 0
CircScrollDelta       = 0.1
CircScrollTrigger     = 0
CircularPad           = 0
PalmDetect            = 1
PalmMinWidth          = 10
PalmMinZ              = 200
CoastingSpeed         = 0
```

These parameters are fully explained in the manpage for *synaptics*, but the most commonly altered values are described in Table 3-3.

Table 3-3. Commonly altered Synaptics driver values

Options	Description	Reason for change
LeftEdge, TopEdge, RightEdge, BottomEdge	Define the border between edge/corner and middle regions of the touchpad	Used to shrink or expand the regions used for scrolling and corner-taps.
PalmDetect, PalmMinWidth, PalmMinZ	Configure the touchpad to ignore broad touches	Prevents accidental touches of the user's palm from registering as touchpad events. PalmDetect enables/disables, PamMinWidth sets the minimum touch diameter that will be considered a palm, and PalmMinZ is the minimum pressure required to register a palm.
RTCornerButton, LTCornerButton, LBCornerButton, RBCornerButton	Define the mouse-button clicks that will be registered when the user touches the corner of the keypad	By default, the top-right corner can be tapped to produce a middle mouse click, and the bottom-right corner can be tapped to produce a right mouse click. If you are finding that these clicks are being accidentally registered, set these button values to zero (0); alternately, you can select a specific button you wish to associate with a corner tap (1=left, 2=middle, 3=right, 4=down, 5=up, 6=left, 7=right)
TapButton1, TapButton2, TapButton3	Define the mouse-button clicks that will be registered when the user taps in the middle region of the touchpad with one, two, or three fingers	If you find that you accidentally tap the touchpad with more fingers than you intend to use, you can change the two- and three-finger tap buttons. To disable a tap altogether, set the appropriate value to 0.
VertScrollDelta, HorizScrollDelta	Define the amount of finger motion required to register a scroll event.	Set these values to adjust the scroll rates, or set them to 0 to disable scrolling altogether. Note that smaller values increase sensitivity. If you're finding that Firefox keeps moving back and forth in its History when you accidentally sweep your finger across the touchpad, try setting HorizScrollDelta to 0.
MaxTapTime	Defines the maximum time (in milliseconds) in which to detect a tap (which is interpreted as a left mouse click).	If tap-to-click drives you bonkers, set this to 0. Otherwise, you can use it to adjust how sensitive your touchpad is to tapping.

To test an option value, use the *synclient* program:

```
$ synclient VertScrollDelta=10
$ synclient PalmDetect=0
```

If you need to find position or pressure values for these options, you can use the monitor (-m) option of *synclient* to experiment:

```
$ synclient -m 100
    time    x    y    z  f  w  l r u d m    multi  gl gm gr gdx gdy
    0.000 3277 2899   0 0  0  0 0 0 0 0  00000000   0  0  0   0   0
    1.247 3687 3172  65 1  5  0 0 0 0 0  00000000   0  0  0   0   0
    1.351 3402 3070   0 0  0  0 0 0 0 0  00000000   0  0  0   0   0
    1.871 3926 3650  62 1  4  0 0 0 0 0  00000000   0  0  0   0   0
    1.975 4337 3339   0 0  0  0 0 0 0 0  00000000   0  0  0   0   0
    2.495 3932 3133   0 0  0  0 0 0 0 0  00000000   0  0  0   0   0
    2.599 3816 3245   1 1  9  0 0 0 0 0  00000000   0  0  0   0   0
    2.703 3810 3286   1 1  7  0 0 0 0 0  00000000   0  0  0   0   0
    2.807 3923 3224   1 1 14  0 0 0 0 0  00000000   0  0  0   0   0
    2.911 3923 3224   0 0  0  0 0 0 0 0  00000000   0  0  0   0   0
    8.423 4018 3986 131 2  5  0 0 0 0 0  00000000   0  0  0   0   0
    8.527 4104 3933 134 2  5  0 0 0 0 0  00000000   0  0  0   0   0
    8.631 4653 3827   0 0  0  0 0 0 0 0  00000000   0  0  0   0   0
...(Ctrl-C to terminate)...
```

In this output, the following options indicate:

x, y, and z
: Position and pressure of touch.

f
: Finger count.

w
: Finger width.

l, r, u, d, m, and multi
: Button state (most touchpads have only the l and r buttons). 0 indicates the button is up; 1 indicates the button is down.

All columns starting with g
: Guest (secondary) pointing device information, such as a finger button.

Once you have tweaked the values to suit your needs, add your preferred values to the Synaptics InputDevice section of the */etc/X11/xorg.conf* file, using the Option keyword:

```
Section "InputDevice"
        Identifier  "Touchpad0"
        Driver      "synaptics"
        Option      "SHMConfig"       "on"
        Option      "VertScrollDelta" "10"
        Option      "PalmDetect"      "0"
EndSection
```

These settings will then take effect when the system is restarted.

How Does It Work?

The Synaptics TouchPad (or Alps GlidePad) device is connected through a PS/2 or USB interface and contains a microcontroller, touch sensor, buttons, and interface electronics. The firmware is programmed to emulate a standard mouse unless (or until) the device driver sends it codes to switch it into native mode.

The Synaptics driver works with the microcontroller in the touchpad to translate user activity into standard mouse signals. There are only 16 types of events that are reported to the X server: button down and button up for buttons 1 through 7, and horizontal and vertical motion. All of the possible tap, press, and slide gestures are translated into combinations of these 16 events.

For example, touching the pad with one finger on the right side (X position greater than RightEdge, and Y position between TopEdge and BottomEdge), and then moving your finger up more than VertScrollDelta units will be interpreted as a vertical scroll action, which will result in a button-down event on button 4, followed by a button-up event on button 4 (this corresponds to rotating the scroll wheel forward one click on a standard mouse).

Not all touchpad models have the hardware or firmware to provide all of the features supported by the driver; for example, most models do not have all of the possible buttons, and some lack multiple-finger or finger-width detection.

What About...

...using a touchpad and a mouse at the same time?

This can be done if the Synaptics device is defined in addition to a traditional mouse, as recommended in the X11 configuration shown in this lab.

...disabling the touchpad automatically when I'm typing?

Even with palm detection, some typists and touchpads register false information during typing (especially true with certain laptop case designs, which transmit case stress to the touchpad). To help in these situations, the Synaptics software includes the *syndaemon* program, which will automatically disable the touchpad when the keyboard is in use. To start this daemon, simply type its name as a command:

```
$ syndaemon
```

Where Can I Learn More?

- The manpages for *synaptics*, *synclient*, and *syndaemon*
- The driver home page: *http://web.telia.com/~u89404340/touchpad/*

3.4   Using Dual Video Output

The video circuits of most laptops support two video outputs: one to the built-in LCD panel and one for external devices. The external output is not enabled by default, but you can switch between the internal and external displays using a function key.

More advanced configurations of the two outputs are supported by some video cards. For example, you can configure a single large desktop spanning both displays, or set up the external display to show a subset of what is shown on the internal display.

How Do I Do That?

Output from one card to multiple monitors is supported only by some drivers. The most commonly used ones are the NVIDIA and ATI proprietary drivers, and the open source Radeon driver. All of these drivers have some limitations; for example, the NVIDIA driver, when used on a laptop, will always configure an external monitor as primary (screen 0), and the ATI drivers permit only general monitor positioning (you can specify that one monitor is to the right of another, but you can't indicate a difference in their vertical alignment).

Configuring dual video on an NVIDIA card

Note that for the changes described in this section to take effect, you will need to restart the X server in one of these ways: changing to runlevel 3 and then back to 5, restarting the system, or terminating the running X server with Ctrl-Alt-Backspace (save your work first!).

First, configure and test your system using the NVIDIA proprietary driver (see Lab 5.3, "Using Repositories"), and then add the highlighted lines to the Device section of your */etc/X11/xorg.conf* file:

```
Section "Device"
        Identifier  "Card0"
        Driver      "nvidia"
        VendorName  "nVidia Corporation"
        BoardName   "NV34 [GeForce FX 5200]"
        BusID       "PCI:1:0:0"

        Option      "TwinView"
        Option      "SecondMonitorHorizSync"  "31.0 - 80.0"
        Option      "SecondMonitorVertRefresh" "50.0 - 75.0"
        Option      "TwinViewXineramaInfo"    "on"

        Option      "MetaModes"               "800x600,1024x768"
        Option      "TwinViewOrientation"     "LeftOf"
EndSection
```

The SecondMonitorHorizSync and SecondMonitorVertRefresh options configure the horizontal and vertical frequency ranges for the second monitor (the settings for the primary monitor are in the Monitor section of the file). The values given here are reasonable for most small monitors. The TwinViewXineramaInfo line configures the driver to inform applications about the fact that the desktop is on two screens, so that windows can be placed intelligently (avoiding dialog boxes that span both screens, for example).

The MetaModes option configures the relative sizes of the two screens; the first screen is always the external display. The TwinViewOrientation specifies the position of the second display relative to the first for the purpose of mouse movement and window positioning (possible values are Above, Below, LeftOf, or RightOf).

For finer control over the monitor relationships, the positions of each monitor may be specified in the MetaModes line as an absolute position within the entire desktop. These values are given in the form +X+Y after each resolution; for example, "800x600+0+0,1024x768+800+0" specifies that the primary monitor is to the left of the secondary monitor and that the two monitors are aligned at the top, and "800x600+1024+168,1024x768+0+0" specifies that the primary monitor is on the right and that the monitors are aligned at the bottom (168 pixels is the difference between the two monitor heights, 768 and 600 pixels).

When using the external monitor connection for projection, it can be convenient to project a subset of what is shown on the laptop's panel. Using the NVIDIA driver, this can be configured by overlapping the two display regions using the MetaModes option. On a laptop with a 1400×1050 display, for example, you can project an 800×600 pixel subset to your audience:

```
Section "Device"
        Identifier "Card0"
        Driver     "nvidia"
        VendorName "nVidia Corporation"
        BoardName  "NV34 [GeForce FX 5200]"
        BusID      "PCI:1:0:0"

        Option     "TwinView"
        Option     "SecondMonitorHorizSync"  "31.0 - 80.0"
        Option     "SecondMonitorVertRefresh" "50.0 - 75.0"
        Option     "TwinViewXineramaInfo"     "on"

        Option     "MetaModes"        "800x600+200+200,1400x1050+0+0"
EndSection
```

When you restart the X server, the GNOME panel bars will be located in the middle of the screen, because the smaller 800×600 subset display is considered "Primary." Drag the panels to the top and bottom of the laptop display. You can then start an application and position the portion of the window that you wish to display into the 800×600 pixel area that starts 200 pixels down and 200 pixels to the right of the upper-left corner of the screen.

This works well with OpenOffice.org Impress in "Normal" mode, which displays three panes, including the current image in the center and a preview of slides on the left (the panes can be rearranged if it is more convenient to see the preview on the right). Reposition the dividing line between the panes and scroll the center pane until the current slide completely fills the external display.

This configuration enables you to preview the slides using the OpenOffice.org preview plane as shown in Figure 3-22 without changing the projected slide. Once you select and then click on a slide, it becomes the current slide and is displayed both in the center plane of the LCD image and on the external projector, shown in Figure 3-23.

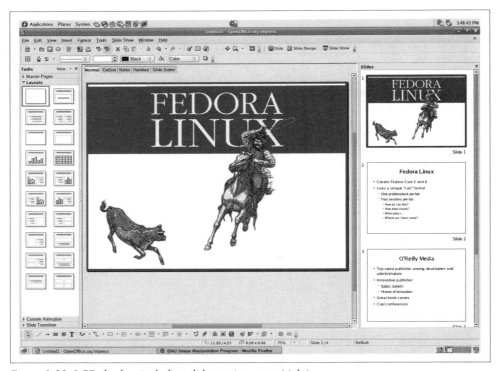

Figure 3-22. LCD display, including slide preview pane (right)

Configuring dual video on an ATI graphics card using the open source driver

First, configure and test your system using the ATI open source driver *radeon*, and then add the lines highlighted in bold to the Device section of your */etc/X11/xorg.conf*:

```
Section "Device"
        Identifier "Card0"
        Driver     "radeon"
        VendorName "ATI"
```

Figure 3-23. Projected 800×600 subset of LCD image, showing only the current slide

```
        BoardName   "ATI 7500"
        BusID       "PCI:1:0:0"

        Option      "MergedFB"        "on"
        Option      "CRT2HSync"       "31.0 - 80.0"
        Option      "CRT2VRefresh"    "50.0 - 75.0"
        Option      "MergedXinerama" "on"

        Option      "MetaModes"       "800x600-1024x768"
        Option      "CRT2Position"    "RightOf"
EndSection
```

The MergedFB option enables dual video output. CRT2HSync and CRT2VRefresh set the horizontal and vertical frequency ranges for the second monitor (the settings for the primary monitor are in the Monitor section of the file), and the MetaModes option sets the resolution of the two displays. MergedXinerama enables sending display hints to applications, and CRT2Position sets the the position of the second display relative to the first for the purpose of mouse movement and window positioning (possible values are Above, Below, LeftOf, or RightOf).

Restart the X server by changing to runlevel 3 and then back to 5, by restarting the system, or by terminating the running X server with Ctrl-Alt-Backspace (save your work first!). When the X server restarts, both displays should be active.

Configuring dual video on an ATI video card using the ATI closed source driver

The ATI closed source driver is configured in much the same way as the other drivers. First, configure and test your system using the ATI closed source driver *fglrx*, and then add the lines highlighted in bold to the Device section of your */etc/X11/xorg.conf*:

```
Section "Device"
        Identifier "Card0"
        Driver     "fglrx"
        VendorName "ATI"
        BoardName  "ATI 7500"
        BusID      "PCI:1:0:0"

        Option     "DesktopSetup"  "0x00000200"
        Option     "HSync2"        "31.0 - 80.0"
        Option     "VRefresh2"     "50.0 - 75.0"
EndSection
```

The DesktopSetup option enables dual video output and specifies that the monitor attached to connector 1 is on the left; change this value to "0x00000201" if the monitors are reversed (it's not always apparent whether the internal or external monitor is attached to connector 1). HSync2 and VRefresh2 set the horizontal and vertical frequency ranges for the second monitor (the settings for the primary monitor are in the Monitor section of the file). The resolutions will automatically be selected from available options by the device driver.

Restart the X server by changing to runlevel 3 and then back to 5, by restarting the system, or by terminating the running X server with Ctrl-Alt-Backspace (save your work first!). When the X server restarts, the two monitors should display two halves of the desktop.

How Does It Work?

The X server contains code to manage two (or more) separate video cards, combining them into a single desktop. However, the X.org server and the configuration file layout were never really designed for multiple outputs from one card controlled by one driver; for example, there is no way to associate more than one Monitor section in the configuration file with a single Device (video card) section.

Some video card drivers have been enhanced to support multiple video outputs, and in order to fit within the X.org configuration file format, the configuration information for the second monitor is placed in the Device section.

There are two ways to use multiple monitors as part of a single display in X:

- Each monitor can be given a distinct Screen number, which enables output to be sent to a specific monitor but prevents windows from spanning displays or being moved from one display to another.

- Use Xinerama, which is named after the old Cinerama movie technology and that combines multiple monitors into a single large display, permitting windows to span monitors and to be moved between monitors.

All of the X.org video card drivers that support multiple video outputs use the Xinerama approach, but the Xinerama extensions used to inform applications of the underlying monitor geometry may be enabled or disabled using configuration options (with the exception of the ATI driver, which does not offer this capability). This information is particularly useful to window managers because it enables the window manager to correctly center dialogs in the middle of the monitor instead of the middle of the virtual desktop, and to make maximized windows fill a monitor instead of spanning monitors.

What About...

...using dual video output with another video driver?

Very few of the other X.org video drivers support multiple video outputs. If you have another driver and want to see the options supported, look for a manpage for your driver. For example, to see the driver options for the Intel 810 adapter:

```
$ man i810
```

Where Can I Learn More?

- The manpages for the *radeon* driver
- *NVIDIA* closed-source driver information from */usr/share/doc/NVIDIA_GLX-1.0/README.txt*

CHAPTER 4

Basic System Management

In order to maintain your system effectively, it's necessary to learn some basic system management skills. This chapter covers these essential skills.

With a small investment in time, you'll be able to adjust your system configuration, keep the filesystem under control, disable unused services, and identify and stop rogue processes. I'll cover the basics of performing these operations using both graphical and command-line tools, both locally and remotely.

4.1   Using the Command Line

Many system management tasks can be performed using either of the graphical user interfaces provided with Fedora (i.e., GNOME or KDE). However, most power users prefer the command line for system management work because they find it faster, more consistent between different versions of Linux, and easier to access remotely. The command line is also called a *shell prompt*, because the commands are processed by a program called a shell; the standard shell on a Fedora system is the Bourne-again shell (*bash*).

How Do I Do That?

If you are logged in to the system through the graphical user interface, access the command line through the terminal program. Select the menu option Applications → Accessories → Terminal (System → Terminal in KDE), or right-click on the desktop background and select Konsole under KDE.

> If you find yourself using the terminal frequently, you can make it easier to launch: right-click on the Terminal option in the application menu and select "Add this launcher to panel." A new panel icon will appear that will launch a new terminal when clicked.

If you have logged in to the system through a character-mode login screen or an SSH login, you will automatically be presented with a command line.

Understanding the shell prompt

The standard shell prompt looks like this:

```
[chris@concord2 ~]$
```

This message is an invitation to enter a command. It shows the name of the user (chris), the computer being used (concord2), and the current working directory within the filesystem (~, meaning the user's home directory). The last character of the prompt, $, indicates that this is a normal user's prompt, as opposed to the system administrator's prompt, which ends with #.

Entering commands

To enter a command, simply type it, and then press Enter to execute it. The output from the command will appear after the command (scrolling the screen if necessary), and when the command is done a new prompt will be printed.

To edit a command line, use the left and right arrow keys to position within the line, and the Backspace and Delete keys to delete characters to the left or right of the cursor, respectively. To insert text, simply type it. You can press Enter with the cursor located anywhere on the line to execute the command. Other editing keys are available; Table 4-1 shows the most useful ones.

Table 4-1. Useful editing keys

Key or key sequence	Description
Left arrow	Move left one character.
Right arrow	Move right one character.
Backspace	Delete the character to the left of the cursor.
Delete	Delete the character under/to the right of the cursor.
Ctrl-U	Delete to the start of the line.
Ctrl-left arrow	Move one word to the left.
Ctrl-right arrow	Move one word to the right.
Esc, D Alt-D	Delete to the end of the current word.
Esc, Backspace Alt-Backspace	Delete to the start of the current word.
Home Ctrl-A	Go to the start of the line.
End Ctrl-E	Go to the end of the line.

Accessing previous commands

You can scroll through the history of previously entered commands using the up and down arrow keys. This enables you to easily re-enter a command, either exactly as you previously entered it or after editing.

You can also search for a previous command by pressing Ctrl-R (for *reverse search*) and then typing a few characters that appear in the command. For example, if you had at some previous point typed cat /etc/hosts and you pressed Ctrl-R and typed hos, the cat /etc/hosts command would appear (providing that no intervening commands contained the letter sequence hos).

Obtaining a root prompt to enter commands as the superuser

The superuser account, *root*, is also called the privileged account, because it is not subject to the security restrictions that are applied to regular user accounts. *root* access is required for many system administration commands. Although it's tempting to use the *root* account all the time on a single-user computer, it is unwise because Fedora assumes that you know what you're doing and won't ask for confirmation if you enter a dangerous command; it will just go ahead and execute it. If you're using the *root* account, an incorrect command can cause a lot more damage than the same command executed in a normal account.

Although you can directly log in as a *root* user, it's usually much safer to take on *root* privilege only when necessary, using the su (switch user) command:

```
$ su
Password: root-password
#
```

The shell prompt will change to end in a pound sign (#) instead of a dollar sign ($) when you are in *root* mode. Press Ctrl-D or type **exit** to drop superuser access and return to your regular shell prompt.

 In this book, I'll use $ to indicate any normal user's prompt, *user*$ to specifically indicate *user*'s prompt, and # to indicate the *root* prompt. Avoid entering commands as *root* unnecessarily!

Linux error messages

Many Linux commands will output a message only if something goes wrong. For example, if you try to remove a file using the *rm* command, no message will be displayed if the file is successfully deleted, but an error message will be generated if the file does not exist:

```
$ rm barbeque
rm: cannot remove `barbeque': No such file or directory
```

Most error messages start with the name of the command that produced the message.

Logging out of a shell prompt

You can leave a shell by pressing Ctrl-D or typing exit. If you are using a terminal window and don't have any programs running, you can simply close the window using the X button on the title bar.

How Does It Work?

The shell prompt is managed by *bash*, the Bourne-again shell. *bash* got its name from the fact that it is a successor to the original Unix shell, *sh*, which is also known as the Bourne shell (after its author, Steve Bourne). *bash* is a command editor, command interpreter, job controller, and programming language.

When *bash* receives a command, it splits it into words and uses *globbing* to expand any ambiguous filenames. *bash* next checks to see if the first word is a built-in command. If not, it treats it as an external command or program and searches a list of directories to find that program. It executes that program, passing the other words to the program as arguments. Almost all Linux commands are external programs.

Linux commands generally accept three types of arguments:

Options
> These start with a hyphen or double-hyphen (- or --) and modify the way the command operates. For example, the ls (list-files) command will include hidden files in its output if the -a argument is given, and will list detailed information about files when the -l option is specified. These options may be used individually, used together in any order, or combined after one hyphen if they all use a single hyphen:
>
> ```
> $ ls -l
> $ ls -a
> $ ls -l -a
> $ ls -a -l
> $ ls -al
> $ ls -la
> ```

Positional arguments
> These have significance according to the order in which they are specified. For example, the cp (copy) command accepts two or more filenames:
>
> ```
> $ cp one two
> ```
>
> *one* is the name of the file being copied, and *two* is the name that will be given to the new copy. If you swap the position of the two arguments, the meaning of the command is changed. Options may be placed before, between, or after positional arguments; usually, the positions of the options don't matter.

Options with a value
> These combine options with positional arguments. An option with a value may be placed before or after other arguments, but the value must be placed directly after the option.

For example, the *ls* command accepts the -w option (width of output), which is specified along with a number indicating the desired width of output in characters. This can be combined with the -a and -1 options in any order, as long as the number immediately follows the -w option:

```
$ ls -a -l -w 60
$ ls -w 60 -al
$ ls -l -w 60 -a
$ ls -l -w60  -a
$ ls -alw60
```

What About...

...accessing a character-mode display when the graphical user interface is running?

Fedora is configured to allow you to log in using a character-mode display even if the graphical user interface is running. In fact, you can log in up to six times, using the same or different user IDs.

The key is *Virtual Terminals* (VTs). There are 12 virtual terminals that can be accessed easily: VT1 through VT6 are configured for character-mode login, VT7 is used for graphical login, and VT8 through VT12 are not normally used.

To switch to a specific VT, press Ctrl-Alt and the function key that corresponds to the virtual terminal you wish to access (Ctrl-Alt-F1 for VT1, Ctrl-Alt-F7 for VT7, etc.).

 There are actually 64 virtual terminals, but virtual terminals above number 12 are not directly accessible from the keyboard and are therefore rarely used.

You can log in on multiple VTs simultaneously and switch back and forth between them. This is particularly useful when you bring up documentation on one VT and enter commands on another.

...finding out where a program is located?

The *type*, *which*, and *whereis* commands all provide information about the location of programs.

type will tell you where a command is located in a verbose way, along with an indication of whether the command location is hashed (stored in the shell for quick reference because the command has already been used recently). If there is more than one command with the same name, the location shown is the first one found using your $PATH:

```
$ type cat
cat is hashed (/bin/cat)
```

which is similar, but shows only the command location:

```
$ which cat
/bin/cat
```

whereis will show you all of the locations for the command (and sometimes there are several, if different versions of the same program are installed), along with the location of its manpage documentation:

```
$ whereis cat
cat: /bin/cat /usr/share/man/man1p/cat.1p.gz /usr/share/man/man1/cat.1.gz
```

...starting graphical programs?

Programs with a graphical user interface are started in exactly the same way as programs with a character-based user interface. GUI-based programs use the DISPLAY environment variable to determine if a graphical display is available and to connect to that display. Some programs, such as *system-config-printer*, will automatically start up with a graphical or a character-based user interface according to the type of display that is available.

...quickly entering a single command?

Typing Alt-F2 will open a Run Application dialog (in KDE, it's called Run Command), which enables you to enter a single command and run it. This is most useful for starting graphical programs that aren't on the menu.

You can also add an applet to your panel bar that does the same thing.

...the difference between commands, utilities, applications, and programs?

There isn't any! Linux does not make any distinction between categories of programs.

...using a different shell?

Fedora offers four different command shells: *csh* (a.k.a. *tcsh*), *bash* (a.k.a. *sh*), *ksh*, and *zsh*. You can temporarily start a different shell just by typing the shell name:

```
$ csh
```

Press Ctrl-D or type **exit** to return to the original shell. You can permanently change your default shell using the chsh (change shell) command:

```
$ chsh
Password: bigsecret
New shell [/bin/bash]: /bin/csh
Shell changed.
```

The password requested is your normal login password; the change will take effect the next time you log in.

chsh requires that you enter the full pathname of the new shell. To see a list of available shells, use *chsh* with the -1 (list) option:

```
$ chsh -l
/bin/sh
/bin/bash
/sbin/nologin
/bin/ksh
/bin/tcsh
/bin/csh
/bin/zsh
```

zsh, *ksh*, and *bash* each use a syntax related to the original Bourne shell (*sh*). *csh* uses a very different syntax, which C programmers often find comfortable.

Where Can I Learn More?

- The *bash*, *chsh*, *csh*, *zsh*, and *ash* manpages

4.2   Accessing Online Documentation

A fully loaded Fedora system includes over 4,700 programs, plus programming interfaces, data files, and graphical tools. To help you learn your way around, over 12,000 files of online documentation are available, with additional documentation available through the Web. Knowing how to access and knowledgeably navigate through this documentation is essential to getting the most out of your Fedora system.

 The phrase *online documentation* refers to both local and Internet-based electronic documentation.

How Do I Do That?

There are five main types of documentation available:

- Manpages
- *info* pages
- The *GNOME Guides* and *KDE Manuals*
- HOWTOs and guides from the Linux Documentation Project
- Text files distributed with applications

Using manpages

Fedora continues the Unix tradition of providing an online version of what were originally loose-leaf printed manuals. These manuals cover the commands, programming interfaces, and data formats used by the system.

The command used to access these online manuals is called *man*, so these documents have come to be known as *manpages*. The majority of Fedora documentation is in this format.

The pages are arranged into sections according to the original binders, using the section numbers described in Table 4-2. The section numbers are used to distinguish different manpages with the same name, such as the manpage for the uname system call (found in section 2) and the uname command (found in section 1). In some cases, a letter or two may be appended to a section number to indicate a subsection (such as 3pm, the manual section containing Perl module library functions).

 A *system call* is a request made of the operating system by an application program.

Table 4-2. Section numbers for manpages

Section	Description
1	User commands
2	System calls
3	Library functions
4	Special files
5	File formats
6	Games
7	Conventions and miscellany
8	Administration and privileged commands

To view the manpage for a particular command, such as *ls*:

```
$ man ls
```

The output will appear as shown in Figure 4-1. You can use the up and down arrow keys and the Page Up/Page Down keys to scroll through the text, or q to quit. You can also type /, enter some text, and press Enter to search for that text within the document; type n (lowercase *n*, for *next*) to search again. ? and N (uppercase *N*) can be used in the same way to search backwards.

To request a manpage from a specific section of the manual, give the section as the first argument and the name of the manpage as the second argument:

```
$ man 2 uname
```

If you don't specify the section, the first section containing a page with the requested name is used—and since there is a uname page in section 1, you won't see the page from section 2 unless you specifically ask for it.

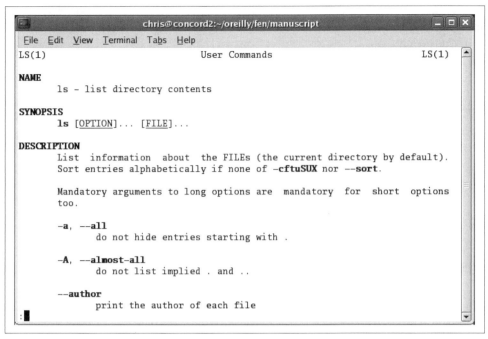

```
 chris@concord2:~/oreilly/fen/manuscript
File  Edit  View  Terminal  Tabs  Help
LS(1)                           User Commands                           LS(1)

NAME
       ls - list directory contents

SYNOPSIS
       ls [OPTION]... [FILE]...

DESCRIPTION
       List  information  about  the FILEs (the current directory by default).
       Sort entries alphabetically if none of -cftuSUX nor --sort.

       Mandatory arguments to long options are  mandatory  for  short  options
       too.

       -a, --all
            do not hide entries starting with .

       -A, --almost-all
            do not list implied . and ..

       --author
            print the author of each file
:
```

Figure 4-1. Online display of a manpage

Finding a manpage

The -k argument of man is used to produce a list of all of the pages that contain a specific keyword in their short descriptions. For example, if you wanted to see all of the manpages that contained the word *calendar* in their summary:

```
$ man -k calendar
Date::Calc             (3pm)  - Gregorian calendar date calculations
Date::Calendar         (3pm)  - Calendar objects for different holiday schemes
Date::Calendar::Profiles (3pm)  - Some sample profiles for Date::Calendar and
                                    Date::Calendar::Year
Date::Calendar::Year (3pm)  - Implements embedded year objects for Date::Calendar
cal                    (1)  - displays a calendar
```

Note that the section number is in parentheses. If you were looking for a calendar command, you could ignore the results from section 3 of the manual (library functions), which leaves just one possibility: the *cal* command. You could then get more information about that command to see if it will do what you need:

```
$ man cal
```

apropos is another name for man -k. To my ear, it has more class!

To see all of the manpages with a specific name in all sections of the manual, use the whatis command:

```
$ whatis uname
uname                    (1)  - print system information
uname                    (2)  - get name and information about current kernel
```

In this case, you can see that there is a page for uname in section 1 and 2 of the manual.

Reading info documents

The GNU project supplies most of its documentation in *info* documents rather than manpages. *info* documents are a unique form of hypertext and are read with a reader program named, not surprisingly, *info*:

```
$ info ls
```

info has many features and can be a bit overwhelming. Each document consists of nodes (analogous to web pages) that are linked together using menu options. The keys listed in Table 4-3 are sufficient for basic navigation.

Table 4-3. Basic navigation in info

Key	Description
Page Up/Page Down	Scroll through the text.
p	Go to the previous node.
n	Go to the next node.
Tab	Jump to the next menu option in the current page.
Enter (when the cursor is on a menu option)	Follow the menu option.
Space	Go to the next page, or next node if there is no more text in the current node.
l	Return to the last node accessed.

To take a guided tour of *info*, type:

```
$ info info
```

Viewing GNOME guides and KDE manuals

GNOME and KDE each provide a general user's guide or manual, with specific chapters (or in some cases, separate manuals) for their various desktop tools.

To access these guides, just press F1 in a GNOME or KDE application. Alternately, select the System → Help (GNOME) or Help (KDE) menu options from the panel bar. The GNOME menu is connected to the GNOME documentation, and the KDE menu is connected to the KDE documentation. You can access the documentation for the other desktop environment from a command prompt; for GNOME documentation, use either of these commands:

```
$ gnome-help
$ yelp
```

For KDE documentation:

```
$ khelpcenter
```

 Each of these tools also provides a graphical user interface for viewing manpages and info documents.

Accessing HOWTOs and guides

The Linux Documentation Project (TLDP) maintains a very helpful set of documents called *HOWTOs*, each of which describes the procedure to accomplish a specific task. They also publish some book-length *guides*. Most of these documents have been translated into multiple languages. However, these documents are generic and do not reflect the default configuration and packaging of Fedora.

The TLDP documentation can be found on the Web at *http://www.tldp.org/*. TLDP also publishes FAQs and maintains links to online versions of the manpages and free Linux magazines.

Viewing text files distributed with applications

Most open source software packages include a small number of text files written by the programmers, which include licensing information, change histories, errata and bug lists, and release notes. In Fedora these miscellaneous documents are placed in */usr/share/doc* and are organized in directories by package name and version. For example, the notes for *dia* (a diagram-drawing application) are available in */usr/share/doc/dia-0.95*.

I find that the easiest way to view these documents is to use a web browser, which enables you to navigate among directories and view documents by simply clicking on them. To do this, just open the Firefox web browser and enter */usr/share/doc* as the location.

To view these files from the shell prompt, change to the directory you wish to view, and then use *ls* to list names of the files and less to view the contents of any text files that interest you. For example, here are the steps you might take to view the *dia* text files:

```
$ cd /usr/share/doc
$ ls -d dia*
dia-0.95  dialog-1.0.20050306
```

```
$ cd dia-0.95
$ ls -l
total 724
-rw-r--r--  1 root root   1578 Aug 16  2004 AUTHORS
-rw-r--r--  1 root root 574015 Aug 17  2004 ChangeLog
-rw-r--r--  1 root root  17992 Mar 12  2004 COPYING
-rw-r--r--  1 root root  11364 Aug 16  2004 custom-shapes
-rw-r--r--  1 root root   1620 Aug 16  2004 diagram.dtd
-rw-r--r--  1 root root   3927 Aug 16  2004 INSTALL
-rw-r--r--  1 root root   4955 Aug 16  2004 KNOWN_BUGS
-rw-r--r--  1 root root  21535 Aug 17  2004 NEWS
-rw-r--r--  1 root root   3444 Aug 16  2004 README
drwxr-xr-x  2 root root   4096 Sep 27 01:13 samples
-rw-r--r--  1 root root   2324 Aug 16  2004 shape.dtd
-rw-r--r--  1 root root    501 Aug 16  2004 sheet.dtd
-rw-r--r--  1 root root   1379 Aug 19  2004 THANKS
-rw-r--r--  1 root root   2545 Aug 16  2004 TODO
$ less KNOWN_BUGS
```

The less command will enable you to scroll through the specified file (*KNOWN_BUGS*) in the same way that you would move through a manpage, using the arrow keys and Page Up/Page Down keys to scroll and q to quit.

Note that this directory also contains a *sample* directory, which includes some sample files for use with the *dia* program.

What About...

...printing a manpage?

The man command's -t option will format a page into PostScript; you can then send the PostScript output to your printer with the command *lpr* using a pipe. This command prints the manpage for *ls*:

```
$ man -t ls | lpr
```

...making a PDF or HTML version of a manpage?

It's easy to convert manpages into PDF or HTML formats.

For PDF, use the -t option with man and then pipe the PostScript output into the *ps2pdf* program. This command places the manpage for *ls* into the file *ls_man_page.pdf*:

```
$ man -t ls | ps2pdf - ls_man_page.pdf
```

The commands to convert a manpage to HTML are more complex:

```
$ zcat $(man --path ls) | man2html | tail +3 > ls_man_page.html
```

This uses man --path to find the compressed, unformatted manual page; *zcat* to decompress the page; *man2html* to convert the page to HTML; and *tail* to strip off the unneeded *httpd* Content-type header.

Where Can I Learn More?

Other sources of information about Fedora and Linux:

* The Fedora Project at RedHat: *http://fedora.redhat.com/*
* The Fedora Project Wiki: *http://fedoraproject.org/wiki/*
* The Fedora Forums: *http://www.fedoraforum.org/*
* Links to Linux-related news at LinuxToday: *http://linuxtoday.com/*
* O'Reilly Network: *http://www.oreillynet.com/*

4.3   Managing Files

A large part of system administration involves dealing with files and directories: creating directories, copying files, moving files and directories around, and deleting them. Fedora provides a powerful set of tools for managing files from the shell prompt as well as graphically.

How Do I Do That?

Linux, like most modern operating systems, uses a tree-like hierarchy to store and organize files. To manage files effectively, extend the hierarchy to organize your data.

Understanding Linux directory names

Fedora's master directory (or *folder*, as it would be referred to by other operating systems) is called the *root directory*; it may contain files and directories. Each of those directories may in turn contain other files and directories.

For each user, one directory is designated as the *home directory*, and that is where that user stores her personal files. Additionally, each *process* (a running copy of a program) has a *current working directory* on the system, which is the directory that it accesses by default unless another directory is explicitly specified.

The root directory is always the same system-wide; the home directory is consistent for a particular user, but varies from user to user; and the current working directory is unique to each process and can be changed anytime.

A *pathname* specifies how to find a file in the file hierarchy. There are three different pathname schemes that can be used, based on the three different starting points (root, home, and current working directory); each scheme specifies the path from the selected starting point to the desired file, separating directory names with the forward slash character (/). These three schemes are summarized in Table 4-4.

Table 4-4. Absolute, Relative, and Relative-to-Home pathnames

Scheme	First characters of pathname	Relative to...	Example
Absolute	/	Root directory	/home/chris/book/chapter/one.odt
Relative-to-Home	~	User's home directory	~/book/chapter/one.odt
	~chris	Home directory of chris	~chris/book/chapter/one.odt
Relative	(Anything other than / or ~)	Current working directory	chapter/one.odt (Assuming that /home/chris/book is the current directory)

The special symbols . (same directory) and .. (parent directory) are useful in pathnames. For example, if your current directory is */home/chris/book*, then *../invitation* refers to */home/chris/invitation*.

Key directories

Fedora uses a standard set of directories derived from historical conventions, the Linux Standard Base (LSB) project, and the kernel. Table 4-5 outlines the key directories and their purpose.

Table 4-5. Key directories in Fedora Core

Directory	Purpose
/bin	Basic binaries (programs) needed to start the system.
/boot	Files used during the boot process, including the boot menu and kernel.
/dev	This directory contains *special files* that are actually connections to devices, such as keyboards, mice, modems, printers, sound cards, and so forth. When you read data from a special file or write data to it, you're actually communicating with the associated device.
/etc	System configuration files (sometimes regarded as the "home directory for the computer").
/home	Users' home directories, for the storage of personal files.
/lib	Libraries.
/lost+found	A directory used to recover files in the event of filesystem damage. Any file that has been disassociated from its name is placed here during filesystem recovery.
/media	External media (floppy disks, USB drives, digital cameras, optical disks) that have been mounted.
/mnt	Historical location for mounting storage devices, many of which have now moved to */media*.
/opt	Optional, add-on software. The definition of add-on software is subjective; if you obtain OpenOffice.org directly from the *openoffice.org* web site, it will be installed here, but if you install the version distributed with Fedora, it will be installed in */usr/bin*.
/proc	Per-process status information plus system information.
/root	Home directory for the *root* user (superuser).
/sbin	Basic system administration binaries.
/selinux	Files for Security Enhanced Linux.

Table 4-5. Key directories in Fedora Core (continued)

Directory	Purpose
/sys	System device information.
/tmp	Temporary file storage.
/usr	User data (years ago, home directories were also stored in /usr).
/usr/bin	The remainder of the standard binaries.
/usr/lib	User libraries.
/usr/libexec	Programs that are not directly executed by the user but that are executed by another application (e.g., graphics demos for the xscreensaver program)
/usr/local	Local files (specific to your system configuration).
/usr/local/bin	Local binaries and scripts.
/usr/sbin	The remainder of the system administration binaries.
/usr/src	Source code for locally built RPM packages and the Linux kernel.
/var	Files that change frequently (variable), including databases, print requests, and logfiles.
/var/log	Various system logfiles.
/var/spool	Files for various queues (spools), such as print queues and file-transfer queues.

Local files refers to files—binaries, scripts, and datafiles—that you have developed and that are not part of Fedora. Separating these files from the rest of the operating system makes it easier to move them to a new system in the future.

Ambiguous filenames

The wildcard characters ? and * can be used for *pattern matching*, which is useful for dealing with several files at a time without individually specifying each filename. ? will match any one character in a filename, and * will match any number of any characters (including none).

Square brackets [ ] can be used to contain a list of characters [123], a range of characters [a-j], or a combined list and range [123a-j]; this pattern will match any *one* character from the list or range. Using an exclamation mark or carat symbol as the first character inside the square brackets will invert the meaning, causing a match with any one character which is *not* in the list or range.

Table 4-6 lists some examples of ambiguous filenames.

Table 4-6. Ambiguous filenames

Filename	Description	Matches	Does not match
a*	Any filename starting with *a*	absolutely.txt a.out albert	Albert backup _abc_
x	Any filename containing an *x*	xylophone.gif nexus old.x	constantinople ALEX

Table 4-6. Ambiguous filenames (continued)

Filename	Description	Matches	Does not match
*[0-9]	Any filename ending in a digit	file3 menu.backup60	file file3a file3.txt 416-555-1212.phone
[Aa]???.txt	Any eight-character file-name starting with *a* or *A* and ending in *.txt*	appl.txt ax42.txt Any1.txt	application.txt a.txt allow.txt
[a-zA-Z][0-9]	Any two-character filename starting with a letter and ending with a digit	a9 G7 N3	No 7G XX Fortran77
[!a-zA-Z]* [^a-zA-Z]*	Any filename that does not start with a letter	9lives.odt _whatever	abc.txt Nevermore

Choosing easy-to-use filenames

Linux filenames can be up to 254 characters long and contain letters, spaces, digits, and most punctuation marks. However, names that contain certain punctuation marks or spaces cannot be used as command arguments unless you place quote marks around the name (and even then there may be problems). Linux filenames are also case-sensitive, so it's productive to adopt a consistent naming convention and stick to it.

Here are my recommendations for Linux filenames:

- Build the names from lowercase letters, digits, dots, hyphens, and underscores. Avoid all other punctuation. Start the filename with a letter or digit (unless you want to specify a hidden file), and do not include spaces.

> Although it makes command-line file manipulation more awkward, more and more users are adding spaces to photo and music filenames.

- Use the single form of words instead of the plural (*font* instead of *fonts*); it's less typing, and you won't have to keep track of whether you chose the singular or plural form.

- Filename extensions (such as *.gif*, *.txt*, or *.odt*) are not recognized by the Linux kernel; instead, the file contents and security permissions determine how a file is treated. However, some applications do use extensions as an indication of file type, so it's a good idea to employ traditional extensions such as *.mp3* for MP3 audio files and *.png* for portable network graphics files.

Listing the contents of directories

The *ls* (list-directory-contents) command will display a list of the files in the current working directory:

```
$ ls
4Suite      crontab       hosts        libuser.conf   nxserver
a2ps.cfg    cron.weekly   hosts.allow  lisarc         oaf
...(Lines snipped)...
```

You can specify an alternate directory or file pattern as an argument:

```
$ ls /
bin    etc    lost+found  mnt   proc  sbin     sys        usr
boot   home   media       net   ptal  selinux  tftpboot   var
dev    lib    misc        opt   root  srv      tmp
$ ls -d a*
a2ps.cfg          alsa          ant.conf      audit.rules
a2ps-site.cfg     alternatives  ant.d         auto.master
acpi              amanda        asound.state  auto.misc
adjtime           amandates     atalk         auto.net
alchemist         amd.conf      at.deny       auto.smb
aliases           amd.net       atmsigd.conf
aliases.db        anacrontab    auditd.conf
```

By default, filenames starting with a dot (.) are not shown. This provides a convenient way to store information such as a program configuration in a file without constantly seeing the filename in directory listings; you'll encounter many dot files and directories in your home directory. If you wish to see these "hidden" files, add the -a (all) option:

```
$ ls -a
```

ls can display more than just the name of each file. The -l (long) option will change the output to include the security permissions, number of names, user and group name, file size in bytes, and the date and time of last modification:

```
$ ls -l
-rw-------  1 chris chris  3962 Aug 29 02:57 a2script
-rwx------  1 chris chris 17001 Aug 29 02:57 ab1
-rw-------  1 chris chris  2094 Aug 29 02:57 ab1.c
-rwx------  1 chris chris   884 Aug 29 02:57 perl1
-rw-------  1 chris chris   884 Aug 29 02:57 perl1.bck
-rwx------  1 chris chris    55 Aug 29 02:57 perl2
-rw-------  1 chris chris    55 Aug 29 02:57 perl2.bck
-rwx------  1 chris chris 11704 Aug 29 02:57 pointer1
-rw-------  1 chris chris   228 Aug 29 02:57 pointer1.c
-rwx------  1 chris chris 12974 Aug 29 02:57 pp1
-rw-------  1 chris chris  2294 Aug 29 02:57 pp1.c
```

 ls -l is so frequently used that Fedora has a predefined *alias* (shorthand) for it: ll.

You can also sort by file size (from largest to smallest) using -S:

```
$ ls -S -l
-rwx------ 1 chris chris 17001 Aug 29 02:57 ab1
-rwx------ 1 chris chris 12974 Aug 29 02:57 pp1
-rwx------ 1 chris chris 11704 Aug 29 02:57 pointer1
-rw------- 1 chris chris  3962 Aug 29 02:57 a2script
-rw------- 1 chris chris  2294 Aug 29 02:57 pp1.c
-rw------- 1 chris chris  2094 Aug 29 02:57 ab1.c
-rwx------ 1 chris chris   884 Aug 29 02:57 perl1
-rw------- 1 chris chris   884 Aug 29 02:57 perl1.bck
-rw------- 1 chris chris   228 Aug 29 02:57 pointer1.c
-rwx------ 1 chris chris    55 Aug 29 02:57 perl2
-rw------- 1 chris chris    55 Aug 29 02:57 perl2.bck
```

The first character on each line is the file type: - for plain files, d for directories, and l for symbolic links.

There are dozens of options to the *ls* command; see its manpage for details.

Displaying and changing the current working directory

To print the name of the current working directory, use the *pwd* (print-working-directory) command:

```
$ pwd
/home/chris
```

To change the directory, use the cd (change-directory) command.

To change to the */tmp* directory:

```
$ cd /tmp
```

To change to the *foo* directory within the current directory:

```
$ cd foo
```

To change back to the directory you were in before the last cd command:

```
$ cd -
```

To change to your home directory:

```
$ cd
```

To change to the *book* directory within your home directory, regardless of the current working directory:

```
$ cd ~/book
```

To change to *jason*'s home directory:

```
$ cd ~jason/
```

Creating and removing directories from the command line

To create a directory from the command line, use the *mkdir* command:

```
$ mkdir newdirectory
```

This will create *newdirectory* in the current working directory. You could also specify the directory name using an absolute or relative-to-home pathname.

To create a chain of directories, or a directory when one or more of the parent directories might not exist, use the -p (path) option:

```
$ mkdir -p foo/bar/baz/qux
```

This has the side effect of turning off any warning messages if the directory already exists.

To delete a directory that is empty, use *rmdir*:

```
$ rmdir newdirectory
```

This will fail if the directory is not empty. To delete a directory as well as all of the directories and files within that directory, use the *rm* (remove) command with the -r (recursive) option:

```
$ rm -r newdirectory
```

 rm -r can delete hundreds or thousands of files without further confirmation. Use it carefully!

Copying files

To copy a file, use the *cp* command with the source and destination filenames as positional arguments:

```
$ cp /etc/passwd /tmp/passwd-copy
```

This will make a copy of */etc/passwd* named */tmp/passwd-copy*. You can copy multiple files with a single *cp* command as long as the destination is a directory; for example, to copy */etc/passwd* to */tmp/passwd* and */etc/hosts* to */tmp/hosts*:

```
$ cp /etc/passwd /etc/hosts /tmp
```

Renaming and moving files

In Linux, renaming and moving files are considered the same operation and are performed with the *mv* command. In either cases, you're changing the pathname under which the file is stored without changing the contents of the file.

To change a file named *yellow* to be named *purple* in the current directory:

```
$ mv yellow purple
```

To move the file *orange* from *jason*'s home directory to your own:

```
$ mv ~jason/orange ~
```

Removing files

The *rm* command will remove (delete) a file:

```
$ rm badfile
```

You will not be prompted for confirmation as long as you are the owner of the file. To disable confirmation in all cases, use -f (force):

```
$ rm -f badfile
```

Or to enable confirmation in all cases, use -i (interactive):

```
$ rm -i badfile
rm: remove regular empty file `badfile'? y
```

-f and -i can also be used with *cp* and *mv*.

 The graphical desktop tools don't directly delete files; they relocate them to a hidden directory named *~/.Trash*, which corresponds to the desktop Trash icon, where they stay until the Empty Trash option is chosen. You can do the same thing from the command line:

```
$ mv badfile ~/.Trash
```

Creating multiple names by linking files

Linux systems store files by number (the *inode number*). You can view the inode number of a file by using the -i option to *ls*:

```
$ ls -i /etc/hosts
3410634 /etc/hosts
```

A filename is cross-referenced to the corresponding inode number by a *link*—and there's no reason why several links can't point to the same inode number, resulting in a file with multiple names.

This is useful in several situations. For example, the links can appear in different directories, giving convenient access to one file from two parts of the filesystem, or a file can be given a long and detailed name as well as a short name to reduce typing.

Links are created using the ln command. The first argument is an existing filename (source), and the last argument is the filename to be created (destination), just like the cp and mv commands. If multiple source filenames are given, the destination must be a directory.

For example, to create a link to */etc/passwd* named *~/passwords*, type:

```
$ ln /etc/passwd ~/passwords
```

The second column in the output from ls -l displays the number of links on a file:

```
$ ls -l electric.mp3
-rw-rw-r--  1 chris chris 23871 Oct 13 01:00 electric.mp3
$ rm zap.mp3
$ ln electric.mp3 zap.mp3
```

```
$ ls -l electric.mp3
-rw-rw-r--  2 chris chris 23871 Oct 13 01:00 electric.mp3
```

Although these types of links, called *hard links*, are very useful, they suffer from three main limitations:

- The target (file being linked to) must exist before the link is created.
- The link must be on the same storage device as the target.
- You cannot link to directories.

The alternative to a hard link is a *symbolic link*, which links one filename to another filename instead of linking a filename to an inode number. This provides a workaround for all three of the limitations of hard links.

The *ln* command creates symbolic links when the -s argument is specified:

```
$ ls -l ants.avi
-rw-rw-r--  1 chris chris 1539071 Oct 13 01:06 ants.avi
$ ln -s ants.avi ants_in_ant_farm.avi
$ ls -l *ants*
-rw-rw-r--  1 chris chris 1539071 Oct 13 01:06 ants.avi
lrwxrwxrwx  1 chris chris       8 Oct 13 01:06 ants_in_ant_farm.avi -> ants.avi
```

Notice that the the link count on the the target does not increase when a symbolic link is created, and that the ls -l output clearly shows the target of the link.

Determining the contents of files

The *file* command will read the first part of a file, analyze it, and display information about the type of data in the file. Supply one or more filenames as the argument:

```
$ file *
fable:        ASCII text
newicon.png: empty
passwd:       ASCII text
README:       ASCII English text
xpdf.png:     PNG image data, 48 x 48, 8-bit/color RGBA, non-interlaced
```

Viewing the contents of text files

You can display the contents of a text file using the cat command:

```
$ cat README
Dia is a program for drawing structured diagrams.
...(more)...
```

 If you accidentally *cat* a non-text file, your terminal display can get really messed up. The *reset* command will clear up the situation:

```
,l*l\<lL,,,<lFL\<<<G\\l<lGRL<l,1\<L,l<lLl\LLLl<
*]US]$$][]UWVS[ j)Eue[^_1PuuuG;re[^_UUSR@t@CuX[USP
[n X[xG hG6QGListxG!GN9Akregator11ApplicationE <L\
L 2hLl,1
[&&*CS@&*_^-&@$#D]$ reset
[chris@concord2 ~]$
```

To display only the top or bottom 10 lines of a text file, use the *head* or *tail* command instead of *cat*.

If the text file is too big to fit on the screen, the *less* command is used to scroll through it.

```
$ less README
```

You can use the up and down arrow keys and the Page Up/Page Down keys to scroll, and the q key to quit. Press the h key for help on other options, such as searching.

Managing files graphically using GNOME

GNOME's file manager is named *Nautilus* and it permits simple drag-and-drop file management.

When you are logged in to GNOME, Nautilus is already running as part of the desktop environment. To open a Nautilus window, double-click on the Home icon on your desktop or select a folder from the Places menu. A window will appear, such as the one shown in Figure 4-2, showing each file as an icon. Emblems overlaid on the icons are used to indicate the file status, such as *read-only*.

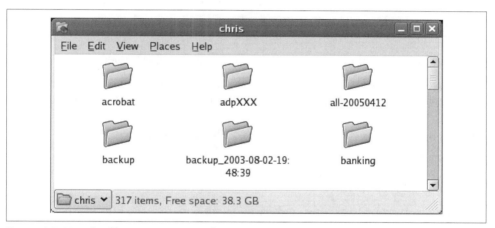

Figure 4-2. Nautilus file management window

By default, Nautilus uses a spatial mode, which means that each directory will open in a separate window, and those windows will retain their position when closed, re-opening at the same location when you access them later.

You can open child directories by double-clicking on them, or you can open a parent directory using the pull-down menu in the bottom-lefthand corner of the window. To deal with more than one directory (for example, for a copy or move operation), open windows for each of the directories and arrange them on the screen so that they are not overlapping.

To manage files, start by selecting one or more files:

- To select a single file, click on it.
- To select several files that are located close together, click on a point to the left or right of the files (which will start drawing a rectangle) and then drag the mouse pointer so that the rectangle touches all of the files you wish to select.
- To select several files that are not adjacent, click on the first one, and then hold Ctrl and click on additional ones.
- To select a consecutive range of files, click on the first file, and then hold Shift and click on the last file.

Once you have selected a file (or files):

- Move the file by dragging it between windows.
- Copy a file by dragging it between windows while holding the Ctrl key.
- Link a file (symbolically) by dragging it between windows while holding the Ctrl and Shift keys.
- Delete a file by dragging it and dropping it on the Trash icon on the desktop, by pressing the Delete key, or by right-clicking and selecting "Move to Trash."
- To rename a file, right-click, select Rename, and then edit the name below the file icon.

You can also use traditional cut, copy, and paste operations on the files:

- To cut a file, press Ctrl-X, or right-click and select Cut. Note that the file will not disappear from the original location until it is pasted into a new location; this effectively performs a move operation.
- To copy a file, press Ctrl-C, or right-click and select Copy.
- To paste a file that has been cut or copied, click on the window of the directory you with to paste into, and then press Ctrl-V or right-click on the window background and select Paste.

You can also perform cut, copy, and paste operations from the Edit menu at the top of the Nautilus window.

Managing files graphically with KDE

KDE's Konqueror is both a file manager and a web browser. Figure 4-3 shows the file manager view. Although at first glance this looks similar to Nautilus, Konqueror offers a larger set of features, most of which are accessed through the toolbar and menus.

To start Konqueror, select Home from the K menu. Unlike Nautilus, Konqueror does not use spatial windows; as you move around the file hierarchy, the same window is reused. To create a second window for drag-and-drop, press Ctrl-N (or select the menu option Location → New Window). Alternately, you can split a window

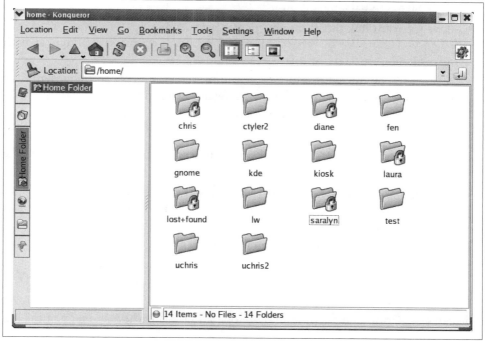

Figure 4-3. Konqueror in file management mode

horizontally or vertically using the Window menu, and then drag and drop between the two panes. To view more information about the files, select the menu option View → View Mode → Detailed List View, which shows information similar to that displayed by ls -l. There are other options on the View Mode menu that are useful in different situations, such as the Photobook view for directories of photographs.

You can change to child directories by double-clicking on them, or you can change to parent directories by using the up-arrow icon on the toolbar. You can also select a directory from the Navigation Panel, shown on the left in Figure 4-3 (the Navigation Panel can be toggled on and off using the F9 key).

To manage files, start by selecting one or more files:

- To select a single file, click on it.
- To select several files that are located close together, click on a point to the left or right of the files (which will start drawing a rectangle) and then drag the mouse pointer so that the rectangle touches all of the files you wish to select.
- To select several files that are not adjacent, click on the first one, and then hold Ctrl and click on additional ones.
- To select a range of files (rectangular region), click on the first file, and then hold Shift and click on the last file.

Once you have selected a file (or files):

- Move, copy, or link the file by dragging it between windows (or window panes). When you drop the file on the destination, a pop-up menu will appear with Move Here, Copy Here, and Link Here options.
- Delete a file by dragging and dropping it on the Trash icon on the desktop, by pressing the Delete key, or by right-clicking and selecting "Move to Trash."
- To rename a file, right-click, select Rename, and then edit the name below the file icon.

As with Nautilus, you can also use traditional cut, copy, and paste operations on the files:

- To cut a file, press Ctrl-X, or right-click and select Cut. Note that the file will not disappear from the original location until it is pasted into a new location; this effectively performs a move operation.
- To copy a file, press Ctrl-C or right-click and select Copy.
- To paste a file that has been cut or copied, click on the window of the directory you wish to paste into, and then press Ctrl-V, or right-click on the window background and select Paste.

You can also perform cut, copy, and paste operations using the Edit menu at the top of the Konqueror window.

How Does It Work?

Matching filenames

Linux shells use a process called *globbing* to find matches for ambiguous filenames before commands are executed. Consider this command:

```
$ ls /etc/*release*
```

When the user presses Enter, the shell converts /etc/*release* into a list of matching filenames before it executes the command. The command effectively becomes:

```
$ ls /etc/fedora-release  /etc/lsb-release  /etc/redhat-release
```

This is different from some other platforms, where the application itself is responsible for filename expansion. The use of shell globbing simplifies the design of software, but it can cause unexpected side effects when an argument is not intended to be a filename. For example, the echo command is used to display messages:

```
$ echo This is a test.
This is a test.
```

However, if you add stars to either side of the message, then globbing will kick in and expand those stars to a list of all files in the current directory:

```
$ echo *** This is a test. ***
bin boot dev etc home lib lost+found media misc mnt net opt proc ptal root sbin
selinux srv sys tftpboot tmp usr var This is a test. bin boot dev etc home lib
lost+found media misc mnt net opt proc ptal root sbin selinux srv sys tftpboot tmp
usr var
```

The solution is to quote the argument to prevent globbing:

```
$ echo "*** This is a test. ***"
*** This is a test. ***
```

The merged file hierarchy

Microsoft Windows uses drive designators at the start of pathnames, such as the *C:* in *C:\Windows\System32\foo.dll*, to indicate which disk drive a particular file is on. Linux instead merges all active filesystems into a single file hierarchy; different drives and partitions are grafted onto the tree in a process called mounting.

You can view the mount table, showing which devices are mounted at which points in the tree, by using the *mount* command:

```
$ mount
/dev/mapper/main-root on / type ext3 (rw)
/dev/proc on /proc type proc (rw)
/dev/sys on /sys type sysfs (rw)
/dev/devpts on /dev/pts type devpts (rw,gid=5,mode=620)
/dev/md0 on /boot type ext3 (rw)
/dev/shm on /dev/shm type tmpfs (rw)
/dev/mapper/main-home on /home type ext3 (rw)
/dev/mapper/main-var on /var type ext3 (rw)
/dev/sdc1 on /media/usbdisk type vfat
    (rw,nosuid,nodev,_netdev,fscontext=system_u:object_r:removable_t,user=chris)
```

Or you can view the same information in a slightly more readable form, along with free-space statistics, by running the *df* command; here I've used the -h option so that free space is displayed in human-friendly units (gigabytes, megabytes) rather than disk blocks:

```
$ df -h
Filesystem            Size  Used Avail Use% Mounted on
/dev/mapper/main-root
                       30G   12G   17G  42% /
/dev/md0              251M   29M  210M  13% /boot
/dev/shm              506M     0  506M   0% /dev/shm
/dev/mapper/main-home
                       48G  6.6G   39G  15% /home
/dev/mapper/main-var   30G   13G   16G  45% /var
/dev/sdc1              63M   21M   42M  34% /media/usbdisk
```

Note that */media/usbdisk* is a flash drive, and that */home* and */var* are stored on separate disk partitions from */*.

What About...

...finding out which files are going to match an ambiguous filename before executing a command?

While the cursor is on or adjacent to the ambiguous filename, press Tab twice. *bash* will display all of the matching filenames, and then reprint the command and let you continue editing:

```
$ ls a* (press Tab, Tab)
a2.html                    all-20090412
a3f1.html
$ ls a*
```

Alternately, press Esc-* and *bash* will replace the ambiguous filename with a list of matching filenames:

```
$ ls a* (press Esc-*)
$ ls a2.html all-20050412 a3f1.html
```

...entering a filename quickly at the shell prompt?

Type the first few characters of the filename, then press Tab. *bash* will fill in the rest of the name (or as much as is unique). For example, if there is only one filename in the current directory that starts with *all*:

```
$ ls all (press Tab)
$ ls all-20090412
```

...using a filename in one command, and then reusing that filename in the next command?

Press Esc-_ (underscore) to copy the last argument from the previous command. For example, to create a directory and then change to that directory:

```
$ mkdir backup-directory-august
$ cd (press Esc, _)
$ cd backup-directory-august
```

Where Can I Learn More?

- The Linux Standard Base project: *http://www.linuxbase.org/*
- The manpages for *bash*, *rm*, *cp*, *mv*, *ls*, *file*, and *less*
- The Konqueror Handbook (press F1 in a Konqueror window)
- The GNOME User's Guide (press F1 in a Nautilus window)

4.4   Basic Text Editing Using vi

Fedora Core, like most other Linux and Unix systems, stores most of its configuration information in text files. These files can be edited using various system administration tools, but they can also be edited by hand using any standard text editor.

vi is one such text editor. Some people love it, and some people hate it, but it has one advantage over just about every other editor available: it's universal. If you know how to use *vi*, you can confidently walk up to just about any Linux or Unix computer in the world and edit text files, so it's a valuable skill. The other nice fact about Vi is that it's not very demanding; you can use it in character mode or graphic mode, over a congested remote connection or with a foreign keyboard, and still get the job done. You can get by with less than a dozen commands to start, and then learn more when you need them.

   vi is pronounced "vee-eye," not "vye" or "six."

How Do I Do That?

To start up the *vi* editor, simply type its name at a shell prompt, optionally providing the name of a file you wish to edit as an argument:

    $ vi *filename*

The screen will clear, and the specified file will be displayed, as shown in Figure 4-4.

Notice that unused lines are marked with a tilde (~) character.

vi modes

vi uses two distinct modes:

- *Normal mode*, where the text keys issue editing commands. This is sometimes called *command mode*.
- *Insert mode*, where text keys insert text into the document.

The lower-left corner of the display shows the current mode: if it says -- INSERT --, then you're in insert mode; otherwise, you're in normal mode.

Moving around

You can move the cursor around using the arrow keys. If your arrow keys don't work (which may be the case if you're using a remote connection from a bad terminal program), you can use the h, j, k, and l keys, as shown in Table 4-7.

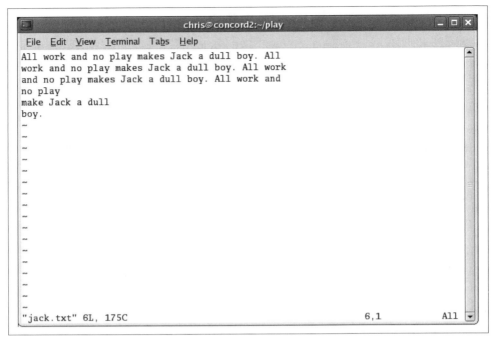

Figure 4-4. Initial vi display

Table 4-7. Basic vi movement commands

Command	Description
Left, h, or Backspace	Move left one character.
Down or j	Move down one line.
Up or k	Move up one line.
Right, l, or Space	Move right one character.
Enter	Move to the start of the next line.
Home, ^, |, or 0 (Zero)	Move to the start of the line.
End, $	Move to the end of the line.
:number Enter	Move to line *number*.
:0 Enter	Move to the start of the file.
:$	Move to the end of the file.
w	Move forward one word.

You can put a number in front of any command to repeat the command. For example, typing 10j will move down 10 lines.

Inserting text

There are several commands for inserting text, as shown in Table 4-8.

Table 4-8. Commands to enter insert mode

Command	Description
i	Insert before the cursor.
I	Insert at the start of the line.
a	Append after the cursor.
A	Append at the end of the line.
o	Open a line after the current line and insert text.
O	Open a line before the current line and insert text.

All of these commands place the editor into insert mode; the only difference is where the cursor is positioned for the inserted text. The word -- INSERT -- will appear in the lower-left corner of the display.

To exit from insert mode and return to normal mode, press Esc. The -- INSERT -- indicator in the lower-left corner of the display will disappear.

Deleting, yanking, and putting: vi's version of cutting, copying, and pasting

vi offers three basic commands for deleting or yanking, as shown in Figure 4-9. *Deleting* is roughly equivalent to cutting in a GUI-based editor, and *yanking* is similar to copying.

Table 4-9. Basic delete and yank commands

Command	Description	Examples
x	Delete one character to the right of the cursor.	x deletes one character to the right of the cursor; 25x deletes the character at the cursor position and 24 characters to the right.
X	Delete one character to the left of the cursor.	X deletes one character to the left of the cursor; 19X deletes 19 characters to the left.
d, followed by a cursor movement	Delete from the cursor position to the indicated position.	dj deletes the current line and the line below; dw deletes one word.
dd	Deletes a line.	dd deletes the current line; 15dd deletes 15 lines.
y, followed by a cursor movement	Yank from the cursor position to the indicated position.	yj yanks the current line and the line below; yw yanks one word.
yy	Yanks a line.	yy yanks the current line; 15yy yanks 15 lines.
p	Puts yanked or deleted text after the cursor. If the text contains any partial lines, it is inserted directly after the cursor; otherwise, it is inserted starting on the next line.	p puts one copy of the yanked text into the document after the cursor; 20p puts 20 copies of the yanked text after the cursor.
P	Puts yanked or deleted text before the cursor. If the text contains any partial lines, it is inserted directly before the cursor; otherwise, it is inserted on the previous line.	P puts one copy of the yanked text into the document before the cursor; 20P puts 20 copies of the yanked text before the cursor.

Searching

Typing / followed by some text (actually, a regular expression) and pressing Enter will search forward in the document. Typing n will repeat the previous search in the forward direction. Typing ? instead of / will search backward instead of forward; N will repeat a search backward.

Searching can be combined with deleting and yanking; for example, d/hello will delete from the cursor position up to the start of the word hello.

Undoing, redoing, and repeating

Pressing u will undo the last operation performed; pressing Ctrl-R will redo it. Typing a dot (.) will repeat the last operation.

Saving and exiting

There are a number of commands available for saving the document and exiting *vi*, as shown in Table 4-10; you must press Enter after these commands.

Table 4-10. Saving text and exiting vi

Command	Description
:w	Write (save) using the current filename.
:w *newfilename*	Write to the file *newfilename* (subsequent :w commands will still write to the original filename).
:w!	Force-write (write even if in read-only mode).
:q	Quit (succeeds only if the document is saved).
:q!	Force quit even if the document isn't saved (abort!).
:wq or :x or ZZ	Write and quit (exit with save).

How Does It Work?

vi is one of a group of programs that uses a terminal-control system called *curses*. *curses* enables an application to manage a character-mode display by positioning the cursor and interpreting keystrokes using a database of information about each terminal—i.e., which codes to send to produce different effects and which codes can be received from the terminal. Fedora's *terminfo* database has entries for about 2,500 different hardware terminals and terminal programs that have been produced through the years.

curses keeps two *buffers*—areas of memory arranged in the same size and layout as the screen—to store the current terminal screen contents and the desired display. When *vi* needs to update the screen, it updates the display buffer; *curses* compares the two buffers to determine the minimum number of commands it can send to the terminal to produce the desired display. It then sends the appropriate codes from the terminal database (*terminfo/termcap*) to update the terminal, copies the display buffer to the terminal buffer, and repeats the process.

The version of *vi* used by Fedora Core is *Vim* (Vi iMproved), which adds many, many features to the traditional *vi* capabilities; the commands covered in this chapter outline only the basics. Vim offers syntax highlighting, macro recording, support for multiple character sets, accents, right-to-left text, and many other features, making it a useful text editor for programming, scripting, and editing system files.

Vim can be configured by creating a *.vimrc* file; for details, type `:help vimrc-intro` within Vim.

What About...

...using vi with a GUI?

If you execute *gvim* instead of *vi*, a window will appear with a full graphical user interface—including pull-down menus and a toolbar—as shown in Figure 4-5. Using the File → Save menu option, clicking on the Save toolbar icon, or typing the *vi* save command (`:w`) will perform the same operation.

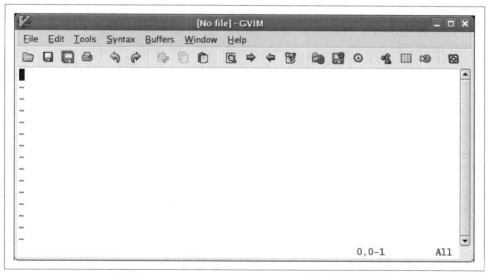

Figure 4-5. gvim: vi with a GUI

...using other text editors?

In addition to *vi*, Fedora ships with a plethora of other text editors, including:

- *nano* (an improved clone of the easy-to-use editor *Pico*)
- *mcedit*

- *joe* (the commands *jstar*, *jmacs*, or *jpico* will start *joe* configured to emulate *WordStar*, *emacs*, or *Pico*).
- *emacs* and *emacs-x*
- *kedit* and *gedit*

All of these text editors are capable of editing just about any text file. Each has its advantages and disadvantages.

Since the choice of editor is very personal, take some time to experiment with each of the editors to see which one you prefer. In any case, I'd recommend knowing the basics of *vi* so that you can always fall back to it if you encounter a situation where your favorite editor is unavailable.

Where Can I Learn More?

- The Vim web site: *http://www.vim.org/*
- The *vi* help file and online tutorial: start *vi*, then type **:help** and press Enter

4.5 Using Runlevels

Fedora can be booted into different *runlevels*, each of which starts a specific collection of software for a particular purpose. The most commonly used are runlevel 3, which starts the system with a character-based user interface, and runlevel 5, which starts the system with a graphical user interface. Table 4-11 lists the standard runlevels.

Table 4-11. Standard runlevels

Runlevel	Description	Purpose
s (or S)	Single-user maintenance mode	Emergency system recovery work
0	Halt	Stops the system
1	Single-user mode	System administration
2	(Multiuser without networking)	(Not normally used)
3	Multiuser, character-mode	Normal system operation without graphical login; useful for servers
4	(Not defined)	(Not normally used)
5	Graphical	Normal system operation with graphical login.
6	Reboot	Restarts the system
7, 8, 9, a, b, c	(Not defined)	Available for custom purposes

The ability to choose the runlevel lets you save system resources (for example, by not running the graphical user interface when it isn't needed) or start the system in a minimal configuration so that you can fix problems.

How Do I Do That?

You can change the runlevel on the fly, or configure your system to start in a different runlevel.

Choosing the runlevel at boot time

The Fedora boot menu can be used to specify the runlevel:

1. Press a key (such as the spacebar) when the Fedora Core boot display appears. This will reveal the boot menu.
2. Select the Fedora Core boot option you wish to use using the arrow keys.
3. Press the letter a (Append). An edit display will appear that allows you to append information to the boot command line.
4. Add a space and then the runlevel to the end of the list of boot options (for example, press space then 3 to select runlevel 3).
5. Press Enter to boot into the runlevel that you've specified.

 If you have configured a GRUB password, you will be prompted to enter it before changing the boot options.

Changing the runlevel after booting

Take the following steps to change the runlevel after booting:

1. Obtain a *root* prompt using the *su* command:

   ```
   $ su
   Password: rootPassword
   #
   ```

2. Use the init command to change to the runlevel of your choice:

   ```
   # init 3
   ```

Changing the default runlevel

System administrators often configure servers to start in runlevel 3, freeing up memory to increase the server's performance.

The default runlevel is controlled by a line in the file */etc/inittab*; to change the default runlevel, edit that file using the *vi* editor:

1. Obtain a root prompt using su.
2. Start *vi* with the */etc/inittab* file:

   ```
   # vi /etc/inittab
   ```

3. Find this line in the file:

   ```
   id:5:initdefault:
   ```

4. Change the second field to the default runlevel of your choice; in this case, I've used 3:

```
id:3:initdefault:
```

Save the file and exit *vi*. The change will take effect next time you boot the system.

Creating entries for different runlevels on the boot menu

The boot menu is configured using the file */boot/grub/grub.conf*. You can edit this file so that options for various runlevels appear on the boot menu:

1. Obtain a *root* prompt.

2. Start *vi* with the */boot/grub/grub.conf*:

   ```
   # vi /boot/grub/grub.conf
   ```

   The file will look something like this:

   ```
   # grub.conf generated by anaconda
   #
   # Note that you do not have to rerun grub after making changes to this file
   # NOTICE:  You have a /boot partition.  This means that
   #          all kernel and initrd paths are relative to /boot/, eg.
   #          root (hd0,1)
   #          kernel /vmlinuz-version ro root=/dev/Main/root
   #          initrd /initrd-version.img
   #boot=/dev/hdc
   default=0
   timeout=5
   splashimage=(hd0,1)/grub/splash.xpm.gz
   hiddenmenu
   title Fedora Core (2.6.17-1.2517.fc6)
           root (hd0,1)
           kernel /vmlinuz-2.6.17-1.2517.fc6 ro root=/dev/Main/root rhgb quiet
           initrd /initrd-2.6.17-1.2517.fc6.img
   title Windows XP
           rootnoverify (hd0,0)
           chainloader +1
   ```

   This example shows two Fedora Core entries for two different kernel versions. There may be additional entries for other operating systems (such as Windows) or additional kernels.

3. Find a Fedora Core entry (the bold lines in the example above)—usually, the one with the latest kernel. Make an identical copy of it immediately after the original location in the file:

   ```
   title Fedora Core (2.6.17-1.2517.fc6)
           root (hd0,1)
           kernel /vmlinuz-2.6.17-1.2517.fc6 ro root=/dev/Main/root rhgb quiet
           initrd /initrd-2.6.17-1.2517.fc6.img
   title Fedora Core (2.6.17-1.2517.fc6)
           root (hd0,1)
           kernel /vmlinuz-2.6.17-1.2517.fc6 ro root=/dev/Main/root rhgb quiet
           initrd /initrd-2.6.17-1.2517.fc6.img
   ```

4. Change the description of the copied section to indicate the runlevel that will be used:

```
title Fedora Core (2.6.17-1.2517_fc6) - Runlevel 3 - Character mode
```

5. On the kernel line, append the runlevel that you wish to use (this will override the default runlevel in *etc/inittab*):

```
kernel /vmlinuz-2.6.17-1.2517.fc6 ro root=/dev/Main/root rhgb quiet 3
```

6. Optionally, change the `default`, `timeout`, or `hiddenmenu` options to suit your tastes.

7. The `default` option specifies which of the menu entries is booted by default; the menu entries are numbered starting at 0, so you could set this line to 1 to boot the second item on the menu automatically:

```
default=1
```

The `timeout` option sets the number of seconds that the menu will be displayed before the default option is automatically chosen. To give the user 30 seconds to decide which boot option to use, change the `timeout` line to read:

```
timeout=30
```

`hiddenmenu` hides the menu until the user presses a key; remove the `hiddenmenu` line to automatically reveal the menu every time the system is booted.

8. Save the file and exit *vi*. The new menu option will appear the next time you boot the system.

How Does It Work?

Once the kernel has fully started up, it runs just one program: *init*. All other software is started directly or indirectly by *init*.

If a runlevel is specified in the kernel boot options, *init* uses that value for the runlevel; otherwise, it obtains a runlevel from the `initdefault` line in *etc/inittab*.

init then looks for a `sysinit` entry in *etc/inittab* and executes the command specified:

```
si::sysinit:/etc/rc.d/rc.sysinit
```

This executes the *etc/rc.d/rc.sysinit* script, which performs some basic system setup common to all runlevels.

Next, *init* examines the *etc/inittab* file, looking for entries that contain the current runlevel in the second field and `wait` or `respawn` in the third field. For runlevel 3, it will find these lines:

```
l3:3:wait:/etc/rc.d/rc 3
1:2345:respawn:/sbin/mingetty tty1
2:2345:respawn:/sbin/mingetty tty2
3:2345:respawn:/sbin/mingetty tty3
4:2345:respawn:/sbin/mingetty tty4
5:2345:respawn:/sbin/mingetty tty5
6:2345:respawn:/sbin/mingetty tty6
```

The first line starts the script */etc/rc.d/rc* with the argument 3. This in turn sequentially executes every script in */etc/rc.d/rc3.d* that starts with the letter S (for *start*); this is how runlevel-specific software and services get started. Scripts in that same directory that start with K (for *Kill*) are used to stop software when switching from the runlevel.

The remaining lines listed start character-mode logins on virtual terminals 1 through 6; the respawn keyword indicates that *init* must restart those programs when they terminate, enabling another user to log in.

What About...

...booting without an /etc/inittab file?

If the file */etc/inittab* doesn't exist, *init* cannot start the system normally. Runlevel S was created specifically for this purpose; it's the only runlevel that doesn't require */etc/inittab*, so it can be a lifesaver if that file is missing or messed up. In fact, *init* doesn't even ask for a password in runlevel S; it takes you directly to a *root* command prompt. This is useful if you've forgotten the *root* password, but presents a huge security risk.

To protect against the unauthorized use of runlevel S, it's a good idea to add a password entry to the boot menu. If you didn't do this during the installation, you can add the password at any time by following these steps:

1. Generate an encrypted password with the *grub-md5-crypt* command:

```
$ grub-md5-crypt
Password: bigsecret
Retype password: bigsecret
$1$f1zo61$j/UEYyBn0e0996w0gjq4k/
```

The previous line in bold is the encrypted (scrambled) version of the password.

2. Next, edit the */boot/grub/grub.conf* file and add this line at the top, substituting the password generated in step 1:

```
password --md5 $1$f1zo61$j/UEYyBn0e0996w0gjq4k/
```

When you boot the system, you will still be able to select a boot menu entry, but to perform any advanced operations (such as appending runlevel information to a boot entry) you will need to enter the password.

...using the GUI in runlevel 3?

Just because runlevel 3 doesn't offer a graphical login screen doesn't mean that you can't use a graphical user interface. If you log in on a character-mode display, you can start the GUI with this command:

```
$ startx
```

To have the GUI start each time you log in, add this command to your *~/.bash_ profile*:

```
exec startx
```

On a server, this gives you the best of both worlds: the GUI doesn't consume any resources when it's not in use, but it can be started quickly any time you need it—useful when you need to look up documentation on a web site, for example.

Where Can I Learn More?

- The manpages for *init* and *inittab*

4.6 Managing and Configuring Services

Fedora starts a number of programs automatically when the system is booted. These *services* (sometimes called *Disk And Execution MONitors*, or *daemons*) perform automatic actions on the local computer and, in some cases, perform operations for remote computers on the network, such as sharing files and serving web pages.

Each service consumes memory and processor time, and each network service may provide a weak spot for an attack against your system. Disabling unused services can reduce your boot time, speed up your system, and reduce your security risk.

How Do I Do That?

Select the menu option System → Administration → Services (in KDE, it is System → Services) to start the *system-config-services tool*, shown in Figure 4-6.

The configuration of the current runlevel is shown by default. Every service with a checkmark in front of it will be started when that runlevel is entered; to add or clear a checkmark, click on the checkbox.

Click on a service name to see a description of that service and its current status (*running* or *stopped*). Click on the Save icon (or File → Save Changes) when you've configured the services to your liking; your changes will take effect next time you change runlevels or boot the system.

You can edit the settings for another runlevel (3, 4, 5, or all three at the same time) using options on the Edit Runlevel menu.

To start, stop, or restart a service immediately, regardless of whether it's configured to start automatically at boot time, click on the service name and then click on the Start, Stop, or Restart icon.

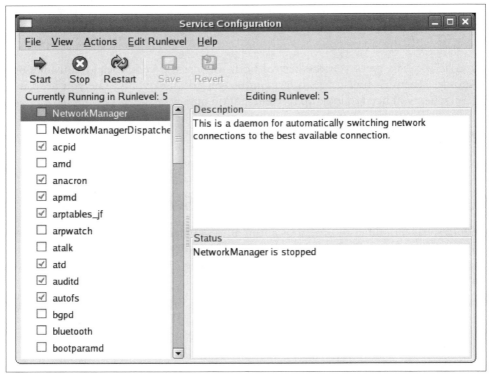

Figure 4-6. Services configuration window

Configuring services using a character user interface

If you're not running a graphical user interface, you can use *ntsysv*, a character-mode program similar to *system-config-services*:

```
# ntsysv
```

This will configure the current runlevel. To configure a different runlevel, use the --level option:

```
# ntsysv --level 4
```

The display shown in Figure 4-7 will appear.

Use the arrow keys to select a service, the spacebar to check/uncheck a service, and Tab to switch between the service list and the buttons. When you are done, press Tab to advance to the OK button and then press Enter.

Configuring services from the command line

The chkconfig command provides an easy way to enable and disable services. The --list option displays the current service configuration:

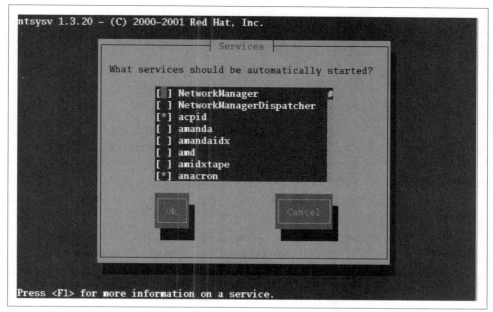

```
ntsysv 1.3.20 – (C) 2000–2001 Red Hat, Inc.
```

```
┌────────────────┤ Services ├────────────────┐
│                                             │
│  What services should be automatically started? │
│                                             │
│      [ ] NetworkManager              #      │
│      [ ] NetworkManagerDispatcher           │
│      [*] acpid                              │
│      [ ] amanda                             │
│      [ ] amandaidx                          │
│      [ ] amd                                │
│      [ ] amidxtape                          │
│      [*] anacron                            │
│                                             │
│        Ok                    Cancel         │
│                                             │
└─────────────────────────────────────────────┘
```

```
Press <F1> for more information on a service.
```

Figure 4-7. The ntsysv display

```
$ chkconfig --list
NetworkManager           0:off   1:off   2:off   3:off   4:off   5:off   6:off
NetworkManagerDispatcher  0:off   1:off   2:off   3:off   4:off   5:off   6:off
acpid                    0:off   1:off   2:off   3:on    4:on    5:on    6:off
amd                      0:off   1:off   2:off   3:off   4:off   5:off   6:off
anacron                  0:off   1:off   2:on    3:on    4:on    5:on    6:off
apmd                     0:off   1:off   2:on    3:on    4:on    5:on    6:off
arptables_jf             0:off   1:off   2:on    3:on    4:on    5:on    6:off
...(Lines snipped)...
```

If you specify a service name, then only the configuration for that service is shown:

```
$ chkconfig --list httpd
httpd                    0:off   1:off   2:off   3:off   4:off   5:off   6:off
```

Note that each of the seven runlevels is shown, even though the configurations for runlevels 0 and 6 are ignored except for K files (since 0 is halt and 6 is reboot).

To enable a service in a runlevel, use the --level option to specify the runlevel along with the on argument:

```
# chkconfig --level 4 httpd on
# chkconfig --list httpd
httpd                    0:off   1:off   2:off   3:off   4:on    5:off   6:off
```

To disable it, use the off argument:

```
# chkconfig --level 4 httpd off
# chkconfig --list httpd
httpd                    0:off   1:off   2:off   3:off   4:off   5:off   6:off
```

To reset a service to its default configuration, use the reset argument. The configuration will be reset for the runlevel you specify, or for all runlevels if you don't include a --level option:

```
# chkconfig --level 4 httpd reset
# chkconfig httpd reset
```

Managing services from the command line

The *service* command is used to manage running services. Two arguments are always used: first, the name of the service being managed, and second, the action that is to be performed. The most common actions are:

start
> Start the service. This will fail if the service is already running.

stop
> Stop the service. This will fail if the service is not running.

restart
> Restart the service by stopping it and then starting it.

reload
> Reload the configuration files for the service after they have been edited.

status
> Display the current status of the service. This will indicate if the service is stopped or running; depending on the service, additional information may be displayed.

For example, to start the web service (named *httpd*):

```
# service httpd start
Starting httpd:                                         [  OK  ]
```

You can then check its status:

```
# service httpd status
httpd (pid 13154 13153 13152 13151 13150 13149 13148 13147 13117) is running...
```

The pid values printed are the process IDs of the web server processes.

To make the web server reload its configuration file after it's been edited:

```
# service httpd reload
Reloading httpd:                                        [  OK  ]
```

Finally, to stop the web server:

```
# service httpd stop
Stopping httpd:                                         [  OK  ]
```

How Does It Work?

Services are managed by scripts in the */etc/rc.d/init.d* directory; the name of each script corresponds to the name of the service. Each runlevel has its own directory named */etc/rc.d/rc<X>.d*, where *<X>* is the runlevel.

If you examine a runlevel directory, you'll see names beginning with K or S, followed by a 2-digit number, followed by a service name:

```
$ ls /etc/rc.d/rc5.d
K01rgmanager                    K36postgresql    K90isicom
K01yum                          K45arpwatch      K92ipvsadm
K02NetworkManager               K46radvd         K94diskdump
K02NetworkManagerDispatcher     K50netdump       S01sysstat
K05innd                         K50snmpd         S04readahead_early
K05saslauthd                    K50snmptrapd     S05kudzu
K09dictd                        K50tux           S06cpuspeed
               ...(Lines snipped)...
K35vncserver                    K85mdmpd         S97messagebus
K35winbind                      K85zebra         S98cups-config-daemon
K36dhcp6s                       K87multipathd    S98haldaemon
K36lisa                         K89netplugd      S99local
K36mysqld                       K89rdisc
```

All of these files are actually symbolic links to service scripts in */etc/rc.d/init.d*, as shown by a long listing:

```
$ cd /etc/rc.d/rc5.d
$ ls -l S90xfs
lrwxrwxrwx  1 root root 13 Oct  5 14:37 S90xfs -> ../init.d/xfs
```

The scripts that start with *S* are used to start services, and the scripts that start with *K* are used to kill (stop) services. *K* scripts are only used when switching between runlevels after the system has been booted.

The digits in the filename are used to control the sequence in which the scripts are executed. This is essential because some services rely on others; for example, the web server relies on the network being up and running, so the network script must be run first.

When you examine the top of a service script, you will find a comment line containing the keyword chkconfig: followed by three arguments:

```
$ head /etc/rc.d/rc5.d/S90xfs
#!/bin/bash
#
# Id:$
#
# xfs:        Starts the X Font Server
#
# Version:    @(#) /etc/init.d/xfs 2.0
#
# chkconfig: 2345 90 10
# description: Starts and stops the X Font Server at boot time and shutdown. \
```

The first argument (2345) is a list of the runlevels in which this service will run by default; this information is used to initially set up the system and to handle *chkconfig*'s reset argument. If the default for this service is to have it turned off in all runlevels, the value - is used. The second argument is the sequence number (00 through 99) for the start link; the value 90 shown here means that the name of the start link will be *S90xfs*. The third argument is the sequence number for the kill link, which in this case yields a kill-link name of *K10xfs*.

When service scripts are called, they are passed a keyword such as start, stop, restart, or reload, indicating the action the script must take.

What About...

...creating my own runlevel?

You can use the *system-config-services* or *chkconfig* tools to create a custom set of services for a runlevel and then use that either as the default runlevel or an option on the boot menu.

This technique is particularly useful on laptops, which may be used in different locations and need different services in each location.

...creating my own service?

To create a service:

1. Create a service script in */etc/rc.d/init.d*. Include a chkconfig line as described in the previous section. (You may want to examine an existing service file to see how it works.)
2. Run the command chkconfig --add *service* to set up the default service links.

You can then configure your service in the same way as any of the other services, using *system-config-services*, *service*, and *chkconfig*.

Where Can I Learn More?

- The manpages for *chkconfig*, *ntsysv*, and *init*

4.7   Managing Users and Groups

In an age of viruses, worms, and identity theft, keeping information private and secure has taken on great importance. Managing user identity creates the framework for system security—even on a single-user system, where a distinction is maintained between using the system as the *normal* user and using the system as the *root* user.

How Do I Do That?

Almost everyone identifies themselves as both an individual and as a member of several groups. Linux uses separate *user* and *group* identities to reconstruct this two-level structure inside the system.

For example, company employee *Richard* might be all of the following:

- A member of the IT department
- Located at the company's Toronto office
- The leader of the team putting together the big sales pitch to Acme, Ltd.
- Part of the Christmas party committee
- A player in the Tuesday evening company soccer league

(And that doesn't even touch on life outside of the company!)

The system administrator configures Richard's account to indicate his many involvements within the company. At the user level, the name *richard* is assigned to him, and a password and home directory are assigned. *richard* is then placed into the groups *it*, *toronto*, *acmeproposal*, *christmas*, and *soccer*.

Fedora Core extends this system using a scheme called *user private group* (UPG), which means that Richard also has his own private group, also named *richard*. UPG makes a lot of sense when you look at permissions.

Managing users graphically

The Fedora GUI tool for managing users and groups is *system-config-users*, which is accessed through the menu under System → Administration → "Users and Groups." After you supply the *root* password, the window shown in Figure 4-8 will appear.

This window has two tabs, one for managing groups and one for managing users.

To add a user, click on the Add User icon. The window shown in Figure 4-9 will be displayed.

Fill in each of the fields:

User Name
> The account name (username) you wish to use (such as *jane*). This is what the user will enter when she logs in to the system. It should be an *opaque string* (no spaces) and consist of letters, digits, dashes, underscores, and periods. Although you can use uppercase characters, traditional user names are all-lowercase for ease of typing.

Full Name
> The actual name of the user, in upper- and lowercase (*Jane Smith*). This information is optional and is used for reference only.

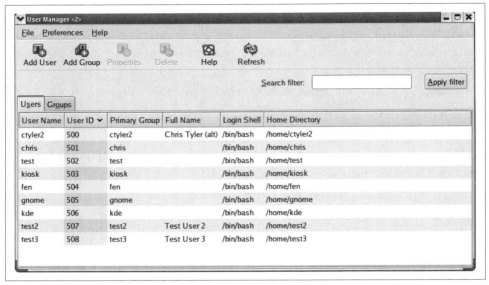

Figure 4-8. The Users and Groups configuration window

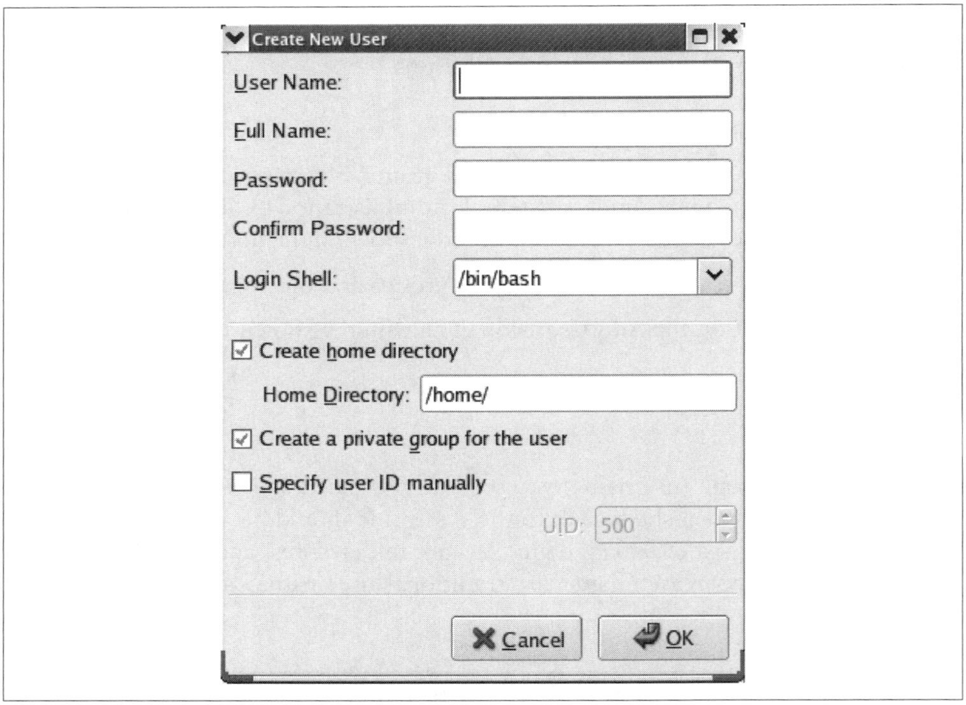

Figure 4-9. The Create New User window

Password and Confirm Password
> Type the new user's password twice.

Login shell
> For most users, this field should be left as is; it can always be changed (using *chsh*) later. If you are creating a user account that will never be used for logging in (such as an account used exclusively for email access or file sharing), select */sbin/nologin* for the shell.

Create home directory
> This should almost always be left checked.

Create a private group for the user
> This enables the Fedora User Private Group scheme (which is a great idea), so it should almost always be left checked.

Specify a user ID manually
> This controls whether the numeric user ID will be automatically or manually assigned. The only time you would want to specify it manually is when you are configuring the same user ID on two systems. In that case, check the box and enter the user ID in the UID field; otherwise, leave it unchecked.

Once you have filled in all of these fields, click OK. You will be returned to the main User and Group configuration window (Figure 4-8).

To edit a user, double-click on the user's name, or highlight the name and click the Properties icon. An edit window will appear with four tabs, enabling you to edit values that cannot be set during the creation of the account; Figure 4-10 shows each of these tabs.

The four tabs are:

User Data
> Contains fields similar to those in the Create New User dialog (Figure 4-9).

Account Info
> Allows you to set an expiry date for the account or lock (disable) the account.

Password Info
> Configures password expiration (also called *password aging*). You can set the number of days before a change is required, to force users to change passwords periodically; the number of days after a change before another change is permitted, to prevent a user from gaming the forced password change by using a temporary password and then immediately switching back to her regular password; how far in advance the user will be warned about an impending password expiry; and the number of days of inactivity permitted before the account is locked as abandoned.

Groups
> This tab is one of the least used, but most useful. Here you configure the groups to which the user belongs. In the case of our fictional example of Richard, you

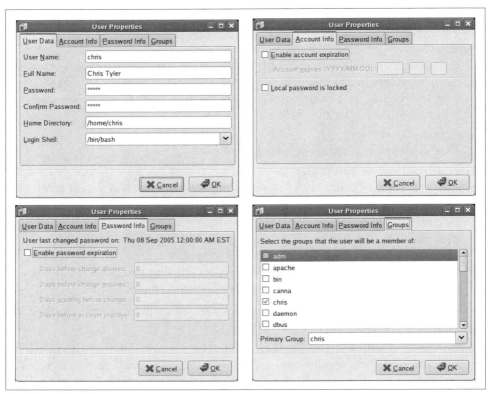

Figure 4-10. The four tabs of the User Properties window

would check the *it*, *toronto*, *acmeproposal*, *christmas*, and *soccer* groups. By default, the user is automatically assigned to a group with the same name as his username. The significance of groups is that they can be used to manage file access.

The value of password aging is debatable; while it does limit the time that a compromised password can be used, forcing a user to change her password too frequently can make it difficult for her to remember the current password, leading to unsafe practices such as writing passwords on sticky notes or choosing weak passwords.

To delete a user account, click on the username and then click on the Delete icon. You will be warned if the user account is active (i.e., if the user is logged in or has processes running), and you will be asked for confirmation. The confirmation dialog has a checkbox that controls whether the user's files will be deleted along with the user account. If you are planning to keep the user's files, it may be better to lock the account than to delete it, so that the user's name continues to show up as the owner of those files (if the account is deleted, the account number is shown instead of the name).

Managing groups graphically

The Group tab of the User Manager window works in exactly the same way as the Users tab. The only fields that appear in the Add Group dialog are for the group name and, if you want to set it manually, the group number. The Properties dialog adds a tab that shows you a list of all of the users on the system, with checkboxes to indicate which ones are in the group.

Adding and managing users from the command line

Fedora provides six utilities for managing users and groups from the command line. For users, there are *useradd*, *usermod*, and *userdel*; for groups, there are *groupadd*, *groupmod*, and *groupdel*.

The express way to add a user is to use *useradd* and then set the new user's password using *passwd*:

```
# useradd jane
# passwd jane
Changing password for user jane.
New UNIX password: bigSecret
Retype new UNIX password: bigSecret
passwd: all authentication tokens updated successfully.
```

useradd accepts a number of options; the most common are shown in Table 4-12. Most of these options can also be used with *usermod* to change an existing user's options.

Table 4-12. useradd options

Option	Description	Notes
-b *directory*	Base for home directories (a directory with the same name as the username will be created in this directory and used as the home directory)	*useradd* only; the default is */home*.
-c *"fullName"*	User comment field; almost always used to hold the user's full name	If the full name contains spaces, quote it.
-d *homedir*	User's home directory	
-e *YYYY-MM-DD*	Account expiry date	
-f *days*	Days of inactivity before the account is considered abandoned and locked	
-g *group*	User's primary group	Default is the user's own group (same name as the username).
-G *grp1,grp2,...*	Supplementary group membership	
-M	Don't create a home directory	*useradd* only.
-m	Create a home directory if it doesn't exist	This is the default action.
-p *cryptpass*	Set encrypted password to *cryptpass*	Useful when copying accounts from an old system configuration.
-s *shell*	Sets the user's shell to *shell*	

Table 4-12. useradd options (continued)

Option	Description	Notes
-u *uid*	Set the numeric user ID to *uid*	Useful when copying accounts from an old system configuration or synchronizing with old NFS servers.
-L	Lock account against login	*usermod* only.
-U	Unlock account and permit login	*usermod* only.

To set Jane's full name when her account is created, execute:

```
# useradd -c "Jane Smith" jane
```

usermod works in a similar way to *useradd*, but is used to adjust the parameters of existing accounts. For example, to change Jane's full name:

```
# usermod -c "Jane Lee" jane
```

As you'd expect, the *userdel* command deletes a user. The -r option specifies that the user's home directory and mail spool (*/var/spool/mail/user*) should also be removed:

```
# userdel -r jane
```

The *groupadd*, *groupmod*, and *groupdel* commands are used in a similar way to create, modify, and delete groups.

To add a group, just specify the name as an argument to *groupadd*:

```
# groupadd groupname
```

The only option commonly used is -g, which lets you manually select the group ID (useful if converting data from an old system):

```
# groupadd -g 781 groupname
```

The *groupmod* command is rarely used, but it will change the numeric group ID (-g) or the name (-n) of an existing group:

```
# groupmod -g 947 groupname
# groupmod -n newname groupname
```

To delete a group, use *groupdel*:

```
# groupdel groupname
```

Managing user passwords from the command line

passwd is used to set a user's password. Used by a normal user, it sets that user's password by asking for the current password and then asking for the new password twice:

```
$ passwd
Changing password for user chris.
Changing password for chris
(current) UNIX password: bigSecret
New UNIX password: newSecret
```

```
Retype new UNIX password: newSecret
passwd: all authentication tokens updated successfully.
```

When used by the *root* user, *passwd* can be used to change the *root* password (the default) or any existing user's password if the username is supplied as an argument. You don't need to know the current password:

```
# passwd
Changing password for user root.
New UNIX password: topSecret
Retype new UNIX password: topSecret
passwd: all authentication tokens updated successfully.
# passwd jane
Changing password for user jane.
New UNIX password: superSecret
Retype new UNIX password: superSecret
passwd: all authentication tokens updated successfully.
```

The *root* user can also delete a password from an account (so a user can log in with just a username):

```
# passwd -d jane
Removing password for user jane.
passwd: Success
```

This must be used carefully because it presents a big security risk. Remember that remote users may be able to connect via SSH, and then they won't need a password either!

To find out the password status of an account, use -S:

```
# passwd -S jane
Empty password.
# passwd -S chris
Password set, MD5 crypt.
```

Managing groups and delegating group maintenance from the command line

The *gpasswd* command can be used to set a group password. This is rarely done. However, it is also used to manage groups and, better yet, to delegate group administration to any user.

To specify the members of a group, use the -M option:

```
# gpasswd -M jane,richard,frank audit
```

In this case, *jane*, *richard*, and *frank* are made members of the *audit* group. Any previous memberships in that group will be obliterated, so only these three users will now be in that group. (Other group memberships held by those users will not be affected.)

You can also add or delete individual group users using the -a and -d options:

```
# gpasswd -a audrey audit
# gpasswd -d frank audit
```

Those commands add *audrey* to the group *audit*, then delete *frank*.

If you delegate group administration to users, they can use the -a and -d options—a great labor-saving idea! Delegation is performed with the -A (administrator) option:

```
# gpasswd -A jane audit
jane$ gpasswd -a matthew audit
```

How Does It Work?

User accounts are controlled by the */etc/passwd* file, which looks like this:

```
root:x:0:0:root:/root:/bin/bash
bin:x:1:1:bin:/bin:/sbin/nologin
daemon:x:2:2:daemon:/sbin:/sbin/nologin
adm:x:3:4:adm:/var/adm:/sbin/nologin
...(Lines snipped)...
fax:x:78:78:mgetty fax spool user:/var/spool/fax:/sbin/nologin
nut:x:57:57:Network UPS Tools:/var/lib/ups:/bin/false
privoxy:x:73:73::/etc/privoxy:/sbin/nologin
chris:x:500:500:Chris Tyler:/home/chris:/bin/bash
diane:x:501:501:Diane Tyler:/home/diane:/bin/bash
jane:x:502:502:Jane Smith:/home/jane:/bin/bash
richard:x:503:503:Richard Lee:/home/richard:/bin/bash
```

The fields in this file are separated by colons. From left to right, they are:

username
> The name of the user account, which shows up in ls -l output and is used to log in to the system. This is sometimes (incorrectly) called the user ID.

password
> The encrypted password used to be stored in this field. For security, it has now been moved to */etc/shadow*.

user ID
> The number identifying this user. Process and file ownership is stored as a number; this field is used to cross-reference the number with a username. The user ID is frequently abbreviated to *uid*. User IDs below 500 are considered *system IDs* and are reserved for system services.

group ID
> The group ID (*gid*) indicates the primary group for this user. It's cross-referenced to a group name through */etc/group*.

comment field
> This field can be used to store any text associated with the user. On Fedora, it's usually used to store the user's full name; the *chfn* and *finger* commands use it to store the user's full name, office location, office phone number, and home phone number, separated by commas.

This field is historically called the *gecos* or *gcos* field because it originally cross-referenced user IDs between the Unix and General Electric Comprehensive Operating System (gecos) at Bell Labs. You'll still find this field documented as `pw_gecos` in Linux library function documentation (for an example, see `man getpwent`).

home directory

At login, the shell changes to this directory automatically, and the `HOME` environment variable is set to this value.

shell

This field specifies the user's default shell.

 For accounts that require a password but should not permit the user to log in, such as an account used only for file sharing or POP/IMAP email access, use the dummy shell `/sbin/nologin`. If the user attempts to log in, the message "This account is currently not available" is displayed, and the user is logged out automatically. To use a different message, place the desired text in the file */etc/nologin.txt*.

Since */etc/passwd* must be readable by everyone so that commands such as `ls -l` can function correctly, the passwords have been moved to a file that is readable only by *root*, named */etc/shadow*, which looks like this:

```
root:$1$45ZWBaPE$XvzhGEj/rA4VDJXdQESiO.:13024:0:99999:7:::
bin:*:13024:0:99999:7:::
daemon:*:13024:0:99999:7:::
adm:*:13024:0:99999:7:::
...(Lines snipped)...
fax:!!:13024:0:99999:7:::
nut:!!:13024:0:99999:7:::
privoxy:!!:13024:0:99999:7:::
chris:$1$hUjsHJUHIhUhu889H98hH.8.BGhhY79:13068:0:99999:7:::
diane:$1$97KJHNujHUkh88JHmnjNyu54NUI9JY7:13024:0:99999:7:::
jane:$1$yuaJsudk9jUJHUhJHtgjhytnbYhGJHy:13024:0:99999:7:::
richard:$1$pIjyfRbKo71jntgRFu3duhU97hHygbf:13024:0:99999:7:::
```

Note that the second field contains an encrypted version of the password. The encryption function, called a *hash*, is not reversible, so it's not possible to take this data and reconstruct the password. When the user enters his password, it is also encrypted; then the two encrypted values are compared.

The other fields in this file contain information used for password aging (expiry).

In a similar way, */etc/group* contains basic information about each group:

```
root:x:0:root
bin:x:1:root,bin,daemon
daemon:x:2:root,bin,daemon
sys:x:3:root,bin,adm
```

```
adm:x:4:root,adm,daemon
...(Lines snipped)...
fax:x:78:
nut:x:57:
privoxy:x:73:
chris:x:500:fen
diane:x:501:
jane:x:502:
richard:x:503:
audit:x:504:jane,richard
soccer:x:505:richard,jake,wilson,audrey,shem,mike,olgovie,newton
toronto:x:506:matthew,jake,wilson,richard,audrey,shem,mike,olgovie,newton,ed,jack
...(Lines snipped)...
```

The fields here are:

group name
> The name assigned to the group.

group password
> A password assigned to the group. This is rarely used, because it's just as easy to add a user into a group as it is to give her the password. The actual password values have been moved to */etc/gshadow*.

group ID
> The numeric value assigned to the group. This file is used to cross-reference group IDs to group names.

supplementary members
> The username of each user in this group, except users who have this group as their primary group (field 4 in */etc/passwd*).

The */etc/gshadow* file contains the actual passwords, plus group administrator information:

```
root:::root
bin:::root,bin,daemon
daemon:::root,bin,daemon
sys:::root,bin,adm
adm:::root,adm,daemon
...(Lines snipped)...
fax:x::
nut:x::
privoxy:x::
chris:!:500::fen
diane:!:501::
jane:!:502::
richard:!:503::
audit:!:504:jane:jane,richard,audrey,matthew
soccer:!:505:richard,jake:richard,jake,wilson,audrey,shem,mike,olgovie,newton
toronto:!:506:ed:matthew,jake,wilson,richard,audrey,shem,mike,olgovie,newton,ed
...(Lines snipped)...
```

The group administrators are in field 4 and group members are in field 5 in this file—so in this case, jane is the group administrator for audit, and jane, richard, andrew, and matthew are group members.

What About...

...the kuser program on the menu?

kuser is a KDE program that provides an alternative to *system-config-user*. The two programs are functional duplicates, but I think *system-config-user* looks better.

...editing the password and group files directly?

It is possible but must be done carefully to avoid leaving the system in an unusable state.

The *vipw* and *vigr* scripts provide the most convenient way of editing these files; *vipw* edits */etc/passwd* and */etc/shadow*, and *vigr* edits */etc/group* and */etc/gshadow*. In both cases, the files will be locked to prevent concurrent changes by another program, and the *vi* editor will be used for editing (the EDITOR environment variable can be used to specify another editor if you'd prefer).

...checking that the password and group files are properly written?

The *pwck* command can be used to check and repair */etc/passwd* and */etc/shadow*:

```
# pwck
user adm: directory /var/adm does not exist
user gopher: directory /var/gopher does not exist
user ident: directory /home/ident does not exist
user torrent: directory /var/spool/bittorrent does not exist
invalid password file entry
delete line `'? y
pwck: the files have been updated
```

grpck performs similar checks on */etc/group* and */etc/gshadow*:

```
# grpck
invalid group file entry
delete line `'? y
invalid group file entry
delete line `ascasdcasdarg asdfasdf'? y
grpck: the files have been updated
```

Where Can I Learn More?

- The manpages for *passwd, useradd, usermod, userdel, groupadd, groupmod, groupdel, vipw, vigr, pwconv, grpconv, crypt (3), passwd (5), shadow (5), group (5),* and *gshadow (5)*

4.8   Control Access to Files

All Linux and Unix systems use *file permissions* or *modes* to control access to files. Fedora extends this with the user-private-group scheme, which simplifies the configuration of permissions for collaboration.

 There are two other mechanisms available for file access control: see Lab 8.2, "Using SELinux" and Lab 8.3, "Using Access Control Lists."

How Do I Do That?

There are three basic file permissions:

read (r)
> Grants permission to access the contents of a file. There are no restrictions on what can be done with the file contents, so read permission includes permission to view or process the contents of the file, as well as permission to copy the file. On a directory, read permission enables the display of the list of files in the directory; without read permission, you can access a file contained in the directory only if you know the exact name of the file.

write (w)
> Grants permission to write to a file; this includes overwriting existing information, append to the end of the file, and truncate (shorten) the file. On a directory, write permission enables the creation and deletion of files within that directory.

execute (x)
> Grants permission to execute the file. If the file is a binary, it can be executed by the kernel; if it is a text file, it is treated as a script. On a directory, execute permission grants access to the contents of the directory (some people refer to execute permission on a directory as *search*, or *passthrough*, permission).

Remember the order: *r w x*.

Each of these three permissions is granted or denied to users in three different *communities*:

user (u)
> The user who owns the file. Initially, this is the user who created the file; it may be changed by the superuser (*root*).

group (g)
> All members of the group that owns the file. Normally, this starts off as the group of the user who created the file. A file's owner may change the group ownership to any group to which she belongs; e.g., if Jane owns the file *foo* and is a member of the *audit* and *toronto* groups, she can make either group own the file.

other (o)
> Everyone else.

The order is significant here, too; you'll want to memorize it: *u g o*.

This gives a total of nine permissions for each file and directory:

- read, write, and execute for the user
- read, write, and execute for the group
- read, write, and execute for other

There are also three special file permissions, as outlined in Table 4-13.

Table 4-13. Special file permissions

Name	Abbreviation	Appearance in ls -l output	Meaning when applied to a file	Meaning when applied to a directory
Set-User-ID	SUID	s in the x column for the *user* if execute permission is enabled, or S if execute permission is disabled.	When executed, the program takes on the user identity of the file's owner.	(No meaning)
Set-Group-ID	SGID	s in the x column for the *group* if execute permission is enabled, or S if execute permission is disabled.	When executed, the program takes on the group identity of the file's group.	All files and subdirectories created in the directory will be owned by the same group that owns the directory. Subdirectories will automatically have their SGID permission enabled.
Sticky bit	Sticky	t in the x column for *other* if execute permission is enabled, or T if execute permission is disabled.	(No meaning)	Files in the directory can be deleted or removed only by their owner (otherwise, anyone with write permission on the directory can delete or rename files in that directory).

The SUID and SGID permissions provide critical abilities. For example, */etc/passwd* and */etc/shadow* are only writable by *root*, but normal users need to be able to change their passwords. The program */usr/bin/passwd* is owned by *root* and has the SUID permission enabled, so it runs with *root* privilege—regardless of who executes it— and is therefore able to change */etc/shadow*.

Viewing the current user, group, and mode from the command line

When *ls* is executed with the -l option, a long and detailed listing of file information is displayed. Here is an example:

```
$ ls -l /etc/aliases.db
-rw-r-----   1 root     smmsp    12288 Oct  6 19:31 aliases.db
```

The first field displayed is -rw-r-----. The first character is reserved for file type information, and the rest of that field contains the file's mode: rw-r-----.

This mode breaks down into three sets of three characters, representing the permissions granted to each of the three communities:

- user: rw-
- group: r--
- other: ---

Notice that these communities are displayed in the *u g o* order mentioned earlier.

The three characters displayed for each of these communities represent read, write, and execute permission; if the permission is denied, a dash is shown, but if the permission is granted, the letter r, w, or x is shown, in that order (*r w x*).

In the preceding example, the permissions granted to the user are *read* and *write* (rw-); the permission granted to the group is *read* (r--); and no permission is granted to other users (---).

In order to correctly interpret the permission, we need to know who the user and group are. The ls -l output shows this information in fields 3 and 4; in this case, the user is *root* and the group is *smmsp*.

Putting this all together, we know that:

- *root* can read and write the file.
- All users in the *smmsp* group can read the file.
- No one else on the system can read, write, or execute the file.

 The permissions on the directories that contain the file also come into play when determining what a user can do with a file. If he does not have execute permission on all of the directories in the path from the root (/) to the file, then he will not be able to access the file, regardless of the permissions on the file itself. Likewise, if he has execute permission on all of those directories, plus write permission on the directory containing the file, then he can delete the file (destroying all the data), even if he can't write to it—and then create a new file with the same name.

Viewing the current user, group, and mode graphically

GNOME's Nautilus file manager normally displays files and directories as icons. To change the display to a list resembling the output of ls -l, select the menu option View → View as List. The default display shows the file name, size, type, and date modified.

You can add the permissions, owner, and group to the display by selecting Edit → Preferences, which presents the File Management Preferences window shown in Figure 4-11. Click on the List Columns tab, and then click on the checkboxes for permissions, owner, and group to include them on the display. You can also use the Move Up and Move Down buttons to change the displayed order of the fields. Click Close when the display is configured to your liking.

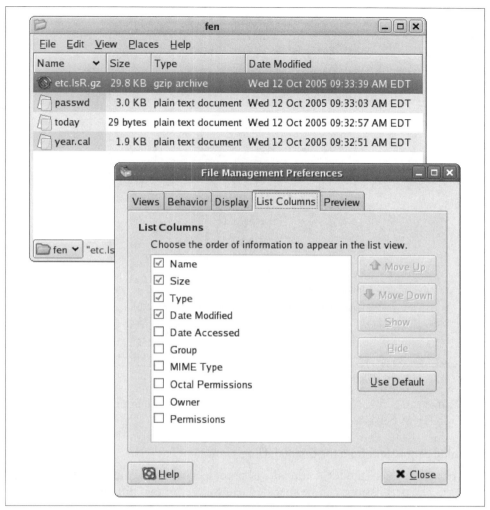

Figure 4-11. Nautilus File Management Preferences window

KDE's Konqueror application provides a similar display when you select View →
View Mode → Detailed List View.

Changing permissions graphically

Right-clicking on a file in Nautilus or Konqueror will bring up the file Properties window shown in Figure 4-12. The Permissions tab within that window contains checkboxes for each of the three permissions in each of the three communities—nine
checkboxes total, plus three for the special permissions (to view the checkboxes in
Konqueror, use the Advanced Permissions button).

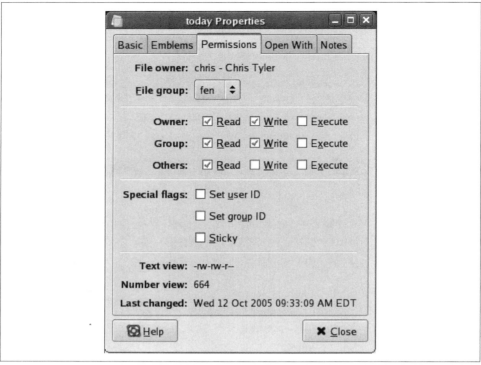

Figure 4-12. Nautilus File Properties window

To change the permissions, simply toggle checkmarks in the appropriate boxes using your mouse. When you're done, click Close.

Changing permissions from the command line

The *chmod* (change-mode) command is used to change permissions from a shell prompt. The permissions can be specified using either of two different syntaxes: relative symbolic notation or octal notation.

Relative symbolic notation uses any combination of the three community letters (*u*, *g*, or *o*) or the letter *a* to indicate all three communities; an operation symbol, which is + to add a permission and - to remove it, or = to exactly set a permission; and finally, one or more permission letters (*r*, *w*, or *x*). Table 4-14 shows some examples of relative symbolic notation; note that multiple operations can be specified using commas as separators (no spaces).

Table 4-14. Relative symbolic notation used by chmod

Notation	Description
u+w	Adds write permission for the user.
o-rwx	Removes read, write, and execute permission for others.

Table 4-14. Relative symbolic notation used by chmod (continued)

Notation	Description
ug+r,o-r	Adds read permission for the user and the group; removes read permission for others.
a-x ugo-x	Removes execute permission for all users.
u=rw,go=r	Sets exactly read and write permission for the user, and only read permission for group and others. The difference between = and + is that = will disable other permissions (such as execute for the user in this example), while + will leave other permissions at their previous value.

Special permissions are specified based on their appearance in ls -l output:

- SUID is specified as u+s.
- SGUID is specified as g+s.
- Sticky is specified as o+t.

Octal notation uses a multidigit number, where each digit represents one community (in *u g o* order). The digit is the sum of values representing each enabled permission:

- 4 for read permission
- 2 for write permission
- 1 for execute permission

Therefore, the octal permission 764 represents read/write/execute for the user (4+2+1=7), read/write for the group (4+2=6), and read for others (4): rwxrw-r--.

When using octal notation, special permissions are given as a fourth digit placed in front of the others; the value of this fourth digit is the sum of 4 for SUID, 2 for SGID, and 1 for Sticky. Octal permission 2770 represents rwxrws---.

To change a permission with *chmod*, specify the permission as the first argument and one or more filenames as the remaining arguments:

```
$ ls -l oreilly
-rw-rw-r--  1 chris chris 40 Oct 12 17:18 oreilly
$ chmod g-w,o= oreilly
$ ls -l oreilly
-rw-r-----  1 chris chris 40 Oct 12 17:18 oreilly
$ chmod 764 oreilly
$ ls -l oreilly
-rwxrw-r--  1 chris chris 40 Oct 12 17:18 oreilly
```

The -R option causes *chmod* to recursively process subdirectories. To remove write permission for others on all files and subdirectories within your home directory, execute:

```
$ chmod -R o-w ~
```

Using group permissions

Users can belong to more than one group, which enables documents to be shared according to group roles.

Previously, we used Richard in group examples; he's a member of the groups *richard*, *it*, *toronto*, *acmeproposal*, *christmas*, *soccer*, and *audit*. Richard's primary group is *richard*, as that is the group listed in his entry in */etc/passwd*. When Richard logs in, the shell starts with its group identity set to the primary group, so any new files or directories created have *richard* as the group owner.

The group identity can be changed at any time using the *newgrp* command, and verified with the `id` command:

```
richard$ id
uid=503(richard) gid=503(richard) groups=503(richard),504(audit),505(soccer),
506(toronto),511(acmeproposal),512(christmas),608(it)
richard$ newgrp audit
richard$ id
uid=503(richard) gid=504(audit) groups=503(richard),504(audit),505(soccer),
506(toronto),511(acmeproposal),512(christmas),608(it)
```

The current group identity (also called *real group ID*) affects only the creation of files and directories; existing files and directories keep their existing group, and a user can access files accessible to any group to which she belongs.

In this case, Richard can access any file that is readable by, say, the *acmeproposal* group, even when his current real group ID is *audit*. However, any files he creates will be owned by the group *audit* and won't be accessible to the *acmeproposal* group.

chgrp modifies the group ownership of an existing file. The group name is given as the first argument, and all other arguments are filenames:

```
$ ls -l report.txt
-rw-r--r--  1 richard richard 3078 Oct 12 19:35 report.txt
$ chgrp audit report.txt
$ ls -l report.txt
-rw-r--r--  1 richard audit 3078 Oct 12 19:35 report.txt
```

A normal user can set the group ownership only to one of the groups to which he belongs, and can change the group ownership only of files that he owns. The *root* user can set the group ownership of any file to any group. Like *chmod*, *chgrp* accepts the `-R` (recursive) option.

Using *chgrp* and *newgrp* is cumbersome. A much better solution is to use the SGID permission on directories, which automatically sets the group ownership.

Richard could create a directory named *game_scores* in his home directory, change the group ownership to *soccer*, and change the permission to `rwxrws---`:

```
richard$ mkdir game_scores
richard$ chgrp soccer game_scores
richard$ chmod u=rwx,g=rwxs,o= game_scores
```

```
richard$ ls -ld game_scores
drwxrws--- 2 richard soccer 4096 Oct 12 19:46 game_scores
```

Everyone in the *soccer* group can access that directory. Because the SGID permission is set, any file created in that directory is automatically owned by the group *soccer* and can be accessed by other group members—exactly what is needed for collaboration within a group. The SGID permission is automatically applied to any directory created within *games_scores*, too.

Default permissions

When a Fedora program asks the Linux kernel to create a new file or directory, that program requests a default set of permissions. OpenOffice.org, for example, requests mode 0666 (rw-rw-rw-) on new files, because it knows that they aren't executable; the C compiler, on the other hand, requests 0777 (rwxrwxrwx) because the output of the C compiler should be an executable program.

This requested permission is limited by the current *umask*, which is an octal value representing the permissions that should *not* be granted to new files. If you want to prohibit anyone in your group from writing to or executing your files, and prevent others from doing anything at all with your files, the permissions that you want to restrict are ----wxrwx. In octal, that translates to 037.

You can set the *umask* with the shell command of the same name:

```
$ umask 037
```

umask by itself displays the current mask value:

```
$ umask
0037
```

This value is inherited by child processes, including all applications started by the shell.

The actual permissions set on a new file will be the permissions requested by the application after the permissions restricted by the *umask* are removed:

```
OpenOffice.org requested permission:   rw-rw-rw-
Permissions restricted by umask:       ----wxrwx
Permission applied to a new file:      rw-r-----
```

The normal *umask* on Fedora systems is 002, which gives full read and write permission to everyone in your group. This works well in group-collaboration directories that have SGID permission set; other group members will be able to edit the files you have created, and vice versa. The beauty of the Fedora user-private-group system is that when you're not in a collaboration directory, new files default to ownership by your private group. This makes group permissions moot, since they apply only to you and are therefore effectively the same as the user permissions.

Changing file ownership

The superuser can change the ownership of a file using the *chown* command:

```
# chown accountfile barbara
```

This is useful when moving files between user accounts (for example, when an employee has left a company).

How Does It Work?

A file's user, group, and mode information is stored in a file's *inode*—a small disk-based data structure containing vital information about a file. The user and group are stored as 32-bit numbers, which means that the maximum GID and UID are both 4,294,967,295 ($2^{32} - 1$). However, some older applications still use 16-bit GID and UID values, so it's best to use IDs under 65,532 ($2^{16} - 4$)—plenty for most systems. IDs under 500 are reserved for system services; this is really just a convention adopted to avoid conflicts, since there is nothing special about user IDs with low numbers.

There is something special about user ID 0, though: it's reserved for the superuser, *root*. It is possible to create multiple accounts with the same ID, and this is sometimes used to create a second superuser account with a different password from the *root* account.

Each process also has a data structure that stores its *real* UID and GID, the *effective* UID and GID (which are different from the real IDs when a SUID or SGID program is running), and the *umask*. This data is copied to child processes automatically, but if the child process is a *bash* or *csh* shell, the *umask* value is reset by the shell startup scripts (*/etc/bashrc* or */etc/csh.cshrc*).

What About...

...viewing file permissions and ownership in the icon view of Nautilus?

You can configure the icon view of Nautilus by selecting Edit → Preferences and going to the Display tab. Up to three fields can be configured, in addition to the filename; by default, the first field is blank, the second field is the file size, and the third field is the date modified. Normally, only the first field is shown beneath each icon, but zooming in and out (using the menu options View → Zoom In and View → Zoom Out) will adjust the amount of information displayed.

This feature is not available in Konqueror.

...changing the group of a file graphically?

The permissions tab of the file properties window in both Nautilus (Figure 4-12) and Konqueror has a drop-down menu that permits you to change the group ownership if you are a member of multiple groups and you own the file.

...deleting someone else's file in /tmp?

/tmp is a special directory used to store temporary files (*/var/tmp* is another). Since this directory is shared among all users, the sticky bit has been set to prevent users from deleting one other's files.

...changing a file's owner and group at the same time?

The *chown* command permits you to specify a group after the username, separated by a colon. To make */tmp/input* owned by the user *barbara* and the group *smilies*, use:

```
# chown barbara:smilies /tmp/input
```

Where Can I Find More Information?

- The manpages for *chmod*, *chown*, *chgrp*, *newgrp*, *id*, *ulimit*, *umask*, and *groups*
- "User Private Groups" in the Red Hat Linux 9 manual: *http://www.redhat.com/ docs/manuals/linux/RHL-9-Manual/ref-guide/s1-users-groups-private-groups.html*

4.9   Managing Processes

A *process* is a running instance of a program. If you run a program twice, two processes are created. In order to manage a Fedora system effectively, you must be able to monitor and control processes.

How Do I Do That?

Fedora provides multiple tools to monitor process activity and resource usage, modify process priority, and terminate processes.

Processes are identified by a *Process ID* (PID) number, which is sequentially assigned. There is a small set of information associated with each process, including:

nice
> A value used to alter a process's scheduling priority, which determines how much CPU time the process receives. The actual priority assigned to a process is calculated based upon this factor, as well as how much CPU time the process has recently received and how many *input/output* (I/O) operations it has recently performed. This value is inherited by child processes.

parent process ID
> The PID of the process that started the process. If the parent process disappears, this is replaced by 1 (the *init* process).

real user ID and effective user ID
> The numeric user ID of the user actually running the program and the effective user running the program. These can be different only when the *suid* mechanism

is active (see Lab 4.8, "Control Access to Files"), although an effective user ID remains in effect when a *suid* program calls a non-*suid* program.

real group ID and effective group ID

The numeric group ID of the group actually running the program and the effective group running the program. These are similar to the real and effective user IDs in that they will be different only when the *sgid* mechanism is active.

umask

The permission mask received from the parent process.

tty

The terminal associated with the program (if applicable). This permits all programs on that terminal to receive a *hangup signal* (HUP) when the terminal connection is lost, which is the case when a telephone modem call is hung up, a terminal window is closed, or a remote access Telnet/SSH session is terminated. This value is inherited by child processes.

It's important to realize that at any particular point in time, most processes are *sleeping* while they wait for some resource to become available. That resource might be a mouse click, a keystroke, a network packet, some data from disk, or a particular time of day.

Monitoring process information graphically in GNOME

The menu item Applications → System Tools → System Monitor will run *gnome-system-monitor* and present the display shown in Figure 4-13.

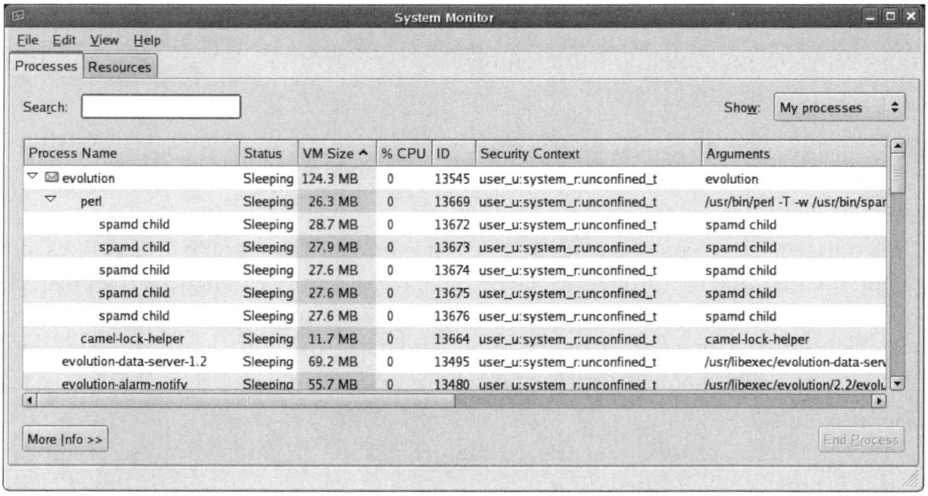

Figure 4-13. GNOME System Monitor window

This display has two tabs:

Processes
> Displays a table of current processes with information about each.

Resources
> Displays scrolling graphs displaying CPU, memory, and swap usage.

By default, the Processes tab displays the name of the program executing, process status (Sleeping or Running), Virtual Memory (VM) size, percentage of CPU time, the SELinux Security Context, and the arguments used on the command line that started the process (including the command name).

The default display shows the most useful information about each process, but to configure the display to your liking, you can:

Add and remove fields
> Select Edit → Preferences to view a list of available fields (columns) with a checkbox for each. Check or uncheck items to add them to or remove them from the list. Close this window when you are done editing the field list.

Reorder and resize columns
> Drag column headings to rearrange the order in which they are displayed. To change a column width, click between it and an adjacent column, and then drag to the desired width.

Sort a column
> Click on a column heading to select that column for the sort sequence. An arrow will appear in the header (as shown on the VM Size column in Figure 4-13); click on the heading again to toggle between ascending and descending sort order.

Filter by process type
> The Show menu lets you select your own processes, all processes on the system, or just the active (running, not sleeping) processes.

To terminate a process, highlight it by clicking on it and then click the End Process button, type Alt-P, or right-click on the process and select End Process. If that doesn't cause the process to terminate within a few seconds, right-click on the process and select Kill Process (or highlight the process and type Ctrl-K).

> You won't be able to terminate processes owned by other users (including system processes) this way because you have insufficient permission. It is possible to run this program as *root*, which will let you terminate any process:
>
> ```
> # gnome-system-monitor
> ```
>
> Terminating the wrong process(es) can leave your system in a partially functioning or unusable state, and it may be necessary to reboot the system to recover. Be careful!

Monitoring process information graphically in KDE

If you're using KDE in Fedora, the menu item System → KSysGuard will start *ksysguard* and display the window shown in Figure 4-14.

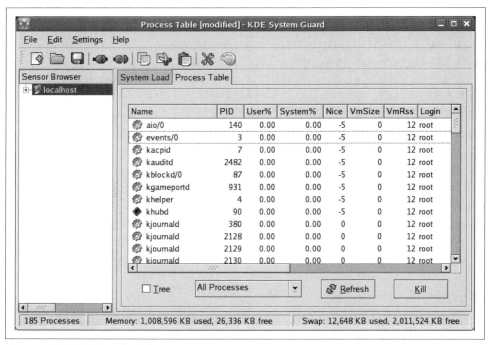

Figure 4-14. KSysGuard window

This tool is very customizable, but the basic display is similar to the GNOME System Monitor, except that the CPU usage is broken down into User% and System%, and the memory size is broken down into VmSize (total process size) and VmRSS (Resident Set Size, the portion of the VmSize currently in memory instead of swap). Use the Process Table tab to monitor and control running processes.

To customize the display, you can:

Show and hide columns

> To remove a column from the display, right-click somewhere within that column (not on the heading) and select Hide Column. To add a column, right-click in an existing column (again, not on the heading), and select Show Column and then the column name you wish to add.

Reorder and resize columns

> Drag column headings to rearrange the order in which they are displayed. To change a column width, click between it and an adjacent column, and then drag to the desired width.

Sort a column

Click on a column heading to select that column for the sort sequence. Click on the heading again to toggle between ascending and descending sort order.

Filter by process type

The pull-down menu at the bottom of the display enables you to choose whether to display all processes, system processes (such as servers), user processes for all users, or just your own processes.

To terminate a process, right-click on the process and select Send Signal → SIG-TERM. If that doesn't cause the process to terminate within a few seconds, highlight the process and then click the Kill button in the lower-right corner of the window (right-click on the process and select Send Signal → SIGKILL).

 Just like the GNOME System Monitor, the KSysGuard program can't terminate processes owned by other users (including system processes) when run by a normal user. To run the program as *root*:

```
# ksysguard
```

KSysGuard can monitor many aspects of system status in addition to the process table; it's also capable of monitoring remote systems. See the KSysGuard Manual for details (press F1 in the KSysGuard window).

Monitoring process information on a character display

A similar tool is available for character-mode displays, named *top*:

```
$ top
```

The output from *top* is shown in Figure 4-15.

Like the graphical process monitors, *top* updates its display regularly—every three seconds by default. You can customize the display using the controls shown in Table 4-15.

Table 4-15. Top customization options

Key	Description
?	Display help.
u	Restrict the display to processes owned by one user.
M	Sort by memory usage.
P	Sort by current CPU usage.
T	Sort by time (cumulative CPU usage).
m	Toggle memory summary on/off.
f	Field-list customization display. You will see a menu of possible fields; press the letter of the field you wish to toggle on/off, then Enter to exit from this display.
o	Field-order customization display. You will see a list of displayed fields; type the uppercase letter for a field to shift the field left on the display, or type the lowercase letter to shift it right. Press Enter to exit this display.

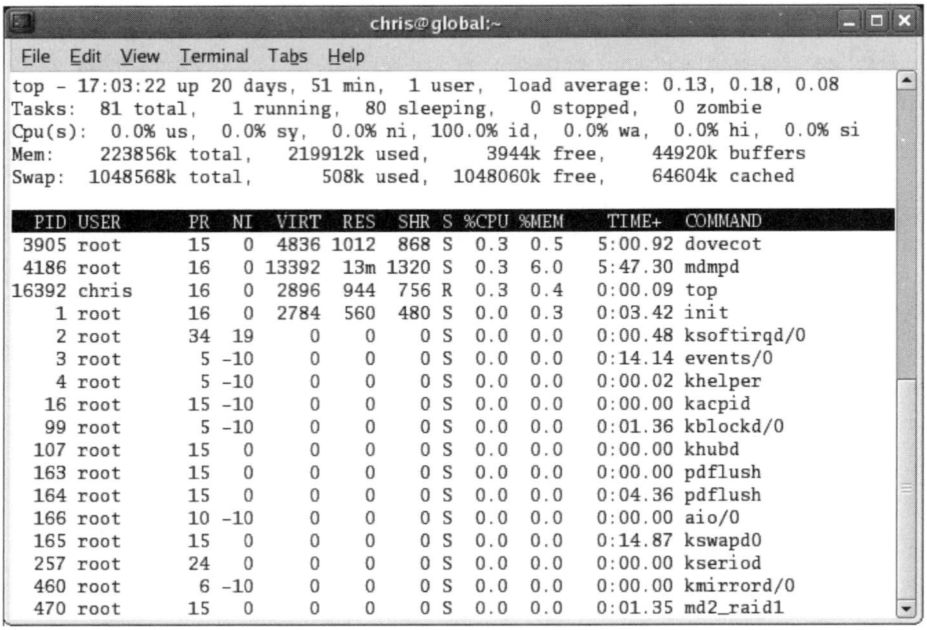

```
                          chris@global:~                        [_][□][x]

 File  Edit  View  Terminal  Tabs  Help
top - 17:03:22 up 20 days, 51 min,  1 user,  load average: 0.13, 0.18, 0.08
Tasks:  81 total,   1 running,  80 sleeping,   0 stopped,   0 zombie
Cpu(s):  0.0% us,  0.0% sy,  0.0% ni, 100.0% id,  0.0% wa,  0.0% hi,  0.0% si
Mem:     223856k total,   219912k used,     3944k free,    44920k buffers
Swap:   1048568k total,      508k used,  1048060k free,    64604k cached

  PID USER      PR  NI  VIRT  RES  SHR S %CPU %MEM    TIME+  COMMAND
 3905 root      15   0  4836 1012  868 S  0.3  0.5  5:00.92 dovecot
 4186 root      16   0 13392  13m 1320 S  0.3  6.0  5:47.30 mdmpd
16392 chris     16   0  2896  944  756 R  0.3  0.4  0:00.09 top
    1 root      16   0  2784  560  480 S  0.0  0.3  0:03.42 init
    2 root      34  19     0    0    0 S  0.0  0.0  0:00.48 ksoftirqd/0
    3 root       5 -10     0    0    0 S  0.0  0.0  0:14.14 events/0
    4 root       5 -10     0    0    0 S  0.0  0.0  0:00.02 khelper
   16 root      15 -10     0    0    0 S  0.0  0.0  0:00.00 kacpid
   99 root       5 -10     0    0    0 S  0.0  0.0  0:01.36 kblockd/0
  107 root      15   0     0    0    0 S  0.0  0.0  0:00.00 khubd
  163 root      15   0     0    0    0 S  0.0  0.0  0:00.00 pdflush
  164 root      15   0     0    0    0 S  0.0  0.0  0:04.36 pdflush
  166 root      10 -10     0    0    0 S  0.0  0.0  0:00.00 aio/0
  165 root      15   0     0    0    0 S  0.0  0.0  0:14.87 kswapd0
  257 root      24   0     0    0    0 S  0.0  0.0  0:00.00 kseriod
  460 root       6 -10     0    0    0 S  0.0  0.0  0:00.00 kmirrord/0
  470 root      15   0     0    0    0 S  0.0  0.0  0:01.35 md2_raid1
```

Figure 4-15. Output from top

To end a process, type k (for *kill*). Type in the process ID and press Enter; *top* will prompt you for the signal to be used. Press Enter to accept the default (15). If the process does not terminate within a few seconds, repeat the procedure with the signal 9.

Displaying process information from the shell prompt

Instead of using *top* to continuously monitor information, you can use the *ps* (process status) command to display a snapshot of the process table at a particular point in time.

By default, *ps* shows only processes executed by you on the current terminal:

```
$ ps
  PID TTY          TIME CMD
14797 pts/1    00:00:00 bash
22962 pts/1    00:00:00 ps
```

This shows the process ID, terminal device (pts/1 means */dev/pts/1*), total amount of CPU time consumed (less than one second in this example), and the command executed. This information alone is rarely useful, so *ps* is almost always used with some arguments.

ps uses options to select the processes to be displayed. The most useful ones are:

-A
-e

All (or everyone's) processes

-u *user*

Processes owned by *user* (which can be a username or numeric user ID)

Other options are used to control the output format:

-f

Displays full information, including the UID, PID, PPID, start time (STIME), terminal (TTY), total CPU time used (TIME), and command (CMD).

-F

Displays extra-full information: everything included in -f, plus the processor number of the CPU the program is running on (PSR) and the approximate kilobytes of RAM used (RSS).

 Like *ls*, the *ps* command has dozens of options. The Fedora version of *ps* can use Unix System V syntax or BSD syntax, so many option letters have two meanings; the one that is used depends on whether the option is specified with or without a hyphen!

To see the full documentation for ps, view the manpage—but be prepared to take some time; it's over 16 pages long!

Terminating processes from the shell prompt

You can terminate processes by command name or by PID. When you terminate a process by name, you save yourself the hassle of looking up the PID, but if there is more than one process of the same name running, you will kill them all.

To kill by command name:

    $ killall xclock

If the process doesn't terminate within a few seconds, add the -KILL argument:

    $ killall -KILL xclock

Note that this will kill only processes of that name that are *owned by you*; you don't have permission to kill other users' processes unless you are *root*. You will see an error message if other users have a process of the same name running, but this will not affect the killing of the processes that you own.

To kill PID 48292:

    $ kill 48292

Again, if that doesn't work within a reasonable period of time, add the -KILL argument:

    $ kill -KILL 48292

How Does It Work?

The Linux kernel has only two basic functions for starting processes: fork( ) and exec( ).

fork( ) makes an exact copy of the current process and starts it running. exec( ) replaces the currently running program with a new program, running in the same process. So to get a new program running, the shell uses fork( ) to create a child process (a copy of the shell) and then uses exec( ) to change the program running in the child process.

When a child process is created, a number of variables are inherited from the parent process, including the real and effective user IDs, the real and effective group IDs, the *umask*, the terminal, the current working directory, and the environment variables.

Processes are generally permitted to run on a CPU until their *timeslice*—the amount of time allocated to them by the scheduling algorithm—is over, at which point another process is scheduled to be run.

However, processes frequently give up the CPU early because they reach a point when they need a resource to continue; this is called *blocking*. This is often due to slow input/output operations; no matter how fast your disk drive is, the CPU is still faster, so when one process is waiting for disk data, another process can be executing.

The difference between your typing speed and your CPU speed is even greater; most people type six characters per second or less, so on a 3 GHz PC, the CPU will average at least 500 million operations between keystrokes.

Since processes are usually waiting for data, it's not uncommon for programs to run for only a few seconds a day. I've been using my X display server heavily all day, and it's accumulated less than 30 minutes of CPU time; my POP3 mail server, which is accessed 600 times and transfers several hundred megabytes of data each day, accumulates less than 20 seconds of CPU time a day.

The 2.6 kernels now used in Fedora do fully preemptive scheduling, which means that when data *does* arrive for a sleeping process, and that sleeping process has a higher priority than the process currently running, the kernel will preempt the running process and immediately schedule the new process for execution (instead of waiting for the currently executing process to reach the end of its timeslice).

The kernel dynamically changes the priority of a process based on the amount of time since it last executed, the amount of time it has executed recently, the amount of I/O it is performing, and the *nice* value.

To terminate a running process, a numeric *signal* is sent to that process. To see all of the available signals, use the -l argument to *kill*, which shows the signal names and numbers:

```
$ kill -l
 1) SIGHUP       2) SIGINT      3) SIGQUIT      4) SIGILL
```

```
 5) SIGTRAP      6) SIGABRT       7) SIGBUS        8) SIGFPE
 9) SIGKILL     10) SIGUSR1      11) SIGSEGV      12) SIGUSR2
13) SIGPIPE     14) SIGALRM      15) SIGTERM      17) SIGCHLD
18) SIGCONT     19) SIGSTOP      20) SIGTSTP      21) SIGTTIN
22) SIGTTOU     23) SIGURG       24) SIGXCPU      25) SIGXFSZ
26) SIGVTALRM   27) SIGPROF      28) SIGWINCH     29) SIGIO
30) SIGPWR      31) SIGSYS       34) SIGRTMIN     35) SIGRTMIN+1
36) SIGRTMIN+2  37) SIGRTMIN+3   38) SIGRTMIN+4   39) SIGRTMIN+5
40) SIGRTMIN+6  41) SIGRTMIN+7   42) SIGRTMIN+8   43) SIGRTMIN+9
44) SIGRTMIN+10 45) SIGRTMIN+11  46) SIGRTMIN+12  47) SIGRTMIN+13
48) SIGRTMIN+14 49) SIGRTMIN+15  50) SIGRTMAX-14  51) SIGRTMAX-13
52) SIGRTMAX-12 53) SIGRTMAX-11  54) SIGRTMAX-10  55) SIGRTMAX-9
56) SIGRTMAX-8  57) SIGRTMAX-7   58) SIGRTMAX-6   59) SIGRTMAX-5
60) SIGRTMAX-4  61) SIGRTMAX-3   62) SIGRTMAX-2   63) SIGRTMAX-1
64) SIGRTMAX
```

Each of these signals has a specific meaning, which can usually be determined from the signal name; for example, SIGHUP is the hangup signal, SIGINT is the interrupt signal (sent when you use Ctrl-C to try to interrupt a program running on a terminal or character-mode VT), SIGFPE is the signal for floating-point exceptions (such as division by zero), and SIGPWR is the signal for a power failure. Most of these signals are generated automatically by the kernel and basic server processes.

In most cases, a process can arrange to *catch* a particular signal and do something; for example, a text editor might save the current file when SIGHUP is received (the connection to the terminal is lost). If the process has not arranged to catch a signal, a default action is taken. In most cases, the default action is to terminate the process, but the default for some signals (such as SIGPWR) is simply to ignore the signal and keep on running.

SIGTERM is used to request that a program terminate itself. Most programs catch this signal and clean up before they terminate, deleting any temporary files, saving data if necessary, informing network peers that they are terminating (where appropriate), and so forth. This is the default signal sent by *top* and *kill*, and the signal sent by the GNOME System Monitor when you specify End Program.

SIGKILL is uncatchable. It always terminates a program. This is useful when you wish to definitely terminate a program, but it doesn't give the program an opportunity to shut down gracefully, so files and network communications may be left in half-finished states, which may cause future problems. For this reason, it should be used as a last resort. SIGKILL is the signal sent by the Kill Program option in System Monitor and the Kill button in KSysGuard.

What About...

...monitoring CPU load continuously?

Both KDE and GNOME provide panel applets that display a continuous graph of the current CPU load, memory usage, and more. To add this applet to your panel bar, right-click on an empty area on the bar and select "Add to Panel." For GNOME, select System Monitor; for KDE, select Applet → KSysGuard. You can configure the display by right-clicking on it and selecting Preferences or Properties.

…starting a process with a lower (or higher) priority than normal?

The *nice* command starts a process with a lower-than-normal priority. The priority can be reduced by any value from 1 to 19 using the -n argument; without -n, the priority is reduced by a value of 10. The command to be run is the only other argument required (any additional arguments are used as arguments to that command):

```
$ nice -n 15 xboard
```

To raise the priority of a process, you must be *root*; supply a negative priority adjustment between −1 (slight boost in priority over normal) to −20 (highest priority):

```
# nice -n -12 xboard
```

…changing the priority of an existing process?

renice is the tool for this:

```
$ xboard &
[3] 27365
$ renice 5 27365
27365: old priority 0, new priority 5
$ renice 2 27365
renice: 27365: setpriority: Permission denied
```

 Note that the value used with the *nice* command is the opposite of what you may usually associate with a priority. Put another way, a nice level of −20 results in a process that isn't very nice to its fellow processes, since it's running at a high priority and hogs the CPU.

Notice that *renice* does not permit the user to increase the priority of a process, even if the user lowered it in the first place. However, *root* can set any priority she chooses:

```
$ renice -5 27365
renice: 27365: setpriority: Permission denied
# renice 2 27365
27365: old priority 5, new priority 2
# renice -5 27365
27365: old priority 2, new priority -5
```

You can also adjust the priority of processes in System Monitor and KSysGuard using the options on the context menu (right-click on the process you wish to adjust).

...starting and managing background processes?

When using the shell, you can start a process in the background by placing an ampersand after the command:

```
$ xboard &
[21771]
$ mc &
[21783]
$
```

The shell will display the PID of the background process, then immediately present a new prompt, permitting you to enter additional commands before the background command has finished executing.

You can display background processes using the jobs command:

```
$ jobs
[1]-  Running              xboard &
[2]+  Stopped              . /usr/share/mc/bin/mc-wrapper.sh
```

Any program that attempts to communicate through the character interface, such as Midnight Commander (*mc*) in this example, will be stopped. Programs that communicate through the graphical user interface, such as *xboard*, are free to do so while running in the background.

To put a stopped command in the foreground so that you can interact with it, use the *fg* command:

```
$ fg 2
```

The argument is the job number as reported by the *jobs* command. You can stop the current foreground process by pressing Ctrl-Z.

To run a stopped process in the background, use the *bg* command:

```
$ fg 1
xboard
...User presses Ctrl-Z...
[1]+  Stopped              xboard
$ jobs
[1]+  Stopped              xboard
[2]-  Stopped              . /usr/share/mc/bin/mc-wrapper.sh
$ bg 1
[1]+ xboard &
$
```

You can use a percent sign and a job number instead of a PID when killing processes:

```
$ kill %1
$
[3]-  Exit 15              xboard
```

Where Can I Learn More?

- Descriptions of each signal: the manpage for *signal(7)*
- The manpages for *bash* (for job control, including *jobs*, *fg*, *bg*, and the version of *kill* that is built into *bash*), *top*, *ps*, and *kill*

4.10 Remote Management Using SSH

It's often useful to be able to log in to a machine remotely to perform some management operation. To enable secure remote access, Fedora provides the Secure Shell (SSH).

How Do I Do That?

SSH consists of two components: *ssh* (the client) and *sshd* (the server). The server is configured automatically when Fedora is installed.

To connect to a Fedora system from another Fedora system (or another Linux system), run the *ssh* client, providing the remote username and hostname (or IP address) as a single argument (*user@host*). For example, to log in to a host with the IP address 10.0.0.1 using the user ID jon:

```
$ ssh jon@10.0.0.1
The authenticity of host '10.0.0.1 (10.0.0.1)' can't be established.
RSA key fingerprint is 1d:dd:20:72:b1:0c:28:90:9a:ff:43:69:03:12:71:02.
Are you sure you want to continue connecting (yes/no)? yes
Warning: Permanently added '10.0.0.1' (RSA) to the list of known hosts.
jon@10.0.0.1's password: AnotherSecret
Last login: Tue Oct 25 23:13:40 2005 from london-office
$
```

The question about the authenticity of the remote host will be asked only the first time you connect. The fingerprint value displayed can be used to verify the identify of the remote host and ensure that you're not being conned by a computer located between you and the computer you're trying to connect to; if you're really paranoid, you can check this value, but for most normal applications this isn't necessary. The fingerprint is cached, though, so if it changes in the future you will be warned. It's necessary to type in **yes** to confirm that you want to continue connecting; **y** won't suffice.

Once you are connected to the remote machine, you can use the shell as you normally would.

Reducing the use of passwords

It's possible to configure *ssh* to enable you to connect from your account on one machine to your account on another machine using public-key cryptography instead of a password. Unfortunately, this means that if your account on one machine is compromised, your account on the other machine will be compromised, too; to prevent this, you can use a *passphrase*, a master password that you enter once per session that permits you to connect multiple times to remote systems without entering a password each time.

To set this up, enter these commands on the client machine (i.e., the machine from which you will be connecting to the remote host):

```
$ ssh-keygen -t dsa
Generating public/private dsa key pair.
Enter file in which to save the key (/home/chris/.ssh/id_dsa):Enter
Enter passphrase (empty for no passphrase):BigSecret
Enter same passphrase again:BigSecret
Your identification has been saved in /home/chris/.ssh/id_dsa.
Your public key has been saved in /home/chris/.ssh/id_dsa.pub.
The key fingerprint is:
3a:f7:e8:88:59:fb:56:f7:0f:55:6b:fe:f6:ec:e2:2c chris@super
$ ssh jon@remoteMachine "cat > ~/.ssh/authorized_keys" <~/.ssh/id_dsa.pub
jon@remoteMachine's password: AnotherSecret
```

 The entire SSH security model revolves around the fact that the private key is private. If you permit access to your private key, the security is completely compromised.

This generates a public key and installs it on the remote system. If you will be connecting to multiple host systems, distribute your key to all of the systems by repeating the previous *ssh* command for each host.

Once the public key is installed on the remote host, you can use the *ssh-add* command to enter your passphrase:

```
$ ssh-add
Enter passphrase for /home/jon/.ssh/id_dsa: BigSecret
Identity added: /home/jon/.ssh/id_dsa (/home/jon/.ssh/id_dsa)
```

 If you're not logged in to your Fedora system through the GUI, you will need to enter this command before using *ssh-add*:

```
$ eval $(ssh-agent)
Agent pid 15431
```

When you log in using the GUI, Fedora starts the *ssh-agent* program automatically.

You can now connect to remote hosts without logging in:

```
$ ssh jon@remoteMachine
Last login: Wed Oct 26 00:20:29 2005 from toronto-office
```

If you wish to run just a single command, you can enter it on the *ssh* command line instead of logging in:

```
$ ssh jon@remoteMachine cal 3 1967
      March 1967
 Su Mo Tu We Th Fr Sa
           1  2  3  4
  5  6  7  8  9 10 11
 12 13 14 15 16 17 18
 19 20 21 22 23 24 25
 26 27 28 29 30 31
```

Using graphical applications remotely

The -X option (uppercase) causes *ssh* to set up an encrypted tunnel for graphical X connections alongside the shell connection. This permits you to start graphical apps on the remote machine and display the output on the local machine (assuming that you're connecting from a graphical session):

```
$ ssh -C -X jon@10.0.0.1
Last login: Wed Oct 26 00:31:42 2005 from parisoffice
$ oowriter
```

In order for this to work, the remote host must have X11Forwarding set to yes in its */etc/ssh/sshd_config* file.

 The -X option may cause remote X clients to be counted as *untrusted* from the point of view of the X server. This is perfect for most purposes, but if you want the remote client to be able to do screen captures (for example, if the remote application is the GIMP and you want to acquire a screenshot), substitute -Y for -X to configure the remote client as *trusted*.

How Does It Work?

SSH uses a variety of ciphers to encrypt your data as it travels across the network. The exact ciphers used can be configured in */etc/ssh/ssh_config* (for the client) and */etc/ssh/sshd_config* (for the server). Configuring a stronger cipher will provide better protection, but will use more CPU power and possibly reduce communication speed; the default settings are a good compromise between security and performance.

Public-key authentication relies upon the fact that two extremely large numbers—the *public key* and *private key*, which are derived mathematically from a single large random number, can be used with cryptographic formulas to encrypt and decrypt data. Anything encrypted with the public key can be decrypted only with the private key (not with the public key or any other number), and anything encrypted with the private key can be decrypted only with the public key. If the private key is kept secret and the public key is distributed to the whole world, then any message that can be decrypted by the public key must have been encrypted with the private key, proving the identity of the sender (*authentication*); any message that is encrypted with the public key can only be decrypted by the private key, ensuring secrecy (*authorization*).

In the case of SSH, the *ssh-keygen* command generates a public/private key pair, placing the private key in ~/.ssh/id_dsa and the public key in ~/.ssh/id_dsa.pub. When the public key is copied to the remote machine and placed in ~/.ssh/authorized_keys, an access request encrypted with the private key can be authenticated using the public key. If the public key is protected with a passphrase, you will be prompted for it each time you connect to a remote machine; to reduce this burden, the *ssh-agent* program can store your passphrase for you. The *ssh-add* command prompts you for your passphrase(s) and hands them over to *ssh-agent* (which is run automatically when the GUI starts up).

SSH is very susceptible to *man-in-the-middle* attacks, where a system between the client and server intercepts communication and presents itself as the client to the server, and the server to the client. However, this type of attack is a lot harder to set up than it would first appear and is rarely encountered. The caching of the host key (presented onscreen in summary format as the *fingerprint*) guards against this after the first contact between the client and server systems has been made.

What About...

...compressing data?

The -C option (note the capital letter!) causes *ssh* to compress data with *gzip* before encryption. This can significantly improve performance in some cases:

```
$ ssh -C jon@10.0.0.1
```

...connecting to a Fedora system from a Windows system using SSH?

To do this, you need a Windows SSH client. There are several available, but for most purposes I'd recommend the free (libre et gratuit) program Putty, downloadable from *http://www.chiark.greenend.org.uk/~sgtatham/putty/*. Of course, you won't be able to use graphical applications unless you've also installed an X server on your windows system—but that's not impossible (see *http://x.cygwin.com/* for one possibility).

...connecting to a Fedora system from a Mac OS X system?

Mac OS X and most other Unix/Linux/BSD-based systems generally have an SSH client installed.

...connecting to my home system from another location?

If you're using a broadband connection with a router or gateway, you'll have to configure the router to pass incoming connections on the SSH port to your Fedora system. Use the router's Applications and Gaming, Port Forwarding, or Servers configuration options to forward TCP/IP port 22 to your Fedora system. Then you can connect to the Fedora system by specifying the address of the gateway system in the *ssh* client arguments.

For example, if the external IP address of the gateway is 1.2.3.4, and the LAN IP address of your Fedora system is 10.0.0.1, configure the router to pass incoming connections on TCP/IP port 22 to 10.0.0.1, and then use the gateway IP address in the client arguments:

```
$ ssh jon@1.2.3.4
```

 You may also need to configure Fedora's firewall to permit SSH connections.

...using public/private keys without a passphrase?

Just leave the passphrase blank when running *ssh-keygen*. This is convenient because you won't need to use *ssh-agent* and *ssh-add*, and can always log in to remote systems without the passphrase. However, it's also dangerous because any attacker who obtains access to your local account will automatically gain access to your remote accounts as well.

Where Can I Learn More?

- The OpenSSH web site: *http://openssh.org/*
- The manpages for *ssh*, *sshd*, *ssh_config*, *sshd_config*, *ssh-agent*, *ssh-add*, and *ssh-keygen*

4.11 Using Shell Redirection and Piping

The Unix/Linux philosophy revolves around the concept of programs as building blocks—each one intended to do one job and do it well. Redirection lets you connect these commands to files, and piping enables you to plug commands together like a child's toy.

How Do I Do That?

Each command has three numbered *file descriptors* that are opened automatically:

standard input (stdin, file descriptor 0)
    The normal input to the program

standard output (stdout, file descriptor 1)
    The normal output from the program

standard error (stderr, file descriptor 2)
    Error messages from the program

By default, these file descriptors are connected to the terminal, if one is available, so standard input comes from the terminal keyboard, and standard output and standard error go to the terminal screen. Programs may open any other connections they need to read or write files, communicate with other local programs, or communicate with programs over the network.

 Connections to the graphical user interface are created by opening a network connection from the program (client) to the X Window server. This is distinct from the three standard file descriptors.

Redirection

To redirect the output of a program to a file, use the greater-than (>) symbol followed by the name of the file:

```
$ cal 7 2006
      July 2006
Su Mo Tu We Th Fr Sa
                   1
 2  3  4  5  6  7  8
 9 10 11 12 13 14 15
16 17 18 19 20 21 22
23 24 25 26 27 28 29
30 31
$ cal 7 2006 >month.txt
$ cat month.txt
      July 2006
Su Mo Tu We Th Fr Sa
                   1
 2  3  4  5  6  7  8
 9 10 11 12 13 14 15
16 17 18 19 20 21 22
23 24 25 26 27 28 29
30 31
```

When you redirect output with >, the previous contents of the file are overwritten. To append (add) to the file, use >>:

```
$ cal 3 2009 >>month.txt
$ cat month.txt
      July 2006
Su Mo Tu We Th Fr Sa
                   1
 2  3  4  5  6  7  8
 9 10 11 12 13 14 15
16 17 18 19 20 21 22
23 24 25 26 27 28 29
30 31
      March 2009
Su Mo Tu We Th Fr Sa
 1  2  3  4  5  6  7
 8  9 10 11 12 13 14
```

```
15 16 17 18 19 20 21
22 23 24 25 26 27 28
29 30 31
```

Error messages are not sent to standard output, so you can still see the messages even when standard output is redirected:

```
$ cal 17 2009 >month.txt
cal: illegal month value: use 1-12
```

To redirect error messages, place the file descriptor number (2) in front of the redirection symbol (> or >>):

```
$ cal 17 2009 2>errors
$ cat errors
cal: illegal month value: use 1-12
```

You can redirect both standard output and standard error:

```
$ cal 17 2009 >month.txt 2>errors
```

To redirect the input of a command, use the less-than sign (<) followed by the filename containing the data you wish to use as the input:

```
$ echo "2^8" >problem
$ bc <problem
256
```

bc is a calculator program. The first command places a numeric expression in the file *problem*; the second line starts *bc*, using *problem* as the input. The output from *bc* is the solution of the expression: 256.

Of course, you can redirect both input and output:

```
$ bc <problem >result
```

Piping

A *pipe* is a mechanism used to connect the standard output of one program to the standard input of another program. To create a pipe, insert the vertical-bar (|) symbol between the two commands:

```
$ mount
/dev/mapper/main-root on / type ext3 (rw)
proc on /proc type proc (rw)
sysfs on /sys type sysfs (rw)
devpts on /dev/pts type devpts (rw,gid=5,mode=620)
/dev/hdc2 on /boot type ext3 (rw)
tmpfs on /dev/shm type tmpfs (rw)
/dev/mapper/main-home on /home type ext3 (rw)
none on /proc/sys/fs/binfmt_misc type binfmt_misc (rw)
/dev/sdb on /media/disk type vfat (rw,noexec,nosuid,nodev,shortname=winnt,uid=503)
$ mount | grep /dev/mapper
/dev/mapper/main-root on / type ext3 (rw)
/dev/mapper/main-home on /home type ext3 (rw)
```

In this example, the output of the *mount* command is used as the input to the *grep* command, which outputs only lines that match the specified pattern. A group of commands connected together with pipe symbols is known as a *pipeline*. You can extend a pipeline by connecting additional commands:

```
$ mount | grep /dev/mapper | sort
/dev/mapper/main-home on /home type ext3 (rw)
/dev/mapper/main-root on / type ext3 (rw)
```

The input to a pipeline and the output from a pipeline may be redirected:

```
$ cut -d: -f1 </etc/passwd|sort|head >output
$ cat output
adm
apache
avahi
beaglidx
bin
chip
chris
daemon
dbus
distcache
```

However, it's essential that the input redirect take place at the start of the pipeline (at the command on the left) and that the output redirection take place at the end (at the command on the right). Consider this *wrong* example:

```
$ cut -d: -f1 </etc/passwd|sort >output|head
```

In this case, it's unclear whether the standard output of sort should be placed in the file *output* or used as the standard input to the head command. The result is undefined (which means *don't do this!*).

How Does It Work?

Redirection is set up by the *bash* shell before the command is executed. If there is a redirection error (such as an invalid filename or a file permission problem), it will be reported by the shell and the command will not be executed:

```
$ cal >foo/bar/baz
bash: foo/bar/baz: No such file or directory
```

 Note that the error message starts with bash, indicating that it was produced by the shell and not by the cal command.

A command is not aware of file redirection unless it has specifically been programed to check the standard file descriptors or perform special operations on them (such as changing terminal characteristics). Redirected file descriptors are inherited by applications that were started by commands; in this example, the *nice* command starts the *cal* command, and *cal* inherits the redirection set up for *nice*:

```
$ nice "cal" >test.txt
$ cat test.txt
     July 2006
Su Mo Tu We Th Fr Sa
                   1
 2  3  4  5  6  7  8
 9 10 11 12 13 14 15
16 17 18 19 20 21 22
23 24 25 26 27 28 29
30 31
```

What About...

...redirecting standard output and standard error to the same destination?

You can use the characters 2>&1 to redirect standard error to the same destination as standard output:

```
$ cal 17 2009 >/tmp/calresult 2>&1
```

Notice that the order of the redirections matters. The preceding command will redirect all output to */tmp/calresult*, but this command will not redirect standard error:

```
$ cal 17 2009 2>&1 >/tmp/calresult
```

The 2>&1 redirection is evaluated first, so standard error is directed to the same destination as standard output (which, at that point, is the terminal); >*/tmp/calresult* then redirects standard output by itself.

This construct can also be used with piping:

```
$ cal 17 2009 2>&1 | head -2
```

This will feed both the standard output and the standard error from *cal* into the standard input of *head*.

...redirecting to a device?

Linux treats most devices as files, so you can redirect data to and from devices easily. This command copies the first 50 lines of the */etc/services* file directly to a parallel printer port:

```
$ head -50 /etc/services >/dev/lp0
```

...splitting a pipe to send data to two destinations?

The *tee* command will receive data on standard input and write one copy to a file and one copy to standard output. This effectively splits a pipe:

```
$ cal -y | tee /tmp/thisyear.txt | head -2
```

To send a copy of the data to the screen, use tee with the device file */dev/tty* (the current terminal):

```
$ cal -y | tee /dev/tty | grep Mo | head -1 >/tmp/dow-header.txt
```

…piping and redirecting data that is not text?

No assumptions are made about the type of data being piped or redirected; in fact, there are many programs that are designed to work with piped graphics, audio, or video data streams. For example, this pipeline will decode a color JPEG image, scale it to half-size, convert it to grayscale, normalize it, convert it back into a JPEG, save a copy as */tmp/final.jpg*, and display the output in a window:

```
$ djpeg /usr/share/wallpapers/floating-leaves.jpg | pnmscale 0.5 |
    ppmtopgm | ppmnorm | cjpeg | tee /tmp/final.jpg | display -
```

Where Can I Learn More?

- The manpage for *bash*

4.12   Writing Simple Scripts

bash command lines can get to be very long, especially when pipes are used. A *script* is a text file that contains shell commands that may itself be executed as a command, providing an easy way to reuse complex sequences of commands. In fact, *bash* provides a complete programming language for use in scripts.

How Do I Do That?

To create a script, simply place commands in a text file. For example, this script will display the ten largest files in the current directory:

```
ls -lS | tail -n +2 | head -10
```

Save this file as *topten*. In order to run the script, you will need to set read and execute permission:

```
$ chmod a+rx topten
```

The script can be executed by specifying the directory and filename (or an absolute pathname):

```
$ ./topten
-rw-r--r-- 1 root root   807103 Jul 12 21:18 termcap
-rw-r--r-- 1 root root   499861 Jul 17 08:08 prelink.cache
-rw-r--r-- 1 root root   362031 Feb 23 08:09 services
-rw-r--r-- 1 root root    97966 Jul 15 11:19 ld.so.cache
-rw-r--r-- 1 root root    92794 Jul 12 12:46 Muttrc
-rw-r--r-- 1 root root    83607 Mar 23 07:23 readahead.files
```

```
-rw-r--r--  1 root root       73946 Jul 13 02:23 sensors.conf
-rw-r--r--  1 root root       45083 Jul 12 18:33 php.ini
-rw-r--r--  1 root root       30460 Jul 13 20:36 jwhois.conf
-rw-r--r--  1 root root       26137 Mar 23 07:23 readahead.early.files
```

The directory name is required because the current directory (.) is not in the list of directories normally searched for commands (called the PATH). To make your script accessible to all users, move it to the */usr/local/bin* directory, which appears by default in everyone's PATH:

```
# mv topten /usr/local/bin
```

Shell and environment variables

bash uses *shell variables* to keep track of current settings. These *shell variables* are private to the shell and are not passed to processes started by the shell—but they can be *exported*, which converts them into *environment variables*, which are passed to child processes.

You can view all shell and environment variables using the *set* command:

```
$ set
BASH=/bin/bash
BASH_ARGC=( )
BASH_ARGV=( )
BASH_LINENO=( )
BASH_SOURCE=( )
BASH_VERSINFO=([0]="3" [1]="1" [2]="17" [3]="1" [4]="release" [5]="i686-redhat-linux-
gnu")
BASH_VERSION='3.1.17(1)-release'
COLORS=/etc/DIR_COLORS.xterm
COLORTERM=gnome-terminal
COLUMNS=172
CVS_RSH=ssh
DBUS_SESSION_BUS_ADDRESS=unix:abstract=/tmp/dbus-
I4CWWfqvE6,guid=e202bd44a31ea8366b20151327662e00
DESKTOP_SESSION=default
DESKTOP_STARTUP_ID=
DIRSTACK=( )
DISPLAY=:0.0
EUID=503
GDMSESSION=default
GDM_XSERVER_LOCATION=local
GNOME_DESKTOP_SESSION_ID=Default
GNOME_KEYRING_SOCKET=/tmp/keyring-FJyfaw/socket
GROUPS=( )
GTK_RC_FILES=/etc/gtk/gtkrc:/home/hank/.gtkrc-1.2-gnome2
G_BROKEN_FILENAMES=1
HISTFILE=/home/hank/.bash_history
HISTFILESIZE=1000
HISTSIZE=1000
HOME=/home/hank
HOSTNAME=bluesky.fedorabook.com
```

```
HOSTTYPE=i686
IFS=$' \t\n'
INPUTRC=/etc/inputrc
KDEDIR=/usr
KDE_IS_PRELINKED=1
LANG=en_US.UTF-8
LESSOPEN='|/usr/bin/lesspipe.sh %s'
LINES=55
LOGNAME=hank
LS_COLORS='no=00:fi=00:di=00;34:ln=00;36:pi=40;33:so=00;35:bd=40;33;01:cd=40;33;01:
or=01;05;37;41:mi=01;05;37;41:ex=00;32:*.cmd=00;32:*.exe=00;32:*.com=00;32:*.
btm=00;32:*.bat=00;32:*.sh=00;32:*.csh=00;32:*.tar=00;31:*.tgz=00;31:*.arj=00;31:*.
taz=00;31:*.lzh=00;31:*.zip=00;31:*.z=00;31:*.Z=00;31:*.gz=00;31:*.bz2=00;31:*.
bz=00;31:*.tz=00;31:*.rpm=00;31:*.cpio=00;31:*.jpg=00;35:*.gif=00;35:*.bmp=00;35:*.
xbm=00;35:*.xpm=00;35:*.png=00;35:*.tif=00;35:'
MACHTYPE=i686-redhat-linux-gnu
MAIL=/var/spool/mail/hank
MAILCHECK=60
OLDPWD=/usr/share/wallpapers
OPTERR=1
OPTIND=1
OSTYPE=linux-gnu
PATH=/usr/lib/qt-3.3/bin:/usr/kerberos/bin:/usr/local/bin:/usr/bin:/bin:/usr/X11R6/
bin:/home/hank/bin
PIPESTATUS=([0]="0" [1]="141" [2]="0")
PPID=3067
PRELINKING=yes
PRELINK_FULL_TIME_INTERVAL=14
PRELINK_NONRPM_CHECK_INTERVAL=7
PRELINK_OPTS=-mR
PROMPT_COMMAND='echo -ne "\033]0;${USER}@${HOSTNAME%%.*}:${PWD/#$HOME/~}"; echo -ne
"\007"'
PS1='$ '
PS2='> '
PS4='+ '
PWD=/etc
QTDIR=/usr/lib/qt-3.3
QTINC=/usr/lib/qt-3.3/include
QTLIB=/usr/lib/qt-3.3/lib
SESSION_MANAGER=local/beige.fedorabook.com:/tmp/.ICE-unix/2621
SHELL=/bin/bash
SHELLOPTS=braceexpand:emacs:hashall:histexpand:history:interactive-comments:monitor
SHLVL=2
SSH_AGENT_PID=2659
SSH_ASKPASS=/usr/libexec/openssh/gnome-ssh-askpass
SSH_AUTH_SOCK=/tmp/ssh-dNhrfX2621/agent.2621
TERM=xterm
UID=503
USER=hank
USERNAME=hank
WINDOWID=58721388
XAUTHORITY=/home/hank/.Xauthority
_=
qt_prefix=/usr/lib/qt-3.3
```

Many of these variables contain settings for particular programs. Some of the common variables used by many programs are shown in Table 4-16.

Table 4-16. Key environment variables

Name	Purpose	Format
DISPLAY	Information on which X display is being used	*hostname:display.screen*
		hostname is the hostname or IP address of the X server or blank for the local host, *display* is the display number, and *screen* is the screen number (optional; the screen number specifies the monitor in a multimonitor, single-person display configuration).
HOME	Home directory	Absolute pathname of the user's home directory.
HOSTNAME	Name of this computer	Fully qualified domain name of the local host.
MAIL	Location of the user's default mailbox	Absolute pathname of the user's mailbox (usually */var/spool/mail/<username>*).
PATH	List of directories to be searched to find a command	Absolute pathnames of directories to be searched, separated by colons.
PS1, PS2	Primary and secondary shell prompts	Plain text. Special characters sequences consisting of \ and a letter are replaced with other information; for example, \w is replaced by the current working directory (see the manpage for *bash* for a complete list).
TERM	Model number of the current terminal	Must correspond to a filename in */usr/share/terminfo/?/**.

To set a shell variable, type the variable name, an equal sign, and the value you wish to assign (all values are treated as text):

```
$ A=red
```

Once a variable has been assigned a value, you can use it in commands, preceded by a dollar sign:

```
$ ls -l red
ls: red: No such file or directory
$ touch $A
$ ls -l red
-rw-r--r-- 1 hank hank 0 Jul 18 15:26 red
```

The *echo* command can be used to view the value of a variable:

```
$ echo $A
red
```

To destroy a variable, use the *unset* command:

```
$ echo $A
red
$ unset A
$ echo $A
$
```

Finally, to make a variable accessible to processes started by the current process, use the *export* command:

```
$ unset A
$ TEST=blue
$ echo $TEST                    # variable is known to the shell
blue
$ bash                          # start a child shell
[hank@beige foo]$ echo $TEST    # variable is not known to child

[hank@beige foo]$ exit          # exit back to parent shell
exit
$ export TEST                    # export the variable
$ echo $TEST                     # value is still known to the shell
blue
$ bash                           # start a new child shell
[hank@beige foo]$ echo $TEST     # exported value is known to the child
blue
```

The PATH value is stored in an environment variable of the same name. Its value can be viewed like any other environment variable:

```
$ echo $PATH
/usr/local/bin:/usr/bin:/bin:/usr/X11R6/bin
```

To add a directory to the existing directories, use $PATH on the righthand side of an assignment to insert the current value of the variable into the new value:

```
$ PATH=$PATH:/home/hank/bin
$ echo $PATH
/usr/local/bin:/usr/bin:/bin:/usr/X11R6/bin:/home/hank/bin
```

You don't need to export PATH in this case because it has already been exported; assigning a new value does not changes its exported status.

Assuming that the *topten* script is saved in */home/hank/bin*, you can now execute it by just typing its name:

```
$ topten
-rw-r--r--  1 root root   807103 Jul 12 21:18 termcap
-rw-r--r--  1 root root   499861 Jul 17 08:08 prelink.cache
-rw-r--r--  1 root root   362031 Feb 23 08:09 services
-rw-r--r--  1 root root    97966 Jul 15 11:19 ld.so.cache
-rw-r--r--  1 root root    92794 Jul 12 12:46 Muttrc
-rw-r--r--  1 root root    83607 Mar 23 07:23 readahead.files
-rw-r--r--  1 root root    73946 Jul 13 02:23 sensors.conf
-rw-r--r--  1 root root    45083 Jul 12 18:33 php.ini
-rw-r--r--  1 root root    30460 Jul 13 20:36 jwhois.conf
-rw-r--r--  1 root root    26137 Mar 23 07:23 readahead.early.files
```

Within a script, you can prompt the user using the echo command, and then use the *read* command to read a line from the user and place it in an environment variable:

```
echo "Please enter your name:"
read NAME
echo "Hello $NAME!"
```

Or you can collect the standard output of a command and assign it to a variable using the $( ) symbols:

```
$ NOW=$(date)
$ echo $NOW
Tue Jul 18 22:25:48 EDT 2006
```

Special variables

There are several *special parameters*, or *special variables*, that *bash* sets automatically; Table 4-17 contains a list of the most important ones.

Table 4-17. Important special variables

Name	Description	Notes
$$	Process ID of the shell	Since process IDs are unique (at any one point in time), this can be used to ensure unique filenames (e.g., */tmp/$$.txt* will never conflict with the same filename used by another copy of the same script).
$0	Name of the script	Useful to generate error messages, and when one script is invoked through more than one name.
$1, $2, $3, ...	Arguments given on the script's command line	The *shift* command will eliminate $1 and then shift all of the parameters accordingly ($2 becomes $1, $3 becomes $2, and so forth).
$#	Number of arguments from the script's command line	If $# is 0, then no options were given on the command line.
$* $@	All of the arguments from the script's command line	When quoted, "$*" becomes a single block of text containing all of the arguments, while "$@" becomes separate words. If the script is called with the arguments "green" and "yellow", then "$*" would evaluate to "green yellow", while "$@" would evaluate to "green" "yellow".
$?	Exit status of the last command	Manpages document the possible exit-status values for most commands.

Control structures

Like most programming languages, *bash* features a number of control structures to enable looping and conditional execution. The three most common control structures are listed in Table 4-18; there is also a C-style for loop that I'll discuss in the next section.

Table 4-18. Common bash control structures

Structure	Notes	Example

for *variable* in *list*
do
   loop-commands
done
	The *variable* is assigned the first value in *list*, and *loop-commands* are executed. The process is then repeated for all of the other values in *list*.	# Set X to 'hosts', then
		# display the filename
		# and file contents.
		# Repeat for 'services'
		for X in hosts services
		do
		  echo "==== $X"
		  cat /etc/$X
		done

if *control-command*
then
   if-commands
[else
   else-commands]
fi
	If the *control-command* succeeds, the *if-commands* are executed; otherwise, the *else-commands* are executed.	# Tell the user if
		# the text 'test'
		# appears in file1
		if grep -q test file1
		then
		  echo "Found it!"
		else
		  echo "Not found."
		fi

while *control-command*
do
   loop-commands
done
	As long as *control-command* executes successfully, *loop-commands* are repeated.	# Display the free
		# disk space every
		# 2 seconds, forever
		while sleep 2
		do
		  df -h
		done

The for..in control structure is great for looping over a range of values. This loop will display the status of the *httpd*, *ftpd*, and *NetworkManager* services:

```
for SERVICE in httpd ftpd NetworkManager
do
     /sbin/service $SERVICE status
done
```

for...in is even more useful when the list of values is specified as an ambiguous filename. In this script, the loop is repeated once for each file in the directory */etc/* that ends in *.conf*:

```
mkdir backup
for FILE in /etc/*.conf
do
     echo "Backing up the file $FILE..."
     cp $FILE backup/
done
```

For the if and while control structures, a *control-command* determines the action taken. The *control-command* can be any command on the system; an *exit status* of zero is considered true and any other exit status is considered false.

For example, the *grep* command exits with a value of zero if a given pattern is found in the file(s) specified or in the standard input. When combined with an if structure, you can cause a program to take a particular action if a pattern is found. For example, this code displays the message "Helen is logged in!" if the output of *who* contains the word helen:

```
if who | grep -q helen
then
    echo "Helen is logged in!"
fi
```

 The exit status of the last command is taken as the exit status of a pipeline, which is *grep* in this case. The -q argument to *grep* suppresses the output—otherwise, matching lines are sent to standard output.

The built-in command *test* can be used to test conditions; the exit status will be zero if the condition is true. The most common conditional expressions are listed in Table 4-19.

Table 4-19. Common bash conditional operators

Operator	Tests whether...	Example using an environment variable
-f *file*	File exists and is a regular file	-f "$A"
-d *file*	File exists and is a directory	-d "$B"
-r *file*	File exists and is readable	-r "$C"
-w *file*	File exists and is writable	-w "$D"
-x *file*	File exists and is executable	-x "$E"
value1 == *value2*	Strings match	"$F" == "red"
value1 != *value2*	Strings don't match	"$G" != "blue"
value1 -eq *value2*	Integer values are equal	"$H" -eq 2
value1 -ne *value2*	Integer values are unequal	"$J" -ne 10
value1 -gt *value2*	*value1* integer value is greater than *value2*	"$K" -gt 25
value1 -ge *value2*	*value1* integer value is greater than or equal to *value2*	"$L" -ge 25
value1 -lt *value2*	*value1* integer value is less than *value2*	"$M" -lt 75
value1 -le *value2*	*value1* integer value is less than or equal to *value2*	"$N" -le 75
expression1 -a *expression2*	*expression1* and *expression2* are both true	"$P" -gt 36 -a "$P" -lt 71
expression1 -o *expression2*	*expression1* or *expression2* (or both) are true	"$P" -lt 12 -o "$P" -eq 50

So if you wanted to print "Too high!" if the value of the variable A was over 50, you would write:

```
if test "$A" -gt 50
then
        echo "Too high!"
fi
```

The variable expression $A is quoted in case A has a null value ("") or doesn't exist—in which case, if unquoted, a syntax error would occur because there would be nothing to the left of -gt.

The square brackets ([]) are a synonym for test, so the previous code is more commonly written:

```
if [ "$A" -gt 50 ]
then
        echo "Too high!"
fi
```

You can also use *test* with the *while* control structure. This loop monitors the number of users logged in, checking every 15 seconds until the number of users is equal to or greater than 100, when the loop will exit and the following pipeline will send an email to the email alias *alert*:

```
while [ "$(who | wc -l)" -lt 100 ]
do
     sleep 15
done
echo "Over 100 users are now logged in!"|mail -s "Overload!" alert
```

Integer arithmetic

bash provides very limited integer arithmetic capabilities. An expression inside double parentheses (( )) is interpreted as a numeric expression; an expression inside double parentheses preceded by a dollar sign $(( )) is interpreted as a numeric expression that also returns a value.

Inside double parentheses, you can read a variable's value without using the dollar sign (use A=B+C instead of A=$B+$C).

Here's an example using a while loop that counts from 1 to 20 using integer arithmetic:

```
A=0
while [ "$A" -lt 20 ]
do
        (( A=A+1 ))
        echo $A
done
```

The C-style increment operators are available, so this code could be rewritten as:

```
A=0
while [ "$A" -lt 20 ]
do
        echo $(( ++A ))
done
```

The expression $((++A)) returns the value of A after it is incremented. You could also use $((A++)), which returns the value of A before it is incremented:

```
A=1
while [ "$A" -le 20 ]
do
        echo $(( A++ ))
done
```

Since loops that count through a range of numbers are often needed, *bash* also supports the C-style for loop. Inside double parentheses, specify an initial expression, a conditional expression, and a per-loop expression, separated by semicolons:

```
# Initial value of A is 1
# Keep looping as long as A<=20
# Each time you loop, increment A by 1
for ((A=1; A<=20; A++))
do
        echo $A
done
```

Note that the conditional expression uses normal comparison symbols (<=) instead of the alphabetic options (-le) used by test.

Don't confuse the C-style for loop with the for...in loop!

Making your scripts available to users of other shells

So far we have been assuming that the user is using the *bash* shell; if the user of another shell (such as *tcsh*) tries to execute one of your scripts, it will be interpreted according to the language rules of that shell and will probably fail.

To make your scripts more robust, add a *shebang* line at the beginning—a pound-sign character followed by an exclamation mark, followed by the full path of the shell to be used to interpret the script (*/bin/bash*):

```
#!/bin/bash
# script to count from 1 to 20

for ((A=1; A<=20; A++))
do
        echo $A
done
```

I also added a comment line (starting with #) after the shebang line to describe the function of the script.

 The shebang line gets its name from *sharp* and *bang*, common nicknames for the #! characters.

An example

Here is an example of a longer script, taking advantage of some of the scripting features in *bash*:

```
#!/bin/bash
#
# number-guessing game
#

# If the user entered an argument on the command
# line, use it as the upper limit of the number
# range.
if [ "$#" -eq 1 ]
then
        MAX=$1
else
        MAX=100
fi

# Set up other variables
SECRET=$(( (RANDOM % MAX) + 1 )) # Random number 1-100
TRIES=0
GUESS=-1

# Display initial messages
clear
echo "Number-guessing Game"
echo "--------------------"
echo
echo "I have a secret number between 1 and $MAX."

# Loop until the user guesses the right number
while [ "$GUESS" -ne "$SECRET" ]
do

        # Prompt the user and get her input
        ((TRIES++))
        echo -n "Enter guess #$TRIES: "
        read GUESS

        # Display low/high messages
        if [ "$GUESS" -lt "$SECRET" ]
        then
                echo "Too low!"
```

```
        fi

        if [ "$GUESS" -gt "$SECRET" ]
        then
                echo "Too high!"
        fi

done

# Display final messages
echo
echo "You guessed it!"
echo "It took you $TRIES tries."
echo
```

This script could be saved as *usr/local/bin/guess-it* and then made executable:

```
# chmod a+rx /usr/local/bin/guess-it
```

Here's a test run of the script:

```
$ guess-it
Number-guessing Game
--------------------

I have a secret number between 1 and 100.
Enter guess #1: 50
Too low!
Enter guess #2: 75
Too low!
Enter guess #3: 83
Too low!
Enter guess #4: 92
Too high!
Enter guess #5: 87
Too high!
Enter guess #6: 85
Too low!
Enter guess #7: 86

You guessed it!
It took you 7 tries.
```

Another test, using an alternate upper limit:

```
$ guess-it 50
Number-guessing Game
--------------------

I have a secret number between 1 and 50.
Enter guess #1: 25
Too low!
Enter guess #2: 37
Too low!
Enter guess #3: 44
Too high!
```

```
Enter guess #4: 40

You guessed it!
It took you 4 tries.
```

Login and initialization scripts

When a user logs in, the system-wide script */etc/profile* and the per-user script *~/.bash_profile* are both executed. This is the default */etc/profile*:

```
# /etc/profile

# System wide environment and startup programs, for login setup
# Functions and aliases go in /etc/bashrc

pathmunge () {
        if ! echo $PATH | /bin/egrep -q "(^|:)$1($|:)" ; then
            if [ "$2" = "after" ] ; then
                PATH=$PATH:$1
            else
                PATH=$1:$PATH
            fi
        fi
}

# ksh workaround
if [ -z "$EUID" -a -x /usr/bin/id ]; then
        EUID=`id -u`
        UID=`id -ru`
fi

# Path manipulation
if [ "$EUID" = "0" ]; then
        pathmunge /sbin
        pathmunge /usr/sbin
        pathmunge /usr/local/sbin
fi

# No core files by default
ulimit -S -c 0 > /dev/null 2>&1

if [ -x /usr/bin/id ]; then
        USER="`id -un`"
        LOGNAME=$USER
        MAIL="/var/spool/mail/$USER"
fi

HOSTNAME=`/bin/hostname`
HISTSIZE=1000

if [ -z "$INPUTRC" -a ! -f "$HOME/.inputrc" ]; then
    INPUTRC=/etc/inputrc
fi
```

```
export PATH USER LOGNAME MAIL HOSTNAME HISTSIZE INPUTRC

for i in /etc/profile.d/*.sh ; do
    if [ -r "$i" ]; then
        . $i
    fi
done

unset i
unset pathmunge
```

This script adds */sbin*, */usr/sbin*, and */usr/local/sbin* to the PATH if the user is the *root* user. It then creates and exports the USER, LOGNAME, MAIL, HOSTNAME, and HISTSIZE variables, and executes any files in */etc/profile.d* that end in *.sh*.

The default *~/.bash_profile* looks like this:

```
# .bash_profile

# Get the aliases and functions
if [ -f ~/.bashrc ]; then
        . ~/.bashrc
fi

# User specific environment and startup programs

PATH=$PATH:$HOME/bin

export PATH
```

You can edit */etc/profile* to change the login process for all users, or *~/.bash_profile* to change just your login process. One useful change that I make to every Fedora system I install is to comment out the if statements for path manipulation in */etc/profile* so that every user has the superuser binary directories in his path:

```
# Path manipulation
#if [ "$EUID" = "0" ]; then
        pathmunge /sbin
        pathmunge /usr/sbin
        pathmunge /usr/local/sbin
#fi
```

 bash comments start with # and are not executed—so *commenting out* code means adding # at the start of selected lines to disable them.

Environment variables are inherited by child processes, so any environment variables set up during the login process are accessible to all shells (and other programs) you start. *bash* also supports the use of *aliases*, or nicknames, for commands, but since these are not inherited by child processes, they are instead placed in the file *~/.bashrc*, which is executed each time a shell starts. If you log in once and then start three shells, *~/.bash_profile* is executed once at login and *~/.bashrc* is executed three times, once for each shell that starts.

This is the default *~/.bashrc*:

```
# .bashrc

# Source global definitions
if [ -f /etc/bashrc ]; then
        . /etc/bashrc
fi


# User-specific aliases and functions
```

As you can see, there aren't any alias definitions in there (but you can add them). The file */etc/bashrc* is invoked by this script, and it contains common aliases made available to all users:

```
# System-wide functions and aliases
# Environment stuff goes in /etc/profile

# By default, we want this to get set.
# Even for noninteractive, nonlogin shells.
umask 022

# Are we an interactive shell?
if [ "$PS1" ]; then
    case $TERM in
        xterm*)
                if [ -e /etc/sysconfig/bash-prompt-xterm ]; then
                        PROMPT_COMMAND=/etc/sysconfig/bash-prompt-xterm
                else
                PROMPT_COMMAND='echo -ne ↵
                    "\033]0;${USER}@${HOSTNAME%%.*}:${PWD/#$HOME/~}";
                    echo -ne "\007"'
                fi
                ;;
        screen)
                if [ -e /etc/sysconfig/bash-prompt-screen ]; then
                        PROMPT_COMMAND=/etc/sysconfig/bash-prompt-screen
                else
                PROMPT_COMMAND='echo -ne "\033_${USER}@${HOSTNAME%%.*}:${PWD/#$HOME/
~}"; echo -ne "\033\\"'
                fi
                ;;
        *)
                [ -e /etc/sysconfig/bash-prompt-default ] && PROMPT_COMMAND=/etc/
sysconfig/bash-prompt-default
            ;;
    esac
    # Turn on checkwinsize
    shopt -s checkwinsize
    [ "$PS1" = "\\s-\\v\\\$ " ] && PS1="[\u@\h \W]\\$ "
fi
```

```
if ! shopt -q login_shell ; then # We're not a login shell
    # Need to redefine pathmunge, it get's undefined at the end of /etc/profile
pathmunge () {
            if ! echo $PATH | /bin/egrep -q "(^|:)$1($|:)" ; then
                    if [ "$2" = "after" ] ; then
                            PATH=$PATH:$1
                    else
                            PATH=$1:$PATH
                    fi
            fi
    }

    for i in /etc/profile.d/*.sh; do
            if [ -r "$i" ]; then
                    . $i
    fi
    done
    unset i
    unset pathmunge
fi
# vim:ts=4:sw=4
```

This script sets up the *umask*, configures a command that will be executed before the
display of each prompt (which sets the terminal-window title to show the user, host,
and current directory), and then executes each of the files in */etc/profile.d* that end in
.sh.

Packages installed on your Fedora system can include files that are placed in */etc/
profile.d*, providing a simple way for each package to globally add aliases or other
shell configuration options. There are a few command aliases defined in these script
files, including:

```
alias l.='ls -d .* --color=tty'
alias ll='ls -l --color=tty'
alias ls='ls --color=tty'
alias vi='vim'
```

If you type **ll** at a command prompt, ls -l will be executed, due to the alias highlighted in the preceding listing:

```
$ ll /
total 138
drwxr-xr-x    2 root root  4096 Jul 17 08:08 bin
drwxr-xr-x    4 root root  1024 Jul 15 11:16 boot
drwxr-xr-x   12 root root  3900 Jul 19 07:56 dev
drwxr-xr-x  102 root root 12288 Jul 18 18:14 etc
drwxr-xr-x    8 root root  4096 Jul 16 22:51 home
drwxr-xr-x   11 root root  4096 Jul 17 07:58 lib
drwx------    2 root root 16384 Jun  9 19:34 lost+found
drwxr-xr-x    4 root root  4096 Jul 18 18:14 media
drwxr-xr-x    2 root root     0 Jul 18 11:48 misc
drwxr-xr-x    6 root root  4096 Jul 15 11:38 mnt
drwxr-xr-x    2 root root     0 Jul 18 11:48 net
drwxr-xr-x    2 root root  4096 Jul 12 04:48 opt
```

```
dr-xr-xr-x  126 root root      0 Jul 18 11:46 proc
drwxr-x---    9 root root   4096 Jul 18 00:18 root
drwxr-xr-x    2 root root  12288 Jul 17 08:08 sbin
drwxr-xr-x    4 root root      0 Jul 18 11:46 selinux
drwxr-xr-x    2 root root   4096 Jul 12 04:48 srv
drwxr-xr-x   11 root root      0 Jul 18 11:46 sys
drwxrwxrwt   98 root root   4096 Jul 19 11:04 tmp
drwxr-xr-x   14 root root   4096 Jul 14 04:17 usr
drwxr-xr-x   26 root root   4096 Jul 14 04:17 var
```

Similarly, if you type **vi** the shell will execute *vim*.

You can create your own aliases using the *alias* command; for example, I like to use l for ls -l, sometimes use *cls* to clear the screen, and like to have machine report the hostname (old habits):

```
$ alias l='ls -l
$ alias cls='clear'
$ alias machine='hostname'
```

Adding the same lines to *~/.bashrc* will make them available every time you start a new shell; adding them to *~/.bashrc* will make them available to all users.

You can see the currently defined aliases by typing **alias** alone as a command:

```
$ alias
alias cls='clear'
alias l='ll'
alias l.='ls -d .* --color=tty'
alias ll='ls -l --color=tty'
alias ls='ls --color=tty'
alias machine='hostname'
alias vi='vim'
```

To destroy an alias, use the *unalias* command:

```
$ unalias machine
$ alias
alias cls='clear'
alias l='ll'
alias l.='ls -d .* --color=tty'
alias ll='ls -l --color=tty'
alias ls='ls --color=tty'
alias vi='vim'
```

How Does It Work?

When the kernel receives a request to execute a file (and that file is executable), it uses *magic number* codes at the start of the file to determine how to execute it. For example, there are magic numbers for standard Executable and Linking Format (ELF) binaries and historical assembler output (*a.out*) binaries; the kernel will use them to set up the correct execution environment and then start the program.

If the first two bytes of the file are #!, which counts as a magic number, the file is treated as a script: a pathname is read from the file starting at the third byte and continuing to the end of the first line. The shell or interpreter program identified by this pathname is executed, and the script name and all arguments are passed to the interpreter.

If a file has no magic number or shebang line, the kernel will attempt to execute it as though the value of the SHELL environment variable were given on the shebang line.

What About...

...interacting with the user through the graphical user interface?

Other scripting languages such as Perl and Python can be used to construct full-scale GUI applications, but the *zenity* program enables a shell script to interact with a GUI user.

zenity presents a simple dialog or information box to the user. There are a number of dialog types available, including information and error boxes, text entry and editing boxes, and date-selection boxes; the type of dialog as well as the messages that appear in the dialog are configured by *zenity* options.

Here is the number-guessing script rewritten to use *zenity* for the user interface:

```
#!/bin/bash
#
# number-guessing game - GUI version
#

# If the user entered an argument on the command
# line, use it as the upper limit of the number
# range
if [ "$#" -eq 1 ]
then
        MAX=$1
else
        MAX=100
fi

# Set up other variables
SECRET=$(( (RANDOM % MAX) + 1 )) # Random number 1-100
TRIES=0
GUESS=-1

# Display initial messages
zenity --info --text \
"I have a secret number between 1 and $MAX. Try and guess it!" \
--title "Guess-It"

# Loop until the user guesses the right number
while [ "$GUESS" -ne "$SECRET" ]
do
```

```
# Prompt the user and get her input
((TRIES++))
GUESS=$(zenity --entry --text "Enter guess #$TRIES:" --title "Guess...")

# Display low/high messages
if [ "$GUESS" -lt "$SECRET" ]
then
        zenity --info --text "Too low!"
fi

if [ "$GUESS" -gt "$SECRET" ]
then
        zenity --info --text "Too high!"
fi

done

# Display final messages
zenity --info --text "You guessed it! It took you $TRIES tries." --title
"Congratulations!"
```

Figure 4-16 shows the *zenity* dialogs produced by this script. Obviously, this user interface is not as refined as one that could be provided by a full-featured GUI application, but it is perfectly suitable for simple interactions.

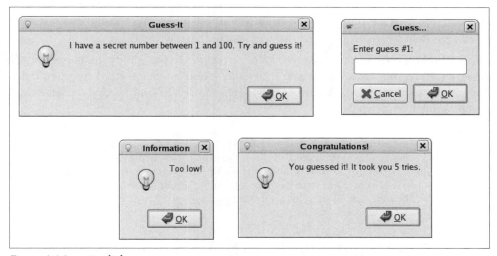

Figure 4-16. zenity dialogs

Where Can I Learn More?

- The manpages for *bash*, *chmod*, and *zenity*

CHAPTER 5

Package Management

One of the advantages of Fedora is the huge amount of software available for it. Finding, installing, updating, and removing this software can be a daunting task, simply due to the amount of software available.

Fortunately, Fedora uses a software management system called *RPM Package Manager* or simply *RPM* (formerly RedHat Package Manager). RPM rolls all of the programs, scripts, documentation, configuration files, and data used by a piece of software into a single file called a *package*. The package also contains metadata describing the package, license, maintainers, and the packages upon which the package depends (for example, a KDE application will need other components of the KDE system to operate).

What RPM doesn't provide is *dependency resolution*: the ability to *automatically* resolve dependency issues. However, the *yum* system builds on RPM to provide this capability, automatically searching external *repositories* to find needed packages and install them automatically.

In this chapter, the sections Lab 5.1, "Querying the Package Management Database" and Lab 5.2, "Installing and Removing Software Using RPM" deal with individual package management from the command line. If you want to go directly to the simplest and most comprehensive way of managing software packages, skip to Lab 5.3, "Using Repositories."

5.1 Querying the Package Management Database

The RPM package management database is an essential source of information about your system. The database is created when the system is installed and is updated whenever packages are added or removed.

As RPM packages are installed on your system, the metadata for those packages is stored in a database that can be queried. If you have a mystery file on your system and want to know where it came from, or want to know which version of a package is installed, or what a package does, an RPM query can answer your question in a few seconds.

How Do I Do That?

The *rpm* program provides access to the RPM database. The `-q` option enables query mode.

The default query takes a package name and tells you whether it is installed and, if so, which version is installed:

```
$ rpm -q selmyscan
package selmyscan is not installed
$ rpm -q httpd
httpd-2.0.54-10.2
```

More advanced queries use two different sets of arguments: one to control which packages are reported in the output, and one to control what is reported about the selected packages.

Table 5-1 describes the most commonly used options for selecting packages.

Table 5-1. RPM query options for package selection

Option	Description
`-a`	Selects all packages.
`-f file`	Selects the package that installed *file*.
`-g pkggroup`	Selects the packages that belong to *pkggroup* (such as *Applications/Productivity*).
`-p pkgfile`	Selects the *uninstalled* RPM package file *pkgfile*, which can be a local filename or an HTTP or FTP URI. Information is retrieved from the package file instead of from the RPM database.
`--triggeredby package`	Selects packages that have scripts that are triggered by the installation or removal of *package*. For example, a mail-client package may have a script that changes its configuration if the local mail server is changed from *sendmail* to *postfix*.
`--whatprovides capability`	Selects packages that provide a certain *capability*, such as the ability to run *perl* scripts.
`--whatrequires capability`	Selects packages that require a *capability*.
`packagename`	Selects a package with the given name.

For example, to find out which package installed the file */usr/lib/libcdda_interface.so*:

```
$ rpm -qf /usr/lib/libcdda_interface.so
cdparanoia-libs-alpha9.8-25
```

Or to find out which packages provide *smtpdaemon* (inbound mail server) capability:

```
$ rpm -q --whatprovides smtpdaemon
sendmail-8.13.4-2
postfix-2.2.2-2
```

Sometimes, though, you need more information than the name and version number of the packages selected. Table 5-2 lists the most common query output options.

Table 5-2. Query output options

Option	Description
--changelog	Shows the package changelog, a list of changes to the various versions of the package (not necessarily to various versions of the software).
-c	Shows the configuration files included in the package.
-d	Shows the documentation files included in the package.
-l	Lists files included in the package.
--filesbypkg	Same as -l, except that the package name is printed in front of each file; useful when multiple packages are selected.
-i	Provides detailed information about the package (package description, license, group, origin, and so forth).
--provides	Lists the capabilities provided by the package.
--requires	Lists the capabilities required to successfully use the package.
--scripts	Displays pre- and post-installation scripts, and pre- and post-uninstallation (removal) scripts.
--triggers	Displays the trigger scripts in the package. Trigger scripts are invoked when another, related package is installed or removed.

When output options and selection options are combined, *rpm* becomes a very powerful tool. For example, to see the description of the package that installed */etc/mail/access*:

```
$ rpm -qif /etc/mail/access
Name        : sendmail                   Relocations: (not relocatable)
Version     : 8.13.4                           Vendor: Red Hat, Inc.
Release     : 2                            Build Date: Fri 06 May 2005 08:35:13 AM
EDT
Install Date: Mon 29 Aug 2005 12:46:19 AM EDT      Build Host: decompose.build.
redhat.com
Group       : System Environment/Daemons   Source RPM: sendmail-8.13.4-2.src.rpm
Size        : 1332268                         License: Sendmail
Signature   : DSA/SHA1, Fri 20 May 2005 01:44:43 PM EDT, Key ID b44269d04f2a6fd2
Packager    : Red Hat, Inc. <http://bugzilla.redhat.com/bugzilla>
Summary     : A widely used Mail Transport Agent (MTA).
Description :
The Sendmail program is a very widely used Mail Transport Agent (MTA).
MTAs send mail from one machine to another. Sendmail is not a client
program, which you use to read your email. Sendmail is a
behind-the-scenes program which actually moves your email over
networks or the Internet to where you want it to go.

If you ever need to reconfigure Sendmail, you will also need to have
the sendmail.cf package installed. If you need documentation on
Sendmail, you can install the sendmail-doc package.
```

To see all of the files installed by the package that installed */usr/lib/libcdda_interface.so*:

```
$ rpm -qlf /usr/lib/libcdda_interface.so
/usr/lib/libcdda_interface.so
/usr/lib/libcdda_interface.so.0
/usr/lib/libcdda_interface.so.0.9.8
/usr/lib/libcdda_paranoia.so
/usr/lib/libcdda_paranoia.so.0
/usr/lib/libcdda_paranoia.so.0.9.8
```

Or to see those files along with the package name:

```
$ rpm -qf --filesbypkg /usr/lib/libcdda_interface.so
cdparanoia-libs          /usr/lib/libcdda_interface.so
cdparanoia-libs          /usr/lib/libcdda_interface.so.0
cdparanoia-libs          /usr/lib/libcdda_interface.so.0.9.8
cdparanoia-libs          /usr/lib/libcdda_paranoia.so
cdparanoia-libs          /usr/lib/libcdda_paranoia.so.0
cdparanoia-libs          /usr/lib/libcdda_paranoia.so.0.9.8
```

To see all of the other capabilities provided by the package that provides the capability *perl*:

```
$ rpm -q --whatprovides perl --provides
APItest.so
B.so
Base64.so
Byte.so
ByteLoader.so
...(Lines snipped)...
perl(warnings::register) = 1.00
re.so
scalar.so
shared.so
threads.so
via.so
perl = 3:5.8.6-15
```

To see the scripts that will be triggered by removing *sendmail*:

```
$ rpm -q --triggeredby sendmail --triggers
triggerpostun scriptlet (using /bin/sh) -- sendmail < 8.10.0
/sbin/chkconfig --add sendmail
triggerpostun scriptlet (using /bin/sh) -- sendmail < 8.11.6-11
/usr/sbin/alternatives --auto mta
```

To list the files in the *uninstalled* RPM package file *a52dec-0.7.4-4.fr.i386.rpm*:

```
$ rpm -qlp a52dec-0.7.4-4.fr.i386.rpm
/usr/bin/a52dec
/usr/bin/extract_a52
/usr/share/doc/a52dec-0.7.4
/usr/share/doc/a52dec-0.7.4/AUTHORS
/usr/share/doc/a52dec-0.7.4/COPYING
/usr/share/doc/a52dec-0.7.4/ChangeLog
/usr/share/doc/a52dec-0.7.4/NEWS
/usr/share/doc/a52dec-0.7.4/README
/usr/share/doc/a52dec-0.7.4/TODO
```

```
/usr/share/doc/a52dec-0.7.4/liba52.txt
/usr/share/man/man1/a52dec.1.gz
/usr/share/man/man1/extract_a52.1.gz
```

If that RPM were on a remote web server or FTP server, you could substitute the URI
for the filename:

```
$ rpm -qlp \
 ftp://ftp.ntua.gr/pub/video/videolan/testing/vlc-0.7.0-test1/rpm/rh9-fc1/rh9-fc1/
vlc/a52dec-0.7.4-4.fr.i386.rpm
/usr/bin/a52dec
/usr/bin/extract_a52
...(Lines snipped)...
```

How Does It Work?

RPM packages are compressed archives of files with metadata. The archive is in *cpio*
format, with *gzip* compression; the metadata is stored in a flexible, easily extensible
format for forward- and (limited) backward-compatibility.

When a package is installed, the metadata is copied to the RPM database. If this
were not done, it would be necessary to keep all of the original package files in storage to find out about installed packages, and queries would run very slowly because
hundreds of files would have to be individually opened and searched.

The RPM database is stored in several files in */var/lib/rpm*. These databases are in the
indexed DBM/GDBM format, which is also used for other configuration databases
such as */etc/aliases.db*; this indexed format permits high-speed searching.

What About...

...converting an RPM to a plain archive?

The *rpm2cpio* command will convert an RPM package to a *cpio* archive:

```
$ rpm2cpio gnome-applet-gvid-0.3-1.i386.rpm > gnome-applet.cpio
```

You can then use *cpio* to examine or install the archive. Note that *rpm2cpio* removes
the gzip compression on the archive contents, so the resulting file is larger than the
original RPM file. If you want to extract a specific file from the archive, you can use
the *cpio* command. However, this is not a good way to install the file, since none of
the scripts and other install-time actions will be performed:

```
$ rpm2cpio gnome-applet-gvid-0.3-1.i386.rpm | cpio -idv
```

...a damaged RPM database?

Use *rpm* with the --rebuilddb option to recover from most forms of database corruption (this can take a while to run). You will need to run it as *root*:

```
# rpm --rebuilddb
```

Where Can I Learn More?

- *Maximum RPM* (an online book about the RPM system—somewhat out of date but still useful), Chapter 5: *http://www.rpm.org/max-rpm-snapshot/*
- The RPM web site: *http://www.rpm.org*
- The manpages for *rpm* and *cpio*

5.2   Installing and Removing Software Using RPM

In addition to queries, *rpm* performs package installation, updating, and removal. As well as copying files to the correct locations (or deleting them), *rpm* checks file integrity, sets permissions, backs up configuration files, and executes scripts within the affected package and other packages that have asked to be notified of changes (trigger scripts). These scripts can in turn start or stop services, modify configuration files, or perform other operations.

How Do I Do That?

rpm provides four options for installing, upgrading, and removing software:

-i *package_file*
> Installs a package that is not currently installed.

-U *package_file*
> Upgrades an existing package version, or installs the package if it is not currently installed.

-F *package_file*
> Freshens an existing installation of the package by upgrading the version. If the package is not currently installed, it remains uninstalled.

-e *package*
> Erases the installed package. Unlike the other options, -e requires a package name (*httpd*), not a package filename (*httpd-2.0.54-10.i386.rpm*).

All of these operations must be performed as the *root* user (unlike queries, which may be performed by anyone). This prevents unwanted software, such as viruses and worms, from being installed in the normal course of activities.

To perform a basic installation of a package, use the -i option and supply the name of a package file:

```
# rpm -i httpd-2.0.54-10.i386.rpm
```

To upgrade the package:

```
# rpm -U httpd-2.0.62-3.i386.rpm
```

In this case, the upgrade would succeed even if *httpd* package weren't already present on the system; it would be installed.

To remove the package:

```
# rpm -e httpd
```

Note that in this case, only the package name is given, not a package filename.

No additional arguments are needed if the installation or removal does not affect any other packages, but frequently a package to be installed will depend on other packages:

```
# rpm -i ogle-0.9.2-1.1.fr.i386.rpm
error: Failed dependencies:
        libdvdread >= 0.9.4 is needed by ogle-0.9.2-1.1.fr.i386
        libdvdread.so.3 is needed by ogle-0.9.2-1.1.fr.i386
        libmad.so.0 is needed by ogle-0.9.2-1.1.fr.i386
```

Likewise, when removing a package, other packages can depend on that package:

```
# rpm -e httpd
error: Failed dependencies:
        httpd-mmn = 20020903 is needed by (installed) mod_auth_kerb-5.0-6.i386
        httpd-mmn = 20020903 is needed by (installed) mod_auth_mysql-2.6.1-4.i386
...(Lines snipped)...
        httpd = 2.0.54-10.2 is needed by (installed) mod_ssl-2.0.54-10.2.i386
        httpd is needed by (installed) squirrelmail-1.4.6-0.cvs20050812.1.fc4.noarch
```

The solution is to add or remove all of the needed packages at the same time (\ indicates that the line is continued):

```
# rpm -i a52dec-0.7.4-4.fr.i386.rpm libdvdcss-1.2.8-2.fr.i386.rpm \
    libdvdread-0.9.4-4.fr.i386.rpm libmad-0.15.0b-3.fr.i386.rpm       \
    ogle-0.9.2-1.1.fr.i386.rpm ogle_gui-0.9.2-1.1.fr.i386.rpm
```

However, each of the other package may have *other* dependencies, which is why repositories are so helpful (see Lab 5.3, "Using Repositories").

Table 5-3 outlines the most common options used when installing or upgrading packages.

Table 5-3. rpm options for installing and upgrading

Option	Description
--excludepath *directory*	Excludes files located in *directory*.
--excludedocs	Excludes documentation files. This will save some space and may be useful on a small system, particularly if another machine is available with the documentation installed.
--force	Enables *rpm* to overwrite files that are part of other packages, reinstall packages already installed, and downgrade instead of upgrade packages.
-v	Verbose; lists each package as it is processed.
-h	Displays hash marks (#) to show the progress of each operation.

Table 5-3. rpm options for installing and upgrading (continued)

Option	Description
--justdb	Updates the RPM database, but doesn't actually install any software.
--nodeps	Turns off checking for dependencies. Be careful using this option; the installed package will usually be unusable.
--noscripts	Prevents installation scripts in the package from running.
--notriggers	Prevents trigger scripts in other packages from running.
--oldpackage	Permits a downgrade instead of an upgrade.
--relocate *olddir=newdir*	Relocates files from one directory subtree to another. Useful if you want your binary files, datafiles, or documentation installed into an unusual location. Many Fedora packages are not relocatable.
--repackage	(Applies to update/freshen only). Repackages the files from the old version of the package so that the upgrade can be undone (rolled back). See Lab 5.4, "Rolling Back a Package Installation, Upgrade, or Removal."
--test	Checks for conflicts and potential problems, but does not make any actual changes to the system.

This command installs *httpd* (Apache) without documentation, using a verbose display with hash marks to show progress:

```
# rpm -ivh --excludedocs httpd-2.0.54-10.i386.rpm
Preparing...                ######################################### [100%]
   1:httpd                  ######################################### [100%]
```

If you later decide that you want the documentation files after all, you can't simply reinstall *httpd*:

```
# rpm -ivh httpd-2.0.54-10.i386.rpm
Preparing...                ######################################### [100%]
        package httpd-2.0.54-10 is already installed
```

But if you add the --force option, the reinstallation will be successful:

```
# rpm -ivh --force httpd-2.0.54-10.i386.rpm
Preparing...                ######################################### [100%]
   1:httpd                  ######################################### [100%]
```

The *httpd* package normally places the DocumentRoot (start of the HTML document tree) in */var/www*; to change this to */usr/share/html*, use the --relocate option:

```
# rpm -ivh --force --relocate /var/www=/usr/share/html/ httpd-2.0.54-10.i386.rpm
Preparing...                ######################################### [100%]
   1:httpd                  ######################################### [100%]
```

The change is recorded in the RPM database, so querying the database will show the actual, installed paths:

```
# rpm -ql httpd
/etc/httpd
/etc/httpd/conf
/etc/httpd/conf.d
/etc/httpd/conf.d/README
/etc/httpd/conf.d/welcome.conf
...(Many lines snipped)...
```

```
/usr/share/html/icons/world1.png
/usr/share/html/icons/world2.gif
/usr/share/html/icons/world2.png
```

 Relocating files does not change configuration files, scripts, or programs that expect files to be located in particular locations. In the *httpd* example just shown, the Apache configuration files (*/etc/httpd/conf/httpd.conf* plus module-specific files in */etc/httpd/conf.d/**) must be edited by hand to reflect the new document root.

The options for erasing software are a subset of the options for installing and upgrading; the most useful options are listed in Table 5-4.

Table 5-4. rpm package-removal (erase) options

Option	Description
--allmatches	Erases all packages matching the name given (useful if more than one version is installed).
--nodeps	Proceeds with the package removal even if doing so will break some dependencies for other packages.
--noscripts	Prevents removal scripts in the package from running.
--notriggers	Prevents trigger scripts in other packages from running.
--repackage	Repackages the files being removed so that the removal can be undone (rolled back). See Lab 5.4, "Rolling Back a Package Installation, Upgrade, or Removal."
--test	Checks for conflicts and potential problems, but does not make any actual changes to the system.

How Does It Work?

RPMs are named using the pattern:

name-version-packagerelease.arch.rpm

in which:

name
> The name of the software in the package.

version
> The software's version number.

packagerelease
> The package version number; if one version of the software has been packaged a few times (for example, with different file locations, scripts, triggers, or sample data), this number is incremented while the software version number is left unchanged.

arch
> The architecture for which the package is compiled (*i386*, *x86-64*, or *PPC*). For packages that are not compiled (such as Perl, PHP, or bash scripts) or packages that contain only data (such as a font set), noarch is used; for source packages, the architecture is set to src.

rpm goes through many steps when performing an installation or upgrade/freshen:

1. The viability of the operation requested is analyzed. *rpm* tests the available disk space, dependencies, installed packages, and package integrity to ensure that the operation can be successfully completed. If not, the user is informed and *rpm* aborts execution.

2. The RPM database is queried to see if any *installation* trigger scripts in other packages are triggered by the installation, and if so, they are executed.

3. The *preinstallation* script in the package is executed.

4. The package files are installed. Required directories are created, relocations are performed, and permissions and ownership are adjusted.

5. The *postinstallation* script in the package is executed.

6. If the operation being performed is not an upgrade or freshen, *rpm* exits because there isn't an older version of the package to uninstall.

7. The RPM database is queried to see if any *uninstallation* trigger scripts in other packages are triggered by the removal of the old package, and if so, they are executed.

8. The *pre-uninstallation* script in the package is executed.

9. If repackaging has been selected, the old package files and metadata are used to construct an RPM, which is placed in */var/spool/repackage*.

10. The obsolete files from the old package are deleted.

11. The *post-uninstallation* script in the package is executed.

12. The RPM database is queried to see if any *post-uninstallation* trigger scripts in other packages are triggered by the removal of the old package, and if so, they are executed.

13. The RPM database is updated to reflect what was done during the transaction.

There are four opportunities for scripts to run. This permits configuration files to be backed up before new packages are installed, services to be stopped before upgrading and restarted after, and configuration data to be copied from the old to the new package. There are also three opportunities for trigger scripts to run.

Each RPM operation is called a *transaction*. All of the packages processed in one operation are called a *transaction set*; this may include a large number of packages. For example, an update transaction could include dozens of packages processed at one time. In the RPM database, a *transaction set identifier* (TID) is used to tie together all of the packages processed in the same transaction set. The TID currently used is the time in seconds since the start of the 1970s (called a *utime*).

What About...

...installing multiple versions of a package?

It's possible, but it can create a lot of problems. The `--force` option is required, and it's probably best to relocate the second installation to avoid file conflicts:

```
# rpm -q httpd
httpd-2.0.54-10.2
# rpm -i --force httpd-2.0.54-10.i386.rpm \
  --relocate /=/var/compare/httpd-old
# rpm -q httpd
httpd-2.0.54-10.2
httpd-2.0.54-10
```

This will install the old version of *httpd* into */var/compare/httpd-old* so that you can compare that installation with the current one.

To remove the packages, you'll either need to specify the full package name including the software and package version numbers (e.g., *httpd-2.0.54-10* instead of *httpd*) to delete one specific version, or use the `--allmatches` option to remove all versions:

```
# rpm -e httpd
error: "httpd" specifies multiple packages
# rpm -e --allmatches httpd
```

Where Can I Learn More?

- *Maximum RPM*, Chapters 2, 3, and 4: *http://www.rpm.org/max-rpm-snapshot/* (somewhat out of date, but useful)
- The manpage for *rpm*

5.3   Using Repositories

RPM is a great package manager, but to really use packages efficiently, you'll need to use RPM along with a repository system so that your Fedora system can access remote libraries of software. Having access to the repository enables the automatic resolution of dependency issues, so that when you select a software package for installation, all required associated software is also installed automatically.

How Do I Do That?

Fedora uses the *yum* repository system. The *apt* system was used in earlier versions of Fedora and is still available, but most of the community's attention has shifted to *yum*, primarily because it supports multiple architectures—useful when running 32-bit software (such as a 32-bit browser, for compatibility with closed-source plug-ins) on a 64-bit system.

Using yum from the command line

Using *yum* to install software is easy; just specify the *install* command and the package name you want installed as an argument:

```
# yum install abe
Setting up Install Process
Setting up repositories
updates-released        100% |=========================|  951 B    00:00
extras                  100% |=========================|  1.1 kB   00:00
base                    100% |=========================|  1.1 kB   00:00
Reading repository metadata in from local files
primary.xml.gz          100% |=========================|  336 kB   00:01
updates-re: ################################################## 987/987
Added 24 new packages, deleted 43 old in 2.06 seconds
Parsing package install arguments
Resolving Dependencies
--> Populating transaction set with selected packages. Please wait.
---> Downloading header for abe to pack into transaction set.
abe-1.0-5.i386.rpm          100% |=========================|  5.1 kB   00:00
---> Package abe.i386 0:1.0-5 set to be updated
--> Running transaction check
--> Processing Dependency: libSDL_mixer-1.2.so.0 for package: abe
--> Restarting Dependency Resolution with new changes.
--> Populating transaction set with selected packages. Please wait.
---> Downloading header for SDL_mixer to pack into transaction set.
SDL_mixer-1.2.6-1.fc4.i38 100% |=========================|  6.9 kB   00:00
---> Package SDL_mixer.i386 0:1.2.6-1.fc4 set to be updated
--> Running transaction check

Dependencies Resolved

=============================================================================
 Package              Arch       Version          Repository       Size
=============================================================================
Installing:
 abe                  i386       1.0-5            extras           2.9 M
Installing for dependencies:
 SDL_mixer            i386       1.2.6-1.fc4      extras           84 k

Transaction Summary
=============================================================================
Install      2 Package(s)
Update       0 Package(s)
Remove       0 Package(s)
Total download size: 2.9 M
```

```
Is this ok [y/N]: y
Downloading Packages:
(1/2): SDL_mixer-1.2.6-1. 100% |=========================| 84 kB   00:03
(2/2): abe-1.0-5.i386.rpm 100% |=========================| 2.9 MB   02:16
Running Transaction Test
```

Notice that *yum* automatically determined that *SDL_mixer* was required, confirmed the installation of both packages with the user before installing, downloaded the software in RPM format, and then installed it.

From this output, you can also see that *yum* started off by updating its list of available packages in each repository and later downloaded the header files for each selected package. A header file contains a package's metadata but not the installation files and scripts (and is therefore much smaller); this lets *yum* determine dependencies and test for file conflicts without downloading the entire package.

To install a package file that is on the local computer (e.g., received in an email from a developer or on a CD) and still take advantage of the repositories to solve dependency problems, use *yum*'s *localinstall* command:

```
# yum localinstall /tmp/frodo-9.6.23-4-i386.rpm
```

Removing software is just as simple as installing it; use *yum*'s *remove* command:

```
# yum remove httpd
Setting up Remove Process
Resolving Dependencies
...(Lines snipped)...

Dependencies Resolved

===============================================================================
 Package              Arch      Version             Repository        Size
===============================================================================
Removing:
 httpd                i386      2.0.54-10.2         installed         2.5 M
Removing for dependencies:
 htdig-web            i386      3:3.2.0b6-5         installed         1.1 M
 httpd-devel          i386      2.0.54-10           installed         466 k
 httpd-devel          i386      2.0.54-10.2         installed         466 k
 httpd-manual         i386      2.0.54-10.2         installed         7.5 M
 ...(Lines snipped)...
 squirrelmail         noarch    1.4.6-0.cvs20050812.1.fc4  installed  8.1 M
 system-config-httpd  noarch    5:1.3.2-2           installed         1.6 M
 webalizer            i386      2.01_10-28          installed         244 k
 wordtrans-web        i386      1.1pre13-10         installed          31 k

Transaction Summary
===============================================================================
Install       0 Package(s)
Update        0 Package(s)
Remove       39 Package(s)
Total download size: 0
```

```
Is this ok [y/N]: n
Exiting on user Command
Complete!
```

Here, the removal of *httpd* would cause dependency failures for 38 other packages, so *yum* offered to remove all 39 packages together. In this case, the user elected not to proceed, so *yum* exited.

yum can also update software:

```
# yum update
Setting up Update Process
Setting up repositories
...(Lines snipped)...

Transaction Summary
===============================================================================
Install      5 Package(s)
Update      19 Package(s)
Remove       0 Package(s)
Total download size: 27 M
Is this ok [y/N]: y
Downloading Packages:
(1/24): bind-utils-9.3.1- 100% |=========================| 146 kB    00:00
(2/24): esound-0.2.36-0.f 100% |=========================| 127 kB    00:00
...(Lines snipped)...
Running Transaction Test
  Repackage : bind-utils                  ###################### [ 0/43]
  Repackage : esound                      ###################### [ 0/43]
...(Lines snipped)...
  Installing: GFS-kernel                  ###################### [22/43]
  Updating   : bind-libbind-devel         ###################### [23/43]
Installed: GFS-kernel.i686 0:2.6.11.8-20050601.152643.FC4.17 cman-kernel.i686
...(Lines snipped)...
pam.i386 0:0.79-9.6 pam-devel.i386 0:0.79-9.6 sudo.i386 0:1.6.8p8-2.3
Complete!
```

For each of the currently installed packages, *yum* checks to see if a newer version exists in any of the repositories and queues the update of those packages plus the installation of any packages required for dependency resolution. After confirming the package set with the user, the packages are downloaded and the update/installation is performed through the RPM system.

To update one specific package (and dependencies), list the package name as an argument:

```
# yum update kernel
```

yum also offers a number of information and miscellaneous options; the most useful are shown in Table 5-5. However, most of these operations are more easily performed using the graphical user interface (GUI).

Table 5-5. Information and miscellaneous commands for yum

Option	Description
`list`	Lists available packages.
`check-update`	Verifies whether any updates are available. An exit code of 100 indicates that updates are ready for installation.
`whatprovides` *capability* `provides` *capability*	Displays the name of any packages that provide the listed *capability*, which may be an RPM-style capability name or a filename.
`search` *keyword*	Searches for a package with *keyword* in the description, summary, packager name, or package name metadata. The search is case-insensitive.
`info` *package*	Displays metadata about *package* (similar to `rpm -qi`).
`deplist` *package*	Displays the dependencies of *package*, including the names of the packages that will resolve those dependencies.
`localinstall` *rpm_file* `localupdate` *rpm_file*	Installs or removes the package contained in the local *rpm_file* and, if necessary, resolves any dependencies using the repositories.
`-C`	Runs the specified command from cache (doesn't contact each repository to check for updates).

Using yum with a GUI

Fedora Core also provides graphical tools for using *yum*. When updates are available for any of the packages on your system, an update icon (which looks like a cardboard box) will appear in the upper GNOME panel. If you place your mouse cursor over this icon, a tool tip message will appear showing the number of available updates, as shown in the upper-right corner of Figure 5-1.

 The *yum-updatesd* service must be running to make the update icon appear.

To install the available updates, right-click on the update icon and select Apply Updates (or select Applications → System Tools → Software Updater, or enter the command *pup*). You will be prompted for the root password, and then the window shown in Figure 5-1 will appear; click "Apply updates" to install the updates listed.

Fedora Core also provides a tool for graphically installing and removing software, named *Pirut* (pronounced "pirate"). To start this program, select the menu option Applications → Add/Remove Software; you will be prompted for the *root* password. *Pirut* offers three main modes of operation, as shown in Figure 5-2; these modes are selected using the buttons on the left side of the window and permit you to search for a specific package (the top window in Figure 5-2), browse by package groups (middle window, along with the window that appears when you click on "Optional packages"), or scroll through a list of all packages (bottom window).

Figure 5-1. The package updater window and notification icon

If the browse-package-groups window looks familiar, you have a good memory. The same display is used for software package customization during installation.

Select the checkbox in front of the packages that you wish to install, and deselect the checkbox of the packages that you wish to uninstall; then click Apply. After confirmation, the selected actions will be performed.

Fedora Extras also provides the *Yumex* tool, which provides an alternate graphical frontend to *yum*.

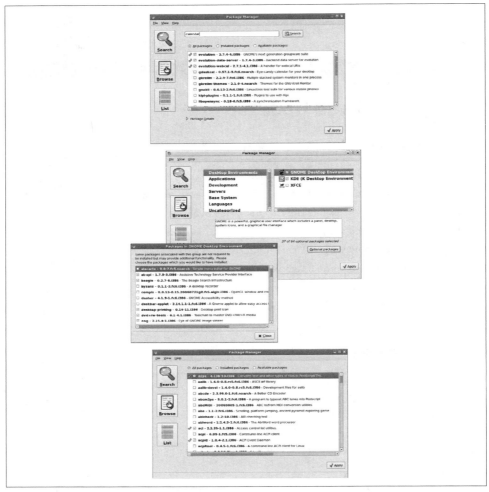

Figure 5-2. The three operating modes of Pirut, the Install/Remove Software tool

Adding repositories

Fedora Core ships with configuration files for the six repositories listed in Table 5-6. The three prerelease repositories are disabled by default, and the rest are enabled.

Table 5-6. Fedora Core repositories

Repository	Enabled by default	Description
base	Y	Fedora Core base packages (same as CD/DVD)
development	N	Prerelease Fedora Core packages (also known as "Rawhide")

Table 5-6. Fedora Core repositories (continued)

Repository	Enabled by default	Description
updates-released	Y	Updates to Fedora Core packages
updates-testing	N	Prerelease update packages
extras	Y	Add-on software for Fedora
extras-development	N	Prerelease add-on software

The repositories are configured by files in */etc/yum.repos.d*. Here is the content of the Fedora Extras file */etc/yum.repos.d/fedora-extras.repo*:

```
[updates-released]
name=Fedora Core $releasever - $basearch - Released Updates
#baseurl=http://download.fedora.redhat.com/pub/fedora/linux/core/updates/$releasever/
$basearch/
mirrorlist=http://fedora.redhat.com/download/mirrors/updates-released-fc$releasever
enabled=1
gpgcheck=1
gpgkey=file:///etc/pki/rpm-gpg/RPM-GPG-KEY-fedora
```

After the section identifier [updates-released], there are several name/value pairs, each on a separate line, joined with equal signs:

name

> The repository name as it will be shown to the user. The variables $releasevar and $basearch are replaced with the distribution release (6) and the system architecture (i386, x86_64, or ppc).

baseurl

> The master URL for the repository.

mirrorlist

> The URL of a text file listing all of the *mirrors* (alternate servers that are loaded from the master server) for the repository. It is better to use a mirrorlist than a baseurl entry to avoid overloading the master server and to provide multiple servers for redundancy.

enabled

> 1 to enable this repository, or 0 to ignore this repository.

gpgcheck

> 1 to enable GPG verification of the origin of the RPM packages served by the repository, or 0 to disable GPG verification. GPG verification tests the package integrity and ensures that the package has not been tampered with (which helps to guard against Trojans and viruses).

gpgkey

> URL of the GPG public key for GPG package verification. This is almost always a *file:///* URL (the key is on the local system).

There are a number of repositories available in addition to the ones preconfigured in Fedora. The maintainer of the Unofficial Fedora FAQ (*http://www.fedorafaq.org/*) also maintains a list of available repositories. You can install configuration files for these repositories with this command:

```
# rpm -Uvh http://www.fedorafaq.org/yum
```

Rerunning this command periodically will update the repository list.

Although this command installs the repository files, most of them are disabled by default. This is because some repositories are not compatible.

The two main add-on repositories groups used in conjunction with the base, updates, and extra repositories are the Livna (*http://rpm.livna.org*) repository, and the RPMforge repositories, a group of repositories that have agreed to work together for compatibility (*http://rpmforge.net*). There have been compatibility issues between these two, so repositories from only one of them should be enabled.

> The Livna repository is located outside of the United States and distributes packages that have license or patent issues that make them ineligible for inclusion in the Fedora or Fedora Extras repositories. This may include usage restrictions (such as personal use only) or U.S. patent encumbrances. Check the licenses *carefully* to ensure that you can legally use the software in your circumstances in your jurisdiction.

The FedoraFaq repository configuration files have *livna* enabled and the other repos disabled by default.

You can manually edit the files in */etc/yum.repos.d/* and change the lines that read:

```
enabled=0
```

to read:

```
enabled=1
```

How Does It Work?

RPM packages contain dependency information that indicates which capabilities are needed by the package and which capabilities are provided by the package. What they don't contain is information about which other packages provide or require those capabilities. Packages can't contain that information because the other packages—the ones that provide and require capabilities—change over time.

yum contains the logic to search repositories based on these capabilities. It can therefore resolve dependencies automatically.

There are three levels of information managed by *yum*: a list of packages available from the repositories, including capabilities provided by those packages; the headers for packages, which contain the metadata for those packages, including the capabilities required by those packages; and the packages themselves, which include both the metadata and the file archive. All of this information is stored in /var/cache/yum.

The first level of information, the list of available files, is updated automatically whenever *yum* (or one of the graphical tools) is started. The second level, headers, is retrieved when *yum* needs to determine dependencies. The actual packages are retrieved only after the decision to install or update the software has been confirmed.

The update icon is managed by the *puplet* monitor, which receives update information from the *yum-updatesd* services over the desktop communication bus (dbus).

What About...

...installing proprietary video drivers?

The Livna repository provides RPM-packaged versions of the ATI and NVIDIA drivers. For the ATI drivers, install *kmod-fglrx* (or *kmod-fglrx-smp* for a multiprocessor/multicore kernel); for the NVIDIA drivers, install *kmod-nvidia* (or *kmod-nvidia-smp*).

For example, to install the NVIDIA drivers on a single-core, single-processor system:

```
# yum install kmod-nvidia
```

Each vendor's video control tools will be installed into the application menus. During the installation, the appropriate changes will be made to the Drivers lines in the X server configuration file /etc/X11/xorg.conf, and those changes will automatically be undone if the proprietary drivers are removed.

 Each proprietary video driver requires a kernel module, so you may need to wait until a day or two after a new kernel is released before upgrading to that kernel.

...installing software to handle proprietary multimedia formats?

Software to play proprietary audio and video formats (such as MP3, WMA, and AVI) is available from the Livna repository. It is not included in Fedora Core because it does not meet the Fedora guidelines (either it is not open source, or it is patent-encumbered).

Once you have enabled the Livna repository, you can install a wide range of audio and video software and decoders (codecs) using the command:

```
# yum install '*mplayer*' '*xmms*' '*xine*'
```

…excluding packages from management by yum?

To exclude packages from *yum*, edit */etc/yum.conf* and add an exclude line. Here is an example (shown in bold); substitute globbing patterns (see Lab 4.3, "Managing Files") that match the packages you wish to exclude:

```
[main]
cachedir=/var/cache/yum
debuglevel=2
logfile=/var/log/yum.log
pkgpolicy=newest
distroverpkg=redhat-release
tolerant=1
exactarch=1
retries=20
obsoletes=1
gpgcheck=1
exclude=*kernel* *xorg*

# PUT YOUR REPOS HERE OR IN separate files named file.repo
# in /etc/yum.repos.d
```

Where Can I Learn More?

- The *yum* project page: *http://linux.duke.edu/projects/yum/*
- The manpages for *pup*, *puplet*, *pirut*, *yum-updatesd*, and *yum-updatesd.conf*
- The *yumex* project page: *http://linux.rasmil.dk/cms/modules/dokuwiki/doku. php?id=yumex:yumex*
- Repository pages for the RPMforge repositories (*http://rpmforge.net/*) and the Livna repository (*http://rpm.livna.org/*)
- Fedora project documentation on managing software with *yum*: *http://fedora. redhat.com/docs/yum/*

5.4   Rolling Back a Package Installation, Upgrade, or Removal

RPM has the ability to save datafiles before erasing them, permitting installations, updates, and removals to be undone through a *rollback* operation. Since it can take a substantial amount of space to save data necessary for a rollback, this feature is not enabled by default—but it's well worth sacrificing some disk space in most cases.

How Do I Do That?

In order to enable rollbacks, it is necessary to enable *repackaging* during the upgrading and removal of software. This can be enabled using command options, but the options have to be used consistently, and it's easy to forget them. Therefore the best approach is to configure both *rpm* and *yum* to use repackaging all the time.

To configure *rpm*, create the file */etc/rpm/macros* and place this line in it:

```
%_repackage_all_erasures 1
```

To configure *yum*, edit */etc/yum.conf* and add the tsflags (*transaction set flags*) line shown in bold here:

```
[main]
cachedir=/var/cache/yum
debuglevel=2
logfile=/var/log/yum.log
pkgpolicy=newest
distroverpkg=redhat-release
tolerant=1
exactarch=1
retries=20
obsoletes=1
gpgcheck=1
exclude=*xorg* *xfree* *XFree* *kernel*
tsflags=repackage

# PUT YOUR REPOS HERE OR IN separate files named file.repo
# in /etc/yum.repos.d
```

The tsflags line may appear anywhere after the [main] tag.

Once you have set this up, any package removal or upgrade (which is actually an installation and a removal performed together) will create a backup of the old data.

You can then roll back to a particular point in time by performing an upgrade with *rpm* and specifying the --rollback option with the time you wish to revert to:

```
# rpm -Uhv --rollback '10 minutes ago'
Rollback packages (+1/-0) to Sat Oct 29 15:23:40 2005 (0x4363cc3c):
Preparing...                ########################################### [100%]
   1:abe                    ########################################### [ 50%]
Cleaning up repackaged packages:
        Removing /var/spool/repackage/abe-1.0-5.i386.rpm:
```

Notice that the rollback installed one package and removed no packages (+1/-0), and that the rollback data was deleted after the rollback.

The format for --rollback values is quite flexible; most reasonable dates and times are interpreted correctly. Here are some examples:

```
# rpm -Uhv --rollback 'last Monday'
# rpm -Uhv --rollback '2 hours ago'
# rpm -Uhv --rollback '10 Jan 2007 16:30'
# rpm -Uhv --rollback 'march 17'
# rpm -Uhv --rollback '9:00 am'
# rpm -Uhv --rollback '4:30 pm last Monday'
# rpm -Uhv --rollback 'yesterday'
```

How Does It Work?

When repackaging is enabled and RPM package updates or removals are performed, the metadata for the package to be removed is combined with the current state of the package's files to create a new RPM package. This is different from the original package used to install the software because it reflects any changes that were made to the package's files. Configuration changes, deleted files, high scores, changes in sample data, and script modifications are all included in the repackaged file. This permits the package to be restored in exactly the same form as it was when it was removed.

However, files that were not in the archive portion of the original RPM package are neither repackaged nor erased—so if you install a package such as MySQL and create files with it (databases, in the case of MySQL), those files will *not* be removed when MySQL is removed, and they *won't* be restored if the package removal is rolled back.

Repackaged files are in standard RPM format, with two exceptions: the transaction ID (date and time of the transaction in seconds since the start of 1970) is recorded in the RPM, and the signatures and hashes are usually invalid because the repackaged files are different from the original files (at least the modification time of the files has changed, and in many cases the contents of one or more files, as well).

What About...

...rolling back a package installation?

Installing a package does not create a repackaged RPM because there are no files already on the system that need to be repackaged. However, the package installation is recorded in the RPM database, and that is enough information for *rpm* to roll back the transaction: it just erases the package.

...rolling back a rollback?

Sorry, there are just too many variables to roll back a rollback! To prevent confusion *rpm* deletes repackaged files once they have been used for rollback.

...seeing what will happen during a rollback, before I decide to do it?

rpm's --test option is very useful for this:

```
# rpm -Uhv --test --rollback "1 minute ago"
Rollback packages (+1/-0) to Sat Oct 29 22:47:27 2005 (0x4364343f):
Preparing...                ######################################### [100%]
Cleaning up repackaged packages:
        Removing /var/spool/repackage/abe-1.0-5.i386.rpm:
```

From the output, you can see that this rollback will result in one package being rein-stalled and no packages being removed (+1/-0). The package being reinstalled can be identified from the clean-up line: it's *abe*.

To proceed with the rollback, execute the command again without the `--test` option:

```
# rpm -Uhv --rollback "1 minute ago"
```

...the disk space used by the rollback files?

Repackaged files are stored in */var/spool/repackage*. The total amount of disk space used is displayed by this command:

```
# du -sh /var/spool/repackage
15M     /var/spool/repackage
```

If you are certain that you won't need to perform a rollback, you can delete these files to free up some disk space:

```
# rm -rf /var/spool/repackage
```

The repackage repository can grow to be fairly large. If you want to store it on another mounted disk, you can configure its directory by adding this line to */etc/rpm/macros*:

```
_repackage_dir     /bigdisk/repackage
```

This will use */bigdisk/repackage* for future repackaging.

However, I prefer to use a symbolic link (see Lab 4.3, "Managing Files"), so that when I look in the default location I'll know where the files have been moved:

```
# mv /var/spool/repackage /bigdisk/repackage
# ln -s /bigdisk/repackage /var/spool/repackage
# ls -la /var/spool/repackage
lrwxrwxrwx  1 root root 18 Oct 31 14:47 /var/spool/repackage -> /bigdisk/repackage
```

Where Can I Learn More?

- The manpage for *rpm* (which covers the `--repackage` option but not `--rollback`)
- The *Linux Journal* article "Transactions and Rollback with RPM": *http://www.linuxjournal.com/article/7034*
- The manpage for *cvs*; see the date format for `-D` for information on the date/time formats accepted by *rpm*'s `--rollback` option

5.5   Automating Updates

One of the main reasons that packages are updated is to correct newly discovered security vulnerabilities. It's important to keep a system up-to-date so that these security vulnerabilities are eliminated as soon as fixes are made available.

Automating system updates makes this easy. Fedora is configured to perform updates automatically; all you need to do is turn this feature on.

How Do I Do That?

Before turning on automatic updates, it's important to verify that *yum* is configured with the right options:

1. Repackaging should be enabled (see Lab 5.4, "Rolling Back a Package Installation, Upgrade, or Removal") so that you can recover from a bad update. Make sure you have plenty of disk space for the repackage repository!

2. Ensure that *yum* is enabled only for the repositories that you wish to automatically update (see Lab 5.3, "Using Repositories").

3. Exclude any packages that you do not wish to update automatically. In particular, think carefully about whether you want the kernel to be updated without your knowledge; such a change won't take effect until the next time the system boots, but changing the kernel can cause some software or services to fail until kernel modules are updated to match the new kernel.

Once you have *yum* configured the way you want, configure *yum-updatesd* to automatically apply updates. The configuration file */etc/yum-updatesd.conf* initially looks like this:

```
[main]
# how often to check for new updates (in seconds)
run_interval = 3600
# how often to allow checking on request (in seconds)
updaterefresh = 600

# how to send notifications (valid: dbus, email, syslog)
emit_via = dbus

# automatically install updates
do_update = no
# automatically download updates
do_download = no
# automatically download deps of updates
do_download_deps = no
```

Change the do_update line to enable the automatic installation of updates:

```
do_update = yes
```

Reload the *yum-updatesd* configuration to activate your changes, either though the services GUI tool or by entering this command:

```
# service yum-updatesd reload
Stopping yum-updatesd:                              [  OK  ]
Starting yum-updatesd:                              [  OK  ]
```

Don't change the emit_via option, or *puplet* will not work.

How Does It Work?

The *yum-updatesd* service polls your configured repositories at regular intervals to determine if updates are available for any of your installed packages. By altering the configuration file, you instruct *yum-updatesd* to install the updated packages that it finds (effectively performing a yum -y update at regular intervals).

What About...

...downloading but not installing updates?

By enabling the do_download and do_download_deps options, you can configure *yum-updatesd* to download available updates and related dependencies without installing them. This enables you to review the list of updates using *Pup* and then install selected updates without further download delay.

To set this up, configure */etc/yum/yum-updatesd.conf* with these options:

```
# automatically install updates
do_update = no
# automatically download updates
do_download = yes
# automatically download deps of updates
do_download_deps = yes
```

...updating a machine when it's booted?

The *yum-updateonboot* package can be used to update a machine whenever it is turned on. This ensures that security patches are automatically applied before the system is used. *yum-updateonboot* can be activated in addition to the automatic 4 a.m. update.

You can install and configure *yum-updateonboot* with these commands:

```
# yum install yum-updateonboot
Setting up Install Process
...(Lines snipped)...
====================================================================
 Package              Arch      Version         Repository    Size
====================================================================
Installing:
 yum-updateonboot     noarch    0.3.1-1.fc4     extras        5.1 k

Transaction Summary
====================================================================
Install      1 Package(s)
```

```
Update         0 Package(s)
Remove         0 Package(s)
Total download size: 5.1 k
Is this ok [y/N]: y
...(Lines snipped)...
Installed: yum-updateonboot.noarch 0:0.3.1-1.fc4
Complete!
# chkconfig --add yum-updateonboot
# chkconfig --level 2345 yum-updateonboot on
```

You can configure *yum-updateonboot* to reboot the system if any of the updates involve the kernel. Edit */etc/sysconfig/yum-updateonboot* and activate the line highlighted here by removing the pound sign (#) at the start of the line:

```
# IF any of these rpms are updated, the yum-updateonboot init script will
# reboot immediately after the yum update.  To keep yum-updateonboot from
# rebooting the system, comment this line out.
REBOOT_RPMS="kernel kernel-smp"

# A list of groups that should be updated at boot.  For each group mentioned
# yum-updateonboot will call 'yum -y groupupdate'  Since group names tend to
# have spaces in them, used a semi-colon to separate the group names
#GROUPLIST="My Group;MyOtherGroup;Some_Group;My Group 4"
```

Where Can I Learn More?

- The *yum* home page: *http://linux.duke.edu/projects/yum/*
- The *yum-updateonboot* README file: */usr/share/doc/yum-updateonboot-0.3.1/ README* (install *yum-updateonboot* first)

5.6   Installing From Source

Although there are thousands of packages available in RPM format ready to be installed on a Fedora system, there is a lot of open source software (*http://opensource.org*) that hasn't been packaged into RPMs. This software can be compiled and installed directly from the source files.

How Do I Do That?

Most open source software follows a certain set of conventions—one that the community has adopted as a de facto standard:

- The software is packaged in compressed tar format (*.tar.gz* or *.tgz*).
- A *configure* script is provided, which analyzes the system (by trying to compile many tiny programs and attempting to locate certain programs and files). After this analysis, a *Makefile* is produced.
- The *Makefile* contains the logic to build and to install the package.

- Basic documentation, including pointers and licensing information, is contained in files with uppercase names such as *README*, *INSTALL*, *TODO*, and *LICENSE*.

To install software distributed this way:

1. Obtain the compressed tar file (or *tarball*) containing the source. You can use a browser to find and download open source software from sites such as *http://sourceforge.net*.

2. Unpack the tarball:

```
$ tar xvzf xmorph_20040717.tar.gz
xmorph-current/
xmorph-current/Makefile.in
xmorph-current/gtkmorph/
xmorph-current/gtkmorph/ChangeLog
xmorph-current/gtkmorph/Makefile.in
xmorph-current/gtkmorph/README
xmorph-current/gtkmorph/Makefile.am
...(Lines snipped)...
```

If the file is compressed with *bzip2* (usually indicated by a filename that ends in *.tar.bz*, *.tar.bz2*, *.tbz*, *.tb2*, or *.tbz2*), use the j option instead of z to decompress:

```
$ tar xvjf xmorph_20040717.tar.bz2
```

> Most tarballs will unpack into their own directory, but some badly packaged ones may not, and unpacking them will leave dozens of files in your current directory. Use *tar*'s t option instead of the x to see the table of contents before unpacking:
>
> ```
> $ tar tvzf xmorph_20040717.tar.gz
> ```

3. Change to the new directory:

```
$ cd xmorph-current
```

4. Review the notes that are provided with the software (such as the *README* and *INSTALL* files).

5. If there is a script named *./configure*, run it:

```
$ ./configure
checking for a BSD-compatible install... /usr/bin/install -c
checking whether build environment is sane... yes
checking for gawk... gawk
...(Lines snipped)...
The Makefile will build morph.
The Makefile will build xmorph.
The Makefile will build gtkmorph.
configure: creating ./config.status
config.status: creating m4/Makefile
config.status: creating po/Makefile.in
config.status: creating Makefile
config.status: creating doc/Makefile
```

```
config.status: creating libmorph/Makefile
config.status: creating morph/Makefile
config.status: creating xmorph/Makefile
config.status: creating gtkmorph/Makefile
config.status: creating glade1/Makefile
config.status: creating glade2/Makefile
config.status: creating tkmorph/Makefile
config.status: creating plyview/Makefile
config.status: creating config.h
config.status: executing depfiles commands
config.status: executing default-1 commands
config.status: creating po/POTFILES
config.status: creating po/Makefile
```

6. Use *make* to build the software using the *Makefile*:

```
$ make
make  all-recursive
make[1]: Entering directory `/tmp/xmorph-current'
Making all in m4
...(Lines snipped)...
if /bin/sh ../libtool --mode=compile gcc -DHAVE_CONFIG_H -I. -I. -I.. \
  -g -O2 -Wall  -DREAL=double -DRGBA_MESH_WARP -g -O2 -Wall -MT \
  my_malloc.lo -MD -MP -MF ".deps/my_malloc.Tpo" \
  -c -o my_malloc.lo `test -f 'my_malloc.c' || echo './'`my_malloc.c; \
then mv -f ".deps/my_malloc.Tpo" ".deps/my_malloc.Plo"; \
else rm -f ".deps/my_malloc.Tpo"; exit 1; \
fi
...(Lines snipped)...
make[2]: Leaving directory `/tmp/xmorph-current'
make[1]: Leaving directory `/tmp/xmorph-current'
```

 If you have a multiprocessor or multicore system, use make -j3, assuming it's not also a multiuser machine and you don't mind two cores/CPUs being utilized at 100 percent.

7. If *make* was successful, use make install to install the software:

```
# make install
Making install in m4
make[1]: Entering directory `/tmp/xmorph-current/m4'
make[2]: Entering directory `/tmp/xmorph-current/m4'
...(Lines snipped)...
mkdir -p -- /usr/local/share/xmorph/pixmaps
cd example; for i in * ;\
        do /usr/bin/install -c -d /usr/local/share/xmorph/example/$i ;\
        for j in $i/* ;\
        do  /usr/bin/install -c -m 644 $j \
           /usr/local/share/xmorph/example/$i; done;\
done
make[2]: Leaving directory `/tmp/xmorph-current'
make[1]: Leaving directory `/tmp/xmorph-current'
```

At this point, the software should be ready to use.

How Does It Work?

A *tarball* is an archive of files created by *tar* (the *tape archiving* program) and usually compressed using *gzip*. By convention, source code tarballs are named *<package-version>.tgz* and all of the files extract into a directory named *<package-version>*; for example, *fen-10.4.tgz* would extract into the directory *./fen-10.4/*.

Since the 1980s, source packages have often contained a script named *configure*; most recent open source projects use versions of this script generated by a tool called GNU *autoconf*. The *configure* script adapts the compilation process for various systems; for example, some Unix systems have multiple C compilers installed, or different versions of libraries such as *malloc*, so *configure* determines what is available and the compiler options that will be needed to compile the software on the current system.

The output of *configure* usually includes one or more *Makefiles* and sometimes a C header file. The *Makefiles* contain the commands necessary to build the software, as well as dependency information; *make* uses this file to perform the least amount of work necessary to build the required output files. Another section of the *Makefile* contains the commands necessary to install the software—performing operations such as copying files and creating directories—and this section is used when the make install command is executed.

The disadvantage of installing software from source is that you lose the benefits of the RPM database. It can be hard to uninstall the software, and you have no record of which version was installed, when it was installed, what dependencies it requires or satisfies, and which files are associated with it. Any updates must be performed manually, and any conflicts that other updates may cause will not be known in advance.

What About...

...packages that are not written in a compiled language?

These packages may still need processing. For example, the manpages may be in a raw format that needs preprocessing, and scripts may need to be adjusted according to where the language interpreter is installed. In most cases, these packages will have a *Makefile*, just like a compiled package.

...packages that don't have a configure script?

The *Makefile* may be sufficiently simple or generic that it will work on a wide range of systems, or you may need to adjust it manually. Look for a file named *INSTALL* or *README* for information on the steps you need to perform to compile and install the software.

Where Can I Learn More?

- The manpages and info pages for *autoconf* and *make*

5.7 Making Your Own RPM Packages

While it's fairly easy to install software from source, it's not much more work to build an RPM package, especially if the original source code is well-written and in a traditional tarball. The extra work will make it much easier to track, update, and remove the software installed on your system.

How Do I Do That?

In order to build an RPM, you need to have the original source tarball plus a *spec file*, which provides most of the metadata for the RPM package and controls how the RPM is built—but before you build any packages, you should customize your RPM environment.

Preparing to build RPMs

RPMs are digitally signed by the packager. Although this is an optional step, it indicates that the package is from a trusted source and provides a way of verifying that no one has tampered with it.

RPM signatures are generated using GNU Privacy Guard (*gpg* or *gnupg*), which can also be used to sign or encrypt email messages. If you have not created a *gpg* key, this is a great time to do so:

```
$ gpg --gen-key
gpg (GnuPG) 1.4.1; Copyright (C) 2005 Free Software Foundation, Inc.
This program comes with ABSOLUTELY NO WARRANTY.
This is free software, and you are welcome to redistribute it
under certain conditions. See the file COPYING for details.

gpg: directory `/home/chris/.gnupg' created
gpg: new configuration file `/home/chris/.gnupg/gpg.conf' created
gpg: WARNING: options in `/home/chris/.gnupg/gpg.conf' are not yet
  active during this run
gpg: keyring `/home/chris/.gnupg/secring.gpg' created
gpg: keyring `/home/chris/.gnupg/pubring.gpg' created
Please select what kind of key you want:
   (1) DSA and Elgamal (default)
   (2) DSA (sign only)
   (5) RSA (sign only)
Your selection? 1
DSA keypair will have 1024 bits.
ELG-E keys may be between 1024 and 4096 bits long.
What keysize do you want? (2048)
Requested keysize is 2048 bits
```

```
Please specify how long the key should be valid.
        0 = key does not expire
     <n>  = key expires in n days
     <n>w = key expires in n weeks
     <n>m = key expires in n months
     <n>y = key expires in n years
Key is valid for? (0) 0
Key does not expire at all
Is this correct? (y/N) y

You need a user ID to identify your key; the software constructs the user ID
from the Real Name, Comment and Email Address in this form:
    "Heinrich Heine (Der Dichter) <heinrichh@duesseldorf.de>"

Real name: Chris Tyler
Email address: <chris@fedorabook.com>
Comment: ENTER
You selected this USER-ID:
    "Chris Tyler <chris@fedorabook.com>"

Change (N)ame, (C)omment, (E)mail or (O)kay/(Q)uit? O
You need a Passphrase to protect your secret key.

Enter passphrase: seeecret
Repeat passphrase: seeecret

We need to generate a lot of random bytes. It is a good idea to perform
some other action (type on the keyboard, move the mouse, utilize the
disks) during the prime generation; this gives the random number
generator a better chance to gain enough entropy.
++++++++++++++++++++++++++++++++++++++++++++++++++.+++++++++++++++++++++++++++.+++
+++++++.+++++++++++++++.+++++++++++++++++++++++++++>++++++++++...............
..........................<+++++...>+++++.......................<.+++++.
++....+++++
We need to generate a lot of random bytes. It is a good idea to perform
some other action (type on the keyboard, move the mouse, utilize the
disks) during the prime generation; this gives the random number
generator a better chance to gain enough entropy.
++++++++++++++++++++++++++++.+++++..+++++++++++++++..++++++++++.+++++.++++++++
+++++++++++++..+++++.+++++++++++++++.++++++++++..+++++++++++++++...+++++.+++
.+++++>.+++++...............+++++^^^^
gpg: /home/chris/.gnupg/trustdb.gpg: trustdb created
gpg: key B2B16060 marked as ultimately trusted
public and secret key created and signed.

gpg: checking the trustdb
gpg: 3 marginal(s) needed, 1 complete(s) needed, PGP trust model
gpg: depth: 0 valid:   1 signed:   0 trust: 0-, 0q, 0n, 0m, 0f, 1u
pub   1024D/B2B16060 2005-11-07
      Key fingerprint = 6283 3FDE 833B D21A 209A  75D2 369E E05E B2B1 6060
uid                  Chris Tyler <chris@fedorabook.com>
sub   2048g/2931B80E 2005-11-07
```

Your *gpg* keys will be created and stored in *~/.gnupg*: the private key in *~/.gnupg/secring.gpg*, and the public key in *~/.gnupg/pubring.gpg*.

The second step in setting up your RPM environment is to create an *~/.rpmmacros* file. This file contains your personal information and controls where RPMs will be built.

Here is a version of the *~/.rpmmacros* file that is fully automatic; it will discover all of the information it needs from your account configuration and *gpg* setup. Type it into a text editor such as *vi* and save it as *.rpmmacros* in your home directory:

```
#
# ~/.rpmmacros file
#
# This gets all necessary information from environment variables and
# system utilities. The first e-mail address on your gnupg keyring
# should be your own.
#

%packager               %(finger -l $LOGNAME|sed -n "s/.*Name: //p")
%distribution           Fedora Core %(tr -dc [0-9] </etc/fedora-release)

# The vendor here is the same as the packager. Use a company or
# organization if appropriate.
%vendor                 %{packager}

%_home                  %(echo $HOME)
%_topdir                %{_home}/rpm
%_tmppath               %{_topdir}/tmp
%_builddir              %{_tmppath}

%_rpmtopdir             %{_topdir}/%{name}
%_sourcedir             %{_rpmtopdir}
%_specdir               %{_rpmtopdir}
%_rpmdir                %{_topdir}/RPMS
%_srcrpmdir             %{_topdir}/RPMS
%_rpmfilename           %%{NAME}-%%{VERSION}-%%{RELEASE}.%%{ARCH}.rpm

%_signature             gpg
%_gpg_path              %{_home}/.gnupg
%_gpgbin                /usr/bin/gpg
%_gpg_name              %(gpg --list-keys|sed -n "s/^uid *//p"|head -1)
```

You can also create this file by manually filling in the values you wish to use:

```
#
# ~/.rpmmacros file
#
# This gets all necessary information from environment variables and
# system utilities. The first e-mail address on your gnupg keyring
# should be your own.
#

%packager               Chris Tyler
```

```
%distribution            Fedora Core 6

# Use an organization or company in the next line if applicable
%vendor                  Chris Tyler

%_home                   /home/chris
%_topdir                 /home/chris/rpm
%_tmppath                /home/chris/rpm/tmp
%_builddir               /home/chris/rpm/tmp

%_rpmtopdir              /home/chris/rpm/%{name}
%_sourcedir              %{_rpmtopdir}
%_specdir                %{_rpmtopdir}
%_rpmdir                 /home/chris/rpm/RPMS
%_srcrpmdir              /home/chris/rpm/RPMS
%_rpmfilename            %%{NAME}-%%{VERSION}-%%{RELEASE}.%%{ARCH}.rpm

%_signature              gpg
%_gpg_path               /home/chris/.gnupg
%_gpgbin                 /usr/bin/gpg
%_gpg_name               Chris Tyler <chris@fedorabook.com>
```

To test that this file has been saved in the correct location and is being correctly interpreted by *rpm*, execute rpm --eval followed by the name of one of the macros:

```
$ rpm --eval "%_gpg_name"
Chris Tyler <chris@fedorabook.com>
$ rpm --eval "%_srcrpmdir"
/home/chris/rpm/RPMS
```

Both versions of this file use the directory *~/rpm* to hold packages being built. Within this directory, there will be:

- A directory for each package being built, named after that package.
- A directory named *tmp*, for temporary files created during the building process.
- A directory named *RPMS*, to hold the final RPM packages.

You'll need to create these directories:

```
$ mkdir -p ~/rpm/RPMS ~/rpm/tmp
```

 The *fedora-rpmdevtools* package provides the *fedora-buildrpmtree* command, which prepares a suitable directory structure within your home directory and creates a very basic *.rpmmacros* file. If you use this command, your RPMs will be built within the directory *~/rpmbuild*.

Creating a spec file

The RPM building process is controlled by a *spec file*. Creating a good spec file is both a science and an art.

To start, create a new directory within *~/rpm* to hold your source tarball and the spec file. In this example, I'm going to package up the game Critical Mass (also called *critter*), available from *http://sourceforge.net/projects/criticalmass*. I'll name the directory after the package:

```
$ mkdir ~/rpm/CriticalMass
```

I'll place the source tarball *CriticalMass-1.0.0.tar.bz2* in this directory. The spec file will also be named after the package: *CriticalMass.spec*.

The first part of any spec file is called the *preamble* and contains the fields, or *tags*, outlined in Table 5-7. Each tag is placed on a line by itself, followed by a colon and the value for that tag.

Table 5-7. Basic preamble tags in a spec file

Tag	Description
Name	Name of the package.
Version	Version of the software in the package (software version).
Release	Release number of the package (package version).
Group	The application group to which the software belongs. See */usr/share/doc/rpm-4.4.2/GROUPS* for a list of possible values.
URL	The software's home page on the Web.
License	The license used for the software (such as GPL or Mozilla).
Summary	A one-line summary of the package description.
Requires	Capabilities needed by the software in order to be successfully installed. Many requirements are automatically determined, so this line is often not needed. Also include in this tag any special capabilities required by install and uninstall scripts (or triggers). If a package name is given as an argument, a version number can be provided, and a comparison can be given (such as gcc >= 4.0 or sendmail =8.13.4).
BuildRequires	Capabilities needed by the software in order to be successfully built, but not needed simply to install the RPM. For example, the *gcc* C compiler may be required to build the RPM package, but not to install it once it has been built.
Provides	Capabilities provided by the package. Like Requires, most of the Provides will be determined automatically.
BuildRoot	Specifies where the package should be installed during the package-building process. Many packages use %{_tmppath}/%{name}-root, which will create a package-specific directory within *~/rpm/tmp*. It is strongly recommended that you do not use /.

This is the initial information for the Critical Mass spec file:

```
Name:          CriticalMass
Version:       1.0.0
Release:       1

Group:         Amusements/Games
Summary:       An arcade-style shoot-em-up game.
License:       GPL
```

```
Source0:        CriticalMass-1.0.0.tar.bz2

URL:            http://sourceforge.net/projects/criticalmass
BuildRoot:      %{_tmppath}/%{name}-root
```

One more tag must be defined—%description—but this tag does not take the *name: value* form. Instead, a description of the package follows on the lines after the tag:

```
%description
CriticalMass is an old-style arcade-style shoot-em-up game with
modern graphics and sound.
```

The description text will be automatically wrapped and formatted to fit available space when it is displayed. To include preformatted text, leave a space at the start of each preformatted line.

After this initial information are seven sections, each identified by a section name:

%prep

> Commands used to prepare the package for building.

%build

> Commands used to build the package from the source (such as *make*).

%install

> Commands to install the software (such as make install).

%check

> Commands to test whether the software built correctly (make test). Optional; many packages do not include this section.

%clean

> Commands to remove temporary files after a build.

%files

> A list of the files that are to be included in the package.

%changelog

> A history of package versions.

The %prep section might include all of the commands that would normally be used to prepare the package:

```
%prep
tar xvjf CriticalMass-1.0.0.tar.bz2
cd CriticalMass-1.0.0
```

However, since most open source packages use some simple variation of the same steps, Fedora's standard RPM setup includes a macro script to do this work for you. It's named %setup; to use it, specify it as the only step in the %prep section of the spec file:

```
%prep
%setup
```

Similarly, the %build stage can use the predefined %configure macro to run *./configure* before *make* is run:

```
%build
%configure
make %{_smp_mflags}
```

The %{_smp_mflags} macro, used as an argument to *make*, will contain the options required to configure the build process for a symmetric multiprocessor system with multiple CPUs *if* the package is being built on an SMP system. (For many applications, this will make no difference).

The %install section installs the files—not into the final destination directories, but into the appropriate directories under the BuildRoot. In this case, since we've defined the BuildRoot as *~rpm/tmp/CriticalMass-root/*, files that would normally be installed into */usr/bin* will be installed into *~rpm/tmp/CriticalMass-root/usr/bin*.

There are two advantages to placing the files into the BuildRoot instead of the final file location: the Fedora system you're using won't get messed up, and since the only files that should be in the BuildRoot are those installed by this package, you can check to see that you can account for all of them.

The %install section often consists of an *rm* command to clear out the BuildRoot, followed by the %makeinstall macro to run make install with the appropriate options to install into BuildRoot instead of the root directory (most, but not all, modern open source packages will respect these options). The whole %install section looks like this:

```
%install
rm -rf %{buildroot}
%makeinstall
```

If you leave out the %check section (which is optional), the next section is %clean—commands to clean up the BuildRoot. This is usually the same *rm* command that was used in the %install section:

```
%clean
rm -rf %{buildroot}
```

At this point, the whole spec file looks like this:

```
Name:        CriticalMass
Version:     1.0.0
Release:     1

Group:       Amusements/Games
Summary:     An arcade-style shoot-em-up game.
License:     GPL

Source0:     CriticalMass-1.0.0.tar.bz2

URL:         http://sourceforge.net/projects/criticalmass
BuildRoot:   %{_tmppath}/%{name}-root
```

```
%description
CriticalMass is an old-style arcade-style shoot-em-up game with
modern graphics and sound.

%prep
%setup

%build
%configure
make %{_smp_mflags}

%install
rm -rf %{buildroot}
%makeinstall

%clean
rm -rf %{buildroot}
```

This file is saved in *~/rpm/CriticalMass/CriticalMass.spec*. Note that the %prep, %build, %install, and %clean sections are pretty generic and could be used with many different packages.

The next section required is a list of files to be included in the package. The easy way to prepare this list is to have *rpmbuild*—the RPM package-building tool—build the package and install it into the BuildRoot, and then see what's there:

```
$ cd ~/rpm/CriticalMass
$ ls
CriticalMass-1.0.0.tar.bz2  CriticalMass.spec
$ rpmbuild -bi CriticalMass.spec
Executing(%prep): /bin/sh -e /home/chris/rpm/tmp/rpm-tmp.54511
+ umask 022
+ cd /home/chris/rpm/tmp
+ LANG=C
...(Lines snipped)...
Checking for unpackaged file(s): /usr/lib/rpm/check-files /home/chris/rpm/tmp/
CriticalMass-root
error: Installed (but unpackaged) file(s) found:
    /usr/bin/Packer
    /usr/bin/critter
    /usr/share/Critical_Mass/lg-criti.xm
    /usr/share/Critical_Mass/resource.dat
    /usr/share/man/man6/critter.6.gz


RPM build errors:
    Installed (but unpackaged) file(s) found:
    /usr/bin/Packer
    /usr/bin/critter
    /usr/share/Critical_Mass/lg-criti.xm
    /usr/share/Critical_Mass/resource.dat
    /usr/share/man/man6/critter.6.gz
```

If your build fails because you need additional software, you must find that software and add it to a BuildRequires line in the spec file.

The -bi argument to *rpmbuild* instructs it to build up to the end of the %install stage. You can see that *rpmbuild* has detected files in BuildRoot that are not included in the package. To see the actual contents of the BuildRoot, you can change to the ~/*rpm*/*CriticalMass* directory and look around:

```
$ cd ~/rpm/tmp/CriticalMass-root
$ find
.
./usr
./usr/bin
./usr/bin/Packer
./usr/bin/critter
./usr/lib
./usr/lib/debug
./usr/lib/debug/usr
./usr/lib/debug/usr/bin
./usr/lib/debug/usr/bin/critter.debug
./usr/lib/debug/usr/bin/Packer.debug
./usr/share
./usr/share/man
./usr/share/man/man6
./usr/share/man/man6/critter.6.gz
./usr/share/Critical_Mass
./usr/share/Critical_Mass/resource.dat
./usr/share/Critical_Mass/lg-criti.xm
./usr/src
./usr/src/debug
```

The *find* command recursively lists all of the files found in the current directory.

From this list of files, you can build the %files section of the spec file. You can safely ignore the files in */usr/lib/debug* and */usr/src* since the RPM system will package these up into a separate debug RPM package automatically.

Among these files, there are some binaries:

```
./usr/bin/Packer
./usr/bin/critter
```

There is also a manpage:

```
./usr/share/man/man6/critter.6.gz
```

plus a data directory and some datafiles:

```
./usr/share/Critical_Mass
./usr/share/Critical_Mass/resource.dat
./usr/share/Critical_Mass/lg-criti.xm
```

The */usr/share/CriticalMass* directory belongs to the package and should be removed when the package is removed. To configure this, you must list only the directory in the %files section of the spec file; the contents of the directory will automatically be included.

Other directories, such as */usr/bin* and */usr/share/man/man6*, also contain files belonging to other packages, so those directories *must not* be included in the %files list; only the individual files in those directories should be included.

Because the RPM package is being built by a regular user—you or me—and our accounts may not exist on the target machine, you must reassign the ownership (and possibly the permissions) of the files using the %defattr directive. %defattr accepts four arguments: the default permission for files, the owner, the group, and the default permission for directories. Use a hyphen for permissions to signify that the existing file permissions should be left untouched:

```
%defattr(-, root, root, -)
```

To set specific attributes for a specific file, use %attr with three arguments (permission, user, group):

```
%defattr(0511, root, nogroup) foofile
```

In addition to files in the BuildRoot, you should also identify files in the top-level directory of the tarball that should be included in the file as documentation; this is done using the %doc directive. When the package is installed, these files will be placed in */usr/share/doc/<packagename-version>*. Good candidates for documentation files include *README, TODO, BUGS, INSTALL, COPYING*, and any other notes the program author has provided. In the case of the CriticalMass software, only the files *COPYING* and *TODO* fit into this category:

```
%doc COPYING TODO
```

In a similar way, the %config directive specifies configuration files that are included in the RPM:

```
%config /etc/master.conf
%config(noreplace) /etc/master.conf
```

When an RPM update is performed, a file marked as %config is replaced with the new version, but the old version is saved as *<filename>.rpmsave*. Files marked as %config(noreplace) are not replaced; the new version of the config file is instead installed as *<filename>.rpmnew*.

> In the case of CriticalMass, there are no configuration files installed by the RPM.

The whole %files section looks like this:

```
%files
%doc COPYING TODO
```

```
./usr/bin/Packer
./usr/bin/critter
./usr/share/man/man6/critter.6.gz
./usr/share/Critical_Mass
```

You can simplify this a bit by using ambiguous pathnames and macros:

```
%files
%doc COPYING TODO
%{_bindir}/*
%{_datadir}/Critical_Mass
%{_mandir}/man?/*
```

Finally, the %changelog section contains entries describing the changes that have been made to the RPM spec file (and, if desired, to the underlying software as well). The entries are placed in reverse chronological order—newest first—and each entry takes the form:

```
* WWW MMM DD YYYY email version
- point form note
- another point
```

with the meaning:

WWW MMM DD YYYY

The date, such as *Sat Jan 1 2006*.

email

The name and email address of the person who made the change, such as *Chris Tyler <chris@fedorabook.com>*

version

The version number in which the change was made (optional).

For example:

```
%changelog
* Mon Nov 7 2005 Chris Tyler <chris@fedorabook.com> 1.0.0-2
- Improved summary

* Sat Nov 5 2005 Chris Tyler <chris@fedorabook.com>
- Initial RPM package.
```

Putting all of this together, the final spec file looks like this (note that I've incremented the release number to be consistent with the information in the %changelog section):

```
Name:       CriticalMass
Version:    1.0.0
Release:    2

Group:      Amusements/Games
Summary:    An arcade-style shoot-em-up game.
License:    GPL

Source0:    CriticalMass-1.0.0.tar.bz2
```

```
URL:          http://sourceforge.net/projects/criticalmass
BuildRoot:    %{_tmppath}/%{name}-root

%description
CriticalMass is an old-style arcade-style shoot-em-up game with
modern graphics and sound.

%prep
%setup -q

%build
%configure
make %{_smp_mflags}

%install
rm -rf %{buildroot}
%makeinstall

%clean
rm -rf %{buildroot}

%files
%defattr(-, root, root)
%doc COPYING TODO

%{_bindir}/*
%{_datadir}/Critical_Mass
%{_mandir}/man?/*

%changelog
* Mon Nov 7 2005 Chris Tyler <chris@fedorabook.com> 1.0.0-2
- Improved summary

* Sat Nov 5 2005 Chris Tyler <chris@fedorabook.com>
- Initial RPM package.
```

To build the final RPM package, use *buildrpm* with the -ba option (build all):

```
$ cd ~/rpm/CriticalMass
$ rpmbuild -ba CriticalMass.spec
Executing(%prep): /bin/sh -e /home/chris/rpm/tmp/rpm-tmp.61308
+ umask 022
+ cd /home/chris/rpm/tmp
+ LANG=C
+ export LANG
...(Lines snipped)...
Checking for unpackaged file(s): /usr/lib/rpm/check-files /home/chris/rpm/tmp/
CriticalMass-root
Wrote: /home/chris/rpm/RPMS/CriticalMass-1.0.0-2.src.rpm
Wrote: /home/chris/rpm/RPMS/CriticalMass-1.0.0-2.i386.rpm
Wrote: /home/chris/rpm/RPMS/CriticalMass-debuginfo-1.0.0-2.i386.rpm
Executing(%clean): /bin/sh -e /home/chris/rpm/tmp/rpm-tmp.76425
+ umask 022
+ cd /home/chris/rpm/tmp
```

```
+ cd CriticalMass-1.0.0
+ rm -rf /home/chris/rpm/tmp/CriticalMass-root
+ exit 0
```

You'll find that *rpmbuild* created three RPM packages and placed them in *~/rpm/RPMS/*:

CriticalMass-1.0.0-2.i386.rpm
> The binary RPM, ready to be installed and used.

CriticalMass-debuginfo-1.0.0-2.i386.rpm
> Debugging info (from the */usr/lib/debug* directory mentioned earlier). This package is rarely used, except by developers.

CriticalMass-1.0.0-2.src.rpm
> A source RPM, which contains the source tarball and spec file. You can use this source RPM to easily generate a new binary RPM for a different type of system (see Lab 5.8, "Rebuilding an RPM Package for a Different Architecture").

The binary RPM—the most useful package, if you just want to play the game—can be installed like any other RPM package:

```
# rpm -i CriticalMass-1.0.0-2.i386.rpm
```

You can also query it like any other package:

```
# rpm -qi CriticalMass
Name        : CriticalMass            Relocations: (not relocatable)
Version     : 1.0.0                         Vendor: Chris Tyler
Release     : 2                         Build Date: Mon 07 Nov 2005 11:59:11 PM
EST
Install Date: Tue 08 Nov 2005 12:07:00 AM EST       Build Host:bluesky.fedorabook.com
Group       : Amusements/Games          Source RPM: CriticalMass-1.0.0-2.src.rpm
Size        : 4474014                      License: GPL
Signature   : (none)
Packager    : Chris Tyler
URL         : http://sourceforge.net/projects/criticalmass
Summary     : An arcade-style shoot-em-up game.
Description :
CriticalMass is an old-style arcade-style shoot-em-up game with
modern graphics and sound.
# rpm -ql CriticalMass
/usr/bin/Packer
/usr/bin/critter
/usr/share/Critical_Mass
/usr/share/Critical_Mass/lg-criti.xm
/usr/share/Critical_Mass/resource.dat
/usr/share/doc/CriticalMass-1.0.0
/usr/share/doc/CriticalMass-1.0.0/COPYING
/usr/share/doc/CriticalMass-1.0.0/TODO
/usr/share/man/man6/critter.6.gz
```

And, of course, you can remove it easily:

```
# rpm -e CriticalMass
```

When you are certain that your RPM package is in good shape, you can digitally sign it:

```
$ rpm --addsign CriticalMass-1.0.0-2.i386.rpm
Enter pass phrase: seeecret
Pass phrase is good.
CriticalMass-1.0.0-2.i386.rpm:
```

How Does It Work?

The default macro definitions for the RPM system are merged from several files when either *rpm* or *rpmbuild* starts:

/usr/lib/rpm/macros
> Standard definitions distributed with the RPM software.

/etc/rpm/macros
> Site-specific macros. Definitions that are local to your system and that should apply to all users should be placed here.

~/.rpmmacros
> Per-user configuration information.

rpmbuild uses the spec file to create a script. This script contains an expansion of all of the macros (such as %configure and %makeinstall) used in the spec file and is executed to prepare the RPM for packaging. (If *rpmbuild* is aborted or encounters a serious error, you will find the script in *~/rpm/tmp/*). This script, in turn, references scripts found in */usr/lib/rpm* to perform some of the processing involved in building a package.

When packages are built by the *root* user, the default RPM directories are used:

/usr/src/redhat/BUILD
> Temporary build files

/usr/src/redhat/RPMS
> Binary and debug RPMs that have been built

/usr/src/redhat/SOURCES
> Source tarballs (as well as patches, RPM icons, and related files)

/usr/src/redhat/SPECS
> Spec files

/usr/src/redhat/SRPMS
> Source RPMs that have been built

Since these directories are writable only by *root*, and it is not recommended that RPMs be built by the *root* user, it's best to use a set of directories within your home directory.

What About...

...creating a desktop menu entry for a packaged program?

To create an entry in the menu, you will need to create a *.desktop* file in */usr/share/applications* and (ideally) an icon in */usr/share/icons*.

In the case of Critical Mass, there is an icon available in the top level of the tarball, so it can be fairly easily copied over to */usr/share/icons* in the %install section of the spec file:

```
mkdir -p %{buildroot}%{_datadir}/icons
install -m 744 critter.png %{buildroot}%{_datadir}/icons/critter.png
```

Creating the *.desktop* file is almost as easy. Here are the contents of a *.desktop* file for Critical Mass:

```
mkdir -p %{buildroot}%{_datadir}/applications

echo "[Desktop Entry]
Name=Critical Mass
Comment=Shoot-em-up Game
Categories=Application;Game
Encoding=UTF-8
Exec=critter
Icon=critter.png
StartupNotify=true
Terminal=False
Type=Application" > %{buildroot}%{_datadir}/applications/CriticalMass.desktop
```

The *.desktop* file identifies all of the information necessary to create an additional entry in the desktop menu (whether KDE or GNOME):

Name
> The name of the menu entry

Comment
> The comment displayed as a tool tip message if you hover over the menu entry with the mouse pointer

Categories
> The menu categories under which this entry will appear

Encoding
> The character encoding used for this entry

Exec
> The name of the command to be executed when this menu entry is selected

Icon
> The name of the icon file

StartupNotify
> Whether this icon supports the *xdg startup notification protocol*, which is used to manage a visual indication that the application is in the process of starting up

Terminal

Whether the application should be run in an terminal window (for nongraphical programs)

Type

Indicates that the program is a standalone application

The extended %install section looks like this:

```
%install
rm -rf %{buildroot}
%makeinstall

mkdir -p %{buildroot}%{_datadir}/icons
install -m 744 critter.png %{buildroot}%{_datadir}/icons/critter.png

mkdir -p %{buildroot}%{_datadir}/applications
echo "[Desktop Entry]
Name=Critical Mass
Comment=Shoot-em-up Game
Categories=Application;Game
Encoding=UTF-8
Exec=critter
Icon=critter.png
StartupNotify=true
Terminal=False
Type=Application" > %{buildroot}%{_datadir}/applications/CriticalMass.desktop
```

It is also necessary to modify the %files section to include the icon and .desktop file:

```
%files
%defattr(-, root, root)
%doc COPYING TODO

%{_bindir}/*
%{_datadir}/Critical_Mass
%{_mandir}/man?/*
%{_datadir}/applications/*
%{_datadir}/icons/*
```

...running a script when a package is installed or removed?

This can be done by specifying a %pre, %post, %preun, or %postun section. The difference between these sections is in when they designate the script to run: before installation (%pre), after installation (%post), before removal (%preun), or after removal (%postun).

As a simple example, if your script contains shared object libraries (.so files), you should run *ldconfig* after installation and after removal:

```
%post
/sbin/ldconfig

%postun
/bin/ldconfig
```

In this case, you should add a Requires tag to the preamble:

```
Requires: /sbin/ldconfig
```

…including an icon to identify the package?

A package icon can be included; graphical installation tools can pick up this icon and display it instead of a generic package icon. Place the icon in the same directory as the tarball, and create an Icon tag in the preamble:

```
Icon: CriticalMass.xpm
```

The icon should be in XPM format. You can use *convert* to make an XPM file from a file in another format:

```
$ convert critter.png critter.xpm
```

…viewing the source code and the spec file for an existing package?

This is an excellent way to learn about writing advanced spec files. You don't even need *root* privileges to open and view the files!

After downloading the source RPM for a package (*.src.rpm* file), install it in the normal way:

```
$ rpm -ivh ImageMagick-6.2.2.0-2.src.rpm
   1:ImageMagick            ######################################### [100%]
```

The files will be installed into *~/rpm/name*—in this case, *~/rpm/ImageMagick*:

```
$ ls ~/rpm/ImageMagick
ImageMagick-5.5.6-mask.patch
ImageMagick-6.2.0-compress.patch
ImageMagick-6.2.1-fixed.patch
ImageMagick-6.2.1-hp2xx.patch
ImageMagick-6.2.1-local_doc.patch
ImageMagick-6.2.1-pkgconfig.patch
ImageMagick-6.2.2-0.tar.bz2
ImageMagick.spec
magick_small.png
```

Where Can I Learn More?

- The Fedora RPM guide: *http://fedora.redhat.com/docs/drafts/rpm-guide-en/* (that's a draft version; the final version is expected to be posted at *http://fedora.redhat.com/docs/rpm-guide-en/*)
- *Maximum RPM*: *http://www.rpm.org/max-rpm-snapshot/*
- *The Fight*, an RPM guide by Matthias Saou: *http://freshrpms.net/docs/fight/*
- IBM DeveloperWorks article on creating RPM packages: *http://www-128.ibm.com/developerworks/library/l-rpm1/*

5.8 Rebuilding an RPM Package for a Different Architecture

Sometimes you'll find an RPM has been prepared that would be perfect for your system—except that the RPM was built for a machine of a different architecture. This can be frustrating, but if you can obtain the source RPM, it's a fairly simple matter to make a binary RPM that is tuned to your system.

How Do I Do That?

Assuming that you have set up your *~/.rpmmacros* file (see Lab 5.7, "Making Your Own RPM Packages"), simply obtain a source RPM file, and then execute *rpmbuild* with the --rebuild option:

```
$ rpmbuild --rebuild
$ rpmbuild --rebuild ImageMagick*.src.rpm
Installing ImageMagick-6.2.2.0-2.src.rpm
Executing(%prep): /bin/sh -e /home/chris/rpm/tmp/rpm-tmp.32955
+ umask 022
+ cd /home/chris/rpm/tmp
...(Lines snipped)...
Executing(--clean): /bin/sh -e /home/chris/rpm/tmp/rpm-tmp.88067
+ umask 022
+ cd /home/chris/rpm/tmp
+ rm -rf ImageMagick-6.2.2
+ exit 0
```

The new RPM packages will be found in *~/rpm/RPMS/*.

How Does It Work?

When rebuilding a package, *rpmbuild* performs the equivalent of a source package installation (rpm -i), followed by a build-all (rpmbuild -ba), and then deletes the source files.

What About...

...editing the spec file before rebuilding?

rpmbuild's --rebuild option is useful only for a direct rebuild without any changes. If you need to edit the spec file, install the source RPM, edit the spec file, and then build the RPM packages normally (see Lab 5.7, "Making Your Own RPM Packages").

Where Can I Learn More?

- The manpage for *rpmbuild*

CHAPTER 6
Storage Administration

Data storage is a critical part of computing. Fedora includes some powerful facilities for managing your data storage. These tools enable you to build high-availability, fault-tolerant storage systems that can be adjusted and tuned while in use, and also enable you to build backup tools that permit automated, self-consistent backups.

6.1 Using Logical Volume Management

Fedora uses the Linux Logical Volume Management (LVM) system by default for disk storage. LVM combines one or more disk partitions, called Physical Volumes (PVs), into a pool of storage called a Volume Group (VG). From this volume group, one or more Logical Volumes (LVs) are allocated. Each LV is used as a block storage device to contain a filesystem or a swapspace.

Here's where the fun begins: LVs can be resized, created, or deleted on the fly, and disks can be added and deleted—while the system is in use!

When changing a storage configuration, it is possible to make a mistake and lose data. Take your time, ensure that you are confident of what each step will do before performing it, and make sure you back up your data before performing any LVM operations.

How Do I Do That?

Fedora Core permits you to manage logical volumes graphically or from the command line.

In the examples given here, the volume-group and logical-volume names recommended in Chapter 1 have been used: the volume group is *main*, and the logical volumes are named *root*, *home*, and *swap*.

If you used the Fedora default names, the main volume group will be named *VolGroup00*, and the logical volumes will be named *LogVol00*, *LogVol01*, and so forth.

Although you can increase or decrease the size of any logical volume at any time, an ext3 filesystem within a logical volume can be reduced in size only when it is not in use (unmounted). If the filesystem is the root filesystem, it is in use whenever the system is running; therefore, the only way to shrink the root filesystem is to use another disk as a temporary root filesystem, which is usually done by running the system from the installation CD in rescue mode (see Lab 10.6, "Using Rescue Mode on an Installation Disc"). There is also a limit to how large a filesystem can grow while in use; growing the filesystem past that point must be done when the filesystem is unmounted.

Managing LVM graphically

Start the LVM administration tool by selecting System → Administration → Logical Volume Management. After you enter the *root* password, the three-panel display shown in Figure 6-1 will appear.

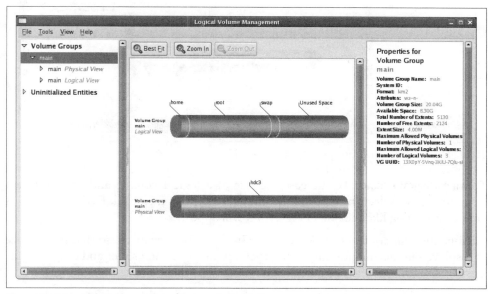

Figure 6-1. Logical Volume Management window

The left pane displays a list of the elements managed by LVM, the middle pane displays the current element in visual form, and the right pane displays a description of the current element.

The element list in the left pane is a collapsing outline. To view the elements within a particular category, click on the small arrow to the left of the category name to rotate it to a downward-pointing position; the elements within that category will be listed immediately below it. For example, to see the logical volumes within the *main* volume group (*VolGroup00* if you used the default Fedora configuration), click on the arrow beside "main Logical View" (or "VolGroup00 Logical View"), and a list of volume groups will appear beneath that line.

The initial display shows the physical (red) and logical (blue) views of the last volume group listed. If you click on a logical volume in the Logical View, the corresponding areas in the physical view are highlighted, as shown in Figure 6-2.

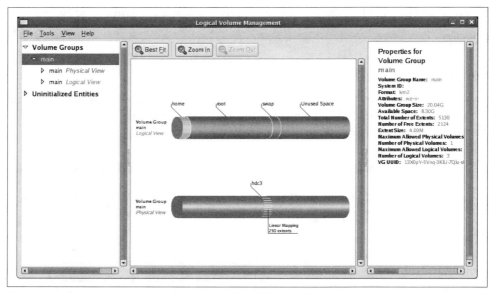

Figure 6-2. Viewing the location of LV data within PVs

Growing a logical volume. To increase the size of a logical volume and the filesystem contained in it, select that LV in the lefthand pane, and then click Edit Properties. A properties dialog like the one in Figure 6-3 will appear.

Change the unit control from Extents to Gigabytes or Megabytes so that the LV size is displayed in meaningful units; then click on the horizontal slider and drag it to the desired size (or type the size into the "LV size" field or click "Use Remaining").

Click OK. The LV will be resized, then the filesystem will be resized, and then the LVM information will be reloaded to update the display. On most systems, this will take just a few seconds.

 If the resize fails with the message "No space left on device," you may have attempted to resize the filesystem past the maximum that can be done while the filesystem is mounted (in use). You can attempt to unmount the filesystem by deselecting the checkbox labeled Mount and then retry the operation (this will always fail for the root filesystem and will usually fail for filesystems containing /var and /home, in which case you may need to use single-user mode).

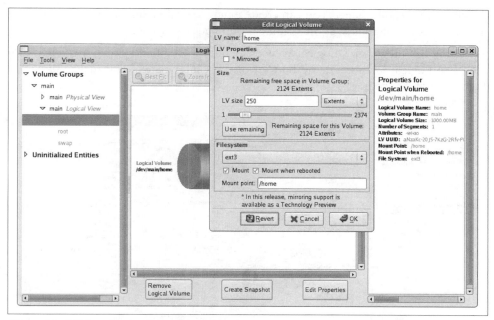

Figure 6-3. LVM properties dialog

Shrinking a logical volume

Shrinking a logical volume using the graphical tool is done exactly the same way as growing it: select the LV you wish to resize, click Edit Properties, enter the new size, and click OK.

The catch is that logical volumes containing ext3 filesystems can be reduced in size only when they are unmounted, so you will be asked if the filesystem may be unmounted during the resize operation. Click Yes.

Whenever the system is booted normally, the root (/) and /var filesystems will be in use, so you will not be able to unmount them, and therefore the resize will fail. You'll need to use a special procedure (detailed shortly) to shrink those filesystems.

The /home filesystem is a different story; if you log in as *root* instead of using a normal user account, the /home filesystem will not be in use, and you can successfully shrink /home. If any non-*root* users have logged in since the system was booted, they may have left processes running, such as the *esound daemon* (esd). These can be terminated with the fuser command:

```
# fuser -k /home/*
/home/chris: 13464c
```

The output shows that the directory /home/chris was in use as the current directory (c) of process 13464. That process is killed, as specified by the -k option. Once this has been done, you can resize the /home directory.

Creating a new logical volume. You can create a new logical volume at any time, as long as there is some free space in the volume group you wish to use.

Select the volume group's Logical View element in the lefthand panel, then click Create New Logical Volume at the bottom of the center panel. The dialog shown in Figure 6-4 will appear.

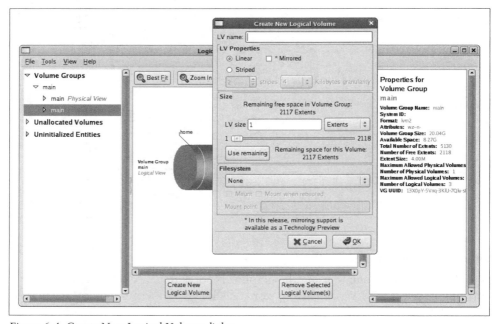

Figure 6-4. Create New Logical Volume dialog

Enter an LV name consisting of letters, digits, and underscores. Change the LV size unit from Extents to Gigabytes (or Megabytes) and enter the desired LV size directly or by using the slider (click the "Use remaining" button to use all of the free space in the PV).

To create a filesystem in this LV, change the Filesystem type control (near the bottom of the dialog) from None to ext3, and select the checkboxes for Mount and "Mount when rebooted." In the "Mount point" field, type the name of the directory where you wish the new filesystem to appear.

For example, to create a 10 GB partition for music and video files, you could enter an LV name of multimedia, set the size to 10 GB, and create an ext3 filesystem with a mount point of */media*.

Click OK. The LV and filesystem will be created and mounted, and you can start using the filesystem immediately.

Creating a snapshot. LVM has the ability to create a *snapshot* of an LV. The snapshot is an exact copy of the LV as it stood when the snapshot was created, but this is an illusion because the snapshot really stores only a copy of data that was changed since the snapshot was created. You can change the data in the origin LV without affecting the snapshot, and change the data in the snapshot without affecting the original LV.

Snapshots enable you to make a self-consistent backup of a filesystem to media such as tape. If you don't use snapshots and you back up an active filesystem containing a database to tape, the database tables would get copied at different times; if the database contained e-commerce data, perhaps the customer table would get copied before the order table. If an order was received from a new customer while the backup was in progress, it is possible that the order table on the tape will include the order but the customer table may not include the new customer. This could lead to severe problems when trying to use the data at a later time. On the other hand, if you take a snapshot and then back that up, the various files will all be in the same state on tape.

In addition, snapshots are useful for self-administered document recovery: if you take a snapshot of your users' files each night and make that snapshot available to them, they can recover from their own mistakes if they mess up a spreadsheet or delete an important document. For example, if you take a snapshot of */home* and make it available as */yesterday/home*, the deleted document */home/jamie/budget.ods* can be recovered as */yesterday/home/jamie/budget.ods*.

Snapshots are also used to test software or procedures without affecting live data. For example, if you take a snapshot of the logical volume containing the */home* filesystem, and then unmount the original filesystem and mount the snapshot in its place, you can experiment with procedures that change the contents of home directories. To undo the results of your experiments, simply unmount the snapshot, remount the original directory, and then destroy the snapshot.

To create a snapshot of a LV using the graphical tool, select the LV in the left pane, and then click on the Create Snapshot button at the bottom of the middle pane. You will see the dialog box shown in Figure 6-5.

This dialog looks a lot like the dialog used to create a logical volume (Figure 6-4), and it should—because a snapshot is a special type of LV. Enter a name for the snapshot; I recommend the name of the origin LV, with -snap added to the end. For example, a snapshot of the *multimedia* LV would be called *multimedia-snap*.

Next, set the size of the snapshot. The snapshot will appear to be the same size as the origin LV; the size setting here is used to reserve disk space to track the differences between the origin LV and the snapshot. Therefore, if you have a 100 GB LV and the data in that LV changes slowly, a 1 GB snapshot might be reasonable; but if the data in that LV changes rapidly, you will need a much larger snapshot size.

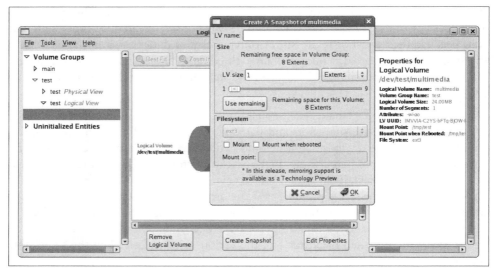

Figure 6-5. Creating a snapshot

Select the Mount and "Mount when rebooted" checkboxes, and then enter the "Mount point" that you wish to use (such as */backup/media*).

You can view the amount of storage used by the snapshot by selecting the snapshot LV in the left pane, then looking at the snapshot usage in the right pane. The usage is reported as a percentage of the total snapshot size and increases as data is changed in the origin or snapshot volumes. If it approaches 100 percent, you can increase the size of the snapshot LV in the same way that you would resize a regular LV.

Removing a logical volume or a snapshot. To permanently remove a logical volume, select it in the left pane, and then click the Remove Logical Volume button at the bottom of the middle pane. A dialog box will appear, asking you to confirm your choice; when you click Yes, the logical volume will be gone forever.

Adding a partition. You can add a partition to a volume group at any time.

The first step is to make the partition a physical volume. Select the disk partition you wish to use under Uninitialized Entities in the left pane, and then click the Initialize Entity button at the bottom of the center pane. A dialog box will warn you of possible data loss; double-check the partition information, and then click Yes if you are certain that you will not lose any critical data.

 Be extremely careful with this option because it will delete all of the data on an entire disk partition. If you select the wrong partition on a dual-boot system, you could wipe out all of the data used by the other operating system (such as Windows).

If the Initialize Entity button is deactivated (grayed-out and unclickable), look in the right pane for the reason that the partition is "Not initializable." The most common reason given is Foreign boot partition, which means that the partition is marked as bootable in the drive's partition table. To correct this, use *fdisk* on the disk containing the partition; for example, run *fdisk* on the disk */dev/sdb* to edit the settings for the partition */dev/sdb1*:

```
# fdisk /dev/sdb
```

fdisk accepts single-letter commands. Enter **p** to print the partition table:

```
Command (m for help): p

Disk /dev/sdb: 8 MB, 8192000 bytes
4 heads, 16 sectors/track, 250 cylinders
Units = cylinders of 64 * 512 = 32768 bytes

    Device Boot      Start        End      Blocks   Id  System
/dev/sdb1    *           1        250        7987+   1  FAT12
```

There is only one partition on this particular disk, and it is bootable (note the * in the Boot column). Use the a (activate) command to toggle the boot flag:

```
Command (m for help): a
Partition number (1-4): 1
```

Then use w to write the partition table to disk and exit:

```
Command (m for help): w
The partition table has been altered!

Calling ioctl() to re-read partition table.
Syncing disks.
```

You can now rerun the graphical LVM administration tool and initialize the partition for use with LVM. This gives you a new physical volume that you can work with.

The next step is to add the new physical volume to the volume group. You'll see the newly initialized partition under Unallocated Volumes in the left pane. Click on it, and then click on the button labeled "Add Volume to existing Volume Group." A menu of volume groups will appear; select the one to add it to, and then click Add.

Once you've added a PV, you can use the extra space to create new logical volumes or grow an existing volume.

Removing a partition. To take a physical volume (partition) out of a volume group, select the PV in the left pane, and then click "Remove Volume from Volume Group." You will be prompted for confirmation (including any move of data to another device), and the PV will be removed (as long as the free space in the VG exceeds the size of the PV; otherwise, removing the PV would destroy data).

Managing LVMs from the command line

Logical volumes are almost always used to contain filesystems (the other common use is to hold swapspace). In essence, an LV serves as a container for a filesystem. This has several ramifications:

- The LV must be created before the filesystem can be created.
- The filesystem must be removed before the LV is destroyed.
- When growing an LV and filesystem, the LV must be grown first.
- When shrinking an LV and filesystem, the filesystem must be reduced first.

Fedora's LVM2 system provides the *lvm* command for administration. Typing **lvm** by itself starts a specialized shell:

```
# lvm
lvm>
```

At the lvm> prompt, you can enter any of the subcommands shown in Table 6-1.

Table 6-1. LVM subcommands

LVM subcommand	Description
vgs	Displays details about volume groups (compact)
pvs	Displays details about physical volumes (compact)
lvs	Displays details about logical volumes (compact)
vgdisplay	Displays details about volume groups (verbose)
pvdisplay	Displays details about physical volumes (verbose)
lvdisplay	Displays details about logical volumes (verbose)
vgcreate	Creates a volume group
vgremove	Removes a volume group
pvcreate	Prepares a block device (such as a disk partition) for inclusion in a volume group by adding a disk label to the start of the block device
pvremove	Wipes out the disk label created by pvcreate
vgextend	Adds a physical volume to a volume group
vgremove	Removes a physical volume from a volume group
pvmove	Migrates data from one physical volume to another
lvcreate	Creates a logical volume or snapshot LV
lvextend	Grows a logical volume
lvreduce	Shrinks a logical volume
lvresize	Grows or shrinks a logical volume
vgscan	Scans block devices for volume groups (necessary when using a rescue-mode boot)

You can also enter any of these subcommands as the first argument on the *lvm* command line:

```
# lvm lvs
  LV          VG   Attr  LSize   Origin Snap% Move Log Copy%
  home        main -wi-ao  1.00G
  multimedia  main -wi-ao 512.00M
  root        main -wi-ao  9.77G
  swap        main -wi-ao  1.00G
```

Symbolic links have been set up from */usr/sbin/<subcommand>* to */usr/sbin/lvm*, so you can just type the name of the subcommand at the regular *bash* shell prompt:

```
# ls -l /usr/sbin/lvs
lrwxrwxrwx 1 root root 3 Mar 20 14:49 /usr/sbin/lvs -> lvm
# lvs
  LV          VG   Attr  LSize   Origin Snap% Move Log Copy%
  home        main -wi-ao  1.00G
  multimedia  main -wi-ao 512.00M
  root        main -wi-ao  9.77G
  swap        main -wi-ao  1.00G
```

 The symbolic links are not available when you are in rescue mode (see Lab 10.6, "Using Rescue Mode on an Installation Disc"), so it's important to remember that you can also use these subcommands as arguments to the *lvm* command (for example, when in rescue mode, type lvm lvdisplay instead of lvdisplay).

LVM device names. Logical volumes can be accessed using any of three different device nodes:

- In the */dev/mapper* directory, the entry named by the pattern *vg-lv*. For example, if the volume group *main* had a logical volume named *home*, it could be accessed using the name */dev/mapper/main-home*.

- There is a separate directory in */dev* for each volume group, and an entry for each logical volume within that directory. Our sample volume could be accessed as */dev/main/home*. These names are slightly shorter to type than the ones in */dev/mapper*, and are actually symbolic links to the longer names.

- Using */dev/dm-<number>*, where *<number>* is a number sequentially assigned when volume groups are initially scanned at boot time (or when the LV is created, if it was created after the last boot). If a volume is the second one found during the *vgscan*, it can be accessed as */dev/dm-1* (the first one found is numbered 0). These names are a bit harder to use, since the VG and LV are not identified; to find the corresponding entry in */dev/mapper*, compare the minor device numbers. You cannot use these names in rescue mode.

In addition to these device node names, some LVM commands allow the volume group and logical volume names to be written as *vg/lv*—for example, *main/ multimedia* refers to the LV *multimedia* within the VG *main*.

Getting information about LVM elements. To discover the VGs present on your system, use the *vgs* command:

```
# vgs
  VG   #PV #LV #SN Attr   VSize  VFree
  main   2   4   0 wz--n- 20.04G 7.78G
```

This shows the volume group name, the number of physical volumes, logical volumes, and snapshots; attributes (see the manpage for *lvm* for details); the volume group size; and the amount of space that is not assigned to a logical volume.

vgdisplay shows the same information as vgs but in a more verbose form:

```
# vgdisplay
  --- Volume group ---
  VG Name               main
  System ID
  Format                lvm2
  Metadata Areas        2
  Metadata Sequence No  51
  VG Access             read/write
  VG Status             resizable
  MAX LV                0
  Cur LV                4
  Open LV               4
  Max PV                0
  Cur PV                2
  Act PV                2
  VG Size               20.04 GB
  PE Size               4.00 MB
  Total PE              5131
  Alloc PE / Size       3140 / 12.27 GB
  Free  PE / Size       1991 / 7.78 GB
  VG UUID               13XOpY-5Vnq-3KlU-7Qlu-sHUc-wrup-zsHipP
```

The VG UUID at the bottom is a unique ID number placed in the disk label of each PV to identify that it is part of this volume group.

 If you have more than one VG present and only want to see information about a specific one, you can specify a volume group name as an argument to *vgdisplay* or *vgs*.

To list the PVs present, use *pvs* or *pvdisplay*:

```
# pvs
  PV         VG   Fmt  Attr PSize  PFree
  /dev/hdc3  main lvm2 a-   20.04G 7.77G
  /dev/sdb1  main lvm2 a-    4.00M 4.00M
# pvdisplay
  --- Physical volume ---
  PV Name               /dev/hdc3
  VG Name               main
  PV Size               20.04 GB / not usable 0
```

```
Allocatable             yes
PE Size (KByte)         4096
Total PE                5130
Free PE                 1990
Allocated PE            3140
PV UUID                 RL2wrh-WMgl-pyaR-bHt4-6dCv-23Fd-kX1gvT


--- Physical volume ---
PV Name                 /dev/sdb1
VG Name                 main
PV Size                 4.00 MB / not usable 0
Allocatable             yes
PE Size (KByte)         4096
Total PE                1
Free PE                 1
Allocated PE            0
PV UUID                 HvryBh-kGrM-c1Oy-yw1v-u8W3-r2LN-5LrLrJ
```

In this case, there are two PVs present: */dev/hdc3* (an IDE hard disk partition) and */dev/sdb1* (a USB disk I was playing with). Both are part of the VG *main*. The display shows the attributes (see man lvm), size, and amount of unallocated space.

In a similar way, you can see logical volume information with *lvs* or *lvdisplay*:

```
# lvs
  LV              VG   Attr   LSize    Origin     Snap%  Move Log Copy%
  home            main -wi-ao   1.00G
  multimedia      main owi-ao 512.00M
  multimedia-snap main swi-a- 128.00M multimedia   0.02
  root            main -wi-ao   9.77G
  swap            main -wi-ao   1.00G
# lvdisplay
  --- Logical volume ---
  LV Name                /dev/main/root
  VG Name                main
  LV UUID                LaQgYA-jiBr-GO2i-y64m-9OfT-viBp-TuZ9sC
  LV Write Access        read/write
  LV Status              available
  # open                 1
  LV Size                9.77 GB
  Current LE             2500
  Segments               1
  Allocation             inherit
  Read ahead sectors     0
  Block device           253:0

...(Lines snipped)...

  --- Logical volume ---
  LV Name                /dev/main/multimedia
  VG Name                main
  LV UUID                f7zJvh-H21e-fSn7-llq3-Ryu1-p1FQ-PTAoNC
  LV Write Access        read/write
  LV snapshot status     source of
```

```
                             /dev/main/multimedia-snap [active]
      LV Status              available
      # open                 1
      LV Size                512.00 MB
      Current LE             128
      Segments               1
      Allocation             inherit
      Read ahead sectors     0
      Block device           253:3

      --- Logical volume ---
      LV Name                /dev/main/multimedia-snap
      VG Name                main
      LV UUID                7U5wVQ-qIWU-7bcz-J4vT-zAPh-xGVN-CDNfjx
      LV Write Access        read/write
      LV snapshot status     active destination for /dev/main/multimedia
      LV Status              available
      # open                 0
      LV Size                512.00 MB
      Current LE             128
      COW-table size         128.00 MB
      COW-table LE           32
      Allocated to snapshot  0.02%
      Snapshot chunk size    8.00 KB
      Segments               1
      Allocation             inherit
      Read ahead sectors     0
      Block device           253:6
```

This display shows the volume group, attributes (again, see man lvm), and logical volume size. Additional information is shown for snapshot volumes and LVs that are being copied or moved between PVs. The Block device shown in the *lvdisplay* output is the major and minor device number.

Growing a logical volume. To increase the size of a logical volume, use the *lvextend* command:

```
# lvextend /dev/main/multimedia --size 1G
  Extending logical volume multimedia to 1.00 GB
  Logical volume multimedia successfully resized
```

Specify the LV device as the first argument, and use the --size option to specify the new size for the volume. Use a numeric size with one of the size suffixes from Table 6-2 as the value for the --size option.

Table 6-2. Size suffixes used by LVM

Suffix	Name	Size	Approximation
k, K	Kibibyte (kilobyte)	$2^{10} = 1{,}024$ bytes	Thousand bytes
m, M	Mebibyte (megabyte)	$2^{20} = 1{,}048{,}576$ bytes	Million bytes
g, G	Gibibyte (gigabyte)	$2^{30} = 1{,}073{,}741{,}824$ bytes	Billion bytes
t, T	Tebibyte (terabyte)	$2^{40} = 1{,}099{,}511{,}627{,}776$ bytes	Trillion bytes

Once you have resized the LV, resize the filesystem contained inside:

```
# resize2fs /dev/main/multimedia
resize2fs 1.39 (29-May-2006)
Resizing the filesystem on /dev/main/multimedia to 1048576 (1k) blocks.
The filesystem on /dev/main/multimedia is now 1048576 blocks long.
```

Note that you do not need to specify the filesystem size; the entire LV size will be used.

If the *resize2fs* fails with the message No space left on device, the new size is too large for the existing allocation tables

Shrinking a logical volume. Before reducing the size of a logical volume, you must first reduce the size of the filesystem inside the LV. This must be done when the filesystem is unmounted:

```
# umount /dev/main/multimedia
```

Next, run a filesystem check to verify the integrity of the filesystem. This is required in order to prevent data loss that may occur if there is data near the end of the filesystem (this is the area that will be freed up by shrinking) and that data is not properly accounted for in the filesystem tables:

```
# fsck -f /dev/main/multimedia
e2fsck 1.38 (30-Jun-2005)
Pass 1: Checking inodes, blocks, and sizes
Pass 2: Checking directory structure
Pass 3: Checking directory connectivity
Pass 4: Checking reference counts
Pass 5: Checking group summary information
/dev/main/multimedia: 11/117248 files (9.1% non-contiguous), 8043/262144 blocks
```

Now use *resize2fs* to reduce the size of the filesystem:

```
# resize2fs /dev/main/multimedia 740M
resize2fs 1.38 (30-Jun-2005)
Resizing the filesystem on /dev/main/multimedia to 189440 (4k) blocks.
The filesystem on /dev/main/multimedia is now 189440 blocks long.
```

Note that *resize2fs* expects the size to be the second argument (there is no --size option as there is with the LVM commands).

The LVM commands accept sizes containing decimals (such as 1.2G), but *resize2fs* does not; use the next smaller unit to eliminate the decimal point (1200M).

Both the filesystem commands and the LVM commands round off sizes to the closest multiple of their internal allocation units. This means that *resize2fs* and *lvreduce* may interpret a size such as 750M slightly differently. In order to avoid the potential

---

disaster of resizing the LV to be smaller than the filesystem, always resize the filesystem so that it is slightly smaller than the planned LV size, resize the LV, and then grow the filesystem to exactly fill the LV. In this case, I'm resizing the filesystem to 740 MB and will resize the LV to 750 MB.

Now that the filesystem has been resized, you can shrink the logical volume:

```
# lvreduce /dev/main/multimedia --size 750M
    Rounding up size to full physical extent 752.00 MB
    WARNING: Reducing active logical volume to 752.00 MB
    THIS MAY DESTROY YOUR DATA (filesystem etc.)
    Do you really want to reduce multimedia? [y/n]: y
    Reducing logical volume multimedia to 752.00 MB
    Logical volume multimedia successfully resized
```

Finally, grow the filesystem to completely fill the logical volume:

```
# resize2fs /dev/main/multimedia
resize2fs 1.38 (30-Jun-2005)
Resizing the filesystem on /dev/main/multimedia to 192512 (4k) blocks.
The filesystem on /dev/main/multimedia is now 192512 blocks long.
```

Creating a new logical volume. The *lvcreate* command will create a new volume:

```
# lvcreate main --name survey --size 5G
    Logical volume "survey" created
```

Next, add a filesystem:

```
# mkfs -t ext3 -L survey -E resize=20G /dev/main/survey
mke2fs 1.38 (30-Jun-2005)
Filesystem label=survey
OS type: Linux
Block size=4096 (log=2)
Fragment size=4096 (log=2)
655360 inodes, 1310720 blocks
65536 blocks (5.00%) reserved for the super user
First data block=0
Maximum filesystem blocks=8388608
40 block groups
32768 blocks per group, 32768 fragments per group
16384 inodes per group
Superblock backups stored on blocks:
        32768, 98304, 163840, 229376, 294912, 819200, 884736

Writing inode tables: done
Creating journal (32768 blocks): done
Writing superblocks and filesystem accounting information: done

This filesystem will be automatically checked every 36 mounts or
180 days, whichever comes first.  Use tune2fs -c or -i to override.
```

The -t *ext3* option specifies the filesystem type, -L *survey* specifies a optional filesystem volume label (to identify the contents), and -E resize=*20G* (also optional) configures a *block group descriptor table* large enough that the filesystem can be grown up to 20 GB while mounted. In this case, 20 GB is four times the initial size of the filesystem; use whatever upper limit seems reasonable for your application (the table will take roughly 4 KB of space for each gigabyte in the filesystem maximum size, so the overhead is minimal).

You can now mount the filesystem and use it. Here I'll use */usr/lib/survey* as the mount point:

```
# mkdir /usr/lib/survey
# mount /dev/main/survey /usr/lib/survey
```

To configure the Fedora system to mount this filesystem every time it is booted, add an entry to the file */etc/fstab*:

```
/dev/main/root          /                       ext3    defaults        1 1
LABEL=/boot             /boot                   ext3    defaults        1 2
devpts                  /dev/pts                devpts  gid=5,mode=620  0 0
tmpfs                   /dev/shm                tmpfs   defaults        0 0
proc                    /proc                   proc    defaults        0 0
sysfs                   /sys                    sysfs   defaults        0 0
/dev/main/swap          swap                    swap    defaults        0 0
/dev/main/home          /home                   ext3    defaults        1 2
/dev/main/multimedia    /tmp/media              ext3    defaults        1 2
/dev/main/survey        /usr/lib/survey         ext3    defaults        1 2
```

The new line (highlighted in bold) contains the filesystem block device, the mount point, the filesystem type, any mount options (defaults specifies the default options, which include mounting the filesystem at boot time), whether the filesystem should be backed up (1 meaning *yes*), and the *fsck* sequence number (2 is for filesystems that should be checked but that are not the root filesystem).

Creating a snapshot logical volume. The *lvcreate* command is also used to create snapshot volumes:

```
# lvcreate -s /dev/main/survey --name survey-snap --size 500M
  Logical volume "survey-snap" created
```

The -s option indicates that this is a snapshot LV. Specify the origin LV as the first positional argument, and use the --name and --size options as you would for a regular *lvcreate* command. However, the value given for the --size option must be the amount of space allocated for tracking the differences between the origin LV and the snapshot LV.

Once the snapshot has been created, it can be mounted and used:

```
# mkdir /usr/lib/survey-snap
# mount /dev/main/survey-snap /usr/lib/survey-snap
```

To have the snapshot automatically mounted when the system is booted, edit the file */etc/fstab* in the same way that you would for a regular filesystem.

To see how much of a snapshot's storage is in use, use *lvs* or *lvdisplay*:

```
# lvs
  LV          VG    Attr   LSize   Origin Snap%  Move Log Copy%
  home        main -wi-ao  1.00G
  multimedia  main -wi-a- 752.00M
  root        main -wi-ao  9.77G
  survey      main owi-ao  5.00G
  survey-snap main swi-ao 500.00M survey   8.27
  swap        main -wi-ao  1.00G
# lvdisplay /dev/main/survey-snap
  --- Logical volume ---
  LV Name                /dev/main/survey-snap
  VG Name                main
  LV UUID                IbG5RS-Tcle-kzrV-Ga9b-Jsgx-3MY6-iEXBGG
  LV Write Access        read/write
  LV snapshot status     active destination for /dev/main/survey
  LV Status              available
  # open                 1
  LV Size                5.00 GB
  Current LE             1280
  COW-table size         500.00 MB
  COW-table LE           125
  Allocated to snapshot  8.27%
  Snapshot chunk size    8.00 KB
  Segments               1
  Allocation             inherit
  Read ahead sectors     0
  Block device           253:7
```

In this case, 8.27% of the snapshot storage has been used, or about 41 MB. If this approaches 100%, you can grow the snapshot LV using *lvextend* in the same way that a regular LV is grown.

Removing a logical volume. To remove a logical volume, unmount it, and then use *lvremove*:

```
# umount /usr/lib/survey-snap
# lvremove /dev/main/survey-snap
Do you really want to remove active logical volume "survey-snap"? [y/n]: y
  Logical volume "survey-snap" successfully removed
```

 Removing an LV is irreversible, so be sure that you're not deleting any important data.

Adding a partition. To set up a partition for use as a physical volume, use the *pvcreate* command to write the LVM disk label, making the partition into a physical volume:

```
# pvcreate /dev/sde1
  Physical volume "/dev/sde1" successfully created
```

If the disk is not partitioned, you can use *fdisk* or (more easily) *parted* to create a partition before running *pvcreate*.

These commands create a single partition that fills the entire disk */dev/sde*:

```
# parted /dev/sde mklabel msdos
# parted -- /dev/sde mkpart primary ext2 1 -1
```

In this case, the partition will be */dev/sde1*.

You can then add that PV to an existing volume group:

```
# vgextend main /dev/sde1
Volume group "main" successfully extended
```

Removing a partition. The *vgreduce* command is used to reduce the size of a volume group by removing a physical volume. It will fail if any space on the PV is in use:

```
# vgreduce main /dev/sdb1
Physical volume "/dev/sdb1" still in use
```

In this case, an attempt to remove */dev/sdb1* from the volume group *main* failed. To move the data off a PV (assuming that there is sufficient space available on other PVs in the volume group), use the *pvmove* command:

```
# pvmove /dev/sde1
/dev/sde1: Moved: 100.0%
```

Depending on the amount of date to be moved, this operation can take quite a while to run. When it is complete, you can remove the physical volume:

```
# vgreduce main /dev/sdb1
Removed "/dev/sdb1" from volume group "test"
```

You can then use that partition for other uses. If you want to erase the LVM disk label, use the *pvremove* command:

```
# pvremove /dev/sde1
Labels on physical volume "/dev/sde1" successfully wiped
```

Managing LVM in single-user mode

Some filesystems, such as those containing */var* or */etc*, may be in use anytime the system is booted normally. This prevents the use of *resize2fs* to shrink ext2 and ext3 filesystems or to grow them large enough to exceed the block group descriptor table.

To use *resize2fs* on these filesystems, you must use runlevel *s*, which is single-user mode. Boot your system, and press the spacebar when the GRUB boot screen appears. Press the A key to append text to the boot line; then type **s** and press Enter. After a few seconds, a root shell prompt will appear (sh-3.1#).

At this shell prompt you can unmount the filesystem, then use *fsck*, *resize2fs*, and *lvreduce* (or *lvextend*). For example, to reduce the size of */home* to 925 MB:

```
sh-3.1# umount /home
sh-3.1# fsck -f /dev/main/home
e2fsck 1.38 (30-Jun-2005)
Pass 1: Checking inodes, blocks, and sizes
Pass 2: Checking directory structure
Pass 3: Checking directory connectivity
Pass 4: Checking reference counts
Pass 5: Checking group summary information
/dev/main/home: 121/256000 files (2.5% non-contiguous), 12704/262144 blocks
sh-3.1# resize2fs /dev/main/home 900M
resize2fs 1.38 (30-Jun-2005)
Resizing the filesystem on /dev/main/home to 230400 (4k) blocks.
The filesystem on /dev/main/home is now 229376 blocks long.
sh-3.1# lvreduce /dev/main/home --size 950M
  Rounding up size to full physical extent 952.00 MB
  WARNING: Reducing active logical volume to 952.00 MB
  THIS MAY DESTROY YOUR DATA (filesystem etc.)
Do you really want to reduce home? [y/n]: y
  Reducing logical volume home to 952.00 MB
  Logical volume home successfully resized
sh-3.1# resize2fs /dev/main/home
resize2fs 1.38 (30-Jun-2005)
Resizing the filesystem on /dev/main/home to 243712 (4k) blocks.
The filesystem on /dev/main/home is now 243712 blocks long.
```

The warning message displayed by *lvreduce* is accurate: if you set the logical volume size smaller than the filesystem size, you will lose data! Be extremely careful when resizing volumes; it's a good idea to back up your data first.

If your system has the default Volume Group and Logical Volume names, substitute the correct name (such as */dev/VolGroup00/ LogVol00*) for */dev/main/home*. The problem is that it's hard to keep the logical volume names straight—which is why I recommend using more meaningful names.

Note that, as before, the filesystem was resized to be slightly smaller than the desired size, then expanded to fill the LV after the LV was resized.

When you're done, type **reboot** or press Ctrl-Alt-Delete to restart the system.

Managing LVM in rescue mode

To reduce or substantially grow the root filesystem, you'll have to boot from a device other than your normal disk. The most convenient way to do this is to boot from the Fedora Core installation media; when the boot screen appears (Figure 1-1), type **linux rescue** and press Enter.

After prompting you for the language (Figure 1-5) and keyboard type (Figure 1-6) the same way it does for a network installation (use the arrow keys and Enter to select the correct value for each), the system will ask if you wish to start the network interfaces, as shown in Figure 6-6. Select No by pressing Tab and then Enter.

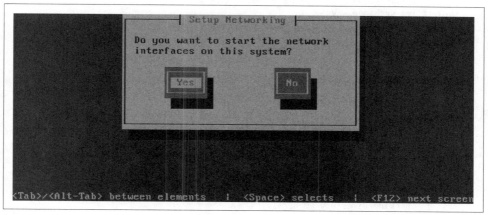

Figure 6-6. Rescue mode network interface dialog

The next screen, shown in Figure 6-7, enables you to select filesystem mounting; select Skip by pressing Tab twice and then pressing Enter.

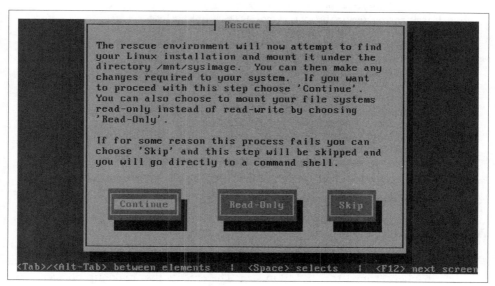

Figure 6-7. Rescue mode filesystem mounting dialog

You will then be presented with a shell prompt (sh-3.1#). The LVM device nodes will not be present until you scan for them and activate them:

```
sh-3.1# lvm vgscan
   Reading all physical volumes. This may take a while...
   Found volume group "main" using metadata type lvm2
sh-3.1# lvm vgchange -ay
   3 logical volume(s) in volume group "main" now active
```

 The LVM device nodes will be created in */dev/mapper/<vg-lv>* and */dev/<vg>/<lv>*. The */dev/dm-<N>* nodes are not created.

You can now resize the *root* partition:

```
sh-3.1# fsck -f /dev/main/root
WARNING: couldn't open /etc/fstab: No such file or directory
e2fsck 1.38 (30-Jun-2005)
Pass 1: Checking inodes, blocks, and sizes
Pass 2: Checking directory structure
Pass 3: Checking directory connectivity
Pass 4: Checking reference counts
Pass 5: Checking group summary information
/dev/main/root: 134009/1532576 files (0.5% non-contiguous), 793321/1531904 blocks
sh-3.1# resize2fs /dev/main/root 5600M
resize2fs 1.38 (30-Jun-2005)
Resizing the filesystem on /dev/main/root to 1433600 (4k) blocks.
The filesystem on /dev/main/root is now 1433600 blocks long.
sh-3.1# lvreduce /dev/main/root --size 5650M
   Rounding up size to full physical extent 5.53 GB
   WARNING: Reducing active logical volume to 5.53 GB
   THIS MAY DESTROY YOUR DATA (filesystem etc.)
Do you really want to reduce root? [y/n]: y
   Reducing logical volume root to 5.53 GB
   Logical volume root successfully resized
sh-3.1# resize2fs /dev/main/root                .
resize2fs 1.38 (30-Jun-2005)
Resizing the filesystem on /dev/main/root to 1449984 (4k) blocks.
The filesystem on /dev/main/root is now 1449984 blocks long.
```

Type **exit** or press Ctrl-D to exit from the rescue-mode shell. The system will then reboot; don't forget to remove the installation media.

How Does It Work?

LVM works by dividing storage space into same-sized pieces called *extents*, which may be anywhere from 1 to 128 MB in size. The extents that make up physical storage are called *physical extents* (PEs); the extents that make up logical volumes are called *logical extents* (LEs).

Obviously, each LE exists as a PE somewhere in the LVM system. A kernel facility called the *device mapper* converts between LE and PE extent numbers. When the physical extents are changed—as the result of a *pvmove*, for example—the logical extent numbers remain the same, providing continuity for the filesystem.

Extents tend to be fairly large—anywhere from 8 KB to 16 GB in size, but typically in the 1 to 128 MB range (32 MB is the default extent size used during installation). Larger extent sizes cause a reduction in the LVM overhead because the extent tables are smaller and need to be consulted less often. However, LVs and PVs must be a multiple of the extent size, so a large size limits granularity. The extent size can be configured when the VG is created, either at boot time or by using the --physicalextentsize argument to *vgcreate*.

A large, efficient extent size is usually too big for effective copy-on-write operation during snapshots, so a smaller *chunk* size is used for copy-on-write management. This can be configured using the --chunksize option to *lvcreate*.

What About...

...taking multiple snapshots of a filesystem?

It is possible to take multiple snapshots of a filesystem. For example, you could have snapshots of */home* for each day in the preceding week, making it even easier for your users to restore their own files in the case of accidental deletion or damage. However, when you have multiple snapshots in place, a single write can trigger a lot of copy-on-write activity—so don't go overboard, or your write performance could really suffer.

...improving performance?

The LVM system has *striping* capability, which spreads data over multiple PVs. Data can be read from multiple PVs simultaneously, increasing throughput in some cases.

To enable striping, use the -i (stripe-count) and -I (stripe-size) arguments to the lvcreate command:

```
# lvcreate main -i 3 -I 8 --name mysql --size 20G
```

The stripe count must be equal to or less than the number of PVs in the VG, and the stripe size (which is in kilobytes) must be a power of 2 between 4 and 512.

You can also select striping in the LV Properties area of the Create New Logical Volume dialog (Figure 6-4).

...LVM mirroring?

To protect data integrity, recent versions of LVM provide a *mirroring* capability, which stores two copies of each physical extent on two different disks. However, this is noted as a *technology preview* capability in Fedora Core 6, meaning that it's at a beta-test stage.

An alternative approach that is stable, proven, and provides a wider range of configuration options is to layer LVM on top of the *md* RAID system (discussed in Lab 6.2, "Managing RAID").

...using LVM with RAID?

LVM can be layered on top of the Linux *md* RAID driver, which combines the flexibility of LVM with striping, mirroring, and advanced error-correction capabilities. See Lab 6.2, "Managing RAID," for details on how this is configured.

...using a raw, unpartitioned disk as a PV?

Although you can use a raw disk as a PV, it's not recommended. The graphical administration tools don't support it, and the amount of space lost to a partition table is minimal (about 1 KB).

...a failing disk drive?

If you suspect that a disk drive is failing, and you want to save the data that is on that drive, you can add a replacement PV to your volume group, migrate the data off the failing (or slow or undersized) disk onto the new PV, and then remove the original disk from the volume group.

To migrate data off a specific PV, use the *pvmove* command:

```
# pvmove /dev/hda3
```

...creating a flexible disk layout?

LVM is all about flexibility—but for absolute maximum flexibility, divide your disk into multiple partitions and then add each partition to your volume group as a separate PV.

For example, if you have a 100 GB disk drive, you can divide the disk into five 20 GB partitions and use those as physical volumes in one volume group.

The advantage to this approach is that you can free up one or two of those PVs for use with another operating system at a later date. You can also easily switch to a RAID array by adding one (or more) disks, as long as 20 percent of your VG is free, with the following steps:

1. Migrate data off one of the PVs.
2. Remove that PV from the VG.
3. Remake that PV as a RAID device.
4. Add the new RAID PV back into the VG.
5. Repeat the process for the remaining PVs.

You can use this same process to change RAID levels (for example, switching from RAID-1 (mirroring) to RAID-5 (rotating ECC) when going from two disks to three or more disks).

Where Can I Learn More?

- The manpages for *lvm, vgcreate, vgremove, vgextend, vgreduce, vgdisplay, vgs, vgscan, vgchange, pvcreate, pvremove, pvmove, pvdisplay, pvs, lvcreate, lvremove, lvextend, lvreduce, lvresize, lvdisplay, lvs*
- The LVM2 Resource page: *http://sourceware.org/lvm2/*
- A Red Hat article on LVM: *http://www.redhat.com/magazine/009jul05/ departments/red_hat_speaks/*

6.2   Managing RAID

Redundant Arrays of Inexpensive Disks (RAID) is a technology for boosting storage performance and reducing the risk of data loss due to disk error. It works by storing data on multiple disk drives and is well supported by Fedora. It's a good idea to configure RAID on any system used for serious work.

How Do I Do That?

RAID can be managed by the kernel, by the kernel working with the motherboard BIOS, or by a separate computer on an add-in card. RAID managed by the BIOS is called *dmraid*; while supported by Fedora Core, it does not provide any significant benefits over RAID managed solely by the kernel on most systems, since all the work is still performed by the main CPU.

 Using *dmraid* can thwart data-recovery efforts if the motherboard fails and another motherboard of the same model (or a model with a compatible BIOS *dmraid* implementation) is not available.

Add-in cards that contain their own CPU and battery-backed RAM can reduce the load of RAID processing on the main CPU. However, on a modern system, RAID processing takes at most 3 percent of the CPU time, so the expense of a separate, dedicated RAID processor is wasted on all but the highest-end servers. So-called RAID cards without a CPU simply provide additional disk controllers, which are useful because each disk in a RAID array should ideally have its own disk-controller channel.

There are six "levels" of RAID that are supported by the kernel in Fedora Core, as outlined in Table 6-3.

Table 6-3. RAID levels supported by Fedora Core

RAID Level	Description	Protection against drive failure	Write performance	Read performance	Number of drives	Capacity
Linear	Linear/Append. Devices are concatenated together to make one large storage area (deprecated; use LVM instead).	No.	Normal.	Normal	2	Sum of all drives
0	Striped. The first block of data is written to the first block on the first drive, the second block of data is written to the first block on the second drive, and so forth.	No.	Normal to normal multiplied by the number of drives, depending on application.	Multiplied by the number of drives	2 or more	Sum of all drives
1	Mirroring. All data is written to two (or more) drives.	Yes. As long as one drive is working, your data is safe.	Normal.	Multiplied by the number of drives	2 or more	Equal to one drive
4	Dedicated parity. Data is striped across all drives except that the last drive gets parity data for each block in that "stripe."	Yes. One drive can fail (but any more than that will cause data loss).	Reduced: two reads and one write for each write operation. The parity drive is a bottleneck.	Multiplied by the number of drives minus one	3 or more	Sum of all drives except one
5	Distributed parity. Like level 4, except that the drive used for parity is rotated from stripe to stripe, eliminating the bottleneck on the parity drive.	Yes. One drive can fail.	Like level 4, except with no parity bottleneck.	Multiplied by the number of drives minus one	3 or more	Sum of all drives except one
6	Distributed error-correcting code. Like level 5, but with redundant information on two drives.	Yes. Two drives can fail.	Same as level 5.	Multiplied by the number of drives minus two	4 or more	Sum of all drives except two

For many desktop configurations, RAID level 1 (RAID 1) is appropriate because it can be set up with only two drives. For servers, RAID 5 or 6 is commonly used.

Although Table 6-3 specifies the number of drives required by each RAID level, the Linux RAID system is usually used with disk partitions, so a partition from each of several disks can form one RAID array, and another set of partitions from those same drives can form another RAID array.

RAID arrays should ideally be set up during installation, but it is possible to create them after the fact. The *mdadm* command is used for all RAID administration operations; no graphical RAID administration tools are included in Fedora.

Displaying Information About the Current RAID Configuration

The fastest way to see the current RAID configuration and status is to display the contents of */proc/mdstat*:

```
$ cat /proc/mdstat
Personalities : [raid1]
md0 : active raid1 hdc1[1] hda1[0]
      102144 blocks [2/2] [UU]

md1 : active raid1 hdc2[1] hda3[0]
      1048576 blocks [2/2] [UU]

md2 : active raid1 hdc3[1]
      77023232 blocks [2/1] [_U]
```

This display indicates that only the raid1 (mirroring) *personality* is active, managing three device nodes:

md0

  This is a two-partition mirror, incorporating */dev/hda1* (device 0) and */dev/hdc1* (device 1). The total size is 102,144 blocks (about 100 MB). Both devices are active.

md1

  This is another two-partition mirror, incorporating */dev/hda3* as device 0 and */dev/ hdc2* as device 1. It's 1,048,576 blocks long (1 GB), and both devices are active.

md2

  This is yet another two-partition mirror, but only one partition (*/dev/hdc3*) is present. The size is about 75 GB.

The designations md0, md1, and md2 refer to *multidevice* nodes that can be accessed as */dev/md0*, */dev/md1*, and */dev/md2*.

You can get more detailed information about RAID devices using the *mdadm* command with the -D (detail) option. Let's look at md0 and md2:

```
# mdadm -D /dev/md0
/dev/md0:
         Version : 00.90.03
   Creation Time : Mon Aug  9 02:16:43 2004
      Raid Level : raid1
      Array Size : 102144 (99.75 MiB 104.60 MB)
     Device Size : 102144 (99.75 MiB 104.60 MB)
    Raid Devices : 2
   Total Devices : 2
 Preferred Minor : 0
     Persistence : Superblock is persistent
```

```
        Update Time : Tue Mar 28 04:04:22 2006
              State : clean
     Active Devices : 2
    Working Devices : 2
     Failed Devices : 0
      Spare Devices : 0

               UUID : dd2aabd5:fb2ab384:cba9912c:df0b0f4b
             Events : 0.3275

    Number   Major   Minor   RaidDevice State
         0       3       1            0   active sync   /dev/hda1
         1      22       1            1   active sync   /dev/hdc1
# mdadm -D /dev/md2
/dev/md2:
            Version : 00.90.03
      Creation Time : Mon Aug  9 02:16:19 2004
         Raid Level : raid1
         Array Size : 77023232 (73.46 GiB 78.87 GB)
        Device Size : 77023232 (73.46 GiB 78.87 GB)
       Raid Devices : 2
      Total Devices : 1
    Preferred Minor : 2
        Persistence : Superblock is persistent

        Update Time : Tue Mar 28 15:36:04 2006
              State : clean, degraded
     Active Devices : 1
    Working Devices : 1
     Failed Devices : 0
      Spare Devices : 0

               UUID : 31c6dbdc:414eee2d:50c4c773:2edc66f6
             Events : 0.19023894

    Number   Major   Minor   RaidDevice State
         0       0       0            -   removed
         1      22       3            1   active sync   /dev/hdc3
```

Note that md2 is marked as degraded because one of the devices is missing.

Creating a RAID array

To create a RAID array, you will need two block devices—usually, two partitions on different disk drives.

If you want to experiment with RAID, you can use two USB flash drives; in these next examples, I'm using some 64 MB flash drives that I have lying around. If your USB drives are auto-mounted when you insert them, unmount them before using them for RAID, either by right-clicking on them on the desktop and selecting Unmount Volume or by using the *umount* command.

The *mdadm* option `--create` is used to create a RAID array:

```
# mdadm --create -n 2 -l raid1 /dev/md0 /dev/sdb1 /dev/sdc1
mdadm: array /dev/md0 started.
```

There are a lot of arguments used here:

`--create`
> Tells *mdadm* to create a new disk array.

`-n 2`
> The number of block devices in the array.

`-l raid1`
> The RAID level.

/dev/md0
> The name of the *md* device.

/dev/sdb1 /dev/sdc1
> The two devices to use for this array.

/proc/mdstat shows the configuration of */dev/md0*:

```
# cat /proc/mdstat
Personalities : [raid1]
md0 : active raid1 sdc1[1] sdb1[0]
      63872 blocks [2/2] [UU]

unused devices: <none>
```

If you have three or more devices, you can use RAID 5, and if you have four or more, you can use RAID 6. This example creates a RAID 5 array:

```
# mdadm --create -n 3 -l raid5 /dev/md0 /dev/sdb1 /dev/sdc1 /dev/sdf1
mdadm: largest drive (/dev/sdb1) exceed size (62464K) by more than 1%
Continue creating array? y
mdadm: array /dev/md0 started.
```

Note that RAID expects all of the devices to be the same size. If they are not, the array will use only the amount of storage equal to the smallest partition on each of the devices; for example, if given partitions that are 50 GB, 47.5 GB, and 52 GB in size, the RAID system will use 47.5 GB in each of the three partitions, wasting 5 GB of disk space. If the variation between devices is more than 1 percent, as in this case, *mdadm* will prompt you to confirm that you're aware of the difference (and therefore the wasted storage space).

Once the RAID array has been created, make a filesystem on it, as you would with any other block device:

```
# mkfs -t ext3 /dev/md0
mke2fs 1.38 (30-Jun-2005)
Filesystem label=
OS type: Linux
Block size=1024 (log=0)
Fragment size=1024 (log=0)
```

```
16000 inodes, 63872 blocks
3193 blocks (5.00%) reserved for the super user
First data block=1
Maximum filesystem blocks=65536000
8 block groups
8192 blocks per group, 8192 fragments per group
2000 inodes per group
Superblock backups stored on blocks:
        8193, 24577, 40961, 57345

Writing inode tables: done
Creating journal (4096 blocks): done
Writing superblocks and filesystem accounting information: done

This filesystem will be automatically checked every 28 mounts or
180 days, whichever comes first.  Use tune2fs -c or -i to override.
```

Then mount it and use it:

```
# mkdir /mnt/raid
# mount /dev/md0 /mnt/raid
```

Alternately, you can use it as a PV under LVM. In this example, a new VG *test* is created, containing the LV *mysql*:

```
# pvcreate /dev/md0
  Physical volume "/dev/md0" successfully created
# vgcreate test /dev/md0
  Volume group "test" successfully created
# lvcreate test --name mysql --size 60M
  Logical volume "mysql" created
# mkfs -t ext3 /dev/test/mysql
mke2fs 1.38 (30-Jun-2005)
...(Lines skipped)...
This filesystem will be automatically checked every 36 mounts or
180 days, whichever comes first.  Use tune2fs -c or -i to override.
# mkdir /mnt/mysql
# mount /dev/test/mysql /mnt/mysql
```

Handling a drive failure

You can simulate the failure of a RAID array element using *mdadm*:

```
# mdadm --fail /dev/md0 /dev/sdc1
mdadm: set /dev/sdc1 faulty in /dev/md0
```

The "failed" drive is marked with the symbol (F) in */proc/mdstat*:

```
# cat /proc/mdstat
Personalities : [raid1]
md0 : active raid1 sdc1[2](F) sdb1[0]
      63872 blocks [2/1] [U_]

unused devices: <none>
```

To place the "failed" element back into the array, remove it and add it again:

```
# mdadm --remove /dev/md0 /dev/sdc1
mdadm: hot removed /dev/sdc1

# mdadm --add /dev/md0 /dev/sdc1
mdadm: re-added /dev/sdc1
# cat /proc/mdstat
Personalities : [raid1]
md0 : active raid1 sdc1[1] sdb1[0]
      63872 blocks [2/1] [U_]
      [>....................]  recovery =  0.0% (928/63872) finish=3.1min speed=309K/
sec

unused devices: <none>
```

If the drive had really failed (instead of being subject to a simulated failure), you would replace the drive after removing it from the array and before adding the new one.

Do not hot-plug disk drives—i.e., physically remove or add them with the power turned on—unless the drive, disk controller, and connectors are all designed for this operation. If in doubt, shut down the system, switch the drives while the system is turned off, and then turn the power back on.

If you check */proc/mdstat* a short while after readding the drive to the array, you can see that the RAID system automatically rebuilds the array by copying data from the good drive(s) to the new drive:

```
# cat /proc/mdstat
Personalities : [raid1]
md0 : active raid1 sdc1[1] sdb1[0]
      63872 blocks [2/1] [U_]
      [=============>.......]  recovery = 65.0% (42496/63872)
            finish=0.8min speed=401K/sec

unused devices: <none>
```

The *mdadm* command shows similar information in a more verbose form:

```
# mdadm -D /dev/md0
/dev/md0:
          Version : 00.90.03
    Creation Time : Thu Mar 30 01:01:00 2006
       Raid Level : raid1
       Array Size : 63872 (62.39 MiB 65.40 MB)
      Device Size : 63872 (62.39 MiB 65.40 MB)
     Raid Devices : 2
    Total Devices : 2
  Preferred Minor : 0
      Persistence : Superblock is persistent

      Update Time : Thu Mar 30 01:48:39 2006
            State : clean, degraded, recovering
```

```
       Active Devices : 1
      Working Devices : 2
       Failed Devices : 0
        Spare Devices : 1

        Rebuild Status : 65% complete

                 UUID : b7572e60:4389f5dd:ce231ede:458a4f79
               Events : 0.34

         Number   Major   Minor   RaidDevice State
            0       8      17         0       active sync   /dev/sdb1
            1       8      33         1       spare rebuilding   /dev/sdc1
```

Stopping and restarting a RAID array

A RAID array can be stopped anytime that it is not in use—useful if you have built an array incorporating removable or external drives that you want to disconnect. If you're using the RAID device as an LVM physical volume, you'll need to deactivate the volume group so the device is no longer considered to be in use:

```
# vgchange test -an
  0 logical volume(s) in volume group "test" now active
```

The -an argument here means *activated: no.* (Alternately, you can remove the PV from the VG using *vgreduce.*)

To stop the array, use the --stop option to *mdadm*:

```
# mdadm --stop /dev/md0
```

The two steps above will automatically be performed when the system is shut down.

To restart the array, use the --assemble option:

```
# mdadm --assemble /dev/md0 /dev/sdb1 /dev/sdc1
mdadm: /dev/md0 has been started with 2 drives.
```

To configure the automatic assembly of this array at boot time, obtain the array's UUID (unique ID number) from the output of mdadm -D:

```
# mdadm -D /dev/md0
/dev/md0:
            Version : 00.90.03
      Creation Time : Thu Mar 30 02:09:14 2006
         Raid Level : raid1
         Array Size : 63872 (62.39 MiB 65.40 MB)
        Device Size : 63872 (62.39 MiB 65.40 MB)
       Raid Devices : 2
      Total Devices : 2
    Preferred Minor : 0
        Persistence : Superblock is persistent

        Update Time : Thu Mar 30 02:19:00 2006
              State : clean
```

```
          Active Devices : 2
         Working Devices : 2
          Failed Devices : 0
           Spare Devices : 0

                    UUID : 5fccf106:d00cda80:daea5427:1edb9616
                  Events : 0.18

        Number   Major   Minor   RaidDevice State
           0       8      17         0       active sync   /dev/sdb1
           1       8      33         1       active sync   /dev/sdc1
```

Then create the file */dev/mdstat* if it doesn't exist, or add an ARRAY line to it if it does:

```
DEVICE partitions
MAILADDR root
ARRAY /dev/md0 uuid=c27420a7:c7b40cc9:3aa51849:99661a2e
```

In this file, the DEVICE line identifies the devices to be scanned (all partitions of all storage devices in this case), and the ARRAY lines identify each RAID array that is expected to be present. This ensures that the RAID arrays identified by scanning the partitions will always be assigned the same *md* device numbers, which is useful if more than one RAID array exists in the system. In the *mdadm.conf* files created during installation by Anaconda, the ARRAY lines contain optional level= and num-devices= entries (see the next section).

If the device is a PV, you can now reactivate the VG:

```
# vgchange test -ay
  1 logical volume(s) in volume group "test" now active
```

Monitoring RAID arrays

The *mdmonitor* service uses the monitor mode of *mdadm* to monitor and report on RAID drive status.

The method used to report drive failures is configured in the file */etc/mdadm.conf*. To send email to a specific email address, add or edit the MAILADDR line:

```
# mdadm.conf written out by anaconda
DEVICE partitions
MAILADDR raid-alert
ARRAY /dev/md0 level=raid1 num-devices=2 uuid=dd2aabd5:fb2ab384:cba9912c:df0b0f4b
ARRAY /dev/md1 level=raid1 num-devices=2 uuid=2b0846b0:d1a540d7:d722dd48:c5d203e4
ARRAY /dev/md2 level=raid1 num-devices=2 uuid=31c6dbdc:414eee2d:50c4c773:2edc66f6
```

When *mdadm.conf* is configured by Anaconda, the email address is set to root. It is a good idea to set this to an email alias, such as raid-alert, and configure the alias in the */etc/aliases* file to send mail to whatever destinations are appropriate:

```
raid-alert: chris, 4165559999@msg.telus.com
```

In this case, email will be sent to the local mailbox chris, as well as to a cell phone.

When an event occurs, such as a drive failure, *mdadm* sends an email message like this:

```
From root@bluesky.fedorabook.com  Thu Mar 30 09:43:54 2006
Date: Thu, 30 Mar 2006 09:43:54 -0500
From: mdadm monitoring <root@bluesky.fedorabook.com>
To: chris@bluesky.fedorabook.com
Subject: Fail event on /dev/md0:bluesky.fedorabook.com

This is an automatically generated mail message from mdadm
running on bluesky.fedorabook.com

A Fail event had been detected on md device /dev/md0.

It could be related to component device /dev/sdc1.

Faithfully yours, etc.
```

 I like the "Faithfully yours" bit at the end!

If you'd prefer that *mdadm* run a custom program when an event is detected—perhaps to set off an alarm or other notification—add a PROGRAM line to */etc/mdadm.conf*:

```
# mdadm.conf written out by anaconda
DEVICE partitions
MAILADDR raid-alert
PROGRAM /usr/local/sbin/mdadm-event-handler
ARRAY /dev/md0 level=raid1 num-devices=2 uuid=dd2aabd5:fb2ab384:cba9912c:df0b0f4b
ARRAY /dev/md1 level=raid1 num-devices=2 uuid=2b0846b0:d1a540d7:d722dd48:c5d203e4
ARRAY /dev/md2 level=raid1 num-devices=2 uuid=31c6dbdc:414eee2d:50c4c773:2edc66f6
```

Only one program name can be given. When an event is detected, that program will be run with three arguments: the event, the RAID device, and (optionally) the RAID element. If you wanted a verbal announcement to be made, for example, you could use a script like this:

```
#!/bin/bash
#
# mdadm-event-handler :: announce RAID events verbally
#

# Set up the phrasing for the optional element name
if [ "$3" ]
then
        E=", element $3"
fi

# Separate words (RebuildStarted -> Rebuild Started)
$T=$(echo $1|sed "s/\([A-Z]\)/ \1/g")
```

```
# Make the voice announcement and then repeat it
echo "Attention! RAID event: $1 on $2 $E"|festival --tts
sleep 2
echo "Repeat: $1 on $2 $E"|festival --tts
```

When a drive fails, this script will announce something like "Attention! RAID event: Failed on */dev/md0*, element */dev/sdc1*" using the Festival speech synthesizer. It will also announce the start and completion of array rebuilds and other important milestones (make sure you keep the volume turned up).

Setting up a hot spare

When a system with RAID 1 or higher experiences a disk failure, the data on the failed drive will be recalculated from the remaining drives. However, data access will be slower than usual, and if any other drives fail, the array will not be able to recover. Therefore, it's important to replace a failed disk drive as soon as possible.

When a server is heavily used or is in an inaccessible location—such as an Internet colocation facility—it makes sense to equip it with a *hot spare*. The hot spare is installed but unused until another drive fails, at which point the RAID system automatically uses it to replace the failed drive.

To create a hot spare when a RAID array is initially created, use the -x argument to indicate the number of spare devices:

```
# mdadm --create -l raid1 -n 2 -x 1 /dev/md0 /dev/sdb1 /dev/sdc1 /dev/sdf1
mdadm: array /dev/md0 started.
$ cat /proc/mdstat
Personalities : [raid1] [raid5] [raid4]
md0 : active raid1 sdf1[2](S) sdc1[1] sdb1[0]
      62464 blocks [2/2] [UU]

unused devices: <none>
```

Notice that */dev/sdf1* is marked with the symbol (S) indicating that it is the hot spare.

If an active element in the array fails, the hot spare will take over automatically:

```
$ cat /proc/mdstat
Personalities : [raid1] [raid5] [raid4]
md0 : active raid1 sdf1[2] sdc1[3](F) sdb1[0]
      62464 blocks [2/1] [U_]
      [=>...................]  recovery =  6.4% (4224/62464) finish=1.5min
speed=603K/sec

unused devices: <none>
```

When you remove, replace, and readd the failed drive, it will become the hot spare:

```
# mdadm --remove /dev/md0 /dev/sdc1
mdadm: hot removed /dev/sdc1
...(Physically replace the failed drive)...
# mdadm --add /dev/md0 /dev/sdc1
mdadm: re-added /dev/sdc1
```

```
# cat /proc/mdstat
Personalities : [raid1] [raid5] [raid4]
md0 : active raid1 sdc1[2](S) sdf1[1] sdb1[0]
      62464 blocks [2/2] [UU]

unused devices: <none>
```

Likewise, to add a hot spare to an existing array, simply add an extra drive:

```
# mdadm --add /dev/md0 /dev/sdh1
mdadm: added /dev/sdh1
```

Since hot spares are not used until another drive fails, it's a good idea to spin them down (stop the motors) to prolong their life. This command will program all of your drives to stop spinning after 15 minutes of inactivity (on most systems, only the hot spares will ever be idle for that length of time):

```
# hdparm -S 180 /dev/[sh]d[a-z]
```

Add this command to the end of the file */etc/rc.d/rc.local* to ensure that it is executed every time the system is booted:

```
#!/bin/sh
#
# This script will be executed *after* all the other init scripts.
# You can put your own initialization stuff in here if you don't
# want to do the full Sys V style init stuff.

touch /var/lock/subsys/local
hdparm -S 180 /dev/[sh]d[a-z]
```

Monitoring drive health

Self-Monitoring, Analysis, and Reporting Technology (SMART) is built into most modern disk drives. It provides access to drive diagnostic and error information and failure prediction.

Fedora provides *smartd* for SMART disk monitoring. The configuration file */etc/smartd.conf* is configured by the Anaconda installer to monitor each drive present in the system and to report only imminent (within 24 hours) drive failure to the *root* email address:

```
/dev/hda -H -m root
/dev/hdb -H -m root
/dev/hdc -H -m root
```

(I've left out the many comment lines that are in this file.)

It is a good idea to change the email address to the same alias used for your RAID error reports:

```
/dev/hda -H -m raid-alert
/dev/hdb -H -m raid-alert
/dev/hdc -H -m raid-alert
```

If you add additional drives to the system, be sure to add additional entries to this file.

How Does It Work?

Fedora's RAID levels 4 and 5 use parity information to provide redundancy. Parity is calculated using the exclusive-OR function, as shown in Table 6-4.

Table 6-4. Parity calculation for two drives

Bit from drive A	Bit from drive B	Parity bit on drive C
0	0	0
0	1	1
1	0	1
1	1	0

Notice that the total number of 1 bits in each row is an even number. You can determine the contents of any column based on the values in the other two columns (A = B XOR C and B = A XOR C); in this way, the RAID system can determine the content of any one failed drive. This approach will work with any number of drives.

Parity calculations are performed using the CPU's vector instructions (MMX/3DNow/SSE/AltiVec) whenever possible. Even an old 400 MHz Celeron processor can calculate RAID 5 parity at a rate in excess of 2 GB per second.

RAID 6 uses a similar but more advanced error-correcting code (ECC) that takes two bits of data for each row. This code permits recovery from the failure of any two drives, but the calculations run about one-third slower than the parity calculations. In a high-performance context, it may be better to use RAID 5 with a hot spare instead of RAID 6; the protection will be almost as good and the performance will be slightly higher.

What About...

...booting from a RAID array?

During the early stages of the boot process, no RAID driver is available. However, in a RAID 1 (mirroring) array, each element contains a full and complete copy of the data in the array and can be used as though it were a simple volume. Therefore, only RAID 1 can be used for the */boot* filesystem.

The GRUB boot record should be written to each drive that contains the */boot* filesystem (see Lab 10.5, "Configuring the GRUB Bootloader")

...mixing and matching USB flash drives, USB hard disks, SATA, SCSI, and IDE/ATA drives?

RAID can combine drives of different types into an array. This can be very useful at times; for example, you can use a USB hard disk to replace a failed SATA drive in a pinch.

...mirroring to a remote drive as part of a disaster-recovery plan?

Daily disk or tape backups can be up to 24 hours out of date, which can hamper recovery when your main server is subject to a catastrophic disaster such as fire, circuit-frying power-supply-unit failure, or theft. Up-to-the-minute data backup for rapid disaster recovery requires the use of a remote storage mirror.

iSCSI (SCSI over TCP/IP) is a *storage area network* technology that is an economical alternative to fiber channel and other traditional SAN technologies. Since it is based on TCP/IP, it is easy to route over long distances, making it ideal for remote mirroring.

Fedora Core includes an *iSCSI initiator*, the software necessary to remotely access a drive using the iSCSI protocol. The package name is *iscsi-initiator-utils*. Obviously, you'll need a remote iSCSI drive in order to do remote mirroring, and you'll need to know the *portal* IP address or hostname on the remote drive.

Create the file */etc/initiatorname.iscsi*, containing one line:

```
InitiatorName=iqn.2006-04.com.fedorabook:bluesky
```

This configures an *iSCSI Qualified Name* (IQN) that is globally unique. The IQN consists of the letters iqn, a period, the year and month in which your domain was registered (2006-04), a period, your domain name with the elements reversed, a colon, and a string that you make up (which must be unique within your domain).

Once the initiator name has been set up, start the *iscsi* server daemon:

```
# service iscsi start
```

You may see some error messages the first time you start the *iscsi* daemon; these can be safely ignored.

Next, use the *iscsiadm* command to discover the volumes (targets) available on the remote system:

```
# iscsiadm -m discovery -tst -p 172.16.97.2
[f68ace] 172.16.97.2:3260,1 iqn.2006-04.com.fedorabook:remote1-volume1
```

 If the remote drive requires a user ID and password for connection, edit */etc/iscsid.conf*.

The options indicate *discovery* mode, *sendtargets* (st) discovery type, and the *portal* address or hostname. The result that is printed shows the IQN of the remote target, including a node record ID at the start of the line (f68ace). The discovered target information is stored in a database for future reference, and the node record ID is the key to accessing this information.

To connect to the remote system, use *iscsiadm* to log in:

```
# iscsiadm -m node --record f68ace --login
```

The details of the connection are recorded in */var/log/messages*:

```
Mar 30 22:05:18 blacktop kernel: scsi1 : iSCSI Initiator over TCP/IP, v.0.3
Mar 30 22:05:19 blacktop kernel:   Vendor: IET       Model: VIRTUAL-DISK     Rev: 0
Mar 30 22:05:19 blacktop kernel:   Type:   Direct-Access                     ANSI
SCSI revision: 04
Mar 30 22:05:19 blacktop kernel: SCSI device sda: 262144 512-byte hdwr sectors (134
MB)
Mar 30 22:05:19 blacktop kernel: sda: Write Protect is off
Mar 30 22:05:19 blacktop kernel: SCSI device sda: drive cache: write back
Mar 30 22:05:19 blacktop kernel: SCSI device sda: 262144 512-byte hdwr sectors (134
MB)
Mar 30 22:05:19 blacktop kernel: sda: Write Protect is off
Mar 30 22:05:19 blacktop. kernel: SCSI device sda: drive cache: write back
Mar 30 22:05:19 blacktop kernel:  sda: sda1
Mar 30 22:05:19 blacktop kernel: sd 14:0:0:0: Attached scsi disk sda
Mar 30 22:05:19 blacktop kernel: sd 14:0:0:0: Attached scsi generic sg0 type 0
Mar 30 22:05:19 blacktop iscsid: picking unique OUI for the same target node name
iqn.2006-04.com.fedorabook:remote1-volume1
Mar 30 22:05:20 blacktop iscsid: connection1:0 is operational now
```

This shows that the new device is accessible as */dev/sda* and has one partition (*/dev/sda1*).

You can now create a local LV that is the same size as the remote drive:

```
# lvcreate main --name database --size 128M
  Logical volume "database" created
```

And then you can make a RAID mirror incorporating the local LV and the remote drive:

```
# mdadm --create -l raid1 -n 2 /dev/md0 /dev/main/database /dev/sdi1
mdadm: array /dev/md0 started.
```

Next, you can create a filesystem on the RAID array and mount it:

```
# mkfs -t ext3 /dev/md0
mke2fs 1.38 (30-Jun-2005)
Filesystem label=
OS type: Linux
Block size=1024 (log=0)
Fragment size=1024 (log=0)
32768 inodes, 130944 blocks
6547 blocks (5.00%) reserved for the super user
First data block=1
Maximum filesystem blocks=67371008
16 block groups
```

```
8192 blocks per group, 8192 fragments per group
2048 inodes per group
Superblock backups stored on blocks:
        8193, 24577, 40961, 57345, 73729

Writing inode tables: done
Creating journal (4096 blocks): done
Writing superblocks and filesystem accounting information: done

This filesystem will be automatically checked every 27 mounts or
180 days, whichever comes first.  Use tune2fs -c or -i to override.
# mkdir /mnt/database
# mount /dev/md0 /mnt/database
```

Any data you write to *mnt/database* will be written to both the local volume and the remote drive.

 Do not use iSCSI directly over the Internet: route iSCSI traffic through a private TCP/IP network or a virtual private network (VPN) to maintain the privacy of your stored data.

To shut down the remote mirror, reverse the steps:

```
# umount /mnt/database
# mdadm --stop /dev/md0
# iscsiadm -m node --record f68ace --logout
```

A connection will be made to the remote node whenever the iSCSI daemon starts. To prevent this, edit the file */etc/iscsid.conf*:

```
#
# Open-iSCSI default configuration.
# Could be located at /etc/iscsid.conf or ~/.iscsid.conf
#
node.active_cnx = 1
node.startup = automatic
#node.session.auth.username = dima
#node.session.auth.password = aloha
node.session.timeo.replacement_timeout = 0
node.session.err_timeo.abort_timeout = 10
node.session.err_timeo.reset_timeout = 30
node.session.iscsi.InitialR2T = No
node.session.iscsi.ImmediateData = Yes
node.session.iscsi.FirstBurstLength = 262144
node.session.iscsi.MaxBurstLength = 16776192
node.session.iscsi.DefaultTime2Wait = 0
node.session.iscsi.DefaultTime2Retain = 0
node.session.iscsi.MaxConnections = 0
node.cnx[0].iscsi.HeaderDigest = None
node.cnx[0].iscsi.DataDigest = None
node.cnx[0].iscsi.MaxRecvDataSegmentLength = 65536
#discovery.sendtargets.auth.authmethod = CHAP
#discovery.sendtargets.auth.username = dima
#discovery.sendtargets.auth.password = aloha
```

Change the node.startup line to read:

```
node.startup = manual
```

Once the remote mirror has been configured, you can create a simple script file with the setup commands:

```
#!/bin/bash
iscsiadm -m node --record f68ace --login
mdadm --assemble /dev/md0 /dev/main/database /dev/sdi1
mount /dev/md0 /mnt/database
```

And another script file with the shutdown commands:

```
#!/bin/bash
umount /mnt/database
mdadm --stop /dev/md0
iscsiadm -m node --record f68ace --logout
```

Save these scripts into */usr/local/sbin* and enable read and execute permission for both of them:

```
# chmod u+rx /usr/local/sbin/remote-mirror-start
# chmod u+rx /usr/local/sbin/remote-mirror-stop
```

You can also install these as init scripts (see Lab 4.6, "Managing and Configuring Services and Lab 4.12, "Writing Simple Scripts").

...using more than one RAID array, but configuring one hot spare to be shared between them?

This can be done through */etc/mdadm.conf*. In each ARRAY line, add a spare-group option:

```
# mdadm.conf written out by anaconda
DEVICE partitions
MAILADDR root
ARRAY /dev/md0 spare-group=red uuid=5fccf106:d00cda80:daea5427:1edb9616
ARRAY /dev/md1 spare-group=red uuid=aaf3d1e1:6f7231b4:22ca60f9:00c07dfe
```

The name of the spare-group does not matter as long as all of the arrays sharing the hot spare have the same value; here I've used red. Ensure that at least one of the arrays has a hot spare and that the size of the hot spare is not smaller than the largest element that it could replace; for example, if each device making up *md0* was 10 GB in size, and each element making up *md1* was 5 GB in size, the hot spare would have to be at least 10 GB in size, even if it was initially a member of *md1*.

...configuring the rebuild rate for arrays?

Array rebuilds will usually be performed at a rate of 1,000 to 20,000 KB per second per drive, scheduled in such a way that the impact on application storage performance is minimized. Adjusting the rebuild rate lets you adjust the trade-off between application performance and rebuild duration.

The settings are accessible through two pseudofiles in */proc/sys/dev/raid*, named *speed_limit_max* and *speed_limit_min*. To view the current values, simply display the contents:

```
$ cat /proc/sys/dev/raid/speed_limit*
200000
1000
```

To change a setting, place a new number in the appropriate pseudo-file:

```
# echo 40000 >/proc/sys/dev/raid/speed_limit_max
```

...simultaneous drive failure?

Sometimes, a drive manufacturer just makes a bad batch of disks—and this has happened more than once. For example, a few years ago, one drive maker used defective plastic to encapsulate the chips on the drive electronics; drives with the defective plastic failed at around the same point in their life cycles, so that several elements of RAID arrays built using these drives would fail within a period of days or even hours. Since most RAID levels provide protection against a single drive failure but not against multiple drive failures, data was lost.

For greatest safety, it's a good idea to buy disks of similar capacity from different drive manufacturers (or at least different models or batches) when building a RAID array, in order to reduce the likelihood of near-simultaneous drive failure.

Where Can I Learn More?

* The manpages for *md*, *mdadm*, *mdadm.conf*, *hdparm*, *smartd*, *smartd.conf*, *mkfs*, *mke2fs*, and *dmraid*
* The manpages for *iscsid* and *iscsiadm*
* The Linux-iSCSI project: *http://linux-iscsi.sourceforge.net*
* The Enterprise iSCSI Target project: *http://iscsitarget.sourceforge.net/*

6.3 Making Backups

Hard disks are mechanical devices. They are guaranteed to wear out, fail, and lose your data. The only unknown is *when* they will fail.

Data backup is performed to guard against drive failure. But it's also done to guard against data loss due to theft, fire, accidental deletion, bad editing, software defects, and unnoticed data corruption.

How Do I Do That?

Before making backups, you must decide:

* What data needs to be backed up
* How often the data needs to be backed up

- How quickly you need to restore the data
- How far back in time you need to be able to restore

Based on this information, you can develop a backup strategy, including a backup technology, schedule, and rotation.

Determining what data to back up

Any data that you want to preserve must be backed up; usually, this does not include the operating system or applications, because you can reinstall those.

Table 6-5 lists some common system roles and the directories that should be considered for backup.

Table 6-5. Directories used for critical data storage in various common system roles

System role	Standard directories	Notes
Database server (e.g., MySQL)	/var/lib/mysql	Stop the database server or use snapshots to ensure consistency between tables.
Web server	/var/www /etc/httpd /home/*/~public_html	Also include any data directories used by web applications.
DNS nameserver	/var/named /etc/named.conf	This information usually changes slowly.
Desktop system, or any system accessed by individual users	/home	Exclude cache directories such as /home/*/.mozilla/firefox/*/Cache.
Samba server	All directories served by Samba	
CUPS print server	/etc/cups	Configuration information only; usually changes slowly.
All systems	/etc	Configuration information for most software and hardware installed on the system.

Determining how often to back up your data

Generally, backup frequency should be decided based on how often (and when) the data changes, and how many changes you are willing to lose.

For example, printer configuration data may be changed only a few times a year, and losing the latest change won't cost much in terms of the work required to re-create that change. Word processing documents may be changed daily, and you may want to ensure that you don't lose more than one day's work (or even a half-day's work); on the other hand, orders on a busy web site may be received every few seconds, and you may decide that you can't live with the loss of more than a few minutes worth of data.

Determine how quickly you will need to restore your data

How long can you live without your data? The answer probably depends on regulatory and operational issues.

Some types of information—such as information about cross-border shipments—must be reported to government agencies on a daily basis, for example, and delays are penalized by fines of thousands of dollars per day. This puts a tremendous amount of pressure on the data-recovery process. On the other hand, personal music and photo collections may not need to be restored until weeks or months after the data loss.

Determine how far back in time you need to restore

Some types of data loss or corruption may not be realized until weeks, months, or years after they have occurred, while others will be immediately obvious. In some cases—when data changes quickly—it may be necessary to be able to restore data to the state it was in on a specific date, while in other cases it's sufficient to be able to restore data to the state that it was in at the end of a particular month.

Decision 1: Incremental versus full backups, and backup rotation

Files may be selected for backup on an *incremental* basis—only files that have been changed since the last backup are selected—or a *full* backup may be performed.

Incremental backups often require significantly less storage space than full backups when dealing with large sets of individual files such as word processing documents because the number of documents that are changed each day is usually fairly small. On the other hand, a small SQL update query may cause all of the files in a database to be modified, nullifying the benefits of incremental backup in that context.

An incremental backup scheme usually involves making full backups periodically and then making incremental backups until the scheduled time of the next full backup. Restoring from an incremental backup therefore requires you to restore a full backup, then restore all of the incremental backups from that point forward. Thus, the time required for a restore operation may be much longer than for a system that uses only full backups. Also, if one of the backups is unusable due to media corruption or damage, you will not be able to reliably perform a full recovery.

Given the choice between full and incremental backups, I recommend using full backups whenever practical.

Decision 2: Decide on the backup media

Cost, capacity, and speed usually drive the selection of backup media. There are many options available:

DVD±R/RW
> DVD is an attractive medium. Fedora includes software to produce compressed optical discs that are automatically decompressed by the kernel when they are read. The compression ratio will depend on the type of data being backed up; text files may compress by 75–90 percent, while data that is already in a com-

pressed format (such as OpenOffice.org documents) may not compress at all. You can reasonably expect 50 percent compression for a typical mix of user files, and 75 percent for databases containing text data; that means a single-sided DVD±R, which costs only a few cents and which has a nominal capacity of 4.7 GB (usable capacity of slightly over 4.3 GB), will hold 8+ GB of regular user files or 16+ GB of database files. DVD is also a fast, random-access medium.

CD-R/RW

Similar to DVD, with a lower storage capacity and wider deployment. Because higher-capacity DVDs are similarly priced (actually, cheaper in some jurisdictions—such as Canada—due to music levies on CDs), DVDs are preferred except when backing up a device such as a laptop that has only a CD-RW drive.

Tape

Tape is by far the most economical choice for high-volume data backup (>10 GB uncompressed), but it still doesn't come cheap. Tape drives can cost more than the disk drives being backed up, and each backup tape can cost 25–50 percent of the price of the corresponding disk storage. Tapes are also fairly slow during search and restore operations due to their sequential nature.

Disk

Hard disks can be used for data backup. USB drives are particularly convenient for this purpose, but removable drive trays can also be used with ATA or SATA drives. Hard drives are fast, but expensive and fragile.

Remote storage

Copying an archive of data to a remote system periodically.

Remote mirror

Making an immediate copy of all data written to the local disk drive provides the ultimate backup, but this approach is complicated and does not by itself guard against data corruption or accidental file deletion. For one approach to remote mirroring, see "…mirroring to a remote drive as part of a disaster-recovery plan?" in the "What About…" section in Lab 6.2, "Managing RAID."

I'm going to focus on DVD and tape storage options in this lab.

Decision 3: Decide on media rotation and storage

When using DVDs, you have the option of selecting DVD±R media, which can only be written once. This provides an inexpensive, compact, and permanent archive through time; assuming one disc per day, a year's worth of discs will take only about 4L of space and cost less than $100.

For tape and DVD±RW media, you'll need to decide on your media rotation strategy. This is a compromise between the number of tapes/discs and how far back in time you wish to restore.

A simple rotation scheme involves buying a set amount of media and rotating through it. For example, 20 discs or tapes used only on weekdays will enable you to restore files to the state they were in during any weekday in the preceding four weeks.

A multilevel scheme permits you to go back farther in time. A simple three-level scheme (known as *Grandfather/Father/Son*) is shown in Table 6-6.

Table 6-6. Grandfather/Father/Son backup scheme with 20 discs/tapes

Level	Media used	Discs or tapes required
A (Son)	Monday–Thursday	4
B (Father)	Three out of every four Fridays	3
C (Grandfather)	Fridays not covered by level B	13

This scheme uses the same 20 discs or tapes, but permits you to restore to:

- Any weekday in the preceding week
- The end of any week in the preceding four weeks
- The end of any four-week period in the preceding year

 Note that level A media will be more frequently used than level B or C media and will therefore need to be replaced more often.

You must also decide where and how you will store your media. Unless the media is stored offsite, a disaster such as fire or theft could result in the loss of both the original storage drives and the backup media, but storing media offsite will slow the restoration process.

Simple backup labeling

There are many ways of labeling backups, but one of the easiest is to create a file named *system-<hostname>* in the root directory immediately before producing the backup, and include that as the first file in the backup volume:

```
# touch /system-$(hostname)
# ls -l /system-*
-rw-r--r--  1 root root 0 Jul  1 01:34 /system-bluesky.fedorabook.com
```

This will identify the originating system name as well as the date and time of the backup (from the file timestamp).

Backing up to DVD

To back up data to DVD, use the *growisofs* command:

```
# growisofs -Z /dev/dvd -RJ -graft-points /etc=/etc /home=/home /system-*
```

This will back up the */etc* and */home* directories to */dev/dvd* (the default DVD recorder). -Z indicates that this is the first session on the disc, and -RJ enables long filename handling compatible with Unix/Linux (Rock Ridge) and Windows (Joliet) systems. The graft-points option permits the backed-up directories to be stored in specific directories on the disc. /etc=/etc and /home=/home specify the directories to be backed up, ensuring that each directory is placed in a directory with the same name on the disc. The argument /system-* places the system label file in the root directory of the DVD.

This command will work with DVD-R, DVD+R, DVD-RW, and DVD+RW media.

To create a compressed DVD, use the *mkzftree* command to create a compressed copy of the origin directories:

```
# mkdir /tmp/zftree
# mkzftree /home /tmp/zftree/home
# mkzftree /etc  /tmp/zftree/etc
```

You will need sufficient disk space to hold the compressed image before it is written to the optical disc.

Then use the -z option to growisofs:

```
# growisofs -Z /dev/dvd -RJz /tmp/zftree /system-*
```

Putting this all together into a script, and mailing the results to the email alias *backup-alert*, we get this:

```
#!/bin/bash
#
# backup-dvd :: backup selected directories to a compressed DVD
#

# List of the directories to be backed up
DIRLIST="/etc /home"

# Create timestamp file
(
rm -f /system-*
touch /system-$(hostname)

# Make directory for compressed backup tree
rm -rf /tmp/zftree 2>/dev/null
mkdir /tmp/zftree
RESULT=0
for DIR in $DIRLIST
do
    mkzftree $DIR /tmp/zftree${DIR}
    RESULT=$(( $? + $RESULT ))
done
```

```
if [ "$RESULT" -eq 0 ]
then

    # Burn the DVD
    growisofs -Z /dev/dvd -RJz /tmp/zftree /system-*

    # Eject the disc
    eject

else

    echo "Skipping burn: file compression failed."

fi

# Delete the zftree
rm -rf /tmp/zftree 2>/dev/null

) 2>&1|mail -s "Backup Log $(hostname)" backup-alert
```

Edit the DIRLIST line so that it contains a list of the directories to be backed up, separated by spaces.

Save this file as */usr/local/bin/backup-dvd* and then make it executable:

```
# chmod u+rx /usr/local/bin/backup-dvd
```

And be sure to create an email alias for the *backup-alert* user in the file */etc/aliases*:

```
backup-alert: chris frank
```

To produce a backup, execute this script:

```
# backup-dvd
```

But it's a better idea to configure the system to run this script automatically every night (see Lab 6.4, "Scheduling Tasks").

Backing up to tape

To back up directories to tape, use the *tape archiver* (*tar*):

```
# tar -cf /dev/st0 /system-* /etc /home
tar: Removing leading `/' from member names
tar: Removing leading `/' from hard link targets
```

In this command, */dev/st0* is the first tape drive, and */etc* and */home* are the directories being backed up.

To perform a compressed backup, add the z (for *gzip* compression) or j (for *bzip2* compression) option:

```
# tar -czf /dev/st0 /system-* /etc /home
tar: Removing leading `/' from member names
tar: Removing leading `/' from hard link targets
```

Here is a script that will perform a tape backup:

```
#!/bin/bash
#
# backup-tape :: backup selected directories to a compressed tape
#

# List of the directories to be backed up
DIRLIST="/etc /home"

# Create timestamp file
(
rm -f /system-*
touch /system-$(hostname)

# Produce the tape
tar -czf /dev/st0 /system-* $DIRLIST

# Eject the tape if possible
mt -f /dev/st0 eject

) 2>&1|mail -s "Backup Log $(hostname)" backup-alert
```

Save this script as */usr/local/bin/backup-tape*.

Like the *backup-dvd* script, this script will send an email report to the email alias *backup-alert*. To include a list of files in the email report, add the -v option to the *tar* command:

```
tar -czvf /dev/st0 /system-* $DIRLIST
```

To produce a backup tape, run the script from the command line:

```
# backup-tape
```

It's best to run this script automatically every night (see Lab 6.4, "Scheduling Tasks").

Restoring files from backups

When restoring from tape, it's a good idea to restore to a location other than the original file location to ensure that critical data is not accidentally overwritten. These commands will perform a full restore of a tape to the directory */tmp/restore*:

```
# mkdir /tmp/restore
# cd /tmp/restore
# tar xvzf /dev/st0
```

To restore only certain files, specify the filenames as arguments to *tar*:

```
# tar xvzf /dev/st0 home/chris/
```

If the file specified is a directory, all of the files and subdirectories in that directory will be restored.

Restoring from disc is easy: just copy the files that you want to the location that you want. You can do this graphically, or you can restore all of the files on the disc:

```
# mkdir /tmp/restore
# cd /tmp/restore
# cp -r /media/CDROM/* .
```

Viewing the table of contents and verifying a backup

To verify that a tape backup is readable, use tar's t option to view a table of contents of the tape:

```
# tar tvzf /dev/st0
-rw-r--r-- root/root      0 2006-07-01 01:34:24 system-bluesky.fedorabook.com
drwxr-xr-x root/root      0 2005-09-23 15:01:38 etc/gconf/
drwxr-xr-x root/root      0 2005-03-02 11:59:15 etc/gconf/gconf.xml.mandatory/
drwxr-xr-x root/root      0 2005-08-29 00:53:34 etc/gconf/1/
-rw-r--r-- root/root    840 2005-03-02 11:59:11 etc/gconf/1/path
drwxr-xr-x root/root      0 2006-03-20 01:33:22 etc/gconf/schemas/
...(Lines skipped)...
```

Since the label file */system-** is the first file on the tape, you can view the originating machine as well as the date and time of the backup by just viewing the first line of the table of contents:

```
# tar tvzf /dev/st0|head -1
-rw-r--r-- root/root      0 2006-07-01 01:34:24 system-bluesky.fedorabook.com
```

To verify that all of the files on an optical disc are readable, use *find* to read each file on the mounted disc:

```
# find /media/cdrecorder -exec cp {} /dev/null \;
```

Only errors will be reported.

How Does It Work?

The *growisofs* command is part of the package *dvd+rw-tools*, which was originally intended for use with DVD+RW media. Since the original design, it has grown to include support for all DVD media formats. It operates as a frontend to the *mkisofs* command, which produces a filesystem in the ISO 9660 format that is the standard for optical media, and then writes the *mkisofs* output to the disc burner.

ISO 9660 is unfortunately limited to eight-character filenames with a three-character extension. The Rock Ridge (RR) extension adds support for long filenames, user and group ownership, and permission mode under Linux; Joliet extensions add similar support for the Windows operating systems. Using the -JR option to *growisofs* causes the created disk to be compatible with both Rock Ridge and Joliet.

mkzftree makes a recursive copy of a directory structure, compressing any files that would benefit from compression during the copy process. The resulting directory structure can be passed to *mkisofs* with the -z option, which will cause *mkisofs* to create additional Rock Ridge records with information about the data compression used. These records in turn enable the kernel's filesystem layer to decompress the files on the fly when reading them from disc.

When backing up to tape, *tar* converts a directory structure to a continuous stream of bytes. A short header contains the pathname, ownership, permissions modes, size, and timestamps for a file, followed by the data for that file; this is repeated for each file in the archive.

The z option to *tar* causes it to start *gzip* and process all data through it. As an alternative, the j option will process the archive stream through *bzip2*, which may offer better compression in some circumstances.

What About...

...using LVM snapshots in a backup script?

You can simply place the appropriate *vgcreate* and *mount* commands at the start of your backup script, and *umount* and *vgremove* commands at the end of the script.

Here is a slightly fancier version of the DVD backup script, which accepts a list of *vg/lv* pairs and creates a compressed DVD backup. Set the LVLIST and SNAPSIZE variables to whatever values you wish to use:

```
#!/bin/bash
#
# backup-dvd :: backup selected directories to a compressed DVD
#

# List of the vg/lv to be backed up
LVLIST="main/home main/var"

# Amount of space to use for snapshots
SNAPSIZE="1G"

# Create timestamp file
(
rm -f /system-*
touch /system-$(hostname)

# Make directory for compressed backup tree
rm -rf /tmp/zftree
mkdir /tmp/zftree

RESULT=0
for VGLV in $LVLIST
do
    echo "========= Processing $VGLV..."

    # Get information about the vg/lv
    VG=$(echo $VGLV|cut -f1 -d/)
```

```
    LV=$(echo $VGLV|cut -f2 -d/)
    SNAPNAME="${LV}-snap"
    OLDMOUNT= \
     $(grep "^/dev/${VGLV}" /etc/fstab|tr "\t" " "|tr -s " "|cut -f2 -d" ")
    NEWMOUNT="/mnt/snap${OLDMOUNT}"

    # Create a snapshot
    lvcreate -s $VGLV --name $SNAPNAME --size $SNAPSIZE
    RESULT=$(( $? + $RESULT ))

    # Mount the snapshot
    mkdir -p $NEWMOUNT
    mount -o ro /dev/${VG}/${SNAPNAME} ${NEWMOUNT}
    RESULT=$(( $? + $RESULT ))

    # Place it in the zftree
    mkdir -p /tmp/zftree$(dirname $OLDMOUNT)
    mkzftree ${NEWMOUNT} /tmp/zftree${OLDMOUNT}
    RESULT=$(( $? + $RESULT ))

    # Unmount the snapshot
    umount $NEWMOUNT

    # Release the snapshot
    lvremove -f ${VG}/${SNAPNAME}
done

if [ "$RESULT" -eq 0 ]
then

    # Burn the DVD
    growisofs -Z /dev/dvd -RJz /tmp/zftree /system-*

    # Eject the disc
    eject

else

    echo "Skipping burn: snapshot or file compression failed."

fi

# Delete the zftree
rm -rf /tmp/zftree 2>/dev/null

) 2>&1|mail -s "Backup Log $(hostname)" backup-alert
```

Each LV to be backed up must have a mount point identified in */etc/
fstab*.

...putting more than one backup on a tape?

The device node */dev/st0* is the default (first) tape drive on the system, configured to rewind after each use. */dev/nst0* is the same device but without the automatic rewind.

In order to position the tape, Fedora provides the *mt* command, described in Table 6-7.

Table 6-7. mt tape control commands

mt command	Description
mt rewind	Rewinds the tape
mt fsf	Forward-skips a file
mt fsf *count*	Forward-skips *count* files
mt bsf	Backward-skips a file
mt bsf *count*	Backward-skips *count* files
mt status	Displays the drive status
mt offline or mt eject	Rewinds and ejects the tape (if possible)

The *mt* command uses */dev/tape* as its default device; create this as a symbolic link to */dev/nst0* if it does not already exist:

```
# ln -s /dev/nst0 /dev/tape
```

You can now create a multibackup tape:

```
# mt rewind
# tar cvzf /dev/tape /home
# tar cvzf /dev/tape /etc
# mt rewind
```

To read a specific backup on a multibackup tape, rewind to the beginning (just to be sure you're at the start), and then skip any files (backups) necessary to reach the archive you want. These commands will access the table of contents for the second archive, for example:

```
# mt rewind
# mt fsf
# tar tvzf /dev/tape
etc/
etc/smrsh/
etc/smrsh/mailman
etc/group-
etc/gnopernicus-1.0/
etc/gnopernicus-1.0/translation_tables/
...(Lines snipped)...
```

...backing up multiple systems onto a central tape archive?

Fedora Core includes *amanda*, a powerful client-server tape backup system that can be used for this purpose. See the *amanda* manpages for details.

Where Can I Learn More?

- The manpages for *st*, *mt*, *tar*, *growisofs*, *mkisofs*, and *amanda*
- CD and DVD Archiving: Quick Reference Guide for Care and Handling (NIST): *http://www.itl.nist.gov/div895/carefordisc/disccare.html*
- Magnetic Tape Storage and Handling: A Guide for Libraries and Archives (NML): *http://www.imation.com/america/pdfs/AP_NMLdoc_magtape_S_H.pdf*

6.4   Scheduling Tasks

Fedora Core can schedule tasks to be run at specific times. This is useful for making backups, indexing data, clearing out temporary files, and automating downloads—and it's easy to set up.

How Do I Do That?

To schedule a task, use *crontab* with the -e option to edit your list of scheduled tasks:

```
$ crontab -e
```

The *vi* editor will start up, and any existing scheduled tasks will appear (if you don't have any scheduled tasks, the document will be blank). Edit the file using standard *vi* editing commands.

Each scheduled task occupies a separate line in this file. Each line consists of five time fields, followed by the command to be executed. In order, the file fields are:

minute
> The number of minutes past the hour, 0–59

hour
> The hour of the day, 0–23

day
> The day of the month, 1–31

month
> The number of the month, 1–12

day of the week
> The day of the week, 0–6 (Sunday to Saturday) or 1–7 (Monday to Sunday), or written out

A time field may contain an asterisk, which means *any*.

Here is an example:

```
30 * * * *    /home/chris/bin/task1
```

The script or program */home/chris/bin/task1* will be executed at 30 minutes past the hour, every hour of every day of every month. Here are some other examples:

```
15 1 * * *      /home/chris/bin/task2
0 22 * * 1      /home/chris/bin/task3
30 0 1 * *      /home/chris/bin/task4
0 11 11 11 *    /home/chris/bin/task5
```

task2 will be executed at 1:15 a.m. every day. *task3* will be executed at 10:00 p.m. every Monday. *task4* will be run at 12:30 a.m. on the first of every month. *task5* will be run at 11:00 a.m. each Remembrance Day (Veteran's Day).

You can use a range (*low-high*), a list of values (*1,2,3*), or */*increment* to specify every *increment* unit. Here are some more examples to illustrate:

```
0,15,30,45 9-16 * * *    /home/chris/bin/task6
*/2 * * * *     /home/chris/bin/task7
0 7 1-7 * 3     /home/chris/bin/task8
```

task6 will be run every 15 minutes (at 0, 15, 30, and 45 minutes past the hour) from 9:00 a.m. to 4:45 p.m. every day. *task7* will be executed every two minutes. *task8* will be executed at 7:00 a.m. on the first Wednesday of each month (the only Wednesday between the first and seventh of the month).

By default, any output (to *stdout* or *stderr*) produced by a scheduled command will be emailed to you. You can change the email destination by including a line that sets the MAILTO environment variable:

```
MAILTO=cronman@gmail.com
30 * * * *      /home/chris/bin/task1
15 1 * * *      /home/chris/bin/task2
0 22 * * 1      /home/chris/bin/task3
```

In fact, you can also set any standard environment variables; the two most useful are SHELL, which overrides the default shell (*bash*), and PATH, which overrides the default path (*/bin:/usr/bin*). Here's an example:

```
PATH=/bin:/usr/bin:/usr/local/bin:/sbin:/usr/sbin
SHELL=/bin/zsh
MAILTO=""
30 * * * *      adjust-network
```

Fedora also provides a system for running scripts on an hourly, daily, weekly, and monthly basis, simply by placing the script into a designated directory. These scripts run as *root*. Table 6-8 shows the time of execution for each directory.

Table 6-8. Scheduled task directories

Directory	Frequency	Time of execution	Task examples
/etc/cron.hourly	Hourly	:01 past each hour	Send/receive *netnews*
/etc/cron.daily	Daily	4:02 a.m. every day	Analyze web logs, rotate logs, delete old temporary files, monitor cryptographic certificate expiry, update installed software

Table 6-8. Scheduled task directories (continued)

Directory	Frequency	Time of execution	Task examples
/etc/cron.weekly	Weekly	4:22 a.m. every Sunday	Clean up old *yum* packages, index manpages
/etc/cron.monthly	Monthly	4:42 a.m. on the first day of every month	(None defined)

Many Fedora packages install files into these directories to schedule tasks; for example, the *webalizer* package installs */etc/cron.daily/00webalizer* to set up automatic web log analysis.

If a task is not performed because the system is off at the scheduled time, the task is performed at the next boot or the next regularly scheduled time, whichever comes first (except for hourly tasks, which just run at the next scheduled time). Therefore, the regularly scheduled maintenance tasks will be still be executed even on a system that is turned on only from (say) 8:00 a.m. to 5:00 p.m. on weekdays.

How Does It Work?

The *cron* server daemon executes tasks at preset times. The *crontab* files created with the *crontab* command are stored in a text file in */var/spool/cron*.

There is also a system-wide *crontab* file in */etc/crontab* and additional *crontab* files, installed by various software packages, in */etc/cron.d*. These *crontab* files are different from the ones in */var/spool/cron* because they contain one additional field between the time values and the command: the name of the user account that will be used to execute the command.

This is the default */etc/crontab* file installed with Fedora Core:

```
SHELL=/bin/bash
PATH=/sbin:/bin:/usr/sbin:/usr/bin
MAILTO=root
HOME=/

# run-parts
01 * * * * root run-parts /etc/cron.hourly
02 4 * * * root run-parts /etc/cron.daily
22 4 * * 0 root run-parts /etc/cron.weekly
42 4 1 * * root run-parts /etc/cron.monthly
```

The entries in this file execute the scripts in the directories listed in Table 6-8. Note that the sixth field is root, meaning that these scripts are executed with *root* permission.

The files in */etc/cron.d* may also be executed by the *anacron* service during system startup (*anacron* takes care of running jobs that were skipped because your computer was not running at the scheduled time). The files */var/spool/anacron/cron.daily*,

/var/spool/anacron/cron.monthly, and */var/spool/anacron/cron.weekly* contain time-stamps in the form *YYYYMMDD* recording when each level of task was last run.

The default */etc/anacrontab* looks like this:

```
# /etc/anacrontab: configuration file for anacron

# See anacron(8) and anacrontab(5) for details.

SHELL=/bin/sh
PATH=/usr/local/sbin:/usr/local/bin:/sbin:/bin:/usr/sbin:/usr/bin
MAILTO=root

1       65      cron.daily              run-parts /etc/cron.daily
7       70      cron.weekly             run-parts /etc/cron.weekly
30      75      cron.monthly            run-parts /etc/cron.monthly
```

The three entries at the end of this file have four fields, specifying the minimum number of days that must have elapsed since a command was last run before it is run again, the number of minutes after *anacron* is started that the command should be executed, the *anacron* label (corresponding to the timestamp filename in */var/spool/anacron*), and the command to be executed. If the specified number of days has elapsed—for example, the weekly tasks have not been executed in more than a week—the *anacron* service starts the appropriate tasks after the specified delay (so, in this example, weekly tasks would be executed approximately 70 minutes after system boot).

What About...

...daylight savings time?

In many parts of the world, *daylight savings time*, or *summer time*, shifts the local time by one hour through the spring and summer months. In most jurisdictions in North America, the local time jumps from 2:00 a.m. to 3:00 a.m. during the spring time change and from 3:00 a.m. to 2:00 a.m. during the autumn time change. The spring time change has been held on the first Sunday in April, but that will change (experimentally) to the second Sunday in March in 2007. The fall time change has been held on the last Sunday in October, which will change to the first Sunday in November in 2007. If the changes do not result in significant energy savings, governments may revert to the traditional dates.

This means that there is no 2:30 a.m. local time on the day of the spring time change, and that 1:30 a.m. local time happens twice on the day of the fall time change.

crond was written to take this issue into account. Jobs scheduled to run between 2:00 and 3:00 a.m. during the spring time change will execute as soon as the time change occurs, and jobs scheduled to run between 1:00 and 2:00 a.m. during the autumn time change will be executed only once.

...using an editor other than vi to edit the crontab?

The environment variable EDITOR can be used to specify a different editor, such as *emacs*, *joe*, or *mcedit*. You can set this variable temporarily by assigning a value on the same command line as the crontab command:

```
$ EDITOR=joe crontab -e
```

It may be useful to edit your *~/.bash_profile* and add this line to permanently specify a different editor:

```
export EDITOR=mcedit
```

...loading the crontab from a file?

When executed without any arguments, the *crontab* command will read the *crontab* configuration from the standard input. You can use this feature to load the configuration from a file:

```
$ crontab </tmp/newcrontab
```

To see the current crontab configuration, use the -l option:

```
$ crontab -l
# Backup ~chris/oreilly/ to bluesky:~chris/backup/ as a tar archive
30 0,12 * * * /usr/local/bin/bluesky-backup-oreilly

# Update the local rawhide repository
0 5 * * * /usr/local/bin/rawhide-rsync
```

Putting these features together, you can create a simple script to edit a crontab configuration:

```
#!/bin/bash
# addtmpclean :: add a crontab entry to clean ~/tmp daily

(crontab -l ; echo "30 4 * * * rm -f ~/tmp/*")|crontab
```

Where Can I Learn More?

* The manpages for *cron*, *crontab(1)*, *crontab(5)*, *anacron*, and *anacrontab*

## CHAPTER 7

Network Services

Fedora, like most Linux and Unix systems, makes no distinction between server and client systems. In fact, many Fedora systems participate in both roles, both serving and consuming information.

It should come as no surprise, then, that Fedora Core ships with a full complement of software for serving everything from web pages and email to files and printer connections. These server packages are based on open standards and interoperate with other platforms, so you can use a Fedora system to serve Windows, Mac, Linux, or Unix clients.

Most Fedora servers are extensively configurable. Configuration information is stored in text files, but the format of the text files varies, and the information in those files goes by different names—*directives*, *statements*, *parameters*, or *options*—depending on the program. Red Hat has developed convenient graphical configuration tools for most of the server configuration files.

Services are programs that constantly run in the background. Services can start automatically when the system starts, but not all services are configured this way by default (see Lab 4.6, "Managing and Configuring Services").

It also might be necessary to adjust your firewall or SELinux configuration to use the services discussed in this chapter (see Chapter 8 for more information).

7.1 Configuring Samba to Share Files with Windows Systems

Fedora can be configured to use Samba to serve files and printers to a wide range of Windows systems using Microsoft-compatible protocols.

Samba can be configured to work with a wide range of Windows versions and to serve resources in many different ways. This lab is focused on sharing files and printers with Windows XP systems in a small workgroup, which is a common scenario in home and small-business networks.

How Do I Do That?

To configure Samba, select the menu option System → Administration → Server Settings → Samba, which will open the window shown in Figure 7-1.

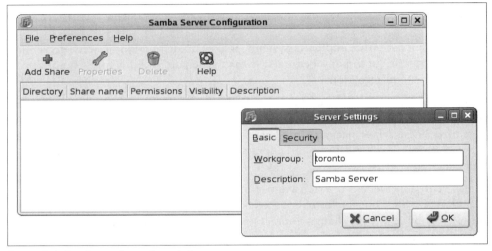

Figure 7-1. Samba configuration window

Click Preferences → Server Settings to open the small window shown at bottom right in Figure 7-1. Enter your local Windows workgroup name into the Workgroup field and click OK. The Samba server will be started automatically.

 See Lab 4.7, "Managing Users and Groups," to create Fedora accounts for your users before enabling Samba access.

Next, select Preferences → Samba Users to bring up the user configuration dialog box shown in Figure 7-2. Click Add User, select an existing Linux user, enter a Windows username (which may be the same as the Linux username), and enter the Samba password of your choice twice. Click OK when you're done.

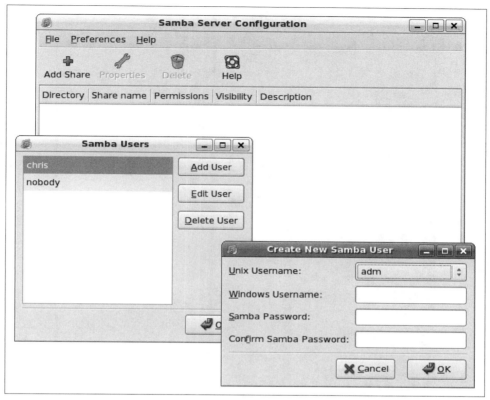

Figure 7-2. Samba user configuration

 If you are using a firewall or have SELinux enforcing turned on, you will need to adjust your security settings to permit remote systems to access the Samba server (see Lab 8.2, "Using SELinux").

Your system will now be visible to local Windows computers; for example, on an XP system, click My Network Places and then "View workgroup computers," and your Fedora system will appear as an icon with the hostname that you have assigned to it, as shown in Figure 7-3. Click on the computer icon to see the folders being shared by the Fedora system (after you enter your Samba user ID and password to authenticate).

The folder labeled *homes* contains the home directory of the authenticated Samba user, and the *Printers and Faxes* folder will contain all of the printers configured on the Fedora system.

Figure 7-3. Windows XP workgroup display showing Samba shares from a Fedora system

Although the Samba configuration tool starts the Samba system, you'll need to enable the Samba service if you want Samba to start every time you boot your system—see Lab 4.6, "Managing and Configuring Services."

Adding additional Samba shares

To share an additional directory, start the Samba configuration tool (System → Administration → Server Settings → Samba) and click the Add button. The window shown in Figure 7-4 will appear.

Under the Basic tab, enter the directory name, the name visible to the Windows systems (i.e., the share name), and a description of what is in the shared directory. Use the checkboxes to configure whether the directory is writable by Windows users, and whether it is visible when the Windows users are browsing using a tool such as Windows Explorer.

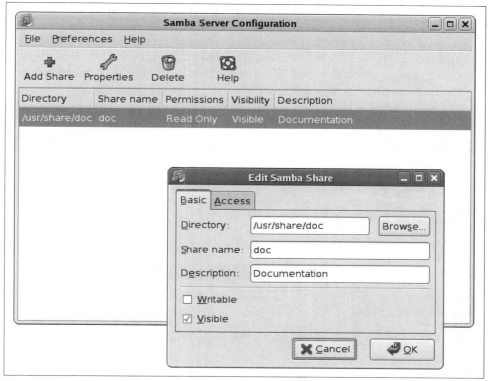

Figure 7-4. Adding a Samba share

Under the Access tab, you can choose to make the directory available to all users, or you can go through the list of Samba users and select the specific ones you want to grant access to it. Click OK when you are done.

 In order for a remote user to access a shared directory through Samba, that directory must have the appropriate permissions and SELinux context.

Accessing Fedora printers from a Windows system

Fedora's default Samba configuration will make all printers available to Windows users. To use a shared Samba printer in Windows XP, follow these instructions.

 Although you can access Fedora printers through Samba printer sharing, it's often faster and easier to access those printers directly through CUPS printer sharing, regardless of the operating system in use.

1. Go to Printers and Faxes and then click "Add a Printer." The Add Printer Wizard will appear. Click Next to get past the introductory message, then select "A network printer, or a printer attached to another computer" for the printer type, and then click Next. Select "Browse for a Printer," and then click Next to see a list of computers on the local Windows network. Double-click on the name of the Fedora system, which will reveal the names of the printers on that system, as shown in Figure 7-5; double-click on the desired printer.

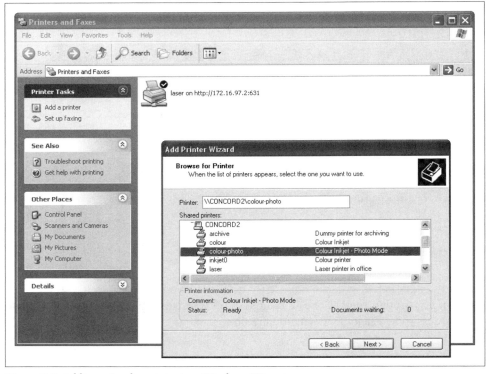

Figure 7-5. Adding a Samba printer to a Windows XP system

2. You may receive a warning about installing printer drivers at this point. Click OK.

3. Select the printer manufacturer and model. Click OK.

 If you do not see the printer listed, you will need to insert the printer's driver CD, click Have Disk, and then select the disk location. When the list of printer models appears, select the one that matches the printer you are installing.

4. If you already have a printer set up on the Windows system, you will be asked if the new printer should become the default. Choose Yes or No, and then click Next.

5. Click Finish.

You will now be able to print to the printer from any Windows application.

Configuring Samba from the command line

You can edit Samba's configuration from the command line instead of using the graphical configuration tool.

Samba's configuration file is */etc/samba/smb.conf*, and it is a regular text file. Like most server programs, Samba has dozens of configuration options, which it calls *parameters*. This configuration file is divided into sections by lines of section names enclosed in square brackets (so, for example, the global configuration section starts with the line [global]). Lines that start with a pound sign (#) are treated as comments and ignored.

The workgroup name and server description are configured at the top of the global section:

```
[global]

# workgroup = NT-Domain-Name or Workgroup-Name
        workgroup = bluesky

# server string is the equivalent of the NT Description field
        server string = Samba Server
```

Set the workgroup name to the value used by the local Windows workgroup or domain. The server string description can be any descriptive value (change the default if you don't want people to know you're running a Linux system). The system name will be the same as the hostname.

By default, only home directories and printers will be shared. To add additional shares, add an additional share section to the end of the configuration file. There are many examples in the configuration file, such as this one:

```
# The following two entries demonstrate how to share a directory so that two
# users can place files there that will be owned by the specific users. In this
# setup, the directory should be writable by both users and should have the
# sticky bit set on it to prevent abuse. Obviously this could be extended to
# as many users as required.
;[myshare]
;   comment = Mary's and Fred's stuff
;   path = /usr/somewhere/shared
;   valid users = mary fred
;   public = no
;   writable = yes
;   printable = no
;   create mask = 0765
```

From this template, you can see the basic format:

[*myshare*]
    Name of the share as it will be seen by the Windows systems.

comment = *Mary's and Fred's stuff*
    The description that will appear when browsing the share.

path = */usr/somewhere/shared*
    The directory to be shared.

valid users = *mary fred*
public = *no*
    Specifies who can access this share: specific users or everyone (public = yes). Either valid users or public should be enabled, but not both.

writable = *yes*
printable = *no*
browseable = *yes*
    Determines what can be done with the share. writable controls whether the remote user can change or create files and directories, printable enables printing (not applicable to a regular directory share), and browseable enables the share to appear when the network user is browsing using a tool such as Windows Explorer.

create mask = *0765*
    Sets the octal permission that is applied to new files.

To allow read-only access to */usr/share/doc*, for example, create this share:

```
[doc]
        comment = Documentation
        path = /usr/share/doc
        writeable = no
        browseable = yes
        guest ok = yes
```

 You will need to adjust the SELinux context of the shared directory (see "Using SELinux" in Chapter 8Lab 8.2, "Using SELinux in Chapter 8).

After editing the configuration file, restart or reload Samba to activate the changes:

```
# service smb reload
Reloading smb.conf file:                          [  OK  ]
```

To add Samba users, you must first create a Linux user account (see Lab 4.7, "Managing Users and Groups"), and then use the *smbpasswd* command with the add option, -a:

```
# smbpasswd -a frank
New SMB password: FranklySpeaking
Retype new SMB password: FranklySpeaking
Added user frank.
```

To change the password, leave out the -a option:

```
# smbpasswd jane
New SMB password: PrimeUser
Retype new SMB password: PrimeUser
```

To delete a user, use the -x option:

```
# smbpasswd -x kim
Deleted user kim.
```

How Does It Work?

Samba uses the Server Message Block (SMB) protocol suite and related protocols and programs developed by Microsoft—more recently grouped under the moniker *Common Internet File System* (CIFS). The name *Samba* is derived from the acronym SMB.

SMB and related protocols have been in use since the 1980s, but have changed significantly through the years. There are many different, incompatible implementations of the protocols present in various versions of Windows, and in particular, there are several ways of authenticating users. Many of Samba's configuration options relate to compatibility and user authentication.

Samba is implemented as two server daemons:

nmbd
> Provides NetBIOS name server services

smbd
> Provides SMB/CIFS services

The graphical configuration tool for Samba is *system-config-samba*.

What About...

...disabling access to printers through Samba?

To prevent Samba from sharing your printers with Windows systems, delete (or comment out) this printer share in */etc/samba/smb.conf*:

```
[printers]
        comment = All Printers
        path = /var/spool/samba
        browseable = no
# Set public = yes to allow user 'guest account' to print
;       guest ok = no
```

```
    ;           writeable = no
                printable = yes
```

Restart or reload Samba to activate the change.

...accessing a Samba share on another Linux machine?

Use the Places → Network Servers option on the GNOME menu (or go to *smb://* in KDE's Konqueror) to browse Windows network shares, including Samba shares.

You can also mount Samba or Windows shares at the command line. To mount the share *bluesky* from the server *pictures* on the mount point */mnt/pictures*:

```
# mount -t smb //bluesky/pictures /mnt/pictures
```

This invokes the *smbmount* command.

Where Can I Learn More?

- The manpages for *samba*, *smb.conf*, *smbd*, *nmbd*, *findsmb*, *smbmount*, and *smbumount*
- The files in */usr/share/samba**, especially */usr/share/samba*/Samba-Guide.pdf* and */usr/share/samba*/Samba-HOWTO-Collection.pdf*
- The Samba web site: *http://www.samba.org/*

7.2   Configuring a DHCP Server

Dynamic Host Configuration Protocol (DHCP) is used to automatically send basic configuration data to computers and network devices. This centralizes network configuration control so that a change in the network layout—such as adding a nameserver or a gateway, or renumbering the network—does not require a visit to every computer in the network. DHCP also provides a convenient method of supplying network configuration information to visiting computers, such as the laptop of a visiting colleague.

When a DHCP client system boots, it effectively shouts a broadcast message to the network: "Does anyone know who I am?" The DHCP server replies, "I know you, you're..." and then proceeds to tell the client its IP address and some combination of other network configuration information, possibly including a hostname, nameserver, timeserver, gateway, and default domain. The information sent by the DHCP server is called a *lease* and is only valid for a set length of time. The client can renew the lease when it expires, in which case it can keep its identity, or, if it disappears from the network and fails to renew the lease, the IP address can be recycled by the DHCP server and assigned to another host.

Most home and small networks are connected to the Internet by a router or gateway device that includes DHCP service capability. However, you may prefer to use the Fedora DHCP server instead because it gives you more configuration options and control over the network configuration.

How Do I Do That?

Before you set up a DHCP server for your network, you must design the network layout that you wish to use.

Private networks—ones that will not be connected to the Internet, or that will be connected through a router or gateway that performs *network address translation* (NAT), or *masquerading*—will use one of the private network ranges defined in RFC 1918, shown in Table 7-1.

Table 7-1. RFC 1918 private network addresses

Range	Number of addresses available	Class-based address breakdown
10.0.0.0–10.255.255.255	16,777,216	1 class A network of 16,777,216 addresses
172.16.0.0–172.31.255.255	1,048,576	16 class B networks of 65,536 addresses each
192.168.0.0–192.168.255.255	65,536	256 class C networks of 256 addresses each

Most small networks use one of the class C networks that start with the 192.168 prefix, yielding 256 addresses. Because two addresses are reserved for broadcast and network messages, that leaves 254 addresses for computers and network devices (such as printers), which is plenty for most homes and small businesses.

DHCP can assign any combination of two address types:

static
> Addresses that are always assigned to a specific computer or network device and never change. Even though these do not change, they are still communicated to the device using the DHCP protocol. Static addresses should be used for any host that other users will need to connect to, such as a web server or printer.

dynamic
> Addresses assigned from a pool on a first-come, first-serve basis. Dynamic addresses are appropriate for computers, such as desktop systems, which will be connecting to remote hosts but will never (or rarely) be a destination for network connections.

Table 7-2 shows a possible network configuration for a home or small office network that will use the network prefix 192.168.1. In this example, available addresses have been divided into four ranges, one each for servers, network devices, desktop and laptop systems, and network infrastructure.

Table 7-2. Example of a small-office network configuration

Address range and purpose	Host address	Name and description	Notes
	0	Network	Reserved address
1–63 Servers	1	*prime* (nameserver, web server)	Traditional nameserver address
	2	*cabinet* (Samba fileserver)	
	3	*chatterbox* (Asterisk phone system)	
	3–63	Future use	
64-127 Network devices (non-computers)	64	*laser1*	Main laser printer
	65	*multifunction1*	Printer-scanner-copier
	66	*webcam1*	Monitors front door
	67–127	Future use	
128–191 Desktop and laptop systems	—	—	Dynamically assigned
192–254 Network infrastructure	192–253	Future use	
	254	*gateway* (router; path to the Internet)	Traditional address for a gateway
	255	Broadcast	Reserved address

DHCP is configured through the text file */etc/dhcpd.conf*, which contains configuration statements and comments. Configuration statements are case-insensitive and are separated by semicolons (;)—whitespace doesn't matter. Some statements create blocks, delimited with curly braces ({}), that contain other statements. Comments start with # and continue to the end of the line.

The *dhcpd.conf* file starts out with global statements; only one is required:

```
ddns-update-style none;
```

This prevents the DHCP server from attempting to update records on the DNS server (which is prohibited by Fedora's default SELinux configuration).

The rest of the configuration statements are placed in a block as part of a subnet statement:

```
subnet 192.168.1.0 netmask 255.255.255.0 {
# Statements that apply only to this subnet...
}
```

These are the most commonly used configuration statements:

`option routers` *192.168.1.254*

The default gateway. Packets destined for a host that is not in your local network are sent to this gateway for forwarding.

`option subnet-mask` *255.255.255.0*

The subnet mask, which is used to determine whether an IP address is on the local network (which determines routing).

`option domain-name-servers` *192.168.1.1*

Nameservers for this subnet (they may be in the subnet, or they may be external). If there is more than one, list them all, separating the IP addresses or hostnames with commas.

`option domain-name` *"fedorabook.com"*

The domain name for machines on this subnet. This is used as the default domain for hostname lookup, so that if a user types a command such as **telnet server42**, the hostname will be looked up (using a nameserver) as *server42. fedorabook.com*.

`option time-offset` *-21600*

The difference (in seconds) between the local time zone and Coordinated Universal Time (UTC). `-21600` indicates a time zone that is six hours behind Greenwich, England (Eastern Standard Time in North America).

`option ntp-servers` *pool.ntp.org*

The hostnames or addresses of any available network time protocol servers. The hostname `pool.ntp.org` accesses a server randomly drawn from a pool of publicly accessible timeservers. You can prepend your ISO country code to select only timeservers in your country; for example, `ca.pool.ntp.org` would randomly select a Canadian timeserver.

`range` *192.168.1.128 192.168.1.191*

The range of address from which dynamic IP addresses will be assigned.

`default-lease-time` *86400*

The normal lease time in seconds. 86,400 seconds corresponds to one day.

`max-lease-time` *172800*

The maximum lease time, in case the client requests a lease that is longer than the default.

To configure static hosts, statements are placed in the block of a host statement:

```
host hostname {
# Statements that apply only to this host...
}
```

These are the statements that are most commonly used in a host block:

`hardware ethernet` *aa:bb:cc:dd:ee:ff*

Determines which Ethernet hardware MAC address will match this host block. This block will be selected if the hostname sent by the DHCP client matches the hostname in the host statement, or if the client's Ethernet card has the same MAC address as the hardware statement.

fixed-address *192.168.1.1*

Specifies the static address for this host.

To configure a network that uses the layout shown in Table 7-2, where the devices have the MAC addresses shown in Table 7-3, you would write this */etc/dhcpd.conf* file:

```
# Sample /etc/dhcpd.conf file

# Don't update DNS
ddns-update-style none;

# The local network is 192.168.1.X
subnet 192.168.1.0 netmask 255.255.255.0 {

        option routers             192.168.1.254;      # Default gateway
        option subnet-mask         255.255.255.0;      # Client netmask
        option domain-name         "fedorabook.com";   # Domain
        option domain-name-servers 172.16.97.1;        # Nameserver is .1
        option time-offset         -21600;             # Eastern Standard Time
        option ntp-servers         pool.ntp.org;       # Timeservers

        default-lease-time         86400;            # 1 day
        max-lease-time             172800;           # 2 days

        # Dynamic configuration

        range 192.168.1.128 192.168.1.191

        # Static configuration for various hosts

        host prime {
            hardware ethernet 00:0c:0d:99:99:99 ;
            fixed-address 192.168.1.1 ;
        }

        host cabinet {
            hardware ethernet 00:0c:0d:aa:aa:aa ;
            fixed-address 192.168.1.2 ;
        }

        host chatterbox {
            hardware ethernet 00:0c:0d:bb:bb:bb ;
            fixed-address 192.168.1.3 ;
        }

        host laser1 {
            hardware ethernet 00:0c:0d:cc:cc:cc ;
```

```
        fixed-address 192.168.1.64 ;
    }

    host multifunction1 {
        hardware ethernet 00:0c:0d:dd:dd:dd ;
        fixed-address 192.168.1.65 ;
    }

    host webcam1 {
        hardware ethernet 00:0c:0d:ee:ee:ee ;
        fixed-address 192.168.1.66 ;
    }

    host gateway1 {
        hardware ethernet 00:0c:0d:ff:ff:ff ;
        fixed-address 192.168.1.254 ;
    }

}
```

Table 7-3. Sample hardware addresses

Hardware MAC address	Hostname
00:0c:0d:99:99:99	*prime*
00:0c:0d:aa:aa:aa	*cabinet*
00:0c:0d:bb:bb:bb	*chatterbox*
00:0c:0d:cc:cc:cc	*laser1*
00:0c:0d:dd:dd:dd	*multifunction1*
00:0c:0d:ee:ee:ee	*gateway1*

Once your configuration has been saved in */etc/dhcpd.conf*, restart *dhcpd* to activate it using the Services graphical tool or this command:

```
# service dhcpd restart
```

If there are errors in your configuration file, *dhcpd* may not start. Check the end of the file */var/log/messages* to see if there are any error messages:

```
# tail -50 /var/log/messages|less
```

If there are no error messages, clients can begin using the *dhcpd* server to obtain their IP addresses.

 You will need to open port 68 UDP in your firewall configuration in order to permit clients to reach *dhcpd*. You should also verify that no other DHCP servers are running on your network (check router and gateway appliances in addition to computers).

If configured to obtain IP information through DHCP, the client systems will contact the DHCP server when they are booted. You can also force them to contact the DHCP server at any time:

- On a Fedora Core 4 or later system, use *dhclient* to configure an Ethernet port using DHCP:

    ```
    # dhclient eth0
    ```

    In this case, the port being configured is eth0, the first Ethernet connection. On other Linux systems, you may need to use *dhcpcd* or *pump* in place of *dhclient*.

- On a Windows system, you can use *ipconfig* to obtain or renew a DHCP lease:

    ```
    C:\> ipconfig /renew

    Windows IP Configuration

    Ethernet adapter 1:

            Connection-specific DNS Suffix  . : fedorabook.com
            IP Address. . . . . . . . . . . : 192.168.1.207
            Subnet Mark . . . . . . . . . . : 255.255.255.0
            Default Gateway . . . . . . . . : 192.168.1.254
    ```

How Does It Work?

Table 7-4 shows the sequence of messages that flow between a DHCP client and a DHCP server during initial negotiation and during lease renewal.

Table 7-4. DHCP messages.

Context		Message type	Origin	Description
Initial negotiation	Lease renewal			
*		DHCPDISCOVER	Client	Client tries to discover the DHCP server.
*		DHCPOFFER	Server	The DHCP server offers its location and possible lease details.
*	*	DHCPREQUEST	Client	The client requests a lease.
*	*	DHCPACK/ DHCPNACK	Server	The server acknowledges (approves) or negatively acknowledges (rejects) the lease request.

Early DHCP messages are sent using UDP to the broadcast address 255.255.255.255. This is necessary because the client does not have an IP address at the start of the negotiation.

dhcpd stores lease information in the file */var/lib/dhcpd/dhcpd.leases* so that if it is stopped and restarted, it still has an idea of what leases are outstanding. In a similar way, *dhclient* stores its lease information in */var/lib/dhcp/dhclient-<eth0>.leases* (where *<eth0>* is the interface name).

What About...

...older clients that use the bootp protocol?

The DHCP server, *dhcpd*, can also manage clients that use the Bootstrap Protocol (BOOTP). However, BOOTP does not use leases, so once an IP address is assigned, it stays assigned *even if the computer using that address is removed from the network*. IP assignments from an address pool are therefore called *automatic* assignments instead of *dynamic* assignments.

To enable *dhcpd* to assign BOOTP addresses, add the dynamic-bootp option to the range statement in */etc/dhcpd.conf*:

```
range dynamic-bootp 192.168.1.128 192.168.1.191
```

Where Can I Learn More?

- The manpages for *dhcpd*, *dhcpd.conf*, *dhclient*, and *dhclient.conf*
- The standard that defines DHCP: RFC 2131, *http://www.ietf.org/rfc/rfc2131.txt*

7.3   Configuring a Domain Name Server

Domain name service (DNS) is like a telephone-directory service for TCP/IP networks. When a program such as a browser or mail server needs to contact a machine for which it has a hostname, it uses DNS to convert that name to a numeric network address. DNS can also do the reverse: convert a numeric address to a hostname.

It is necessary to have DNS set up before you can serve data to the Internet. Although you can contract for DNS service from an external provider, Fedora Core provides a nameserver that you can easily set up to provide your own DNS capability.

How Do I Do That?

Fedora provides the *named* domain name server, which is the Berkeley Internet Name Domain (BIND). *named* serves two roles:

authoritative nameserver
> Serves name information about one or more domains to other servers.

caching nameserver
> Provides name lookups for client programs such as web browsers by contacting other nameservers. This information is cached in local storage in case it is requested again in the near future.

 The Fedora package called *bind* contains the *named* service.

The *named* service is not run by default. Once you configure it to run (see Lab 4.6, "Managing and Configuring Services"), it will act as a caching nameserver:

 If you just want to use *named* as a caching nameserver, you can skip to the section entitled "Using your nameservers locally."

To configure *named* as an authoritative nameserver for your domain, you just have to give it the information about your domain that you want it to serve to other systems. Usually at least two authoritative nameservers are set up for each domain; one is configured as the *master*, and the others are *slaves*. Changes to the DNS data are made on the master, and the slaves update themselves periodically.

You can configure an authoritative nameserver graphically or by editing configuration files and datafiles.

Configuring named graphically

Select the menu option System → Administration → Server Settings → Domain Name Server. After you enter the *root* password, the window shown in Figure 7-6 will appear.

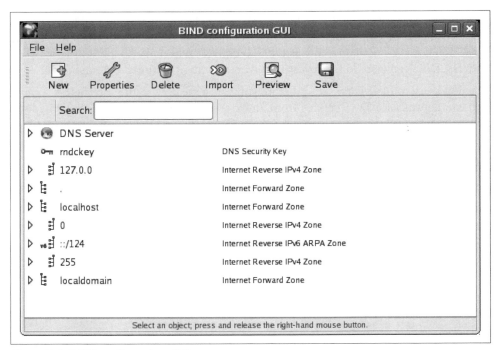

Figure 7-6. BIND configuration GUI

The user interface of this tool is unique! It does not behave in the same way as other graphical configuration tools, so take your time when using it.

To add a *zone*—which can be a complete domain or a subdomain—click on the DNS Server entry to highlight it, click the New button, and then select "zone" from the menu that appears. Figure 7-7 shows the small dialog box that appears.

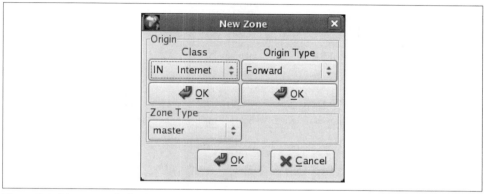

Figure 7-7. New Zone dialog box

Click OK under Class, and then click OK under Origin Type. The dialog's controls will change to let you type in the Forward Zone Origin, as shown in Figure 7-8. Enter the name of the domain with a period at the end—for example, `fedorabook.com`.

Figure 7-8. Zone Origin entry

Click OK to create the zone. The window in Figure 7-9 will appear. Don't be alarmed by the number of controls!

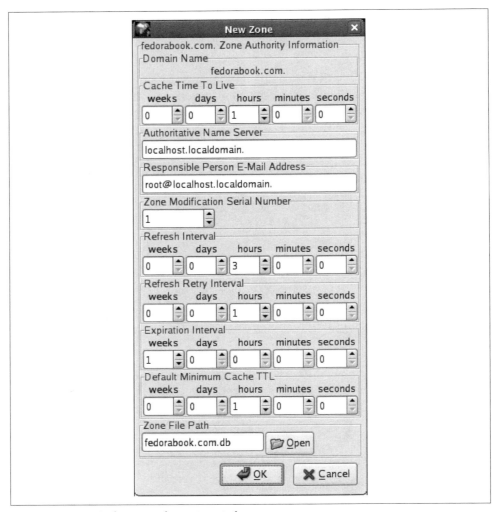

Figure 7-9. Zone Authority configuration window

This window sets several overall values for the zone. Many of these are time values:

Cache Time to Live (TTL)

The maximum length of time that information should be cached by a client or remote nameserver. A higher value will result in a lower volume of DNS requests for your server to process and fewer delays for your users, but when you change a DNS entry, it will take longer to be "noticed" by other systems. A minimum value of three days is recommended once your configuration is stable (RFC 1912); the default value of one hour is appropriate during initial setup and during periods of frequent changes.

Refresh Interval, Refresh Retry Interval, and Expiration Interval

These values configure communication between a master and a slave system. The Refresh Interval specifies how often the slave should get an update from the master, the Refresh Retry Interval specifies how long the slave should wait before retrying a refresh if it is unsuccessful, and the Expiration Interval specifies how long a slave can go without an update before it should stop responding to requests.

Default Minimum Cache TTL

The name of this field is somewhat misleading because the usage has changed. It is now used to indicate how long a *negative* response should be cached by a remote machine; in other words, this is the minimum length of time that a remote machine should wait before asking again if a domain exists. In this graphical configuration tool, this value also sets the default TTL for the rest of the records within this zone.

Leave these values at their defaults to start. If you are setting up DNS for a heavily used domain, you should go back and change the Cache Time to Live to the three-day recommended minimum (or longer) once you've confirmed that your configuration works correctly; you'll also need to change the TTL on each resource record in this zone (which I will come to in a minute).

Beside the time fields, there are only four pieces of information to fill in:

Authoritative Name Server

The hostname of the nameserver computer. If the host is in this zone, you can enter the hostname without the domain name portion (e.g., just *bluesky* for *bluesky.fedorabook.com*); otherwise, enter the fully qualified domain name followed by a period (the hostname and domain name together, such as *ns.global. proximity.on.ca.*).

Responsible Person E-mail Address

The email address of the person responsible for managing DNS, followed by a period (if the address is in this zone, you can enter just the username, such as *jessica*). Ideally, this address should *not* be inside the zone that you're defining because people may want to use this address to reach you to tell you that something is wrong with the domain—and that same problem may prevent mail from reaching you.

Zone Modification Serial Number

Any number can be used here, but it must be increased every time this zone's DNS information is updated. Most sites use one of these two approaches:

- A straight serial number, initially set to 1, incremented by one each time the zone information is changed. This graphical configuration tool will automatically increment this serial number when required.

- The date and a sequence number in *YYYYMMDDSS* format, where *YYYYMMDD* is the year/month/day and *SS* is the sequence number of changes made on that date. For example, 2009021702 indicates the second change made on February 17, 2009. If you're going to use this format, you'll have to remember to update the serial number whenever you make a change.

Zone File Path

The name of the file that will store information for this zone. Use the default value for this field.

Click OK to save this information. You will see the domain listed in the main window, as in Figure 7-10; click on the arrow to the left of the domain name to see the entries within that domain.

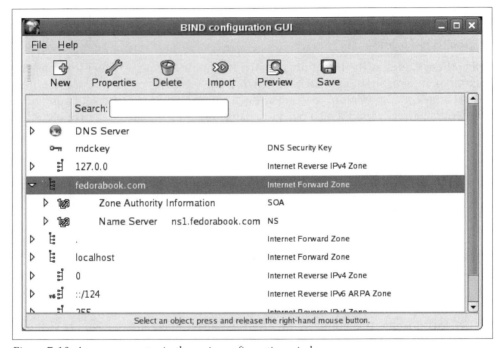

Figure 7-10. A new zone entry in the main configuration window

Note that two entries have been created: a Start of Authority (SOA) record, which contains basic information about the domain, plus an NS record, which contains information about the authoritative nameserver for the zone.

You'll now need to add *resource records* (RR) for the machines in this zone. Most domains need four types of records:

A

Defines the address for a hostname. Every host in the zone needs an A record; the next three record types are used *in addition* to an A record.

CNAME

Enables the use of nicknames for hosts. These records translate a host nickname into a *canonical name* (true hostname).

MX

Defines a mail exchanger (SMTP server) within the domain.

NS

Identifies a nameserver for the zone.

To add these records, highlight the new zone you've created, click the Add button, and select the record type from the drop-down list that appears. One of the four windows shown in Figure 7-11 will appear, according to the type of resource record you are adding.

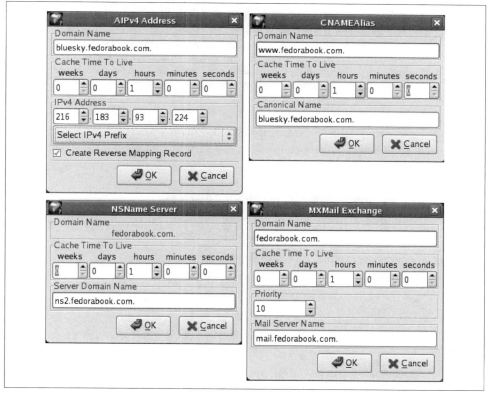

Figure 7-11. Resource record windows

- For an A record, insert the hostname in the Domain Name field and the IP address in the IPv4 Address field.
- For a CNAME record, insert the nickname in the Domain Name field and the full name of the host in the Canonical Name field.

- For an NS record, insert the hostname of the nameserver in the Server Domain Name field.

- For an MX record, leave the Domain Name as it is written. If you have more than one mail exchanger for your domain (perhaps a master and a backup email server), enter a priority for each server; lower numbers take precedence over higher numbers. Enter the hostname of the mail server in the Mail Server Name field.

 Make sure that an A record exists for each hostname mentioned in CNAME, NS, and MX records.

These hosts don't have to be in the same zone or domain; for example, it's possible for email and name service to be handled by a host outside that domain. In that case, the A record will not appear in this zone but *must* appear in the zone for that domain.

For example, if the mail server for *fedorabook.com* was *global.proximity.on.ca*, then the MX record could point to that host. There would be no A record for *global.proximity.on.ca* within the *fedorabook.com* zone, but there would have to be one within the *proximity.on.ca* zone (which might be on a different nameserver altogether).

Once you have entered all of the resource records you want, click Save to save the information. If *named* is already running, it will be reloaded so that the changes take effect immediately.

Configuring named through configuration files and datafiles

named can also be configured by directly editing the configuration files and datafiles, which is the approach used by many experienced users.

The overall operation of *named* is controlled by the file */etc/named.conf*. This is the default configuration installed by the BIND package:

```
//
// named.conf for Red Hat caching-nameserver
//

options {
        directory "/var/named";
        dump-file "/var/named/data/cache_dump.db";
        statistics-file "/var/named/data/named_stats.txt";
        /*
         * If there is a firewall between you and nameservers you want
         * to talk to, you might need to uncomment the query-source
         * directive below.  Previous versions of BIND always asked
         * questions using port 53, but BIND 8.1 uses an unprivileged
         * port by default.
         */
        // query-source address * port 53;
```

```
};

//
// a caching-only nameserver config
//
controls {
        inet 127.0.0.1 allow { localhost; } keys { rndckey; };
};

zone "." IN {
        type hint;
        file "named.ca";
};

zone "localdomain" IN {
        type master;
        file "localdomain.zone";
        allow-update { none; };
};

zone "localhost" IN {
        type master;
        file "localhost.zone";
        allow-update { none; };
};

zone "0.0.127.in-addr.arpa" IN {
        type master;
        file "named.local";
        allow-update { none; };
};

zone "0.0.0.0.0.0.0.0.0.0.0.0.0.0.0.0.0.0.0.0.0.0.0.0.0.0.0.0.0.0.0.0.ip6.arpa" IN {
        type master;
        file "named.ip6.local";
        allow-update { none; };
};

zone "255.in-addr.arpa" IN {
        type master;
        file "named.broadcast";
        allow-update { none; };
};

zone "0.in-addr.arpa" IN {
        type master;
        file "named.zero";
        allow-update { none; };
};

include "/etc/rndc.key";
```

The options section sets up the basic file and directory locations for the server. controls limits which machines can control *named* (in this case, only programs running on the localhost, and only if they have the correct security key); and the include line at the end accesses that encryption key from another file and causes *named* to act as though it's included in this file.

The rest of this file consists of zone sections. The first zone section is for the entire Internet and refers to the file */var/named/named.ca*, which contains the names and addresses of the master domain name servers, called the *root servers*. The extension *.ca* stands for *cache*.

 If you have the package *bind-chroot* installed, then prepend the directory */var/named/chroot/* to pathnames throughout this chapter. For example, */var/named* would become */var/named/chroot/var/named*, and */etc/named.conf* would become */var/named/chroot/etc/named.conf*.

bind-chroot is a package intended to increase the security of the nameserver. It is considered obsolete, since SELinux now provides similar protection.

The remaining zone sections are used to resolve standard requests, such as the address of *localhost* and *localhost.localdomain* (always 127.0.0.1), and the reverse of those requests.

To create a new zone, add it to the end of this file (you can copy an existing zone entry and then modify it):

```
zone "fedorabook.com" IN {
        type master;
        file "fedorabook.com.db";
        allow-update { none; };
};
```

This specifies the name of the zone (exactly the same as the name of the domain) and the file in which this zone's information can be found. You can enter any filename you want, but names based on the domain and ending with .db or hosts—such as *fedorabook.com.db* or *fedorabookhosts*—are traditional.

Next, create the file for the zone. This is a standard text file with a very exact syntax.

The file starts with the default TTL for the zone:

```
$TTL 3D
```

The value here represents three days. You can use any combination of numbers suffixed with W, D, H, M, or S (representing units of weeks, days, hours, minutes, and seconds) concatenated together, or you can specify the time in seconds; some examples are shown in Table 7-5.

Table 7-5. named time values

Entry	Description	Equivalent number of seconds
3D	3 days	259,200
1D12H 36H	1 day and 12 hours (or 36 hours)	129,600
2W	2 weeks	1,209,600
1D10M	1 day and 10 minutes	87,000

The zone file then contains the Start of Authority (SOA) resource record:

```
@       SOA     ns1     chris.global.proximity.on.ca. (2007201702,3D,1H,3D,1H)
```

The @ sign means "this zone", and SOA is the record type. The values are the author-itative master nameserver (*ns1*), followed by the administrative email contact, with the @ converted to a period (therefore, usernames containing periods cannot be used for administrative contacts).

 All hostnames and domain names in a zone file will have the name of the zone added to the end of them *unless* they end with a period. Thus, in this example, bluesky (with no period) would be interpreted as bluesky.fedorabook.com, as would bluesky.fedorabook.com with no period: bluesky.fedorabook.com.fedorabook.com.

The values in parentheses at the end of the record are the serial number and the time values for this record. It's helpful (and common practice) to split this information across several lines and add comments to label which time value is which:

```
@       SOA     ns1     chris.global.proximity.on.ca. (
                2007201702   ; serial number
                3D           ; refresh
                1H           ; retry
                3D           ; expire
                1H )         ; minimum
```

Notice that comments start with a semicolon. The time values used here are the same ones configured using the graphical tool.

The rest of the zone file contains resource records. We need NS records to indicate the nameservers for this domain:

```
        IN      NS      bluesky
        IN      NS      darkday
```

The first field is blank; the line must be indented at least one space. The next field value, IN, specifies that these records are related to the Internet (TCP/IP address family). NS indicates the record type (nameserver), and the last field is the hostname of the nameserver.

We also need A records to indicate the IP address of each computer:

```
bluesky IN      A       216.183.93.224
darkday IN      A       216.183.93.225
```

The first field in each record is the hostname, followed by the address family (IN) and the record type (A), and then the IP address.

Next we have MX records for mail exchangers:

```
        IN      MX      10 bluesky
        IN      MX      20 global.proximity.on.ca.
```

These have a blank first field, followed by the address family (IN) and record type (MX), followed by the mail server priority (lower numbers are higher priority), and then the mail server hostname.

Note that *global.proximity.on.ca* is outside of this zone, so the hostname is written as a fully qualified domain name (FQDN) ending with a period.

We also need some aliases for common hostnames:

```
mail    IN      CNAME   bluesky
ftp     IN      CNAME   darkday
www     IN      CNAME   bluesky
ww      IN      CNAME   bluesky
wwww    IN      CNAME   bluesky
```

These records are like A records, except that the record type is set to CNAME and the last field contains the canonical (true) hostname.

It is possible to override the default TTL by inserting it between the address family (IN) and the record type in each record. For example, you could set the TTL for the last CNAME record to five minutes:

```
wwww    IN  5M  CNAME   bluesky
```

Putting this all together and adding some comments gives us the complete zone file:

```
; Zone file for 'fedorabook.com'

; Default TTL is 1 hour
$TTL    1H

; Start of authority
@       SOA     ns1     chris.global.proximity.on.ca. (
                2007201705  ; serial number
                3D          ; refresh
                1H          ; retry
                3D          ; expire
                1H )        ; minimum

; Nameservers
        IN      NS      bluesky
        IN      NS      darkday
```

```
; Addresses of hosts
bluesky IN       A       216.183.93.224
darkday IN       A       216.183.93.225

; Mail exchangers
        IN       MX      10 bluesky
        IN       MX      20 darkday

; Nicknames/aliases
mail    IN       CNAME   bluesky
www     IN       CNAME   bluesky
ww      IN       CNAME   bluesky
wwww    IN       CNAME   bluesky
```

The filename for this data is */var/named/fedorabook.com.db*, to match the file entry
that we made in */etc/named.conf*.

Testing DNS entries

Once you have your DNS entries configured, reload the *named* service. The end of
the system message logfile, */var/log/messages*, will look something like this:

```
Mar  4 22:14:58 core5 named[10977]: starting BIND 9.3.2 -u named
Mar  4 22:14:58 core5 named[10977]: found 1 CPU, using 1 worker thread
Mar  4 22:14:58 core5 named[10977]: loading configuration from '/etc/named.conf'
Mar  4 22:14:58 core5 named[10977]: listening on IPv4 interface lo, 127.0.0.1#53
Mar  4 22:14:58 core5 named[10977]: listening on IPv4 interface eth0, 172.16.97.
100#53
Mar  4 22:14:58 core5 named[10977]: command channel listening on 127.0.0.1#953
Mar  4 22:14:58 core5 named[10977]: zone 0.in-addr.arpa/IN: loaded serial 42
Mar  4 22:14:58 core5 named[10977]: zone 0.0.127.in-addr.arpa/IN: loaded serial
1997022700
Mar  4 22:14:58 core5 named[10977]: zone 255.in-addr.arpa/IN: loaded serial 42
Mar  4 22:14:58 core5 named[10977]: zone 0.0.0.0.0.0.0.0.0.0.0.0.0.0.0.0.0.0.0.0.
0.0.0.0.0.0.0.0.ip6.arpa/IN: loaded serial 1997022700
Mar  4 22:14:58 core5 named[10977]: zone fedorabook.com/IN: loaded serial 2007201705
Mar  4 22:14:58 core5 named[10977]: zone localdomain/IN: loaded serial 42
Mar  4 22:14:58 core5 named[10977]: zone localhost/IN: loaded serial 42
Mar  4 22:14:58 core5 named[10977]: running
Mar  4 22:14:58 core5 named[10977]: zone fedorabook.com/IN: sending notifies (serial
2007201705)
```

If there is an error in your zone file, an error message will appear here. Read the error
message carefully, and then edit your zone file to correct the error and try again (the
most common errors are simple syntax errors in the configuration or zone files).

Once *named* has started without errors, test the nameserver using the *dig* command:

```
$ dig  bluesky.fedorabook.com  @localhost  any

; <<>> DiG 9.3.2 <<>> bluesky.fedorabook.com @localhost any
; (1 server found)
;; global options:  printcmd
;; Got answer:
```

```
;; ->>HEADER<<- opcode: QUERY, status: NOERROR, id: 43031
;; flags: qr aa rd ra; QUERY: 1, ANSWER: 1, AUTHORITY: 2, ADDITIONAL: 1

;; QUESTION SECTION:
;bluesky.fedorabook.com.              IN      ANY

;; ANSWER SECTION:
bluesky.fedorabook.com. 3600   IN     A       216.183.93.224

;; AUTHORITY SECTION:
fedorabook.com.          3600   IN     NS      bluesky.fedorabook.com.
fedorabook.com.          3600   IN     NS      darkday.fedorabook.com.

;; ADDITIONAL SECTION:
darkday.fedorabook.com. 3600   IN     A       216.183.93.225

;; Query time: 17 msec
;; SERVER: 127.0.0.1#53(127.0.0.1)
;; WHEN: Sat Mar  4 22:18:08 2006
;; MSG SIZE  rcvd: 108
```

The argument @localhost tells *dig* to use the local nameserver instead of the one your machine is normally configured to use. The any argument instructs *named* to report any information that it finds about the requested server or domain (the default is to show only A records). You can substitute a record type such as soa or mx to see those specific resource records.

The line highlighted in bold the output shows the correct address for the requested hostname, which proves that *named* is configured correctly.

You can also test the nameserver with the *host* or *nslookup* commands (don't include the @ sign in front of the nameserver name *localhost* when using these commands):

```
$ host  bluesky.fedorabook.com  localhost
Using domain server:
Name: localhost
Address: 127.0.0.1#53
Aliases:

bluesky.fedorabook.com has address 216.183.93.224
Using domain server:
Name: localhost
Address: 127.0.0.1#53
Aliases:

$ nslookup  bluesky.fedorabook.com  localhost
Server:         localhost
Address:        127.0.0.1#53

Name:    bluesky.fedorabook.com
Address: 216.183.93.224
```

To test the caching capabilities of the nameserver, look up a hostname that is not in any of your local zones:

```
$ dig  fedora.redhat.com  @localhost

; <<>> DiG 9.3.2 <<>> fedora.redhat.com @localhost
; (1 server found)
;; global options:  printcmd
;; Got answer:
;; ->>HEADER<<- opcode: QUERY, status: NOERROR, id: 41999
;; flags: qr rd ra; QUERY: 1, ANSWER: 1, AUTHORITY: 3, ADDITIONAL: 0

;; QUESTION SECTION:
;fedora.redhat.com.                  IN       A

;; ANSWER SECTION:
fedora.redhat.com.       300    IN       A        209.132.177.50

;; AUTHORITY SECTION:
redhat.com.              600    IN       NS       ns1.redhat.com.
redhat.com.              600    IN       NS       ns2.redhat.com.
redhat.com.              600    IN       NS       ns3.redhat.com.

;; Query time: 401 msec
;; SERVER: 127.0.0.1#53(127.0.0.1)
;; WHEN: Sat Mar  4 22:28:53 2006
;; MSG SIZE  rcvd: 105
```

Configuring a slave nameserver

Once you have configured a master nameserver for a zone, you can configure
another computer to fetch the zone information from that master nameserver and
serve it to other machines. This can be done to share the workload for extremely
busy domains or (more often) to provide some redundancy in case the master server
is down or unreachable.

 There is little point configuring a second nameserver if all of your services (mail server, web server, and so on) are on one server and that is
the same machine that runs your master nameserver, because a failure
or overload on that system would effectively cripple the other services
along with the nameserver (and there is no value in being able to reach
a server that can't provide service).

This type of nameserver is called a *slave*, but it is still considered authoritative for the
domain if there is an NS record for it in the zone.

 You may need to adjust your SELinux configuration to use slave zones
(see Lab 8.2, "Using SELinux").

To configure a slave nameserver graphically, start the graphical configuration tool
(Figure 7-6), highlight the DNS Server entry, click on the New icon, and then click
on the Zone option from the pull-down list. Create the zone in the same way you did

on the master server, but set the Zone Type to "slave." Click OK, and the window shown in Figure 7-12 will appear.

Figure 7-12. Slave zone configuration window

Click on IPV4 Address, and the window will change to include fields for the IP address, as shown in Figure 7-13.

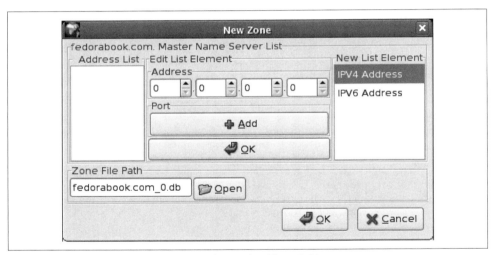

Figure 7-13. Slave zone configuration window with address fields

Enter the IP address of the master nameserver, and then click on the upper OK button followed by the lower OK button. Click on the Save button on the main window, and the slave zone will be created.

To configure a slave zone by editing the configuration files, add a section to /var/ named.conf that looks like this:

```
zone "fedorabook.com" IN {
        type slave;
        file "fedorabook.com.db";
        masters { 216.183.93.224; };
};
```

The zone and file values are the same as for a master zone. The type must be set to slave, and the masters value is a semicolon-separated list of zone master nameservers, enclosed in curly braces.

Once you have configured the slave zone, restart or reload *named* on the same machine. The initial zone transfer should be recorded in */var/log/messages*:

```
zone fedorabook.com/IN: Transfer started.
transfer of 'chris.com/IN' from 216.183.93.224#53:
        connected using 47.52.6.120#55096
zone fedorabook.com/IN: transferred serial 2
```

Using your nameservers locally

Once the nameserver is working, you can configure your local clients to use it:

- If the computers on your local network have been manually configured with their IP information, change the nameserver IP address to that of the machine running *named*. Edit the file */etc/resolv.conf*, or for Fedora Linux systems, use the menu option System → Administration → Network (the *system-config-network* tool, also known as *neat*) and adjust the entries in the DNS tab. For other operating systems, use the appropriate network configuration tool (such as the Microsoft Windows Control Panel).

- If the computers on your local network are configured to get their IP information through the DHCP protocol, and the DHCP server is on a gateway or router device, program the DHCP settings on that gateway or router so that the IP address of your *named* server is used as the domain name server. Consult the device documentation for configuration information.

- If the computers on your local network are configured to get their IP information through the DHCP protocol, and you're using your Fedora system as the DHCP server, add the nameserver to your DHCPD configuration file.

If you configure only your local clients to use your nameserver, any zones that you have configured are accessible only to those clients.

Serving domain information to the Internet

In order to make your domain information accessible to other systems on the Internet, it is necessary to register your domain and give the IP address of your nameserver(s) to your domain registrar.

There are many registrars available; to find one, simply search for "domain registration" on any search engine. Be sure to read the fine print of the registrar's contract because some registrars will try to lock you into their service by charging you exorbitant transfer fees if you try to switch to another registrar at a later date.

Most registrars now offer a myriad of different packages with domain forwarding, web hosting, or email management features. If you are planning to do your own web serving and email hosting, you can forgo those features and sign up for the most basic registration service. Give the IP address of all of your *named* servers to your registrar as the nameservers for your domain.

Once your domain registration is complete, the nameservers for your *top-level domain* (TLD)—such as .com or .org—will start forwarding queries about your domain to *your* nameservers. It takes a short while for your domain information to circulate to all of the nameservers for your TLD, so be patient!

To test whether your domain name service is accessible to the Internet, use the *dig* command with your ISP's nameserver:

```
$ dig somehost.yourdomain.com @nameserver.yourisp.com
```

Reverse mapping

DNS is also capable of performing *reverse mapping*, which translates an IP address into a domain name. However, unless your ISP has provided you with a block of IP addresses that is a power of 256—that is, either 256, 65,536, or 16,777,216 addresses—reverse mapping is particularly difficult to set up. If you really need reverse mapping controlled by your nameserver, you'll need to find out how your ISP has configured this and whether they are willing to delegate the reverse mapping to you.

If you have a small number of Internet-accessible hosts, most ISPs prefer to enter your hostnames and IP addresses into their reverse-mapping tables rather than go through the arduous task of connecting a portion of their reverse map to your nameserver.

How Does It Work?

Domain name service is based on the concept of *referrals*. When a client program (such as a web browser) needs to convert a hostname into an IP address, it uses query functions in a *resolver library*. The resolver looks in the local hosts file (*/etc/hosts* on Fedora, other Linux, Unix, and Mac OS X systems; *c:\windows\system32\drivers\etc\hosts* on Windows 2000, Windows Server 2003, and Windows XP), and if the hostname is not found in that file, it queries one of the caching nameservers specified in the operating system's network configuration. On a Fedora system (like most other Linux and Unix systems) the nameservers to be used are listed in */etc/resolv.conf*.

 The Linux resolver uses the file */etc/nsswitch* to determine possible ways of resolving a hostname to an IP address. The default configuration is to check */etc/hosts* first, and then try DNS.

The caching nameserver first checks its cache to see if it already has the answer to the query, and if it does, it returns that answer to the client. Otherwise, it contacts one of the *root nameservers* (listed in */var/named/named.ca*) by sending a UDP packet to port 53. The root nameserver sends back a reply referring the caching nameserver to the authoritative nameserver for the appropriate top-level domain (TLD). The caching nameserver then sends another query, this time to the TLD nameserver, which replies with a referral to the next nameserver down the chain. This happens recursively until a nameserver that knows the answer is found—or until the possibilities are exhausted and a nameserver finally returns an NXDOMAIN (nonexistent domain) response.

Slave zones are transferred from master zones when the master zone notifies the slave of the need for an update, or when an update is mandated by the refresh time value in the zone's SOA record. The transfer is always initiated by the slave side.

In addition to the resource records discussed in this lab, DNS supports a number of other record types that can be used to serve information, such as host hardware and OS configuration, geographical locations, email server authorization (Sender Policy Framework), and more, but these records are much less commonly used.

Reverse address resolution is performed by reversing the bytes of the dotted-quad IP address and using that as a domain name within the *in-addr.arpa* TLD. The resource record returned is a pointer (PTR) record.

For example, to discover the hostname of *216.183.93.224*, a query is made for *224. 93.183.216.in-addr.arpa*:

```
$ dig  224.93.183.216.in-addr.arpa  ptr

; <<>> DiG 9.3.1 <<>> 224.93.183.216.in-addr.arpa ptr
;; global options:  printcmd
;; Got answer:
;; ->>HEADER<<- opcode: QUERY, status: NOERROR, id: 10860
;; flags: qr rd ra; QUERY: 1, ANSWER: 1, AUTHORITY: 1, ADDITIONAL: 1

;; QUESTION SECTION:
;224.93.183.216.in-addr.arpa.     IN      PTR

;; ANSWER SECTION:
224.93.183.216.in-addr.arpa. 38204 IN    PTR     global.proximity.on.ca.

;; AUTHORITY SECTION:
93.183.216.in-addr.arpa. 38204  IN      NS      ns1.scratchtelecom.com.

;; ADDITIONAL SECTION:
ns1.scratchtelecom.com. 172567  IN      A       216.183.93.250

;; Query time: 1 msec
;; SERVER: 127.0.0.1#53(127.0.0.1)
;; WHEN: Sun Mar  5 00:21:39 2006
;; MSG SIZE  rcvd: 133
```

The *host* or *nslookup* commands will automatically convert an IP address into this type of query:

```
$ host  216.183.93.224
224.93.183.216.in-addr.arpa domain name pointer global.proximity.on.ca.

$ nslookup  216.183.93.224
Server:         127.0.0.1
Address:        127.0.0.1#53

Non-authoritative answer:
224.93.183.216.in-addr.arpa      name = global.proximity.on.ca.

Authoritative answers can be found from:
93.183.216.in-addr.arpa nameserver = ns1.scratchtelecom.com.
ns1.scratchtelecom.com  internet address = 216.183.93.250
```

The Fedora graphical configuration tool for DNS is called *system-config-bind*.

What About...

...changing from one nameserver to another?

Be sure that you never leave an obsolete nameserver active. For example, if your name service was provided by an ISP and you take over the name service, ensure that the ISP's nameserver no longer contain entries for your domain; otherwise, customers of that ISP may not be able to reach your system because they will receive obsolete DNS information.

Where Can I Learn More?

- The manpages for *named* and *named_selinux*; *dig*, *nslookup*, and *host*; *nsswitch.conf*, *hosts*, and *resolv.conf*
- The *BIND 9 Administrator's Reference Manual* in PDF format (*/usr/share/doc/bind-9.3.2/arm/Bv9ARM.pdf*) or HTML format (*file:///usr/share/doc/bind-9.3.1/arm/Bv9ARM.html*)

7.4   Configuring a CUPS Print Server

The Common Unix Printing System (CUPS) printer daemon can also be used as a print server, enabling other computers on the local network to access the printers it controls.

How Do I Do That?

Start the Printer Configuration tool shown in Figure 7-14. Highlight the printer you wish to share, select the checkbox labeled Shared, and then click Apply.

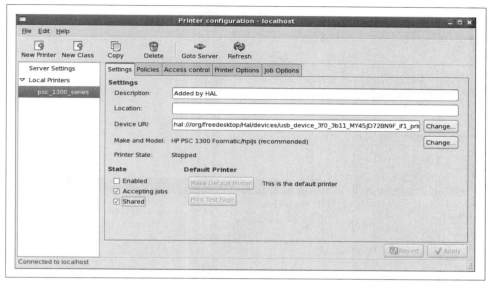

Figure 7-14. Printer configuration: sharing properties

Next, click on Server Settings on the lefthand side and select the checkbox labeled "Share published printers connected to this system." Click Apply.

You will need to open the IPP port 631 (`ipp:tcp`) in your firewall configuration (see Lab 8.1, "Prevent Unwanted Connections").

Your printer will now be accessible to other systems.

Accessing a CUPS printer from Windows XP

To add a CUPS printer to a Windows XP system, select "Printers and Faxes" from the Start menu and click on "Add a printer." The Add Printer Wizard will appear.

Click Next to advance past the introduction. On the next page, select "A network printer, or a printer attached to another computer," and click Next. The window shown in Figure 7-15 will appear.

Select "Connect to a printer on the Internet or on a home or office network," and enter a URI in this form:

```
http://server:631/printers/printername
```

Replace *server* with the hostname of the CUPS server if the Windows system can resolve that hostname using DNS; if you haven't configured DNS, use the IP address instead. Replace *printername* with the name of the printer as it is known to CUPS.

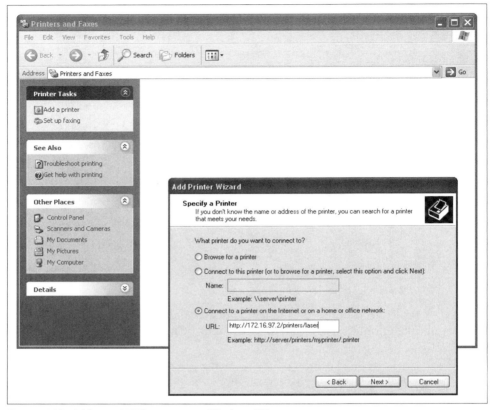

Figure 7-15. Adding a CUPS printer to a Windows XP system

Click Next.

Select the manufacturer and printer model, and click Next (or, if the printer drivers are on a CD, click "Have a Disk" and select the disk location). Then click Finish to set up the printer. You can now use the CUPS printer from any Windows applications.

How Does It Work?

CUPS uses the Internet Print Protocol (IPP), which is based on the same HTTP protocol used by the Web. One shared virtual directory is mapped to each printer.

The CUPS configuration files are stored in */etc/cups*, and the format of the main configuration file */etc/cups/cupsd.conf* is very similar to the Apache configuration file (discussed in Lab 7.5, "Using the Apache Web Server"). Printer sharing is therefore enabled and disabled using Allow and Deny directives in the same way that they would be used to control access to an Apache directory. For example, global access to the printer *laser0* could be configured like this:

```
<Location /printers/laser0>
    Order Deny,Allow
    Allow From All
</Location>
```

What About...

...a client that uses the older LPD protocol?

If you wish to share the printer with a client that knows only the older Line Printer Daemon (LPD) protocol, such as an older Linux/Unix system or a Windows NT system, you will need to install the *cups-lpd* package.

To enable the service, start the Services tool (System → Administration → Services), select the On Demand Services tab, select the checkbox labeled "cups-lpd," and click Save. You can also enable the service by editing */etc/xinetd.d/cups-lpd*, which looks like this:

```
# default: off
# description: Allow applications using the legacy lpd protocol
# to communicate with CUPS
service printer
{
        disable = yes
        socket_type = stream
        protocol = tcp
        wait = no
        user = lp
        server = /usr/lib/cups/daemon/cups-lpd
}
```

Change the `disable` line to the following:

```
disable = no
```

Save the file and restart the *xinetd* service:

```
# service xinetd restart
Stopping xinetd:                                    [  OK  ]
Starting xinetd:                                    [  OK  ]
```

LPD printer sharing requires the printer port 515 (`printer:tcp`) to be opened in your firewall.

LPD emulation is enabled globally; there is no provision to share only some printers, or to share only with certain clients.

...configuring sharing from the command line?

Fedora does not provide a facility for configuring printer sharing from the command line. The only available option is to edit */etc/cups/cupsd.conf* and insert the appropriate

Allow and Deny directives (or, if you're accessing from a remote system, you may want to use X tunneling via SSH—see Lab 4.10, "Remote Management Using SSH").

Where Can I Learn More?

- The CUPS manual: *http://localhost:631/documentation.html*
- The manpage for *cups-lpd*

7.5   Using the Apache Web Server

Apache is the most widely used web server and is a standard part of Fedora Core. One of the reasons that it has garnered a majority market share is that it is highly configurable and can therefore meet a wide range of web-serving needs. Despite the number of options available, Fedora Core ships Apache with a default configuration that is ready to meet most basic web-serving needs.

How Do I Do That?

Before configuring Apache, it's a good idea to make a backup copy of the original configuration file:

```
# cp /etc/httpd/conf/httpd.conf /etc/httpd/conf/httpd.conf-original
```

Starting Apache

Apache is not enabled by default. To start it, use the Services tool or enter this command:

```
# service httpd start
```

To ensure that Apache starts each time the system is booted, enable the *httpd* service.

Whenever the Apache configuration is changed, you must instruct Apache to reload its configuration:

```
# service httpd reload
```

Alternately, you can use the Restart button in the Services tool.

Testing Apache

Using a web browser on the machine running Apache, access the web location *http://localhost/*. You will see the test page shown in Figure 7-16.

Once you can view this web page on the server, you can attempt to access the page from a remote system using the IP address of the server (such as *http://192.168.100.1/*), or, if DNS has been set up to allow it, the server's hostname (e.g., *http://fedorabook.com/*).

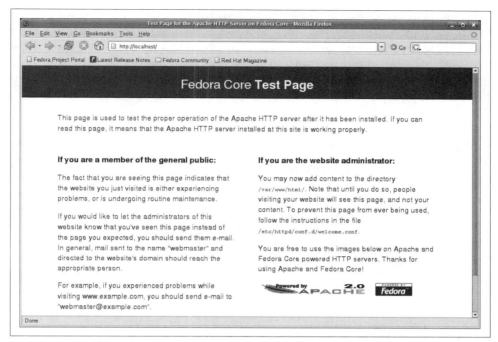

Figure 7-16. Apache test page confirming operation of the web server

 If you can access the web page on the server but not from a remote system, then the firewall configuration may require adjustment.

Installing your own web content

Once the web server is running, place the content you wish to serve in the directory */var/www/html*. The default page for each directory is *index.html*; once you have created */var/www/html/index.html*, the test page (Figure 7-16) will no longer appear.

Create subdirectories within */var/www/html* to create any directory structure you want. These directories will be reflected in the URLs accessible through the web server. For example, you could create the directory */var/www/html/photos/*:

```
# mkdir /var/www/html/photos
```

That directory will be accessible using the URI *http://<hostname>/photos/*.

Changing the default configuration

The default Apache configuration serves all web content from one directory: */var/www/html*. To perform more advanced web serving, the default configuration needs to be modified.

Apache can be configured by using Fedora's graphical configuration tool or by editing configuration files, but you can't alternate between the two approaches. Most experienced Apache administrators prefer to directly edit the configuration file because it provides direct access to all of Apache's features and because it is more convenient when accessing a remote server. However, Fedora's graphical configuration tool is quite powerful and is a good place to start if you're not familiar with Apache setup.

Configuring Apache graphically

To configure Apache graphically, select System → Administration → Server Settings → HTTP (or in KDE, Administration → Server Settings → HTTP). The *httpd* configuration dialog, a simple tabbed window (shown in Figure 7-17), will appear.

Figure 7-17. Graphical configuration tool for Apache httpd

Start with the Main tab and enter the server name and webmaster's email address. The server name must contain only alphanumeric characters; it will be used as a hostname and combined with the current domain name to build a fully qualified domain name (FQDN).

 The webmaster's address is displayed in server error messages and could be harvested by web spiders, so it is a good idea to use a disposable email alias and change it frequently to thwart spammers.

The Available Addresses area is used only if you wish to prevent the web server from using some network interfaces, or if you wish to use a nonstandard TCP/IP port (the default for HTTP is port 80). This is usually left at the default setting.

The Virtual Hosts tab shown in Figure 7-18 is used to configure Apache to respond to requests for multiple web sites—for example, *www.fedorabook.com* and *www. tylers.info*. By default, a single entry is present, labeled Default Virtual Host.

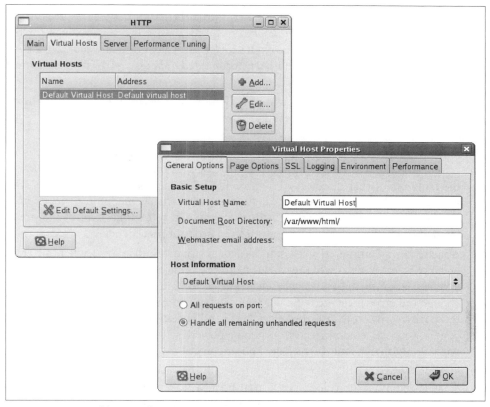

Figure 7-18. Virtual host configuration

To edit an existing entry or add a new entry, use the Edit or Add buttons. In either case, the window shown on the right of Figure 7-18 will appear, with these tabs:

General Options

> Enter the name of the virtual host (this information is only for your reference, so you can be as descriptive as you want), the Document Root directory that will store documents for this host, and the webmaster email address (if different from the default).

If you choose a Document Root that is not within */var/www/html* and have SELinux active, you will need to change the security context of that directory (see Lab 8.2, "Using SELinux").

In the Host information area, choose a host type:

- Specify "Default virtual host" if only one host is being used.
- For each virtual host sharing a common IP address—the most common type of virtual host—select "Name-based virtual host" and enter the IP address, hostname (e.g., *www.fedorabook.com*), and aliases and misspellings for the hostname (e.g., *fedorabook.com*, *ww.fedorabook.com*, *wwww.fedorabook.com*, *toronto.fedorabook.com*, and *www.toronto.fedorabook.com*). The aliases must be separated by spaces.
- For each virtual host with a unique IP address, select "IP based virtual host" and enter the host IP address and name.

Page Options

When Apache receives a request for a directory (such as *http://www.fedorabook. com/example/*), it will search that directory for files that can serve as an index to the contents of that directory. Traditionally, the index is named *index.html*, but you may wish to use other names, such as *index.php*, *home.html*, or *index.htm*. Use the Directory Page Search List area of this tab to configure all of the possible names for the index file, in your desired order of precedence.

Apache is preconfigured with standard pages that are displayed when an error occurs. To override any of these pages and present a custom error message, highlight the page in the Error pages list and click Edit. A dialog box will appear; change the error message behavior from Default to File and enter the location of the page you wish to use (or select URL and specify the local URL of the web page). You can customize the footer displayed at the bottom of default error pages using the Default Error Page Footer control.

Logging

Apache maintains two logs per virtual host: a *transfer log*, which records what was sent to clients, and an *error log*, which records any problems encountered. By default, all virtual hosts will share one pair of logs, but to analyze statistics separately for each virtual host, you'll need to specify separate logfiles for each. To do this, change the "Log to file" name for the Transfer Log from logs/ access_log to a name that includes an indication of the virtual hostname, such as logs/*fedorabook*_access_log. Do the same for the Error log, changing logs/ error_log to logs/*fedorabook*_error_log. Alternately, you can consolidate logs from several servers using *syslog* by selecting the Use System Log option and entering the hostname or IP address of the *syslog* server.

The default logfile format does not contain *referrer* information, so you can't tell where your visitors are coming from or how they're navigating your site. To add this information, select the checkbox "Use custom logging facilities" and set the "Custom log string" to combined.

Performance

This tab should actually be named Permission, since it controls what is permitted in web directories. Click on the Edit button in the Default directory options section to edit the options for the virtual host's Document Root directory; available permission options include ExecCGI (run scripts), FollowSymLinks (follow symbolic links to files), Includes (process server-side include directives in files), IncludesNOEXEC (process server-side includes, except scripts), Indexes (use index files such as *index.html* when a directory is requested), MultiViews (enable content negotiation such as automatic language or image-type selection), and SymLinksIfOwnerMatch (follow symbolic links if the link and the target are owned by the same user).

To set the permissions for a particular directory, click the Add button in the lower part of the window (or, if the directory is already listed, click the Edit button). Enter the directory name in the Directory field at the bottom of the window and set the Options checkboxes for the options you wish to enable in this directory. By default, all remote computers (hosts) will have access to the content in this directory; the Allow and Deny list options can be used to permit (or deny) access only from certain hosts. The hosts can be identified by hostname (*fedorabook.com*), partial domain name (*.com*), IP address (*192.168.100.1*), or IP address and netmask or bit count (*192.168.100.0/255.255.255.0*, or the equivalent *192.168.100.0/24*).

To enable the use of *.htaccess* files, select the checkbox labeled "Let .htaccess override directory options."

There is also a tab for SSL—used for secure, encrypted web serving—and a tab for Environment, which is used to pass information to web scripts, but the options on those tabs are not used for basic web serving.

Once the virtual host is configured, click OK to return to the main HTTP configuration window (Figure 7-17).

The Server and Performance Tuning tabs in the main HTTP configuration window do not normally require adjustment.

After configuring Apache, click OK to save your configuration (a confirmation dialog may appear).

Directly editing Apache's configuration file

The main Apache configuration information is stored in */etc/httpd/conf/httpd.conf*. Additional configuration information is stored in the directory */etc/httpd/conf.d/*. Per-module configuration files are automatically installed and removed along with Apache modules and web applications such as SquirrelMail.

httpd.conf is a regular text file and can be edited with any standard text editor. As mentioned earlier, I strongly recommended that you make a backup copy of this file before each change:

```
# cp /etc/httpd/conf/httpd.conf /etc/httpd/conf/httpd.conf.backup-1
```

httpd.conf contains a number of *directives*, each of which consists of a name and one or more values, listed on a single line with a space after the name and each of the values. The directive names are not case-sensitive, but some of the values are. Values must be quoted if they contain spaces.

These directives are all equivalent:

```
ServerRoot /etc/httpd
ServerRoot "/etc/httpd"
ServerRoot '/etc/httpd'
SERVERROOT /etc/httpd/
serverroot /etc/httpd
```

To add a comment line, place a pound sign at the start of the line:

```
# Note: /etc/httpd is the standard Fedora server root.
```

 Comments must be on a line by themselves.

Directives are global unless they are placed in a *container*, which limits the scope to which the directive applies. For example, the `<Directory>` container causes the contained directives to be applied only to a specific directory (and its subdirectories); here, the directives apply only to the contents of */var/www/html*:

```
<Directory "/var/www/html">
        Options Indexes Includes FollowSymLinks
        AllowOverride None
        Allow from all
        Order allow,deny
</Directory>
```

Configuring the server root and document root. The `ServerRoot` directive sets the directory that contains all files related to the Apache server—including configuration files, logs, modules, and runtime information—except the actual content being served. By default, all relative paths specified in *httpd.conf* are relative to this directory. The default is */etc/httpd*:

```
ServerRoot "/etc/httpd"
```

The `DocumentRoot` directive sets the directory for files being served. Fedora's default is */var/www/html*:

```
ServerRoot "/var/www/html"
```

Changing DocumentRoot will require you to change the SELinux context of the new document root directory.

Configuring the server administrator, IP address and port, and server name. The directive named ServerAdministrator specifies an email address that can be used to reach the person responsible for running the web server. This address appears on certain error pages. This should be a valid address so that your web visitors can contact you if necessary, but since it can be harvested by web spiders, it is a good idea to use a disposable email address and change it regularly. The default value is root@localhost and should always be changed:

```
ServerAdministrator webmaster@fedorabook.com
```

The IP address and port are configured with the Listen directive. The web server will normally listen to port 80 on all available network interfaces:

```
Listen 80
```

If necessary, you can specify an alternate port, or a specific IP address and a port:

```
Listen 8000
Listen 192.168.10.1:8000
```

The ServerName directive configures the name of the server and is necessary only if you are using a value different from the machine's fully qualified domain name:

```
ServerName www.fedorabook.com
```

Configuring access. Apache uses directory containers to control access to directories on your system. The root directory is configured first:

```
<Directory />
    Options FollowSymLinks
    AllowOverride None
</Directory>
```

The Options directive is critical: it specifies what is permitted in these directories. In this case, all access to the root directory and all subdirectories—in other words, the entire system—is prohibited except as the destination of symbolic links.

The next directory container loosens up the restrictions for */var/www/html* and its subdirectories:

```
<Directory "/var/www/html">
    Options Indexes FollowSymLinks
    AllowOverride None
    Order Allow,Deny
    Allow from all
</Directory>
```

The values for the Options directive are selected from this list:

All
> The default, which permits everything except for MultiViews.

ExecCGI
> Permits execution of scripts.

FollowSymLinks, SymLinksIfOwnerMatch
> If FollowSynLinks is specified Apache will follow symbolic links which lead to or from this directory. If SymLinksIfOwnerMatch is specified, the link and the target must be owned by the same user.

Includes, IncludesNoExec
> Files may *include* other files, with or without the ability (Includes and IncludesNoExec, respectively) to execute those other files. Files that use this feature must have a name ending in *.shtml* and may include directives such as `<!--#include virtual="footer.html" -->` or `<!--#exec cmd="/usr/bin/cal" -->` to include the *footer.html* file or the output of the cal command, respectively.

Indexes
> An *index.html* file usually serves as the index for a directory. If it is not present, and the Indexes option is enabled, Apache will generate an appropriate index page when required, listing the contents of the directory. If you do not wish your web visitor to know the contents of your directories, do not use this option.

MultiViews
> Enables Apache to search for appropriate content based on file type, encoding, and language. For example, if the MultiViews option is in effect, Apache will select between *index.html.en* (English) and *index.html.fr* (French) files when *index.html* is requested, using the browser's language preference to select the most appropriate file.

Order, Allow, and Deny are directives that work together to define which remote users may access the directory. Order sets the order in which the Allow and Deny directives are used, and the value must be Allow,Deny or Deny,Allow (the default). The Allow and Deny directives accept a list of full or partial domain names, IP addresses, or IP addresses and netmask or network bit count.

For example, to enable access only from computers on your internal network, assuming your network is 12.200.X.X:

```
Order Allow,Deny
Allow from 12.200.0.0/16
Deny from all
```

On the other hand, you could enable access only from computers that are not in your internal network:

```
Order Deny,Allow
Deny from 12.200.0.0/255.255.0.0
Allow from all
```

Or you could exclude access from specific domains:

```
Order Deny,Allow
Deny from .gov ourcompetition.com
Allow from all
```

The `AllowOverride` directive enables the use of a hidden file, *.htaccess*, which may be placed in directories to override the configuration of that directory and subdirectories. Although there are several possible values for this directive, it is normally set to `None` (no overrides are permitted) or `AuthConfig` (the *.htaccess* file can control whether a user ID and password are required to access the content of that directory).

The next set of directory containers configure special permissions for the *icon*, *cgi-bin*, and *error* directories in */var/www*:

```
<Directory "/var/www/icons">
    Options Indexes MultiViews
    AllowOverride None
    Order Allow,Deny
    Allow from all
</Directory>

<Directory "/var/www/cgi-bin">
    AllowOverride None
    Options None
    Order Allow,Deny
    Allow from all
</Directory>

<Directory "/var/www/error">
    AllowOverride None
    Options IncludesNoExec
    AddOutputFilter Includes html
    AddHandler type-map var
    Order Allow,Deny
    Allow from all
    LanguagePriority en es de fr
    ForceLanguagePriority Prefer Fallback
</Directory>
```

These directories are not within the normal `DocumentRoot` and are instead made accessible through the use of `Alias` and `ScriptAlias` directives:

```
Alias /icons/ "/var/www/icons/"
ScriptAlias /cgi-bin/ "/var/www/cgi-bin/"
Alias /error/ "/var/www/error/"
```

These directives make the indicated directories appear to exist within the document tree; for example, a request for *http://<hostname>/icons/text.png* is fulfilled using the file */var/www/icons/text.png* (instead of */var/www/html/icons/text.png*). This permits */var/www/html* to remain uncluttered by icons, scripts, and error messages.

Since */cgi-bin/* is aliased using a `ScriptAlias` directive, it is assumed that all files in that directory are actually scripts (executable programs) rather than document files, regardless of their extension. In the default configuration, this is the only directory that may contain scripts, so you only have to look in one place to check for script vulnerabilities.

Enabling personal web pages. To permit each user to maintain her own web directory, find the UserDir section of *httpd.conf:*

```
<IfModule mod_userdir.c>
    #
    # UserDir is disabled by default since it can confirm the presence
    # of a username on the system (depending on home directory
    # permissions).
    #
    UserDir disable

    #
    # To enable requests to /~user/ to serve the user's public_html
    # directory, remove the "UserDir disable" line above, and uncomment
    # the following line instead:
    #
    #UserDir public_html

</IfModule>
```

Comment out the line that reads UserDir disable and uncomment the line which reads UserDir public_html:

```
<IfModule mod_userdir.c>
    #
    # UserDir is disabled by default since it can confirm the presence
    # of a username on the system (depending on home directory
    # permissions).
    #
    #UserDir disable

    #
    # To enable requests to /~user/ to serve the user's public_html
    # directory, remove the "UserDir disable" line above, and uncomment
    # the following line instead:
    #
    UserDir public_html

</IfModule>
```

Then uncomment the container section <Directory /home/*/public_html>:

```
    #
    # Control access to UserDir directories. The following is an example
    # for a site where these directories are restricted to read-only.
    #
    <Directory /home/*/public_html>
        AllowOverride FileInfo AuthConfig Limit
        Options MultiViews Indexes SymLinksIfOwnerMatch IncludesNoExec
        <Limit GET POST OPTIONS>
```

```
        Order allow,deny
        Allow from all
    </Limit>
    <LimitExcept GET POST OPTIONS>
        Order deny,allow
        Deny from all
    </LimitExcept>
</Directory>
```

Each user can then create a *~/public_html* directory and place her own personal content in that directory.

 If you have SELinux enabled, each user will need to execute this command to make his content accessible to Apache:

```
$ chcon -R -t httpd_sys_content_t ~/public_html
```

Alternately, users can make their *public_html* content accessible to both Apache and Samba (see Lab 8.2, "Using SELinux").

Using virtual hosts. Virtual hosting permits one web server to serve web pages for multiple hostnames. There are two ways of detecting which host a browser is trying to connect to: the web server can respond to multiple IP addresses and serve different content based on which IP address is used (IP-based virtual hosts), or the web server can serve the content based on the Host: header sent by the browser (name-based virtual hosts).

To configure named-based virtual hosts—the most common type—uncomment the NameVirtualHost directive in the *httpd.conf* file:

```
NameVirtualHost *:80
```

If you're using a port other than 80, enter it on this line.

Next, create a VirtualHost container for each virtual host. There is an example in the comments near the end of the *httpd.conf* file:

```
#<VirtualHost *:80>
#    ServerAdmin webmaster@dummy-host.example.com
#    DocumentRoot /www/docs/dummy-host.example.com
#    ServerName dummy-host.example.com
#    ErrorLog logs/dummy-host.example.com-error_log
#    CustomLog logs/dummy-host.example.com-access_log common
#</VirtualHost>
```

Copy and uncomment these lines, substituting the correct values for these directives:

ServerAdmin
  Insert the email contact for the administrator for this virtual host.

DocumentRoot
  Enter the document root for this virtual host. If you're using SELinux, it is easiest to use subdirectories of */var/www/html* for the virtual host document roots.

ServerName, ServerAlias

The main name of the web server and any assigned nicknames, respectively. These names must appear in the DNS entries for this host. It's a good idea to include common misspellings within your domain name, such as *ww. fedorabook.com* and *wwww.fedorabook.com*.

 Your DNS configuration must include all of the hostnames used for ServerName and ServerAlias or be configured with a wildcard hostname (*).

ErrorLog, CustomLog

Set these to the name of the logfiles you wish to use for errors and for normal access, respectively. At the end of CustomLog, specify the logfile format combined so that referrer information is included in your logfile.

A completed virtual host container will look like this:

```
<VirtualHost *:80>
    ServerAdmin webadministrator@fedorabook.com
    DocumentRoot /var/www/html/fedorabook
    ServerName fedorabook.com
    ServerAlias www.fedorabook.com ww.fedorabook.com wwww.fedorabook.com
    ErrorLog logs/fedorabook-error_log
    CustomLog logs/fedorabook-access_log combined
</VirtualHost>
```

Enabling CGI scripts in every directory

Fedora's default Apache configuration permits CGI scripts only in the */cgi-bin/* script alias directory, */var/www/cgi-bin/*. This makes it easy to keep an eye on all of the scripts, and many webmasters prefer this.

However, on a complex site with different web applications running, it is often desirable to group files by application, allocating one directory for each application and building a structure within that directory for the scripts, HTML, stylesheets, and multimedia files, rather than mixing the scripts for all of the applications together into a single directory.

To enable CGI scripts in every directory, uncomment the AddHandler directive for the *.cgi* extension in *httpd.conf*:

```
AddHandler cgi-script .cgi
```

Then add ExecCGI to the Options directive for the DocumentRoot:

```
<Directory "/var/www/html">
    ...
    Options Indexes FollowSymLinks ExecCGI
    ...
</Directory>
```

Apache will then treat any file with a *.cgi* extension as a script.

If you want individual users to be able to run scripts, do the same for the ~/*public_html*
directories:

```
<Directory /home/*/public_html>
    ...
    Options MultiViews Indexes SymLinksIfOwnerMatch IncludesNoExec ExecCGI
    ...
</Directory>
```

CGI scripts in users' ~/*public_html* directories will execute with that
user's permission and will therefore be able to read and write any files
that the user can read and write. This can be a huge security risk
because a single web script can expose any file, email, or database on
your system which that user can normally access.

In order to reduce the risk of a script that has been maliciously compromised, scripts that are writable by group or other users or contained in directories that are writable by group or others will not be
executed by Apache, and an error message will be logged in /*var/log/*
httpd/suexec.

Password-protecting content

Apache can be configured to password-protect content using two files: a password
file and an .*htaccess* file.

Note that passwords are sent in unencrypted form over the network
unless you use a secure (SSL) connection, so the security provided by
this option is minimal.

First, configure Apache to permit the use of .*htaccess* files for authentication configuration. If you're using the graphical configuration tool, select the checkbox labeled
"Let .htaccess files override directory options."

To configure this without using the graphical tool, add the AuthConfig keyword to
the AllowOverride line in the appropriate directory container within *httpd.conf*:

```
<Directory "/var/httpd">
    ...
    AllowOverride AuthConfig
    ...
</Directory>
```

This option is enabled by default for ~/*public_html* directories.

An .*htaccess* file is similar to an *httpd.conf* file, but it is placed in the directory that
you wish to protect. Here is an example:

```
AuthType     Basic
AuthName     "team scores"
AuthUserFile /etc/httpd/team_scores_password
Require      valid-user
```

The four directives in this file are required for basic password protection:

AuthType
> Specifies the authentication type to be used. Basic indicates that a simple user ID/password pair will be used.

AuthName
> Describes the type of data being protected by the password. Most browsers will include this text in the password dialog, as shown in Figure 7-19.

AuthUserFile
> The name of the password file.

Require
> Normally set to valid-user, permitting any user with a valid password to access the protected content.

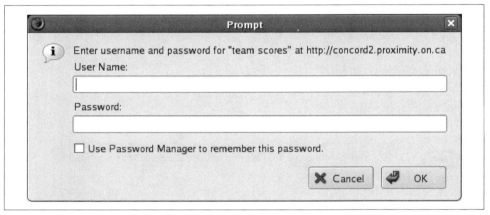

Figure 7-19. Browser dialog box showing the AuthName value

For security, the password file must be located outside of the directories served by Apache. It is managed with the *htpasswd* command; to create the file and set the first password, use the -c option and provide the password filename and user ID as arguments:

```
# htpasswd -c /var/httpd/team_scores_password chris
New password: bigsecret
Re-enter new password: bigsecret
Adding password for user chris
```

Once the file has been created, leave out the -c option, or you'll erase existing entries:

```
# htpasswd /var/httpd/team_scores_password diane
New password: neverguess
Re-type new password: neverguess
Adding password for user diane
```

If you prefer, you can include the password at the end of command line—which works well for scripts—by adding the -b option:

```
# htpasswd -b /var/httpd/team_scores_password frank TheBestPitcher
Adding password for user frank
```

 If other users are logged in to the system, there is a small chance that they will be able to discover these passwords if you set them using the -b option because the command line is visible in the output of the ps command (although very briefly).

If you enter an existing user ID instead of a new one, the old password will be updated instead of creating a new record:

```
# htpasswd -b /var/httpd/team_scores_password diane new-secret
Updating password for user diane
```

.htaccess files have traditionally been used for access control, and they work well for ~/public_html directories because users can configure them on their own. For directories in your document root, it's just as easy to place the authentication directives in a directory container in httpd.conf:

```
<Directory /var/www/html/scores/>
    AuthType        Basic
    AuthName        "team scores"
    AuthUserFile    /etc/httpd/team_scores_password
    Require         valid-user
</Directory>
```

How Does It Work?

Apache is the most widely used web server software in the world. It is actively developed by the Apache Software Foundation (http://apache.org) and can be scaled from a static personal web site on a desktop-class computer to a extremely high-volume database-backed web site running on clusters of computers.

In order to meet such a wide range of needs, Apache can be configured using over 370 distinct directives. Although many different graphical configuration tools have been developed, none of them can configure all directives or handle all possible deployment scenarios for the software.

The Fedora graphical configuration tool for Apache is named system-config-httpd. The options entered into the configuration dialogs are saved in XML and then converted into a working httpd.conf by using the XSLT transformation stylesheet /usr/share/system-config-httpd/httpd.conf.xsl. You can customize that file to change the generated httpd.conf file.

The actual Apache server program is /usr/sbin/httpd. It can be started or stopped with the service command or system-config-services, which use the Fedora-specific script file */etc/rc.d/init.d/httpd*; it can also be started and stopped with Apache tool */usr/sbin/apachectl*, but the SELinux security context will be different.

Apache listens on the configured ports and waits for incoming connections from client software such as web browsers. Once a connection is established, the client sends a *request*, plus additional headers with information such as the client software version and preferred languages and encodings, followed by a blank line. The server responds with a result code, additional headers, a blank line, and then the content requested (or an error message). In its most basic form, the conversation goes something like this (the request is shown in bold; the response headers are in italic, and the rest of the listing is the body of the response):

```
GET /testfile.html HTTP/1.1
Host: www.fedorabook.com

HTTP/1.1 200 OK
Date: Wed, 01 Mar 2006 02:49:54 GMT
Server: Apache/2.2.0 (Fedora)
Last-Modified: Mon, 27 Feb 2006 21:25:54 GMT
ETag: "f0518-4a-5b0edc80"
Accept-Ranges: bytes
Content-Length: 85
Connection: close
Content-Type: text/html; charset=UTF-8

<html>
<head><title>Test</title></head>
<body>
<i><p>Success!</p></i>
</body>
</html>
```

In an elementary configuration, Apache is responsible for mapping the web namespace to the local filesystem namespace, performing access control and logging, collecting the requested resource (either by reading a file or executing code), and sending the resource to the client.

What About...

...interpreting the Apache logfiles?

Logfiles come in two forms: access logs and error logs. An *access log* in the default *common* format contains entries like these (all on one line):

```
24.43.223.54 - - [28/Feb/2006:22:01:33 -0500] "GET / HTTP/1.1" 200 956
```

The fields here are the IP address of the remote host (24.43.223.54); the remote user login name (-); the authenticated username on the local system (-, because the user did not authenticate); the date, time, and time zone of the request ([28/Feb/2006:22:01:33 -0500]); the request string (GET / HTTP/1.1); the status code returned to the client (200, meaning OK); and the number of bytes sent to the client (956).

If you use the *combined* log format, the entries will look like this:

```
24.43.223.54 - - [28/Feb/2006:22:01:33 -0500] "GET / HTTP/1.1" 200 956 "http://www.
fedorabook.com/index.html" "Mozilla/5.0 (X11; U;
Linux i686; en-US; rv:1.7.12) Gecko/20060202 Fedora/1.0.7-1.2.fc4 Firefox/1.0.7"
```

The additional fields are the referring page, which linked to or contained the information requested (`http://www.fedorabook.com/index.html`), and the *user agent* header, which describes the client software (Firefox on a Fedora system in this case). The user agent information is interesting, but the *referrer* information is critical if you want to analyze where your visitors are coming from, which pages they visit first, and how they progress through your web site.

The error logfile contains entries like this:

```
[Tue Feb 28 22:01:33 2006] [error] [client 24.43.223.54] File does not exist: /var/
www/html/favicon.ico
```

This indicates the date and time, the fact that this is an error, the client IP address, and the detail of the error.

...using a more secure authentication scheme than Basic?

The problem with basic authentication is that the user ID and password travel in plain text across the network. Anyone snooping on the network can see the password.

A slightly better approach is to use digest authentication, which hashes the password before sending it across the network. This is still not nearly as secure as encrypting the connection.

To use digest authentication, use the same authentication configuration as you would for basic authentication, but substitute Digest for the AuthType:

```
AuthType        Digest
AuthName        "prices"
AuthUserFile    /var/www/digest
Require         valid-user
```

Create the password file using the *htdigest* command instead of *htpasswd*. *htdigest* requires one additional argument in front of the username, called the *realm*; copy the value from the AuthName directive and use it for the realm. Here is an example:

```
# htdigest -c /var/www/digest prices chris
Adding password for chris in realm prices.
New password: confidentialpassword
Re-type new password: confidentialpassword
# htdigest /var/www/digest prices diane
Adding user diane in realm prices
New password: bigsecret
Re-type new password: bigsecret
```

htdigest does not accept the -b option used with *htpasswd*.

Where Can I Learn More?

- The Apache documentation from the Apache Software Foundation is on their web site at *http://httpd.apache.org/docs/2.2/* and on the web server of any Fedora system at *http://<hostname>/<manual>* (to disable access to the manual, remove */var/www/manual*).

- The manpages for *httpd*, *htpasswd*, *htdigest*, and *httpd_selinux*.

7.6   Configuring the sendmail Server

sendmail is a robust email server. Like Apache, it has an enormous number of configuration options to handle many different service scenarios, even though many of these scenarios are pretty rare. With a small amount of configuration, sendmail can be configured to handle most mail-serving tasks.

How Do I Do That?

Fedora's default sendmail configuration will:

- Start the *sendmail* service at each boot
- Accept mail from local users for local mailboxes and place it in those mailboxes
- Accept mail from local users for remote systems, place it in a queue, and attempt to deliver it directly to the remote mail hosts

This configuration may or may not work for you, depending on how you are connected to the Internet.

Preparing to configure sendmail and activating changes

To configure sendmail easily, install the *sendmail-cf* package:

```
# yum install sendmail-cf
```

Changes to the sendmail configuration are made to the file */etc/mail/sendmail.mc*. However, this isn't the sendmail configuration file! Instead, it's a file that is used to *generate* the sendmail configuration file, */etc/mail/sendmail.cf*.

To generate a new *sendmail.cf* file:

```
# cd /etc/mail
# make
```

This must be done after each change is made to *sendmail.mc*. Reload the *sendmail* server to make your changes take effect:

```
# service sendmail reload
```

(You can also use the Restart button in the Services tool.)

Configuring sendmail to use a mail relay

Some Internet Service Providers (ISPs) block email traffic to all mail servers except their own. This is intended to block viruses that set themselves up as a mail server, but it also interferes with Fedora's default sendmail configuration, which expects to be able to send email directly to the destination system.

To configure sendmail to send your outbound email through your ISP's mail server, find the line in */etc/mail/sendmail.mc* that contains the word SMART_HOST:

```
dnl # Uncomment and edit the following line if your outgoing mail needs to
dnl # be sent out through an external mail server:
dnl #
dnl define(`SMART_HOST',`smtp.your.provider')
```

In this file, dnl means *discard to newline*, which effectively turns this line into a comment. Uncomment the SMART_HOST line by removing the dnl and then replace *smtp.your.provider* with the name of your ISP's mail server:

```
define(`SMART_HOST',`mailserver.yourisp.com')
```

Configuring sendmail to accept inbound email

Fedora's standard sendmail configuration does not accept email from remote systems, a feature that must be enabled if the system is going to act as an Internet email host.

To enable remote inbound connections, locate the line in *sendmail.mc* that contains the loopback address 127.0.0.1:

```
dnl # The following causes sendmail to only listen on the IPv4 loopback address
dnl # 127.0.0.1 and not on any other network devices. Remove the loopback
dnl # address restriction to accept email from the internet or intranet.
dnl #
DAEMON_OPTIONS(`Port=smtp,Addr=127.0.0.1, Name=MTA')dnl
```

Add dnl to the start of this line to comment it out:

```
dnl DAEMON_OPTIONS(`Port=smtp,Addr=127.0.0.1, Name=MTA')dnl
```

sendmail will then accept connections on all network interfaces and deliver mail that is addressed to a user on the local host. For example, if the hostname is *bluesky.fedorabook.com*, then email addressed to *chris@bluesky.fedorabook.com* will be delivered to the mailbox of the local user *chris*, which is */var/spool/mail/chris*.

To configure sendmail to accept mail for other destinations, add those destinations to the file */etc/mail/local-host-names*:

```
# local-host-names - include all aliases for your machine here.
```
fedorabook.com
mailserver.fedorabook.com
global.proximity.on.ca

 Remember to enable inbound connections on port 25 (SMTP) in your firewall configuration.

Using aliases

There are many standard email addresses that people expect to be able to use: *webmaster* to reach the person responsible for the web server and content, *abuse* to report spam problems, *info* as a general information contact, and so forth. Mail sent to these standard addresses can be redirected to the mailbox of chosen users through the sendmail *alias* facility.

Aliases are configured in the file */etc/aliases*, which looks like this:

```
#
#  Aliases in this file will NOT be expanded in the header from
#  Mail, but WILL be visible over networks or from /bin/mail.
#
#       >>>>>>>>>      The program "newaliases" must be run after
#       >> NOTE >>     this file is updated for any changes to
#       >>>>>>>>>      show through to sendmail.
#

# Basic system aliases -- these MUST be present.
mailer-daemon:  postmaster
postmaster:     root

# General redirections for pseudo accounts.
bin:            root
daemon:         root
adm:            root
...(Lines snipped)...
info:           postmaster
marketing:      postmaster
sales:          postmaster
support:        postmaster


# trap decode to catch security attacks
decode:         root

# Person who should get root's mail
#root:          marc
```

You'll notice that all of the standard aliases are redirected to *root*—but on most systems, no one checks the *root* mailbox, so you should start by defining who is to receive mail addressed to *root*. Uncomment the last line of this file and replace marc with a valid user ID:

```
root:           chris
```

 Run the *newaliases* command after each edit to the */etc/aliases* file to ensure that the changes are put into effect immediately:

```
# newaliases
/etc/aliases: 76 aliases, longest 10 bytes, 765 bytes total
```

Next, change any aliases that you do not wish to redirect to *root*, sending the mail to the user of your choice:

```
info:           sam
marketing:      frida
sales:          angela
support:        henry
```

Destination mailboxes do not have to be local:

```
abuse:          hotline@global.proximity.on.ca
```

And it's possible to specify multiple destinations for an alias, separated by commas:

```
webmaster:      frank, jason@fedorabook.com
```

This opens up the possibility of using aliases to create simple mailing lists. For example, all of your sales people could be reached through one address:

```
sales-team:     angela, sue, mike, olgovie, george

sysadmins:      nancy43252345234@hotmail.com,
                scott84353534534@gmail.com,
                george
```

Note that alias destinations can be on multiple lines.

You can create as many aliases as you want, whenever you want. Aliases are handy for creating *disposable email addresses*. I create batches of made-up addresses from time to time and use them when I register for a conference or web site, or when I enter a contest:

```
daa:            chris
dab:            chris
dac:            chris
dad:            chris
dae:            chris
daf:            chris
```

When I use one of these addresses, I record who I gave it to, and if I see spam arriving with that address, then I know who has been abusing my personal information. I can discontinue receiving mail at that address simply by removing the offending alias from the *aliases* file.

 This strategy is also effective when publishing email addresses on a web site: simply change the address on the web site periodically, using a different disposable email address each time. If a spammer harvests your email address from the web page, it will be useful to them only for a short time.

Configuring virtual users

Aliases (and regular user accounts) have one critical limitation: they apply to all of the domains for which sendmail is accepting mail. If you have a server that is accepting mail for *fedorabook.com* as well as *global.proximity.on.ca*, and you define an alias or create a user account named *chris*, then mail to *chris@fedorabook.com* and mail to *chris@global.proximity.on.ca* will end up in the same mailbox.

To overcome this limitation, use the */etc/mail/virtusertable* file to define where mail to each address should be sent. Each line in this file consists of an address, a space, and the destination. Here is an example:

```
chris@fedorabook.com            chris
chris@global.proximity.on.ca    chris7895378943683897@gmail.com
```

 Note that the syntax for */etc/mail/virtusertable* differs from the syntax for */etc/aliases*: there are no colons, and only one destination address may appear in each entry.

virtusertable also permits the redirection of entire domains, by leaving out the username portion of the email address:

```
joe@fedorabook.com      joseph
frank@fedorabook.com    frank265897e93456738@hotmail.com
@fedorabook.com         chris
```

The last entry will redirect all mail to the *fedorabook.com* domain to the local user *chris*, except for mail addressed to *joe@fedorabook.com* or *frank@fedorabook.com* (because they are listed first, and the file is processed in the sequence given).

Like */etc/mail/sendmail.mc*, the *virtusertable* file must be processed before it is used:

```
# cd /etc/mail
# make
```

Configuring Masquerading

sendmail includes *masquerading* capability, which enables outbound mail to be modified so that it looks like it came from another system. This is commonly used to remove hostname information from the email address. To configure *bluesky. fedorabook.com* so that outbound mail appears to be from *user@fedorabook.com* instead of *user@bluesky.fedorabook.com*, locate the MASQUERADE_AS line in */etc/mail/sendmail.mc*:

```
dnl # The following example makes mail from this host and any additional
dnl # specified domains appear to be sent from mydomain.com
dnl #
dnl MASQUERADE_AS(`mydomain.com')dnl
```

Uncomment the MASQUERADE_AS line and replace mydomain.com with the domain name you wish to use:

```
MASQUERADE_AS(`fedorabook.com')dnl
```

 Masquerading is not applied to email from the *root* and *mailer-daemon* users because those addresses are used for error messages. If several machines in a domain were masquerading with the same name, it would not be possible to determine where the error messages were originating.

How Does It Work?

Fedora's email system, like most others, is divided into three parts:

mail transport agent (MTA)
> Transports mail between systems. *sendmail* is the default MTA.

mail delivery agent (MDA)
> Delivers mail to local users, optionally performing filtering or sending vacation replies ("Jane is away from the office until Monday; she will read and reply to your mail when she returns"). Fedora uses *procmail* in this role.

mail user agent (MUA)
> The email client that interacts with the user. A Fedora user can choose from many different MDAs, including Evolution, Thunderbird, SquirrelMail, and the text-based *mail* command.

Originally written when a wide range of email transportation schemes were in use, sendmail is designed to route mail through and between these different systems, each with their own address format and message queuing system. Because of this heritage, sendmail has a sophisticated and complex configuration system, but many of the configuration options are not used for Internet email servers.

sendmail is now used almost exclusively with the Simple Mail Transport Protocol (SMTP), which is a human-readable transfer protocol that uses TCP/IP connections on port 25. You can use *telnet* to connect to an SMTP server and manually send mail if you want:

```
$ telnet concord2.proximity.on.ca smtp
Trying 127.0.0.1...
Connected to concord2.proximity.on.ca (127.0.0.1).
Escape character is '^]'.
```

```
220 concord2.proximity.on.ca ESMTP Sendmail 8.13.5/8.13.5; Thu, 2 Mar 2006 13:07:11 -
0500
EHLO fedorabook.com
250- concord2.proximity.on.ca Hello concord8.proximity.on.ca [127.0.0.1], pleased to
meet you
250-ENHANCEDSTATUSCODES
250-PIPELINING
250-8BITMIME
250-SIZE
250-DSN
250-ETRN
250-AUTH DIGEST-MD5 CRAM-MD5
250-DELIVERBY
250 HELP
MAIL From: chris@fedorabook.com
250 2.1.0 chris@fedorabook.com... Sender ok
RCPT To: chris@concord2.proximity.on.ca
250 2.1.5 chris@concord2.proximity.on.ca... Recipient ok
DATA
354 Enter mail, end with "." on a line by itself
Subject: Greetings!
Date: Thu, Mar 2006 12:08:11 -0500

Hi there -- just dropping you a quick note via
telnet. Hope your day is going well.

-Chris
.
250 2.0.0 k22I7BTo016133 Message accepted for delivery
QUIT
221 2.0.0 concord2.proximity.on.ca closing connection
```

Notice the blank line separating the email headers from the message body—just like HTTP transfers. The HTTP format is derived from the email format.

You can also send mail by sending it to the standard input of a *sendmail* process:

```
$ /usr/bin/sendmail chris@concord2.proximity.on.ca
Subject: Test II

Did you remember to renew the domain registration?
If not, please take care of this before next Tuesday.
[Ctrl-D]
```

Outbound mail is queued in */var/spool/mqueue/*. Inbound mail is delivered via *procmail* to users' mailboxes in */var/spool/mail/*. The mailboxes are simply text files containing all of the messages concatenated end to end; this format is sometimes called *mbox format*.

The */etc/mail/sendmail.mc* file used for configuration is an *m4* macro file. It is interpreted by the *m4* command using files in */usr/share/sendmail-cf/m4/* to build */etc/mail/sendmail.cf*. While it is possible to construct the *sendmail.cf* file by hand, it's typically eight times as long as the *sendmail.mc* file and uses a very cryptic structure. Here's a snippet:

```
R< > $+                     $: < > < $1 <> $&h >        nope, restore +detail

R< > < $+ <> + $* >         $: < > < $1 + $2 >          check whether +detail
R< > < $+ <> $* >           $: < > < $1 >               else discard
R< > < $+ + $* > $*              < > < $1 > + $2 $3      find the user part
R< > < $+ + $* >            $#local $@ $2 $: @ $1        strip the extra +
R< > < $+ >                 $@ $1                        no +detail
R$+                         $: $1 <> $&h                 add +detail back in
```

Most system administrators would much rather deal with *sendmail.mc* than *sendmail.cf*.

What About...

...using an alternate MTA?

Postfix is an alternate MTA shipped as part of Fedora. For most users, sendmail will work well, but if you are familiar with Postfix configuration you may want to use it instead.

You can easily switch between sendmail and Postfix using the *alternatives* command:

```
# alternatives --config mta

There are 2 programs which provide 'mta'.

  Selection    Command
-----------------------------------------------
*+ 1           /usr/sbin/sendmail.sendmail
   2           /usr/sbin/sendmail.postfix

Enter to keep the current selection[+], or type selection number: 2
```

You can also switch graphically, using the *system-switch-mail* command available through the menu option System → Administration → Mail Transport Agent Switcher (this requires the somewhat obscure package *system-switch-mail*). The window shown in Figure 7-20 will be displayed; select the MTA you wish to use and click OK.

...fetching mail from a remote mailbox?

If you're using Fedora at a location that does not have a permanent Internet connection with a static IP address, incoming email cannot be delivered directly to sendmail. Instead, you'll have to arrange for the email to be delivered to mailboxes on another system and then pick up the mail from that system.

Many MUAs such as Evolution will directly access remote mailboxes, but sometimes you want to have that mail flow through the local mail system so that alias handling and *procmail* processing take place.

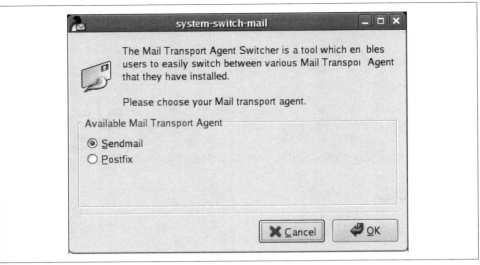

Figure 7-20. The Mail Transport Agent Switcher tool.

Fetchmail can retrieve mail from a remote mailbox and feed it to sendmail on the local system. To configure Fetchmail, create the file *~/.fetchmailrc* using a text editor. Here is a simple configuration:

```
# Check for email at five-minute (300-second) intervals
set daemon 300

# Poll the system fedorabook.com using the POP3 protocol
poll fedorabook.com with protocol POP3:

        # Describe how the usernames on this machine relate
        # to the usernames on fedorabook.com
        user chris here is chris.tyler there, password "FedoraRules!"
        user diane here is diane.tyler there, password "BiggestSecret";
```

This will fetch the mail for two users from one server using the Post Office Protocol, Version 3 (POP3). Fetchmail can retrieve mail using many different protocols and has an uncommonly readable configuration syntax; consult its extensive manpage for the gritty details.

Once you have set up the *~/.fetchmailrc* file, execute the *fetchmail* command:

```
$ fetchmail
```

It will run in the background until you stop it by running *fetchmail* with the -q option:

```
$ fetchmail -q
fetchmail: background fetchmail at 8025 killed.
```

To make *fetchmail* run automatically whenever you log in, place it in your *~/.bash_profile*.

Where Can I Learn More?

- The manpages for *sendmail*, *procmail*, *procmailrc*, *fetchmail*, *procmailex*, and *postfix* (check the See Also section for a long list of other manpages related to *postfix*)
- The files in the */usr/share/doc/sendmail**, */usr/share/doc/fetchmail**, */usr/share/doc/procmail**, and */usr/share/doc/postfix** directories
- The *sendmail* web site: *http://www.sendmail.org*
- The *fetchmail* web site: *http://www.catb.org/~esr/fetchmail*
- The *procmail* web site: *http://www.procmail.org*
- The *postfix* web site: *http://www.postfix.org*
- RFC 2142 defines a standard list of aliases that should exist on any Internet server: *http://www.ietf.org/rfc/rfc2142.txt*

7.7   Configuring IMAP and POP3 Email

Having mail delivered to the system mailboxes in */var/spool/mail* is fine—as long as the users are using an MUA running on the Fedora system. If a user is running his MUA on another system—Evolution on another Fedora system in the local network, or perhaps Outlook on a Windows machine—then the user needs IMAP or POP3 access to the remote mailbox.

How Do I Do That?

Fedora's Dovecot server provides IMAP and POP3 access.

When freshly installed, Dovecot will not successfully start. Dovecot requires security certificates to enable encrypted communications. There are three solutions to this problem:

Buy a certificate
> A certificate is *signed* by a *certificate authority* (CA), who—theoretically—is trusted by both the client and server. The CA certifies that the parties to whom certificates are issued are who they say they are, therefore eliminating the possibility of a malicious party between the client and the server masquerading as the server.

Buying a certificate is not covered in this lab.

Create your own certificate

Because there is no way to verify the authenticity of the certificate (whether unsigned or self-signed) with a third party, most client programs will present a warning dialog every time a certificate of this type is encountered. However, the connection will still be encrypted.

Disable encryption

In all cases—whether encryption is disabled or not—Dovecot will accept unencrypted connections. If you are in a secure environment (for example, where the only client connecting to the Dovecot server is SquirrelMail on the local machine, or connections are made over a reasonably secure LAN such as a wired home network), you may decide to forgo encryption altogether.

Creating your own certificate

First, edit the file */etc/pki/dovecot/dovecot-openssl.cnf* and find the CN= and emailAddress= lines:

```
[ req ]
default_bits = 1024
encrypt_key = yes
distinguished_name = req_dn
x509_extensions = cert_type
prompt = no

[ req_dn ]
# country (2 letter code)
#C=FI

# State or Province Name (full name)
#ST=

# Locality Name (eg. city)
#L=Helsinki

# Organization (eg. company)
#O=Dovecot

# Organizational Unit Name (eg. section)
OU=IMAP server

# Common Name (*.example.com is also possible)
CN=imap.example.com

# E-mail contact
emailAddress=postmaster@example.com
```

```
[ cert_type ]
nsCertType = server
```

Edit these two lines to contain the hostname of the system and the mail administrator's email address:

```
# Common Name (*.example.com is also possible)
CN=bluesky.fedorabook.com

# E-mail contact
emailAddress=postmaster@fedorabook.com
```

Then generate the certificates:

```
# SSLDIR=/etc/pki/dovecot /usr/share/doc/dovecot-1.0/examples/mkcert.sh
```

Disabling Encryption

To disable encryption, edit */etc/dovecot.conf* and locate the ssl_disable line:

```
# Disable SSL/TLS support.
#ssl_disable = no
```

Uncomment this line and change the value to *yes*:

```
# Disable SSL/TLS support.
ssl_disable = yes
```

Starting Dovecot

Start the *dovecot* service using the Services tool or from the command line:

```
# service dovecot start
```

If you are going to use IMAP or POP3 remotely, you will need to open some ports in your firewall. For IMAP, open ports for the IMAP and IMAPS services (TCP ports 143 and 220); for POP3, open the POP3 and POP3S ports (TCP ports 110 and 995).

On the other hand, if you will be using the IMAP and POP3 services only with local applications such as SquirrelMail or local MTAs such as Evolution, you should close the IMAP and POP3 ports on your firewall.

How Does It Work?

Dovecot enables MUAs to access mailboxes over a network connection using the POP3 or IMAP protocols. POP3 is primarily used to fetch mail from a mailbox so that it can be used elsewhere; IMAP is used to manipulate email messages and folders while leaving them on the server.

Like SMTP, POP3 is a human-readable protocol, and you can use *telnet* to manually conduct a POP3 session to see how it works:

```
$ telnet bluesky.fedorabook.com pop3
Trying 172.16.97.102...
```

```
Connected to 172.16.97.102 (172.16.97.102).
Escape character is '^]'.
+OK Dovecot ready.
USER chris
+OK
PASS bigsecret
+OK Logged in.
LIST
+OK 2 messages:
1 615
2 609
.
RETR 1
+OK 616 octets
Return-Path: <root@localhost.localdomain>
Received: from localhost.localdomain (localhost.localdomain [127.0.0.1])
        by localhost.localdomain (8.13.5/8.13.5) with ESMTP id k232Hf26026693
        for <chris@localhost.localdomain>; Thu, 2 Mar 2006 21:17:41 -0500
Received: (from root@localhost)
        by localhost.localdomain (8.13.5/8.13.5/Submit) id k232HfOb026692
        for chris; Thu, 2 Mar 2006 21:17:41 -0500
Date: Thu, 2 Mar 2006 21:17:41 -0500
From: Jason Smith <root@localhost.localdomain>
Message-Id: <200603030217.k232HfOb026692@localhost.localdomain>
To: chris@localhost.localdomain
Subject: Book Cover

Nice!
.
QUIT
+OK Logging out.
```

IMAP is also human-readable, but a bit more complex.

In its default configuration, Dovecot uses the input mailboxes in */var/spool/mail* as the IMAP INBOX folder and the POP3 data source. This ensures that other applications (such as a local MUA like Evolution) can be used to access the same messages.

What About...

...IMAP folders other than the INBOX?

Dovecot creates these in the user's home directory.

Where Can I Learn More?

- The Dovecot web site: *http://dovecot.org*
- The Dovecot Wiki: *http://wiki.dovecot.org*
- Documentation in */usr/share/doc/dovecot**
- The manpages for *openssl*, the library that handles encryption for *dovecot*

7.8 Configuring Webmail

When you're on the move, it's nice to have consistent access to your email. If you set up SquirrelMail, you'll be able to access your email from any web browser.

How Do I Do That?

Before you set up SquirrelMail, you'll need a working Apache configuration and the Dovecot IMAP server.

If you're using SELinux, you must permit web scripts to create network connections. Use the graphical SELinux configuration tool or enter this command:

```
# setsebool -P httpd_can_network_connect 1
```

If Apache was running before you installed SquirrelMail, you'll need to restart or reload it so that it notices the SquirrelMail `alias` directive:

```
# service apache reload
```

Unless you have other computers on your local network that need to access IMAP, you can restrict remote access to the IMAP server using Fedora's firewall facilities.

You can now use SquirrelMail by accessing *https://<hostname>/webmail*. The web page shown in Figure 7-21 should appear.

If you are using the default Apache SSL certificate (which is automatically up by default), you will get a warning from your browser when you first connect using *https*.

You can instead access *http://<hostname>/webmail* to avoid that warning message, but your passwords and email may be read if someone intercepts your network communication.

Once you enter your user ID and password, the main inbox display will appear, as shown in Figure 7-22.

How Does It Work?

SquirrelMail is a set of PHP scripts that reside in the directory */usr/share/squirrelmail*. The file */etc/httpd/conf.d/squirrelmail.conf* contains an `Alias` directive, which aliases that directory to *http://<hostname>/webmail*. When a user attempts to log in, the PHP scripts contact the local Dovecot IMAP server and tries to log in with the same user ID and password. Because the authentication information is passed directly to the IMAP server, SquirrelMail doesn't need an authentication mechanism of its own. Once connected to the IMAP server, SquirrelMail accesses your mailbox contents, reformats the messages into web pages, and passes them back to Apache for delivery to the browser.

Figure 7-21. SquirrelMail login page

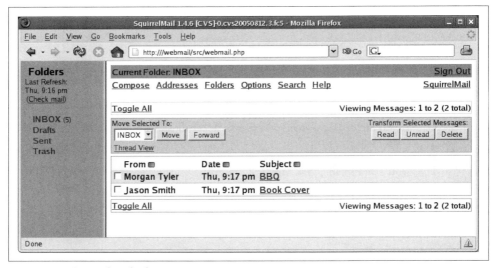

Figure 7-22. SquirrelMail inbox page

SquirrelMail also installs a daily cron job through the file */etc/cron.daily/ squirrelmail.cron*; this cron job cleans up any temporary files that have been left lying around for more than 10 days.

What About...

...changing the SquirrelMail configuration?

You can change individual user preferences using the Option link within the SquirrelMail web interface.

Global SquirrelMail configuration is performed by running the script */usr/share/squirrelmail/config/conf.pl*. You will be greeted with a menu:

```
# /usr/share/squirrelmail/config/conf.pl
SquirrelMail Configuration : Read: config.php (1.4.0)
---------------------------------------------------------------
Main Menu --
1.  Organization Preferences
2.  Server Settings
3.  Folder Defaults
4.  General Options
5.  Themes
6.  Address Books
7.  Message of the Day (MOTD)
8.  Plugins
9.  Database
10. Languages

D.  Set pre-defined settings for specific IMAP servers

C   Turn color off
S   Save data
Q   Quit

Command >>
```

Type the number or letter of the option you wish to configure; then press Enter and follow the instructions on the screen. For example, to change the default theme:

```
Command >> 5
SquirrelMail Configuration : Read: config.php (1.4.0)
---------------------------------------------------------------
Themes
1.  Change Themes
      Default                        Plain Blue
      Sand Storm                     Deep Ocean
  ...(Lines snipped)...
      Random (Changes every login)   Midnight
      Penguin
2.  CSS File :

R   Return to Main Menu
C   Turn color off
S   Save data
Q   Quit

Command >> 1
Define the themes that you wish to use.  If you have
added a theme of your own, just follow the instructions
(?) about how to add them.  You can also change the
default theme.
[theme] command (?=help) > ?
.-------------------------.
| t       (detect themes) |
```

```
| +            (add theme) |
| - N      (remove theme) |
| m N      (mark default) |
| l          (list themes) |
| d               (done) |
`-------------------------'
[theme] command (?=help) > l
  *  0.  Default                         (../themes/default_theme.php)
     1.  Plain Blue                      (../themes/plain_blue_theme.php)
     2.  Sand Storm                      (../themes/sandstorm_theme.php)
     3.  Deep Ocean                      (../themes/deepocean_theme.php)
     4.  Slashdot                        (../themes/slashdot_theme.php)
...(Lines snipped)...
    31.  Midnight                        (../themes/midnight.php)
    32.  Alien Glow                      (../themes/alien_glow.php)
    33.  Dark Green                      (../themes/dark_green.php)
    34.  Penguin                         (../themes/penguin.php)
[theme] command (?=help) > m 32
[theme] command (?=help) > d
SquirrelMail Configuration : Read: config.php (1.4.0)
---------------------------------------------------------
Themes
1.   Change Themes
        Default                          Plain Blue
        Sand Storm                       Deep Ocean
...(Lines snipped)...
        Random (Changes every login)     Midnight
        Alien Glow                       Dark Green
        Penguin
2.   CSS File :

R    Return to Main Menu
C    Turn color off
S    Save data
Q    Quit

Command >> s
Data saved in config.php
Press enter to continue... [Enter]
Command >> q
Exiting conf.pl.
You might want to test your configuration by browsing to
http://your-squirrelmail-location/src/configtest.php
Happy SquirrelMailing!
```

...browsers that don't support JavaScript or ECMAScript?

SquirrelMail has been designed to work regardless of whether JavaScript is enabled.

Where Can I Learn More?

- The SquirrelMail web site: *http://www.squirrelmail.org/*
- The documentation files in */usr/share/doc/squirrelmail**

7.9 Creating Databases and Accounts on a MySQL Server

MySQL is an open source database system that has become very popular due to its high performance, lightweight design, and open source license.

Many software packages, including web applications such as the Serendipity blog software (*http://www.s9y.org/*), use MySQL to store data. In order to use these programs, you will need to create a MySQL database and access account.

How Do I Do That?

First, you'll need to select names for your database and access account; for this example, let's use *chrisblog* for the database name and *chris* for the access account. Both names should start with a letter, contain no spaces, and be composed from characters that can be used in filenames.

To create the database and account, use the *mysql* monitor program:

```
# mysql
Welcome to the MySQL monitor.  Commands end with ; or \g.
Your MySQL connection id is 2 to server version: 5.0.18

Type 'help;' or '\h' for help. Type '\c' to clear the buffer.

mysql> create database chrisblog;
Query OK, 1 row affected (0.01 sec)

mysql> grant all privileges on chrisblog.* to 'chris'@'localhost'
identified by 'SecretPassword';
Query OK, 0 rows affected (0.00 sec)

mysql> quit
Bye
```

 Make sure that the *mysqld* service is running!

You can then enter the database, access account, and password information into the configuration of whatever software will use MySQL.

MySQL recommends that you add a password to *root's* access of the MySQL server. You can do that with these commands (\ indicates that text continues on the following line):

```
# /usr/bin/mysqladmin -u root password 'Secret'
# /usr/bin/mysqladmin -u root -h $(hostname) \
password 'Secret'
```

Secret is the *root* password that you wish to use. After you enable the *root* password, you'll need to use the -p option to mysql so that you are prompted for the password each time:

```
# mysql -p
```

For example, to install Serendipity:

1. Download the Serendipity software from *http://www.s9y.com* and place it in the */tmp* directory.

2. Unpack the Serendipity software in the */var/www/html* directory:

```
# cd /var/www/html
# tar xvzf /tmp/serendipity*.tar.gz
```

3. Access that directory through a web browser at *http://<hostname>/serendipity*. You will see the initial verification page shown in Figure 7-23.

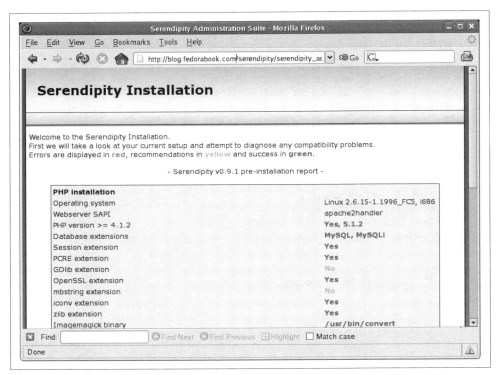

Figure 7-23. Serendipity Installation verification page

If there are any permission errors, correct them using the instructions on the page and then click the Recheck Installation link at the bottom of the page. Once the check is successful, click on the Simple Installation link.

4. As shown in Figure 7-24, enter the database, hostname, access account (database user), and password that you created in the MySQL database. Fill in the other fields, such as the blog title and the username and password you wish to use to administer the blog, using values of your choosing. Click on the Complete Installation link at the bottom of the page.

5. Figure 7-25 shows the confirmation page that appears. Click on the link labeled "Visit your new blog here" to see your initial blog page, shown in Figure 7-26.

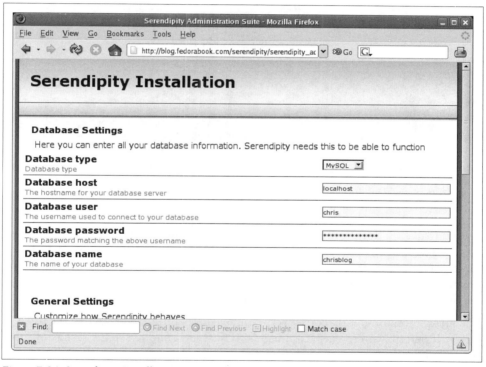

Figure 7-24. Serendipity Installation page

How Does It Work?

MySQL is a Structured Query Language (SQL) database server. It provides rapid access to large sets of structured data, such as customer lists, sports scores, student marks, product catalogs, blog comments, or event schedules. The MySQL database runs as a server daemon named *mysqld*, and many different types of software can connect to the server to access data.

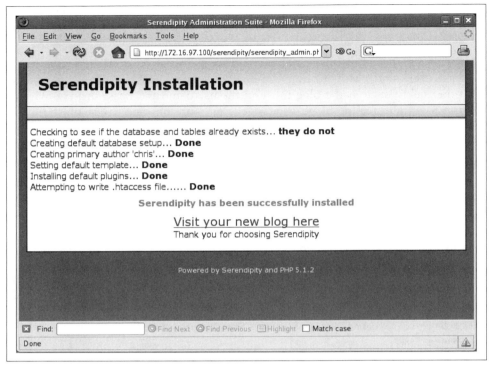

Figure 7-25. Serendipity Installation confirmation page

Connections to the database server are made through the network socket */var/lib/mysql/mysql.sock* (local connections) or on the TCP port 3306 (remote connections). If the MySQL server is running on the same machine as your application, you should leave port 3306 closed in your firewall configuration, but you must open it if you separate the MySQL server and the application onto different machines (which you might do for performance reasons if you're using the database heavily).

The *mysql* monitor command is a very simple command-line interface to the MySQL server. It permits you to enter commands to the server and to see the results of those commands on your screen.

MySQL data is stored in */var/lib/mysql*; each database is stored in a separate subdirectory.

What About...

...creating my own scripts and programs that access MySQL data?

Most scripting and programming languages have modules to access MySQL data. For example, you can use the database driver (DBD) module *DBD::mysql* to access the basic *database interface* (DBI) abstraction layer to work with databases in Perl.

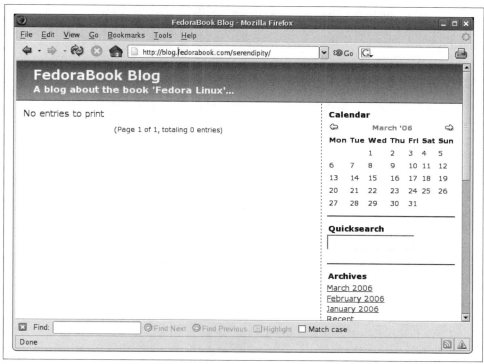

Figure 7-26. Serendipity blog front page

For details on writing software that accesses a MySQL database, see Chapter 22 in the MySQL documentation (*http://dev.mysql.com/doc/refman/5.0/en/apis.html*).

Where Can I Learn More?

- The manpages for *mysqld*, *mysql*, *mysqladmin*, *mysqldump*, and *mysqlshow*
- The MySQL manual: *http://www.mysql.com/doc*
- Documentation on the Perl DBI module: `perldoc DBI`
- Documentation on the PHP MySQL functions: *http://ca.php.net/mysql*

7.10   Installing and Configuring a Wiki

A *Wiki* is a series of web pages that can be easily edited using only a web browser—a simple and convenient way of producing a collaborative web site. Perhaps the most impressive examples of Wikis are those operated by the Wikimedia Foundation (*http://wikimedia.org*), including Wikipedia, the Wiktionary, and WikiBooks.

Fedora Extras includes the Wiki software used by the Wikimedia Foundation, named MediaWiki. Once installed, it can be configured and ready for use in a few minutes.

How Do I Do That?

MediaWiki requires a MySQL server. *yum* won't automatically install a MySQL server when you install MediaWiki because MySQL isn't truly a dependency: the database server doesn't have to be on the same computer—but for a small installation, that makes the most sense.

To configure MediaWiki, start your web server (if it's not already running) and then, using a browser on the same computer as the MediaWiki software, go to *http:// localhost/mediawiki/*. You will see an introduction page like that in Figure 7-27, informing you that the software must be configured before use.

Figure 7-27. MediaWiki before initial configuration

To configure the software, click on the link provided. The page shown in Figure 7-28 will appear.

This page presents the results of some initial configuration tests, followed by a form that you must fill in with configuration information. The fields on this form are:

Site name
> Input an opaque string (no spaces and no punctuation marks) of letters and numbers for the name of your Wiki.

Contact email
> Enter an email address that can be used to contact the Wiki administrator. It is probably best to use an email alias here.

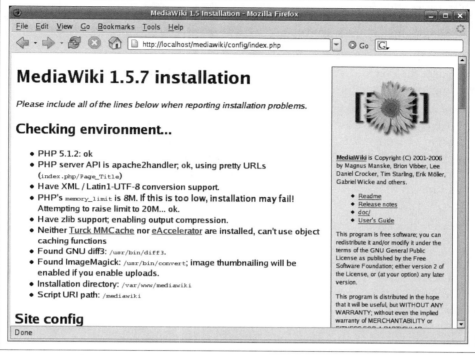

Figure 7-28. MediaWiki configuration page

Language

> The language for the Wiki prompts and messages (the content can be in any language, regardless of the value you choose here).

Copyright/license metadata

> The license that will be used to tag the Wiki contents. You can choose not to tag your pages with license information, or you can use one of two types of open content licenses: GNU Free Documentation License (GNU FDL) or a Creative Commons license. If you are not sure what to use, select "no license metadata."

Sysop account name and password

> Enter the username of the system operator (*sysop*) or Wiki administrator. This user does not have to have a Fedora login account. The password must be entered twice to verify that it is typed correctly.

Shared memory

> Use a memory cache system for performance acceleration. This is not necessary for small installations.

E-mail (general)

> Enable all email operations. In almost all cases, this should be left on.

User-to-user e-mail

Enable users to send mail to each other; whether this makes sense depends on the intended use of your Wiki.

E-mail notification

Select the events that trigger an automatic notification email. Use the middle setting for most small-to-medium Wikis.

E-mail address authentication

If enabled, this feature sends a *token* to the email address of newly registered users to verify that the email address is valid. This presents a minor inconvenience to your users, but prevents email from being sent to invalid addresses and, more importantly, prevents a user from entering someone else's email address.

MySQL server

Leave this set to localhost if the MySQL server is on the same computer as the MediaWiki software.

Database name, DB username, and DB password

The name of the MySQL database, and the username and password for the MySQL access account, respectively. Leave the default values for the Database name and the DB username, and make up a new password (twice) for the DB password.

Database table prefix

If you are running more than one instance of MediaWiki, set this to a unique value for each instance. Otherwise, leave this field blank.

Database charset

Leave this value set to "Backwards-compatible UTF-8."

Super user and Password

The MySQL database and access account for the Wiki can be created by hand, or you can enter the user ID and MySQL password for the database administrator here, and MediaWiki will create the database and access account automatically.

 This is the MySQL administrator account (*root*) and the MySQL password for that account; do not enter the Fedora *root* password!

Once you have entered this information, click the Install button at the bottom of the page. You will see a confirmation page.

At this point, copy the configuration file from the *config* directory to the main *mediawiki* directory:

```
# cp -v /var/www/mediawiki/config/LocalSettings.php /var/www/mediawiki
`/var/www/mediawiki/config/LocalSettings.php' ->    `/var/www/mediawiki/
LocalSettings.php'
```

You can now click the link at the bottom of the confirmation page or go to *http://<hostname>/mediawiki/* to view the front page of the Wiki.

The only other customization that is necessary is to install a new logo image. The image should be 155 pixels wide and 135 pixels tall and in *.gif*, *.png*, or *.jpg* format. Edit */var/www/mediawiki/LocalSettings.php* and find the line that reads:

```
$wgLogo            = "$wgStylePath/common/images/wiki.png";
```

Change the path on the righthand side of the equal sign to the path of your image location, relative to the Apache Document Root. For example, if your image is in */var/www/mediawiki/images/draft-cover.png*, edit this line to read:

```
$wgLogo            = "/mediawiki/images/draft-cover.png";
```

You can then edit the front page of your Wiki by clicking on the "edit" link at the top of the page; changes are made using the same Wikitext format used on Wikipedia. Figure 7-29 shows a fully configured MediaWiki installation.

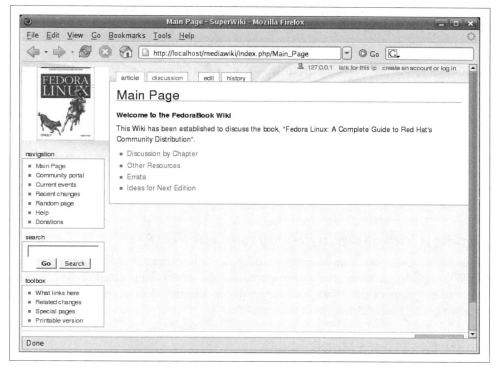

Figure 7-29. Configured MediaWiki front page

How Does It Work?

MediaWiki is written as a collection of PHP scripts, with some Perl scripts for maintenance functions. The Fedora Extras MediaWiki package installs these files in */var/www/mediawiki*, which is within the default Apache Document Root. The file */etc/httpd/conf.d/mediawiki.conf* limits access to the *mediawiki* subdirectories, ensuring that only a browser on the same machine as the server can access the configuration page and making several other directories inaccessible through the Web.

All of the Wiki content is stored in the MySQL database for fast, index-based access. Users indicate how they want text to appear by using Wikitext markings; most of these are converted to HTML when the page is displayed, but some (such as --~~~, which is converted to the user's name) are translated when the page is saved.

What About...

...changing the appearance of the Wiki?

You can alter the appearance of the Wiki by editing the value of $wgDefaultSkin in */var/www/mediawiki/LocalSettings.php*. This variable must be set to the name of one of the skin files in */var/www/mediawiki/skins/*; for example, to use the *simple* skin, place this line in the *LocalSettings.php* file:

```
$wgDefaultSkin="simple";
```

Additional skins are available from the Wikimedia "Gallery of user styles" (*http://meta.wikimedia.org/wiki/Gallery_of_user_styles*).

...using a logo that isn't rectangular?

Use a graphics tool such as the GIMP to create an image with transparency, so that the page background shows through the portions of the 155×135 logo rectangle that are not occupied by your logo image. For example, if you had an oval image, the space between the outer edge of the logo and the edge of the logo rectangle would be transparent. Save your image in PNG format.

...moving or deleting a page, or protecting a page against edits?

All of these operations can be performed by the sysop user. Go to the main page of the Wiki and log in using the sysop username and password created during the initial configuration of the Wiki, and you will see additional tabs on the top of each page for protecting, deleting, and moving.

Where Can I Learn More?

- The MediaWiki web page: *http://www.mediawiki.org*
- The files in */usr/share/doc/mediawiki*/docs*
- The Wikipedia Cheatsheet, which describes the Wikitext format on a reference card: *http://upload.wikimedia.org/wikipedia/commons/0/05/Cheatsheet-en.pdf*

7.11 Configuring an FTP Server

File Transfer Protocol (FTP) is a long-established Internet protocol for downloading files. In Fedora, you can use the Very Safe FTP program, *vsftp*, to serve data via FTP.

How Do I Do That?

To serve content via FTP, just install the *vsftpd* package and place the content that you wish to make publicly available in the */var/ftp* directory.

 If you are using a firewall, you will need to open the FTP ports in the firewall.

To view the contents of */var/ftp* with a browser, go to *ftp://<hostname>/*. To access files in a home directory, use the URL *ftp://<user>@<hostname>/* (the browser will ask for your password) or *ftp://<user>:<password>@<hostname>/*.

To access the contents of */var/ftp* using a command-line FTP client program, log in as *anonymous* and use your email address as your password:

```
$ ftp
ftp> open ftp.fedorabook.com
Connected to 172.16.97.100.
220 (vsFTPd 2.0.4)
530 Please login with USER and PASS.
530 Please login with USER and PASS.
KERBEROS_V4 rejected as an authentication type
Name (ftp.fedorabook.com:chris): anonymous
Password: chris@fedorabook.com
230 Login successful.
Remote system type is UNIX.
Using binary mode to transfer files.
ftp> ls
227 Entering Passive Mode (172,16,97,100,237,192)
150 Here comes the directory listing.
drwxr-xr-x    2 0        0            4096 Mar 09 16:41 fedora-core-5
drwxr-xr-x    2 0        0            4096 Mar 09 16:41 fedora-core-6
drwxr-xr-x    2 0        0            4096 Mar 09 16:41 fedora-linux
drwxr-xr-x    2 0        0            4096 Mar 09 16:42 images
drwxr-xr-x    2 0        0            4096 Mar 09 04:46 pub
drwxr-xr-x    2 0        0            4096 Mar 09 16:41 rawhide
226 Directory send OK.
ftp> cd images
250-This directory contains images for the book "Fedora Linux".
250-
250 Directory successfully changed.
ftp> ls *http*
227 Entering Passive Mode (172,16,97,100,240,225)
150 Here comes the directory listing.
```

```
-rw-r--r--   1 0        0            49931 Mar 09 16:44 fen-chapter07-system-config-
httpd-tab2.png
-rw-r--r--   1 0        0            27119 Mar 09 16:44 fen-chapter07-system-config-
httpd.png
226 Directory send OK.
ftp> get fen-chapter07-system-config-httpd-tab2.png
local: fen-chapter07-system-config-httpd-tab2.png remote: fen-chapter07-system-
config-httpd-tab2.png
227 Entering Passive Mode (172,16,97,100,214,160)
150 Opening BINARY mode data connection for fen-chapter07-system-config-httpd-tab2.
png (49931 bytes).
226 File send OK.
49931 bytes received in 0.017 seconds (2.9e+03 Kbytes/s)
ftp> quit
221 Goodbye.
```

To access a home directory using an FTP client, enter the user ID and password of the Fedora account.

vsftpd is configured using the files in */etc/vsftpd*. The main configuration file is */etc/vsftpd/vsftpd.conf* and permits all local users (except for system users such as *root*, *bin*, and so forth) to have read/write access to their home directories, and all anonymous users to have read-only access to */var/ftp*.

These are the most commonly changed configuration entries, along with the default values (as set in the Fedora default configuration file or in the program's internal defaults):

anonymous_enable=*YES*
Enables anonymous login. Change the value to NO to disable access to */var/ftp*.

write_enable=*YES*
Permits file uploads.

anon_upload_enable=*NO* and anon_mkdir_write_enable=*NO*
Permits anonymous users to upload files and create directories. write_enable=YES must also be present and at least one of the directories in */var/ftp* must be writable in order for this to work.

dirmessage_enable=*NO* and message_file=*.message*
Enables the display of descriptive messages when a user enters a directory; this is usually used to explain the directory contents, usage instructions, contact information, or copyright and licensing details. There is an example of this in the character-mode transfer shown earlier, highlighted in bold. The text of the message is normally contained in the file *.message* within the directory, but the filename may be set to any value you choose. Some client programs will display these messages to the remote client, and some—such as the Firefox web browser—will not.

`banner_file=`*filename*
> Configures a file that contains a banner message that will be sent to clients when they connect to the server.

`ascii_upload_enable=`*NO* and `ascii_download_enable=`*NO*
> FTP has the ability to automatically change end-of-line characters to compensate for differences between Linux/Unix, Windows, and Macintosh computers using ASCII mode. The author of *vsftpd*, Chris Evans, considers this to be a bug in the protocol rather than a feature, and it is true that ASCII mode has mangled many, many binary files. If you want to use ASCII mode, enable these options.

`ls_recurse_enable=`*NO*
> Controls the use of recursive directory listings. Some very nice clients, such as *ncftp*, assume that this is enabled.

`use_localtime=`*NO*
> Enables the display of times in the local time zone instead of GMT.

You can restrict FTP access to specific local users by adding their usernames into the file */etc/vsftpd/ftpusers* or */etc/vsftpd/user_list*.

How Does It Work?

FTP is a disaster from a security perspective, since transmitted data (including the username and password) are sent in plain text and can be intercepted by anyone snooping on the network. Nonetheless, it's a useful protocol for the public download of large files.

vsftp was designed from the ground up to be as secure as possible because many of the preceding FTP servers were notoriously insecure. It uses simple code along with techniques such as changing the root directory (*chroot*) to limit the damage that can be caused if the server is compromised.

FTP is a very old protocol—so old, in fact, that in its original form, it predates TCP/IP! In order to work around some network transport limitations, traditional FTP uses *two* connections between the client and the server: one for data and one for controlling commands and responses. The control connection originates at the client, and the data connection originates at the server. For years this architecture has caused headaches in firewall configuration.

FTP also supports *passive* (PASV) operation, which uses a single connection for both control and data. Almost all modern client programs support passive operation as the default mode of operation, as an automatic fallback option, or as a manually configured option.

vsftpd logs data transfers in the file */var/log/xferlog*.

What About...

...secure FTP?

There are two types of secure FTP:

SFTP

> An FTP extension to the secure shell (SSH) protocol. This is installed by default on Fedora systems as part of the SSH service; the command name is *sftp*. SSH also provides secure copy (*scp*), which is in many cases more convenient than SFTP.

FTPS

> FTP over the Secure Socket Layer (SSL). SSL is a general encryption layer that can be used to protect many types of connections, including HTTP, IMAP, and POP3 (which are known as HTTPS, IMAPS, and POP3S when used with SSL). I recommend the use of SFTP over FTPS, but *vsftpd* is capable of handling FTPS connections if security certificates are installed; refer to the *vsftpd* documentation for details.

Where Can I Learn More?

- The manpages for *vsftpd*, *vsftpd.conf*, and *ftp*
- The manpages for *sshd*, *scp*, and *sftp*
- RFC 959: *http://www.ietf.org/rfc/rfc0959.txt*

7.12   Analyzing Web and FTP Logs

Fedora provides the Webalizer tool for analyzing Apache and *vsftp* logfiles, but the default configuration works only with the default Apache virtual host. With a few minutes of configuration, Webalizer can analyze the logfiles off all of your Apache virtual hosts as well as your *vsftp* server.

How Do I Do That?

The default configuration for Webalizer analyzes the default Apache logfile at 4:02 a.m. each day, as long as that logfile is not empty. The results can be read by using a browser on the same machine and accessing *http://localhost/usage/*, which displays the report page. A sample report page is shown in Figure 7-30.

Analyzing virtual host logfiles

> This configuration assumes that your Apache virtual host logfiles are named */var/log/httpd/<virtualhostname>-<access_log>* and are in combined format.

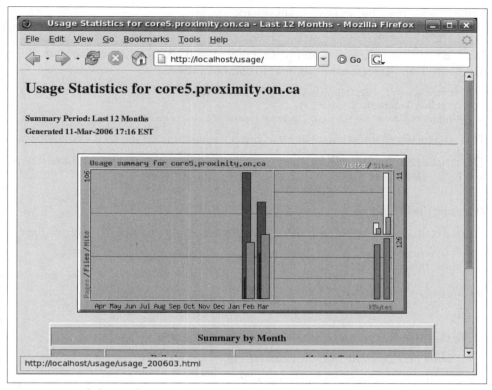

Figure 7-30. Webalizer web usage report

To configure Webalizer to analyze your virtual host logfiles each day, create the file
/etc/cron.daily/00webalizer-vhosts:

```
#! /bin/bash
# update access statistics for virtual hosts

CONF=/etc/httpd/conf/httpd.conf

for NAME in $(sed -n "s=^[^#]*CustomLog logs/\([^ ]*\)-.*=\1=p" $CONF)
do

    mkdir /var/www/usage/$NAME
    chmod a+rx /var/www/usage/$NAME

    LOG=/var/log/httpd/${NAME}-access_log

    if [ -s $NAME ]
    then
      exec /usr/bin/webalizer -Q  -o /var/www/usage/$NAME $LOG
    fi

fi
```

Make this file readable and executable by *root*:

```
# chmod u+rx /etc/cron.daily/00webalizer-vhosts
```

Next, edit */etc/webalizer.conf* and place a pound-sign character (#) at the start of the HistoryName and IncrementalName lines to comment them out:

```
#HistoryName      /var/lib/webalizer/webalizer.hist
...(Lines snipped)...
#IncrementalName        /var/lib/webalizer/webalizer.current
```

This will ensure that a separate analysis history is maintained for each virtual host.

The virtual host logfiles will be analyzed every morning at 4:02 a.m., and the reports will be accessible at *http://localhost/usage/<virtualhostname>*.

Analyzing the FTP logfile

To analyze the *vsftp* logfile each day, create the file */etc/cron.daily/00webalizer-ftp*:

```
#! /bin/bash
# update access statistics for ftp

if [ -s /var/log/xferlog ]; then
   exec /usr/bin/webalizer -Q -F ftp -o /var/www/usage/ftp /var/log/xferlog
fi
```

Make this file readable and executable by *root*:

```
# chmod u+rx /etc/cron.daily/00webalizer-ftp
```

Then create the directory */var/www/usage/ftp*:

```
# mkdir /var/www/usage/ftp
# chmod a+r /var/www/usage/ftp
```

Make sure that you have made the changes to */etc/webalizer.conf* noted previously.

Your FTP usage statistics will now be analyzed each day at 4:02 a.m. along with your web statistics. The reports will be accessible at *http://localhost/usage/<ftp>*.

Accessing the usage statistics from another location

It's often inconvenient to access the usage statistics from the same machine that is running Apache. To make the statistics password-protected and accessible from any system, edit the file */etc/httpd/conf.d/webalizer.conf* to look like this:

```
#
# This configuration file maps the Webalizer log-analysis
# results (generated daily) into the URL space. By default
# these results are only accessible from the local host.
#
Alias /usage /var/www/usage

<Location /usage>
    Order deny,allow
```

```
      Allow from ALL
      AuthType           Basic
      AuthName           "usage statistics"
      AuthUserFile       /var/lib/webalizer/passwd
      Require            valid-user
  </Location>
```

Create the password file with the *htpasswd* command:

```
# htpasswd -c /var/lib/webalizer/passwd chris
New password: NeverGuess
Re-type new password: NeverGuess
Adding password for user chris
```

 The SELinux context of the directory containing the password file must be changed in order for this to work:

```
# chcon -t httpd_sys_content_t /var/lib/webalizer/
```

The statistics reports should now be accessible using a web browser on any computer.

How Does It Work?

The script */etc/cron.daily/00webalizer* is started once a day (at around 4:02 a.m.) by *crond*. This script in turn starts up Webalizer; the default configuration file (*/var/webalizer.conf*) is preset to analyze the main Apache logfile (*/var/log/httpd/access_log*) and place the results in */var/www/usage*.

The script file *00webalizer-vhosts* obtains the virtual host log filenames from */etc/httpd/conf/httpd.conf* and runs Webalizer on each logfile after the main logfile has been processed. *00webalizer-ftp* does the same thing for the *vsftp* logfile, */var/log/xferlog*.

The web directory */var/www/usage* is initially protected by the file */var/httpd/conf.d/webalizer.conf* so that Apache will serve it only to a browser running on the same computer.

Webalizer analyzes web files and logfiles to determine usage patterns; it can process the Apache common and combined logfile formats, and the *wuftp* logfile formats (which is the same format used by *vsftp*). It stores the generated statistics for the last year in the file *webalizer.hist*, and stores partial statistics for the current reporting period (month) in the file *webalizer.current*. The data from previous runs of the program is retrieved from those files and combined with data from the current logfile to generate the reports. By default, *webalizer.hist* and *webalizer.current* are stored in */var/lib/webalizer*; the changes to the configuration file cause these files to be stored in the output directories so that each report has its own, separate copy of these files.

The generated reports are saved as HTML pages and PNG graphics.

Where Can I Learn More?

- The manpages for *webalizer*, *cron*, and *crontab*
- The Webalizer web site: *http://webalizer.org/*
- Information on the Apache logfile format: *http://httpd.apache.org/docs/2.2/logs.html*
- Information on the wu-ftp/vsftp logfile format: *http://www.wu-ftpd.org/man/xferlog.html*

## CHAPTER 8

Securing Your System

System security maintenance is an essential task when running a computer, but it's never been particularly glamorous or fun. The basic goal of system security is to ensure that the system provides the services it is supposed to provide, cannot be subverted to do things it was not intended to do, and to ensure that the services remain available for use.

Effective security requires a multipronged approach, and Fedora provides effective tools to secure your system in several different ways:

- Filtering of network traffic
- System activity logging and automatic monitoring tools
- Discretionary access controls such as permissions and access control lists
- Mandatory access controls through SELinux
- Intrusion-detection tools and immutable file attributes to detect and prevent file alteration
- Tools to delegate specific system administration privileges to different users

Together with automated software updates, these tools enable you to efficiently maintain your system security.

8.1   Prevent Unwanted Connections

Most Fedora systems are connected to a TCP/IP network. You can guard against unwanted inbound connections to your system by using the built-in firewall.

How Do I Do That?

To adjust the Fedora firewall graphically, select the menu option System → Administration → "Security Level and Firewall." After you enter the *root* password, the window shown in Figure 8-1 will appear.

Figure 8-1. Firewall configuration tool

The control at the top of this window enables and disables the firewall. When the firewall is enabled, the lower portion of this window can be used to permit connections to your system for selected services; simply select the checkboxes for the desired services. SSH should remain selected to permit secure remote administration.

To permit connections to services that are not listed, click on the triangle for "Other ports." The display will change to reveal an additional section, as shown in Figure 8-2.

To add additional ports, click the Add button, and the window shown on the right side of Figure 8-2 will pop up. Enter the port number or the service name, select TCP or UDP for the protocol, and click OK.

 A list of most of the common services and their corresponding port numbers can be found in the file */etc/services*.

When the firewall is configured to your liking, click OK.

Configuring the firewall in text mode

Enter this command:

```
# lokkit
```

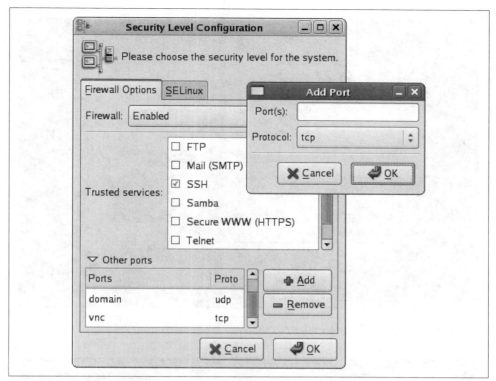

Figure 8-2. Configuring other ports

The screen displayed in Figure 8-3 will appear. Use the Tab key to navigate among fields, the spacebar to select and deselect checkboxes, and Enter or the spacebar to activate buttons.

Enable or disable the firewall using the checkboxes. To customize the types of connections that are permitted through the firewall, tab to the Customize button and press Enter. The customization screen shown in Figure 8-4 will appear.

The Trusted Devices and MASQUERADE Devices checkboxes are applicable only to systems with multiple network connections. Do not select either of those options on a system with a single network interface.

The Trusted Devices checkbox will *disable* firewall protection for the selected interface!

Use the Allow Incoming checkboxes to select the services that will be permitted to connect to your system through the firewall. In almost all cases, SSH should be selected to permit secure remote connections for system administration.

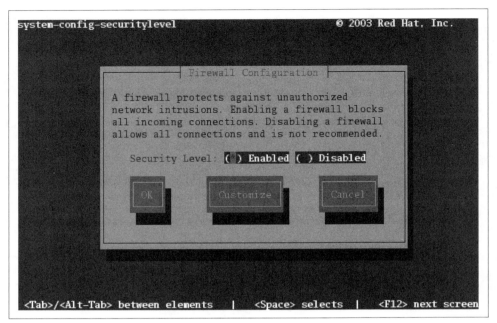

Figure 8-3. Lokkit firewall configuration screen

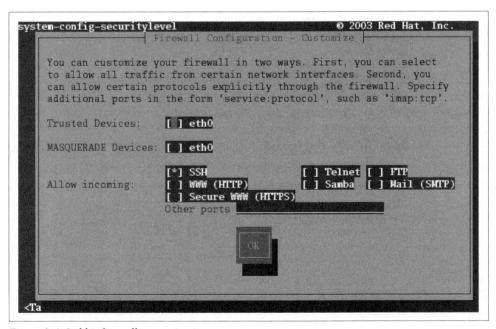

Figure 8-4. Lokkit firewall customization screen

To allow incoming connections to services that are not listed, enter the port number or service, followed by a colon (:), and the protocol (TCP or UDP) into the "Other ports" field at the bottom of the screen. You will need to separate multiple entries with a space or comma. For example, to permit incoming connections to the VNC service as well as to a custom UDP service running on port 64447, use:

```
vnc:tcp 64447:udp
```

Select OK to return to the main screen (Figure 8-3); select OK on that screen to save your settings and exit.

Temporarily disabling the firewall from the command line

To disable the firewall until the next reboot, stop the *iptables* service:

```
# service iptables stop
```

To reset your firewall to the configured settings, restart the *iptables* service:

```
# service iptables restart
```

How Does It Work?

The Fedora firewall uses the kernel's *iptables* capability, which can filter packets based on their source, destination, port, protocol, contents, and current connection state.

To view the current *iptables* configuration, use the -L option:

```
# iptables -L
Chain INPUT (policy ACCEPT)
target      prot opt source        destination
RH-Firewall-1-INPUT  all  --  anywhere       anywhere

Chain FORWARD (policy ACCEPT)
target      prot opt source        destination
RH-Firewall-1-INPUT  all  --  anywhere       anywhere

Chain OUTPUT (policy ACCEPT)
target      prot opt source        destination

Chain RH-Firewall-1-INPUT (2 references)
target      prot opt source        destination
ACCEPT      all  --  anywhere      anywhere
ACCEPT      icmp --  anywhere      anywhere       icmp any
ACCEPT      ipv6-crypt--  anywhere anywhere
ACCEPT      ipv6-auth--  anywhere  anywhere
ACCEPT      udp  --  anywhere      224.0.0.251    udp dpt:mdns
ACCEPT      udp  --  anywhere      anywhere       udp dpt:ipp
ACCEPT      tcp  --  anywhere      anywhere       tcp dpt:ipp
ACCEPT      all  --  anywhere      anywhere       state RELATED,ESTABLISHED
ACCEPT      tcp  --  anywhere      anywhere       state NEW tcp dpt:ssh
REJECT      all  --  anywhere      anywhere       reject-with icmp-host-prohibited
```

There are four *chains* of rules defined here:

INPUT

> Filters packets that are inbound to this system.

FORWARD

> Filters packets that are passing through the system. This applies only if there is more than one network interface and IP forwarding is turned on to pass packets between the interfaces (for example, in a system serving as a router).

OUTPUT

> Filters packets that are outbound from this system.

RH-Firewall-1-INPUT

> This is the chain of rules configured by the firewall system. Notice that this chain is included into the chains for INPUT and FORWARD.

 In this example, IPP (Internet Print Protocol, used by CUPS), MDNS (multicast DNS, used by Avahi), and SSH connections are all permitted; only SSH was configured for the firewall, demonstrating that not all services are configured through the firewall configuration tools.

Since the policy for each chain is ACCEPT, flushing (clearing) the rules will result in all packets being accepted. This is exactly what the iptables -F command does, which is executed when the *iptables* service is stopped.

The graphical firewall configuration tool is *system-config-securitylevel* (which, in recent versions, also handles SELinux configuration). The character-based version is *system-config-securitylevel-tui*, which is also known as *lokkit*. Both of these tools save the firewall configuration in */etc/sysconfig/system-config-securitylevel* and, from that configuration, derive a set of *iptables* rules that are saved in */etc/sysconfig/iptables*. That file, in turn, is used by the *iptables* service (*/etc/init.d/iptables*) to configure the firewall; options that control the operation of the *iptables* service are stored in */etc/sysconfig/iptables-config*.

iptables is actually an unusual service. Most other services—such as *cups*, *httpd*, or *gpm*—have a server process that begins running when the service is started and that is stopped when the service is stopped; *iptables*, on the other hand, just configures the *iptables* facility in the kernel when the service is started or stopped, so there's no actual process running when the firewall is active.

What About...

...more complex firewall rules?

The firewall interface provided by Fedora's *system-config-securitylevel* supports only the filtering of inbound (and forwarded) packets and is quite simple. However, the *iptables* mechanism supports much more complex filtering. Fedora Extras provides several alternate tools for firewall configuration, including *firestarter*, *fwbuilder*, and *shorewall*.

Where Can I Learn More?

- The manpages for *iptables*
- The home page for *iptables* at *http://netfilter.org*

8.2   Using SELinux

Security Enhanced Linux (SELinux) is installed and enabled by default in Fedora Core. SELinux controls what a program is and is not allowed to do, enforcing security policy through the kernel. This prevents an attacker from using a compromised program to do something it was not intended to do.

Although SELinux can at times be challenging to configure, it dramatically improves protection against some common system attacks—so a little bit of effort can pay off in a big way.

How Do I Do That?

SELinux is managed using the same graphical tool used to manage the firewall. Click System → Administration → "Security Level and Firewall" to start it, then select the SELinux tab, shown in Figure 8-5.

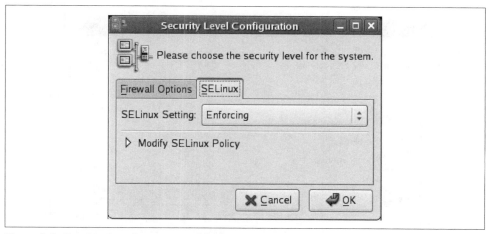

Figure 8-5. Graphical configuration tool for SELinux

There are three possible values for SELinux Setting:

Enforcing

Fully enables SELinux. Any attempted operation that violates the current security policy is blocked.

Permissive

Enables SELinux security checks but does not enforce the security policy; operations that violate the current security policy are permitted, but an error message is logged to record the event. This is useful if you have previously disabled SELinux and want to evaluate the potential impact before you enable it.

Disabled

Completely disables SELinux.

If you enable SELinux (using Enforcing or Permissive mode), expand the Modify SELinux Policy section by clicking the triangle. The SELinux policy configuration categories will appear, as shown in Figure 8-6.

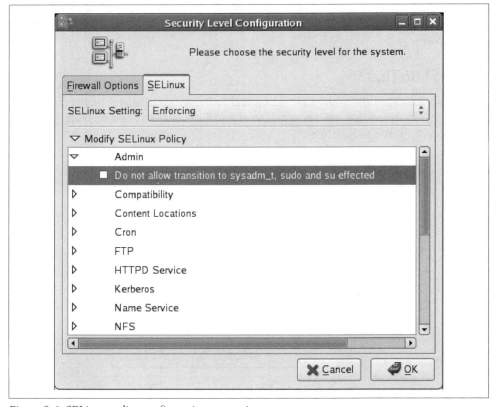

Figure 8-6. SELinux policy configuration categories

Each of these categories contains a number of options (represented as checkboxes) called *booleans*. Each boolean may be set on (checked) or off (unchecked).

To expand the options in any category, click on the arrow in front of that category. In Figure 8-6, the Admin category has been expanded, and the window width has been resized to fully show each option.

After selecting or deselecting booleans as desired, click OK. Changes in boolean values will take effect immediately, but changing the SELinux setting to or from Disabled will take effect only when the system is booted.

Configuring SELinux from the command line

SELinux can also be configured very easily from the command line. To enable SELinux, edit the file */etc/selinux/config* and set the SELINUX value to enforcing, permissive, or disabled:

```
# This file controls the state of SELinux on the system.
# SELINUX= can take one of these three values:
#       enforcing - SELinux security policy is enforced.
#       permissive - SELinux prints warnings instead of enforcing.
#       disabled - SELinux is fully disabled.
SELINUX=enforcing
# SELINUXTYPE= type of policy in use. Possible values are:
#       targeted - Only targeted network daemons are protected.
#       strict - Full SELinux protection.
SELINUXTYPE=targeted
```

Changes made to this file will take effect when the system is booted. If SELinux is enabled, you can use the *getenforce* command to view the current mode, and you can use the *setenforce* command to immediately switch between enforcing and permissive modes:

```
# getenforce
Enforcing
# setenforce permissive
# getenforce
Permissive
# setenforce enforcing
# getenforce
Enforcing
```

Boolean values—corresponding to the checkboxes in the graphical Security Level configuration tool—can be viewed with the *getsebool* command, using the -a option to see all values:

```
$ getsebool -a
NetworkManager_disable_trans --> off
allow_cvs_read_shadow --> off
allow_execheap --> off
allow_execmem --> on
...(Lines snipped)...
ypserv_disable_trans --> off
```

```
ypxfr_disable_trans --> off
zebra_disable_trans --> off
```

You can also specify a specific boolean:

```
$ /usr/sbin/getsebool httpd_enable_cgi
httpd_enable_cgi --> on
```

To temporarily set a boolean value, use the *setsebool* command:

```
# setsebool httpd_enable_cgi 1
# setsebool httpd_enable_homedirs=0
```

Notice that the on/off state of the boolean is expressed numerically, with 1 representing on and 0 representing off. Also note that the boolean name and value may be specified as two arguments (first example), or they may be specified as a single argument, joined with the = symbol (second example). If you use the second form, you can set multiple booleans with one command:

```
# setsebool httpd_enable_cgi=1 httpd_enable_homedirs=0
```

Changes made to boolean values with *setsebool* take effect immediately but are not permanent; they will reset at the next boot. To make them permanent, add the -P argument:

```
# setsebool -P httpd_enable_cgi=1
```

Determining which booleans to modify

The default boolean settings for SELinux are reasonable for most systems, but they may need to be changed to relax the security policy for specific applications.

For example, by default, web scripts are not permitted to communicate through the network; this prevents an untrusted script from somehow transferring private data to another host. But if your web scripts need to connect to an IMAP email server or an SQL database such as MySQL or PostgreSQL, you'll need to set the appropriate boolean.

In this case, you can find the boolean in the graphical interface by expanding the HTTPD Service category and looking through the options. Select the checkbox for the boolean labeled "Allow HTTPD scripts and modules to connect to the network."

There is also a manpage provided for each of the most popular servers protected by SELinux. These manpages are named *service*_selinux; for example, to access a description of the SELinux booleans that affect *httpd*, view the httpd_selinux manpage:

```
$ man httpd_selinux
```

 To see a list of all the service-specific manpages for SELinux, enter the command:

```
$ apropos _selinux
```

In the BOOLEAN section you will find this text:

```
httpd scripts by default are not allowed to connect out to the network.
   This would prevent a hacker from breaking into you httpd  server
   and attacking other machines.  If you need scripts to be able to
   connect you can set the httpd_can_network_connect boolean on.

setsebool -P httpd_can_network_connect 1
```

To translate between the descriptions shown in the graphical Security Level Configuration tool and the boolean names used by *setsebool* and *getsebool*, use the file */usr/share/system-config-securitylevel/selinux.tbl*, which looks like this:

```
unlimitedUtils _("Admin") _("Allow privileged utilities like hotplug and insmod to
run unconfined.")
unlimitedRC _("Admin") _("Allow rc scripts to run unconfined, including any daemon
started by an rc script that does not have a domain transition explicitly
defined.")
unlimitedRPM _("Admin") _("Allow rpm to run unconfined.")
staff_read_sysadm_file _("Admin") _("Allow staff_r users to search the sysadm home
dir and read files (such as ~/.bashrc)")
direct_sysadm_daemon _("Admin") _("Allow sysadm_t to directly start daemons")
...(Lines snipped)...
```

Each line consists of the boolean name used by *setsebool*/*getsebool*, followed by the configuration category and the description used by the Security Level Configuration tool.

Use *grep* with a server name, boolean name, or a description from the configuration tool to quickly find values in this file:

```
$ cd /usr/share/system-config-securitylevel
$ grep httpd selinux.tbl
httpd_enable_cgi _("HTTPD Service") _("Allow HTTPD cgi support")
httpd_can_network_connect _("HTTPD Service") _("Allow HTTPD scripts and modules to
connect to the network.")
httpd_enable_homedirs _("HTTPD Service") _("Allow HTTPD to read home directories")
httpd_ssi_exec _("HTTPD Service") _("Allow HTTPD to run SSI executables in the same
domain as system CGI scripts.")
httpd_builtin_scripting _("HTTPD Service") _("Allow HTTPD to support built-in
scripting")
httpd_disable_trans _("HTTPD Service") _("Disable SELinux protection for httpd
daemon")
httpd_suexec_disable_trans _("HTTPD Service") _("Disable SELinux protection for http
suexec")
httpd_unified _("HTTPD Service") _("Unify HTTPD handling of all content files.")
httpd_tty_comm _("HTTPD Service") _("Unify HTTPD to communicate with the terminal.
Needed for handling certificates.")
$ grep "Allow ftp to read/write files in the user home directories" selinux.tbl
ftp_home_dir _("FTP") _("Allow ftp to read/write files in the user home directories")
$ grep unlimitedRPM selinux.tbl
unlimitedRPM _("Admin") _("Allow rpm to run unconfined.")
```

Table 8-1 contains some of the most commonly altered SELinux booleans.

Table 8-1. Commonly altered SELinux booleans

Boolean name	Description in system-config-securitylevel	Reason for altering	Default value
`allow_ptrace`	Allow *sysadm_t* to debug or ptrace applications.	Permit *root* to use tools such as *gdb* for debugging.	Off
`allow_execmod`	Allow the use of shared libraries with Text Relocation.	Required to use Adobe Flash browser plug-in and Sun Java.	Off
`allow_ftp_anon_write`	—	Permits the FTP server to write to files labeled with type `public_content_rw_t`, described in Table 8-2.	Off
`httpd_can_network_connect`	Allow *httpd* scripts and modules to connect to the network.	Enables web scripts to connect to databases and mail servers.	Off
`httpd_enable_homedirs`	Allow *httpd* to read home directories.	Enables the use of *~/public_html* for personal web pages.	Off
`httpd_tty_comm`	Unify *httpd* to communicate with the terminal. Needed for handling certificates.	Enables the use of certificates with passphrases (requires the passphrase to be entered on the terminal).	Off
`allow_httpd_anon_write`	—	Permits Apache to write to files labeled with type `public_content_rw_t` (see Table 8-2).	Off
`named_write_master_zones`	Allow *named* to overwrite master zone files.	Required for *dhcpd* updating of zones.	Off
`nfs_export_all_ro`	Allow reading on any NFS filesystem.	Enables NFS file sharing (read-only).	Off
`nfs_export_all_rw`	Allow read/write/create on any NFS filesystem.	Enables NFS file sharing (read/write).	Off
`use_nfs_home_dirs`	Support NFS home directories.	Allows home directories (such as */home/chris*) to be imported from an NFS server.	Off
`samba_enable_home_dirs`	Allow Samba to share users' home directories.	Allows *homes* shares in *smb.conf*.	Off
`use_samba_home_dirs`	Allow users to log in with CIFS home directories.	Allows home directories (such as */home/chris*) to be imported from a Samba or Windows server.	Off
`allow_samba_anon_write`	—	Permits Samba to write to files labeled with type `public_content_rw_t`.	Off
`spamassasin_can_network`	Allow Spam Assassin daemon network access.	Enables the use of real-time blackhole lists (RBLs) by Spam Assassin.	Off
`ssh_sysadm_login`	Allow SSH logins as *sysadm_r: sysadm_t*.	Allows *root* login via SSH (otherwise, you'll need to log in as a regular user and then use *su*). This may be required if you're running remote backups via SSH.	Off
subsystem`_disable_trans`	Disable SELinux protection for *subsystem*.	Use this as a last alternative. It's better to disable SELinux protection for one subsystem than to turn it off entirely.	Off

Using file labels

SELinux uses file labels to specify an SELinux *context* for each file. To display the context labels, use the -Z or --context options to *ls*:

```
$ ls -Z /etc
-rw-r--r--  root    root    system_u:object_r:etc_t           a2ps.cfg
-rw-r--r--  root    root    system_u:object_r:etc_t           a2ps-site.cfg
drwxr-xr-x  root    root    system_u:object_r:etc_t           acpi
-rw-r--r--  root    root    system_u:object_r:adjtime_t       adjtime
drwxr-xr-x  root    root    system_u:object_r:etc_t           alchemist
-rw-r--r--  root    root    system_u:object_r:etc_aliases_t   aliases
-rw-r-----  root    smmsp   system_u:object_r:etc_aliases_t   aliases.db
drwxr-xr-x  root    root    system_u:object_r:etc_t           alsa
drwxr-xr-x  root    root    system_u:object_r:etc_t           alternatives
-rw-r--r--  root    root    system_u:object_r:etc_t           anacrontab
-rw-------  root    root    system_u:object_r:etc_t           at.deny
-rw-r--r--  root    root    system_u:object_r:automount_etc_t auto.master
-rw-r--r--  root    root    system_u:object_r:automount_etc_t auto.misc
-rwxr-xr-x  root    root    system_u:object_r:automount_etc_t auto.net
-rwxr-xr-x  root    root    system_u:object_r:automount_etc_t auto.smb
...(Lines snipped)...
```

The context label displayed on each line contains the text system_u:object_r: followed by the file type assigned to the file. In the output above, the *aliases* file has been given the file type etc_aliases_t (which is unique to that file), indicating that the SELinux policy treats that file specially.

 All file types end in _t for easy identification.

Files contained in your home directory are usually given the type user_home_t. The default policy will not permit web pages in *~/public_html* to be accessed through the web server, even if the httpd_enable_homedirs boolean is turned on, unless the files being shared have the type httpd_sys_content_t. To change file contexts, use the *chcon* command:

```
$ chcon -R -t httpd_sys_content_t ~/public_html
```

The -R option causes *chcon* to recursively change the context of directories within *~/public_html*, and -t httpd_sys_content_t sets the file type.

The file context types most commonly used with *chcon* are shown in Table 8-2.

Table 8-2. Common nondefault file context types

Type	Description	Examples
httpd_sys_content_t	Files that may be served by *httpd*	Web pages, graphics, CSS files, client-side ECMAScript/JavaScript
httpd_sys_script_exec_t	CGI scripts that may be executed by *httpd*	Web scripts written in any external scripting language (e.g., scripts written in Perl when you are not using *mod_perl*)

Table 8-2. Common nondefault file context types (continued)

Type	Description	Examples
`httpd_unconfined_script_exec_t`	CGI scripts that will not be constrained by SELinux	Dangerous!—but may be required for some complex CGI scripts
`httpd_sys_script_ro_t`	Datafiles that may be read (but not written) by CGI scripts	Static CGI script datafiles
`httpd_sys_script_ra_t`	Datafiles that may be read and appended (but not overwritten or truncated) by CGI scripts	Script logfiles, guestbooks, nonrevisable order queues, survey and quiz records
`httpd_sys_script_rw_t`	Datafiles that may be read/written by CGI scripts	User profiles, session status, and other CGI datafiles
`samba_share_t`	Enables sharing of the file by Samba (not required for home directories)	Group Samba shares
`public_content_t`	Enables sharing of the file (read only) by Samba, *httpd*, NFS, and *rsync*	Files shared by multiple servers
`public_content_rw_t`	Enables sharing of the file (read/write) by Samba, *httpd*, FTP, and *rsync*	Files shared and updatable through multiple servers

 A file label that has been changed manually may be changed back to the default value during a relabeling (discussed in the next section).

For example, if you have created the */var/samba* directory and are using it for Samba group shares, it will need to be labeled with the type `samba_share_t`:

```
# chcon -R -t samba_share_t /var/samba
```

To make that the default context label for */var/samba*, edit */etc/selinux/targeted/contexts/files/file_contexts.local* to contain this line:

```
/var/samba(/.*)?        system_u:object_r:samba_share_t
```

The first field contains a regular expression specifying that this entry will match any filename starting with /var/samba. The context label in the second field (which must include the `system_u:object_r:` portion) configures the default label for files that match the regular expression.

Relabeling the system

Some caution is in order: you may end up with a system where many file labels are wrong if you update your SELinux policy, mount your filesystems without SELinux support enabled (perhaps during rescue mode), or go wild with *chcon*. To relabel your system, you should create the empty file */.autorelabel* and then boot the system:

```
# touch /.autorelabel
# shutdown -r now
```

During system startup, your files will be relabeled to default values, except for files labeled with a type listed in */etc/selinux/targeted/contexts/customizable_types*. The relabeling operation will typically take a few minutes on a desktop system or small server, and could take much longer on a large server or very old computer.

Viewing and interpreting SELinux messages

SELinux policy messages are sent to *syslog* and usually end up in */var/log/messages*. To find them among the other messages, search for the string avc:

```
# grep avc: /var/log/messages
May  2 16:32:56 laptop3 kernel: audit(1146601976.667:289): avc:
denied  { getattr } for  pid=23807 comm="httpd" name="public_html" dev=dm-1
ino=192237 scontext=user_u:system_r:httpd_t:s0
tcontext=user_u:object_r:user_home_t:s0 tclass=dir
```

Here we see that an access request was denied between a subject with an *scontext* of user_u:system_r:httpd_t:s0 and a *tcontext* of user_u:object_r:user_home_t:s0 for the *tclass* dir (a filesystem directory). The additional fields provide a bit more information: the attempted operation was *getattr* (get attributes), the process ID of the subject was 23807, the command executing was *httpd*, the directory name was *public_html*, the storage device was *dm-1*, and the inode number was 192237.

The fact that the storage device name starts with *dm* (which stands for *device mapper*) indicates that the directory is stored in a logical volume. You can find the device number from a detailed listing of the device node:

```
$ ls -l /dev/dm-1
brw-r----- 1 root disk 253, 1 Apr 29 08:57 /dev/dm-1
```

The output indicates that the device number is 253, 1. Compare this with the device nodes in */dev/mapper*:

```
$ ls -l /dev/mapper
total 0
crw------- 1 root root  10, 63 Apr 29 08:57 control
brw-rw---- 1 root disk 253,  1 Apr 29 08:57 main-home
brw-rw---- 1 root disk 253,  3 Apr 29 08:57 main-remote
brw-rw---- 1 root disk 253,  0 Apr 29 08:57 main-root
brw-rw---- 1 root disk 253,  4 Apr 29 08:57 main-test
brw-rw---- 1 root disk 253,  2 Apr 29 08:57 main-var
```

According to this output, */dev/dm-1* corresponds to */dev/mapper/main-home*, which refers to the logical volume *home* within the volume group *main*. The *mount* command shows the mount point for this volume:

```
$ mount
/dev/mapper/main-root on / type ext3 (rw)
proc on /proc type proc (rw)
sysfs on /sys type sysfs (rw)
devpts on /dev/pts type devpts (rw,gid=5,mode=620)
/dev/hdc2 on /boot type ext3 (rw)
tmpfs on /dev/shm type tmpfs (rw)
```

```
/dev/mapper/main-home on /home type ext3 (rw)
none on /proc/sys/fs/binfmt_misc type binfmt_misc (rw)
sunrpc on /var/lib/nfs/rpc_pipefs type rpc_pipefs (rw)
automount(pid10695) on /net type autofs (rw,fd=4,pgrp=10695,minproto=2,maxproto=4)
```

We know that the directory filename is *public_html*, but we don't know the full pathname of the directory. Passing the mount point and inode number to *find* will reveal the pathname:

```
# find /home -xdev -inum 192237
/home/chris/public_html
```

 The -xdev argument limits the search to a single filesystem.

So now we know that *httpd* (Apache) was unable to access the directory */home/chris/public_html*.

The command *audit2why* will attempt to decode SELinux error messages:

```
# grep avc: /var/log/messages|audit2why
May  2 16:32:56 laptop3 kernel: audit(1146601976.667:289): avc:  denied  { getattr }
for  pid=23807 comm="httpd" name="public_html" dev=dm-1 ino=192237 scontext=user_u:
system_r:httpd_t:s0 tcontext=user_u:object_r:user_home_t:s0 tclass=dir
        Was caused by:
                Missing or disabled TE allow rule.
                Allow rules may exist but be disabled by boolean settings;
                check boolean settings.
                You can see the necessary allow rules by running audit2allow
                with this audit message as input.
```

This explanation is not very informative, but it does tell us that there is no type enforcement rule to allow this access, and that may be because of a boolean setting. Viewing the manpage for *httpd_selinux* gives information about the necessary boolean setting, along with the required context label:

```
httpd by default is not allowed to access users home directories.
If you want to allow access to users home directories you  need  to
set the httpd_enable_homedirs boolean and change the context of the
files that you want people to access off the home dir.

setsebool -P httpd_enable_homedirs 1
chcon -R -t httpd_sys_content_t ~user/public_html
```

Issuing the commands given in the manpage fixes the problem. Here I've substituted the actual user's name into the *chcon* argument:

```
# setsebool -P httpd_enable_homedirs
# chcon -R -t httpd_sys_content_t ~chris/public_html
```

Fedora Core 6 includes the first release of the *setroubleshoot* tool, which provides a desktop notification of AVC denials as well as a GUI program for analyzing AVC messages. To use this tool, install the *setroubleshoot* package.

How Does It Work?

The Linux kernel provides the Linux Security Module (LSM) interface to enable additional access controls to be added to operations. These interfaces provide connections, or *hooks*, into the system call code used by processes to request that the kernel perform an operation, such as opening a file, sending a signal to another process, or binding to a network socket.

SELinux uses these hooks to permit or deny requests made by a process (*subject*) on a resource (such as a file, network socket, or another process, called an *object*). These controls are called *mandatory access controls* (MAC) because they enforce a consistent security policy across the entire system. This stands in contrast to the traditional Unix/Linux file permissions, which are considered *discretionary access controls* (DAC) because the access settings are left to each user's discretion.

SELinux does not override permissions; access to a resource must be permitted by all security mechanisms—including SELinux, permission modes, ACLs, mount options, and filesystem attributes—before it will be granted.

An SELinux policy defines the rules used to make each access decision. There are three inputs into each decision: the security context of the source subject, and the security context and class of the target object.

Each security context consists of four parts: a *user*, a *role*, a *type*, and a *sensitivity*. In order to track this information, SELinux assigns a label to each subject and object.

You can view the context of processes by using the -Z (or --context) argument with the *ps* command:

```
$ ps -e -Z
LABEL                          PID TTY       TIME CMD
system_u:system_r:init_t         1 ?       00:00:02 init
system_u:system_r:kernel_t       2 ?       00:00:00 ksoftirqd/0
system_u:system_r:kernel_t       3 ?       00:00:00 watchdog/0
system_u:system_r:kernel_t       4 ?       00:00:00 events/0
...Lines snipped...
user_u:system_r:unconfined_t 24168 pts/2   00:00:00 bash
user_u:system_r:unconfined_t 24228 pts/2   00:00:00 ps
user_u:system_r:unconfined_t 24229 pts/2   00:00:00 tail
```

This information is also displayed by the GNOME System Monitor, as shown in Figure 8-7.

If you've added the System Monitor applet to your GNOME panel, clicking on it will start the GNOME System Monitor. You can also start it using the menu entry Applications → System Tools → System Monitor, or by typing the command **gnome-system-monitor**.

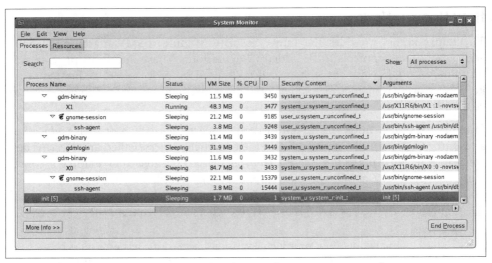

Figure 8-7. GNOME System Monitor display showing the security contexts of processes

The label on the *init* process (highlighted in Figure 8-7) indicates that the user is system_u, the role is system_r, and the type is init_t. The sensitivity is not shown in this output. This label defines the source security context (*scontext*) because the *init* process is a source of system access requests.

_t indicates a type, _r indicates a role, and _u indicates a user.

When *init* attempts to read the configuration file */etc/inittab*, the label on that file defines the target security context (*tcontext*):

```
$ ls -Z /etc/inittab
-rw-r--r-- root      root      system_u:object_r:etc_t         /etc/inittab
```

Context labels on files are stored in the file's attributes, and therefore SELinux can be used only on filesystems that support these attributes: ext2, ext3, and XFS. Other filesystems, such as ReiserFS, JFS, ISO9660, and VFAT do not support these attributes yet.

You can view the context labels as a file attribute using the *getfattr* command, specifying the security.selinux attribute name:

```
# getfattr -n security.selinux /etc/hosts
getfattr: Removing leading '/' from absolute path names
# file: etc/hosts
security.selinux="system_u:object_r:etc_t:s0\000"
```

 The last portion of the security.selinux attribute is the *sensitivity level*, which is used only for *multilevel security* (MLS) and *multicategory security* (MCS). The \000 at the end of the attribute indicates an ASCII NUL character, used to delimit the end of the attribute in traditional C style.

The target class (*tclass*) associated with the object being accessed is determined by the type of object (and in some cases, how it is being accessed); in this example, where *init* is attempting to access */etc/inittab*, the *tclass* is file. Therefore the SELinux policy is checked to see if access is permitted for an *scontext* of system_u: system_r:init_t, a *tcontext* of system_u:object_r:etc_t, and a *tclass* of file. To speed access, SELinux rules are cached in an area of memory called the *access vector cache*—which explains why SELinux error messages are labeled avc.

The Fedora project has three policies available:

targeted

> The default policy installed with Fedora Core. This policy is targeted for the protection of the most frequently attacked portions of the system, including most network services. Programs that are not targeted are unconstrained by SELinux.

strict

> This policy denies every action except those explicitly permitted. Although this should be more secure than the targeted policy, it's hard to create a policy that encompasses all possible configurations of all programs that can be installed on a Fedora system, and attempting to use this policy has frustrated many system administrators into turning off SELinux altogether. In other words, the targeted policy is often more secure simply because it's more likely to be used.

MLS

> Experimental policy to support multilevel security (MLS). This is important for some government certifications and is not widely used outside of government. (The future MCS framework appearing in the targeted policy will use specific features of MLS for a type of discretionary access control).

In the default targeted policy, the *role* element of the security context is not used (all subjects are system_r, and all objects are object_r), and very few users are defined (just system_u, user_u, and root).

SELinux policies are difficult and time-consuming to write, and even more difficult to write well. Nonetheless, they have to be customized to suit the particular needs of each site. The SELinux booleans provide a compromise between complexity and flexibility, by enabling policy options to be configured without editing, compiling, and retesting the policy code.

The SELinux technology was originally developed by the U.S. National Security Agency (NSA), with several partner organizations. The kernel components of SELinux have been incorporated into the main Linux kernel releases. The Fedora project utilizes those kernel components along with customized policy and some user tools (such as versions of *ls* and *ps* that include the -Z options, and SELinux-specific tools such as *chcon* and *getenforce*, and the graphical configuration tool *system-config-securitylevel*). Red Hat is a major contributor to SELinux development.

What About...

...using the strict or MLS policies?

These alternate policies are provided as RPM packages and are installed using *yum*:

```
# yum install selinux-policy-strict selinux-policy-mls
```

Switch between the installed policies using the graphical configuration tool (system-config-securitylevel from the command line, or System → Administration → "Security Level and Firewall" from the menu). When more than one policy is installed, a drop-down menu for Policy Type appears on the SELinux tab, as shown in Figure 8-8. When you change the policy, the warning dialog shown at bottom left of Figure 8-8 will appear, informing you that the policy change will cause the filesystem to be relabeled. Click Yes to approve the relabeling, and then click OK in the Security Level Configuration window. Reboot to activate the new policy.

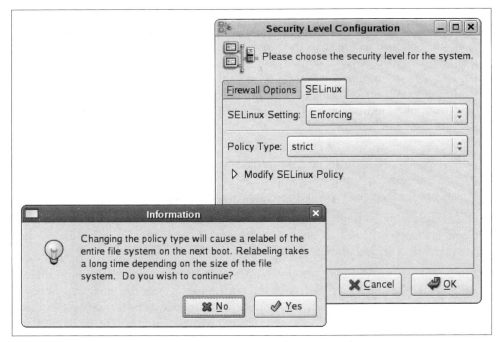

Figure 8-8. Selecting policy using the Security Level Configuration tool

To change the policy from the command prompt, edit */etc/selinux/config* and change the SELINUXTYPE value to the policy of your choice (targeted, strict, or mls):

```
# This file controls the state of SELinux on the system.
# SELINUX= can take one of these three values:
#       enforcing - SELinux security policy is enforced.
#       permissive - SELinux prints warnings instead of enforcing.
#       disabled - SELinux is fully disabled.
SELINUX=enforcing
# SELINUXTYPE= type of policy in use. Possible values are:
#       targeted - Only targeted network daemons are protected.
#       strict - Full SELinux protection.
SELINUXTYPE=mls

# SETLOCALDEFS= Check local definition changes
SETLOCALDEFS=0
```

Then create the empty file */.autorelabel* to ensure that the filesystem will be relabeled when the system is booted:

```
# touch /.autorelabel
```

Reboot to activate the change.

 Fedora development is focused on the targeted policy. Changing the policy may lead to a number of unexpected system problems!

...booting with SELinux disabled?

If you have SELinux enabled, but your system cannot boot successfully due to an SELinux problem, you may need to temporarily disable it while you investigate.

To boot with SELinux disabled, append selinux=0 to the boot options.

Where Can I Learn More?

- The manpages for *selinux*, *getsebool*, *setsebool*, *getenforce*, *setenforce*, *sestatus*, *semanage*, *selinuxenabled*, *restorecon*, *getfattr*, and *audit2why*
- The manpage for *<subsystem>_selinux* (for example, the manpage for *samba_selinux* for details of SELinux protection provided for the Samba server)
- The Fedora Wiki SELinux page: *http://fedoraproject.org/wiki/SELinux*
- The setroubleshoot Wiki page: *http://fedoraproject.org/wiki/SELinux/setroubleshoot*
- The NSA SELinux web site: *http://www.nsa.gov/selinux/index.cfm*
- The SELinux project on Sourceforge: *http://selinux.sourceforge.net/*
- The SELinux symposium web site: *http://www.selinux-symposium.org/*
- The NSA SELinux FAQ: *http://www.nsa.gov/selinux/info/faq.cfm*
- The Fedora SELinux FAQ: *http://fedora.redhat.com/docs/selinux-faq/*

- The Unofficial SELinux FAQ: *http://www.crypt.gen.nz/selinux/faq.html*
- The home page of Tresys, a company that has done extensive work on SELinux policy development: *http://www.tresys.com/*
- The Linux Security Modules web site: *http://lsm.immunix.org/*

8.3   Using Access Control Lists

Unix/Linux permission modes are very simple; they don't cover all security needs. But, because they are simple, they are actually *used*, which is more than can be said for many other access control technologies.

But sometimes permissions just don't cut it, and a better system of discretionary access control is needed. *Access control lists* (ACLs) enable you to specify exactly which users and groups can access a file and in what ways.

How Do I Do That?

In order to use ACLs on a filesystem, that filesystem must be mounted with the `acl` mount option. To check whether this option is active, use the *mount* command:

```
$ mount
/dev/mapper/main-root on / type ext3 (rw)
proc on /proc type proc (rw)
sysfs on /sys type sysfs (rw)
devpts on /dev/pts type devpts (rw,gid=5,mode=620)
/dev/hdc2 on /boot type ext3 (rw)
tmpfs on /dev/shm type tmpfs (rw)
/dev/mapper/main-home on /home type ext3 (rw)
none on /proc/sys/fs/binfmt_misc type binfmt_misc (rw)
sunrpc on /var/lib/nfs/rpc_pipefs type rpc_pipefs (rw)
automount(pid10695) on /net type autofs (rw,fd=4,pgrp=10695,minproto=2,maxproto=4)
```

 If you kept the default volume group and logical volume names during installation, you may see device paths such as */dev/mapper/VolGroup00-LogVol01*.

The mount options are shown in parentheses; none of these filesystems were mounted with the `acl` option.

To add the acl mount option to a filesystem that is already mounted, use the *mount* command with the `remount` option:

```
# mount -o remount,acl /home
# mount -o remount,acl /
# mount
/dev/mapper/main-root on / type ext3 (rw,acl)
proc on /proc type proc (rw)
sysfs on /sys type sysfs (rw)
```

```
devpts on /dev/pts type devpts (rw,gid=5,mode=620)
/dev/hdc2 on /boot type ext3 (rw)
tmpfs on /dev/shm type tmpfs (rw)
/dev/mapper/main-home on /home type ext3 (rw,acl)
none on /proc/sys/fs/binfmt_misc type binfmt_misc (rw)
sunrpc on /var/lib/nfs/rpc_pipefs type rpc_pipefs (rw)
automount(pid10695) on /net type autofs (rw,fd=4,pgrp=10695,minproto=2,maxproto=4)
```

Note that the *home* and / filesystems are now mounted with the acl option. To
make this option the default for future mounts of these filesystems, edit the file */etc/
fstab* and add it to the fourth column for these filesystems:

/dev/main/root	/	ext3	defaults,**acl**	1	1
LABEL=/boot	/boot	ext3	defaults	1	2
devpts	/dev/pts	devpts	gid=5,mode=620	0	0
tmpfs	/dev/shm	tmpfs	defaults	0	0
proc	/proc	proc	defaults	0	0
sysfs	/sys	sysfs	defaults	0	0
/dev/main/swap	swap	swap	defaults	0	0
/dev/main/home	/home	ext3	defaults,**acl**	1	2

Once the filesystem has been mounted with the correct option, the *getfacl* (get file
ACL) command can be used to view the ACL of a file:

```
$ touch test
$ ls -l test
-rw-rw-r-- 1 chris chris 0 May  6 20:52 test
$ getfacl test
# file: test
# owner: chris
# group: chris
user::rw-
group::rw-
other::r--
```

The ACL displayed by *getfacl* exactly matches the permissions shown by *ls*: the user
who owns the file (*chris*) can read and write the file, users in the group that owns the
file (*chris*) can read and write the file, and all of the other users of the system can
only read the file.

Each entry in the ACL consists of three components separated by colons:

type

> The keyword user, group, mask, or other. This may be abbreviated to u, g, m, or o
> when setting or changing ACL entries.

qualifier

> The name of the user or group affected by this entry. User type entries with an
> empty qualifier apply to the user that owns the file; group type entries with an
> empty qualifier apply to the group that owns the file. mask and other entries
> always have an empty qualifier.

permissions

The permissions granted by the entry; any combination of r (read), w (write), and x (execute). When displayed by the *getfacl* command, the permissions are always shown in *rwx* order, and permissions that are not granted are replaced with a dash.

To modify the ACL, use the *setfacl* command with the -m (modify) option. This command will limit the user *thomas* to just reading the file *test*:

```
$ setfacl -m user:thomas:r test
$ getfacl test
# file: test
# owner: chris
# group: chris
user::rw-
user:thomas:r--
group::rw-
mask::rw-
other::r--
```

This additional ACL entry shows up on a line of its own. Notice that a mask entry is now displayed, showing the maximum permission available to users and groups identified by a qualifier; this mask value corresponds to the group permission of the traditional Linux permission mode, as displayed by *ls*.

When *ls* is used to display detailed file information, the output is slightly modified:

```
$ ls -l test
-rw-rw-r--+ 1 chris chris 0 May  6 20:52 test
```

The + after the file permissions indicates that an ACL is in effect in addition to the permissions shown.

Changing the file mode using the chmod command alters the ACL mask value:

```
$ chmod 644 test
$ ls -l test
-rw-r--r--+ 1 chris chris 0 May  6 20:52 test
$ getfacl test
# file: test
# owner: chris
# group: chris
user::rw-
user:thomas:r--
group::rw-                    #effective:r--
mask::r--
other::r--
```

The new group permission has been set to r-- (read-only), and this is also used as the mask value. Because the mask is more limiting than the group value in the ACL, the group permission has effectively changed to r--, as indicated by the #effective: r-- comment in the output.

This works both ways; changing the mask using *setfacl* also changes the group permission, as displayed by *ls*:

```
$ ls -l test
-rw-r--rwx+ 1 chris chris 0 May  6 20:52 test
$ setfacl -m mask::rw test
$ ls -l test
-rw-rw-rwx+ 1 chris chris 0 May  6 20:52 test
$ getfacl test
# file: test
# owner: chris
# group: chris
user::rw-
user:thomas:r--
group::rw-
mask::rw-
other::rwx
```

On the other hand, changing the default group ACL entry affects both that entry and the mask value:

```
$ setfacl -m g::r test
$ ls -l test
-rw-r--r--+ 1 chris chris 0 May  6 20:52 test
$ getfacl test
# file: test
# owner: chris
# group: chris
user::rw-
user:thomas:r--
group::r--
mask::r--
other::r--
```

 The g::r argument is a short form for group::r.

To change multiple ACL entries at one time, separate them by commas:

```
$ setfacl -m u:diane:rw,u:jim:r,g::r,m::rw test
$ getfacl test
# file: test
# owner: chris
# group: chris
user::rw-
user:thomas:r--
user:diane:rw-
user:jim:r--
group::r--
mask::rw-
other::r--
```

To set a new ACL, discarding the previous ACL completely, use the --set argument instead of -m:

```
$ setfacl --set u::rw,u:diane:r,u:thomas:r,u:gord:rw,u:jim:r,m::rw,g::-,o::- test
$ getfacl test
# file: test
# owner: chris
# group: chris
user::rw-
user:thomas:r--
user:diane:r--
user:gord:rw-
user:jim:r--
group::---
mask::rw-
other::---
```

Note the use of - to indicate no permissions in the ACL entries for group and other.

When using --set, it is necessary to specify at least the permission for the file's owner, the file's group owner, and others, because these will be used to construct the legacy permission mode. Leaving one of those entries out results in an error message:

```
$ setfacl --set u:diane:r,g::- test
setfacl: test: Malformed access ACL `user:diane:r--,group::---,mask::r--':
Missing or wrong entry at entry 1
```

To remove an ACL entry, use the -x option to *setfacl* and specify one or more ACL entries by the type and qualifier components (leave out the permissions):

```
$ getfacl test
# file: test
# owner: chris
# group: chris
user::rw-
user:thomas:r--
user:diane:r--
user:gord:rw-
user:jim:r--
group::---
mask::rw-
other::---
$ setfacl -x user:gord test
$ getfacl test
# file: test
# owner: chris
# group: chris
user::rw-
user:thomas:r--
user:diane:r--
user:jim:r--
group::---
mask::r--
other::---
```

Setting the default ACL for new files

Each file has an *access ACL*, but directories can additionally have a *default ACL* that is used as the default for new files and subdirectories created within that directory.

The default ACL is displayed when *getfacl* is run with the -d option. Initially the default ACL is empty:

```
$ getfacl .
# file: .
# owner: chris
# group: chris
user::rwx
group::rwx
other::r-x

$ getfacl -d .
# file: .
# owner: chris
# group: chris
```

To set the default ACL, use the *setfacl* command with the -d option:

```
$ setfacl -d --set u::rw,u:thomas:rw,g::r,m::rw,o::- .
$ getfacl -d .
# file: .
# owner: chris
# group: chris
user::rw-
user:thomas:rw-
group::r--
mask::rw-
other::---
```

This ACL will then be applied automatically to new files:

```
$ touch trial
$ getfacl trial
# file: trial
# owner: chris
# group: chris
user::rw-
user:thomas:rw-
group::r--
mask::rw-
other::---
```

Copying and moving files with their ACLs

To copy an ACL when copying a file, use the -p argument to cp:

```
$ getfacl demo
# file: demo
# owner: chris
# group: chris
user::rw-
```

```
group::rw-                          #effective:r--
mask::r--
other::---

$ cp -p demo demo2
$ getfacl demo2
# file: demo2
# owner: chris
# group: chris
user::rw-
group::rw-                          #effective:r--
mask::r--
other::---
```

When moving a file (with mv), the ACL is automatically preserved:

```
$ mv demo2 demo3
$ getfacl demo3
# file: demo3
# owner: chris
# group: chris
user::rw-
group::rw-                          #effective:r--
mask::r--
other::---
```

Copying an ACL from one file to another

It can be a lot of work setting up a complex ACL with many entries. To simplify the reuse of ACLs, *setfacl* provides the --set-file option, which sets an ACL from a text file. This file can be created by redirecting the output of *getfacl*, providing an easy way to copy an ACL from one file to another. This example writes the ACL from the file *demo* to the file */tmp/acl*, and then applies that ACL to the file *bar*:

```
$ getfacl demo >/tmp/acl
$ setfacl --set-file /tmp/acl bar
$ getfacl bar
# file: bar
# owner: chris
# group: chris
user::rw-
user:thomas:r--
user:diane:r--
user:gord:rw-
user:jim:rw-
group::rw-
mask::rw-
other::---
```

Since --set-file accepts the filename - for standard input, you can also pipe the output of *getfacl* into *setfacl* to copy an ACL without using an intermediate file:

```
$ getfacl demo | setfacl --set-file - bar
```

Improving the appearance of ACL listings

getfacl provides a --tabular option, which presents the output in a format that is somewhat easier to read than the default output:

```
$ getfacl bar
# file: bar
# owner: chris
# group: chris
user::rw-
user:thomas:r--
user:diane:r--
user:gord:rw-                        #effective:r--
user:jim:rw-                         #effective:r--
group::rw-                           #effective:r--
mask::r--
other::---

$ getfacl --tabular bar
# file: bar
USER    chris    rw-
user    thomas   r--
user    diane    r--
user    gord     rW-
user    jim      rW-
GROUP   chris    rW-
mask             r--
other            ---
```

Notice that permissions that are not effective due to the mask value are shown in (the name inserted into the qualifier column is the file's owner and group owner).

It can be convenient to create an alias for viewing the tabular output:

```
$ alias showacl='getfacl --tabular'
```

 Don't name this alias getfacl, or you won't be able to copy ACLs between files; tabular output cannot be used as input to *setfacl*.

How Does It Work?

ACLs are stored in a compressed format in a file's extended attributes, just like SELinux context labels. They can be viewed with the command *getfattr* using the name system.posix_acl_access:

```
$ getfattr -n system.posix_acl_access yearend.ods
# file: yearend.ods
system.posix_acl_access=0sAgAAAAEABgD/////AgAEAPYBAAACAAQA9wEAAAIABg
D4AQAAgAGAPoBAAAEAAYA/////xAABgD/////IAAAAP////8=
```

Obviously, the output of *getfacl* is much more useful!

Like SELinux labels, ACLs work only on filesystems that support extended attributes, and therefore cannot be used on filesystems such as VFAT and ISO9660.

On an ext2 or ext3 filesystem, all of the extended attributes must fit into one *block*, as defined at the time that the filesystem was created. To determine the block size of a filesystem, use *dumpe2fs*:

```
# dumpe2fs /dev/mapper/main-home | grep 'Block size'
dumpe2fs 1.38 (30-Jun-2005)
Block size:               4096
```

In this case, the block size is 4,096 bytes (4 KB); the SELinux context, ACL, and any other extended attributes must fit within that 4 KB limit.

When an ACL is changed, a new block is allocated, the new ACL is written to that block, and then the old block is freed. If no blocks are available on the filesystem (or if the user doesn't have access to any more blocks, which may be the case if you have enabled per-user storage quotas), then the ACL cannot be changed.

Modification of an ACL may only be performed by the owner of the file and the superuser (*root*).

What About...

...adjusting ACLs graphically?

Unfortunately, Fedora Core does not include any tools that permits ACLs to be viewed or adjusted graphically.

...saving and restoring the ACLs of a file subtree?

The -R option to *getfacl* produces a recursive listing of all files in the named directory. *setfacl* has a --restore option that will use such a recursive listing to set the ACLs of a group of files. This can be used to save and restore ACLs—useful if a number of files are being transported between systems, or backed up and restored from tape or optical disk.

For example, this command creates a file named *acl.txt* that contains all of the ACLs for all files and subdirectories in the current directory:

```
$ getfacl -R . >acl.txt
```

The entire directory can be copied to a CD or DVD, backed up to tape or a USB flash drive, or saved in a tarball and sent to another system. To restore the ACLs at a later date:

```
# setfacl --restore acl.txt
```

If the *setfacl* command is run as *root*, the ownerships and group ownerships will also be reset to their original values.

...a version of tar that supports ACLs?

Fedora Core provides the *star* package, which is an advanced replacement for *tar*. *star* can back up and restore ACLs along with files when the *exustar* archive format is used and the -acl option is specified. For example, to back up the */home* directory with ACL information:

```
# star cvzf /tmp/home-backup.star.gz -acl artype=exustar /home
a /home/ directory
a /home/john/ directory
a /home/john/.bash_logout 24 bytes, 1 tape blocks
a /home/john/.bash_profile 191 bytes, 1 tape blocks
a /home/john/.bashrc 124 bytes, 1 tape blocks
a /home/john/.gtkrc 120 bytes, 1 tape blocks
...(Lines snipped)...
```

To restore from this archive:

```
# star xvzf /tmp/home-backup.star.gz artype=exustar -acl
star: WARNING: skipping leading '/' on filenames.
Release     star 1.5a69 (i386-redhat-linux-gnu)
Archtype    exustar
Dumpdate    1146974078.733347 (Sat May  6 23:54:38 2006)
Volno       1
Blocksize   20
x home/ directory
x home/john/ directory
x home/john/.bash_logout 24 bytes, 1 tape blocks
x home/john/.bash_profile 191 bytes, 1 tape blocks
x home/john/.bashrc 124 bytes, 1 tape blocks
x home/john/.gtkrc 120 bytes, 1 tape blocks
...(Lines snipped)...
```

Where Can I Learn More?

- The manpages for *acl(5)*, *getfacl*, and *setfacl*
- The manpages for *star* and *spax*

8.4 Making Files Immutable

Because the *root* user can override permissions, file permissions alone are not enough to ensure that a file will not be changed. But when a file is made *immutable*, it cannot be changed by anyone.

How Do I Do That?

To make a file immutable, use the *chattr* (change attribute) command to add the i attribute to the file:

```
# chattr +i foo
# date >>foo
```

```
bash: foo: Permission denied
# mv foo baz
mv: cannot move `foo' to `baz': Operation not permitted
# rm foo
rm: cannot remove `foo': Operation not permitted
```

You can find out if the i attribute has been set by using the *lsattr* (list-attribute) command:

```
# lsattr foo
----i-------- foo
```

The presence of the i in the output indicates that the file *foo* has been made immutable.

Removing the i attribute causes the file to act normally again:

```
# chattr -i foo
# date >>foo
# mv foo baz
# rm baz
# ls baz
ls: baz: No such file or directory
```

How Does It Work?

The immutable capability is provided by the ext2/ext3 filesystems. Each file has an immutable flag that is part of the ext2/ext3 file attributes; when set, the ext2/ext3 code in the kernel will refuse to change the ownership, group, name, or permissions of the file, and will not permit writing, appending, or truncation of the file.

By making configuration files and programs immutable, you can provide a small measure of protection against change. This can be used to guard against accidental changes to configuration files. It can also prevent a program from being subverted to change files it should not; although SELinux provides similar protection, you may add software to your system that is not covered by the SELinux targeted policy.

 Do not attempt to upgrade or remove software packages if you've made any of the files belonging to those packages immutable! Doing so may render your system unusable. Be particularly careful if you are using immutable files on a system that has automatic *yum* updates enabled.

What About...

...making an entire subtree immutable?

The -R option to *chattr* causes it to operate recursively over all of the files and subdirectories within a directory:

```
# chattr -R +i /etc
```

...other file attributes that might be useful?

Although a number of file attributes have been defined for ext2/ext3 filesystems, very few of the interesting ones have been implemented! For example, attributes have been defined to enable per-file automatic data compression, automatic zeroing (enhanced security erasure) of deleted files, and save-for-undeletion, but none of those features have been implemented so far.

But there is one other attribute that is occasionally useful: the *append-only* attribute, a. When applied to a file by chattr, this attribute provides all of the protection of the immutable attribute, except that it remains possible to append data to the file. This is ideal for logfiles, because it makes it impossible to alter or erase data that has been placed in the logfile.

Where Can I Learn More?

- The manpages for *chattr* and *lsattr*

8.5   Using sudo to Delegate Privilege

Sometimes it's useful to delegate superuser privilege to a Fedora user; however, giving him the superuser password gives him total control of the system. The *sudo* system enables superuser privilege to be delegated on a program-by-program basis.

How Do I Do That?

There are two parts to *sudo*: the */etc/sudoers* file, which controls who can do what, and the *sudo* command, which enables authorized users to run commands with superuser privilege.

To configure */etc/sudoers*, use the *visudo* utility, which will start *vi* so that you can edit the file. When you are done, it checks the syntax before installing it. If there is a syntax error, *visudo* will prompt you for a course of action; to see the available options, enter a question mark:

```
# visudo
>>> sudoers file: syntax error, line 17 <<<
What now? ?
Options are:
  (e)dit sudoers file again
  e(x)it without saving changes to sudoers file
  (Q)uit and save changes to sudoers file (DANGER!)

What now? x
```

To enable the user *chris* to run the *netstat* and *ifconfig* commands as the superuser, add this entry to the *sudoers* file:

```
chris ALL=/bin/netstat,/sbin/ifconfig
```

This entry contains the username, the computers (in this case, ALL) on which this user can execute this command (useful if the *sudoers* file is shared among several machines, either through a file-sharing protocol or by copying the file), and a list of commands that may be executed as *root*.

Be careful selecting the commands to include in the list: if any of the commands permit access to the shell, the user will be able to execute anything!

Once this change has been made, the user *chris* can use *sudo* to execute the *netstat* command using the -p option (which requires superuser privilege to operate correctly):

```
chris@bluesky$ sudo netstat -ap
Password: bigsecret
Active Internet connections (servers and established)
Proto Recv-Q Send-Q Local Address        Foreign Address  State      PID/Program
name
tcp        0      0 *:sunrpc             *:*              LISTEN 1488/portmap
tcp        0      0 laptop3:smtp         *:*              LISTEN 1724/sendmail
tcp        0      0 laptop3:x11-ssh-offset *:*            LISTEN 20494/2
tcp        0      0 *:42365              *:*              LISTEN 507/rpc.statd
tcp        0      0 *:http               *:*              LISTEN 21393/httpd
...(Lines snipped)...
```

Notice that a password is requested; this is the user's password, not the *root* password.

The user can also execute *ifconfig*:

```
$ sudo /sbin/ifconfig eth2 down
```

The full pathname of the command (*/sbin/ifconfig*) is required because */sbin* is not in the user's normal search path.

It is reasonable idea to add */sbin* and */usr/sbin* to everyone's search path, since it makes both *sudo* and *su* more useful and provides easy access to the nonprivileged modes of the administration utilities.

This time, no password is requested because it's been less than five minutes since the last time *sudo* asked for the user's password. To disable the password request entirely, add the keyword NOPASSWD: after the equal sign in the *sudoers* entry:

```
chris ALL=NOPASSWD:/bin/netstat,/sbin/ifconfig
```

By default, *sudo* enables the execution of the listed commands as *root*; to enable execution as another user, place that user's name in parentheses after the equal sign in the configuration entry. For example, to permit *chris* to run the script */usr/local/bin/ checkstatus* as the user *scott*:

```
chris ALL=(scott) NOPASSWD:/usr/local/bin/checkstatus
```

chris can then use *sudo* with the -u option to specify the desired user ID:

```
$ sudo -u scott checkstatus
```

Replacing the command list with the word ALL will include all commands. For example, this entry permits *chris* to execute any command or script as *root*:

```
chris ALL=ALL
```

 Permitting unrestricted access to all commands through *sudo* is equivalent to giving away the *root* password. A *root* user can compromise the system at very basic levels, making it impossible to later secure the system, even if you cut off that user's access.

For convenience, you can define groups of users, hosts, or commands and then reference those in entries. This is done by using the User_Alias, Host_Alias, and Cmnd_Alias statements.

For example, to define a group of administrators and permit them to run the *ifconfig* and *route* commands as *root* on any of a group of desktop systems, you could use a configuration file like this:

```
User_Alias  ADMINS=sally,harry,jason
Host_Alias  ADMINDESKTOPS=yellow.fedorabook.com,orange.fedorabook.com
Cmnd_Alias  NETCONFIG=ifconfig,route

ADMINS ADMINDESKTOPS=NETCONFIG
```

How Does It Work?

The *sudo* program executes with *root* privilege. If you view the permissions on the binary, you will see that the *set-user-ID* permission bit is enabled (note the s in the user community permissions):

```
$ ls -l /usr/bin/sudo
---s--x--x 2 root root 106832 Feb 12 04:41 /usr/bin/sudo
```

Since this bit is set and the file is owned by *root*, it executes with *root*'s privilege.

sudo checks the */sbin/sudoers* file to determine if and how it should run the requested command. It requests a password if necessary, and then either denies execution or changes the effective user ID to the specified value (or leaves it as *root*) and executes the requested command.

When the user is prompted for—and successfully enters—her password, *sudo* updates a timestamp file in */var/run/sudo*. The next time *sudo* is executed, the timestamp is checked, and if it is less than five minutes old, the user is not prompted for her password again. The timestamp is then updated.

The value of *sudo* lies in the ability to permit a user to execute specific commands with privilege. However, it's easy to accidentally misconfigure *sudo* to permit more access than intended.

For example, if you wish to permit *frank* to view text files owned by *jenny*, you could create the *sudoers* entry:

```
frank ALL=(jenny) NOPASSWD:/usr/bin/less
```

But the *less* command permits the user to access the shell by typing !, and *frank* can use this loophole to execute any command as though he were *jenny*:

```
frank$ sudo -u jenny less /home/jenny/.bash_profile
...(Normal output of less)...
!
$ id
uid=508(jenny) gid=508(jenny) groups=508(jenny)

$ mail -s boss@fedorabook.com
Subject: I Quit
I quit because you are a hateful, mean boss.
-Jenny
.
Cc: Enter
$ rm -rf /home/jenny/*
$ exit
...(Normal output of less)...
```

It can be useful to configure *sudo* for ALL commands for users that already have the *root* password because it encourages good practice, especially when used without the NOPASSWD option. The benefits of this configuration are:

- A user can assume *root* privilege from time to time only when it is necessary, operating without *root* privilege the majority of the time. Compared to the use of a *root* shell, this practice reduces the likelihood that a command will accidentally be executed with privilege.

- If the user steps away from the display while a shell is open, *root* access is not exposed.

- The user must enter a password to escalate privilege but does not have to enter the password for each individual privileged command in a series.

- The act of typing *sudo* in front of privileged commands serves to remind the user to check the command carefully.

What About...

...changing the password timeout?

By default, *sudo* won't prompt the user for their password as long as they have entered it successfully in the last five minutes. To change this value, add this entry to the top of the */etc/sudoers* file:

```
Defaults timestamp_timeout=2
```

The value for this timeout is expressed in minutes.

...voluntarily giving up the password timestamp?

The user can voluntarily give up the timestamp at any time using the -k option:

```
$ sudo -k
```

This is useful if the terminal will be unattended for a while.

...disabling the root password entirely (like a Debian or Ubuntu system)?

The Fedora community has discussed this idea and ultimately opted to keep a *root* password. Fedora's *consolehelper* PAM configuration relies on a *root* password, and using a *root* password can in some cases provide one additional obstacle to gaining superuser access.

Where Can I Learn More?

- The manpages for *sudo*, *sudoers*, and *visudo*

8.6 Configuring PAM and consolehelper

Fedora uses the Pluggable Authentication Module (PAM) system to handle user authentication and identity changes. As the name implies, PAM is modular and configurable, enabling you to change the authentication (and authorization) setup on your system without programming.

How Do I Do That?

PAM configuration files are stored in */etc/pam.d*, with one file per configured service. Each file is written in plain text and consists of at least three fields separated by spaces. The entries in these files are divided into four categories according to the first field, which identifies the *module type*. Possible values are:

auth
:   Authentication configuration (determining who is logging in).

account
:   Non-authentication-based access control, such as restricting activities by time of day.

password
:   Password changes or other authentication token updates (such as recording a new retinal scan or fingerprint).

session
:   Setup of the post-login session and environment.

The entries for a given module type are executed in sequence. For example, when performing authentication, the modules listed on the `auth` lines are executed in sequence.

The second field in each entry is called the *control flag* and determines the action taken when the module succeeds or fails. Possible values are:

`required`

> The module must succeed for the module type to succeed. Regardless of whether the module fails or succeeds, processing will continue with the next line (other modules of the same module type will be executed), but at the end of all of the processing, a failure will be recorded.

`requisite`

> The module must succeed for the module type to succeed. If it fails, processing stops immediately. If it succeeds, processing continues with the next line.

`sufficient`

> If the module succeeds, then the module type succeeds and processing stops immediately. If it fails, processing continues with the next line.

`optional`

> The module is executed, but the failure or success of the module is ignored.

`include`

> In place of a module name, another configuration file is given. All of the lines of the same type from that configuration file are treated as if they were present in this configuration file.

 It is also possible to use a complex expression as a control flag, but this feature is not used in the default Fedora Core configuration.

The remaining fields on the line contain the name of the module and any arguments to it (except when the control flag is `include`, in which case the third argument is the included file).

Here's an example. This is the content of */etc/pam.d/sshd*, the configuration file for the SSH server daemon:

```
#%PAM-1.0
auth       include     system-auth
account    include     system-auth
password   include     system-auth
session    include     system-auth
session    required    pam_loginuid.so
```

Authentication is carried out by the first line, which includes all of the auth lines from the file */etc/pam.d/system-auth*, which looks like this:

```
#%PAM-1.0
# This file is auto-generated.
```

```
# User changes will be destroyed the next time authconfig is run.
auth        required    pam_env.so
auth        sufficient  pam_unix.so nullok try_first_pass
auth        requisite   pam_succeed_if.so uid >= 500 quiet
auth        required    pam_deny.so

account     required    pam_unix.so
account     sufficient  pam_succeed_if.so uid < 500 quiet
account     required    pam_permit.so

password    requisite   pam_cracklib.so try_first_pass retry=3
password    sufficient  pam_unix.so md5 shadow nullok try_first_pass use_authtok
password    required    pam_deny.so

session     required    pam_limits.so
session     required    pam_unix.so
```

The first line highlighted in bold executes the *pam_env.so* module (*/lib/security/pam_env.so*), which sets up environment variables according to the configuration file */etc/security/pam_env.conf*. The next lines use the *pam_unix.so* module to perform traditional Unix password checking, then deny access if the password check does not succeed.

In this configuration, the *pam_succeed_if.so* lines do nothing! (They are used when a network authentication scheme is in effect, though.)

These are the account entries, as included into the *sshd* configuration file from the *system-auth* file:

```
account     required    pam_nologin.so
account     required    pam_unix.so
account     sufficient  pam_succeed_if.so uid < 500 quiet
account     required    pam_permit.so
```

The *pam_nologin.so* module checks for the existence of the file */etc/nologin* and, if present, prevents anyone except *root* from logging in. This is useful during periods of system maintenance.

The contents of */etc/nologin* will be displayed as a message to the user in a dialog box when he attempts to log in using the graphical user interface. In the case of a character-mode login, the file will be displayed but the screen will be cleared immediately, making it nearly impossible to read the message. The SSH daemon will not display the message at all.

The *pam_unix.so* module (in this account mode) performs password maintenance checking, to see if the user should be forced to change her password, warned of imminent expiry, or locked out of the system. Finally, the *pam_permit.so* module sets up a default action of permit for the account section of the file.

The password portion of the configuration controls password changes:

```
password    requisite    pam_cracklib.so try_first_pass retry=3
password    sufficient   pam_unix.so md5 shadow nullok try_first_pass use_authtok
password    required     pam_deny.so
```

The first line executes *pam_cracklib.so* to ensure that any newly set password is sufficiently complex, and the second line updates the password files on the system. The last line ensures that a failure is recorded if the password update is not successful.

Finally, we have the session entries, which set up the environment and perform logging after the user has authenticated:

```
session    required    pam_limits.so
session    required    pam_unix.so
session    required    pam_loginuid.so
```

The first two lines are included from */etc/pam.d/system-auth*, while the last line is from */etc/pam.d/sshd*.

The *pam_limits.so* module can be used to configure *ulimit* values according to */etc/security/limits.conf*, but the default version of that file contains only comments. You can use this module to limit the amount of memory, CPU time, simultaneous logins, or other resources available to specific users.

The *pam_unix.so* module (in session mode) simply logs the fact that the user has authenticated using the *syslog* facility. The last module, *pam_loginuid.so*, records the fact that this is an initial login (as opposed to a switch of user ID performed using *su* or *sudo*).

Using an authentication server

Fedora can authenticate against an authentication server instead of (or in addition to) the local user and password database (*/etc/passwd*, */etc/shadow*, */etc/group*, and */etc/gshadow*). Usable authentication and user information services include Kerberos, LDAP, Hesiod (DNS), Winbind (local Windows domain), and SMB (Windows domain server).

To use an established authentication server, select the desktop menu option System → Administration → Authentication or run the command *system-config-authentication*. The window shown in Figure 8-9 will appear. Select the User Information or Authentication tab, and then select the checkbox for the server type you wish to use. Click the Configure button to the right of the server type to enter the parameters specifically required by that server type (for example, for NIS you will need to enter the NIS domain and the server name).

Click OK. *system-config-authentication* will then write a new version of the file */etc/pam.d/system-auth*.

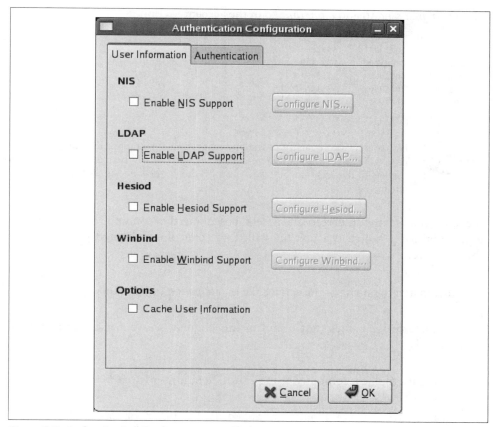

Figure 8-9. Authentication Configuration window

 Using the Authentication Configuration tool will undo any customization that you have made in */etc/pam.d/system-auth*.

Authentication can also be configured from the command line using *authconfig*.

Adding a PAM module: restricting access by time and user

We can tighten up the security of the system by adding additional modules into the configuration file. For example, you can restrict SSH access to certain times of day using the *pam_time.so* module.

 Before editing any PAM configuration file, make a backup copy. You should also keep a *root* shell open in a virtual terminal or terminal window in case your changes accidentally lock you out of the system. Test the new configuration thoroughly before closing the *root* shell!

Edit */etc/pam.d/sshd* to add *pam_time.so* in the account section:

```
#%PAM-1.0
auth       include     system-auth
account    required    pam_time.so
account    include     system-auth
password   include     system-auth
session    include     system-auth
session    required    pam_loginuid.so
```

 Notice that the sequence of the lines is critical; if you place the *pam_time.so* line after the file *system-auth* is included, it will be ignored for users with IDs less than 500 (such as root) due to the *pam_succeed_if.so* line in *system-auth*.

The *pam_time.so* module restricts access based on the contents of the file */etc/security/time.conf*, which is a text file with four semicolon-delimited fields per line. The fields are:

service
> Must match the name of the service file in */etc/pam.d* (sshd in this example).

tty
> Terminal device names (not useful in this context, so we'll use * to match all terminals).

users
> A list of usernames, combined using ! (not), & (and), or | (or).

times
> A list of days (any combination of Su, Mo, Tu, We, Th, Fr, or Sa—or Wk for weekdays, Wd for weekends, or Al for all days) concatenated to a range of times, expressed in 24-hour format (such as 0600-1800 for 6 a.m. to 6 p.m., local time).

 The default */etc/security/time.conf* contains extensive notes on the line format.

To prevent all users other than *root* from connecting via SSH during evenings and weekends, place these lines in */etc/security/time.conf*:

```
# Limit ssh for non-root users to 8 am to 5 pm on weekdays
sshd;*;!root;Wk0800-1700
```

Note that if there is no line in */etc/security/time.conf* that applies to a particular connection, it is permitted by default. These restrictions also apply only when a user logs in; once logged in, the user may stay connected for as long as he chooses.

To place a time restriction on all types of login—whether through SSH, a local character-mode virtual terminal, or the GUI—place the entry for the *pam_time.so* module in */etc/pam.d/system-auth* instead of */etc/pam.d/sshd*:

```
#%PAM-1.0
# This file is auto-generated.
# User changes will be destroyed the next time authconfig is run.
auth        required        pam_env.so
auth        sufficient      pam_unix.so nullok try_first_pass
auth        requisite       pam_succeed_if.so uid >= 500 quiet
auth        required        pam_deny.so

account     required        pam_time.so
account     required        pam_unix.so
account     sufficient      pam_succeed_if.so uid < 500 quiet
account     required        pam_permit.so

password    requisite       pam_cracklib.so try_first_pass retry=3
password    sufficient      pam_unix.so md5 shadow nullok try_first_pass use_authtok
password    required        pam_deny.so

session     required        pam_limits.so
session     required        pam_unix.so
```

You can then create separate rules for each type of user access in */etc/security/time.conf*:

```
# Character-mode login - Only root is permitted (any time).
login;*;!root;!Al0000-2400

# Remote login via ssh - Root is always permitted, other
# users are permitted 8 am to 5 pm on weekdays.
sshd;*;!root;Wk0800-1700

# Graphical-mode login - Not available to root.
gdm;*;root;!Al0000-2400

# Switching user via 'su' command - not permitted unless
# switching -to- the root user. Note that the root user
# can switch to any other user because of the pam_rootok.so
# module line in /etc/pam.d/su
su;*;!root;!Al0000-2400
```

Automatic blacklisting of sites trying a brute-force password attack

The PAM module *pam_abl.so* from Fedora Extras provides the ability to blacklist (block access from) users and hosts that repeatedly send an incorrect password. This is useful in guarding against brute-force password attacks, where a remote system will simply try to log in over and over again with different password guesses until it is successful.

This module will not work successfully with *gdm* (graphical logins), so it must not be added to *system-auth*. To protect SSH logins (the best use of this module), add an entry for *pam_abl.so* module to */etc/pam.d/sshd*:

```
#%PAM-1.0
auth        required        pam_abl.so config=/etc/security/pam_abl.conf
auth        include         system-auth
```

```
account    include     system-auth
password   include     system-auth
session    include     system-auth
session    required    pam_loginuid.so
```

The file */etc/security/pam_abl.conf* is installed by the *pam_abl* RPM and contains this configuration:

```
# /etc/security/pam_abl.conf
# debug
host_db=/var/lib/abl/hosts.db
host_purge=2d
host_rule=*:10/1h,30/1d
user_db=/var/lib/abl/users.db
user_purge=2d
user_rule=!root:10/1h,30/1d
```

The *host_rule* line controls which hosts may be blacklisted and the number of failed login attempts that must be registered before blacklisting; the default configuration specifies that any host (*) may be blacklisted for more than 10 login failures in one hour (10/1h), or more than 30 login failures in one day (30/1d). The user_rule line similarly blacklists any user except *root* (!root) who has 10 failed login attempts in one hour or 30 failed login attempts in one day.

The host_purge and user_purge lines configure how quickly a blacklist entry is revoked; the default for both is two days.

When a login failure is recorded, the *pam_abl.so* module updates its database. You can query the database using the *pam_abl* command:

```
# pam_abl
Failed users:
    <none>
Failed hosts:
    <none>
```

Initially, no failed login attempts are recorded. As login failures occur, *pam_abl* will count and report them (in parenthesis):

```
# pam_abl
Failed users:
    jane (1)
        Not blocking
Failed hosts:
    darkday (1)
        Not blocking
```

Eventually, access from the host or user will be blocked:

```
# pam_abl
Failed users:
    jane (11)
        Blocking users [!root]
Failed hosts:
    darkday (11)
        Blocking users [*]
```

To re-enable access from a specific host or by a specific user, use the `--okhost` or `--okuser` arguments to *pam_abl*:

```
# pam_abl --okhost darkday
# pam_abl
Failed users:
    jane (11)
        Blocking users [!root]
Failed hosts:
    <none>
```

PAM and consolehelper

Fedora uses the *consolehelper* program to control access to a number of system administration tools. It's *consolehelper* that asks you for the *root* password when you use many of the configuration menu options such as System → Administration → Network (or, equivalently, run *system-config-network* from the shell).

If you examine the *system-config-network* file, you'll see that it is actually a symbolic link to *consolehelper*:

```
$ type system-config-network
system-config-network is /usr/bin/system-config-network
$ ls -l /usr/bin/system-config-network
lrwxrwxrwx 1 root root 13 Mar 20 14:57 /usr/bin/system-config-network
            -> consolehelper
```

When *consolehelper* is invoked with another command name, it uses the PAM configuration in */etc/pam.d* with the same name as the command entered. If the user runs *system-config-network*, then the PAM configuration */etc/pam.d/system-config-network* is invoked, which looks like this:

```
#%PAM-1.0
auth          include          config-util
account       include          config-util
session       include          config-util
```

This includes */etc/pam.d/config-util*, which contains these lines:

```
#%PAM-1.0
auth          sufficient       pam_rootok.so
auth          sufficient       pam_timestamp.so
auth          include          system-auth
account       required         pam_permit.so
session       required         pam_permit.so
session       optional         pam_xauth.so
session       optional         pam_timestamp.so
```

The auth configuration will succeed if the current user is *root* (*pam_rootok.so*) or there is a recent timestamp file present (*pam_timestamp.so*). Failing that, the traditional Unix password authentication is performed (via the included *system-auth* file).

The timestamp file that *pam_timestamp.so* checks is created by the last line, which invokes the *pam_timestamp.so* module in session mode. In other words, if the user successfully authenticates to the system as root in order to use one tool, she is permitted to run other tools without typing in her password for the next few minutes.

Once the authentication has succeeded, *consolehelper* consults the file with the same name as the originally entered command in the directory */etc/security/console.apps*; in this example, the file would be */etc/security/console.apps/system-config-network*, which contains:

```
USER=root
PROGRAM=/usr/sbin/system-config-network
SESSION=true
```

This instructs *consolehelper* to run */usr/sbin/system-config-network* as the *root* user after performing the PAM session initialization (using the session lines in the PAM configuration file).

You can adjust the PAM configuration to suit your needs. For example, to allow regular users to run *system-config-network* without entering the *root* password, edit the auth line in */etc/pam.d/system-config-network* to use the permissive *pam_permit.so* module instead of including the *config-util* file:

```
#%PAM-1.0
auth          sufficient       pam_permit.so
account       include          config-util
session       include          config-util
```

It's often convenient to enable the console user—the person physically logged on to the system keyboard and display—to run any of the programs controlled by *consolehelper* without entering the *root* password. To do this, edit */etc/pam.d/config-util* and add this line:

```
#%PAM-1.0
auth          sufficient       pam_rootok.so
auth          sufficient       pam_timestamp.so
auth          sufficient       pam_console.so
auth          include          system-auth
account       required         pam_permit.so
session       required         pam_permit.so
session       optional         pam_xauth.so
session       optional         pam_timestamp.so
```

 This will permit the current console owner to execute the configuration tools regardless of where he is executing them. For example, if the user *joe* is logged in on the console (either graphically or using a character-mode login), then *joe* can execute configuration tools both at the console and through a remote connection.

How Does It Work?

PAM is simply a group of libraries used by applications. Each PAM-aware application uses those libraries to perform authentication, account control, the management of passwords (or other tokens), and session setup.

Each PAM module is a shared object (*.so*) file conforming to the PAM specification. These files are stored in */lib/security* and are accessed when needed according to the configuration files in */etc/pam.d*.

What About...

...other PAM modules?

There are many PAM modules included in Fedora Core. For documentation, refer to the PAM Administrator's manual in */usr/share/doc/pam-*/html/*. Some PAM modules not documented in that manual have their own manpages; use `apropos pam_` to see a list of all of them.

There are also a number of PAM modules available on the Internet and from hardware vendors, designed to support authentication using biometric devices, smart tokens, and more.

...permitting the console user to use su without a password?

Edit */etc/pam.d/su* to add this line:

```
#%PAM-1.0
auth            sufficient      pam_rootok.so
# Uncomment the following line to implicitly trust users in the "wheel" group.
#auth           sufficient      pam_wheel.so trust use_uid
# Uncomment the following line to require a user to be in the "wheel" group.
#auth           required        pam_wheel.so use_uid
auth            sufficient      pam_console.so
auth            include         system-auth
account         include         system-auth
password        include         system-auth
session         include         system-auth
session         optional        pam_xauth.so
```

Then create the file */etc/security/console.apps/su*:

```
# touch /etc/security/console.apps/su
```

You can now use *su* at the console without entering the *root* password.

 This is, obviously, a security risk.

Where Can I Learn More?

- The manpages for *pam*, *consolehelper*, *userhelper*, and *authconfig*
- The PAM administrator's guide: */usr/share/doc/pam*/html*
- The manpages for the PAM modules (use the command `apropos pam_` to see a list of all of them); not all of the PAM modules have a manpage

8.7   Logging

It's important to know what is going on on your system. Fedora provides a standardized, network-based logging system and tools to automatically monitor and trim logfiles. Understanding and using these tools effectively will allow you to keep your finger on the pulse of your system with minimal effort.

How Do I Do That?

The *syslog* facility collects and routes messages in a Fedora system. The file */etc/syslog.conf* configures the message routing; the default version of the file looks like this:

```
# Log all kernel messages to the console.
# Logging much else clutters up the screen.
#kern.*                                                  /dev/console

# Log anything (except mail) of level info or higher.
# Don't log private authentication messages!
*.info;mail.none;authpriv.none;cron.none                /var/log/messages

# The authpriv file has restricted access.
authpriv.*                                              /var/log/secure

# Log all the mail messages in one place.
mail.*                                                  -/var/log/maillog

# Log cron stuff
cron.*                                                  /var/log/cron

# Everybody gets emergency messages
*.emerg                                                          *

# Save news errors of level crit and higher in a special file.
uucp,news.crit                                          /var/log/spooler

# Save boot messages also to boot.log
local7.*                                                /var/log/boot.log
```

On the left side of each entry is a pattern that consists of selectors. Each *selector* contains one or more facilities (separated by commas), then a period, and then one or more levels (again, separated by commas).

The *facility* indicates the origin of the log entry. Possible values are shown in Table 8-3.

Table 8-3. Facility values to indicate the origin of the log entry

Value	Description
authpriv	Security, authentication, or authorization systems.
cron	Task scheduler (*crond* and *atd*).

Table 8-3. Facility values to indicate the origin of the log entry (continued)

Value	Description
daemon	Server daemons that don't have a category of their own.
ftp	File-transfer-protocol daemon.
kern	Kernel messages.
local0, local1, local2, local3, local4, local5, local6, *and* local7	Reserved for custom use on a distribution-by-distribution or site-by-site basis. Fedora uses local7 to log boot messages.
lpr	Printing system.
mail	Electronic mail.
news	Net news (Usenet).
syslog	Messages from *syslogd* itself.
user	User-level messages.
uucp	Unix-to-Unix copy messages (rarely used).

The *level* consists of a priority level and can be any of the values listed in Table 8-4, in increasing order of severity.

Table 8-4. Priority-level values, in order of severity

Value	Description
debug	Informational software debugging messages.
info	General informational messages.
notice	Important normal messages that do not indicate an error or problem.
warning	Information about an unusual or impending situation.
err	Error messages, indicating that something is wrong.
crit	Critical conditions indicating imminent danger.
alert	Serious, emergency problems.
emerg	Emergency situation: the system is in crisis and failing.

Specifying a level means any message of that level or higher (more severe), so the selector kern.crit would match messages from the kernel with a priority of crit, alert, or emerg. To match only crit, an equal sign is added: kern.=crit. An exclamation mark negates a match: kern.!crit matches kernel messages with a priority below crit, while kern.!=crit matches all kernel messages except those with a priority of crit.

An asterisk indicates that the facility or level should be ignored. Therefore, authpriv.* matches messages from the authpriv facility regardless of the priority, and *.info matches messages from any facility which are at the info level or higher. Multiple facilities or priorities can be matched using commas (indicating an OR operation), so mail,local3.* matches any message from the mail or local3 facilities.

Multiple selectors may be included in one entry, separated by semicolons, which indicates an AND operation. The special priority none matches no messages from the specified facility. Therefore *.crit;kern.none matches all messages that are of crit priority or higher, unless they come from the kernel.

On the right side of each entry in */etc/syslog.conf* is a destination for the messages. The destination may be:

An absolute pathname
> Messages are placed in the specified file. The pathname may also point to a named pipe, providing a method for passing messages to another program, or to a device such as a terminal (such as */dev/tty3*) or a printer (*/dev/lp0*). Adding a hyphen in front of a pathname will prevent *syslogd* from flushing the buffers to disk after each write, a performance-eating behavior that increases the chance that a message describing the cause of a crash will make it onto the disk.

@host
> Messages are forwarded to *syslogd* on the remote *host*.

user,user,user,...
> Messages are written to the terminals of any of these users who are currently logged in.

*
> Messages are written to the terminals of all logged-in users.

The order of the lines in the configuration file does not matter; every line is checked against each incoming message, so messages may be sent to multiple destinations.

The default configuration file routes messages according to Table 8-5; as you can see, */var/log/messages* is the prime source of information about the state of the system.

Table 8-5. Message routing as configured in the default syslog configuration file

Type of message	Destination
Everything except mail, authentication, and cron messages, with a priority of info or higher	*/var/log/messages*
Authentication messages (which may contain private information)	*/var/log/secure*
Mail	*/var/log/maillog*
Cron	*/var/log/cron*
All messages of emerg level or higher	The terminals of all logged-in users
UUCP and news messages of crit level or higher	*/var/log/spooler*
Boot messages	*/var/log/boot.log*

Interpreting /var/log/messages

The */var/log/messages* logfile contains entries similar to this:

```
May 31 10:40:58 laptop3 dhclient: DHCPREQUEST on eth0 to 172.16.97.254 port 67
May 31 10:40:58 laptop3 dhclient: DHCPACK from 172.16.97.254
```

```
May 31 10:40:58 laptop3 dhclient: bound to 172.16.97.100 -- renewal in 34387
    seconds.
May 31 20:14:05 laptop3 dhclient: DHCPREQUEST on eth0 to 172.16.97.254 port 67
May 31 20:14:05 laptop3 dhclient: DHCPACK from 172.16.97.254
May 31 20:14:05 laptop3 dhclient: bound to 172.16.97.100 -- renewal in 41631
    seconds.
```

Each entry consists of a date, time, hostname (laptop3 in this example), program name or other prefix (dhclient), and a text message. Note that the facility and priority are not recorded in the logfile.

Since the */var/log/message* file can be very large, it's worthwhile using a tool such as *grep* to search for specific records. For example, you can view all of the kernel messages with the command:

```
$ grep kernel /var/log/messages
May 30 04:23:08 bluesky kernel: SELinux: initialized (dev hdd, type iso9660),
    uses genfs_contexts
May 31 20:48:40 bluesky kernel: atkbd.c: Unknown key pressed (translated
set 2, code 0x85 on isa0060/serio0).
May 31 20:48:40 bluesky kernel: atkbd.c: Use 'setkeycodes e005 <keycode>'
    to make it known.
May 31 21:14:54 bluesky kernel: cdrom: This disc doesn't have any tracks I
    recognize!
```

Creating your own logfile entries

You can generate *syslog* messages using the *logger* command-line tool. Simply provide your text as arguments:

```
$ logger Added host lightning to /etc/hosts
```

The message recorded in */var/log/messages* contains the username as the prefix:

```
Jun  1 02:32:59 darkday chris: Added host lightning to /etc/hosts
```

It's convenient to log information about changes you have made on the system in this way, entering them as you work. Your notes will be interleaved with system-generated log messages, making it easy to see the relationship between the changes that you have made and any messages that start or stop appearing in the log as a result.

By default, *logger* uses the facility user and the priority notice. You can override this using the -p option, and you can override the insertion of the username by supplying an alternate tag with the -t option:

```
$ logger -p local1.crit -t cooling Stopped water pump
```

Which would result in this message being logged:

```
Jun  1 09:54:49 darkday cooling: Stopped water pump
```

An alias can be used to simplify logging from the command line:

```
$ alias note='logger -p local4.notice'
$ note Ran yum update
```

If you are logging a message that contains metacharacters, surround the message with quotation marks.

By adding a custom rule to */etc/syslog.conf*, the messages sent to the local1 facility can be placed in their own file (in addition to being logged in */var/log/messages*):

```
local1.*                    /var/log/cooling
```

The security context of any new logfiles must be set to the same context as */var/log/ messages*:

```
# touch /var/log/cooling
# ls -Z /var/log/messages /var/log/cooling
-rw-r--r--  root     root     user_u:object_r:var_log_t      /var/log/cooling
-rw-------  root     root     system_u:object_r:var_log_t    /var/log/messages
# chcon system_u:object_r:var_log_t /var/log/cooling
# chmod 0600 /var/log/cooling        # Optional!
# ls -Z /var/log/messages /var/log/cooling
-rw-------  root     root     system_u:object_r:var_log_t    /var/log/cooling
-rw-------  root     root     system_u:object_r:var_log_t    /var/log/messages
```

Keeping an eye on logs

The -f option to *tail* provides a convenient way to watch messages that are being appended to a file and is perfect for use with logfiles:

```
# tail -f /var/log/messages
Jun  1 08:47:14 darkday kernel: hub 1-0:1.0: over-current change on port 1
Jun  1 08:47:14 darkday kernel: hub 1-0:1.0: port 2 disabled by hub (EMI?), re-
enabling...
Jun  1 08:47:14 darkday kernel: hub 1-0:1.0: over-current change on port 2
Jun  1 08:47:14 darkday kernel: usb 1-2: USB disconnect, address 4
Jun  1 08:47:14 darkday kernel: usb 1-2: new low speed USB device using uhci_hcd and
address 5
Jun  1 08:47:14 darkday kernel: usb 1-2: configuration #1 chosen from 1 choice
Jun  1 08:47:14 darkday kernel: input: Logitech USB-PS/2 Optical Mouse as /class/
input/input4
Jun  1 08:47:14 darkday kernel: input: USB HID v1.10 Mouse [Logitech USB-PS/2 Optical
Mouse] on usb-0000:00:1f.2-2
Jun  1 09:54:49 darkday cooling: Water temperature exceeds 70C
Jun  1 09:54:49 darkday cooling: Water temperature exceeds 85C
...(Additional lines are displayed as they are added to the logfile)...
```

 /var/log/messages is normally readable only by *root*. Although making it readable by other users may reveal a small amount of information about your system (reducing security), it can also reduce the amount of time spent in superuser mode (which, in turn, increases security). To make the *messages* file accessible to everyone:

```
# chmod a+r /var/log/messages
```

This *tail* command will display the last 10 lines in the file, and then additional lines within a second of the time that they are appended to the file. It can be left running

---

in a terminal window in the corner of the screen while you perform system administration tasks.

Configuring remote logging

The *syslog* service was designed to facilitate remote logging. This is very useful in two circumstances:

- In the event of a successful system intrusion, an attacker will often edit or delete logfiles to erase any record of his presence. If messages are logged to a remote server, it becomes more difficult to erase the trail because the attacker then needs to successfully attack the machine recording the log in addition to the system originally compromised.

- In a network, it is convenient to gather logs in one place for centralized analysis. This lets you stay on top of the state of many systems from one location.

To configure a *syslog* network server, edit that host's */etc/sysconfig/syslog* file, which initially looks like this:

```
# Options to syslogd
# -m 0 disables 'MARK' messages.
# -r enables logging from remote machines
# -x disables DNS lookups on messages recieved with -r
# See syslogd(8) for more details
SYSLOGD_OPTIONS="-m 0"
# Options to klogd
# -2 prints all kernel oops messages twice: once for klogd to decode, and
#    once for processing with 'ksymoops'
# -x disables all klogd processing of oops messages entirely
# See klogd(8) for more details
KLOGD_OPTIONS="-x"
#
SYSLOG_UMASK=077
# set this to a umask value to use for all logfiles, as in umask(1).
# By default, all permissions are removed for "group" and "other".
```

Change the SYSLOGD_OPTIONS line to include -r (remote logging):

```
SYSLOGD_OPTIONS="-m 0 -r"
```

Then restart *syslogd*:

```
# service syslog restart
Shutting down kernel logger:                               [  OK  ]
Shutting down system logger:                               [  OK  ]
Starting system logger:                                    [  OK  ]
Starting kernel logger:                                    [  OK  ]
```

 Ensure that your firewall configuration permits connections on UDP port 514.

Next, edit the file */etc/syslog.conf* on the machines that will be forwarding log messages to the *syslog* server, and add this line:

```
*.*                      @syslogserver
```

This will forward all messages to the remote host *syslogserver* (which may be an IP address or hostname). Restart *syslogd* to activate the changes.

> It's important to leave local logging turned on in case the *syslog* server is unavailable, so don't remove the lines that write to the local logfiles.

The result will be a combined log containing entries from both the *syslog* server and the host that is forwarding its log messages:

```
Jun  1 02:52:33 darkday named[13255]: starting BIND 9.3.2 -u named
Jun  1 02:52:33 darkday named[13255]: found 1 CPU, using 1 worker thread
Jun  1 02:52:33 darkday named[13255]: loading configuration from '/etc/named.conf'
Jun  1 02:52:33 darkday named[13255]: listening on IPv4 interface lo, 127.0.0.1#53
Jun  1 02:52:33 darkday named[13255]: listening on IPv4 interface eth0, 172.16.97.
100#53
Jun  1 02:52:33 darkday named[13255]: command channel listening on 127.0.0.1#953
Jun  1 02:52:33 darkday named[13255]: zone 0.in-addr.arpa/IN: loaded serial 42
Jun  1 02:52:33 darkday named[13255]: zone 0.0.127.in-addr.arpa/IN: loaded serial
1997022700
Jun  1 02:52:33 darkday named[13255]: zone 255.in-addr.arpa/IN: loaded serial 42
Jun  1 02:52:33 darkday named[13255]: zone 0.0.0.0.0.0.0.0.0.0.0.0.0.0.0.0.0.0.0.0.
0.0.0.0.0.0.0.0.0.0.ip6.arpa/IN: loaded serial 1997022700
Jun  1 02:52:33 darkday named[13255]: zone localdomain/IN: loaded serial 42
Jun  1 02:52:33 darkday named[13255]: zone localhost/IN: loaded serial 42
Jun  1 02:52:33 darkday named[13255]: running
Jun  1 02:57:22 bluesky chris: VNC service configured, restarting xinetd
Jun  1 02:57:29 bluesky xinetd[15394]: Exiting...
Jun  1 02:57:29 bluesky xinetd[15452]: xinetd Version 2.3.13 started with libwrap
loadavg options compiled in.
Jun  1 02:57:29 bluesky xinetd[15452]: Started working: 1 available service
```

Notice that this log contains entries from *darkday* (the *syslog* server) as well as from *bluesky* (which is forwarding log messages to *darkday*). Notice also the system administrator's note on *bluesky*, stating the reason that *xinetd* was being restarted.

> If the *syslog* server can't convert the IP address on a message into a hostname, the message will be logged with the IP address in the hostname field. Add the corresponding entry to */etc/hosts* to make the logfile more readable.

Automated log watching

There's not much point in collecting all this information if the logs are never read, but reading logfiles is boring, tedious work. Fortunately, the *logwatch* package automates this process, sending a daily summary email to alert you to important log entries.

The daily summary is emailed to *root* on the local machine. Email to the *root* user should be redirected to a specific user or users by the */etc/aliases* file. Edit this file and uncomment the entry for root found at the the end, inserting the name of a user who is responsible for administering the system (or a list of people separated by commas). In this example, all mail for *root* is redirected to *chris@fedorabook.com*:

```
# Person who should get root's mail
root:           chris@fedorabook.com
```

Here is a typical daily *logwatch* summary:

```
From:     root <root@bluesky.fedorabook.com>
To:       root@bluesky.fedorabook.com
Subject: LogWatch for bluesky.fedorabook.com
Date:     Wed, 31 May 2006 04:02:17 -0400


################### LogWatch 7.1 (11/12/05) ###################
         Processing Initiated: Thu Jun  1 02:52:14 2006
         Date Range Processed: yesterday
                              ( 2006-May-31 )
                              Period is day.
       Detail Level of Output: 10
               Type of Output: unformatted
            Logfiles for Host: bluesky.fedorabook.com
##############################################################


-------------------- httpd Begin -----------------------
A total of 3 unidentified 'other' records logged
GET /level/16/exec/-///pwd HTTP/1.0 with response code(s)
   2 404 responses
POST /garethjones/photos/--WEBBOT-SELF-- HTTP/1.0 with response code(s)
   1 404 responses
GET http://bluesky.fedorabook.com/foo HTTP/1.1 with response code(s)
   1 404 responses


-------------------- httpd End -------------------------



-------------------- SSHD Begin ------------------------

 Users logging in through sshd:
    chris:
       172.16.97.2: 3 times

-------------------- SSHD End --------------------------



-------------------- Disk Space Begin ------------------------

Filesystem                    Size  Used Avail Use% Mounted on
/dev/mapper/main-root         9.5G  2.9G  6.1G  33% /
/dev/hda1                      99M  9.7M   84M  11% /boot
/dev/mapper/main-home         4.9G   24M  4.7G   1% /home
```

```
-------------------- Disk Space End ------------------------

##################### LogWatch End #########################
```

This report will vary according to the services you have installed, but it provides a simple, easy-to-scan summary of log entries that may warrant attention. It also provides a summary of free disk space; if you methodically review these email messages, you won't be caught unaware when your storage needs start to inch upward.

Log rotation

Logfiles can grow to be massive. The Fedora *logrotate* package automatically moves historical log data into history files and keeps a limited number of history files on hand.

logrotate is configured through the master configuration file */etc/logrotate.conf*:

```
# see "man logrotate" for details
# rotate log files weekly
weekly

# keep 4 weeks worth of backlogs
rotate 4

# create new (empty) logfiles after rotating old ones
create

# uncomment this if you want your logfiles compressed
#compress

# RPM packages drop log rotation information into this directory
include /etc/logrotate.d

# no packages own wtmp -- we'll rotate them here
/var/log/wtmp {
    monthly
    create 0664 root utmp
    rotate 1
}

# system-specific logs may be also be configured here.
```

The most frequently altered lines are highlighted in bold: *logrotate* is initially configured to rotate logs every week and to save the last four historical logfiles in addition to the current log. If you have a lot of storage and wish to keep more history, edit the rotate line to increase the number of history files maintained, or change the `weekly` line to `monthly` to reduce the frequency of history snapshots (which can make it easier to analyze patterns over a longer period of time without merging data from several files).

The default configuration results in five separate message files being present on the system:

```
$ ls -l /var/log/messages*
-rw------- 1 root root  86592 Jun  1 02:49 /var/log/messages
-rw------- 1 root root  85053 May 30 02:03 /var/log/messages.1
-rw------- 1 root root 105491 May 26 23:51 /var/log/messages.2
-rw------- 1 root root  74062 May  7 04:12 /var/log/messages.3
-rw------- 1 root root 286194 May  2 13:00 /var/log/messages.4
```

 logrotate also uses per-logfile configuration files in */etc/logrotate.d*. These files are installed by various RPM packages that generate log-files.

How Does It Work?

The main system logging utility is named *syslog*. It is network-based and uses a server daemon, *syslogd*, which receives messages from all sorts of system programs through the Unix domain socket */var/log*. These messages are matched against the lines in */etc/syslog.conf* and written to the selected destinations.

Kernel messages are stored in a buffer that is read by a helper daemon named *klogd*, either by reading the file */proc/kmesg* or by using a kernel system call. *klogd* then forwards these messages to *syslogd* for inclusion in the system logs.

A *syslog* network server listens to UDP port 514 and processes any messages received there through the normal routing decisions.

One significant problem with the *syslog* implementation is that there is absolutely no authentication performed. Any application can log any message with any facility and priority. Therefore it is relatively easy to spoof log messages or to create a denial-of-service attack by sending huge numbers of logfile entries, eventually filling all available disk space and making it impossible to log further events. (For this reason, it is a good idea to use a separate filesystem for */var/log*).

The *logwatch* and *logrotate* programs are activated by cron through their entries in */etc/cron.daily*.

What About...

...sending log messages to a program?

The standard Fedora *syslog* program does not support output to a program such as a mailer. However, you can easily write a script that reads a logfile using the *tail* command and outputs new log entries to a program.

This example emails log messages to a pager or cell phone text service:

```
#!/bin/bash

DESTINATION=8885551234@pagercompany.example.com
```

```
tail -0f /var/log/messages|
while read LINE
do
        echo $LINE|
        mail $DESTINATION
done
```

To use this script, place it in the file */usr/local/bin/log-mail* and add read and execute permissions:

```
# chmod u+rx /usr/local/bin/log-mail
# log-mail
```

 You may want to use this script with a lower-volume logfile than */var/log/messages*, especially if you pay for each pager message.

To filter messages by content, place a *grep* command between the tail and while lines in the script.

You can also have log output read to you over the system's speakers:

```
#!/bin/bash

logger -t log-speak "Starting log reading."
sleep 0.3

tail -1f /var/log/messages|
while read LINE
do
        # The sed expressions remove the date/time and PIDs
        # from messages to shorten the text.
        echo $LINE|
        sed     -e "s/^.\{17\}[^ ]*//" \
                -e "s/\[.*\]//g"|
        festival --tts
done
```

...outputting to a named pipe?

A named pipe is a special type of file that can be used to pass messages between two programs. While *syslog* supports writing to named pipes, the default SELinux security policy prohibits it.

To output to a named pipe, you must first disable SELinux protection for *syslogd* by setting the syslogd_disable_trans boolean and then create the named pipe with *mkfifo*:

```
# setsebool -P syslogd_disable_trans=1
# mkfifo /var/log/messagepipe
```

Next, create an entry in */etc/syslog.conf*, placing a pipe symbol in front of the destination pathname:

```
*.*                     |/var/log/messagepipe
```

Restart *syslogd*. You can then follow the message output with a simple file read:

```
# service syslog restart
Shutting down kernel logger:                      [  OK  ]
Shutting down system logger:                      [  OK  ]
Starting system logger:                           [  OK  ]
Starting kernel logger:                           [  OK  ]
# cat /var/log/messagepipe
...(Messages appear as they are logged)...
```

...logging messages from printers, routers, and other network devices?

Most network hardware offers the option of logging messages to a *syslog* server. Simply enter the IP address of your *syslog* network server into the configuration settings of the device.

...using patterns within the message text to determine message routing?

The *syslog-ng* package from Fedora Extras can be used in place of the standard *syslogd* and *klogd* programs. It uses a different configuration file syntax, and it supports message-text matching and message routing to programs.

 The original *syslogd* and *klogd* programs are from the package *sysklogd*.

Where Can I Learn More?

- The manpages for *syslogd*, *syslog.conf*, *klogd*, *logrotate*, and *logwatch*
- The home page for *logwatch*: *http://www.logwatch.org*

8.8   Detecting File Changes with AIDE

The Advanced Intrusion Detection Environment (AIDE) is a program that takes a "fingerprint" of system files so that changes in those files can be detected. You can use it to detect a system intrusion, accidental file overwrites, and file corruption.

How Do I Do That?

To initialize the AIDE fingerprint database, execute it with the `--init` option:

```
# aide --init

AIDE, version 0.11

### AIDE database at /var/lib/aide/aide.db.new.gz initialized.
```

It will take several minutes to run. When it is finished, a fingerprint database will be saved as */var/lib/aide/aide.db.new.gz*. Rename it to */var/lib/aide/aide.db.gz* to make it the active AIDE database:

```
# mv /var/lib/aide/aide.db.new.gz /var/lib/aide/aide.db.gz
```

Once the fingerprint database is configured, you can check for file changes using the --check argument:

```
# aide --check
AIDE found differences between database and filesystem!!
Start timestamp: 2006-06-01 12:50:01

Summary:
  Total number of files:      127172
  Added files:                2
  Removed files:              0
  Changed files:              4


---------------------------------------------------
Added files:
---------------------------------------------------

added:/root/.xauthOVekVw
added:/root/.xauthcvqPrt


---------------------------------------------------
Changed files:
---------------------------------------------------

changed:/root
changed:/root/.lesshst
changed:/bin
changed:/bin/date


---------------------------------------------------
Detailed information about changes:
---------------------------------------------------


Directory: /root
  Mtime    : 2006-06-01 09:51:05        , 2006-06-01 11:43:23
  Ctime    : 2006-06-01 09:51:05        , 2006-06-01 11:43:23

File: /root/.lesshst
  Mtime    : 2006-06-01 10:57:21        , 2006-06-01 12:47:34
  Ctime    : 2006-06-01 10:57:21        , 2006-06-01 12:47:34

Directory: /bin
  Mtime    : 2006-03-21 00:18:37        , 2006-06-01 12:49:18
  Ctime    : 2006-03-21 00:18:37        , 2006-06-01 12:49:18

File: /bin/date
```

```
Size      : 54684                              , 2003
Bcount    : 128                                , 16
Permissions: -rwxr-xr-x                        , -rws--x--x
Mtime     : 2006-02-11 01:43:13               , 2006-06-01 12:49:18
Ctime     : 2006-03-21 00:11:18               , 2006-06-01 12:49:32
Inode     : 1986165                            , 1977386
MD5       : sGkOBZz1ixmfifDWyS5PNw==          , RUhh+HqFShK4bABDxePEtw==
SHA1      : mY4z3oD64L+e36a7s2LQ32E4k+8=      , NAkwdOkIO5k8svWFerYN5k8C1tO=
```

 A copy of this report is automatically saved in */var/log/aide.log*.

In this case, AIDE has detected a change in */bin/date* and in */root/.lesshst* (the history for the less command). The change to *date* is of particular note because that is a commonly used program, and the new version is configured with the set-user-ID bit set, meaning that any user typing **date** will execute a program with superuser privileges.

Since some files are expected to change in specific ways, the qualities that AIDE checks for each file and directory are configurable. Table 8-6 summarizes the default configuration.

Table 8-6. Default AIDE fingerprint configuration

Pathnames	Fingerprint qualities
/boot /bin /sbin /lib /opt /usr /root /etc/exports /etc/fstab /etc/passwd /etc/group /etc/gshadow /etc/shadow	Permissions inode number Number of links User Group Size Time of last modification Time of creation or last inode modification Block count MD5 checksum SHA1 checksum
All other files in /etc (except /etc/mtab, which is not checked)	Permissions inode number User Group
/var/log	Permissions Number of links User Group

AIDE is configured using the text file *etc/aide.conf*; the default contents of this file are:

```
# Sample configuration file for AIDE.

@@define DBDIR /var/lib/aide

# The location of the database to be read
database=file:@@{DBDIR}/aide.db.gz

# The location of the database to be written
#database_out=sql:host:port:database:login_name:passwd:table
#database_out=file:aide.db.new
database_out=file:@@{DBDIR}/aide.db.new.gz

# Whether to gzip the output to database
gzip_dbout=yes

# Default
verbose=5

report_url=file:/var/log/aide.log
report_url=stdout
#report_url=stderr
#NOT IMPLEMENTED report_url=mailto:root@foo.com
#NOT IMPLEMENTED report_url=syslog:LOG_AUTH

# These are the default rules
#
#p:       permissions
#i:       inode:
#n:       number of links
#u:       user
#g:       group
#s:       size
#b:       block count
#m:       mtime
#a:       atime
#c:       ctime
#S:       check for growing size
#md5:     md5 checksum
#sha1:    sha1 checksum
#rmd160:  rmd160 checksum
#tiger:   tiger checksum
#haval:   haval checksum
#gost:    gost checksum
#crc32:   crc32 checksum
#R:       p+i+n+u+g+s+m+c+md5
#L:       p+i+n+u+g
#E:       Empty group
#>:       Growing logfile p+u+g+i+n+S

# You can create custom rules like this
```

```
NORMAL = R+b+sha1
DIR = p+i+n+u+g

# Next decide what directories/files you want in the database

/boot    NORMAL
/bin     NORMAL
/sbin    NORMAL
/lib     NORMAL
/opt     NORMAL
/usr     NORMAL
/root    NORMAL

# Check only permissions, inode, user and group for /etc, but
# cover some important files closely
/etc     p+i+u+g
!/etc/mtab
/etc/exports    NORMAL
/etc/fstab      NORMAL
/etc/passwd     NORMAL
/etc/group      NORMAL
/etc/gshadow    NORMAL
/etc/shadow     NORMAL

/var/log    p+n+u+g

# With AIDE's default verbosity level of 5, these would give lots of
# warnings upon tree traversal. It might change with future versions.
#
#=/lost\+found    DIR
#=/home          DIR
```

Most of this file consists of *selection lines*, which contain two fields. The first field is used to specify files to process or, if prepended with !, files to exclude from processing. This field is evaluated as a regular expression, so the pattern /lib will match any filename starting with /lib, including files such as /lib/lsb/init-functions.

 These regular expressions are treated as if they have ^ prepended (they match only at the start of filenames). To exactly match one filename, append $:

> /var/log/messages$ >

The $ prevents this selection line from matching the *logrotate* history files (such as */var/log/messages.1*).

The second field is a list of fingerprint qualities, drawn from the list included in the file as comments, separated with + characters. The values NORMAL and DIR are configured as group definitions, permitting easy reference to commonly used combinations of fingerprint qualities. In this case, NORMAL is defined as R+b+sha1, meaning the predefined fingerprint-qualities group R, block count, and SHA1 checksums. R in turn means permissions, inode number, number of links, user, group, size, modification time, creation/inode change time, and MD5 checksum.

To add additional files to be fingerprinted, append entries to this file. For example, to verify that your web pages have not changed, append:

```
/var/www/html    NORMAL
```

How Does It Work?

AIDE works by recording the fingerprint qualities in its database file as plain text (though the file is normally compressed using *gzip*). Here is a sample of a fingerprint database:

```
@@begin_db
# This file was generated by Aide, version 0.11
# Time of generation was 2006-06-01 10:57:23
@@db_spec name lname attr perm bcount uid gid size mtime ctime inode lcount md5 sha1
/etc 0 541 40755 0 0 0 0 0 713153 0 0 0
/sbin 0 4029 40755 32 0 0 12288 MTEOMjkxODMyMg== MTEOMjkxODMyMg== 1880129 2 0 0
/root 0 4029 40750 16 0 0 4096 MTEOOTE2OTg2NQ== MTEOOTE2OTg2NQ== 1296641 8 0 0
/usr 0 4029 40755 16 0 0 4096 MTEOMjg5MjIzOA== MTEOMjg5MjIzOA== 1782881 14 0 0
...(Lines snipped)...
/boot/grub/grub.conf 0 16317 100600 4 0 0 599 MTEOMjg5NTcwNw== MTEOMjg5NTcwNw== 2011
1 zvjoV7HEEv/lHBdWPRNK9g== xJ2OrD9u9dqn9n3M2y/iKgxzoHk=
/boot/grub/reiserfs_stage1_5 0 16317 100644 20 0 0 9056 MTEOMjg5NTcwOA==
MTEOMjg5NTcwOA== 2022 1 3QMuqfoxpKu/nMsBGE554Q== 6fWY3Yrk7M4+aWOvoaqzOIxyQY8=
/boot/grub/jfs_stage1_5 0 16317 100644 18 0 0 8032 MTEOMjg5NTcwOA== MTEOMjg5NTcwOA==
2020 1 6favoJt1WCIN/dnckuHbfQ== aIlm2nFM9bVJSaE/rwLYehLgpRQ=
@@end_db
```

When run with the -C option, *aide* simply calculates a new fingerprint and compares the value with the old fingerprint, reporting any discrepancies.

What About...

...an intruder altering the fingerprint database?

This is a very real possibility. To guard against this, the fingerprint database should be recorded on read-only media (such as a CD-R), stored on a different system, or stored on removable media that the system administrator can secure against alteration.

...automating AIDE scans?

To automate daily AIDE scans, create the file */etc/cron.daily/50aide* with these contents:

```
#!/bin/bash

/usr/sbin/aide --check 2>&1|mail -s "AIDE scan results" root
```

Make the file executable by *root*:

```
# chown root /etc/cron.daily/50aide
# chmod u+rx /etc/cron.daily/50aide
```

An AIDE scan will then be performed daily, and the results will be mailed to *root* on the local system (or the user who receives *root* mail, as defined in */etc/aliases*).

Where Can I Learn More?

- The manpages for *aide* and *aide.conf*
- The AIDE online manual: *http://www.cs.tut.fi/~rammer/aide/manual.html*

CHAPTER 9
The Fedora Community

Despite the fact that it is supported and heavily financed by Red Hat, Fedora is truly a community project with a global scope. Effectively participating in that community is an important part of using Fedora.

9.1   Participating in the Fedora Mailing Lists

Red Hat runs a large number of mailing lists for Fedora, which are the communication lifeblood of the Fedora projects and are the starting point for communicating with and becoming involved in the Fedora community.

How Do I Do That?

The Red Hat mailing lists are accessed through the web page *http://www.redhat.com/ mailman/listinfo*; the Fedora lists have names starting with "fedora-". Clicking on a list title will take you to a page where you can join the list or view archives of previous messages sent to the list.

The list archives are useful in two ways:

- You can get a sense of the scope of discussion on the list and the volume of messages.
- If you have a specific issue you wish to discuss, you can see any discussion that has already transpired on that same topic.

Once you find a list that looks interesting to you, sign up by entering your email address, name, and password (twice), and then select digest or individual emails and click Subscribe.

 Consider using a disposable email address for your subscription because this address will be made public and will probably eventually receive some spam. See Lab 7.6, "Configuring the sendmail Server."

Receiving messages in digest form reduces the volume of email to one or two large messages a day; the nondigested form will pepper your mailbox with many small messages but will make it is easier to respond to one specific message.

 Even though Fedora is used internationally, the Fedora mailing lists are in English, which serves as the lingua franca of the open source community. The exceptions are the lists used by translation projects, which are usually in the target language.

Your subscription request will generate an email like this one:

```
Mailing list subscription confirmation notice for mailing list
fedora-devel-list

We have received a request for subscription of your email address,
"chris@fedorabook.com", to the fedora-devel-list@redhat.com mailing
list.
To confirm that you want to be added to this mailing list, simply
reply to this message, keeping the Subject: header intact. Or visit
this web page:

 https://www.redhat.com/mailman/confirm/fedora-devel-list/f1a901557

Or include the following line -- and only the following line -- in a
message to fedora-devel-list-request@redhat.com:

 confirm f1a901557

Note that simply sending a `reply' to this message should work from
most mail readers, since that usually leaves the Subject: line in the
right form (additional "Re:" text in the Subject: is okay).

If you do not wish to be subscribed to this list, please simply
disregard this message. If you think you are being maliciously
subscribed to the list, or have any other questions, send them to
fedora-devel-list-owner@redhat.com.
```

To confirm the subscription, click on the link or send a reply email without editing the subject line. You'll receive a confirmation email:

```
Welcome to the fedora-devel-list@redhat.com mailing list!

To post to this list, send your email to:

 fedora-devel-list@redhat.com

General information about the mailing list is at:

 https://www.redhat.com/mailman/listinfo/fedora-devel-list
```

```
If you ever want to unsubscribe or change your options (eg, switch to
or from digest mode, change your password, etc.), visit your
subscription page at:

 https://www.redhat.com/mailman/options/fedora-devel-list
      /chris%40fedorabook.com

You can also make such adjustments via email by sending a message to:

 fedora-devel-list-request@redhat.com

with the word `help' in the subject or body (don't include the
quotes), and you will get back a message with instructions.

You must know your password to change your options (including changing
the password, itself) or to unsubscribe. It is:

 superSecret

Normally, Mailman will remind you of your redhat.com mailing list
passwords once every month, although you can disable this if you
prefer. This reminder will also include instructions on how to
unsubscribe or change your account options. There is also a button on
your options page that will email your current password to you.
```

Keep this email! To unsubscribe or change your digest option, go to the link contained in this message and enter your chosen password.

Posting on the mailing list

When posting messages on the mailing list, you must send from the same address that you used to subscribe to the list, or your message will be rejected.

Since your message will be read by hundreds or even thousands of people around the world, succinct, detailed, and informative messages are highly regarded, and off-topic and time-wasting messages are disparaged. This doesn't mean that you have to be an expert to post; most lists welcome messages from community members of all skill levels. Since most list members will only ever know you by your writing, the quality of that writing plays a key role in establishing your reputation within the community.

Start your message with a clear subject line (remember that your messages are being archived by topic). "ACPI problem with Kernel 2.6.43" is a good title; "Power problem" is too vague, and "Please help!" is completely uninformative.

The body of your message should contain a concise comment, suggestion, request for help, or announcement. Write in plain text; avoid the use of HTML, which bloats the message, since that bloat will be multiplied by the hundreds or thousands of inboxes in which your message will take residence. Tiny code fragments or extracts from logfiles or configuration files that illuminate the discussion should be included; long portions of code, screenshots, logfiles, complete configuration files, or sample data should be posted on the Web with a link to them included in your message.

Be sure to review any logfiles, configuration files, or screenshots for confidential information before posting them publicly.

When replying to a previous posting in nondigest mode, leave enough of the previous poster's comments as a quotation so that the reader will know what you're replying to. Place your reply at the *end* of the quoted text:

```
Mary Eleanor wrote:
> When I change the hostname, I can't open
> new windows on the GUI display. Does anyone
> know what causes this?

It's due to the fact that the new hostname breaks
the cross-reference to authorization information
("magic cookies") in the ~/.Xauthority file. Before
you change the hostname, execute this command:

    xhost +localhost

That will turn off authorization checking for
GUI programs on the same computer as the display.
```

Signature blocks are welcome, but should not exceed four lines in total; one or two lines is ideal. Bear in mind that any information you post will be permanently and publicly archived, so think carefully about any personal information (phone numbers, place of employment, instant messaging IDs) revealed in your signature block.

If you are replying to a message that is part of a digest, it is important to edit your reply so that the subject line relates to the message to which you are replying and not to the entire digest. For example, here is the first part of a digest message on the *fedora-devel-list*:

```
From:       fedora-devel-list-request@redhat.com
Reply-to:   fedora-devel-list@redhat.com
To:         fedora-devel-list@redhat.com
Subject:    fedora-devel-list Digest, Vol 20, Issue 40
Date:       Thu, 27 Oct 2005 08:38:38 -0400 (EDT)

Send fedora-devel-list mailing list submissions to
   fedora-devel-list@redhat.com

To subscribe or unsubscribe via the World Wide Web, visit
   https://www.redhat.com/mailman/listinfo/fedora-devel-list
or, via email, send a message with subject or body 'help' to
   fedora-devel-list-request@redhat.com

You can reach the person managing the list at
   fedora-devel-list-owner@redhat.com

When replying, please edit your Subject line so it is more specific
than "Re: Contents of fedora-devel-list digest..."
```

```
Today's Topics:

    1. Re: Problems installing rawhide and reporting thereof
    2. Re: Problems installing rawhide and reporting thereof
    3. Re: Problems installing rawhide and reporting thereof
    4. Re: Problems installing rawhide and reporting thereof
    5. Re: Encouraging the use of multiple packaging systems on one
         systems, and the resulting problems
    6. initrd stage: CAP_SYS_RAWIO on /dev/iscsictl fails . help
    7. Re: rawhide report: 20051025 changes
    8. Re: initrd stage: CAP_SYS_RAWIO on /dev/iscsictl fails . help
    9. rawhide report: 20051027 changes (Build System)
   10. UTF-8 & imap folder name handling
```

If you reply to the digest, the subject line will read "Re: fedora-devel-list Digest, Vol 20, Issue 40." Change this to the subject of the particular posting to which you are replying; for example, if you are replying to message 10, set the subject to "Re: UTF-8 & imap folder name handling."

You'll also have to do some editing to include only some quoted text from the original message (ideally including the poster's name) and no text from the other postings in the digest.

How Does It Work?

The Fedora lists are managed by Mailman (the GNU mailing-list manager software), which in turn is available as part of Fedora Core.

Mailing lists are used for communication because they are easy to use, asynchronous (users don't have to be logged in at the same time, which is important when crossing time zones), and not very bandwidth-intensive. They are also very flexible on the client side, providing access from a wide range of software and network configurations.

What About...

...posting to a mailing list when a disposable email address is used to subscribe to the list?

You will need to create an email account configuration that lets you post *from* the alias address. This requires an email client that can handle multiple sending accounts.

To use the Evolution client to send email from a disposable address, add a new account under Edit → Preference with your name and the disposable email address, a receiving server type of None, and a sending server type of Sendmail. When sending a message to the list, select the disposable email address from the pull-down list labeled From in the mail composition window.

...subscribing to a Fedora list in nondigest mode without having the list messages cluttering up my email inbox?

Use your email client's filtering capabilities to move all of the list-related email to a separate mailbox. This will make it easy to scan the subject lines of the list postings and reply to individual messages without touching your main mailbox.

To configure this using Evolution, select the menu option Tools → Filter and create a new rule: if the message's sender contains the name of your list (such as *fedora-devel-list*), then move the message to a folder that you have created (such as *fedora-devel*).

Where Can I Learn More?

- The Fedora Project communication page can be found at *http://fedoraproject.org/wiki/Communicate*
- The Red Hat mailing lists: *http://www.redhat.com/mailman/listinfo*
- The Fedora mailing-list guidelines are located at *http://fedoraproject.org/wiki/MailinglistGuidelines*
- The Mailman web page: *http://www.list.org*
- The Mailman documentation in */usr/share/doc/mailman**

9.2   Using IRC

Internet Relay Chat (IRC) is a network-based, multiserver chat/instant message system. While mailing lists provide asynchronous communication, IRC provides almost-immediate, synchronous communication. You can use it to participate in online planning meetings, discuss development, or exchange support advice.

How Do I Do That?

There are many different IRC client programs available.

To use the IRC client XChat, select the menu option Applications → Internet → IRC, or run the command *xchat*. The window shown in Figure 9-1 will appear.

XChat will propose a first, second, and third nickname based on the username and actual name (GECOS field) of the account you're using. Edit these values if desired, select the FreeNode network, and click Connect. Figure 9-2 shows the main XChat window and introductory message that will appear.

To join a specific channel, select the menu option Window → Channel List. When the channel-list window shown in Figure 9-3 appears, enter *fedora* into the Regex Match field and click Apply. Select the channel you wish to join from the list and click Join Channel.

Figure 9-1. XChat server-list window

The main XChat window will now show a list of users down the right side and a tab containing your selected channel at the bottom of the screen, as in Figure 9-4. In some cases, the server will redirect you to an alternate channel such as *fedora-join-instructions* to assist you with registering or authenticating.

If you have never connected to the FreeNode network with your selected nickname, enter this command in the field at the bottom of the XChat window:

```
/msg nickserv register yourSecretPassword
```

This will send a private message to the *nickserv* program to register your nickname with the specified password.

 Don't use your system password for IRC because it could be read by a third party. Create a separate password exclusively for use with IRC.

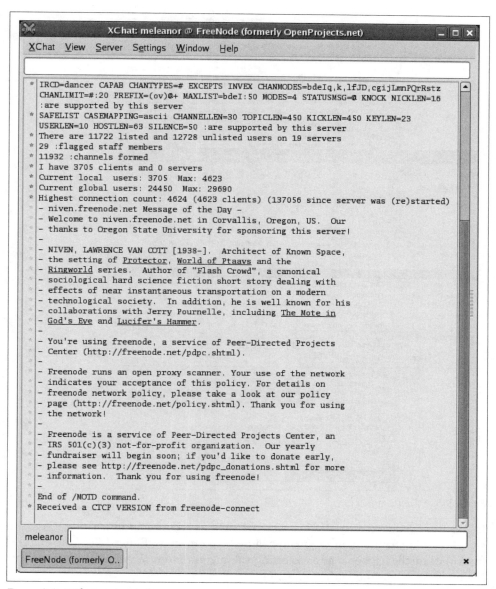

```
*   IRCD=dancer CAPAB CHANTYPES=# EXCEPTS INVEX CHANMODES=bdeIq,k,lfJD,cgijLmnPQrRstz
    CHANLIMIT=#:20 PREFIX=(ov)@+ MAXLIST=bdeI:50 MODES=4 STATUSMSG=@ KNOCK NICKLEN=16
    :are supported by this server
*   SAFELIST CASEMAPPING=ascii CHANNELLEN=30 TOPICLEN=450 KICKLEN=450 KEYLEN=23
    USERLEN=10 HOSTLEN=63 SILENCE=50 :are supported by this server
*   There are 11722 listed and 12728 unlisted users on 19 servers
*   29 :flagged staff members
*   11932 :channels formed
*   I have 3705 clients and 0 servers
*   Current local  users: 3705  Max: 4623
*   Current global users: 24450  Max: 29690
*   Highest connection count: 4624 (4623 clients) (137056 since server was (re)started)
-   niven.freenode.net Message of the Day -
-   Welcome to niven.freenode.net in Corvallis, Oregon, US.  Our
-   thanks to Oregon State University for sponsoring this server!
-
-   NIVEN, LAWRENCE VAN COTT [1938-].  Architect of Known Space,
-   the setting of Protector, World of Ptaavs and the
-   Ringworld series.  Author of "Flash Crowd", a canonical
-   sociological hard science fiction short story dealing with
-   effects of near instantaneous transportation on a modern
-   technological society.  In addition, he is well known for his
-   collaborations with Jerry Pournelle, including The Mote in
-   God's Eye and Lucifer's Hammer.
-
-   You're using freenode, a service of Peer-Directed Projects
-   Center (http://freenode.net/pdpc.shtml).
-
-   Freenode runs an open proxy scanner. Your use of the network
-   indicates your acceptance of this policy. For details on
-   freenode network policy, please take a look at our policy
-   page (http://freenode.net/policy.shtml). Thank you for using
-   the network!
-
-   Freenode is a service of Peer-Directed Projects Center, an
-   IRS 501(c)(3) not-for-profit organization.  Our yearly
-   fundraiser will begin soon; if you'd like to donate early,
-   please see http://freenode.net/pdpc_donations.shtml for more
-   information.  Thank you for using freenode!
-
    End of /MOTD command.
*   Received a CTCP VERSION from freenode-connect
```

meleanor |

FreeNode (formerly O..   ✕

Figure 9-2. XChat main window

If you're visiting the FreeNode network with a nickname that you have already registered, authenticate to *nickserv* by typing:

```
/msg nickserv identify yourSecretPassword
```

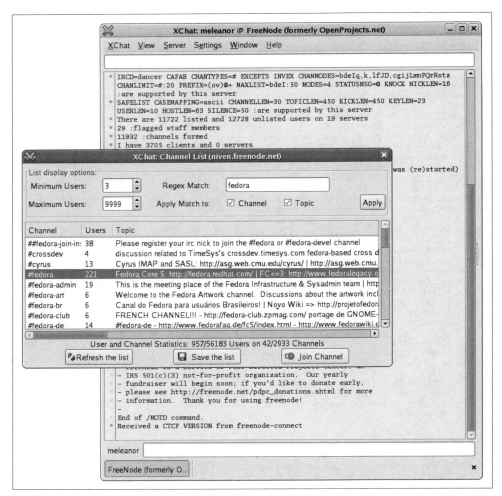

Figure 9-3. XChat channel list

If you were redirected to another channel such as *fedora-join-instructions*, you can switch to the channel you originally wanted to join now. Either select the channel from the list that appears after selecting the menu option Window → Channel List (Figure 9-3), or use the /join command:

/join #fedora

You can now view messages in the large pane of the XChat window or enter messages in the text field at the bottom of the window. To find out about a specific user, right-click on that username and select the name from the pop-up list that will appear. XChat will display basic information about that user.

To send a private message to another user, use the /msg command:

/msg susan Have you installed FC6 on your new laptop yet?

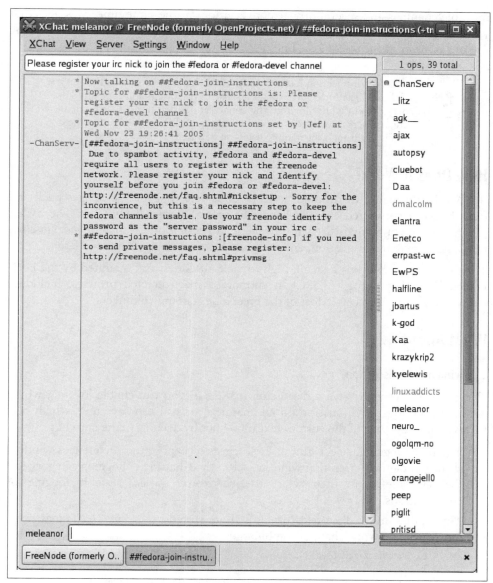

Figure 9-4. XChat connected to a channel

In the message pane, when on a public channel, outbound private messages are identified by angle-brackets pointing at the username:

```
>olgovie< | I don't think that will work.
```

When other users send a private message to you, that message will appear in a separate tab at the bottom of the screen. The label text on a tab will turn red if there are unread messages on that tab, providing you with an easy way of monitoring multiple channels and several private conversations at the same time. Messages that you enter while a private tab is active are automatically private, even without the use of /msg *user* at the start of the line.

 IRC communication has a unique flavor. It's a good idea to lurk on a channel for a little while to get a sense of the discussion tone and key players before jumping into the conversation. Because IRC is immediate, answers to questions may not be as carefully reasoned out as those received through the mailing lists—so beware!

How Does It Work?

IRC works through a distributed network of servers that relay messages back and forth between connected clients—hence the name *Internet Relay Chat*. The XChat program is one of many IRC clients available in Fedora; others include *mozilla-chat*, EPIC, Irssi, *ninja*, Konversation, and the multiprotocol clients Gaim and *naim*.

The FreeNode network is a small, high-capacity IRC network operated by the Peer-Directed Projects Center (PDPC) in support of peer-directed projects, including many open source projects. Most of the FreeNode staff are volunteers.

What About...

...saving an IRC discussion?

There are two ways to save a discussion in XChat: you can enable logging, which automatically logs all discussion on all channels, or you can save text, which performs a one-time save of the current text (300 lines by default) in the current topic:

- To enable logging, select Edit → Preferences to expose the preferences window shown in Figure 9-5. In that window, select the Chatting → Logging category (on the left side), and then select the checkbox labeled "Enable logging of conversations."

  The logfiles are in plain-text format and are stored in *~/.xchat2/xchatlogs*, with one log per network/channel combination:

  ```
  $ cd ~/.xchat2/xchatlogs
  $ ls
  FreeNode (formerly OpenProjects.net)-##fedora-join-instructions.log
  FreeNode (formerly OpenProjects.net)-#fedora.log
  FreeNode (formerly OpenProjects.net)-freenode (formerly openprojects.net).log
  ```

- To save the current text in the current channel, use the menu option Window → Save Text.

 Since each log filename contains special characters and spaces, you will need to quote the filename when using it in a command:

```
$ grep ctyler "FreeNode (formerly OpenProjects.net)-#fedora.log"
```

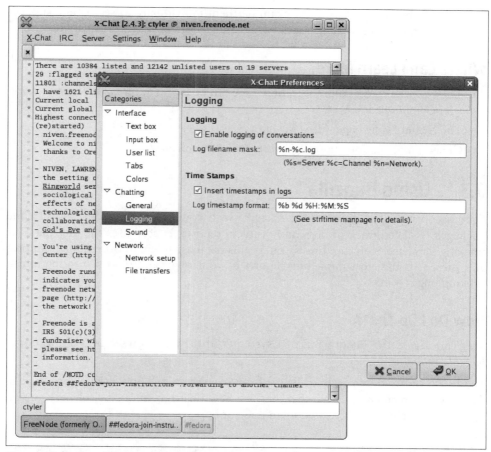

Figure 9-5. XChat preferences window

…other ways of accessing IRC?

From time to time, you may want to connect to IRC from a computer that does not have an IRC client when you don't have administrative permission to install one—at a friend's house or a library, for example.

The ChatZilla extension to Firefox offers a chat client that runs within the Firefox browser. Since some systems permit users to install extensions without superuser privilege, you may be able to use this approach. Within Firefox, select Tools → Extensions to bring up the Extensions window, and then click the Get More Extensions link in the corner of that window to go to the Firefox Extensions web site. Browse to or search to find the ChatZilla extension, the click the Install Now button. Confirm the installation on the dialog that appears; when the extension has finished installing, restart Firefox, then click Tools → ChatZilla.

The other option is to use a *webchat* client through your web browser. Web sites offering webchat clients come and go; a few minutes of searching with Google will find several, but you will need to examine them individually to see if they support connecting to the FreeNode network (where the Fedora channels are hosted).

Where Can I Learn More?

- The Fedora Project communication page can be found at *http://fedoraproject.org/ wiki/Communicate*
- The XChat home page: *http://xchat.org/*
- General information about IRC: *http://www.irchelp.org/*

9.3   Using Bugzilla

Fedora consists of thousands of packages, with complex interactions between the packages. To keep track of bugs and problem reports, Fedora uses the Bugzilla bug-tracking database. You can directly query this database to get information about past and present issues, to submit bug reports of your own, and to add information to existing bug reports.

How Do I Do That?

You can access the Fedora Bugzilla system with a web browser by visiting *http:// bugzilla.redhat.com*.

Figure 9-6 shows the main Bugzilla page, on which you will find a Quick Seach field. There, you can enter a bug number that you have heard mentioned elsewhere, or you can enter some keywords related to an issue or bug.

Figure 9-6. Bugzilla main page

In the Bugzilla system, the word *bug* is used loosely; any issue, patch, enhancement request, or trouble report is called a bug.

The Query tab provides a more precise way of searching, as shown in Figure 9-7. Using that interface, you can narrow your search to a specific package in a particular version of Fedora Core or Fedora Extras. For options that are even more detailed, click on the Advanced tab.

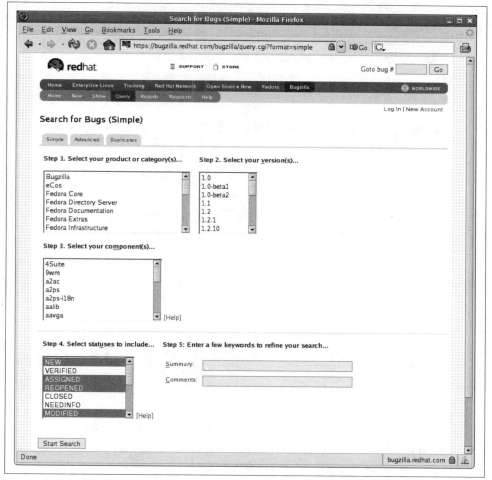

Figure 9-7. Bugzilla query page

Your query will yield a list of matching bugs with their summaries, as shown in Figure 9-8. Clicking on a bug number will display a detailed description of the bug, as in Figure 9-9. The description includes the product, version, and package information, plus a detailed text description of the bug. Additional comments may be added by the originator of the report, the maintainer of the package in question, or any other registered user of Bugzilla.

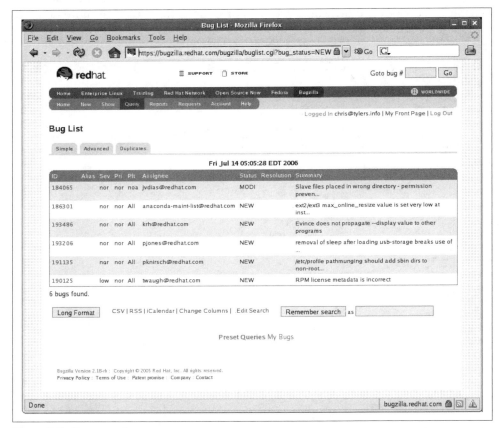

Figure 9-8. Query results

 If your query produces no matches, Bugzilla will helpfully inform you that "Zarro boogs" were found.

Creating a Bugzilla account

In order to add to the comments on existing bugs or to report new bugs, you must have a Bugzilla account. To create an account, click the New Account link in the

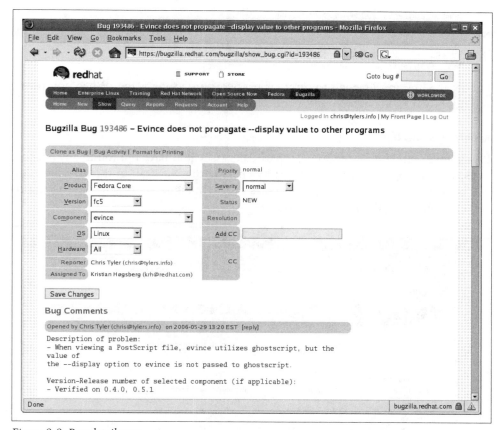

Figure 9-9. Bug detail page

upper-right corner of the page, and then enter your email address and your full name.

You may want to use a disposable email address because the address will be made public (see Lab 7.6, "Configuring the sendmail Server," for more on disposable email addresses).

Bugzilla will send you an email containing a temporary password:

```
From:     bugzilla@redhat.com
To:       jdoe@fedorabook.com
Subject:  Your Bugzilla password.
Date:     Fri, 14 Jul 2006 05:37:36 -0400

To use the wonders of Bugzilla, you can use the following:
```

```
E-mail address: jdoe@fedorabook.com
      Password: J8sCuid79D
```

```
To change your password, go to:
https://bugzilla.redhat.com/bugzilla/userprefs.cgi
```

Follow the link in the email to set your password to a sane value. When you revisit Bugzilla, you can log in to your account using your email address and password.

Reporting a new bug

If you have searched for reports of a particular issue and have not found any existing bugs, you can open a new bug report by clicking the New tab in the gray bar. You will be presented with a list of products, as shown in Figure 9-10; select the appropriate one from the Fedora portion of the list.

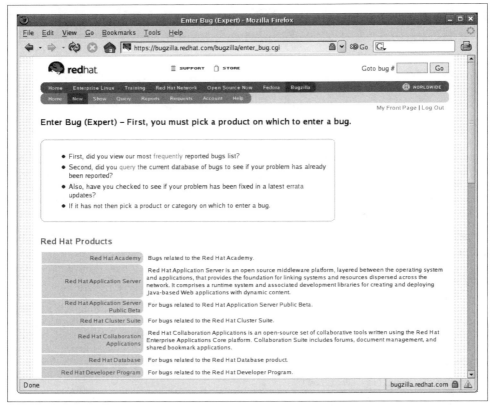

Figure 9-10. Bugzilla product list

Bugzilla will then present you with the main bug-entry form, as shown in Figure 9-11. Select the product version that you are using, and then select the component (package).

Figure 9-11. Bugzilla new bug-detail form

If the package you want is not in the component list, you may have selected the wrong product—for example, you may have selected Fedora Core for a package that is actually in Fedora Extras. Use the Back button on your browser to return to the product list and try another product.

Select a platform and severity (the default is usually correct for both), and then enter a summary (title) for the bug. Choose one that succinctly describes the bug.

Now enter the bug Description. Use as many of the preplaced headings as possible ("Description of problem," "How reproducable," "Steps to reproduce," "Expected results," "Actual results"). Ideally you should provide clear, step-by-step instructions that will reliably provoke symptoms that demonstrate the bug, as well as any relevant details about your system and use context.

You also have the options of attaching a file (such as a configuration file or logfile) and marking the bug as a security-sensitive bug, which is not posted publicly.

Click on Submit to file the bug report. You will be given a Bugzilla bug number that will enable you to rapidly find the bug for follow-up in the future.

Each bug has a status that is initially set to New. This status will change as the bug is reviewed, assigned, commented upon, and eventually resolved. Each time a comment is added or the status changes, you will receive an email.

How Does It Work?

Bugzilla was written by the Mozilla project to track bugs in the Mozilla browser and related software. It has since been adopted (and adapted) by a number of other open source projects, including the GNOME and KDE desktops. It's written in Perl, uses Apache for the web server, and can be used with either a MySQL or PostgreSQL database for bug storage and tracking.

What About...

...receiving less (or more) email from Bugzilla?

If you log in to Bugzilla and select the Account tab, you will see a preferences screen (which in turn has an E-mail tab). In that page, you will find controls that let you fine-tune the circumstances under which Bugzilla will send you email.

...a bug that's not really a bug?

You can add a comment to an existing bug that you have created and change its status. For example, if you find out that a bug that you reported is actually correct behavior, you can close the bug as resolved, setting the resolution indicator to NOTABUG. In your comment, you can explain the reason for the status change.

...a bug due to problems in the upstream code?

Since Fedora is a *distribution*, most of the code comes from other projects (such as GNOME, Apache, and OpenOffice.org). In many cases, the resolution of a bug will really be the responsibility of the upstream project.

If you know that a particular problem is due to a code defect or issue with the underlying program code, rather than Fedora's packaging of that code or the interaction of that code with other Fedora packages, it is a good idea to register the bug in that project's Bugzilla database and add a cross-reference to the Fedora bug record. To facilitate this, there is a control labeled External Bug References on the Bugzilla entry screen; select the upstream Bugzilla system from the pull-down list and enter the bug number from that system.

...referring to a Bugzilla bug on the mailing lists or in IRC?

By convention, numbers prefixed with "BZ" are interpreted as Bugzilla numbers.

Where Can I Learn More?

- The Fedora Bugzilla Reporting Guidelines: *http://fedoraproject.org/wiki/BugsAndFeatureRequests*
- The Red Hat Bugzilla help page: *https://bugzilla.redhat.com/bugzilla/page.cgi?id=redhatfaq.html*
- The home page of the Bugzilla project: *http://www.bugzilla.org/*

9.4   Running Rawhide

If you're interested in seeing the evolving future shape of Fedora Core and assisting with testing, you can run Rawhide, the constantly changing development version of Fedora Core.

How Do I Do That?

First, a warning is in order. As the original Rawhide announcement noted:

> Raw Hide Can Be a Bit Tough to Chew on So Run at Your Own Risk (and Enjoyment)
>
> These releases have not been quality tested by Red Hat's Quality Assurance team. They may not boot. If they boot, they may not install. If they install, they may not do anything other then waste CPU cycles. If anything breaks, you most assuredly own the many fragments which will be littered across your floor.
>
> It may not be possible to upgrade from Fedora Core to Raw Hide, from Raw Hide to Fedora Core, or from Raw Hide to Raw Hide! If a stable upgrade path is important to you, please do not use Raw Hide.
>
> DO NOT USE THESE RELEASES FOR ANY WORK WHERE YOU CARE ABOUT YOUR APPLICATION RUNNING, THE ACCURACY OF YOUR DATA, THE INTEGRITY OF YOUR NETWORK, OR ANY OTHER PURPOSE FOR WHICH A RESPONSIBLE HUMAN WOULD USE A COMPUTER. (But then again what would be the fun of hacking Linux if there wasn't some risk involved. ;-)....)

In other words, you should run Rawhide only on a secondary computer dedicated to testing because it's far from stable.

Most Rawhide systems are updated daily. The nature of the development process ensures that features will break one day and then start working again a few days later. Menu options will shift around, and from time to time, your system will not boot normally. You may be frustrated, but you'll never be bored when running Rawhide!

There are two ways to install Rawhide: by upgrading from a released version of Fedora Core, or by installing Rawhide directly.

Updating Fedora Core to Rawhide

Rawhide is really just a *yum* repository of development packages. The repository information is distributed with Fedora Core but is disabled.

Edit the file */etc/yum.repos.d/fedora-development.repo* to enable the *development* repository by editing the first enabled line under [development] (highlighted in bold here) to read enabled=1:

```
# These packages are untested and still under development. This
# repository is used for updates to test releases, and for
# development of new releases.
#
# This repository can see significant daily turnover and major
# functionality changes which cause unexpected problems with other
# development packages. Please use these packages if you want to work
# with the Fedora developers by testing these new development packages.
#
# fedora-test-list@redhat.com is available as a discussion forum for
# testing and troubleshooting for development packages in conjunction
# with new test releases.
#
# fedora-devel-list@redhat.com is available as a discussion forum for
# testing and troubleshooting for development packages in conjunction
# with developing new releases.
#
# More information is available at http://fedoraproject.org/wiki/Testing
#
# Reproducible and reportable issues should be filed at
# http://bugzilla.redhat.com/.
#
# Product: Fedora Core
# Version: devel

[development]
name=Fedora Core - Development
#baseurl=http://download.fedora.redhat.com/pub/fedora/linux/core/development/
$basearch/
mirrorlist=http://fedora.redhat.com/Download/mirrors/fedora-core-rawhide
enabled=1
gpgcheck=0

[development-debuginfo]
name=Fedora Core - Development - Debug
#baseurl=http://download.fedora.redhat.com/pub/fedora/linux/core/development/
$basearch/debug/
mirrorlist=http://fedora.redhat.com/Download/mirrors/fedora-core-rawhide-debug
enabled=0
gpgcheck=0

[development-source]
name=Fedora Core - Development - Source
#baseurl=http://download.fedora.redhat.com/pub/fedora/linux/core/development/SRPMS/
mirrorlist=http://fedora.redhat.com/Download/mirrors/fedora-core-rawhide-source
enabled=0
gpgcheck=0
```

You can optionally enable the *development-debuginfo* and *development-source* repositories as well, by setting enabled=1 there as well.

Next, disable all of the other repositories by setting enabled=0 in their respective */etc/yum.repos.d/*.repo* files. When you're done, enter these commands to confirm that only the development repositories are enabled:

```
# cd /etc/yum.repos.d
# grep enabled *.repo | grep 1
fedora-development.repo:enabled=1
```

If you see other repository files listed, edit those files to disable the additional repositories.

Once you have set up the repositories, use *yum* to perform an update:

```
# yum update
Setting up Update Process
Setting up repositories
development                    100% |=========================| 1.1 kB    00:00
Reading repository metadata in from local files
Resolving Dependencies
--> Populating transaction set with selected packages. Please wait.
---> Downloading header for newt-perl to pack into transaction set.
newt-perl-1.08-9.2.2.i386 100% |=========================| 9.2 kB    00:00
---> Package newt-perl.i386 0:1.08-9.2.2 set to be updated
---> Downloading header for words to pack into transaction set.
words-3.0-8.1.1.noarch.rp 100% |=========================| 4.0 kB    00:00
...(Lines snipped)...
```

Once you have completed the update, reboot the system. Update the system frequently (daily updates are recommended) by rerunning yum update.

Installing Rawhide directly

Rawhide can also be directly installed using the Fedora network installation method.

Using a browser, select a nearby Fedora mirror server from the list at *http://fedora.redhat.com/Download/mirrors.html* and verify that it contains the *os/development* directory for your architecture (not all mirrors carry Rawhide) and that the development tree is reasonably up-to-date (i.e., that some of the files in the *os/Fedora/RPMS* directory are timestamped within the last 48 hours).

From the *images* directory on the mirror, download the *boot.iso* file and burn it to a CD or DVD, or download the *diskboot.img* file and copy it to a USB flash drive (see Lab 10.3, "Preparing Alternate Installation Media").

Boot the target system from this disc or USB flash drive and perform a normal HTTP or FTP installation from the mirror that you selected (see Chapter 1).

When installed in this way, the development repository is automatically enabled. Use *yum* to update the system periodically—usually on a daily basis:

```
# yum update
```

It's not uncommon to see the *yum* update fail due to dependency issues. Usually the issues will be solved by the next Rawhide update, and the *yum* command will succeed the next day. It's recommended that you run *yum* manually rather than using the *yum* daily update service so that you can see the error messages explaining any conflicts.

It's a good idea to periodically reinstall Rawhide from scratch to eliminate the "cruft" that accumulates with frequent unclean updates.

Creating a local Rawhide mirror

If you're using Rawhide heavily—testing it on several systems, for example—and you have a broadband Internet connection, it's worthwhile maintaining your own local development mirror.

The *rsync* tool provides a convenient method of mirroring the development repository. To use it, select an *rsync* URI from the mirror list at *http://fedora.redhat.com/ Download/mirrors.html*. Finding the correct directory within the *rsync* server may take a bit of experimentation because various mirror sites use different directory layouts. Use the *rsync* command to explore content on the mirror server:

```
$ rsync -v rsync://ftp.muug.mb.ca/
Welcome to MUUG Online Network Access, courtesy of the
Manitoba Unix User Group.

For any questions, problems, or concerns about this site,
please send e-mail to: <ftp@muug.mb.ca>.

Look under the /pub directory and subdirectories for files to download.

We are now also maintaining a mirror of selected sites (or a subset
thereof), in the /mirror directory.  Look at the README file there
for details on what is being mirrored.

ftp              MUUG Online FTP area (more Gigs than you want to download!)
pub              MUUG Online pub area (more Gigs than you want to download!)
mirror           Mirror of various sites (more Gigs than you want to download!)
redhat           ftp.redhat.com mirror (more Gigs than you want to download!)
redhat-contrib   ftp.redhat.com mirror, contrib directory
redhat-updates   updates.redhat.com mirror
fedora           fedora.redhat.com mirror, top-level directory
fedora-linux-core       fedora.redhat.com mirror, core directory
fedora-linux-core-updates        fedora.redhat.com mirror, updates directory
fedora-linux-core-development    fedora.redhat.com mirror, development directory
fedora-linux-core-test  fedora.redhat.com mirror, (beta) test directory
fedora-linux-extras     fedora.redhat.com mirror, extras directory
```

In this case, the introductory message indicates that *fedora-linux-core-development* contains the development tree. Use *rsync* again to view the contents of that directory:

```
$ rsync -v rsync://ftp.muug.mb.ca/fedora-linux-core-development/
Welcome to MUUG Online Network Access, courtesy of the
```

```
Manitoba Unix User Group.
...(Lines snipped)...

drwxrwsr-x       4096 2006/07/13 18:43:37 .
-rw-r--r--       3101 2003/11/04 12:23:24 README
drwxr-xr-x       4096 2006/07/13 15:21:37 i386
drwxrwsr-x       4096 2006/07/13 15:21:33 source

sent 117 bytes  received 544 bytes  440.67 bytes/sec
total size is 3101  speedup is 4.69
```

 Don't omit the final / on the *rsync* URI.

The *i386* directory is the one we're interested in (it looks like you'd have to use a different mirror for other architectures):

```
$ rsync -v rsync://ftp.muug.mb.ca/fedora-linux-core-development/i386/
Welcome to MUUG Online Network Access, courtesy of the
Manitoba Unix User Group.
...(Lines snipped)...

drwxr-xr-x       4096 2006/07/13 15:21:37 .
drwxr-xr-x      81920 2006/07/13 15:37:52 debug
drwxrwsr-x       4096 2006/07/12 08:09:49 iso
drwxrwsr-x       4096 2006/07/13 15:49:37 os

sent 123 bytes  received 530 bytes  145.11 bytes/sec
total size is 0  speedup is 0.00
```

The presence of the *debug*, *iso*, and *os* subdirectories indicates that this is the directory we're looking for.

Armed with that information, create a script, */usr/local/bin/rawhide-rsync*, on a stable (non-Rawhide) system with 10 GB or more free storage space:

```
#!/bin/bash
#
# rawhide-rsync :: script to mirror the Fedora rawhide repo locally
#

MAILTO=alert                        # Person/alias to receive reports
DIR=/var/www/html/rawhide           # Mirror directory
URI=rsync://mirrorhost/directory/   # Rsync URI

if tty -s             # If being run interactively, show progress
then
        XCMD='tee /dev/tty'
else
        XCMD='cat'
fi
```

```
(
  cd $DIR || exit 2 # Abort if the cd fails (important!)

  rsync --recursive --delete -v $URI . 2>&1

  echo
)|$XCMD|mail $MAILTO -s "Rawhide Rsync Report"
```

Ensure that *httpd* and *rsync* are installed on the target system, and create a directory to hold the development mirror (replace *user* with the name of the non-*root* user account that you will be using to run the *rawhide-repo* script):

```
# mkdir -p /var/www/html/rawhide/
# chown user /var/www/html/rawhide
# chmod a+rx /var/www/html/rawhide
```

Finally, run the script:

```
$ rawhide-rsync
Welcome to MUUG Online Network Access, courtesy of the
Manitoba Unix User Group.

For any questions, problems, or concerns about this site,
please send e-mail to: <ftp@muug.mb.ca>.

Look under the /pub directory and subdirectories for files to download.

We are now also maintaining a mirror of selected sites (or a subset
thereof), in the /mirror directory.  Look at the README file there
for details on what is being mirrored.

receiving file list ... done
debug/ElectricFence-debuginfo-2.2.2-20.2.2.i386.rpm
debug/ElectricFence-debuginfo-2.2.2-20.2.i386.rpm
debug/GConf2-debuginfo-2.14.0-2.1.i386.rpm
...(Lines snipped)...
os/repodata/repoview/zsh-html-0-4.2.5-1.2.2.html
os/repodata/repoview/zulu-support.group.html

sent 15296418 bytes received 706808440 bytes 166633.17 bytes/sec
total size is 8112656832 speedup is 11.23
```

The server and the local *rsync* program will compare notes and modify the files and directories on the local system to match the server. The first time the script is run, it will transfer the entire repository, and the speedup value will be 1.0. In subsequent runs, the speedup value will indicate the amount of time saved over transferring the entire repository (the preceding example indicates that the transfer took $1/11.23$ of the time that a full transfer would take).

 There is a high rate of change in the development repository, and from time to time, most or all of the repository will be freshly rebuilt, resulting in very large transfers. If you have a transfer-limited or capped Internet account and run the *rawhide-rsync* script often, be careful that you don't accidentally exceed your transfer limits.

You can now automate the *rsync* process by adding a *crontab* entry. Using the non-root account that will be performing the mirroring, edit the *crontab*:

```
$ crontab -e
```

Modify the *crontab* file to start the *rawhide-rsync* script at a convenient time:

```
# Update the local rawhide repo
0 5 * * * /usr/local/bin/rawhide-rsync
```

The *rawhide-rsync* reports will be mailed to you on a daily basis.

 The *rawhide-rsync* reports are each over half a megabyte! Consider deleting them after reviewing the end of each report for errors.

To verify that the local mirror is accessible through HTTP, connect with a browser. For example, if the host containing the mirror were *bluesky*, you'd point your browser to *http://bluesky/rawhide*, on which you would see the *Fedora*, *iso*, and *image* directories.

Using a local Rawhide mirror

To install from a local Rawhide mirror, simply specify that mirror during the installation process.

To use the local mirror for *yum* updates, edit */etc/yum.repos.d* on the Rawhide system, commenting out the mirrorlist entry and adding a baseurl entry pointing to the local mirror:

```
[development]
name=Fedora Core - Development
#baseurl=http://download.fedora.redhat.com/pub/fedora/linux/core/development/
$basearch/

# This line is commented by the addition of # at the start
# of the line, which disables the use of repositories on the standard
# mirrorlist
#mirrorlist=http://fedora.redhat.com/Download/mirrors/fedora-core-rawhide

# This line directs yum to the local mirror
baseurl=http://bluesky/fedora/os/

enabled=1
gpgcheck=0
```

Rawhide-related mailing lists

The *fedora-devel-list* and *fedora-test-list* discuss Rawhide-related developments and issues, and include automated reports describing changes that have been made to Rawhide packages.

How Does It Work?

Rawhide is a standard *yum* repository. Package maintainers submit package source to the Fedora build system, which builds the packages periodically and emails a report to the *fedora-devel-list* and *fedora-test-list*. The report looks like this:

```
Date:      Fri, 14 Jul 2006 09:28:29 -0400
From:      buildsys@redhat.com
Subject:   rawhide report: 20060714 changes
To:        fedora-devel-list@redhat.com, fedora-test-list@redhat.com
Message-ID: <200607141328.k6EDSTJ5031177@hs20-bc2-6.build.redhat.com>

New package xorg-x11-drv-amd
  Xorg X11 AMD Geode video driver


Updated Packages:

ImageMagick-6.2.8.0-1.1
-----------------------
* Wed Jul 12 2006 Jesse Keating <jkeating@redhat.com> - 6.2.8.0-1.1
- rebuild

anaconda-11.1.0.57-1
--------------------
* Thu Jul 13 2006 David Cantrell <dcantrell@redhat.com> - 11.1.0.57-1
- Fix unknown error on shadow file (#196705, clumens)
- Removed inet_calcGateway (clumens)
- Don't guess gateway address in text network UI (#197578, clumens)
- Change iutil.copyFile calls to shutil.copyfile (clumens)
- Removed DRI enable/disable code from xsetup (clumens)
- Removed copyFile, getArch, memInstalled, and rmrf from iutil (clumens)
- Don't pass command as first argument to subprocess calls (clumens)
- Added network debugging mode for readNetConfig( ) in loader
- Removed "BOOTP" string from loader network config UI
- Added new dialog for network device config in stage2 (katzj)
- Write gateway address to correct struct in manualNetConfig
- Removed IP_STRLEN macro since that's moved to libdhcp
- Link and compile libisys with libdhcp
- Added back 'confignetdevice' and 'pumpnetdevice' in iutil
- Removed isys_calcNetmask and isys_calcNS (clumens)
- Added xkeyboard-config to fix VT switching (katzj)

...(Lines snipped)...

Broken deps for i386
---------------------------------------------------------------
  anaconda-runtime - 11.1.0.57-1.i386 requires syslinux
  gnucash - 2.0.0-2.1.i386 requires libgsf-gnome-1.so.114
  mkbootdisk - 1.5.3-2.1.i386 requires syslinux
  perl-suidperl - 4:5.8.8-6.1.i386 requires perl = 4:5.8.8-6
  systemtap - 0.5.8-2.1.i386 requires libdw.so.1(ELFUTILS_0.120)
```

```
Broken deps for ia64
----------------------------------------------------------
  gnucash - 2.0.0-2.1.ia64 requires libgsf-gnome-1.so.114( )(64bit)
  perl-suidperl - 4:5.8.8-6.1.ia64 requires perl = 4:5.8.8-6
  systemtap - 0.5.8-2.1.ia64 requires libdw.so.1(ELFUTILS_0.120)(64bit)

...(Lines snipped)...
```

The report lists new and removed packages, the latest changelog entries from updated packages, and a list of broken dependencies for each architecture. Developers, package maintainers, and testers review this report daily, discussing the results on the mailing lists.

The build system places the resulting RPMs on a master server, where they are periodically retrieved by the mirror servers and made accessible to the world. Individual systems use the standard *yum* client and transfer protocols (HTTP or FTP) to access files on the mirror servers.

The *rsync* tool works by comparing files and directories on the client and server systems and transferring only the files that have changed. This comparison can use combinations of file-modification timestamp, file size, and checksum, depending on the command-line options selected.

What About...

...testing upcoming Fedora Core versions without performing a network installation or update?

The Fedora Core project produces at least three test releases before each Fedora Core release. These test releases are effectively clean snapshots of Rawhide released in ISO form; they can be installed from optical disc using the same method as Fedora Core releases (see Chapter 1 and Lab 10.3, "Preparing Alternate Installation Media").

You will find announcements of test releases on the Fedora web site and the *fedora-announce-list*. The test releases may be downloaded from *test* directories in the Fedora mirror servers; the releases are numbered in increments of 0.01 starting with a version number that is 0.1 less than the upcoming Fedora Core version number— so Fedora Core 7 test 1 will be found in the directory *test/6.90*, and FC7t2 will be in *test/6.91*.

...using other repositories with the Rawhide development repository?

That's not usually recommended. Repositories such as Livna (and even Fedora Extras) do not update their packages to work with new Fedora Core releases until just before the official release of a new Fedora Core version.

Where Can I Learn More?

- The Fedora Testing Guide: *http://www.fedoraproject.org/wiki/Testing*
- The manpages for *yum* and *rsync*
- List of Fedora mirrors: *http://fedora.redhat.com/Download/mirrors.html*
- Torrent trackers for Fedora Core, including test releases: *http://torrent.fedoraproject.org/*
- The BitTorrent home page: *http://bittorrent.com/*

9.5   Participating in Fedora Projects

Within the Fedora Community, there are many different projects aimed at developing and improving various aspects of Fedora Linux. Regardless of your skill set, interests, or experience, there is probably a role that is perfect for you in one of the projects. Becoming directly involved in a Fedora project contributes back to the Fedora community and can build your skill and reputation.

How Do I Do That?

A list of Fedora Projects is maintained at *http://fedoraproject.org/wiki/Projects*. Each project has separate standards and requirements for participation, so a good place to start is by reading the project outline to determine the participation requirements, then joining the relevant mailing lists to meet and get to know other project members.

Here are some projects to consider:

Fedora Documentation

The Fedora Docs project (*http://fedoraproject.org/wiki/DocsProject*) produces release notes, installation and configuration guides, and other documentation, and is always looking for writers, editors, and readers willing to provide feedback. Other members of the Fedora Docs team develop the tool chain used to manage the documentation and transform it into various forms.

Fedora Translation

Since Fedora software is used globally, messages and controls within the software, documentation, and web sites all require translation into many languages. The Fedora Translation project exists to do this translation and to develop and refine the tools necessary to manage translated text. The Fedora Translation web site is found at *http://fedoraproject.org/wiki/L10N*.

 L10N in the Translation URI stands for *localization* (translation into specific languages). *I18N* stands for *internationalization* (technologies that enable use of software in multiple locales). The numbers in the abbreviations refer to the quantity of letters removed.

Fedora Extras

If you have RPM packages that aren't included in Fedora Core or Fedora Extras, you can become a Fedora Extras contributor and make those packages available to other Fedora users. The Fedora Extras project has set up strict standards and a rigorous review process to protect the quality of the Extras repository, so participating in this project requires a certain level of skill and commitment. To streamline the process, Fedora Extras uses a sponsorship process, which pairs experienced members with newcomers during their first package submission. The web site *http://fedoraproject.org/wiki/Extras/Contributors* describes the process of becoming a Fedora Extras contributor.

What About...

...Fedora-related projects that have sprung up outside of the official Fedora community?

There are a number of Fedora-related projects that are not part of the official Fedora project, and these projects are also staffed by volunteers:

Derivative distributions
> There are over 60 Linux distributions derived from Fedora Linux, and yet others that are derived from Red Hat Enterprise Linux (Red Hat's enterprise Linux distribution, which shares a common root with Fedora). These distributions tailor Fedora to meet specific community, linguistic, or hardware requirements.

Other repositories
> The Livna, ATrpms, and RPMforge repositories interoperate with the Fedora Core and Extras repositories (although not necessarily with each other).

The Fedora Unity project
> Fedora Unity provides web sites with guides and technical notes on various Fedora-related issues. It also produces what it terms *respins* of the Fedora Core CDs and DVDs, incorporating updates released since the official Fedora Core release dates.

Where Can I Learn More?

- The Fedora projects page: *http://fedoraproject.org/wiki/Projects/*
- Linux distributions derived from Fedora: *http://distrowatch.com/dwres.php?resource=independence#fedora*
- External repositories: *http://rpm.livna.org/*, *http://atrpms.net/*, and *http://rpmforge.net/*
- The Fedora Unity Project: *http://fedoraunity.org/*

CHAPTER 10

Advanced Installation

There are thousands of different computer configurations, and thousands of different ways in which computers are used. The Fedora installer, Anaconda, is up to the challenge: although the default installation procedure is straightforward, Anaconda can also perform automated installations, set up complex storage layouts involving RAID and LVM, handle different types of installation media and network installation servers, and provide a rescue mode for the recovery of disabled systems.

This chapter deals with these advanced installation features. It also looks at GParted, a partition resizing tool, and GRUB, the bootloader used by Fedora that can be extensively customized.

10.1   Resizing a Windows Partition

Many computers are sold with some version of Microsoft Windows preinstalled, claiming the entire disk. In order to install Fedora in a dual-boot configuration, it is necessary to reduce the size of the Windows partition to free up some space.

How Do I Do That?

Fedora does not provide a good tool for resizing Windows partitions. Fortunately, there is a very good open source tool available, GParted.

   Always back up your data before adjusting partitions.

Download the 26 MB GParted LiveCD from *http://gparted.sourceforge.net/livecd.php* and burn it onto a CD or DVD. Insert the disc into the system to be resized, and then start (or restart) the system; the screen shown in Figure 10-1 will appear.

   You may need to adjust the BIOS boot options to force the system to boot from the disc.

Figure 10-1. GParted LiveCD boot screen

Press Enter. The system will ask you to select your language, as shown in Figure 10-2, and then to select the keyboard type, as shown in Figure 10-3.

Figure 10-2. Language selection screen

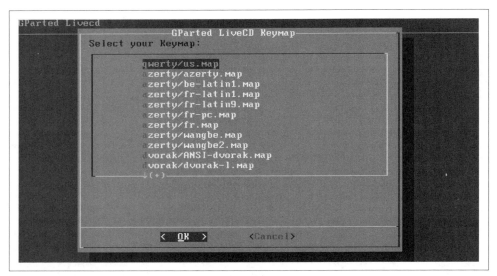

Figure 10-3. Keyboard selection screen

The software will then prompt you for your display resolution, as shown in Figure 10-4; select the default unless you're using an old monitor.

 Do not select 640×480 resolution; the GParted window will not fit on the screen.

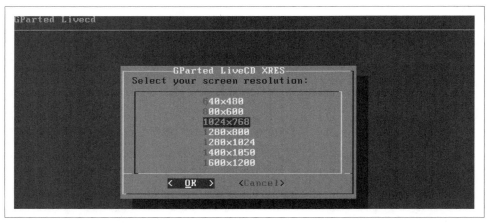

Figure 10-4. Display resolution selection screen

You should also select the default for the display color depth, as shown in Figure 10-5, unless you find that the default does not work with your system.

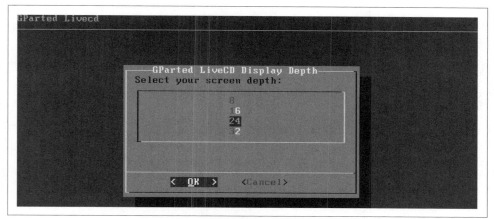

Figure 10-5. Display color-depth selection screen

The GParted screen in Figure 10-6 will now appear, displaying a list of all of the partitions on the first hard disk drive. If you wish to edit the partitions on another drive, click on the drive menu in the upper-right corner of the screen and select that drive.

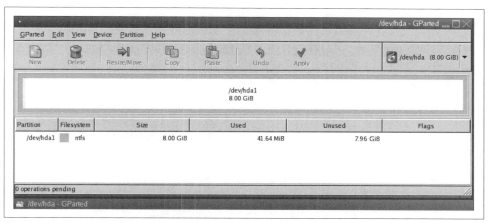

Figure 10-6. GParted main window

Click on the partition that you wish to resize, and then click on the Resize/Move button at the top of the window. In the resizing dialog shown in Figure 10-7, select the new size for the partition by dragging the end of the partition, by entering the new partition size, or by entering the amount of free space that you wish to have after repartitioning. Click Next.

The resize option will appear in a list of queued tasks at the bottom of the main window. Click the Apply button at the top of the window, and then click Apply on the confirmation dialog shown in Figure 10-8.

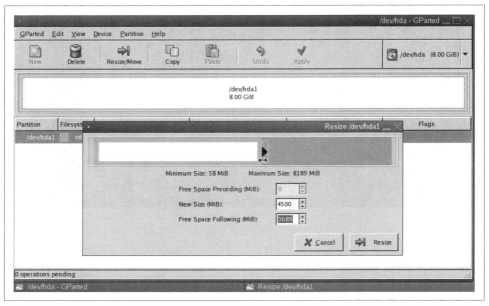

Figure 10-7. Entering a new partition size

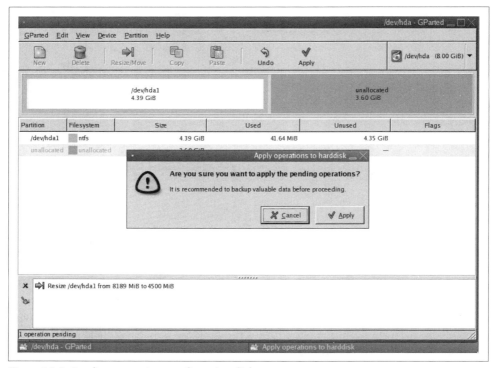

Figure 10-8. Pending-operations confirmation dialog

A progress display will appear while the partition is resized; click Close when the resize has finished.

Close the GParted window; then right-click on the display background and select Reboot.

How Does It Work?

The GParted LiveCD is a combination of open source software from several separate projects: the *libparted* partition-manipulation libraries from the GNU *parted* partition editor, filesystem-manipulation utilities from various filesystem projects, the GParted GNOME graphical *parted* interface, and a Live CD version of Slackware Linux.

The GParted LiveCD boots using a process very similar to the Fedora Core installation disc. Once the kernel and *initrd* (ramdisk) are loaded, startup scripts request the language, keyboard, resolution, and color-depth information, and then start Xvesa, a version of the X Window server that communicates with the graphics card through lowest-common-denominator standards set by the Video Electronics Standards Association (VESA). This enables the use of almost any modern video card in a low-performance mode (perfectly acceptable for this application) without requiring card-specific drivers.

The only application started is the GParted graphical interface, which communicates with other tools as necessary to perform requested tasks. Windows uses two different filesystem types: FAT32, a simple filesystem based on the original DOS 2.0 filesystem, and NTFS, an advanced filesystem with a database-like structure. Filesystem manipulation is handled by tools from the *dosfstools* and *linux-ntfs* packages. Then partition resizing is accomplished using the *linux-ntfs* tools or *libparted* libraries (depending on the partition type).

What About...

...one or two small partitions that appear at the end of my disk drive?

Those partitions are for system diagnostic software and for returning your system to a factory-fresh state, and are especially common on notebook computers. It is best to leave those partitions alone.

Where Can I Learn More?

- The GParted web site: *http://gparted.sourceforge.net/*
- The *parted* web site: *http://www.gnu.org/software/parted/*
- The *linux-ntfs* project: *http://www.linux-ntfs.org/*
- The *dosfstools* distribution site: *ftp://ftp.uni-erlangen.de/pub/Linux/LOCAL/dosfstools/*

10.2   Configuring RAID and LVM During Installation

Fedora Core's default storage layout works well for many systems, but one approach doesn't suit all situations. The Anaconda installer lets you configure complex storage layouts incorporating RAID and LVM to suit advanced needs.

Back up any important data on your disk drive(s) before installing Fedora Core!

Be sure to read Chapter 6 before reading this lab.

How Do I Do That?

Start a normal installation as described in Chapter 1. When you get to the disk and partition strategy screen shown in Figure 10-9, choose "Create custom layout" and select the checkbox for each of the disk drives that you wish to use.

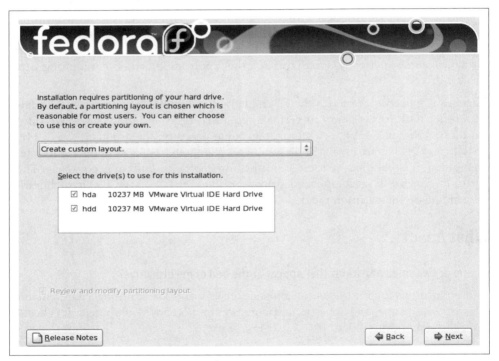

Figure 10-9. Selecting a custom layout as the partitioning strategy

Click Next to proceed to the Disk Druid screen shown in Figure 10-10, which gives an overview of the drive partitions in the top portion of the screen; the details of drive partitions, RAID devices, and LVM configuration in the lower portion of the screen; and action buttons in the center.

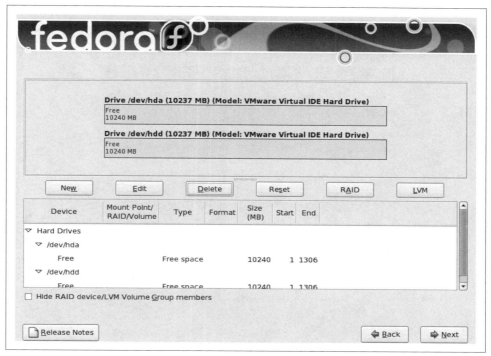

Figure 10-10. Disk Druid screen

Start by scrolling through the partition list in the lower half of the window. Delete any existing partition that you no longer want by clicking on the partition to select it and then clicking the Delete button; confirm the deletion in the warning dialog that appears.

Creating a boot filesystem

The GRUB bootloader used by Fedora can boot only from simple disk partitions, not Logical Volumes or RAID stripes. However, when a RAID 1 (mirroring) array contains a filesystem, each partition that is an element of that array contains a full copy of the filesystem, and GRUB can boot from that.

Therefore, if you're using RAID levels other than RAID 1, or if you're using LVM, you must create a separate boot filesystem. The mount point for this filesystem is */boot*, and the recommended size is 100 MB.

If you are not using RAID, create a small partition to hold the boot filesystem. In Disk Druid click the New button, which will bring up the Add Partition dialog shown in Figure 10-11. Enter a mount point of */boot*, deselect the checkboxes for all of the drives except the first one, and then click Next. This will create a 100 MB ext3 partition on the first disk drive.

If you are using RAID, follow the steps in the next section to create a boot partition.

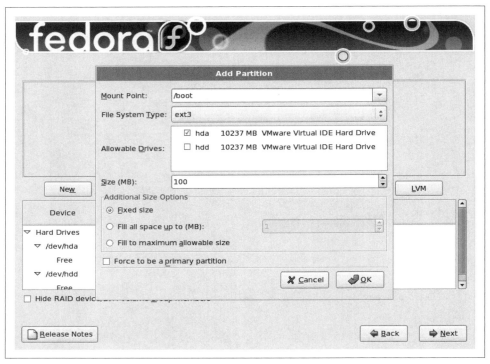

Figure 10-11. Add Partition window

Creating RAID devices

Table 10-1 shows RAID level recommendations for various numbers of disk drives. (Table 6-3 describes the RAID levels supported by Fedora.)

Table 10-1. RAID recommendations based on the number of same-sized disk drives

# of disk drives	Possible RAID levels	Recoverable failure	Notes
1	Cannot use RAID	None	
2	RAID 0	None	Improves performance but also increases the risk of data loss. It provides storage capacity equal to two drives.
	RAID 1	1 drive	Provides storage capacity equal to one drive. *This is the only RAID level that can be used for the /boot filesystem.*
3	RAID 5	1 drive	Provides storage capacity equal to two drives.
4 or more	RAID 5 with no hot spares	1 drive	Provides storage capacity equal to the number of drives minus one.
	RAID 5 with hot spare(s)	1 drive at a time to a sequential maximum failure of 1 + the number of hot spares	Provides storage capacity equal to the number of drives minus the number of hot spares minus one.

Table 10-1. RAID recommendations based on the number of same-sized disk drives (continued)

# of disk drives	Possible RAID levels	Recoverable failure	Notes
	RAID 6 with no hot spares	2 drives	Provides storage capacity equal to the number of drives minus two.
5 or more	RAID 6 with hot spare(s)	2 drives at a time to a maximum of 2 + the number of hot spares	Provides storage capacity equal to the number of drives minus the number of hot spares minus two.

To create a RAID array (device), you must first create the partitions that will make up the elements of the array. Start by creating a RAID 1 boot partition of about 100 MB on each drive. Although it's tempting to create a giant RAID partition to use the rest of the space, I recommend that you divide the space on each drive into five partitions of roughly equal size. For example, if you are using 120 GB disk drives, create five partitions of 24 GB; if you are using 10 GB drives, create five partitions of 2 GB. Combine these partitions into five RAID arrays, each incorporating one partition from each drive, and then combine those five RAID arrays into a single volume group. The advantage to this approach is that it enables you to migrate to a different RAID level as long as a minimum of 20 percent of the VG space is free (see Lab 6.1, "Using Logical Volume Management").

To create a partition to serve as a RAID array element, click the New button in Disk Druid's main window. The Add Partition dialog will appear, as in Figure 10-12.

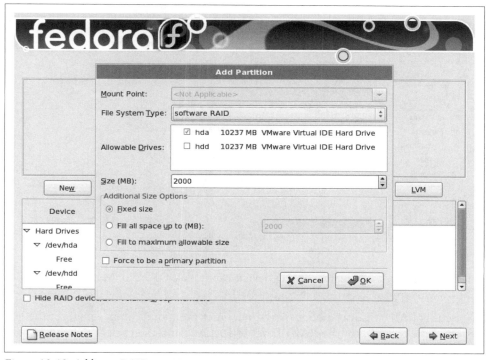

Figure 10-12. Adding a RAID partition

Another way to create a RAID partition is by clicking on the RAID button; the dialog in Figure 10-13 will appear, asking what you want to do next. Select the option "Create a software RAID partition" and click OK.

For the File System Type, select "software RAID." Deselect all of the Allowable Drives checkboxes except one to indicate the drive on which you wish to create the partition. Enter the Size in megabytes, and select "Fixed size." Click OK to proceed.

Repeat this process to create partitions for the other elements of the RAID array on other drives. For example, when creating a 2 GB RAID 1 array that spans two drives, create a 2 GB software RAID partition on each of the two drives.

Once you have created all of the partitions for the array, click the RAID button to view the RAID Options window, as shown in Figure 10-13.

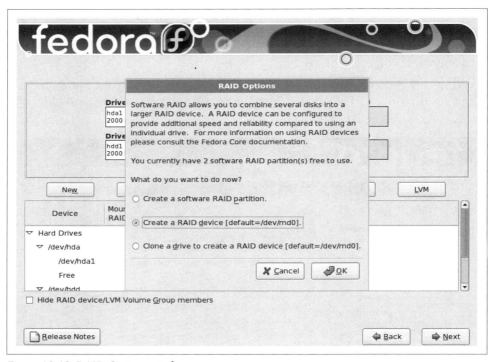

Figure 10-13. RAID Options window

Select the option to "Create a RAID device" and click OK. The Make RAID Device window will appear, as shown in Figure 10-14.

To use this RAID array as a boot filesystem, enter the mount point */boot*, set the File System Type to ext3, set the RAID Level to RAID 1, and then select the checkboxes

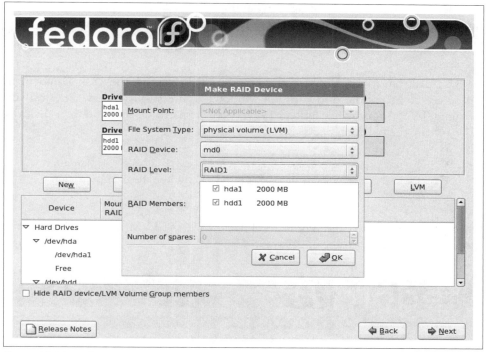

Figure 10-14. Make RAID Device window

of the RAID partitions that will serve as elements of the array. Click OK to create the filesystem.

 When creating a RAID array, use partitions that are exactly or almost exactly the same size because the size of the smallest element defines the amount of space that will be used in each of the elements; any differences between the size of the smallest element and the sizes of each of the other elements is wasted space.

To create a RAID array that will serve as a Physical Volume in an LVM Volume Group, set the File System Type to "Physical volume (LVM)," select the RAID Level, and select the checkboxes of the RAID partitions that will serve as elements of this array. Click OK to create the array.

Creating an LVM layout

Whether you're using RAID or not, LVM is the best way to set up partitioning: the overhead is minuscule, and the flexibility that it buys is valuable.

In order to configure LVM during installation, you need to create one or more partitions that will serve as physical volumes. There are two ways to do this:

- Use RAID arrays as physical volumes, following the instructions in the previous section.

- Use disk partitions as physical volumes. Click New in the Disk Druid main screen to access the Add Partition window (Figure 10-11). Select "Physical volume (LVM)" for the File System Type, enter the partition size, and then click OK to create the partition.

 It usually doesn't make sense to combine RAID and disk partition PVs in the same volume group because you will lose the data protection provided by the RAID array.

Once you have created the physical volumes, click the LVM button. The window shown in Figure 10-15 will be displayed.

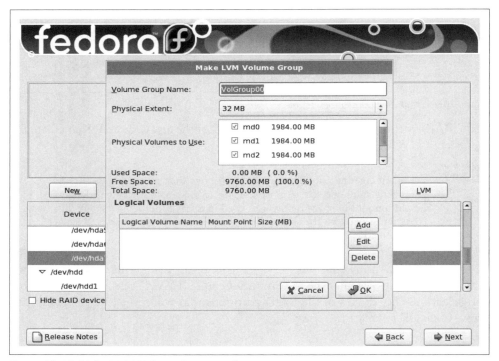

Figure 10-15. Make LVM Volume Group window

Enter a descriptive volume group name, such as *main* for your primary volume group. The default physical extent size is 32 MB, which is a reasonable choice for most applications. If you have a good reason to use a different extent size, set it now because it cannot be easily changed after installation.

Reducing the physical extent size increases the size of the LVM data structures but gives a finer granularity for assigning storage to logical volumes. Increasing the physical extent size slightly reduces the LVM overhead, increasing performance.

Select the checkbox of all of the physical volumes you wish to use in this volume group.

The next step is to create a logical volume to hold each filesystem you wish to create. Table 10-2 contains a list of recommended filesystems.

Table 10-2. Recommended filesystems for Fedora Core

Mount point	Recommended size	Notes
/	10 GB	Required
/home	10 GB or more, depending on how much data your users will be personally storing	Strongly recommended for any system where users will be logging in on the console or via remote SSH access (e.g., desktop systems, servers with personal user accounts), and systems that are acting as file servers for personal files such as a Samba server (see Lab 7.1, "Configuring Samba to Share Files with Windows Systems"). By separating the users' home directories onto a separate filesystem, you can reinstall the operating system in the future without affecting users' files.
/var	2 GB to 1 TB depending on the applications in use	The /var filesystem holds data that is variable but that is not stored in the users' home directories—for example, databases, email, web pages, and queued print requests. Creating a separate filesystem segregates it for backup and makes it easier to reinstall the operating system without affecting this data.

To create each logical volume and filesystem, click the Add button at the bottom of the screen to access the Make Logical Volume window shown in Figure 10-16.

Enter the chosen Mount Point and a descriptive logical volume name; then enter the desired size (leaving the File System Type set to the default, "ext3"). Click OK to return to the Make LVM Volume Group window; note that the LV size you entered is rounded to a multiple of the physical extent size in the Logical Volumes display.

Repeat this process for the other logical volumes.

It is best to leave some space within the VG unassigned so that you can use LVM snapshots and so that you can add space to a crowded filesystem without having to unmount another filesystem to reduce its size.

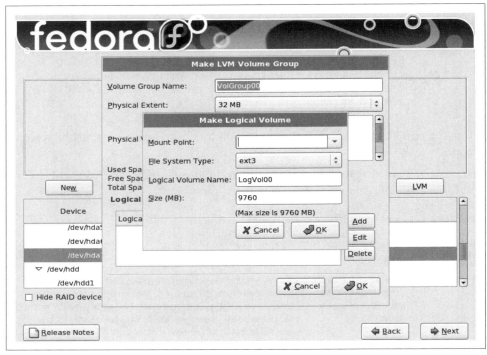

Figure 10-16. Make Logical Volume window

Finally, create a swap LV by clicking on the Add button in the Make LVM Volume Group window; when the Make Logical Volume window appears (Figure 10-16), set the File System Type to "swap," and enter the desired swap size. Although traditional wisdom dictates a swap size twice as large as the system memory, it's reasonable to give a system with more memory less swapspace, and a system with less memory more swapspace. If in doubt, use the traditional figure as a starting point, since it can be changed later. The swapspace should be at least as large as the installed RAM (Disk Druid will warn you if it is not).

Once you have configured all of the logical volumes, click OK in the Make LVM Volume Group window, and then click Next in the main Disk Druid window. Proceed with the installation as outlined in Chapter 1.

How Does It Work?

Like most of the Fedora system administration tools, Disk Druid (and Anaconda) are largely written in Python and interface with other open source tools such as *parted*, *libparted*, and *lvm*.

The purpose of Disk Druid is to improve the installation experience by taking care of many of the partitioning, RAID configuration, and LVM setup details automatically.

While other partitioning tools such as *fdisk* and *parted* require the user to keep track of partition numbers and starting and ending locations, and to use cylinders as a unit of measure, Disk Druid handles partition numbering automatically (even including drive selection, where appropriate).

On a PC, the first sector of each disk drive stores a Master Boot Record (MBR). The last 64 bytes of the MBR contain a *partition table*, which can hold a maximum of four entries; each entry contains a starting and ending cylinder number, boot flag, and partition type code. If more than four partitions are required, one of the MBR entries is configured to point to an *extended partition*, which contains its own *extended partition table*. The extended partition table can contain a maximum of one partition entry and one additional extended partition entry, both of which must be located within the extended partition. In this way, any number of partitions may be created.

What About...

...disk partitions on non-PC systems?

There are many different types of *disklabels*, or disk partition table types, used on different types of systems. Of particular note for Fedora users is the fact that Mac systems use a different, more capable disk partition table. *parted* is able to display, create, and manipulate nine different types of disklabels, including those for IBM AIX Unix systems, Macs, PCs (called *msdos* in the *parted* documentation), Sun systems, and many others.

Where Can I Learn More?

- The manpages for *parted*, *fdisk*, *lvm*, and *mdadm*
- The Anaconda project page: *http://fedora.redhat.com/projects/anaconda-installer/*
- The Anaconda Wiki page: *http://fedoraproject.org/wiki/Anaconda*

10.3 Preparing Alternate Installation Media

The Fedora Core installation process is usually booted from CD or DVD, but it may also be booted from a USB flash disk or hard disk drive, or from a PXE boot server.

In addition, Fedora Core permits the use of an FTP or HTTP server as the package source during installation.

These alternate installation media must be specially prepared before use.

How Do I Do That?

Before preparing alternate boot media, check that the target system can boot from the media you wish to use. Examine the BIOS of the system on which Fedora will be installed to see if it supports booting from a USB flash drive or a PXE server; if not, select a different installation medium.

Preparing a USB drive

To configure a USB drive for booting, download the USB boot image by selecting a mirror site from the web page *http://fedora.redhat.com/Download/mirrors.html* and going to that mirror with a web browser. Select the directory for the desired Fedora Core version number (e.g., *6*), then the directory for your machine architecture (*i386*, *PPC*, or *x86_64*), then select the *os* directory, and then select the *images* subdirectory. Download the file named *diskboot.img* (you can also find this in the */images* directory of the Fedora Core DVD or the first disc of the CD set).

 The directory layout varies slightly among the mirror sites.

Once you have obtained the *diskboot.img* file, transfer it to your USB flash drive using a Linux system. First, insert the drive into the system; you should see an icon appear on the desktop.

 This procedure will wipe out everything on your USB flash drive! Back up the drive contents before proceeding.

Use the *df* command to determine the drive's device name:

```
$ df -h
Filesystem            Size  Used Avail Use% Mounted on
/dev/mapper/main-root
                       30G   14G   15G  48% /
/dev/md0              251M   41M  197M  18% /boot
/dev/shm              506M     0  506M   0% /dev/shm
/dev/mapper/main-home
                       14G  6.6G  7.0G  49% /home
/dev/mapper/main-var   65G   56G  8.0G  88% /var
/dev/hdb1              99M   24M   71M  26% /mnt/oldboot
/dev/hdb3             109G   75G   29G  73% /mnt/oldroot
/dev/hda6              14G  4.1G  8.5G  33% /mnt/x-root
/dev/sdb1            8.0M  6.4M  1.7M  80% /media/usbdisk1
```

In this case, the device name is */dev/sdb1*. Unmount that device:

```
# umount /dev/sdb1
```

(Notice that there is only one *n* in *umount*.)

Now copy the boot image to the USB flash drive:

```
# dd if=diskboot.img of=/dev/sdb1
16384+0 records in
16384+0 records out
```

Flush the system disk buffers to ensure that the data is written out to the drive before you unplug it:

```
# sync
```

The USB flash drive is now ready for booting. Insert the drive into the target system, turn it on, and use the BIOS options to specify that the system is to be booted from the USB drive; the rest of the process will be identical to booting from a CD or DVD.

When you're done using the drive to install Fedora Core, you'll find that it looks like an 8 MB drive, regardless of its actual drive capacity. To restore its full capacity, format it with a FAT32 filesystem:

```
# mkdosfs /dev/sdb1
mkdosfs 2.10 (22 Sep 2003)
```

Preparing a network installation server

You can use any FTP, HTTP, or NIS server for network installation, but of these three, HTTP is the easiest to set up and has the least overhead.

You'll need the full set of installation files. You can copy the entire contents of the DVD (or each of the five CDs) to a directory shared by your web server:

```
# mkdir /var/www/fedora
# cp -R /media/discname /var/www/fedora
```

Replace */media/diskname* with the disc mount point (see the output of *df*).

Instead of copying the files, you could leave the DVD in your drive (this won't work with CDs, since you need several of them) and create a symbolic link from your web server's document root to the DVD mount point:

```
# ln -s /media/disk /var/www/html/fedora
```

Since the DVD's filesystem does not support file attributes—necessary to assign an SELinux context—you will have to disable SELinux enforcement for HTTPD before using it to serve files from a DVD.

Alternatively, you can download the files directory to your web server directory. Go to the web page *http://fedora.redhat.com/Download/mirrors.html*, select an *rsync*, HTTP, or FTP mirror site for download, and download the entire distribution (all of the files and subdirectories in the *os* directory for your platform).

The directory layout varies from mirror to mirror. Use a browser to connect to your selected mirror site to confirm the directory names for the following commands.

On an existing Fedora Core system, you can do this by first creating a directory that is web-accessible:

```
# mkdir /var/www/fedora
```

Then fetch all of the files into that directory:

```
# cd /var/www/fedora
# wget -nH --cut-dirs=4 -r http://less.cogeco.net/pub/fedora/linux/core/6/
```

Note that the URL here is taken from the mirror list, but has the Fedora Core release number (6) added to the end (replace this URL with that of a mirror close to you). The --cut-dirs=4 option removes four leading directory names (*pub/fedora/linux/core*) from the retrieved files before saving them.

The downloaded tree will include the ISO files. If you'd rather not download them, use the -X option when you run *wget*:

```
# cd /var/www/fedora
# wget -nH -X '/*/*/*/*/*/iso' --cut-dirs=4 -r \
    http://less.cogeco.net/pub/fedora/linux/core/6/
```

(The \ indicates that the command continues on the next line; you can leave it out and type everything on one line.)

The downloaded directory indexes will be saved as files starting with *index.html*; these can be deleted using the *find* command:

```
# find /var/www/fedora -name 'index.html*' -print -exec rm {} \;
```

The wget command can also be used with FTP sites:

```
# cd /var/www/fedora
# wget -X '/*/*/*/*/*/iso' -nH -X index.html --cut-dirs=4 -r \
    ftp://ftp.muug.mb.ca/pub/fedora/linux/core/5/
```

To fetch files from an *rsync* mirror, use the *rsync* command:

```
# cd /var/www/fedora
# rsync -v --recursive rsync://fedora.cat.pdx.edu/fedora-linux-core/4 .
```

 Don't miss the . at the end of the line!

Ensure that the *httpd* service is started (see Lab 7.5, "Using the Apache Web Server"), and then start the installation on the target system using your choice of boot media (disc, PXE boot, or USB drive).

Preparing a PXE Boot Server

To configure a PXE boot server, you will need the *tftp-server*, *xinetd*, *system-config-netboot*, and *dhcp* packages. You will also need a working network installation server, as described in the previous section.

 Before configuring a PXE Boot Server, confirm that the installation target machines use the PXE protocol for network booting.

To configure the PXE server, select the menu option System → Administration → Server Settings → Network Booting Service. The window shown in Figure 10-17 will be displayed.

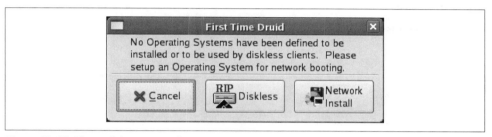

Figure 10-17. Network boot-type selection

Click on the Network Install button, and the Network Installation Dialog in Figure 10-18 will appear.

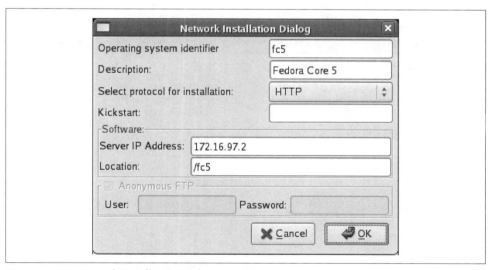

Figure 10-18. Network Installation Dialog

Enter fc6 as the operating system identifier, type an easily readable description of the OS to be installed, select the protocol for installation, and then enter the IP address and the server directory in which the software is installed. Leave the Kickstart field blank (even if you're using a Kickstart file). Click OK to proceed.

You will now see the main window of the netboot configuration tool, shown in Figure 10-19. This window is used to associate the operating system identifier of the configuration you just created (fc6) with a particular range of IP addresses.

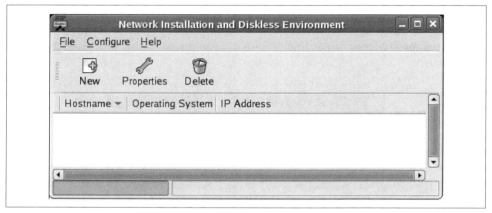

Figure 10-19. Main netboot configuration window

Click New to add a new IP entry in the dialog shown in Figure 10-20. To configure one specific computer, enter that computer's hostname or IP address; to configure an entire subnet, enter the subnet.

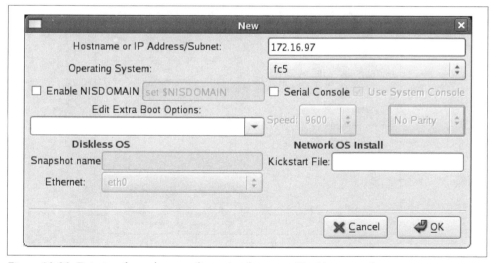

Figure 10-20. Entering the netboot configuration for a new IP address or subnet

The format for entering the subnet is a bit unusual; you must enter just the network part of the address. For example, the IP address 172.16.97.32 with a netmask of 255. 255.255.0 yields a network number of 172.16.97 and a host number of 32, so you would enter 172.16.97 into the IP Address Subnet field.

If you have created more than one network installation profile, select the correct value for the Operating System field. Enter the Kickstart URL, if any, into the Kickstart File field, and then click OK.

The main *system-config-netboot* window will show the new entry; you can now close the window.

The next step is to configure a DHCP server using the file */etc/dhcpd.conf*. In addition to the regular configuration options, you will need to add one additional statement. If you don't otherwise need DHCP, use this minimal configuration file:

```
# /etc/dhcpd.conf file for PXE booting

ddns-update-style none;
subnet 192.168.1.0 netmask 255.255.255.0 {
        range 192.168.1.16 192.168.1.250;
        filename "linux-install/pxelinux.0";
}
```

The additional statement (highlighted in bold) identifies the name of the file to be loaded via TFTP. *linux-install/pxelinux.0* is the Linux bootloader; the path is relative to */tftpboot* on the server.

 You can run the DHCP and TFTP servers on different machines if you add a next-server line to the DHCP configuration:

```
        next-server 192.168.1.3;
```

This configures the next phase of the boot process to use the TFTP server at the IP address 192.168.1.3.

Do not run more than one DHCP server on your LAN. If you have a DHCP server on a router or gateway device, disable it while using the PXE boot server.

Finally, configure the *tftp* Xinetd service and start the *xinetd* and *dhcpd* services (see Lab 7.2, "Configuring a DHCP Server").

To use the PXE boot server, start the target system and select Network Boot using the BIOS options. A boot display similar to that shown in Figure 10-21 should appear.

The system will then proceed with the normal Fedora Core installation process.

Figure 10-21. PXE boot process

How Does It Work?

All Fedora Core boot media use one of the bootloaders from the *isolinux/syslinux/pxelinux* family. These programs have been specifically tailored for booting from optical disk, removable disk drives, and PXE boot servers. Each of them uses text files to configure the available boot options.

The USB boot image *diskboot.img* is a complete image of a bootable 8 MB VFAT (MS-DOS FAT with long filenames) filesystem. This filesystem contains the *isolinux* bootloader, the kernel, the *initrd* ramdisk image, and configuration files.

The Intel Preboot Execution Environment (PXE) specification is used for network booting of Fedora systems. The PXE boot process uses the *pxelinux* bootloader, which is retrieved from */tftpboot/linux-install/pxelinux.0* on the TFTP server. Once it is running, *pxelinux* searches for an appropriate configuration file in */tftpboot/linux-install/pxelinux.cfg*, first trying for a file named with the hardware MAC address of the target system's Ethernet adapter, then a series of filenames generated from the target's IP address written in hexadecimal, and then finally the file *default*.

The *system-config-netboot* tool is executed when you select the menu option System → Administration → Server Settings → Network Booting Service. It creates a file in */tftpboot/linux-install/pxelinux.cfg* named according to the network address specified in the GUI. For example, if the user specifies a certain configuration for the IP network 192.168.1, the configuration is stored in the file */tftpboot/linux-install/pxelinux.cfg/C0A801* because 192.168.1 in decimal corresponds to C0A801 in hexadecimal.

system-config-netboot obtains the *pxelinux* bootloader, Linux kernel, and *initrd* files from the specified network installation server (the *pxelinux* bootloader is found in the */images* directory on the network installation server).

A network installation server is not intended to provide boot files for the installation, so its only purpose is to provide the package files and other information needed to install Fedora Core after the installation environment has loaded. While FTP, NFS, and HTTP are all available, NFS and FTP use multiple ports (NFS actually relies on multiple server programs), whereas HTTP uses a single server on a single port.

What About...

...installing from a public HTTP or FTP server?

It is possible to install directly from a public Fedora Core HTTP or FTP mirror; simply enter the mirror URL as the server for the HTTP or FTP installation methods. However, doing so generates a lot of Internet traffic, resulting in a long installation time, and the likelihood of a network error aborting the entire installation partway through is higher than it would be on a local LAN. If you are going to install more than once, it's a better idea to download the files onto a local machine for speed.

...booting the installer from a mini-CD?

The normal Fedora Core CD 1 is too large to fit on a mini-CD, but the boot image in */images/boot.iso* on that CD (or the Fedora Core mirror servers) is under 8 MB in size and will easily fit on an 8 cm mini-CD or a "business card" CD.

...booting the installer from floppy disk?

Unfortunately, the Fedora Core installation boot files are now too large to fit on a 1.44 MB floppy disk. However, you may be able to use the 8 MB USB disk image file (*diskboot.img*) with a larger removable disk, such as a Zip or LS-120 disk.

...configuring a PXE installation from the command line?

Although *system-config-netboot* is recommended for PXE configuration, you can also use the *pxeos* and *pxeboot* commands to configure PXE from the command line.

To configure a version of Fedora Core for PXE booting:

```
# pxeos -a -i "Fedora Core 6" -p HTTP -D 0 -s 192.168.1.2 -L /fedora fc6
```

These are the arguments used:

-a
    Add to the existing configuration

-i "Fedora Core 6"
    The descriptive identification for this entry

-p *HTTP*

> Installation protocol (can be HTTP, FTP, or NFS)

-D 0

> Sets this up as an installation instead of a diskless boot

-s *192.168.1.2*

> The HTTP, FTP, or NFS server address

-L */fedora*

> The pathname on the server; in this example, the -p, -s, and -L options combine to be equivalent to *http://192.168.1.2/fedora*

fc6

> The operating system identifier

To configure specific hosts to use the *fc6* boot image:

```
# pxeboot -a -0 fc6 192.168.1
```

This will configure all hosts that have an IP address beginning with 192.168.1 to use the *fc6* configuration. To configure the use of a Kickstart file (see the next lab), add the option -K followed by the Kickstart URL.

Where Can I Learn More?

- The manpages for *dd*, *httpd*, *mkdosfs*, *rsync*, *wget*, *system-config-netboot*, *dhcpd*, *dhcpd.conf*, *tftpd*, *pxeos*, and *pxeboot*
- The HTML documentation for *system-config-netboot*: *file:///usr/share/doc/system-config-netboot-0.1.38/index.html*
- The *syslinux* home page (which includes the *isolinux* and *pxelinux* bootloaders): *http://syslinux.zytor.com/*
- The Intel PXE specification: *http://download.intel.com/design/archives/wfm/downloads/pxespec.pdf*

10.4   Installing with Kickstart

In a normal Fedora Core installation, Anaconda asks a number of questions before beginning the actual installation procedure, which then runs without any user intervention (except for changing CDs, if that is the chosen installation method).

Kickstart is a Fedora installation option that uses a text file to supply basic configuration information so that Anaconda can skip all of the questions normally asked during installation.

How Do I Do That?

To use Kickstart, you must create a Kickstart file using any regular text editor. A Kickstart file contains a number of options, one per line, with arguments.

These options are required:

auth or authconfig

> Configures the authentication system. For normal password authentication, use the arguments --enableshadow --enablemd5.

bootloader

> The GRUB installation location and password. For an upgrade, use --upgrade; for a new installation, use --location=mbr --md5pass=*encryptedpassword* (I cover how to generate encrypted passwords shortly).

lang

> Selects the language to be used during installation. Possible values are listed in */usr/share/system-config-language/locale-list*; for U.S. English, use the argument en_US.

keyboard

> The keyboard type to be used. Specify us for a standard North American English keyboard, or use one of the codes found in */usr/lib/python2.4/site-packages/rhpl/keyboard_models.py* (such as cf for Canadian French).

rootpw

> The *root* password. Use the arguments --iscrypted *encryptedpassword*.

timezone

> The time zone for the system. The third column of */usr/share/zoneinfo/zone.tab* lists possible values, such as America/Toronto or Asia/Shanghai. Add the argument --utc if the system clock is in UTC (recommended except when the system is dual-boot and you are in a time zone that has daylight savings time).

To encrypt a password for the bootloader and *root* access, use the *openssl* command:

```
$ openssl passwd -1 -salt "RaNDoMjuNk" "MySecretPassword"
$1$RaNDoMju$OSOp7cTCbvCJ2ITUfcovM1
```

Replace *RaNDoMjuNK* with any garbage characters you want to use, and *MySecretPassword* with the desired password. Cut and paste the result into the Kickstart file as the encrypted password.

Here is a basic configuration using these options:

```
auth --enableshadow --enablemd5
bootloader --location=mbr --md5pass=$1$RaNDoMju$OSOp7cTCbvCJ2ITUfcovM1
lang en_US
keyboard us
rootpw --iscrypted $1$RaNDoMju$OSOp7cTCbvCJ2ITUfcovM1
timezone America/Toronto
```

Next, specify the installation source and networking:

cdrom

> Installation from the first optical disk drive on the system (CD or DVD).

url

> HTTP or FTP installation. Use the argument --url http://*host/directory* or --url ftp://*host/directory* to specify the location of the installation files.

nfs

> NFS installation. Use --server=*ip_address* and --dir=*directory* to specify the server host and directory that contain the installation files.

harddrive

> Installation from a VFAT or ext2/ext3 partition on a local hard drive. Use the arguments --partition=*partitionId* and --dir=*/directory* to specify the location of the installation files. The *partitionId* must be one of the hard drive device names from Table 1-4, with the partition number appended without the */dev/* directory (for example, *hda2* for partition 2 on the IDE/ATA primary slave drive).

network

> Configures IP networking for the installed system. If the system already has networking enabled (for example, because it booted from a PXE server), then that configuration is used for the rest of the installation, but if no network configuration has been set up for the installation and one is required, this configuration is used.

> The argument --bootproto=*method* sets the network configuration method: dhcp, bootp, or static. If you specify static, use the options --ip=*ip_address* --netmask=*subnetmask* --gateway=*router_ip* --nameserver=*nameserver_ip* to configure the network interface. If you have more than one network interface, use the --device=*devicename* option; to configure the interface to be inactive at boot, use --onboot=off.

Note that the directory specified for the url or nfs options must contain the *fedora* directory of the installation tree; in other words, it must be equivalent to the root directory of the Fedora Core CD or DVD.

To specify HTTP as the installation method on a system with two network interfaces—one configured with DHCP and one with a static IP—use a configuration like this:

```
url --url=http://192.168.1.2/fc6/
network --bootproto=dhcp    --device eth0
network --bootproto=static --device eth1 \
    --ip 10.2.97.33 --netmask=255.255.255.0
```

 If a Kickstart option line ends with \, it is continued on the next line.

If you are using Kickstart to perform an upgrade instead of an installation, use the upgrade option. Otherwise, use these options to lay out the storage:

zerombr

> Clears any invalid partition tables. Use this option with just one argument: yes.

autopart

> Sets up the default partition structure, which includes a /boot filesystem and a volume group with logical volumes for swap and the root filesystem. If part options are also present, they will selectively override the default setup for the same mount point.

clearpart

> Clears existing partition table entries. Use the argument --all to clear all partitions, --linux to clear all Linux partitions, --drives=*drive1,drive2* to specify the drive or drives to be cleared, and --initlabel to enable the creation of disk labels (partition tables) on empty drives.

part or partition

> Creates a disk partition. Provide an option identifying the mount point (such as /boot) or one of the keywords swap, raid.*NN*, or pv.*NN*, where *NN* is a RAID or physical volume number (01–99). Then use the arguments --size=*size* and --maxsize=*maxsize* to set the minimum and maximum partition sizes in megabytes, and --grow to indicate that the filesystem can be expanded to fill the maximum size if it is specified (or all of the remaining free space if a maximum is not specified). --ondrive=*drive* can be used to force the use of a particular drive; use drive names from Table 1-4. Use --fstype=*filesystem* to configure the filesystem type (ext2, ext3, or vfat).

raid

> Creates a RAID device from partitions defined with the part option. Use the argument --level=*raidlevel* to set the RAID level to 0, 1, 5, or 6, and the argument --device=*devicename* to set the RAID device name (such as md0 or md12). If the array will have hot spares, specify the number of hot spares with the argument --spares=*S*. Set the filesystem type with --fstype=*filesystem*, and then list the mount point (or swap for a swap device, or pv.*NN* for physical volume number *NN*). Finally, list the partition names (raid.*NN*) that will make up the elements of this array.

volgroup

> Creates a volume group. Supply the volume group name (such as main) and a list of physical volumes (pv.*NN*) as arguments.

logvol

> Creates a logical volume. Use the --vgname=*volumegroup* argument to select the volume group, --size=*size* to set the LV size in megabytes, and --name=*lvname* to set the name. Specify the mount point (or swap for a swap partition) as a separate argument.

For example, if you had a system with two 200 GB disks (as the master IDE/ATA drives on the primary and secondary disk controllers) with RAID 1 and LVM (see Lab 6.2, "Managing RAID"), the storage layout options would look like this:

```
# General partitioning options
clearpart --all --initlabel --drives=hda,hdc
```

```
zerombr yes

# Partitions
# Two IDE disk drives, hda and hdc
part raid.01 --size 100    --ondrive=hda
part raid.02 --size 40000 --ondrive=hda
part raid.03 --size 40000 --ondrive=hda
part raid.04 --size 40000 --ondrive=hda
part raid.05 --size 40000 --ondrive=hda
part raid.06 --size 1      --ondrive=hda --grow

part raid.07 --size 100    --ondrive=hdc
part raid.08 --size 40000 --ondrive=hdc
part raid.09 --size 40000 --ondrive=hdc
part raid.10 --size 40000 --ondrive=hdc
part raid.11 --size 40000 --ondrive=hdc
part raid.12 --size 1      --ondrive=hdc --grow

# RAID arrays
# Six RAID arrays, all RAID 1:
# - one is 100 MB /boot array
# - five are 40GB PV arrays
#   (4 * 40000 MB, remaining space in last array)
raid /boot --device md0 --level=RAID1 raid.01 raid.07 --fstype ext3
raid pv.01 --device md1 --level=RAID1 raid.02 raid.08
raid pv.02 --device md2 --level=RAID1 raid.03 raid.09
raid pv.03 --device md3 --level=RAID1 raid.04 raid.10
raid pv.04 --device md4 --level=RAID1 raid.05 raid.11
raid pv.05 --device md5 --level=RAID1 raid.06 raid.12

# Volume Group 'main'
volgroup main pv.01 pv.02 pv.03 pv.04 pv.05

# LVs for root (10GB), /home (35GB), /var (35GB), and swap (1GB),
# leaving about 20 GB available for snapshots and future expansion
# of the LVs
logvol swap  --vgname=main --size=1024  --name=swap
logvol /     --vgname=main --size=10000 --name=root --fstype=ext3
logvol /home --vgname=main --size=35000 --name=home --fstype=ext3
logvol /var  --vgname=main --size=35000 --name=var  --fstype=ext3
```

You can now specify the user interface mode during installation:

text

Install in full-screen text mode.

cmdline

Install in text mode without the full-screen display.

interactive

Present the normal interactive prompts at the start of the installation process, but use the values from the Kickstart file as the defaults. The user can then override the values.

autostep

> Run through the interactive prompts automatically, like a slideshow; this may be helpful for debugging.

You can also include instructions on how the final user interface is to be configured:

skipx

> Don't configure the X Window System.

xconfig

> Although you can specify many arguments for the X Window configuration, in most cases it's best to let Anaconda discover your hardware configuration by probing. Set the screen resolution with --resolution=WxH, and set the maximum color depth with --depth=24. To configure the system to start in runlevel 5 instead of runlevel 3 (see Lab 4.5, "Using Runlevels"), use the argument --startxonboot.

Putting these options together for a text based, hands-off installation configured so that the installed system will start up with a graphical login prompt (1024×768 resolution, 16-million-color display), use:

```
text
xconfig --startxonboot --depth=24 --resolution=1024x768
```

Next comes security:

firewall

> Configures the network firewall. Use --enabled to turn the firewall on or --disabled to turn it off. If you have multiple network interfaces and don't want to firewall some of them, use a --trust=ethN argument for each unprotected interface. To permit connections on particular ports, use the argument --port=port:proto,port:proto, or select a combination of the abbreviations --http, --smtp, --ftp, --telnet, and --ssh.

selinux

> Disables SELinux if used with the --disabled argument, or produces warning messages but does not enforce security policy if --permissive is specified.

This is a typical configuration:

```
firewall --enabled --port=5900:tcp --ssh --http --smtp
```

 TCP port 5900 is the port used for VNC.

You can now specify what should happen after the installation is complete:

firstboot

> Enables the interactive post-installation configuration during the first boot of the new system. Normally, this is not performed after a Kickstart installation. Use

the --enable option to enable a normal first-boot session or --reconfig to enable additional settings to be changed (including the keyboard, language, and network settings).

poweroff

Turns the system off after installation (if the system can be turned off by the kernel).

halt

Halts the system after installation but doesn't turn the power off.

reboot

Restarts the computer after installation. If the installation media is still present or you used PXE booting to start the installation process, this may lead to an endless cycle of installations.

To shut the system down and allow for reconfiguration when the system is first turned on, use:

```
firstboot --reconfig
poweroff
```

At the very end of the Kickstart file, place the option %packages, followed by a list of packages to be installed, one per line. To see the available package names, look in the *Fedora* directory of the installation tree (e.g., the installation DVD or network installation server). Instead of selecting packages individually, you can choose groups of packages as shown in Table 10-3.

Table 10-3. Package groups available in Fedora Core 6

Category	Available package groups
Desktop environments	@gnome-desktop @kde-desktop
Applications	@authoring-and-publishing @editors @engineering-and-scientific @games @graphical-internet @graphics @office @sound-and-video @text-internet
Development	@development-libs @development-tools @eclipse @gnome-software-development @java-development @kde-software-development @legacy-software-development @ruby @x-software-development

Table 10-3. Package groups available in Fedora Core 6 (continued)

Category	Available package groups
Servers	*@dns-server* *@ftp-server* *@legacy-network-server* *@mail-server* *@mysql* *@network-server* *@news-server* *@printing* *@server-cfg* *@smb-server* *@sql-server* *@web-server*
Base system	*@admin-tools* *@base* *@base-x* *@dialup* *@dns-server* *@java* *@legacy-software-support* *@system-tools*
Languages	*@arabic-support* *@assamese-support* *@bengali-support* *@bulgarian-support* *@chinese-support* *@croatian-support* *@czech-support* *@estonian-support* *@gujarati-support* *@hebrew-support* *@hindi-support* *@hungarian-support* *@japanese-support* *@korean-support* *@polish-support* *@punjabi-support* *@romanian-support* *@russian-support* *@serbian-support* *@slovak-support* *@slovenian-support* *@tamil-support* *@thai-support* *@ukrainian-support*

Use * to select all available packages (dependencies and conflicts permitting). On the other extreme, use the special package group @core to install a very minimal, text-based system (almost too small to be usable but a good starting point for very compact systems) or @base to install a small text-based system with enough basic software to be useful.

To exclude a package, prepend a minus sign:

```
-hdparm
```

For example, if you wanted GNOME, office applications, Samba, printing capability, support for Russian, the GIMP graphics editor, and the Tomboy note program, place these lines at the end of the Kickstart file:

```
%packages
@gnome-desktop
@office
@smb-server
@printing
@russian-support
gimp
tomboy
```

Putting this all together, we get this Kickstart file:

```
auth --enableshadow --enablemd5
bootloader --location=mbr --md5pass=$1$RaNDoMju$OSOp7cTCbvCJ2ITUfcovM1
lang en_US
keyboard us
rootpw --iscrypted $1$RaNDoMju$OSOp7cTCbvCJ2ITUfcovM1
timezone America/Torontourl --url=http://192.168.1.2/fc6/

url --url=http://192.168.1.2/fc6/
network --bootproto=dhcp   --device eth0
network --bootproto=static --device eth1 \
    --ip 10.2.97.33 --netmask=255.255.255.0

# General partitioning options
clearpart --all --initlabel
zerombr yes

# Partitions
# Two IDE disk drives, hda and hdc
part raid.01 --size 100    --ondrive=hda
part raid.02 --size 40000 --ondrive=hda
part raid.03 --size 40000 --ondrive=hda
part raid.04 --size 40000 --ondrive=hda
part raid.05 --size 40000 --ondrive=hda
part raid.06 --size 1      --ondrive=hda --grow

part raid.07 --size 100    --ondrive=hdc
part raid.08 --size 40000 --ondrive=hdc
part raid.09 --size 40000 --ondrive=hdc
part raid.10 --size 40000 --ondrive=hdc
part raid.11 --size 40000 --ondrive=hdc
part raid.12 --size 1      --ondrive=hdc --grow

# RAID arrays
```

```
# Six RAID arrays, all RAID 1:
# - one is 100 MB /boot array
# - five are 40GB PV arrays
#   (4 * 4000 MB, remaining space in last array)
raid /boot --device md0 --level=RAID1 raid.01 raid.07 --fstype ext3
raid pv.01 --device md1 --level=RAID1 raid.02 raid.08
raid pv.02 --device md2 --level=RAID1 raid.03 raid.09
raid pv.03 --device md3 --level=RAID1 raid.04 raid.10
raid pv.04 --device md4 --level=RAID1 raid.05 raid.11
raid pv.05 --device md5 --level=RAID1 raid.06 raid.12

# Volume Group 'main'
volgroup main pv.01 pv.02 pv.03 pv.04 pv.05

# LVs for root (10GB), /home (35GB), /var (35GB), and swap (1GB),
# leaving about 20 GB available for snapshots and future expansion
# of the LVs
logvol swap  --vgname=main --size=1024  --name=swap
logvol /     --vgname=main --size=10000 --name=root --fstype=ext3
logvol /home --vgname=main --size=35000 --name=home --fstype=ext3
logvol /var  --vgname=main --size=35000 --name=var  --fstype=ext3

text
xconfig --startxonboot --depth=24 --resolution=1024x768

firewall --enabled --port=5900:tcp --ssh --http --smtp

firstboot --reconfig
poweroff

%packages
@gnome-desktop
@office
@smb-server
@printing
@russian-support
gimp
tomboy
```

Using a Kickstart file

To use a Kickstart file, make it accessible to the installation target system by placing it on an HTTP, FTP, or NFS server, or put it on a floppy disk.

To use a Kickstart file on floppy disk, add ks=floppy to the boot string encountered when booting from a USB key or optical disc:

```
: linux ks=floppy
```

It is assumed that the Kickstart file is named *ks.cfg*, that it is in the root directory of the floppy disk, and that the floppy disk is formatted with an MS-DOS (VFAT) or ext2 filesystem.

To make the Kickstart file available through the web server on a Fedora Core system, use these commands (assuming that the file is named *ks.cfg* and is in the current directory):

```
# mkdir -p /var/www/kickstart
# cp ks.cfg /var/www/kickstart
```

You can then access the Kickstart file by URL at the installation boot prompt:

```
: linux ks=http://192.168.1.2/kickstart/ks.cfg
```

(Replace *192.168.1.2* with the actual address of your server.) However, when booting from a PXE boot server, no boot prompt is provided. Instead, you must configure the Kickstart file by entering the URL into the *system-config-netboot* window for a particular IP address or range (Figure 10-20) or using the -K argument to the *pxeboot* command:

```
# pxeboot -a -O fc6 192.168.1 -K http://192.168.1.2/kickstart/ks.cfg
```

How Does It Work?

Fedora's Anaconda installer is written in Python and uses a library called the Red Hat Python Library, or *rhpl*. Before commencing the installation process, Anaconda must load the data structures that control the installation. These data structures can be filled with data from user input or from the Kickstart file.

What About...

...creating a Kickstart file using a graphical tool?

Fedora Core provides the *system-config-kickstart* utility for graphically editing a Kickstart file. Unfortunately, the version of *system-config-kickstart* shipped with Fedora Core 6 has some show-stopping bugs that cause it to create defective Kickstart files, and it is not able to configure LVM systems. However, you can use it to create a rough Kickstart file to use as a starting point for further customization.

...creating a Kickstart file that dynamically adjusts according to properties of the installation target?

Kickstart files can include a script that is run before installation, and the output of that script can be included into the Kickstart configuration.

For example, to configure swapspace to be double the memory size, you can add this script to the Kickstart file:

```
%pre

# Calculate twice the size of the installed memory, in MB
MEM=$(cat /proc/meminfo|sed -n "s/MemTotal: *\([0-9]\+\) kB/\1/p")
```

```
SIZE=$(( $MEM * 2 / 1024 ))

# Create the file /tmp/swap.cfg
echo  "logvol swap --vgname=main --size=$SIZE --name=swap" >/tmp/swap.cfg
```

The %pre option identifies this part of the file as a preinstallation script. Place this script at the end of the Kickstart file; it will produce the file */tmp/swap.cfg* containing the appropriate *logvol* line for the swap partition.

You can then replace the swap partition line in the Kickstart file with an option that refers to the */tmp/swap.cfg* file using %include:

```
# LVs for root (10GB), /home (35GB), /var (35GB), and swap (RAM * 2),
# leaving about 20 GB available for snapshots and future expansion
# of the LVs.
%include /tmp/swap.cfg
logvol /      --vgname=main --size=10000 --name=root --fstype=ext3
logvol /home --vgname=main --size=35000 --name=home --fstype=ext3
logvol /var  --vgname=main --size=35000 --name=var  --fstype=ext3
```

 Preinstallation scripts cannot change the installation source.

...performing customization after installation?

The Kickstart file can also include a script that is run after installation, using the %post option. Here is an example:

```
% post

# Add aliases to /etc/bashrc:
echo "alias l='ls -l'" >>/etc/bashrc
echo "alias cls='clear'" >>/etc/bashrc

# Change the login welcome message for text consoles
echo "Welcome to Fedora Core!" >/etc/issue

# Place a copy of acceptable-use-policy.txt
# in /etc/skel so that it will be copied to each
# new user's home diretory.
cd /etc/skel
wget http://192.168.1.2/text/acceptable-use-policy.txt

# Configure httpd to start automatically on boot
/sbin/chkconfig httpd on
```

 Post-installation scripts cannot reliably use hostnames; any IP addresses must be specified numerically.

...installing a system with the same configuration as another, previously installed system?

Whenever you install a system, the configuration used for that system is written into the file */root/anaconda-ks.cfg*. This is a standard Kickstart file with the disk layout commented out (every line has a # prepended). If you uncomment the disk layout and then use this as the Kickstart file for another system, it will produce an identical configuration (note that the hardware must be sufficiently similar for this to work).

Where Can I Learn More?

- The *RHEL 4 System Administration Guide* (see Chapter 1; RHEL uses a version of Anaconda similar to that used by Fedora): *http://www.redhat.com/docs/manuals/enterprise/RHEL-4-Manual/sysadmin-guide/*
- "Hands-Off Fedora Installs with Kickstart," by Ethan McCallum: *http://www.linuxdevcenter.com/pub/a/linux/2004/08/19/kickstart.html*
- The Fedora Wiki page with information on Kickstart: *http://fedoraproject.org/wiki/AnacondaKickstartIntegration*

10.5   Configuring the GRUB Bootloader

GRUB is a powerful bootloader that can be used to boot Linux, Windows, DOS, and other operating systems as well as the Xen virtualization system. By mastering its configuration file and command-line options, you can configure GRUB to boot exactly the way you want.

How Do I Do That?

GRUB is configured through the file */boot/grub/grub.conf*; typical contents of this file look like this:

```
# grub.conf generated by anaconda
#
# Note that you do not have to rerun grub after making changes to this file
# NOTICE:  You have a /boot partition.  This means that
#          all kernel and initrd paths are relative to /boot/, eg.
#          root (hd0,0)
#          kernel /vmlinuz-version ro root=/dev/main/root
#          initrd /initrd-version.img
#boot=/dev/hda
default=0
timeout=5
splashimage=(hd0,1)/grub/splash.xpm.gz
hiddenmenu
title Fedora Core (2.6.31-1.3420_fc6)
  root (hd0,1)
  kernel /vmlinuz-2.6.31-1.3420_fc6 ro root=/dev/main/root rhgb quiet
```

```
    initrd /initrd-2.6.31-1.3420_fc6.img
title Other
    rootnoverify (hd0,0)
    chainloader +1
```

This configuration file specifies two menu options, identified by the `title` keywords: Fedora Core and Windows (which Anaconda labels `Other` by default). Lines that start with a pound sign are comments. The first lines after the initial comments set up the appearance of the bootloader at startup time:

`default=0`

Configures the first `title` entry as the default entry (they are numbered starting at 0)—in this case, Fedora Core.

`timeout=5`

Sets the delay in seconds before the default entry is booted.

`splashimage=(hd0,1)/grub/splash.xpm.gz`

Loads a graphical background for the boot display.

`hiddenmenu`

Does not display the boot menu unless the user presses a key during the timeout period, in which case all of the available operating system entries are shown.

The filename given in the `splashimage` line is in a special, GRUB-specific form: `(hd0,1)` specifies the first hard disk, second partition (*/dev/hda2* in Linux terminology), and `/grub/splash.xpm.gz` identifies the pathname on that drive. Because */dev/hda1* is normally mounted on */boot*, the full pathname within the Fedora system is */boot/grub/splash.xpm.gz*.

 GRUB numbers partitions starting at 0, while Linux numbers them starting at 1.

The remainder of this file configures the two menu options. The first one consists of these four lines:

```
title Fedora Core (2.6.31-1.3420_fc6 )
    root (hd0,1)
    kernel /vmlinuz-2.6.31-1.3420_fc6 ro root=/dev/main/root rhgb quiet
    initrd /initrd-2.6.31-1.3420_fc6.img
```

Each line provides specific information:

`title Fedora Core (2.6.31-1.3420_fc6)`

The title displayed on the menu. The number in parentheses is the kernel version number; since it's standard practice to keep the second-most-recent kernel installed when the kernel is updated, just in case the new kernel does not boot properly, this information enables you to identify which kernel is newer.

`root (hd0,1)`

The root filesystem for the boot process, written using GRUB notation. Note that this may not be the root directory of the Fedora Core installation; it's usually the filesystem mounted at */boot* when the system is running.

`kernel /vmlinuz-2.6.31-1.3420_fc6 ro root=/dev/main/root rhgb quiet`

The kernel location within the root filesystem, plus boot options. These boot options specify that the root filesystem for Linux is */dev/main/root* (logical volume *root* in volume group *main*), and the *root* filesystem will be mounted read-only (ro), that the Red Hat Graphical Boot (rhgb) display is enabled, and that noncritical kernel boot messages will be suppressed (quiet).

`initrd /initrd-2.6.31-1.3420_fc6.img`

The location of the *initrd* ramdisk file. This file contains a compressed filesystem image that contains all of the files other than the kernel necessary for the initial phases of the Fedora system startup, including device drivers, programs, and scripts.

The other `title` entry is simpler:

```
title Other
        rootnoverify (hd0,0)
        chainloader +1
```

The lines in this entry invoke the Windows Stage 2 bootloader, found at the start of the Windows partition:

`rootnoverify (hd0,0)`

Similar to the root option in the Fedora Core entry, except that this partition will not be mounted, and therefore files cannot be accessed within the partition by GRUB.

`chainloader +1`

Specifies that the boot process should be turned over to the bootloader found in sector 1 of the partition.

Customizing the GRUB menu

You can directly edit the GRUB configuration file to change the appearance of the boot process.

To eliminate the boot menu entirely and directly boot the default entry, set the timeout value to zero:

```
timeout=0
```

This is a useful setting for end-user, single-boot systems with a stable kernel. On the other hand, if you have several operating systems installed, it may be convenient to remove the `hiddenmenu` line and use a longer timeout:

```
timeout=20
```

To turn the timeout off and wait indefinitely for the user to select the operating system, remove the timeout line from the file.

Using your own splash image

You can also customize or replace the boot image to include your company logo or a personalized message.

Use the GIMP graphics editor to create a 640×480 image. Reduce the number of colors by using the GIMP menu option Image → Mode → Indexed and selecting 14 colors.

 When converting an existing image to 14 colors, the result may look better if you select the No Dithering option, especially if the original image contains large areas of solid color. If you are creating a new image, select the indexed mode before you start drawing.

Save the image in the */boot/grub* directory, using the file extension *.xpm.gz*.

Another way to generate a splash image is to convert an existing landscape-oriented digital photo or a desktop wallpaper file using the ImageMagick *convert* program:

```
# convert -resize 640x480 -colors 14 photo.jpg /boot/grub/new_splash.xpm.gz
```

Finally, edit the splashimage line to point to your new creation:

```
splashimage=(hd0,1)/grub/new_splash.xpm.gz
```

An example of a modified splash image is shown in Figure 10-22.

Creating additional boot entries

Creating additional boot entries is simply a matter of entering additional lines with the options that you want.

For example, you could create two separate entries for Fedora Core—one for runlevel 5 (GUI) and one for runlevel 3 (text mode):

```
title Fedora Core - Graphical Login (2.6.31-1.3420_fc6)
   root (hd0,1)
   kernel /vmlinuz-2.6.31-1.3420_fc6 ro root=/dev/main/root rhgb quiet
   initrd /initrd-2.6.31-1.3420_fc6.img
title Fedora Core - Text Login (2.6.31-1.3420_fc6)
   root (hd0,1)
   kernel /vmlinuz-2.6.31-1.3420_fc6 ro root=/dev/main/root rhgb quiet 3
   initrd /initrd-2.6.31-1.3420_fc6.img
```

These two options are identical except for the descriptions on the title lines and the addition of the number 3 to the end of the kernel line for text-mode entry.

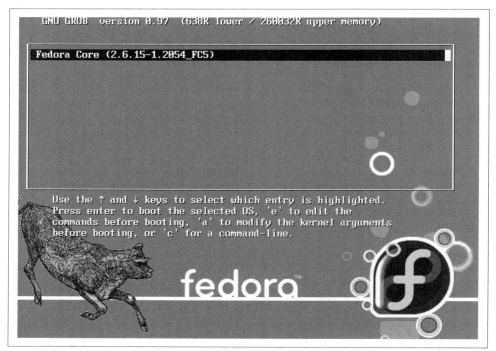

Figure 10-22. Modified splash image

 Installing a new kernel RPM will add an additional boot option and make it the default. If you are using *yum* to perform updating, a maximum of two versions of the kernel will be installed at once (configurable in */etc/yum/pluginconf.d/installonlyn.conf*), so old kernel versions and their corresponding GRUB entries may be removed from the menu by *yum* when updating.

Installing GRUB's boot record from Fedora

Anaconda normally installs the GRUB boot record on the first disk drive automatically.

There are two situations where it may be necessary to manually install GRUB on an existing system:

- When you're using a RAID 1 */boot* partition, Anaconda will install the Grub boot record only on the first disk drive. Having a mirrored copy of */boot* won't help if the first disk drive fails and you can't boot from the second drive—a situation easily remedied by installing the GRUB boot record on the second drive as well.

- When your boot record is corrupted or overwritten by another program, such as an installer for another operating system, you may need to manually install the GRUB boot record again.

The easiest way to install GRUB is to use the *grub-install* script:

```
# grub-install --root-directory=/boot /dev/hda
Installation finished. No error reported.
This is the contents of the device map /boot/boot/grub/device.map.
Check if this is correct or not. If any of the lines is incorrect,
fix it and re-run the script `grub-install'.

(fd0)    /dev/fd0
(hd0)    /dev/hda
(hd1)    /dev/hdb
(hd2)    /dev/hdc
(hd3)    /dev/sdb
```

The `--root-directory` argument specifies the root directory for the boot files and should be used only if */boot* is a mount point for a separate boot partition. The drive argument at the end of the line (*/dev/hda*) specifies the hard drive that GRUB will be installed on.

grub-install uses Linux disk names, such as */dev/hdc*, instead of Grub disk names such as (hd2).

Installing GRUB's boot record from a GRUB DVD or floppy disk

Sometimes the GRUB boot record gets damaged, making it impossible to boot the system normally. It may be necessary to boot from a GRUB DVD or floppy disk to fix this type of problem.

To create a GRUB DVD on a Fedora system (obviously not the one that won't boot!), enter these commands:

```
# cd /usr/share/grub/
# growisofs -Z /dev/cdrom -R -b stage2_eltorito -no-emul-boot
    -boot-load-size 4 -boot-info-table i386-redhat
```

Type the entire *growisofs* command on one continuous line.

To create a bootable floppy instead of a DVD:

```
# cd /usr/share/grub/i386-redhat
# cat stage1 stage2 >/dev/fd0
```

It's worthwhile keeping a GRUB DVD or floppy with your system manuals just in case you ever find that you can't boot your system due to bootloader problems.

Boot your system with this disc or floppy. A GRUB command prompt will appear, as shown in Figure 10-23.

```
    GNU GRUB  version 0.95  (638K lower / 260032K upper memory)

[ Minimal BASH-like line editing is supported.  For the first word, TAB
  lists possible command completions.  Anywhere else TAB lists the possible
  completions of a device/filename.]

grub> _
```

Figure 10-23. GRUB command prompt from a CD/DVD boot

At this prompt, search for your *stage1* file:

```
grub> find /boot/grub/stage1

Error 15: File not found

grub> find /grub/stage1
 (hd0,0)
```

If your boot files are in your root filesystem, GRUB will find */boot/grub/stage1*, but if you have a separate */boot* partition, GRUB will find */grub/stage1*. In the previous example, the partition (hd0,0) contains the *stage1* file.

Make this partition your *root* partition:

```
grub> root (hd0,0)
 Filesystem type is ext2fs, partition type 0x83
```

Now instruct GRUB to set up the boot record on that drive:

```
grub> setup (hd0)
 Checking if "/boot/grub/stage1" exists... no
 Checking if "/grub/stage1" exists... yes
 Checking if "/grub/stage2" exists... yes
 Checking if "/grub/e2fs_stage1_5" exists... yes
 Running "embed /grub/e2fs_stage1_5 (hd0)"... 15 sectors are embedded.
succeeded
 Running "install /grub/stage1 (hd0) (hd0)1+15 p (hd0,0)/grub/stage2 /grub/grub
.conf"... succeeded.
Done
```

 Note that the *setup* command was given the drive (hd0) instead of the partition (hd0,0) to install the boot record at the start of the drive instead of the start of the boot partition.

You can now remove the GRUB disc/floppy and boot directly from the hard drive.

Editing boot options

To temporarily override a GRUB menu option, select a menu option on the boot menu using the up/down arrow keys, and then press E (for edit). The screen shown in Figure 10-24 will be displayed.

> If you have a bootloader password configured, you will be prompted for it at this point.

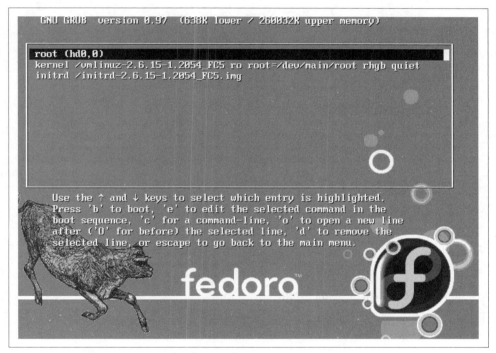

Figure 10-24. Selecting a menu-entry line to edit

Use the arrow keys to select the line you wish to edit, and then press E again. You can now move across the line using the arrow keys, as shown in Figure 10-25. Type new text to insert it into the line, or use the Backspace/Delete keys to remove text. Press Enter when done.

Press Enter to accept your changes or Esc to undo them. In either case you will return to the menu-entry display shown in Figure 10-24; press B to boot, or press Esc to return to the boot menu.

Figure 10-25. Edit a line in a menu entry

As a shortcut, if you are adding boot options only to an existing menu entry, select the entry using the up/down arrow keys, then press A (for append). You can then type the additional option(s), such as a runlevel. Press Enter to proceed with booting or Esc to cancel and return to the boot menu.

Installing or changing a GRUB password

To protect against the unauthorized use of runlevel 5 or other boot options, it's a good idea to add a password entry to the boot menu. If you didn't do this during the installation, you can add the password at any time by following these steps:

Generate an encrypted password with the *grub-md5-crypt* command:

```
$ grub-md5-crypt
Password: bigsecret
Retype password: bigsecret
$1$f1z061$j/UEYyBn0e0996w0gjq4k/
```

The line in bold at the bottom of the listing is the encrypted (scrambled) version of the password.

Next, edit the */boot/grub/grub.conf* file and add this line at the top, substituting the password you just generated:

```
password --md5 $1$f1z061$j/UEYyBn0e0996w0gjq4k/
```

When you boot the system, you will still be able to select a boot menu entry, but to perform any advanced operations (such as appending runlevel information to a boot entry), you will need to enter the password.

How Does It Work?

GRUB actually consists of four pieces of software, plus some utilities:

stage 1
> The boot record. This tiny piece of code is less than 512 bytes long.

stage 1.5
> Additional drivers for filesystems, such as ext2, to enable GRUB to find the *stage 2* files.

stage 2
> The standalone GRUB command shell and menu program.

/sbin/grub
> A version of the GRUB command shell that can be executed inside a running Fedora system.

During boot, the system BIOS loads *stage 1* as the boot record and executes it, which then loads *stage 1.5* (if necessary) and finds *stage 2*. *stage 2* then seeks out the GRUB configuration file *menu.lst* (a symbolic link to *grub.conf*, which the Fedora developers apparently consider to be a better name).

The GRUB command shell supports over three dozen commands; most of these are never used except by experts and developers. Instead, most users interact with the GRUB menu.

The *grub.conf* file permits a set of boot options to be presented to the user as a menu entry, removing most of the complexity from the user's view.

A typical Linux entry in *grub.conf* sets the root filesystem, which is mounted by GRUB to enable access to the kernel and other boot drives. The entry also specifies the name of the kernel and *initrd* ramdisk to be loaded into memory, and also indicates any configuration options that are to be passed to the kernel.

What About...

...an archive of GRUB splash images?

The author of the splash-image code maintains a small gallery of tested splash images at *http://ruslug.rutgers.edu/~mcgrof/grub-images/images/* and an archive at *http://ruslug.rutgers.edu/~mcgrof/grub-images/images/working-splashimages/*.

This works well. Simply add the entries for the other Linux distributions to the active */boot/grub/grub.conf* (or */boot/grub/menu.lst*) file. This can be done by specifying that the second Linux distribution install GRUB at the start of that distribution's root file-system partition instead of placing it in the master boot record for the drive. Then copy the */boot/grub/grub.conf* entries from the second Linux distribution to the first one.

Where Can I Learn More?

- The Grub manual: *http://www.gnu.org/software/grub/manual/* (also installed as an *info* document in Fedora Core)
- The Grub web site: *http://www.gnu.org/software/grub/*
- The sample configuration file */usr/share/doc/grub-0.95/menu.lst*
- The manpage for *convert*

10.6   Using Rescue Mode on an Installation Disc

The Fedora Core installation DVD—or disc 1 of the CD set—can be used to boot into a *rescue mode*, which lets you access a Fedora system installed on a hard disk without booting from that hard disk. This can be used to recover from many types of system failure or badly misconfigured startup scripts.

How Do I Do That?

Inset your Fedora installation disc (DVD or CD 1) into the system and boot from it. At the boot prompt, enter:

```
boot: linux rescue
```

You will be presented with the standard language and keyboard menus (see Figures 1-5 and 1-6 in Chapter 1), and then the question shown in Figure 10-26 will be displayed.

If you want to be able to transfer files to and from the system (for example, to back up critical data), answer Yes; otherwise, answer No. If you answer Yes, the standard network configuration dialog will appear, enabling you to select DHCP network configuration or manually enter the network details.

Figure 10-27 shows the next screen, which offers to mount your hard disk directories for you. If you need to access files on your hard disk, select Continue; if you need to access files on your hard disk but want to avoid the possibility of damaging any files, select Read-Only; and if you do not want to mount the hard disk filesystems (for example, because you want to work on the filesystems first, resizing or repairing them), select Skip.

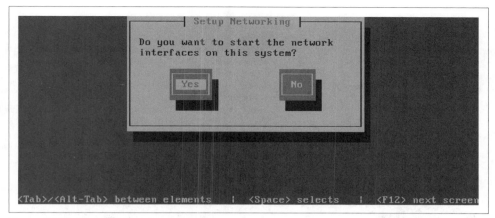

Figure 10-26. Network interface question

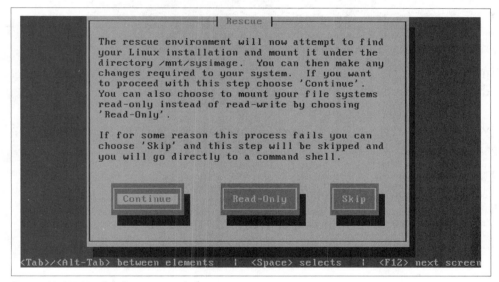

Figure 10-27. Hard disk mounting dialog

Figure 10-28 shows the final dialog that will be displayed before a root shell is opened, which informs you whether the hard disk filesystems were mounted. Select OK to proceed to a *root* shell.

A minimal environment is available in the rescue-mode shell, providing access to the most important system administration commands.

If you requested that the hard disk filesystems be mounted, the mount point will be */mnt/sysimage*, and the mounts will be cascaded properly. Therefore, if you have separate */boot* and */home* filesystems, they will be mounted under */mnt/sysimage/boot* and */mnt/sysimage/home*.

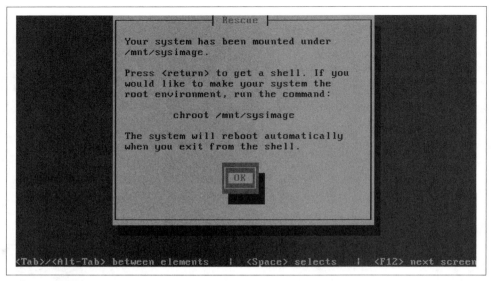

Figure 10-28. Final dialog before the rescue-mode shell

If you selected a read/write mount, you can temporarily make the root directory of the hard disk your root directory using the *chroot* command:

```
sh-3.1# chroot /mnt/sysimage
```

You can now access directories in their usual locations (*/etc*, */home*, and so forth), and you'll have access to all of the software installed on the hard disk.

 When you issue the *chroot* command, you will no longer be accessing the software on the installation disc. Therefore, if the commands installed on the hard disk filesystems are corrupted or damaged, you will be using the corrupted or damaged versions. Likewise, if the software on your hard disk is newer than the software on the installation disc, you will be using the newer versions.

Press Ctrl-D (for done) to exit from the *chroot* shell and return to the normal rescue shell.

If you chose not to mount your hard disk filesystems, any LVM volume groups on your hard disks will be inaccessible. To access the VGs, issue these commands:

```
sh-3.1# lvm vgscan
 Reading all physical volumes. This may take a while...
 Found volume group "main" using metadata type lvm2
sh-3.1# lvm vgchange -ay
 2 logical volumes in volume group "main" now active
```

You can then access the logical volumes as */dev/<pv>/<lv>* (for example, */dev/main/ root*).

When you are finished with the shell, press Ctrl-D. The system will automatically reboot.

How Does It Work?

Rescue mode uses the same Linux kernel, *initrd* ramdisk, and device probing that are used during the installation process to create a minimal work environment using only software loaded from the installation disc. The same code that is used to detect and mount existing Fedora partitions for an upgrade installation is used to mount the partitions during rescue mode.

The *chroot* command changes the definition of the *root* directory for one process—in this case, a shell—and any processes started by that shell. Changing the *root* directory effectively changes the PATH so that the software installed in the *chroot* environment (software on the hard disk) is used while the *chroot* is active. When you exit from the *chroot* shell, the root directory reverts to the root directory of the installation session, which is a ramdisk.

What About...

...copying files to or from another machine while in rescue mode?

The *scp* command is available in rescue mode and can be used to copy files to or from another Fedora system (or other Linux host). You must enable the network interfaces in order for this to work.

To copy a file from an FTP or HTTP server, use *wget*:

```
sh-3.1# wget http://192.168.1.2/help.txt
```

...using a GUI while in rescue mode?

Unfortunately, there's not enough of the supporting infrastructure in place in rescue mode to support the use of a GUI.

...accessing software from the hard disk without using chroot?

Set your path to include directories on the mounted hard disk filesystems:

```
sh-3.1# PATH=$PATH:/mnt/sysimage/bin:/mnt/sysimage/usr/bin:
    /mnt/sysimage/sbin:/mnt/sysimage/usr/sbin:/mnt/sysimage/usr/local/bin
```

 Type this command on one line.

Where Can I Learn More?

- The Fedora Core Installation Manual: *http://fedora.redhat.com/docs/fedora-install-guide-en/fc6/*
- The manpages for *chroot*, *wget*, *scp*, and *lvm*

10.7   Installing Xen Virtual Machines

Xen is a technology that permits one physical computer to act as two or more virtual machines (or *domains*). Each domain is isolated from other domains, so administration privilege can be safely delegated; you can designate a system administrator for one domain and give him the *root* password for total control of that system, confident that he will not be able to touch the configuration of other domains.

Virtualization technology is also very helpful when testing multiple software versions or configurations, and since virtual machines can be migrated between physical systems, it provides a lot of flexibility for server deployment and management.

To use Xen, you must install a special kernel and utilities on your existing Fedora system, which then becomes your primary domain (*Domain-0*). You can then install Fedora on as many additional domains as you want.

How Do I Do That?

To set up for Xen, install the *kernel-xen* and *xen* packages using *Pirut* or this command:

```
# yum -y install kernel-xen xen
```

Reboot your system. When the GRUB boot screen appears, press the spacebar to display the boot menu. Select the new xen kernel using the cursor keys, and then press Enter to boot.

 To make your system boot the Xen kernel by default, edit */boot/grub/grub.conf* (see Lab 10.5, "Configuring the GRUB Bootloader")

You can confirm that you are running the Xen kernel by using the *uname* command:

```
# uname -r
2.6.17-1.2564.fc6xen
```

The *xend* service should also be running, which you can confirm using the *service* command:

```
# service xend status
service xend is running
```

The Fedora installation that you are using is *Domain-0*, the master domain. Additional virtual machines, called *guest domains*, must be installed from a network installation server. If you do not have one, you can quickly set up one within *Domain-0* by inserting a Fedora Core DVD and typing:

```
# yum -y install httpd
...(Lines snipped)...
# setenforce 0
# ln -s /media/disk /var/www/html/fedora
# service httpd start
Starting httpd:                                        [ OK ]
```

 The setenforce command just shown disables SELinux protection for your system, which presents a security risk. Re-enable SELinux as soon as you are finished using the network installation server:

```
# setenforce 1
```

To start the guest domain installation:

```
# xenguest-install
What is the name of your virtual machine? fedora
 How much RAM should be allocated (in megabytes)? 256
 What would you like to use as the disk (path)? /var/xen/fedora
 How large would you like the disk to be (in gigabytes)? 2
 Would you like to enable graphics support (yes or no) no
 What is the install location? http://192.168.2.48/fedora
```

The name of the virtual machine can be any value that meets the requirements for a filename. The disk path and size requested are used to set up a file that will act as the hard disk for the guest domain. The install location is the URL of the network installation server; if you're using an HTTP server on *Domain-0*, use the full IP address of that system instead of the loopback address 127.0.0.1 (since, inside a guest domain, the loopback destination is the guest domain itself, not *Domain-0*).

A regular Fedora installation will now start in text mode within the guest domain. After prompting you for the language and keyboard, the installer will give you the option of continuing with a text mode installation or using VNC for a graphical installation, as shown in Figure 10-29.

 This message indicates that the installer was unable to start X. This is normal, since the guest domain does not have a video card.

Choose one of the two options:

- To continue in text mode, press Enter.
- To use VNC, press Tab, and then press Enter. The installer will prompt you to create a VNC password and will then start a VNC server. This message will be displayed on the screen:

```
Starting VNC...
The VNC server is now running.
```

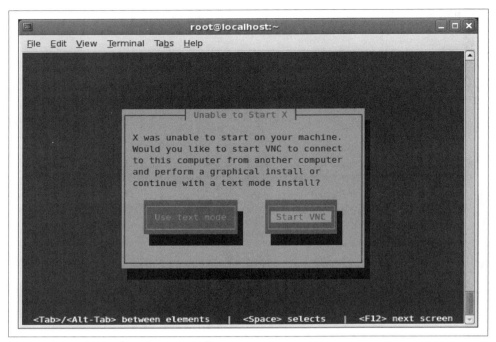

Figure 10-29. Text mode and VNC installation options

```
Please connect to 192.168.2.112:1 to begin the install...
Starting graphical installation...

Press <enter> for a shell
```

Use the *vncviewer* program to connect to the indicated address and port:

```
$ vncviewer 192.168.2.112:1
```

A window will appear showing the normal Fedora graphical installation display.

You can then proceed with a regular Fedora installation into the guest domain. When the installation is finished, you can start your guest domain with this command:

```
# xm create fedora
Using config file "/etc/xen/fedora".
Going to boot Fedora Core (2.6.17-1.2517.fc6xen)
  kernel: /vmlinuz-2.6.17-1.2517.fc6xen
  initrd: /initrd-2.6.17-1.2517.fc6xen
Started domain fedora
```

This will boot the guest domain. You can view the current domains using xm list:

```
# xm list
Name                       ID Mem(MiB) VCPUs State  Time(s)
Domain-0                    0      510     2 r-----   247.8
fedora                      5      256     1 -b----     9.5
```

This display shows that the domains *Domain-0* and *fedora* are both running, and displays the domain ID number, memory, virtual CPUs, and CPU usage in seconds for each domain.

So what's going on in the guest domain? Good question! You can see the guest console by using xm console:

```
# xm console fedora
```

The first time your guest domain boots, you will see a text version of the *firstboot* configuration.

 To start a guest domain and connect to its console immediately, use xm create with the -c (console) option:

```
# xm create -c fedora
```

After the first boot, you may find it just as easy to use SSH to connect to the guest domain as though it were a remote server:

```
$ ssh -X 192.168.2.112
```

The -XC option enables the remote display of X clients, so that you can use graphical administration tools such as *system-config-printer* within the guest domain and display the window on your *Domain-0* screen.

To shut down a guest domain, either initiate a shutdown within the domain (for example, by executing the *shutdown* command), or use the xm shutdown command in *Domain-0*:

```
# xm shutdown fedora
```

The shutdown will take up to a few minutes, just like the shutdown of a physical system. If a guest domain is stuck in an unrecoverable state, you can forcefully stop it (although this is the equivalent of turning off the power on the virtual machine, so it may result in data loss):

```
# xm destroy fedora
```

How Does It Work?

Xen boots a small program called a *hypervisor* before booting *Domain-0*. The hypervisor masks the underlying hardware and presents a modified virtual environment to each domain. *Domain-0* has direct access to certain hardware, such as network interface cards and other peripherals, and the standard device drivers are used to access those devices.

Inside *Domain-0*, a service daemon named *xend* provides monitoring and control functions for the guest domains and communication between the guest domains and certain types of hardware (such as network interfaces).

The Xen environment is different from the normal PC environment, and the operating system must be modified to run in this special environment; this is called *paravirtualization* because it requires some cooperation on the part of the guest operating system. The advantage to this approach is higher performance and the ability to control the guest operating system in certain ways (such as sending the guest OS a shutdown message when xm shutdown is used).

Xen is developed as an open source project; XenSource is a company formed by the original Xen researchers to offer an enhanced, commercially supported version of Xen.

The Fedora Xen guest installation tool, *xenguest-install*, is a Python script that interfaces with Fedora's Anaconda system and *python* libraries. The configuration files generated by *xenguest-install* are stored in */etc/xen*.

What About...

...starting Xen guest domains automatically at boot time?

Xen configuration files created with *xenguest-install* are installed in */etc/xen*, and the filenames match the guest domain names. If these files are symlinked to the */etc/xen/auto* directory, they will be started automatically at boot time by the *xendomains* service.

For example, to start the *fedora* guest domain automatically at each boot, link its configuration file using ln -s:

```
# ln -s /etc/xen/fedora /etc/xen/auto
```

...hardware support for virtualization?

CPU makers are starting to build support for virtualization into their CPUs. AMD's technology is named Pacifica, while Intel's is named VT-X. Xen can take advantage of either technology to boost performance and to provide full virtualization to unmodified operating systems.

...using other network or storage configurations?

Xen is very configurable, but the Fedora Xen guest installation script handles only a small subset of the possibilities. To use alternate configurations it is necessary to manually edit the configuration files in */etc/xen* (see the Xen documentation and the sample configuration files in */etc/xen* for details).

...booting other operating systems?

It is possible to install other Linux distributions and (soon) other operating systems into guest domains, but they must be installed manually; Fedora's Xen installer only works with Fedora Core at this point. For information on installing other Xen guests, see the XenSource web site (*http://www.xensource.com*) and the documentation for the Xen guest you wish to install.

Microsoft Windows and other unmodified operating systems can be used as Xen guests only with hardware virtualization support.

…monitoring the resource usage and activity of Xen domains?

Xen provides the *xentop* tool for domain monitoring, shown in Figure 10-30. As the name implies, it provides a *top*-like display of domain activity, updated every three seconds.

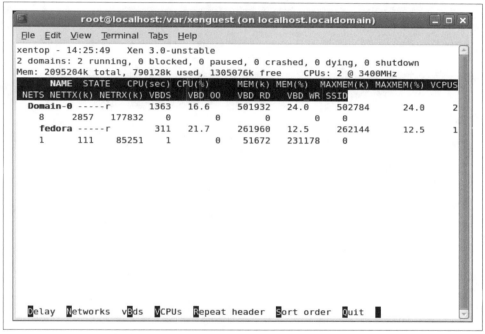

Figure 10-30. Xentop display

Fedora Core also includes the Virtual Machine Manager (*virt-manager*) application, but the version released with Fedora Core 6 is at a very early stage of development. It is designed to provide an effective way of managing virtual machines through a graphical user interface; you can follow development on the fedora-xen list (see Lab 9.1, "Participating in the Fedora Mailing Lists").

Where Can I Learn More?

- The Fedora Virtualization Project: *http://fedora.redhat.com/projects/virtualization/*
- The XenSource web site: *http://www.xensource.com/*
- The Xen Wiki: *http://wiki.xensource.com/xenwiki/*

Index

Symbols

A

We'd like to hear your suggestions for improving our indexes. Send email to *index@oreilly.com*.

G

M

m4 command, 428
MAC addresses, 125, 378, 379
MAC (mandatory access controls), 473
Mac systems (Apple), 5, 235
magic numbers, 257
mail command, 427
mail delivery agent (MDA), 427
MAIL environment variable, 244
mail exchangers, 387, 392
mail facility level, 505
mail transport agent (MTA), 427, 429
mail user agent (see MUA)
MAILADDR line (mdadm.conf), 339
mailing lists
    overview, 522–527
    Rawhide-related, 547
    referring to Bugzilla bugs, 540
Mailman software, 526, 527
MAILTO environment variable, 361
Main tab (Apache), 406
make install command, 288, 289
Makefiles, 286, 288, 289
%makeinstall macro, 303
man command, 165, 169
man2html command, 169
mandatory access controls (MAC), 473
man-in-the-middle attacks, 235
manpages
    finding, 166, 167
    overview, 164–165
    printing, 169
    section numbers for, 165
    SELinux booleans, 466
masquerading, 375, 426
master boot record (MBR), 103, 567
master nameservers
    configuring named nameservers, 385
    configuring slave nameservers, 395, 396
    defined, 382
maximize icon, 45
max-lease-time statement (DHCP), 377
MaxTapTime value (Synaptics driver), 149
mbox format, 428
MBR (master boot record), 103, 567
mcedit text editor, 189, 364
MCS (multicategory security), 474, 475
md0 device node, 333
md1 device node, 333
md2 device node, 333
MDA (mail delivery agent), 427
mdadm command
    creating RAID arrays, 335
    handling drive failures, 336, 337
    monitoring RAID arrays, 339, 340
    overview, 333
    restarting RAID arrays, 338
    setting up hot spare, 341
    stopping RAID arrays, 338
mdadm.conf files, 339
mdmonitor service, 339
MDNS (multicast DNS), 462
mdstat file, 333, 336, 339
/media directory, 171
MediaWiki, 444–447
MergedFB option (xorg.conf), 155
MergedXinerama option (xorg.conf), 155
message_file entry (vsftpd file), 450
messages file, 143
Metacity window manager, 49, 53
metadata
    packages and, 260, 264, 279
    repackaging and, 282
MetaModes option (xorg.conf), 153, 155
method keyword, 10, 11
Microsoft fonts, 90
minimize icon, 45
minute field (scheduling tasks), 360
mirroring
    as backup media, 351
    development repository, 544–547
    disaster recovery and, 344–347
    LVM support, 329
    RAID arrays and, 333, 345
    shutting down, 346
mirrorlist name/value pair
        (fedora-extras), 277
mkdir command, 176
mkfs command, 103
mkisofs command, 356
mkzftree command, 353, 356
MLS (multilevel security), 474, 475
MLS policy (SELinux), 475, 476
/mnt directory, 171
modem dial-up connections, 133
modes, controlling file access, 212–221
Modes section (xorg.conf), 69
modprobe command, 143
Module section (xorg.conf), 69
module-type field (PAM), 493
Monitor section (xorg.conf), 69, 73
monitoring
    CPU load continuously, 229
    process information from shell
        prompt, 226

monitoring (*continued*)
    process information in KDE, 224–225
    process information on character
        displays, 225–226
    processing information in
      •   GNOME, 222–224
    RAID arrays, 339, 341
monitors
    displaying, 44
    nonstandard, 73
    xorg.conf file and, 68
month field (scheduling tasks), 360
mount command
    acl option, 478
    backup script and, 357
    grep command and, 239
    remount option, 478
    showing mount point, 471
    viewing devices, 183
    viewing mtab file, 100
mouse
    multiple, 73
    problems with, 15
    touchpad and, 151
Moving option (kwin), 63
Mozilla browser, 540
/msg command, 530
mt command, 359
MTA (mail transport agent), 427, 429
mtab file, 100
MUA (mail user agent)
    considerations, 431
    defined, 427
    Dovecot servers and, 433
    remote mailboxes, 429
multicategory security (MCS), 474, 475
multidevice nodes, 333
multilevel security (MLS), 474, 475
multimedia keyboards, 55
multimedia-snap, 313
MultiViews permission, 409, 412
mv command, 176, 177
MX record, 387, 388, 392
mysql monitor program, 439, 442
MySQL server
    booleans and, 466
    Bugzilla support, 540
    creating databases and
        accounts, 439–443
    MediaWiki support, 444, 446
mysqld service, 439, 441

N

name name/value pair (fedora-extras), 277
Name tag (spec file), 294
named nameserver
    configuring graphically, 382–388
    configuring via configuration/data
        files, 388–393
    IP addresses, 397, 398
    overview, 381–382
    testing, 393
named pipe, 514
named_write_master_zones boolean, 468
nameserver keyword (resolv.conf), 140
nameservers
    changing, 400
    defined, 126
    domain information to Internet and, 397
    loopback address, 127
    root, 399
    using locally, 397
    (see also master nameservers; slave
        nameservers)
NameVirtualHost directive, 415
nano text editor, 189
NAT (network address translation), 375
National Security Agency (NSA), 476
Nautilus (GNOME)
    adding/removing fonts, 87–88
    changing permissions, 215–216
    customizing, 51, 53
    managing files graphically, 179, 180
    viewing permissions, 220
Navigation Panel (Konqueror), 181
neat tool, 397
Nero program, 7
netmasks
    by IP address class, 137
    routing and, 123, 139–140
    wlan interfaces and, 137
netstat command, 489, 490
network address translation (NAT), 375
Network Configuration window
    changing device configurations, 120–126
    configuring DNS and Hosts
        table, 126–127
    depicted, 118
    saving network configuration, 128
Network Device Control window, 130, 131
Network Installation dialog, 571
network option (Kickstart), 578
network profiles, 131

OUTPUT chain of rules, 462
ownership
    changing for files, 220, 221
    killall command and, 227

P

P command (vi editor), 187
p command (vi editor), 187
package icons, 306
packages
    building, 290–306
    building for different architectures, 307
    defined, 260
    excluding from automatic updates, 284
    Fedora Core support, 582, 583
    installing multiple versions, 270
    removing, 266, 268
    upgrading, 266–267
package-version.tgz, 289
Packard, Keith, 96
packet routing, 145
Page Down key, 165, 179
Page Options tab (Apache), 408
Page Up key, 165, 179
PalmDetect value (Synaptics driver), 149
PalmMinWidth value (Synaptics driver), 149
PalmMinZ value (Synaptics driver), 149
PAM (Pluggable Authentication
        Module), 493–503
pam_abl.so module, 499, 500
pam_cracklib.so module, 496
pam_env.so module, 495
pam_limits.so module, 496
pam_loginuid.so module, 496
pam_nologin.so module, 495
pam_permit.so module, 495, 502
pam_time.so module, 498
pam_unix.so module, 495, 496
Panel Animation setting (Hiding section), 59
panel bar (panel), 41
panel icons, 43
Panel-Hiding Buttons setting (Hiding
        section), 59
panels
    adding, 50
    adding items to, 58
    customizing GNOME, 50, 51
    customizing KDE, 57–60
    deleting, 50, 58
    deleting applications from, 58
    deleting items from, 50
    expanding, 51

GNOME/KDE support, 41
    hiding, 51
    icon support, 43
    moving items around, 50
    setting properties, 51, 58
    setting size of, 51
parameters, 371
paravirtualization, 606
parentheses ( ), 166, 249
parity, 343
part option (Kickstart), 579
parted command, 325
parted tool, 567
partition option (Kickstart), 579
partition table, 567
partitioning/partitions
    adding, 314–315, 324
    flexible disk layout and, 330
    layout for, 22–27
    options supported, 20, 21
    RAID arrays and, 334, 561
    removing, 315, 325
    resizing, 552–557
    USB devices and, 100, 101–103
passive (PASV) operation, 451
passphrase, 233, 236
passthrough permission, 212
passwd command, 205, 206, 207
passwd file, 208–209
password aging, 203, 204, 209
password field (passwd file), 208
Password Info tab (User Properties
        window), 203
passwords
    Apache server and, 417–419
    basic authentication and, 421
    boot menu and, 194
    bootloader, 26, 37
    brute-force attacks, 499, 501
    Bugzilla support, 537
    changing for Samba users, 373
    changing periodically, 203
    changing timeouts, 492
    email address as, 449
    giving up timestamp, 493
    GRUB bootloader, 596
    IRC and, 528
    maintenance checking, 495
    managing from command line, 206, 207
    MySQL recommendations, 439
    protecting statistics, 454
    recommendations, 30

wireless adapters, firmware and, 142–143,
146
wireless extensions, 145
wireless networks
airplane mode, 114
configuring, 131
configuring from command line, 137–139
port forwarding feature, 144
wlan interfaces, 136, 146
workplace/desktop switcher, 43
WPA encryption keys, 134
:wq command (vi editor), 188
write (w) permission, 212–214, 219
write_enable entry (vsftpd file), 450
wuftp log format, 455

X

X command (vi editor), 187
x command (vi editor), 187, 188
X tunneling, 404
X Window System
additional resources, 48, 73
controlling display access, 122
fast pasting, 46
font support, 93
interoperability, 41
x86_64 architecture, 5
xboard program, 231
xchat command, 527–528, 530, 532
xconfig option (Kickstart), 581
xDSL, 133
Xen virtual machines, 588, 602–608
xend service, 602, 605
xendomains service, 606
xenguest-install.py tool, 606
xentop tool, 607
Xfce desktop, 48, 114
XFS filesystem, 474
Xinerama monitor, 157
xinetd service, 403, 573
xm console command, 605
xm list command, 604
xm shutdown command, 605, 606
XML, 419
X.org configuration file format, 156, 157
xorg.conf file
additional resources, 73
ATI cards, 154–156
configuration information in, 68–72
configuring touchpads, 147–148

nonstandard monitors, 73
NVIDIA cards, 152, 153
Option keyword, 150
xpdf program, 79
XPM format, 306
XSLT transformation stylesheet, 419
xterm command, 95
Xvesa, 557

Y

y command (vi editor), 187
yum tool
additional resources, 38
Anaconda installer and, 37
automating updates, 284–286
immutable files and, 488
Rawhide and, 541, 543
repositories and, 270–280
rollback operations, 281
RPM package format and, 3, 260
SELinux and, 476
Xen support, 602
Yumex tool, 276
yum-updateonboot package, 285, 286
yum-updatesd services, 279, 284
yy command (vi editor), 187

Z

Zarro boogs, 536
zcat command, 169
zenity program, 258, 259
zerombr option (Kickstart), 578
Zone File Path value (zones), 386
Zone Modification Serial Number value
(zones), 385
zones
configuring named nameserver, 390–391
creating, 390–393
defined, 383
DNS values, 384–387
reverse mapping and, 399
zsh shell, 163
ZZ command (vi editor), 188

About the Author

Chris Tyler is a computer consultant and a professor of computer studies at Seneca College in Toronto, Ontario, Canada where he teaches courses on programming, Linux system administration, and the X Window System. Over the last 22 years, he has programmed a wide range of systems in more than two dozen languages. In 1996 he started focusing on database-backed web development and has been using Red Hat Linux and Fedora Core ever since. He blogs from time to time on the O'Reilly Network (*http://oreillynet.com*) and his own web site (*http://chris.tylers.info*).

Colophon

The image on the cover of *Fedora Linux* is a cowboy roping a calf. In the Old West, horseback cowboys entrapped and retrieved fugitive cattle with the help of a lasso, or lariat, a rigid noose that could be tossed over a wayward animal's neck and easily tightened with a pull of the rope. The stiffness of the rope ensured that the noose maintained its wide aperture in midair.

Today, this activity is an official rodeo event called *tie-down roping*, sanctioned by the Professional Rodeo Cowboys Association. In this competition, a calf is released from a narrow holding pen, referred to as the *bucking chute*, into the rodeo arena. After giving his conquest a brief head start, the cowboy chases after the calf on his specially trained horse and attempts to rope it as quickly as possible. He then must expeditiously tip the animal on its side, a maneuver known as *flanking*, and use another tiny piece of rope, the *pigging string*, to bind together any three of its four legs. If the calf is unable to break free from its fetters in six seconds or less, the cowboy's attempt is a success, and his official time is registered. Leading professional ropers can ensnare and immobilize a calf in approximately seven seconds.

The cover image and chapter opening graphics are from the Dover Pictorial Archive. The cover font is Adobe ITC Garamond. The text font is Linotype Birka; the heading font is Adobe Myriad Condensed; and the code font is LucasFont's TheSans Mono Condensed.

Better than e-books

Buy *Fedora Linux* and access the digital
edition FREE on Safari for 45 days.

Go to www.oreilly.com/go/safarienabled
and type in coupon code 7DD4-6RAC-4S6T-1VCP-RTXJ

Search
thousands of
top tech books

Download
whole chapters

Cut and Paste
code examples

Find
answers fast

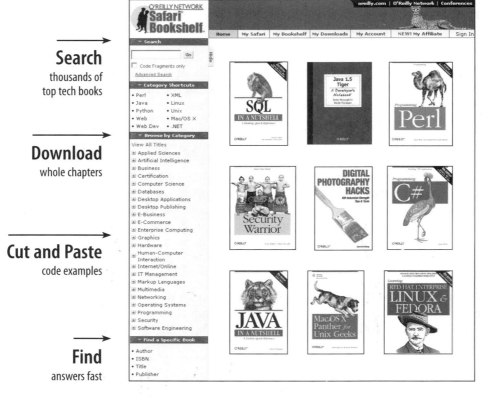

Search Safari! The premier electronic reference
library for programmers and IT professionals.